P9-CKJ-927

Modern

ENGLISH HANDBOOK

ROBERT M. GORRELL
University of Nevada

CHARLTON LAIRD
University of Nevada

Second Edition

Englewood Cliffs, N. J.

PRENTICE-HALL, INC.

©—COPYRIGHT, 1953, 1956, BY

PRENTICE-HALL, INC.

Englewood Cliffs, N. J.

ALL RIGHTS RESERVED. NO PART OF THIS BOOK
MAY BE REPRODUCED IN ANY FORM, BY MIMEO-
GRAPH OR ANY OTHER MEANS, WITHOUT PER-
MISSION IN WRITING FROM THE PUBLISHERS.

LIBRARY OF CONGRESS
CATALOG CARD NO.: 56-9005

First printing..............May, 1956
Second printing..........August, 1956
Third printing...........January, 1957
Fourth printing...........June, 1958

PRINTED IN THE UNITED STATES OF AMERICA

59418

PREFACE

It's puzzling work, talking is. —GEORGE ELIOT

Using English is puzzling work, but this book assumes that it is less puzzling than it has sometimes been made to seem and that it becomes least puzzling when studied by principles rooted in language habits. Our book, therefore, is based on the following principles:

(1) Writing is the use of language for expression and for communication; much attempted writing fails because the writer begins writing before he has something to say.

(2) Good writing—as manifested in word choice, in sentence structure, and in the broader aspects of composition—must be based upon clear thinking.

(3) A mastery of writing can be acquired most quickly and thoroughly through improvement rather than correction; so-called errors disappear only when the writer learns to construct a sentence well.

(4) A study of any grammar promotes skill in the use of language, but to be most helpful, the grammar studied should describe the language to which it is peculiar. The student of English derives the greatest benefit from the study of *English* grammar, not the grammar of another language—not even that of one so excellent as Latin.

(5) Usage is the basis of idiom, and hence eventually the basis of language. It determines standards, but the varying degree of respect paid to tradition at various language levels is a part of usage. The important difference between "It is not true" and " 'Tain't so" is not that one is right and the other wrong or that the "best" people use one and not the other. The important difference is that the expressions have different effects on readers or listeners; that they convey different meanings.

To the authors, this approach has seemed successful. Students are aware that they are studying something important, something not to be dismissed as "just commas." Students improve faster under this system than under some others because they are learning to write,

[iii

not merely to "correct" weak sentences, which will remain weak after they are corrected. This method helps the teacher, too, because the student who learns to think will outgrow many infelicities and require less correction. To promote these ends, we have given more than usual attention to such subjects as development and predication.

On the other hand, our presentation of materials does not reflect a disregard for established practice. We have preserved the conventionally accepted grammatical terms and the more tenable of the common grammatical concepts, even though the resulting mixture may occasionally seem inconsistent. Similarly, we have restricted our discussion and our examples mainly to standard written English.

The book has been planned as an organized program of study, but we have tried to make each section independent and to provide cross references so that sections can be considered in any order.

We are grateful for many helpful criticisms and suggestions. Among those who read the original manuscript and gave valuable help are Donald W. Lee, University of Pittsburgh; Thomas Elliott Berry, West Chester State Teachers College; William Wight, University of Miami; and Edward Calver. We are grateful for the discussions and suggestions of Mr. William A. Pullin, of Professor Clark Emery of the University of Miami, and of Professor Thomas Clark Pollock, Dean of Washington Square College, New York University, who provided especially useful comments on the manuscript and gave us the benefits of his research in student spelling. We are grateful for careful criticism and suggestions for the revision from Professor David Reed, University of California; Professor Ferris Cronkhite, Cornell University; Professor Hans H. Andersen, Oklahoma Agricultural and Mechanical College. We thank the staff of Prentice-Hall, Inc., for constant guidance and careful editing, especially Mr. Donald Hammonds, Miss Mary F. Sherwood, and Mr. William W. Worcester. Our colleagues at the University of Nevada have given us innumerable helpful suggestions. From several generations of students we have gained good as well as horrible examples, but, more important, we have had occasional evidence that the teaching of English is not entirely futile. To our wives, Johnnie Belle Gorrell and Helene Laird, we are grateful for patience and for practical assistance; we had need for both.

ROBERT M. GORRELL
CHARLTON LAIRD

A NOTE ON THE REFERENCE SYSTEM

Modern English Handbook attempts to combine several approaches to composition: positive instruction in rhetoric and logic; a summary of modern attitudes toward grammar and usage; and specific guides for theme correction, not only for common slips in usage but for weaknesses in organization and development. As a result the book requires a more elaborate system of key symbols than will suffice for a manual intended only for spelling, mechanics, and simpler grammatical concepts. The teacher will find some symbols not available in most books—19, *Emphasis,* or 20, *Predication,* for instance— and a few old favorites may appear in unexpected places. The authors have tried, however, to make the reference machinery flexible and convenient for rapid use. The following observations may help the teacher adapt the text to his course and his system of marking papers.

(1) The book is planned for an organized program, but sections are kept relatively independent and provided with cross references; thus subjects may be considered in any order.

(2) To facilitate revision, the teacher may wish to assign section 46 early in the course, perhaps when the first themes are returned.

(3) Three distinct systems of symbols can be used independently or in conjunction: (a) reference to sections by numbers outlined in chart on front endpapers; (b) reference to sections by copyreading symbols and abbreviations outlined on front endpapers and listed alphabetically on back endpapers; (c) reference by number index to rhetorical sections outlined on the back of the front endpapers.

(4) All these systems are flexible; the teacher may refer to a general subject or to a specific treatment, according to his philosophy of teaching and the time available for theme reading. He may use the general symbols in the shaded boxes of the chart, the more specific numbers or symbols in the other boxes, or their still more specific subdivisions marked in the text. For example, a sentence with the wrong clause subordinated can be marked simply *S* for sentence

structure, *22* or *Sub* to refer to the section on subordination, *22b* or *Sub b* to refer to the section exactly, or 22-3 to suggest that the student study the paragraph on subordination and emphasis.

(5) The teacher can often save time by encircling words in the paper, instructing students to look in the index or glossary (47) for anything so marked.

(6) The teacher can often save the time required to write comments by using references not keyed in some books. For example, a paper or paragraph lacking factual development can be criticized by a reference to 6, *Using Facts*.

(7) Many topics would logically be treated in more than one place; we have placed main discussions of such topics where they encourage the understanding of the student, with cross references to them. The teacher may wish to note the following locations especially:

(a) The use of a comma rather than a period or semicolon, the so-called comma fault, is discussed as a question of sentence structure, joining clauses, in 18c.

(b) Omission of the comma between independent clauses joined by a co-ordinating conjunction may be marked *18b* or *Run-on b* or *39a* or *Com a* but is discussed mainly in 18 in connection with joining clauses.

(c) Faulty end punctuation may be marked *38* or *EP,* but failure to use a period at the end of a sentence is discussed mainly in connection with the structure of the complete sentence, 17 and 18.

(d) Illogical comparison is discussed as an aspect of parallelism and can be marked *21d* or *Comp*; incomplete comparisons are considered types of incomplete constructions and can be marked *25d* or *Inc Comp.*

(e) Shifts in person, time, and place are treated as aspects of point of view in 13, with cross references to related sections on verbs and pronouns. General shifts in structure are discussed as problems of predication in 20e.

(f) Uses of the apostrophe and hyphen are considered spelling problems and can be marked by references to *42a* or *Apos* and *42b* or *Hy.*

ACKNOWLEDGMENTS

The authors wish to thank the following for their permission to reproduce material in this handbook:

The Atlantic Monthly: the selections from Jacques Barzun, "What Is Teaching?" 174 (December, 1944); James B. Conant, "Force and Freedom," 183 (January, 1949); David L. Cohn, "Who Will Do the Dirty Work?" 183 (May, 1949); and "Moonlight and Poison Ivy," 183 (January, 1949); J. Roswell Gallagher, "There Is No Average Boy," 183 (March, 1949); Hilary St. George Saunders, "Can France Come Back?" 183 (March, 1949). Used by permission of *The Atlantic Monthly.*

Brandt & Brandt: the selection from *Inside Europe* by John Gunther, copyright, 1936, by John Gunther, published by Harper & Brothers, and used by permission of Brandt & Brandt.

Dodd, Mead & Company: the selection from *Life and Literature* by Lafcadio Hearn, copyright, 1917, by Mitchell McDonald, and used by permission of Dodd, Mead & Company.

Doubleday & Company, Inc.: the selection from *The Old Wives' Tale* by Arnold Bennett, used by permission of Doubleday & Company, Inc.; the selections from *Rain* by W. Somerset Maugham, used by permission of Doubleday & Company, Inc.

E. P. Dutton & Co., Inc.: the selection from *The French Revolution* by Nesta H. Webster, used by permission of E. P. Dutton & Co., Inc.

Farrar, Straus & Cudahy, New York, Cassell and Company, Ltd., London, and Robert Graves: the selection from *Occupation Writer* by Robert Graves, copyright, 1950, by Robert Graves, and used by permission of the above.

Harcourt, Brace and Company, Inc.: the selection from *Book of Bays* by William Beebe, copyright, 1942, by Harcourt, Brace and Company, Inc., and used by permission of Harcourt, Brace and Company, Inc.; the selection from *Abraham Lincoln: The Prairie Years* by Carl Sandburg, copyright, 1926, by Harcourt, Brace and Company, Inc., and used by permission of Harcourt, Brace and Company, Inc.

Harper & Brothers: the selection from *You Can't Go Home Again* by Thomas Wolfe, used by permission of Harper & Brothers.

Harvard University Press: the selection from *Philosophy in a New Key* by Susanne K. Langer, copyright, 1942, 1951, and used by permission of the Harvard University Press.

Houghton Mifflin Company: the selection from *Letters of Henry Adams* by Worthington C. Ford, used by permission of the Houghton Mifflin Company; the selection from *Convention and Revolt in Poetry* by John Livingstone Lowes, used by permission of the Houghton Mifflin Company; the selections from *Patterns of Culture* by Ruth Benedict, used by permission of the Houghton Mifflin Company; the selection from *The Heart of Thoreau's Journals,* edited by Odell Shepard, used by permission of the Houghton Mifflin Company.

Indiana University Press: the selection from *The Old Northwest: Pioneer Period, 1815–1840* by R. Carlyle Buley, copyright, 1951, and used by permission of the Indiana University Press.

John Lane, The Bodley Head, Limited: the selection from *Heretics* by G. K. Chesterton, used by permission of John Lane, The Bodley Head, Limited, London.

The Macmillan Company: the selection from *The Way of All Flesh* by Samuel Butler, used by permission of The Macmillan Company; the selection from *Science and the Modern World* by A. N. Whitehead, used by permission of The Macmillan Company; the selection from *The Mind of Primitive Man* by Franz Boas, used by permission of The Macmillan Company; the selection from *Men of Destiny* by Walter Lippmann, used by permission of The Macmillan Company; the selection from "Misspelling in the Twelfth Grade" (*Teachers Service Bulletin in English*) by Thomas Clark Pollock, used by permission of The Macmillan Company; the selection from *Modern English and Its Heritage* by Margaret Bryant, used by permission of The Macmillan Company.

Oxford University Press: the selection from *Man: A History of the Human Body* by Sir Arthur Keith, copyright, 1912, and used by permission of Oxford University Press; the selections from *The Classical Tradition* by Gilbert Highet, copyright, 1949, and used by permission of Oxford University Press; the selection from *Under the Sea Wind* by Rachel L. Carson, copyright, 1941, by Rachel L. Carson, and used by permission of Oxford University Press.

Penguin Books, Inc.: the selection from *Our Language* by Simeon Potter, used by permission of Penguin Books, Inc.

Philosophical Library: the selection from the preface written by George Bernard Shaw to *The Miraculous Birth of Language* by Richard Albert Wilson, used by permission of the Philosophical Library.

Prentice-Hall, Inc.: the selection from *Thinking Straight: A Guide for Readers and Writers* by Monroe C. Beardsley, copyright, 1950, 1956, and used by permission of Prentice-Hall, Inc.

G. P. Putnam's Sons: the selection from *An Almanac for Moderns* by

Donald Culross Peattie, copyright, 1935, by Donald Culross Peattie, and used by permission of G. P. Putnam's Sons.

Charles Scribner's Sons: the selection from *Of Time and the River* by Thomas Wolfe, used by permission of Charles Scribner's Sons; the selection from *How to Write Short Stories* by Ring Lardner, used by permission of Charles Scribner's Sons.

Simon and Schuster: the selection from *Men of Art* by Thomas Craven, copyright, 1931, and used by permission of Simon and Schuster, Publishers.

Viking Press, Inc.: the selection from *Sea of Cortez* by John Steinbeck and Edward F. Ricketts, copyright, 1941, and used by permission of the Viking Press, Inc.; the selection from *Winesburg, Ohio* by Sherwood Anderson, copyright, 1919, and used by permission of the Viking Press, Inc.

H. W. Wilson Company: the selection from *Readers' Guide to Periodical Literature,* used by permission of the H. W. Wilson Company.

CONTENTS

I. Organizing a Composition

II. Developing and Controlling an Idea

III. Paragraphs and Continuity

IV. The Basic Sentence Pattern

22. Subordination 260

Subordination and style, 260. Subordination to show relationships, 261. Subordination and emphasis, 261. Subordination and contexts, 262. Repeated subjects and subordination, 264. Illogical or upside-down subordination, 265.

23. Modifiers; Methods in Subordination 269

Modifying expressions, 269. Subordination and modification, 270. Types of modifiers, 271. Word order of modifiers, 272. Fixed modifiers, 273. Sentence and clause modifiers, 274. Position or fixed modifiers, 276. "Squinting" modifiers, 277. "Dangling" introductory modifiers, 277. "Dangling" concluding verbal phrases, 280. "Split" constructions, 281. Position of modifier-connectives, 284.

24. Reference 292

Meaning and word reference, 292. Signals of reference; pronouns, 293. Patterns of reference, 294. Reference to general ideas, 295. Reference and position of antecedents, 297. General pronoun reference, 298. Reference with impersonal constructions, 299. Word reference in restatements, 299. Reference with modifiers, 300. Shifts of meaning, 302. Reference of substitute verb forms, 303.

25. Incomplete Constructions and Sentence Patterns 310

Economy with verbs, 311. Omission of prepositions, 312. Omission of subordinating words, 313. Omissions in comparisons, 313.

VI. Selection of Forms; Function Words

26. Parts of Speech 321

Form changes in English grammar, 321. Parts of the sentence; parts of speech, 323.

27. Noun Expressions 327

Uses of noun expressions, 327. Types of noun expressions, 328. Verbal nouns, 328.

VII. Words

VIII. Mechanics

IX. The Research or Investigative Paper

I. Organizing a Composition

First catch the rabbit . . .

If the manager of a large grocery store merely stacked his goods on the shelves in the order in which packages appeared at his back door, he would save himself a good deal of thought and trouble; but he would soon drive both his clerks and his customers either to other stores or to distraction. Soap flakes might appear above canned spinach flanked by cartons of eggs and jars of peanut butter. The manager would not know what to order from the wholesaler, and he might find his store full of canned artichoke hearts and completely without salt. For a time, shopping might be a novel adventure, an exploration of uncharted country, but it would soon become a chore.

The manager, therefore, if he wants to stay in business, does not present his merchandise in any such helter-skelter fashion. He buys and arranges various articles according to a plan. He buys what he needs, and he may arrange his goods according to a variety of purposes. He may, for example, group all breakfast foods in one place and all canned fruits or all spices in another. He arranges items, in other words, according to a kind of logic, according to resemblances which simplify finding individual articles. He may also, however, violate this kind of logic to put an overstocked article into a prominent position, a position of emphasis, where it will sell more rapidly at a reduced price. Or he may arrange unrelated items in a window because they have attractive packages. But he always works with a plan, a purpose.

The writer, in many ways, faces the same problems as the store manager. He has at his disposal a great wealth of material which he may discuss. He has his experience, which includes his attitudes and ideas as well as what has happened to him. It includes knowledge of other people. It includes information about a family, a school, a community. Furthermore, the writer can supplement such experience by observation, by reading, and by specific research. Like the store manager, however, he must use this material according to a plan if he is to communicate successfully.

As the store manager must consider his needs and purposes when he makes his orders to the wholesaler, the writer must think about the main plan and purpose of his paper as he searches his memory or studies his reference books. If he knows what he is trying to do in his writing, he can ask himself questions which will dredge up facts and examples from his experience. And as the store manager then displays his goods according to definite purposes, the writer organizes his facts and ideas to do what he wants them to do. He groups details which are related; he emphasizes details which have special importance. As the writer thinks systematically about his topic, he finds that he can no longer indulge in the common student lament, "I have nothing to say." He finds that as soon as he begins thinking in terms of a plan and purpose he has more than enough to say.

Language is man's greatest invention, the tool with which, more than any other, he has built his civilization. It is also the most important tool with which most of us build our lives. It is most useful when it is used purposefully. The first section, therefore, concerns the development of writing with a plan and purpose: limiting a topic, unifying material about a main idea, analyzing, classifying, and arranging.

1. THE THEME TOPIC; SOMETHING TO WRITE ABOUT

[For Guide to Revision, see page 7]

*A theme topic should reflect what the writer knows
about and wants to discuss; it should be limited by
the writer's specific plan and purpose.*

Everyone has something to write about. He has gone to school,
had a job, traveled, known people, built a model airplane, played
hookey, read a book, or held opinions. He has experience and
knowledge and attitudes which can be the material for writing. And
he draws on them constantly for verbal communication, which is
basically like writing.

Friends gather after midnight in a dormitory room. Most of the
group have something to say, and much of the time they interest one
another. A student home from a play rehearsal starts to tell what
happened. Before he has finished, someone else has thought of a
high school play rehearsal and has his anecdote ready. Others pick
up the thread. But one student with no story to tell says that dramatics is a waste of time and should not be allowed to divert students
from the more serious business of studying chemistry. Someone calls
on his experience for a story which he thinks justifies the value of
plays. Someone else quotes his psychology book on the values of
recreation. Someone describes a very bad high school production to
show that amateur plays threaten the future of drama. The argument turns into a discussion of the idiosyncrasies of various dramatic
coaches and finally drifts off into enthusiastic if unreasoned views
on the heroine of a current moving picture.

The discussion probably produced no conversational triumphs.
In the cold permanence of ink and paper, many of the comments
would seem feeble, but the stuff of writing was there. The students
had something to express, something to write about, and the discussion contained subjects for a dozen college themes.

1-1 The theme

In a sense, the college theme is an artificial exercise. It is written for a course, often on an assigned subject, to be handed in on a certain day, and to be scrutinized by an instructor with a red pencil and a grade book. Actually, it is much less artificial than it may seem. Most of the writing done in real life is subject to equally arbitrary specifications. A letter or a newspaper editorial or a report on a business inspection trip or a political speech or a legal brief usually has its subject dictated by orders or circumstances. The deadlines of the world are just as rigorous as those of the classroom, and editors or juries or vice presidents are more ruthless critics than are instructors.

1-2 Limiting the topic

The topic has much to do with the success or failure of a theme. If the writer picks a subject which he knows or will study and then selects some aspect of that subject which can be handled in the space available, he has started right. If not, he is certain to have trouble. Even with an assigned subject, a writer must select and restrict before he writes. He must narrow his field by breaking down a subject into more specific topics (see 3-1), selecting constantly according to his interests and knowledge.

For example, a student recalls that he has been thinking about extracurricular activities in college and decides to write on the subject. He realizes that "Extracurricular Activities in College" is too broad for a 750-word paper. He decides to narrow the topic by considering one activity. He breaks the general subject into athletics, music, drama, social affairs, campus politics. He might, of course, have thought of more subtopics, but he knows something of campus politics. "Campus Politics," however, is not specific enough for a relatively short paper. The student considers various aspects of campus politics: graft in campus politics, relations of campus politics to academic work, methods for succeeding in campus politics, the value of campus politics. He decides on the last, but as he considers ways in which campus politics is valuable, he discovers that he still has more to say than he can put into one paper, and he sees he must break down his topic again. Re-examining his ideas, he finds that he considers campus politics valuable to the nation as training in democracy, valuable to the school, and valuable to the individual student.

4]

He sees that these subtopics partially overlap, but he also sees the advantage of separating them and selecting one for his paper. Because he feels he is best able to discuss the value of politics to the student, he works down to a topic specific enough so that he can hope to do something with it: "Campus Politics as Education." The process, then, whereby a specific topic can be drawn from a general subject is roughly pictured in the following chart:

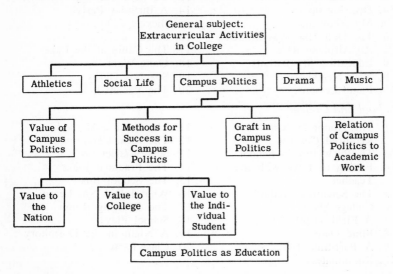

The final title may differ from the descriptive topic which the writer selects for his own guidance. But the topic to which he restricts his thinking must be narrow enough to be manageable and descriptive enough to guide the writer. In other words, the writer, even as he selects his topic, must consider what he can say about it. He need not proceed as formally as the chart above suggests, but he must ask himself questions, deciding what he is best qualified to discuss. As he does, he directs his attention toward the kind of topic in which he is interested, about which he has some knowledge, and which he can develop in the space alloted.

1-3 Suggestions for theme topics

Only the writer can select his topic because only he can know the basis on which he wants to limit his subject. Sometimes, however, a general list suggests subjects the student can consider and raises questions he can ask himself about them. The following list is intended to suggest general ideas and help the writer think of subjects which he can restrict to workable topics:

Childhood Experiences

1. Learning to Swim
2. My First Fish
3. Grandmother's Pantry
4. Dressing up
5. My Allowance
6. The Doll That Was Broken
7. An Airplane Ride
8. Educating My Parents
9. New Neighbors
10. Piano Lessons

11. Learning about Religion
12. Playing Soldier
13. Our Old Car
14. A Birthday Party
15. Bicycle Riding
16. Secret Societies
17. The Cabin at the Lake
18. Gang Wars
19. Soapbox Derby
20. The Vacant Lot

School and College

1. The Honor System
2. Required Courses
3. The New Boy in School
4. Falling in Love with the Teacher
5. The Scientific Method
6. College Slang
7. A Field Trip
8. Blind Date
9. A Part-time Job
10. Roommates

11. The Lecture Method
12. The Ideal Class
13. School Elections
14. The Practical Joker
15. The School Bus
16. What I Did Not Learn
17. The Dressing Room
18. School Play
19. A Night in the Dormitory
20. Class Party

People

1. The College Politician
2. The Village Bum
3. A Teacher I Remember
4. The Juvenile Delinquent
5. The House Mother

6. The School Bully
7. The Minister
8. The Boss
9. My Favorite Relative
10. An Honest Man

Information

1. Picking Cotton
2. The Canning Factory
3. Editing a School Paper
4. How to Take a Picture
5. Driving a Hot Rod
6. How to Take Notes
7. How to Sell Magazines
8. Impressing the Opposite Sex
9. How to Plan a Meal
10. How to Be Dull at Parties

11. Fun with Music
12. Decorating a College Room
13. How to Grow Peanuts
14. How to Train a Pup
15. Baby Sitting as a Business
16. How to Fail a Course
17. Buying Clothes Economically
18. How to Milk a Cow
19. How to Cook Possum
20. How a Force Pump Works

Problems

1. Is Television a Threat to Education?
2. Should Some Books Be Banned from the Market?
3. Should National Officials Be Nominated in Party Conventions?
4. Should College Football Players Be Subsidized?
5. Should Congressional Lobbying Be Allowed?
6. Do Fraternities and Sororities Help or Hinder Education?
7. Should Colleges Require a Course in American History?
8. Should Professional Courses in College Include Liberal Arts Subjects?
9. Should Radio and Television Advertising Be More Strictly Supervised?
10. Are Radio Commercials Necessary?
11. Is the United States a Democracy?
12. Should Protestant Church Denominations Be Merged?
13. Should Labor Strikes Be Outlawed?
14. What Is Success?
15. Are Extracurricular Activities Being Overemphasized in College?
16. Should Colleges Require Military Training of All Students?
17. Is Television Improving?

Opinions, Attitudes, Beliefs

1. Religion and the College Student
2. A Low-cost Housing Project
3. The Values of Modern Music
4. The Importance of Good Grooming
5. My Favorite Newspaper Column
6. My Favorite Childhood Reading
7. The Power of Words in the Modern World
8. The Values of a College Education
9. A Change I Would Make in University Rules
10. One Plank That Should Be in Any Party Platform
11. The Importance of the Poet in the Modern World
12. Women's Participation in Politics
13. My Views on Required Attendance at Classes
14. How Library Service Could Be Improved
15. The Best Moving Picture of the Year
16. Sensible Fashions for Men and Women

1 The theme topic   **Top**

GUIDE TO REVISION:

> *Restrict the topic of the paper so that it can be adequately developed in the allotted space.*

Many student themes are doomed at the outset. They attempt what is almost impossible. They try to discuss in 500 words "The

Culture of the Middle West"; they strive in a page or two to analyze "America's Foreign Policy" or "University Education in America." These are, of course, worthy general subjects, but they are topics for books or series of books, not for short essays. A theme on any one of them would be only a string of unsubstantiated generalities.

The writer must limit himself, must focus on the aspect of his general subject to which he can make an individual contribution. He might, for example, narrow a subject like "The Culture of the Middle West" geographically, restricting his topic to the culture of one state or further to the culture of a city or a section of a city. He might narrow the subject still more to various aspects of culture—the literature or the religion or the art of a restricted area. Religion could then be restricted to some attitude toward religion. A possible working topic might be "Fundamentalism in Religion in Midtown, Michigan."

Original	*Revision*
Fishing	How to Tie a Fly
Interesting People I Have Known	My Temperamental Music Teacher
Athletics	How to Play First Base
Photography	Photographing against the Sun
Newspapers in the United States	The Editorial Attitude of *The Daily News* toward Expansion of the School System
War Between the States	A Problem in Tactics at the Battle of Bull Run

EXERCISE 1

A. From the following list of subjects select those appropriate for treatment in a theme 500 to 1000 words long:

1. Ideal Communities in New York State in the Nineteenth Century
2. My First Lost Tooth
3. Should Medicine Be Socialized?
4. How to Poison Coyotes
5. How to Ride a Subway
6. The Monroe Doctrine
7. A Major Weakness of the Sales Tax
8. Prejudice in a Small Town
9. Making a Coal Mine Safe
10. Clam Chowder

B. Narrow any five of the following general subjects to topics suitable for themes 500 to 1000 words long; for each construct a chart like the one on page 5 to show possible stages in the breakdown:

1. Snobs
2. College Sports
3. Moving Pictures
4. Automobiles
5. Hairdressing

6. Farming
7. Poetry
8. Congress
9. Summer Jobs
10. Southern Hospitality

C. All American libraries use some system of breaking down subjects into smaller compartments so that books can be arranged according to subject. Many American libraries use the Dewey Decimal System, which breaks the subjects of the world into ten main fields, each of these into ten fields, and so forth. Your library uses this or a similar system and has a chart describing it posted for your convenience. The following exercise assumes that your library uses the Dewey system, but it can be adapted to whatever system your library uses:

Find out the ten fields of knowledge recognized in the ten main divisions of the Dewey system. Select one subdivision under each of these main divisions; that is, select ten in all. Then narrow each of these subdivisions until it would be suitable for a theme of 500 to 1000 words.

D. By using the card catalogue in the library, or by browsing in a book store or among library shelves which are open to you, select five books whose subjects you can infer. For each book think of the title of a 750-word paper, which is either part of the general subject of the book, or closely related to it. For instance, for Rachel Carson's *The Sea Around Us* you could propose a theme title, "How to Dive for Abalone," or "A Glimpse through a Glass-bottomed Boat." Donald Day's *Woodrow Wilson's Own Story* might suggest "If I Mentioned Wilson, Father Started Shouting."

2. UNITY; THE MAIN IDEA

[For Guide to Revision, see page 16]

Unify a composition by focusing attention on a main idea or central plan.

We select a topic because we have something to say about it—even when we are fulfilling class assignments. We read *Paradise Lost* and decide that Milton does not sound like the puritan he is called in the introduction to the poem. We have something to say about Milton and his poetry. We listen to a radio commentator discussing foreign affairs, and find we have something to say about the State Department. We read a newspaper report of traffic deaths, and decide we have something to say about driving habits. We experience a month of college social life and find we want to talk about it—describe it, criticize it, suggest changes, praise it. We do not necessarily have new or clever or sensational ideas about a subject, but we have some ideas.

Almost any unit of writing, then, from a sentence to a book, centers about a main idea. The main idea may be a highly important interpretive statement or a highly personal point of view. Frederick Jackson Turner in his influential essay on *The Significance of the Frontier in American History* marshals evidence to support the view that:

> . . . the existence of an area of free land, its continuous recession, and the advance of American settlement westward, explain American development.

Well-known facts of history are seen in a new light when interpreted on the basis of this central idea. On the other hand, Robert Louis Stevenson in an entirely different kind of essay, *Walking Tours,* offers no profound conclusions; he holds his facts together with a central theme that walking tours, well conducted, are a source of genuine

10]

delight and satisfaction. But both essays give clear evidence that the writers had thought about the central meaning of what they had to say, and had selected and organized their material with a main idea or purpose in mind.

2-1 Stating the main idea

Even while he is selecting his topic, the writer should ask himself searchingly what he wants to say about his topic, why he wants to say it, and what is his attitude toward it. A student planning a theme should think about his purpose and his main idea as he collects material, and before he begins writing *he should phrase his main idea in a complete sentence.*

For example, if a student adopted "Campus Politics as Education" as a topic for a theme, before beginning to write he would need to think about his attitude toward his subject, about his purpose in writing the paper, about his main idea. He might adopt a controversial point of view and phrase his main idea as:

> Campus politics provides the opportunities for practical education that are lacking in formal courses in political science.

Another student might phrase his main idea as:

> Campus politics, because it deals with artificial situations and insignificant problems, has no place in an educational institution.

A third student might decide that he could take no controversial stand, that he wanted to describe, not argue; but he would still need to state his main idea as a guide to his planning:

> Campus politics is sometimes educational and sometimes a waste of time, but it is almost always exciting for the student participating in it.

As he writes, the writer may, of course, change his mind or collect new evidence which will result in a modification of his main idea; but until he can tie himself down to some tentative view, he has not thought enough. Before he starts he should be able to make a statement of the main idea which has the following qualities:

(1) It should be a complete sentence. The statement should not be merely a wordier version of the topic.

(2) It should be specific, the more specific the better. "This paper describes a house I knew in my childhood" only postpones the necessary thinking. "An old house had an important influence on my childhood" is better. "An old house in our block, because it reminded me of the man in the Chas. Adams cartoons, gave me a horror of dark rooms" is still better.

(3) It should be exact; an inexact statement usually results from cloudy thinking. For instance, the first topic mentioned above might have been phrased as follows: "Campus politics provides more opportunities for practical education than all the formal courses in political science in the university." This is a possible subject, but the student probably has no intention of writing on it. Has he taken "all the formal courses in political science"? Probably not, and even if he has he probably has no intention of contrasting them systematically with what a student can learn from campus politics.

2-2 Main idea and unity

A motion picture camera man photographing a crowd faces a problem like the writer's. He attempts to present a large number of details in such a way that they will make a unified impression. He often provides views from a distance which give a general over-all impression of the large scene, then turns his camera to details, to pictures of individual characters and smaller scenes; and almost always he helps his audience to keep these more concentrated scenes in order by focusing attention on some central object. A tree or a building or an important character becomes a focal point, and the camera swings back to it and then away from it so that the audience can keep the great mass of details in order by relating them to this point of focus. Similarly, the skillful writer keeps his reader's attention turned toward a main idea or to central objects which he can use as focal points.

These focal points are important in every stage of the writing, from planning to proofreading. Any alert mind constantly receives new suggestions, continually sees new implications in familiar material, but not all suggestions, however enticing they may be, are useful when they appear. A student may decide to write a paper arguing that fraternities often harm campus politics by using the methods of machine politicians. He remembers that one of the finest men on the campus had been defeated for office because he refused to join a fraternity; several fraternities had combined to elect an inferior candidate. He begins his paper with this story. Then he remembers that the fraternity machine had triumphed partly because it could afford to plaster the campus with advertising. He writes a paragraph on campaign posters. Next he remembers that his group in high school once elected Jimmie Good over Henry Maibie by using on its posters the slogan, "We want a Good president, and we don't mean Maibie." But this slogan, he recalls, had been based on a pun in his mathematics class, and accordingly the student turns to a discussion of the witty remarks of the mathematics teacher—and is by this time completely off the subject. He has failed to concentrate on his main idea, his controlling purpose.

2-3 Devices for unity

Usually the main idea or central proposition, stated in the topic sentence (see 14-3), becomes the focal point of the paper, the unifying device. A student writing a theme on the educational value of student self-government might take as his theme sentence a statement that student government provides experience in democracy. He could then unify his paper by relating subsidiary facts and arguments to this thesis.

Often, however, other devices help to keep the reader's attention in focus, as in Thomas Henry Huxley's famous essay *On a Piece of Chalk.* The main idea of the essay is that the earth "has been the theatre of a series of changes," that physical characteristics and living inhabitants of the earth have been affected by evolution. The essay is unified around a specific example, around the story of the changes embodied in a piece of chalk.

Similarly, Esmé Wingfield Stratford labels a chapter of his *History of British Civilization* "Gothic Christianity." He wishes to describe the particular qualities of the growth of religious ardor in England about the thirteenth century. To unify his chapter he relates his ideas to the development of the Gothic architecture which distinguished English cathedrals built during the period. These cathedrals become a symbol for the thesis of the chapter.

A student theme on the value of student self-government uses a similar device for unity. Its central thesis is that student government improves efficiency and justice in handling student affairs. Its title, however, is *The Bookstore,* and the arguments in the paper are unified about a story of how a student government acquired a university bookstore and improved its service and management. The paper makes such general points as these: students are better aware of their own needs than other groups; they are capable of sensible management; they are stimulated by the challenge of the problems of regulating their own affairs. The paper connects all these by relating them to the specific instance of the development of the bookstore.

Unity can be furthered by keeping the reader's attention focused. A textbook explanation of the working of a gasoline engine provides a good example. The explanation follows the fuel from the storage tank through the carburetor into the cylinders and finally, as waste, out the exhaust. By explaining the working of each part of the engine in terms of its effect on the fuel, the writer makes a clear and unified explanation. An account of the workings of the houses of Congress gains unity by centering attention on the progress of a bill from its original drafting through readings and committee reports and votes and conferences to its final signing.

Some devices for unity are more artificial than these, invented solely to hold the composition together. A bridge game unifies one mystery novel, for instance; it has no relation to the plot of the story, but ties it together. The murder takes place during a bridge game, and subsequent events are talked about, sometimes whimsically, as if they were parts of a game. A chapter in which the women characters do some expert investigating is called "Queens Are Trumps"; the device gets mixed in a chapter called "One-eyed Jacks Wild," but the book returns to the original game and concludes with "The Last Trick." Even so contrived a device as this may unify writing.

2-4 The précis and the main idea

The précis, a useful sort of writing for many purposes, can serve the student writer to study the main idea as the core of a composition. The word *précis* is French, related to our word *precise* and to a Latin word which meant "cut off in front." A good précis embodies the idea of both words; it is "cut off" in the sense that it is intended to give the essence in brief compass of a longer piece of writing, and it should be as precise as a relatively brief restatement can be. Its origin suggests its character. The précis arose from reports sent back by diplomatic representatives abroad, and if the student will put himself in the position of a representative of the State Department in a foreign country he should recognize the qualities of a good précis.

14]

Consider, for instance, the position of a diplomatic attaché in a South American capital who fears a revolution accompanied by an attack from a neighboring country. The State Department will want his opinion of the situation, but it will also need evidence divorced from opinion, because any decision must take into account both the countries, factions within the countries, international organizations, and a host of other governments, along with a variety of interests, including our own. Decisions will be made in Washington, and those who decide will need accurate and proportioned understanding of the situation in Latin America. Right decisions require reliable information, but time may not permit lengthy reports—revolutions may not wait. Accordingly, the attaché prepares précis of all important documents, and as he writes he must be as objective and penetrating as possible, endeavoring to reflect his originals accurately, without distortion or bias, while losing nothing vital, as a small mirror can reflect a large room without distortion or omission. In words, the accuracy of the mirror is not possible, but for a précis, precision is still the ideal.

Now, to understand the précis we might write a précis of the previous paragraph. First, of course, we must read the passage carefully and be sure we understand it. Next we must understand the parts of the paragraph, and in restating, preserve the relative importance of each in the whole. We must not be content with skimming through, picking a phrase here and there. We must shrink the whole, by grasping its essence and expressing the result in our own words. A précis might read about as follows:

> The précis can promote the study of the main idea in composition. It reflects the etymological relationships of the word, since it should be both precise in statement and reduced in size, and it reflects also the origin of the précis as a concise diplomatic report. It maintains the ideal of a diplomatic representative endeavoring to present his government with a reduced, proportioned reflection of the more extensive evidence before him, evidence which must be shrunk to promote quick decisions and kept accurate and unbiased to encourage right decisions.

We might notice that the idea of the précis is essentially that of the original, that it preserves the order of the original, the main parts of the original, and even preserves roughly the proportions of the original.

2 *Unity; the main idea*   **U**

GUIDE TO REVISION:

> *Write a statement of the main idea of the theme and then reorganize and rewrite the paper so that it is unified.*

Any piece of writing should have unity of purpose and material; that is, it should depend upon and give expression to a main idea or should keep the reader's attention focused by some other unifying device.

2a *Unity about a main idea*   **U a**

The writer's best device for achieving unity is to settle on a main idea which he can express in a complete statement and then keep his attention constantly focused on it (see also 14-3, 15, especially on unity in the paragraph). A paper without a main idea is almost certain to become a purposeless jumble.

Original

READING

It is said that we learn to read in order to learn by reading. And because reading is the greatest individual means of acquiring knowledge, it is easy to understand why the person who lets himself hang back in the shadows of illiteracy can never attain anything in life worth shouting about.

Many of the happiest hours of my childhood were passed in reading. I can remember when I found my father's discarded stories of Frank Merriwell in a box in the garage and found them more exciting than the batch of comic books I had acquired. It was from those books that I learned how much fun reading could be. I used to push myself back into a corner of the

Revision

READING TO LEARN

There are so many reasons for reading that we sometimes overlook the obvious one—that reading is our most important single means of acquiring knowledge. We talk nostalgically of childhood hours spent with Frank Merriwell among the head-hunters, or we cite the emotional power of a great poem, and we forget some of the more pedestrian uses of printed language.

Even our most common day-to-day activities require some ability in reading. The worker has to read signs to drive his car to the plant in the morning. The careful shopper reads labels as she compares the quality of the products she is considering. Telegrams, memoranda, letters are read every second, and

Original (Cont.)

garage and sit for hours while Frank Merriwell struck out the entire Harvard team or rescued Elsie from the head-hunters.

Many people I know say that they do not like to read. I do not understand their point of view, because most of the knowledge of the world can be acquired from reading. In some countries of the world today people are not so fortunate, because there is no freedom of the press and they cannot acquire knowledge so easily. In America we need only to read in order to become educated.

A reader should not be content to read something he is already an authority on, but he should tackle books about subjects of which he is relatively ignorant. It is true that a good book can teach you a lesson, one which you can profit from, if you will stop and think how pleasant and easy it is to read. . . .

[The paper continues in much the same vein. Much is wrong with it, but at the bottom of most of the trouble is the absence of a main idea. One cannot say that the paper wanders from the point; there just is no point. To begin with, the title is too broad; it needs to be narrowed. Then the writer needs to decide what he wants to say about reading and start over.]

There was an oval mirror on one wall with a heavy black frame containing fat angels carved into the wood. On the large, massive walnut dresser were a silver brush and comb. There was a faint tinge of violet perfume hanging over the room. A bad print of a Rosa Bon-

Revision (Cont.)

important matters turn on the communication they carry. Lives often depend on the ability of a military officer to read orders accurately. Our daily lives turn on communication, much of which requires skillful reading.

Almost equally important is our use of reading to acquire more general but equally practical information. We read to find out how to bake a cake or make a model airplane or identify a horned lark. Words describe the cast of a play, tell us when and where to find a meeting, help us order a meal or catch a train. More complex reading can make a student an expert in chemistry or philosophy. And in a very real sense, reading can make a democracy work. Only reading can create an informed electorate in a world as complex as ours.

In still another way, however, reading is the route to valuable information. By reading literature we begin to learn what life is about. . . .

[With a main idea—that reading is necessary because it is our most important means of acquiring knowledge—the theme makes more sense. The topic is still too broad, but the writer can collect illustrative details because he knows what he is trying to illustrate.]

Everything in the room seemed somehow to exhale the faint scent of violet that hung over the room. The oval mirror, framed heavily with fat angels carved into blackened wood, the silver brush and comb on the massive walnut dresser, the faded lace curtains, the high

Original (Cont.)

heur picture was hanging on the wall over the high walnut bed. Faded lace curtains bordered the high, narrow windows.

[*Merely putting the details together gives a unity of effect; their selection gives the reader a general notion of the room. The reader could, however, be helped still more to see how the details are related.*]

I like Walt Kelly's comic strip, *Pogo.* One of my favorite characters is Albert the Alligator; good old lazy Albert is somewhat of a big, conceited show-off. And of course everybody loves Pogo. As for Deacon Muskrat and the Buzzard, they are anything but lovable, though they are not so short tempered as Albert, who though he is loyal to his friends and even sentimental on occasion will sometimes throw a towering tantrum. His friend, Churchy La Femme. . . .

[*This composition, although it shows some promise, threatens to become confused—as well as slipshod in its diction—because the writer reveals no plan to give it unity.*]

Revision (Cont.)

walnut bed, the bad print of a Rosa Bonheur picture all seemed part of the mildly sickening perfume.

[*The reviser has selected one of the details and made it a kind of symbol for the whole room, using it as a unifying device to pull all the details together.*]

Walt Kelly's comic strip, *Pogo,* gains part of its charm from the fact that each of the swamp creatures becomes a satire on some recognizable type of human being. Albert the Alligator is an irresponsible but genial ne'er-do-well, a lazy, rather cowardly show-off, short-tempered enough to throw a towering tantrum, but loyal to his friends and even, on occasion, sentimental. Deacon Muskrat, on the other hand. . . .

[*With the unifying idea that each of Walt Kelly's creatures can be equated with a human type, the writer can give order and unity to his composition.*]

2b Stating the proposition   **U b**

Inaccurate expression of the main idea misleads the reader and even confuses the writer, because a clumsily phrased statement usually reflects careless thinking. Often a main idea is obscure because the writer allows minor issues, which he never intends to develop, to appear in the statement of his proposition.

Original

(1) *The success of the American educational system can be traced directly to freedom of speech.* American instructors are not mouthpieces

Revision

America, unlike Hitler's Germany, enjoys freedom of speech. The man in the street is granted by constitutional law the privilege

Original (Cont.)

for the government. (2) Their job is to teach a sound doctrine, one not influenced by a person or group of persons. (3) And what about the students? (4) Very few students have ever been condemned for expressing their ideas in the classroom. (5) *In Germany, when Hitler was dictator, the fellow who dared criticize the system of government was promptly executed or rushed to a concentration camp.* (6) It is not like that in this great land of ours. (7) The man in the street is granted by constitutional law the privilege of saying what he pleases without fear of prosecution. (8) Newspapers in the United States are at liberty to present their readers with local, national, and world news without dictation from the government. (9) Radio broadcasting, though censored to a certain degree by the Federal Communications Commission, is another example of freedom of speech in this country.

[*This paragraph from a student theme fails, partly because it does not fulfill what the first sentence seems to promise. The reader assumes he will learn how freedom of speech has caused the success of education. He learns something else. Probably the writer did not intend this sentence as a proposition, but he has written as if he did;* (5) *may be pertinent to other parts of the theme, but it does not fit here.*]

Revision (Cont.)

of saying what he pleases without fear of prosecution. Education is generally free from censorship. Instructors in America are not mouthpieces for the government. Their job is to teach a sound doctrine, one not influenced by a person or group. And very few students have ever been condemned for expressing their ideas in the classroom. Newspapers in the United States are at liberty to present their readers with local, national, and world news without dictation from the government. Radio broadcasting, though censored to a certain degree by the Federal Communications Commission, provides another example of freedom of speech.

[*The writer's selection of details suggests that he probably intended the paragraph's main purpose to be the presentation of evidence that freedom of speech exists in America. Perhaps in another place he intends to show also that this freedom distinguishes America from other nations, such as Hitler's Germany. The revision supplies a proposition which seems to be the one intended, and then lists the details, which were already available in the paragraph to support the proposition;* (5) *and* (6) *of the original are reduced to parts of the opening sentence.*]

EXERCISE 2

A. Criticize the following main ideas. Which are suitable for student themes?

   1. TOPIC: Learning American History from Stamps.
      MAIN IDEA: Collecting American stamps is a painless but profitable way to learn the facts of American history.

2. TOPIC: I Want to Live in a City.
   MAIN IDEA: Advantages and disadvantages of life in the city.

3. TOPIC: Sutphen's Mansion.
   MAIN IDEA: An hour wandering through the ruins of the old mansion makes one feel a sense of loss for a way of life that has disappeared from the South.

4. TOPIC: Orientation.
   MAIN IDEA: This theme will show various problems of the freshman at a large university and how his courses are different from his high school work and something should be done to remedy the situation.

5. TOPIC: Yellow Creek.
   MAIN IDEA: A description of Yellow Creek as it wanders through rich fields and thick woods to the swimming hole where I spent many happy hours.

6. TOPIC: Dormitory Life.
   MAIN IDEA: To show what life is like in a dormitory.

7. TOPIC: Ballet.
   MAIN IDEA: I would expect to give a brief sketch of the invention, history, and development of ballet, say something about the recent popularity of ballet in this country, the leading ballet companies, stars, choreographers, new ballets like *Age of Anxiety,* movies like *The Red Shoes,* writers like Agnes de Mille, etc., and give some of my own opinions of ballet as an art, based on my lessons in ballet.

8. TOPIC: Woodchucks as Game Animals.
   MAIN IDEA: Hunting woodchucks provides good sport; woodchucks are plentiful, never out of season, and, properly dressed, the flesh is excellent.

9. TOPIC: Becky Thatcher's Home.
   MAIN IDEA: When we visited Hannibal, Mo., we went to see it.

10. TOPIC: United Nations.
    MAIN IDEA: Show how it is basic.

11. TOPIC: Sweaters.
    MAIN IDEA: Uses of sweaters in a girl's wardrobe. Many kinds. Sizes, colors, styles, etc. What will go with what? How many a girl ought to have? Styles. Yarns from which made.

12. TOPIC: The New Automobiles.
    MAIN IDEA: What the new models are like, and what I think the trend next year is likely to be.

13. TOPIC: Engineering.
    MAIN IDEA: Engineering as a profession.

14. TOPIC: Future of Mexico.

      MAIN IDEA: Although Mexico has great natural resources, the republic is so backward that in a world dominated by technology she can have no promising future without closer ties with the United States or with some other modern power.

15. TOPIC: Urban Transportation.

      MAIN IDEA: What my city needs most is a better transportation system.

B. From the list below, select any five general subjects. Then, (*a*) narrow each of the five to a topic which might be managed in a theme of about 500 words, and (*b*) for each restricted topic write a sentence stating a main idea which you might develop if you were to write a theme on the topic.

1. Musical Instruments
2. Advertising
3. Mountain Scenery
4. Radio and Television Programs
5. Magazines
6. Regional Prejudices
7. Materials for Clothing
8. Desserts
9. College Courses
10. Methods of Transportation

C. Examine the current number of a well-written magazine—*Harper's Magazine, The Atlantic Monthly, The Reporter*—or a collection of essays which your instructor designates. Choose three essays, and endeavor to state as accurately as you can the main idea of each.

D. What is the main idea of the first section of this book (pp. 3-7)? Criticize each of the following as statements of the main idea, and then try to write a better statement yourself.

1. Everyone has something to write about.
2. Fitting your idea to your space.
3. Considering all the factors involved, the subject should have a basic foundation suitable to existing conditions.
4. Narrowing a topic is a hard but necessary job.
5. Suit the idea to the topic, the topic to the idea.

E. Write a précis of pages 319-20 of this book, or of another selection chosen by your instructor, or write a précis of one of your earlier themes. You should reduce the original to about a quarter or a third, or to no more than half at most.

3. ANALYSIS

[For Guide to Revision, see page 25]

To explain anything complex, analyze and discuss its parts.

Analysis is the orderly breaking down of a subject into its parts. It is one of the basic ways in which we use our minds to understand, and accordingly it is one of the essentials of good writing and speaking. Once we have analyzed a subject, we understand it better, and we are ready to approach it systematically or to select one part from many parts for special attention.

3-1 Scientific and literary analysis

Roughly speaking, analysis is of two sorts: scientific or formal, and literary or informal. The first, scientific analysis, attempts to be complete and exact. A biologist, for instance, endeavors to make an analysis account for every sort of bird, plant, fish, animal, or reptile. He establishes the families, the subfamilies, the genuses, and the species, and continues his subdivisions until every known sort of creature is accounted for. For example, the Canadian lynx, which clearly belongs in the cat family or Felidae, is placed within the genus Lynx and becomes *Lynx canadensis* to distinguish it from *Lynx rufus,* the bay lynx. If a new sort of lynx were now to be discovered, a Canadian lynx but different from previous known lynxes of the species, a new category within *Lynx canadensis* would be required to differentiate it from the first. This sort of analysis is useful in bringing permanent order into a complex subject, but it is necessarily exacting and time consuming.

Literary or informal analysis is less exacting, and is usually used for practical and relatively immediate ends. The same ornithologist who spends his lifetime endeavoring to correct and complete the classification of Pacific Ocean birds may open a lecture as follows: "Birds which frequent the Hawaiian Islands represent several aquatic species in such families and subfamilies as the Sternidae, the Pelecanidae, the Sulidae, but I am concerned this morning with only *Pterodroma phaeopygia sandwichensis,* the Hawaiian race of the dark-rumped petrel." He is using literary analysis. He feels no obligation to enumerate all the main categories of Pacific birds or to pursue any category to its final subdivision. He has said enough to indicate that there are a number of sorts of birds and to center attention upon the subject of his lecture. A lecturer in history may say, "Land fighting in the War Between the States divides roughly into campaigns in the East and those in the West. The western campaigns were important, but by the very nature of Southern population distribution they could never be decisive." He has been systematic so far as he has gone, but he will certainly feel no obligation to analyze either campaign to the last skirmish—he would have few students left if he did—and he has provided, in his word *roughly,* for the fact that he has ignored minor actions like raids into the North and Indian action in the far West. Furthermore, some subjects are not amenable to scientific analysis. A lecturer on recent American literature, for instance, might mention the Southern school of novelists, the Midwestern regionalists, the proletarian novelists, the psychological novelists, the novelists concerned with race problems. This rough, informal analysis would be adequate for his purposes, but it is not, because of the nature of the material, a scientific analysis. What would the lecturer do, for instance, about a novel written by a Southern writer and concerned with psychological problems of a Negro steel worker? Literary or informal analysis is not so detailed nor so systematic as scientific analysis, but it is much more common, and for most purposes, more useful. In this book we shall be concerned with some common types of literary or informal analysis.

3-2 Structural analysis

A writer analyzing the government of the United States could begin by considering three branches: legislative, executive, and judiciary. In a section treating each of these branches he could analyze further, perhaps dividing the discussion of the executive branch into chapters on the President, the cabinet, and executive bureaus. Or a student explaining a printing press might discuss in turn the feeding device,

[23

the inking mechanism, and the impression mechanism. A writer discusses the weather by dividing his topic into discussions of each of the "seven American airs." Another discussing jet-propulsion units breaks his topic down by discussing each of four types of power units. A historian approaches his problem by analysis, titling a chapter "The Three Great Divisions of Christendom at the Close of the Sixteenth Century." Or a writer discusses how a teacher conducts a class:

> Let me explain. The three basic ways are the lecture, the discussion group, and the tutorial hour. In a lecture, a silent class is addressed, more or less like a public meeting. In a discussion group, comprising from five or six to not more than thirty students, the members of the class speak freely, putting or answering questions on points which the teacher organizes so as to form a coherent account of some topic. It may be that for this purpose discussion by the class is broken at intervals by lecturettes from him. In a tutorial hour, the instructor is really holding a conversation, usually with one student, certainly with not more than three or four. This is in the best sense a free-for-all and it presupposes a good stock of knowledge on the part of the students.
>
> —JACQUES BARZUN, *What Is Teaching?*

Here the writer analyzes the topic, breaking it into three basic methods.

3-3 Chronological analysis

Analysis may divide on the basis of time or the order of events. A writer explains a process by analyzing it into major steps and discussing each. In three paragraphs in *Typee,* for example, Herman Melville tells how to make tappa, discussing one stage of the process in each paragraph; the opening sentences of the paragraphs reveal his method:

> In the manufacture of the beautiful white tappa generally worn on the Marquesan Islands, the preliminary operation consists in gathering a certain quantity of the young branches of the cloth-tree. . . .
>
> When the substance is in a proper state for the next process, it betrays evidences of incipient decomposition; . . .
>
> When the operation last described has been concluded, the new-made tappa is spread out on the grass to bleach and dry, and soon becomes of a dazzling whiteness.

A historian may describe an event in history by analyzing it into periods:

> From England's point of view, the French Revolution can be considered in three stages: the first in which a new spirit was aroused in

France, the second which saw the force of the movement unleashed on Europe, and the third in which France became the enemy of England.

The process by which the subject of a composition is narrowed is usually only the process of analysis (see 1-2). The writer says, in effect, this subject is composed of these and these and these parts, but on this occasion I shall discuss only this one.

3 Analysis   **An**

GUIDE TO REVISION:

> *Rewrite, using analysis to break down a subject and indicating in the writing the results of the analysis.*

Analysis is only one method of organization useful to the writer, but it is basic. It is especially useful in short papers dealing with part of a large subject. By indicating the basis of his analysis and the particular materials chosen for treatment, the writer can show that he understands a complex subject and also can indicate the relationship of his particular subject to the whole. He can, for instance, admit that students choose a particular college for many reasons, but he can at the same time point out that on this occasion he proposes to discuss only the impact of family tradition on a student's choice.

3a Analysis for unity and organization   **An a**

Analysis is often the cure for weaknesses in organization or for lack of unity. Failure to analyze leads to overuse of judgments, general rather than specific writing, or obscurity.

Original

What is a hot rod? Ask this question of the average person. It is almost a certainty that he will picture it as an old vintage roadster less fenders and paint. Furthermore, he will think that the driver is incompetent. In reality, the hot rod has changed tremendously during the past decade, even if the public's conception of it has not.

The public is unaware that the

Revision

What is a hot rod? Most people would answer this question by describing an old-vintage roadster, lacking fenders, paint, and a competent driver. Actually a modern hot rod is a complex automobile, embodying a series of improvements over the ordinary stock car.

A hot rod varies most obviously from an ordinary car in the structure of its body. The body of a hot

[25

Original (*Cont.*)

present-day hot rod is really a complex mechanism, involving a good deal of hard work on the part of the boy constructing it. It is really a complete rebuilding of many of the most important parts of a car, not just a heap of junk put in temporary running order.

Such things as the body and engine are thoroughly overhauled and put into shape for greater speed and better lines. The car, therefore, is made lighter and more compact. Moreover, the engine is a better engine than the original car because it has greater horsepower. The hot rod does not look like an ordinary car, but it does not look like a dilapidated car either. Hot rods often resemble more nearly the custom-built sport cars that one sometimes sees.

It is a mistake to look on the hot rod as a dangerous toy for careless boys, because it is not that. It is really good training for young men to work with hot rods, because they can feel pride in accomplishing a good job of remodeling.

[*The weaknesses of this theme can be described in many ways: the main idea is forgotten as the paper wanders from point to point; there are too many unsubstantiated judgments; statements are general and not specific. Analysis provides one way of avoiding most of those difficulties. If the writer would break his subject into its parts, he would bring order into his composition and would probably find he could use specific material to substantiate his judgments.*]

Revision (*Cont.*)

rod is likely to begin as that of a discarded light car; the 1932 Ford is a popular model. Such a body is first rebuilt so that it sits several inches down over the chassis and lowers the center of gravity of the car. Then excess parts of the body, especially chrome ornaments, are removed, and the doors are welded shut and smoothed in to fit the lines of the rest of the body.

More important to the actual running of the car, however, are the extensive changes in the running gear. The hot rod builder improves wheels, axles, brakes, and differential assembly as extensively as his pocketbook will allow; safety requires some changes. He must, for example, change the size of the wheels and use regulation high-speed tires. He must install modern brakes, either hydraulic or disc type. He may lower the center of gravity by dropping the front axle, and he may change the differential to an assembly with a lower ratio.

Changes in the engine vary with the ingenuity and patience of the builder, but they provide the extra speed characteristic of the modern hot rod. They may be as fundamental as a modernized carburetor or as nonessential as chrome plate on the exhaust manifold, but improvements in the engine increase the power of the average motor by thirty-five to fifty horsepower.

Changes like these, rather than those the public imagines, distinguish the modern hot rod from the ordinary car.

[*By analyzing the hot rod, breaking the subject into three main groups, the writer finds something to say.*]

3b *Making analysis clear*   An b

Analysis can be used to limit a subject (see 1-2), but the reader should know how the subject is broken down, and usually what has been eliminated. Since analysis is one of the natural mental processes, writers often use it unconsciously and may fail to make the reader aware of the thinking behind the writing.

Original

Prior to the Communist occupation there were more than four million Christians of all denominations in China. Matthew Ricci, S.J., who arrived in the sixteenth century was one of them. . . .

[*The writer has used analysis, although not in an orderly manner, and he has not made the basis of his analysis clear.*]

Revision

Christianity has been introduced into China three times, but the missionary ventures of the seventh and thirteenth century proved abortive. Not until Matthew Ricci, S.J., arrived in 1582 to replant the faith of the West did Christianity play a leading part in Chinese life. . . .

[*The chronological analysis is now clear to the reader.*]

EXERCISE 3

A. Select any five of the following topics and list parts, types, or elements of each revealed by structural analysis:

1. A university	8. Socialism
2. A newspaper	9. Snobbishness
3. A football team	10. Fashion
4. A gasoline engine	11. A cement mixer
5. A corporation	12. A garden
6. A radio program	13. A farm
7. The gland system of human beings	14. Tolerance
	15. Courtesy

B. Select any three of the following topics and list stages or steps in each revealed by chronological analysis:

1. The beginning of the War Between the States	8. A hunt
2. Getting a newspaper ready for the press	9. Harvest day
3. Making camp	10. Learning to swim
4. Building a tree house	11. Organizing a club
5. Preparing for a test	12. Planning a campaign for a school election
6. Organizing a party	13. Registration day
7. A storm	14. Fraternity or sorority pledging
	15. Decorating for a dance

C. Examine the textbook in another of your courses for the manner in which the author has used analysis, and write a 250-word account of your findings. For instance, in a text in American history, chrono-logical analysis may provide the basis for the main periods, but the War Between the States may be divided into military and diplomatic history, and the military history divided again into the war in the East and the war in the West. Chapters on "The Rise of Industrialism" and "The Role of the Frontier" may deal with the same time but result from an analysis of great movements. Be sure to note whether analysis has been used to restrict the topic. For instance, in a history book the history of literature might be omitted on the theory that the student will probably take a course in literature.

4. CLASSIFICATION

[For Guide to Revision, see page 32]

To put ideas into order, classify, co-ordinate, and subordinate.

In writing, as in business or science or card games or philosophy—in almost any activity involving more than one part—we show relationships by classifying. A self-service grocery store, trying to make its thousands of items easily available to customers, collects all its produce in one section of the store, has a counter for meat, one for canned fruit, and another for canned vegetables. A university trying to convey to students a seemingly infinite variety of information classifies knowledge into "subjects" taught by different departments. A newspaper with hundreds of items clicking in over the press-service wires arranges its presentation in different sections of national news, local news, editorials, sports, society.

4-1 The basis of classification

Classification relies on similarities and differences. For example, considering all living things on earth, we could observe that some are similar in that they have four feet. We could group them as quadrupeds. But within this class, brought together because of a particular similarity, we would also find differences, and distinguish cows, horses, sheep, pigs, and lions. Furthermore, each of these subclasses could again be subdivided—cows into Guernseys, Jerseys, Holsteins, Herefords, and so forth.

The same items may also be grouped in a number of ways by using different points of similarity as the basis of classification. Consider the following items: fire truck, bluebird, violet, yellow convertible, goldfinch, poinsettia, sunflower, blue bicycle, cardinal. They can obviously be classified as shown on the following page.

Vehicles	Birds	Flowers
fire truck	bluebird	violet
yellow convertible	goldfinch	poinsettia
blue bicycle	cardinal	sunflower

But a painter might very well classify them by colors:

Red	Blue	Yellow
fire truck	blue bicycle	yellow convertible
cardinal	bluebird	goldfinch
poinsettia	violet	sunflower

The students in a classroom may be classified by the registrar as freshmen, sophomores, juniors, and seniors; by a minister as Baptists, Catholics, Episcopalians, Methodists; by the instructor as A-students, B-students, C-students; by the football coach as potential spectators, potential halfbacks, potential linemen; by a boy in the back row as men and potential "dates." The important consideration is that *material can be classified on only one basis at one time.* The women in a class may be classified on the color of their hair as blondes, brunettes, and redheads. The redheads can be reclassified on the basis of their grades, and the B-student redheads can be classified into Pan Hellenics, members of local sororities, and independents. They cannot be classified on any two of these bases at one time, since some students would belong to both classes and some to neither.

The interests of the classifier determine the basis for the classification. There is an old story of a college dean who had to deal with a parrot that had become a nuisance in a dormitory, even though its presence did not violate any existing rule. "I suggest," he told the owner of the offending bird, "that you dispose of your parrot before I am forced to classify it as a dog or a radio."

4-2 Co-ordination and subordination

Classification reveals or establishes two basic relationships between ideas: co-ordination and subordination. When the chemist lists under the heading *elements* aluminum, argon, arsenic, calcium, chromium, copper, oxygen, nitrogen, and zinc, he implies that all of these items are equal or parallel in some way and that they are also secondary in some way to the general concept, element. In other words, the individual elements are co-ordinate, but they are all subordinate to the general idea of elements.

30]

Co-ordination, then, is the process by which items are put into the same class, are shown to be equal or parallel or similar in some way, to possess certain common qualities (see also 21).

Subordination is the process by which items are relegated to a secondary or inferior position, are shown to be dependent on some larger concept or to be aspects of it (see also 22).

Items may, of course, be co-ordinated and subordinated in a variety of ways according to the user's purpose. The chemist, for instance, may be concerned with chromium, copper, and zinc not as elements but as metals. He may therefore think of them as subordinate to metals and co-ordinate not only with one another but with brass, which is not an element.

4-3 Classification and writing

All writing can be thought of as a process of classification, of co-ordination and subordination of materials. The writer reorganizes details, reorders them. He gains individuality in his work because he works his ideas over in his own mind and presents them with his own emphasis and interpretation. He reveals new relationships by showing that one idea is dependent on another, and one fact is parallel to another. Whether he is constructing a single sentence or a two-volume work, he is constantly occupied with co-ordination and subordination.

Consider, for example, the following sentence.

> Although the old man and his wife lived in filth and squalor in a tiny shack, the twenty-two sleek Holsteins relaxed in concrete splendor in a spacious, freshly painted barn.

The first clause, *Although . . . tiny shack,* is subordinate to the rest of the sentence; the sentence is mainly concerned with the living conditions of the cows, and it mentions the old man and his wife as a way of accenting the relative grandeur of the cows' quarters. The writer might have reversed the relationship.

> Although the twenty-two sleek Holsteins relaxed in concrete splendor in a spacious, freshly painted barn, the old man and his wife lived in filth and squalor in a tiny shack.

The contrast remains, but reversal of the subordination shifts the emphasis; the sentence is primarily about the plight of the old man and his wife. (For further discussion of co-ordination and subordination in the sentence see 21, 22.)

The plan of a longer unit of composition involves the same processes. Consider the following paragraph about the career of Henry Plantagenet, son of Henry II of England:

> His career had been wild and criminal. He had rebelled against his father again and again; again and again he had been forgiven. In a fit of remorse he had taken the cross, and intended to go to Jerusalem. He forgot Jerusalem in the next temptation. He joined himself to Lewis of France, broke once more into his last and worst revolt, and carried fire and sword into Normandy. He had hoped to bring the nobles to his side; he succeeded only in burning towns and churches, stripping shrines, and bringing general hatred on himself. Finding, we are told, that he could not injure his father as much as he had hoped to do, he chafed himself into a fever, and the fever killed him.
>
> —JAMES ANTHONY FROUDE, *Life and Times of Thomas Becket*

The writer subordinates a series of co-ordinate details to a general topic.

Still longer units are organized in the same way (see 3-2, 3-3, 5-5). The idea of the paragraph above is, in turn, made subordinate in the essay to a general view of the temper of twelfth-century England, which the writer says can be revealed by "characteristic incidents, particular things which men representative of their age indisputably did." The paragraph reveals a group of those "characteristic incidents." It is subordinate to the general purpose of the writer in describing the whole culture; it is, however, co-ordinate with a number of other descriptions of incidents serving the same purpose.

4 Classification   Class

GUIDE TO REVISION:

> *Revise, classifying, co-ordinating, and subordinating details according to a system suggested by the main idea or purpose of the theme.*

The writer who records material in the order in which it occurs to him usually reveals more about his own mental processes than about his subject. Facts and ideas must be classified so that the reader can see how they are related to one another.

4a Classifying material   **Class a**

Original

The income taxes of the United States should not be increased because there is no reason for them to be increased. If the government was not so extravagant, it would have enough money to cover all expenses. There would even be money to spare. The government does not have to build fertilizer plants and ice-skating rinks in Europe with American tax money. Of course, much of the money goes into military expenses, and people may say that we have to be ready to defend ourselves from possible aggression. But that is no reason for such wastes as sending sleeping bags to the troops in Alaska which would not protect in temperatures more than a little below freezing. If the representatives of our government want to put money in such investments, they should do so with their own finances, not with the people's money. Expense accounts of these representatives also show where some of the money is going. And some of the high salaries in the armed forces, paid to so-called experts who no longer have anything to do, might be saved. Just as some of the money being spent to keep government representatives living in luxury in Germany could be saved. I know of one instance of an army camp in this country also which was kept inactive for several years. Finally the government had it torn down. Then only about a year later it was entirely rebuilt, just about as it had been before. The money being spent for such things as pensions and unemployment insurance

Revision

The income taxes of the United States should not be increased. Instead, the government should curtail its expenditures and get along on its present income. Waste and extravagance should be eliminated.

Obviously we can cut our expenditures abroad. We have built fertilizer plants and ice-skating rinks in Europe with American tax money. We have built hospitals and other facilities, which ought to be the responsibility of the people benefiting from them. Furthermore, we are using American tax money to keep government representatives living in luxury in Germany.

Expenses in our own country are as bad. Expense accounts of our representatives in Washington show where some of our tax money is going. More of our money is being poured into payments for pensions and unemployment insurance. Many of the people receiving these payments are not deserving; they are just using the government because they are too lazy to work.

Much of the money, of course, goes into military expenses, and people may say that we have to be ready to defend ourselves from possible aggression. But we can do away with waste in the armed services. We could save some of the salaries paid by the armed forces to so-called experts who no longer have anything to do. There is no reason for such waste as sending sleeping bags to Alaska which would not protect in temperatures a little below freezing. I know of one army camp in this country which was kept

Original (Cont.)

in this country might also be decreased. And so might the money being spent abroad for such things, like rebuilding hospitals and other facilities which ought to be the responsibility of the people in those countries. Furthermore, many of the people receiving pensions and unemployment insurance are just using the government as a racket, just because they are too lazy to work. That is why I say if the government was not so extravagant the taxes would not have to be raised.

[*No amount of reorganizing could make this theme convincing. It needs more facts to develop it; it needs to be more specific (see 6, 7). Even the material that has been collected is not used effectively— mainly because it is not classified. The paper reads as if the writer had jotted thoughts down in the order in which they popped into his head.*]

Revision (Cont.)

inactive for several years. Finally the government had it torn down. Then only about a year later it was entirely rebuilt, just about as it had been before.

If even the extravagances outlined above could be eliminated, the government could operate without increasing taxes.

[*The material could be classified in more than one way, but the opening sentence of the original suggests a classification based upon three sorts of extravagances:*

1. *Extravagances in expenditures abroad.*

2. *Extravagances in domestic spending.*

3. *Extravagances in military expenditures.*

Reorganized on the basis of these classifications, the paper can be understood. It is still not convincing because the evidence is inadequate (see 10b).]

4b Cross-ranking   Class b

Items in each rank must be classified on a single basis. Otherwise classes overlap, and the material of the paper is confused rather than organized. Apples cannot be classified as green, yellow, red, small, winter; the bases for classifications differ—color, size, time of ripening—and the classes overlap. Small apples may be green, winter apples may be red, and yellow apples may be small.

Original

During the period 1932–1936, the government of the United States created a large number of temporary bureaus and agencies. In this paper I shall be concerned with the question of why some of the supposedly temporary agencies were accepted permanently. I shall con-

Revision

During the period 1932–1936, the government of the United States created a large number of temporary bureaus and agencies. In this paper I shall be concerned primarily with the question of why some agencies were accepted permanently whereas others were soon

Original (*Cont.*)

sider four groups of agencies: agricultural agencies, financial agencies, agencies established after 1936, and agencies that exist today . . .

[*The classification is unsatisfactory because classes have been established on different bases. The first two depend on matter the agencies dealt with; the third is based on time of establishment of the agency, and the fourth on permanence of the agency. The material needs to be reclassified on a consistent basis—probably a basis indicated by the central purpose of the paper.*]

Revision (*Cont.*)

abandoned. I shall consider the agencies in four groups: those abandoned after a short trial, those replaced by other agencies, those abandoned because their purpose was accomplished, and those still in existence.

[*The classification of the final sentence is changed to one which depends on a single principle—the permanence of the agencies. The basis for classification in the revision is the one suggested by the paragraph's statement of the purpose of the paper.*]

4c Subordinating material   **Class c; Sub**

The writer should not let minor matters occupy major attention in space or position. Subordinate matter should usually not appear at the end of a composition or at the end of a paragraph. If subordinate matter appears at the beginning as part of an introduction, the writer should make clear that the subordinate matter is subordinate. Within the body of a work the writer should keep minor subjects from running away with the composition, and should make clear in one way or another what he conceives to be important and what subordinate. For subordination within sentences, see 22.

Original

My grandmother gave me an electric lantern for Christmas. It was an expensive one, but Grandmother was spending her first Christmas with us for several years, and she wanted to give each of us children something nice. The result was metal-edged skis and bindings for my younger brother, Jim, what looked like a bucket of cologne for my sister, Jinny, and for me a lot of camping things, including the lantern. It is an amazing gadget. It has a big, long-

Revision

When I received an electric lantern as a Christmas present, I discovered that a revolution has taken place in what used to be known as "flashlights." I recall that the old advertisements used to read, "The light that says, 'There it is.'" That is, a flashlight used to be an emergency implement, but the new electric lantern is a source of light adaptable to almost any need. Mine has a big, long-burning battery, and two lamps and two lenses, one to diffuse light in the

[35

Original (Cont.)

burning battery, and two lamps and two lenses, one to light the adjacent area, one to send forth a beam that looks like the headlight of a train. Likewise, it has two handles, one a bail, one a hand grip. It will sit on a table, hang on a wall, and do either in several different positions. When I found out how that lantern would work, I remembered that the old advertisements used to read, "The light that says, 'There it is.'" That is, the old flashlight was an emergency implement. The new electric lantern is adaptable to almost any need.

[*If the subject is the new type of electric lantern, acquiring the lantern should be subordinated to the lantern itself.*]

Michigan Avenue in Chicago has changed in a half century from heavy, stodgy elegance to light but impressive strength. Old pictures of the avenue show dumpy though durable buildings, fronted with massive stone, looking down on a line of elegant carriages. Today the buildings are taller and airier. Glass, brick, terra cotta, and modern composition surfaces have replaced the cumbersome stone, and the buildings themselves soar with long clean lines high into the air. The pavement below is wider, and whizzing with traffic. The trees are gone, too. But then, the trees a half century ago were not very big anyhow. The lamp posts were also shorter.

[*The most effective portion of any paragraph, the close, is here*

36]

Revision (Cont.)

adjacent area, one to send forth a beam that looks like the headlight of a locomotive. Furthermore, it has two handles, one a bail, one a hand grip. It will sit on a table, hang on a wall, turn upside down on its own axis, and send almost any kind of light you want in almost any direction.

[*The revision saves everything that concerns the lantern, but subordinates the Christmas festivities, keeping only enough to explain how the writer became suddenly aware of what has happened to electric lanterns.*]

Michigan Avenue in Chicago has changed in a half century from heavy, stodgy elegance to light but impressive strength. Old pictures of the avenue show dumpy though durable buildings, fronted with massive stone, looking down on elegant carriages, rows of spindling trees, and squat, ornate lamp posts. Today the buildings are taller and airier. Glass, brick, terra cotta, and modern composition surfaces have replaced the cumbersome stone, and the buildings themselves soar with long, clean lines high into the air. The pavement below is wider, smoother, studded with stop lights, and whizzing with traffic. Chicago has become a modern city.

[*The unimportant details have been sorted back into the paragraph where they belong, and a*

Original (*Cont.*)	*Revision* (*Cont.*)
inappropriately used for minor and not very significant details.]	*new close points up the significance of the previous development. Subordinate details have been given a subordinate position.*]

EXERCISE 4

A. Make two separate classifications for the items in each of the following groups, classifying each time on a different basis (Be sure to classify on only one basis at a time):

1. canned peas, frozen pears, canned peaches, a can of wax, a dozen clothes pins, 10 pounds of potatoes, a dozen oranges, frozen peaches, a can of kitchen cleanser.

2. baseball, tennis, swimming, basketball, diving, skiing.

3. advanced economics, freshman chemistry, beginning history, physics seminar, beginning German, first-year Italian, freshman biology, senior French.

B. Indicate one item in each of the following classifications which is inconsistent because it has not been classified on the same basis as the other items:

1. Books *into* novels, collections of poems, collections of short stories, leather-bound books, collections of plays, histories, textbooks.

2. Shoes *into* leather shoes, canvas shoes, horse shoes.

3. Dresses *into* evening dresses, afternoon dresses, sports dresses, cotton dresses, dinner dresses.

4. Criminals *into* burglars, murderers, incorrigibles, arsonists, embezzlers.

5. Literature *into* novels, poetry, drama, pastorals, short fiction.

C. Rewrite the following passage, improving it by changing the subordination and co-ordination. Try to decide which are the main statements to be co-ordinated, which are subordinate to them, and which subordinate in a secondary degree. First, of course, you will need to decide upon a basis of classification.

Calvin Coolidge did have a sense of humor, a salty Vermont wit. Very few people liked it much. George Washington was a great general and a great president. He had dignity, but apparently not much sense of humor. William Howard Taft is said to have been a very genial man in private, but he was also a very heavy man, and thus in public life he was more frequently the butt of humor than the creator of it. Most of our presidents, if they do not illustrate the assertion, "The people expect their statesmen to be solemn asses," give us little reason to suppose that a sense of humor is a political asset.

Woodrow Wilson had a sense of humor, which he used in his scholarly writing and in the privacy of his home. John Adams and John Quincy Adams were men of subtle mind, but they seem not to have enjoyed laughing. Adlai Stevenson, who convulsed his audiences when he was campaigning against the then General Eisenhower, was defeated, whether because of his humor or in spite of it. Of the early presidents, only Thomas Jefferson seems to have enjoyed a joke, a very quiet joke well screened from public view. Theodore Roosevelt was perhaps not subtle enough to have much humor; as Professor T. V. Smith has said, "He exclaimed 'bully' from the larynx more often than he laughed from the belly." Franklin Roosevelt used his humor sparingly and for calculated effects. When Peter Cartwright, a frontier evangelist, was campaigning against Lincoln for Congress, he accused Lincoln of not knowing where he wanted to go because he would stand neither with those who were certain they would go to heaven nor with those who expected to go to hell. "I aim, of course, to go to Congress," Lincoln drawled. Presidents like Zachary Taylor and Andrew Jackson were blunt, almost humorless men. Even Madison and Monroe were notably solemn. Abraham Lincoln, whose sense of humor became legend, offers the only notable exception to the general rule that our presidents have not been characterized by their sense of humor. Some presidents seem to have had some sense of humor, but hesitated to use it in politics, or in any connection suggestive of state affairs. Harding probably lacked the liveliness of mind either to engender or to appreciate much humor.

D. Examine an article in a good magazine approved by your instructor or a selection from your book of models which he designates. Determine the author's main idea, and from it the basis on which he has classified his material. Then notice which paragraphs are co-ordinate with each other and which are subordinate to some other paragraph. Some paragraphs will be co-ordinate with certain paragraphs but subordinate to others. Write a report of your findings.

5. ORGANIZATION; THE OUTLINE

[For Guide to Revision, see page 47]

Organization, planned in the outline, reveals the relationships among ideas, the essentials of the composition.

The arrangement of material defines relationships. The positions of paragraphs, sentences, and words convey meaning. In the sentence, order is the basic device for indicating grammatical relationships. In larger units of composition, material can be ordered, after analysis and classification, on the basis of a main idea, to reveal relationships which can be classified generally as chronological, spatial, and logical.

5-1 Chronological organization

In the following sentences, order shows a chronological relationship:

> A yellow convertible flashed by the billboard and screamed around the curve. A traffic policeman wheeled his motorcycle from its hiding place and roared into the highway.

Because one sentence precedes the other, the reader assumes that the event it describes precedes the other event. Reversing the order of the sentences would reverse the order of events and save a fine for the driver of the convertible.

Any record of happenings can almost always be planned around related times—often by the simple procedure of putting first things first. The following description of Mary Stuart's preparation for execution is organized in this way:

> She laid her crucifix on her chair. The chief executioner took it as a perquisite, but was ordered instantly to lay it down. The lawn veil was lifted carefully off, not to disturb the hair, and was hung upon the rail. The black robe was next removed. Below it was a

petticoat of crimson velvet. The black jacket followed, and under the jacket was a bodice of crimson satin. One of her ladies handed her a pair of crimson sleeves, with which she hastily covered her arms; and thus she stood on the black scaffold with the black figures all around her, blood-red from head to foot.

        —JAMES ANTHONY FROUDE, *History of England*

5-2 Spatial organization

Order can show relationship in space as well as in time. To help the reader picture relative positions, the writer reflects spatial arrangement by the arrangement of his sentences. For example, a writer describing a scene can arrange details in the order in which they meet his eye.

> The ship turned sharply and steamed slowly in. It was a great landlocked harbour big enough to hold a fleet of battleships; and all around it rose, high and steep, the green hills. Near the entrance, getting such breeze as blew from the sea, stood the governor's house in a garden. The Stars and Stripes dangled languidly from a flag staff.
>   —SOMERSET MAUGHAM, *Rain*

Consider a passage describing a London churchyard.

> As I stand peeping in through the iron gates and rails, I can peel the rusty metal off, like bark from an old tree. The illegible tombstones are all lop-sided, the grave-mounds lost their shape in the rains of a hundred years ago, the Lombardy Poplar or Plane-Tree that was once a drysalter's daughter and several common-councilmen, has withered like those worthies, and its departed leaves are dust beneath it.
>   —CHARLES DICKENS, *The Uncommercial Traveller*

Dickens continues the passage, enumerating other details of the scene as they are observed from the position established in the opening sentence.

5-3 Logical organization

Order also reveals or enforces various kinds of relationships which might generally be called "logical." For example, we suggest that details belong to the same class just by mentioning them at the same time. Or we reveal a relationship like causation by order. Consider the following two sentences:

> The army was soon in a state of complete disorganization. The central command found itself unable to issue a single sensible order.

This suggests that the confusion of the army caused the confusion of its commanders. Reverse the order of the sentences.

> The central command found itself unable to issue a single sensible order. The army was soon in a state of complete disorganization.

The responsibility shifts.

The paragraph below relies upon a more complex pattern of logical relationships.

> (1) Nor can one easily discover any extraordinary personal accidents without which the Duce might have lived and died a blacksmith's boy in Forli. (2) It is quite possible, as Bertrand Russell has pointed out, that the revolution in Russia might never have occurred had not a German general permitted Lenin to travel across Germany in a sealed train. (3) It is quite probable that Soviet Russia would have never had a Five-Year-Plan had not Trotsky succumbed to a fit of pique and refused to attend Lenin's funeral. (4) The Dollfuss dictatorship in Austria was, as we shall see, made possible because a socialist deputy went to the bathroom during a crucial parliamentary vote. (5) Such personal accidents, which play a large part in history, are not prominent in Mussolini's life. (6) He made his own luck. (7) His career has been a growth, steady and luxuriant, like that of some monstrous weed.
>
> —JOHN GUNTHER, *Inside Europe*

It opens with a general statement (1), proceeds with specific illustrations of one aspect of the general statement (2), (3), and (4), describes the relationship of the illustrations to the general statement (5), and then concludes by restating and expanding the opening statement (6) and (7).

5-4 The outline

For the word, for the paragraph, for the whole composition, various devices are available which can be used to show classifications and relationships. For the whole composition, the most useful tool for these purposes is the outline. With it, the writer can organize his material, co-ordinating it, subordinating it, arranging it. With the outline he can also test the results of his organization.

Student writers often resist the suggestion that they should write from an outline. An outline, they insist, is too limiting; it "stifles inspiration." Usually such students either have the wrong notion of what an outline should be or have found that outlining requires clear thinking, and they do not want to think. Actually, an outline provides the easiest method of doing preliminary thinking well, and good writing requires clear thinking. An outline is a means of saving time—provided the writer is trying to write well.

All writing not formless and unconvincing requires some plan, even in its smallest units, and the outline is essentially a memorandum of that plan. For a single paragraph or a short theme, one may keep his plan in mind without a written record, and an experienced writer knows basic patterns so well that he can compose still larger units without a written outline. A skilled carpenter can put together a set of bookshelves without a blueprint. But a contractor is not likely to start construction on a house without a set of carefully worked-out plans. A writer working seriously will not proceed without an outline.

The outline is a means to an end, not an end in itself. It is practical. It should therefore have the most useful form the writer can devise. For a paragraph or two or for an answer to an essay question on an examination, a few scribbled headings may be sufficient. For longer compositions, however, the writer should follow the procedures described below because they will produce the kind of outline which will help most in writing.

5-5 Classification, co-ordination, and subordination in the outline

A statement of the main idea (see 2-1) is the first stage in the construction of an outline. It provides the basis for classification, and guides the co-ordinating and subordinating of details. It should constitute a complete sentence. The writer thinking through a possible theme on "Women at State University" tentatively decides that he wants to show that "At State University women do not have rights and privileges equal to those of the men." He begins his outline with this statement.

He then jots down ideas; let us assume that he produces something like the following:

1. Rules requiring women to live in dormitories
2. Rules regulating hours women must come in at night
3. The paragraph in the University Catalogue concerning equal rights for all students
4. Women in student-body offices
5. Men's lounge in Union Building, but no women's lounge

6. As many girls on campus as men
7. Women not willing to assert their rights
8. Rules requiring women to eat in dining hall
9. Swimming pool privileges
10. Rules on leaving campus
11. Intercollegiate athletics
12. College women just as responsible as college men
13. More married students
14. The time Anne Wilkins was expelled but the boy who was equally guilty was not
15. Girls not interested in student government
16. Gymnasium and athletic facilities
17. Modern women taking equal responsibilities in the world
18. Military service of women

The list is a beginning, a record of random thoughts about a subject; it is not a record of organized thinking. To organize his material, the writer needs to analyze his subject and classify his details.

He may do so in a more or less systematic way. He may ask himself: What are the principal parts or aspects of the life of women on the campus, and which of these do I wish to consider? That is, he may start by analyzing his subject and stating a main idea which can be used as the basis of classification. Or, he can start by examining his jottings to see whether he can observe any general groups and classifying material under general headings. He can check his findings later by asking himself whether the headings he gets do or do not constitute an adequate analysis. As a matter of practice, of course, most writers use analysis and classification pretty much unconsciously as twin means of restricting a subject, ordering it, and developing it.

The student may now appropriately look over his jottings. If he is to write on discriminations against women at State University, some material is obviously inappropriate and can be thrown out, items 4 and 13, for instance. On the other hand, items 1 and 2 begin a list of discriminatory rules. Items 5 and 9 suggest a class of inequalities in university facilities. Items 3 and 6 might suggest a class of reasons why there should be equality. Item 7 might suggest a class which would require new material, reasons for inequalities. Some items would seem inappropriate to the main idea and should therefore be stricken out. The list, then, could be rearranged and expanded by classification somewhat as follows:

[43

Rules that discriminate against women

  1. Rules requiring women to live in dormitories
  2. Rules regulating hours women must come in at night
  8. Rules requiring women to eat in dining hall
10. Rules on leaving campus
14. Expulsion of Anne Wilkins (Might fit here as example of use of rules)
     Rules for sororities stricter than those for fraternities (The writer thinks of a new point as he is making the classification.)

Inequalities in university facilities

  5. Men's lounge in Union Building
  9. Swimming pool privileges
11. Intercollegiate athletics
16. Gymnasium and athletic facilities

Reasons why there should be equality

  3. The statement of the University Catalogue
  6. As many girls on campus as men
12. College women just as responsible as college men
17. Modern women taking equal responsibilities in the world
18. Military service of women

Causes for inequalities

  7. Women not willing to assert their rights
15. Girls not interested in student government
     Tradition in colleges and world
     Prevalence of men in administration and on faculties
     Old prejudices against educating women
     (The writer adds new items.)

Such classification is the beginning of an outline, but the writer must still give the outline form by considering the classes in terms of the main idea and in terms of the proposed length of his paper. Strictly speaking, only the first two of the classes listed above apply to the proposed subject. Reasons for equality and causes of inequalities could be incorporated, but they would expand the paper beyond manageable length. The writer therefore limits his main headings to:

    I. Rules that discriminate against women
    II. Inequalities in University facilities

He then subordinates details to these main headings, thinks of further details to support his ideas, and chooses an order for his topics.

The writer should never hesitate to add to his outline any kind of note that may help him later. Often as he works he has useful ideas for a transition, for a striking introduction, for an incident for illustration, for an apt phrase. He can jot them down on his outline so that he will not forget to use them in the appropriate places.

5-6 Indicating subordination

The degrees of subordination are conventionally indicated in an outline by indenting and by labeling subdivisions alternately with numbers and letters. The standard form is shown below.

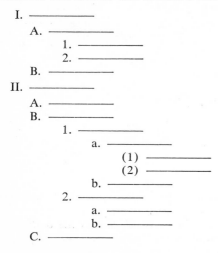

5-7 The complete outline

The final outline, then, includes a statement of the main idea, a note on the introduction and conclusion, and a summary of the main topics to be discussed in the body of the paper, with relationships between them indicated by numbers and indentation. The following outline might be developed from the materials collected above for a paper on "Women in State University."

Outline

STATEMENT OF MAIN IDEA: At State University, women do not have rights and privileges equal to those of the men.

INTRODUCTION: Use the statement in the University Catalogue that all students have equal rights and privileges and point out that the paper will show the statement to be false.

[A detail that the writer recalled when first thinking about the topic seems to provide a possible introduction. The writer gives himself a reminder.]

I. Rules that discriminate against women
  A. Dormitory rules (begin paragraph with story of expulsion of Anne Wilkins)

[Again the writer sees a place to use a detail and makes a note.]

[The writer sees need for classification more detailed than in preliminary organization.]

    1. Rules requiring women to live in dormitories
    2. Rules on hours
    3. Registration and signout system
    4. Rules forbidding leaving dormitory and campus
  B. Sorority rules—regulations stricter than those for fraternities

[The expansion of point B is not illogically made a single subdivision.]

  C. Rules requiring women to eat in dining hall
    1. Expense of dining hall
    2. Quality of food
II. Inequalities in University facilities. (Possible transition pointing out that above rules can be justified on ground that they are for students' "own good" but that other inequalities cannot.)

[A lengthy note for future use records an idea that occurs to the writer as he makes the outline.]

  A. Social facilities
    1. Lack of meeting places for women's organizations

[Co-ordination of topics is indicated by parallel form.]

    2. Lack of a room comparable to the Men's lounge in the Union Building
  B. Athletic facilities
    1. Lack of women's activity comparable to men's intercollegiate athletic program

2. Lack of equal swim-
ming-pool privileges
3. Restriction on women's
use of gymnasium

CONCLUSION: Use idea that there
are as many women on the campus
as men, that they will have equal
responsibilities in the world, and
that they should have equal rights
and privileges in college.

[*A possible conclusion is suggested by another of the groups
of details rejected in preparing the
body of the outline.*]

5-8 Using the outline

The outline is a working guide (see 15-1). It should be used but
should not be followed slavishly. Obviously a writer cannot visualize
a paper perfectly. He will change his mind as he works out paragraphs and sentences, and he will think of new material. He should
use his outline as a preliminary sketch, constantly subject to revision
and expansion as the writing proceeds.

5 Organization; the outline   Org

GUIDE TO REVISION:

*Rewrite to improve organization. Usually revision of
the outline is a first step.*

Faulty organization almost always results from a combination of
difficulties, including faulty classification (see 4), lack of proper subordination (see 4-2, 4-3), inadequate development (see II), and
lack of a main idea (see 2). Usually the writer should go back to the
outline stage and reorganize and rewrite the entire paper.

5a Clear planning   Org a

Every piece of writing should have a clear, orderly plan.

Original

A word not only indicates an
object but can also suggest an
emotional meaning. The essence of
poetry depends upon words that
arouse the emotions of the reader.

Revision

A word not only "means"; it conveys emotion. If we refer to a dog
as a *mongrel,* we objectively define
his pedigree, but we also reveal an
attitude toward the dog.

[47

Original (*Cont.*)

An experiment may be conducted to prove how much words mean in poetry. Replace the emotionally filled words with neutral ones, and all the poetic value will be knocked out of the poem by the change. Politicians are apt at changing the public's opinion merely by the use of words. "Bolshevik," "Fascist," "reactionary," "revolutionary" are examples of emotional words used by politicians. Emotional words find their place in poetry but are out of place in modern science where exact thinking is required. The scientist wants only the facts. He does not want to be swayed by words, only facts. This type of straight scientific thinking results in new discoveries. Science has worked hard ridding their books and discussions of emotional words; politics should do the same. The use of emotional words makes it hard for us to think straight in national and social problems. If clear unemotional words were used by people in the government, it would benefit our civilization. People would then be able to form their opinions by facts, not words.

Emotion-filled words are used not only by politicians but also by critics. By the use of words a critic can sway the public opinion against a writer, simply because he does not like the work.

We need to be careful not to form opinions on emotionally filled words.

[*The student theme printed above contains many inaccuracies in writing; as a review exercise, the student might profitably see how many errors he can find in it.*

Revision (*Cont.*)

The emotional meanings of words are useful, especially if the writer's purpose is to sway opinion. Poetry, for example, depends on words that arouse the emotions of the reader, as anyone may demonstrate if he will replace the emotion-filled words of a poem with neutral ones; all the poetic value will be knocked out of the poem by the change.

Emotional words have their place in poetry, but they are misleading when we are concerned with facts and not with attitudes. The scientist, for example, wants facts; he does not want to be swayed by words. He has worked to rid his books and discussion of emotional words, and by straight scientific thinking has made important discoveries. Politicians have not done the same. They are apt at changing the public's opinion merely by the use of such emotional words as *Bolshevik, Fascist, reactionary,* or *revolutionary.* They prevent straight thinking about national and social problems. If people in the government would use clear, unemotional words, we could form opinions on facts, not words, and society would benefit.

Emotional words can present a danger as well as an advantage, and we need to be careful not to form opinions on emotion-filled words.

[*The theme is still undeveloped, in spite of the addition of an illustration or two. But it does come nearer than the original to showing how ideas are related. The revision involved first of all a new outline:*

Original (Cont.)

Worse, the paper lacks any clear plan. An attempt to outline the theme reveals its weakness, for a meaningful outline proves to be almost impossible. An attempt might look like this:

INTRODUCTION: *Words have emotional as well as denotative meaning.*

    I. Importance of emotional words to poetry
    II. Use of emotional words by politicians
    III. Avoidance of emotional words by scientists
    IV. Dangers of emotional words in politics
    V. Use of emotional words by critics

CONCLUSION: *We need to be careful in using emotion-filled words.*

Topic II is out of order. The outline reveals the lack of classification of material and the failure to subordinate minor to major topics. The writer needs to make a new outline and rewrite the entire theme.]

Revision (Cont.)

STATEMENT OF MAIN IDEA: *Emotion-filled words are a handicap to scientific thinking.*

INTRODUCTION: *Words not only "mean"; they convey emotions.*

    I. Usefulness of emotional words
      A. Usefulness in swaying opinions
      B. Usefulness in poetry
    II. Dangers of emotional words
      A. Danger in science
      B. Danger in politics

CONCLUSION: *We should avoid emotion-filled words to form opinions.*

The new outline classifies topics under two main headings and organizes the paper around a central idea. It changes the illogical order revealed by the original outline. The writing follows the outline, corrects the obvious errors in accuracy, revises many of the sentences, and leaves out the undeveloped and nonessential example of the critic.]

5b Proportion   Org b

Inadequate planning leads to badly proportioned compositions. The writer who puts words on paper without a good outline may find that he has used half his space without reaching the center of his topic. He may become so much interested in a single example that he has no space for other topics. A writer must apportion his space so that secondary matters do not steal space needed for main ideas. The following outline of a 2,000-word investigative paper reveals the difficulty:

Original

MARIJUANA AND JUVENILE
DELINQUENCY

STATEMENT OF MAIN IDEA: Marijuana is not an important cause of juvenile delinquency in our society.

  I. The history of marijuana
      A. American Indians
      B. Europe
      C. The United States
 II. Methods of growth and preparation of marijuana
      A. Growth of the hemp plant
          1. Ease of cultivation
          2. Extent of cultivation
      B. Extraction of the drug
      C. Commercial uses of the plant
III. Use and effects of marijuana
      A. Methods of taking drug
      B. Characteristic behavior of users
      C. Question of habit formation
 IV. Use of drugs by juveniles
      A. Methods of distribution of marijuana
      B. Control of distribution
      C. Marijuana and music
      D. Studies of extent and use
          1. Government statistics
          2. Recent studies of New York schools

CONCLUSION: Marijuana is not one of the major causes of juvenile delinquency in the United States today.

[*The outline suggests that the paper will be mainly a superficial discussion of questions not pertinent to the main idea, and when the writer comes to the final section he will have used most of his space.*

50]

Revision

MARIJUANA AND JUVENILE
DELINQUENCY

STATEMENT OF MAIN IDEA: Marijuana is not an important cause of juvenile delinquency in our society.

INTRODUCTION: Current concern about use of marijuana by juveniles and widespread opinion that it is a major cause of juvenile delinquency

  I. Use of drugs by juveniles
      A. Methods of distribution of marijuana
          1. Distribution by amateurs
          2. Professional dope rings
      B. Marijuana and music
      C. Control of distribution
          1. Control by schools and welfare groups
          2. Law enforcement
      D. Cost of drugs to juveniles
      E. Studies of extent of use
          1. Government statistics
          2. Recent studies of New York schools
 II. Effects of marijuana on juveniles
      A. Characteristic behavior of users of drug
          1. Actions while under influence of drug
          2. Aftereffects
      B. Habit formation

CONCLUSION: Marijuana is not one of the major causes of juvenile delinquency in the United States today.

[*The revised outline needs further development, but at least it improves proportions, omitting the first two sections of the original*

Original (*Cont.*)

Sections I, II, and III are out of proportion. Part IV is the central part of the paper, and the remainder should be omitted or reduced.]

Revision (*Cont.*)

and suggesting development of the sections pertinent to the main idea.]

5c Specific topics in outline   Org c

An outline is useless unless it includes topics specific enough to help in the actual writing. An outline which is merely a statement of vague intentions only postpones the problem of thinking of specific materials; it indicates that the writer has not planned.

Original

GETTING A DEER

I. Planning the hunt
   A. Reasons
   B. Methods
II. Finding the deer
   A. Methods
   B. Incidents
III. The kill
   A. Incidents
   B. Results

[*The writer has done almost nothing to plan his paper beyond deciding on what is apparently a chronological arrangement in three main stages. There is no main idea. And none of the material has been classified or arranged. One suspects that the writer has just not thought much about what the "methods" and "incidents" are.*]

Revision

GETTING A DEER

STATEMENT OF MAIN IDEA: A deer hunt does not always turn out as planned.

I. Planning the hunt scientifically
   A. Consulting maps and marking our route
   B. Studying migrations of the deer
   C. Investigating weather conditions
II. Hunting the deer
   A. Following our plans
      1. The loss of the maps
      2. Losing the trail
      3. The unexpected storm
   B. Giving up the hunt and trying to find the way to the car
III. The kill
   A. Appearance of the deer
   B. Our surprise and inability to get our guns ready
   C. A lucky shot
   D. Our discovery that we are only 200 yards from the road

[*The revision more nearly prepares the writer to start the paper; it suggests more specifically what the "reasons" and "methods" are to be.*]

5d Subdivisions which analyze   Org d

The subdivisions of each part of an outline should make up an analysis of the heading above them. That is, A, B, and C should, taken together, represent a complete breakdown of I; 1, 2, 3, and 4 should represent a complete breakdown of A, and so on.

Original

B. Problems peculiar to portraiture
   1. Problems peculiar to men
   2. Problems peculiar to children
   3. Problems of indoor lighting
[*This is not a logical subdivision (see 4b). Women are omitted, and indoor lighting is not parallel with human beings. If the writer wishes to treat lighting with portraiture, his outline should look something like the following:*
B. *Problems crucial in portraiture*
   1. *Problems involving sitters*
      a. Men
      b. Women
      c. Children
   2. *Problems involving lighting.*]

Revision

B. Problems peculiar to portraiture
   1. Problems peculiar to men
   2. Problems peculiar to women
   3. Problems peculiar to children
[*All three types of sitters have been provided for and made co-ordinate, and the illogical entry involving lighting has been relocated elsewhere in the outline or dropped.*]

5e Single subdivisions   Org e

Since the outline records logical subordination and co-ordination, it should not include single subdivisions. There should be no *I* without a *II,* no *A* without a parallel *B,* and so on. The presence of a single subdivision is a symptom of faulty planning; the topic of the single subdivision should be incorporated in the heading above it, relocated, or balanced with a parallel subdivision.

Original

I. Misleading television commercials
   A. Singing commercials
      1. The soap singers
   B. Commercials making false claims
      1. Cigarette advertisements
      2. Advertisements for patent medicines
II. Long commercials

Revision

A. Singing commercials—the soap singers
[*In this first revision the single topic is included as part of A, as an illustration, not a division.*]

A. Singing commercials
   1. The soap singers
   2. The beer songs

52]

Original (Cont.)

[*The single topic under A should be relocated or supplemented. Division into one is impossible.*]

Revision (Cont.)

[*In the second revision another illustration is introduced to develop the topic more fully.*]

5f Parallel topics   **Org f**

Co-ordinate items, those of the same rank or class, have the same kind of letter or number preceding them. Co-ordination should be further indicated by giving the items parallel form. The parallel form helps the writer to avoid showing false relationships in his final composition.

Original

I. Selecting a camp site
  A. Finding water
  B. The ground should be flat
  C. Insects a danger
  D. Are there rules against camping?

[*The inconsistencies in form suggest that the writer is not quite aware that the topics are parallel.*]

Revision

I. Selecting a camp site
  A. Finding water
  B. Choosing flat ground
  C. Finding a place free from insects
  D. Observing camping restrictions.

[*The parallel form aids rather than misleads the writer.*]

EXERCISE 5

A. Comment on the weaknesses of the following outlines:

    TOPIC: Satire in Moving Picture Cartoons
    STATEMENT OF MAIN IDEA: The satire in cartoons which appear today on the moving picture screen.

   I. Introduction
     A. Increasing tendency toward satire in the cartoons
  II. Caricatures of human beings
     A. Caricatures of types
       1. The man who loses his temper
         a. Donald Duck
       2. The pedant
         a. Examples
       3. Sentimental lovers
         a. Examples
     B. Particular individuals may appear in cartoons
  III. Satire on situations in life
     A. Domestic life
     B. National affairs

[53

IV. Conclusion
    A. General quality of satire
    B. Conforms to attitudes already present in most people

TOPIC: Success in the American University

STATEMENT OF MAIN IDEA: To write about success at the university.

  I. Introduction
    A. The purpose of a university
      1. Details of the purpose
      2. Further details
    B. The organization of a university
      1. Schools and colleges
      2. The campus
      3. The administration
      4. Registrar's office, comptroller, etc.
      5. Fraternities and sororities
    C. Types of students in a university
      1. Men
      2. Women
      3. Foreign students
      4. Negro students
      5. "Barbs"
      6. Alumni organizations
 II. Methods of attaining success in a university
    A. Attaining social success
      1. Fraternities and sororities
      2. Dances
      3. Games and athletic events
      4. Snack bars, soda fountains, etc.
        1. Make new friends, get dates, etc.
      5. The library
      6. Contacts which will be valuable in afterlife
    B. Athletic successes
      1. Major sports
      2. Minor sports
      3. Passing your courses
        1. Choosing courses you can pass
          a. Advice about choosing courses
III. Conclusion
    A. Success in college and social activity

B. Below are preliminary notes for a theme on *Education for Women Today*. They are not complete and are not necessarily pertinent or sufficiently specific. Using the list as a start, select a main idea for a possible theme and then construct an outline for it, using the notes which are pertinent. You will probably need to eliminate some notes, revise others, and add new ones to fit your main purpose.

1. Beauty shop apprenticeship
2. Teacher-training courses
3. Liberal arts training
4. Special course for social workers
5. Nurses' training
6. Laboratory technology for women
7. Preparation for life
8. Home economics
9. Courses in preparation for marriage
10. General culture
11. Business courses
12. The importance of English composition for the secretary
13. Number of women in college last year
14. Adult education
15. Music and dancing schools
16. Business colleges
17. The old-fashioned finishing school
18. Women in industry

C. Below are numbered sentences which might be arranged into a short essay describing the group of sea animals which includes squids and octopuses. Make an outline which arranges the sentences in the order they might have in a theme. Do not copy the statements; refer to them by number.

1. Among the animal's most interesting characteristics is its system of jet propulsion.
2. With this jet engine the cephalopod attains extraordinary speed.
3. They are octopuses, cuttlefish, and squids, and they are remarkable organisms in a variety of ways.
4. Among the thousands of creatures that inhabit the oceans of the world none is more interesting than those known as *Cephalopoda* or "head-footed ones."
5. The cephalopod can protect itself not only with its speed and remarkable strength for its size; it also has two physical properties with which it can become almost invisible.
6. Some of the tiny, slim varieties streak through the water as fast as flies move through the air.
7. They can leap from the water and dart by so fast that the eye cannot follow them.
8. Cephalopods may not live up to all the fantastic yarns about them told by ancient mariners, but they are certainly among the most interesting of the animals of the sea.

9. First, it has developed the technique of the smoke screen long before modern navies.

10. The cephalopod is encased in a long, slim cloak, with a muscular collar that rings its neck and a funnel that sticks up in front.

11. Larger varieties, it is estimated, move over the surface of the ocean faster than the fastest speedboat.

12. The cephalopods have little ink sacs which manufacture and store ink, and they can squirt sepia cloud screens to shield them from their enemies.

13. It can then close the collar and squeeze its body suddenly and violently.

14. Swimming on its belly, the octopus or squid can pump water into its body cavity through the space between this collar and its neck.

15. They also can hide themselves because of their chameleon-like ability to change colors.

16. The water shoots out the funnel, propelling the animal backward.

17. The propulsion system of the squid or octopus is no more remarkable than its special devices for defense.

18. They can turn purple when annoyed, or on white sand they can pale to near invisibility.

D. Use the following as a main idea: "The story of the letter *A* reflects the history of the alphabet." Construct a suitable outline by classifying, co-ordinating, and subordinating. Reject any material not pertinent, and note any main divisions which need to be further divided or developed, and any details which have no general heading.

Changes in Latin
Sounds of the various letters
Early known forms of *A*
Introduction—story of how I learned letter *A*
Changes during the Middle Ages leading to modern upper-case *A*
Lost Greek forms of *A*
Greek reversal of the letter
Development of North Semite *A* into Phoenician *A*
The North Semites and the earliest known form of *A*
Modern upper-case *A* from the medieval book hand
Difference between *a* and *an*
Contributions of medieval Irish scribes to modern upper case *A*
Changes in Greek
Interesting details about *U* and *V*
Medieval and modern forms of the letter
Influence of Greek "boustrophedon" writing on *A*
Symbol for Egyptian sacred bull as possible ancestor of *A*
Contributions of medieval French scribes to modern upper-case *A*

Hypothetical origins of *A*
Modern upper-case *A* from medieval court hand
Developments in classical times
Babylonian aleph as possible ancestor of *A*
Pre-classical history of *A*

II. Developing and Controlling an Idea

Men are but children of larger growth.—JOHN DRYDEN

Students often excuse the infrequency of their letters home by protesting that they have nothing to say. Then they prove their point by going on in this fashion:

> Most of my courses are very good, but some are better than others. The house is old but very pleasant. It is enjoyable, especially because of the many good friends I have made. Studying is encouraged at the house, and the study table every night is valuable for me. Everything is fine, although I am not sure my allowance will be enough for the rest of the month.

Even a mother might yawn over this. The writer has introduced topics and stated opinions, but he has said little about them. He has not developed his ideas. He has indicated only that he has plenty to say if he would take the trouble to think it out.

To develop an idea, the writer thinks about his subject, raises questions a reader may want answered, and answers them. He searches in his experience or in the library to substantiate or illustrate his main idea. To make a letter from the generalities above, the writer could ask himself why some courses are better than others; he might recall details describing the house, characterize his new friends, or tell how the "study table" operates. He might even gain practically by thinking of reasons for the inadequacy of the allowance. Development of a topic begins with disciplined thinking.

In other words, the writer looks into his mind or into the library to get facts, details, illustrations, examples which will develop his ideas. The process resembles selecting facts from a file drawer, with the writer's statement of his main idea and his outline helping him to know which headings to look under. If he selects materials according to a plan, his writing will make sense; if not—if he merely dumps out the file drawer and takes a handful of scattered material— he is likely to reveal little but the confusion in his mind. The writer must learn both to develop an idea and to control its development.

We have already observed some of the techniques for developing and controlling an idea. Analysis and classification, for example, are useful not only in planning a work but also in developing it. The writer, however, must also know the uses of facts and of judgments, must know the relative merits of general and specific statements, must know how to illustrate, how to provide adequate, relevant evidence, how to control his ideas logically. This section of the book discusses techniques for managing a composition after it has passed the stage of initial planning.

6. USING FACTS

[For Guide to Revision, see page 63]

Unsubstantiated judgments do not develop an idea;
judgments convince only when supported by facts.

We have all heard the kind of fruitless conversation which is a string of vociferously maintained opinions:

> "Joe Louis was never any good. Tunney was better."
> "You're crazy. He was the best champion we ever had."
> "Oh, no, he wasn't. Dempsey could have knocked him out any day in the week."
> "Oh, no, he couldn't. Dempsey was a bum."

This kind of dialogue, obviously ineffective as communication, is charactertistic of small boys and cannot lead to much except a fist fight. But a great many student papers fail primarily because the writer relies almost exclusively on judgments like those in the dialogue, rather than on facts.

6-1 Distinguishing fact and judgment

A writer must learn to distinguish clearly between facts and judgments.

Compare the following sets of statements:

JUDGMENT: Martha is a bad girl.
FACT: Martha took two pieces of candy without asking.

JUDGMENT: Snidhart is a murderer.
FACT: Two witnesses saw Snidhart shoot twice at the cashier who died in the hospital this morning.

JUDGMENT: Smith's dog kills sheep.
FACT: I saw Smith's dog kill a sheep.

JUDGMENT: College football is on the way out.
FACT: In many major universities football costs are increasing more rapidly than gate receipts.

[61

The judgments are opinions, decisions, pronouncements. They characterize or classify; they express approval or disapproval; they make a general statement. Their truth or falsity cannot finally be demonstrated. The facts are true; they report what has happened or exists; they result from measurement or observation or calculation; they can be verified.

Most statements, however, cannot be distinguished so sharply as these examples. A comment like "I believe that Martha is a bad girl" can be called fact—presumably the writer knows what he believes— but it obviously includes a judgment. Or a primarily factual statement like "We saw the murderer Snidhart shoot the cashier" includes a judgment in the label *murderer*. Furthermore, judgments are not always so nearly final as those above. They often are plausible opinions which provoke thought or lead to factual development:

> A little learning is a dangerous thing.
> Athletics are a valuable part of an educational program.

Many statements are somewhere between, seemingly factual but not clearly verifiable. They often introduce substantiating evidence or illustrative fact.

> The trouble with youth is that it belongs to those who are too young to enjoy it.

> College football has ceased to have any relation to education.

Obviously, not all statements can be clearly classified, but fact and judgment can generally be distinguished as products of different kinds of thinking with different uses in writing.

6-2 Limiting the use of judgments

Judgments are deceptively easy to come by. We hear them all about us, and often, especially if we think uncritically, we accept them because other people do. When we need to put words on paper, judgments and opinions often occur to us first, but they impair writing unless they introduce factual material. Facts are harder to collect than judgments, but judgments are useless without them.

Furthermore, accepted at face value, judgments impede the writer because they tend to bring his thinking to a dead end. In serious writing, judgments as nearly final as those cited above leave the reader only two choices: agreement or denial. Confronted by "John is a fool" a reader can only agree or say, "He is not." The judgment opens no further discussion. It begins by settling the matter. Such a judgment, in other words, is so sweeping that it cannot be substantiated, even by evidence that John behaved foolishly. The writer can only reassert his opinion, and repetition does not convince. The successful writer, therefore, recognizes the limited usefulness of judgments, preferring statements which he can develop with facts.

6 Using facts   **Facts**

GUIDE TO REVISION:

> *Rewrite, omitting or revising unsubstantiated or un-illustrated judgments and supplying facts.*

Often the writer who cannot finish a paper because he "has said everything he knows" is partly right; he has blocked his progress by overusing judgments. Judgments and opinions, of course, are often useful in writing; but when they are so nearly conclusive that the writer cannot logically support them, he can only fill his page by repeating his old judgments or thinking up new ones. Usually the sweeping judgment is unnecessary, and the writer can avoid his problem by abandoning the judgment, or making it less inclusive and using a generalization which he can hope to illustrate with facts. If he says "American teachers are uneducated," he may shock his readers into interest, but he also makes logical development of his paper almost impossible. How can he obtain convincing data on all teachers? Unless he wishes merely to repeat judgments, he must modify his assertion by suggesting that he means "many teachers" and "inadequately educated"; and when he modifies in this way, only a rather obvious comment remains. If he makes his general statement more specific—for instance, "Many American teachers have not been trained for the jobs they are required to do"—he opens the way for illustration. Then he can develop his paper by marshaling the facts he knows and by looking up new material.

6a Undeveloped judgments   Facts a

Original

College education is much too expensive in America, and it is getting worse every day. Many deserv-

Revision

The cost of a college education in the United States has almost doubled in the last fifteen years. It

[63

Original (*Cont.*)

ing students either have to postpone college indefinitely or work so much of the time that they neglect their studies. If democracy is to survive, the government must provide some method for enabling more capable students to get college educations. Scholarship awards are unfair because they put a premium on memory and mental ability and not on character and need. If our country is to survive, something must be done about this problem.

[*It is no wonder that this paper stopped short of the required number of words; except for the second sentence, the paragraph is made up of judgments, none of them substantiated or illustrated. Furthermore, the judgments are so broad that they discourage development. The writer should begin by abandoning the unnecessary judgments.*]

Revision (*Cont.*)

is no longer easy for a young man to save enough from his paper route and a job in the soda fountain on Saturdays to see him through four years at a university. Tuition costs in many private institutions have doubled, and many state universities have had to increase fees substantially. The textbook that cost $5.00 a few years ago is likely to be $10.00 or $12.00 now. Inflated food prices have affected college cafeterias, and even the soft drink or cup of coffee which used to provide a couple of hours of afternoon recreation for a nickel is now ten or fifteen cents. . . .

[*The revision narrows the scope of the paragraph; instead of broad judgments, it uses a general factual statement which can be illustrated. It leaves the writer with a chance to develop his topic.*]

6b Repetitive judgments

Facts b

Original

The old Union Building at Winnemac University must be replaced. We must have a modern building which will be worthy of an institution like Winnemac. The present building is a disgrace and a shame, far from providing any beneficial college atmosphere. Both inside and out the building is inadequate. It does not, even in the most elementary way, fulfill the needs of student body and faculty. The building stands out on the campus like a sore thumb.

[*The writer of this paper also had trouble finishing, probably because there seemed to be a limit to the number of times he could say*

Revision

The old Union Building at Winnemac University is not meeting the needs of the student body. There are now about 8,000 students in residence, but the cafeteria seats only 75 at a time. The dance floor is so small that a hundred couples crowd it; as a result Union dances are becoming more and more unpopular. The bookstore is so crowded that it cannot keep texts in stock. Furthermore, many important activities are entirely neglected. No rooms are available for meetings of student or faculty groups. There is no space for accommodation of guests of the University. There is no theater, no

Original (*Cont.*)

*the same thing in different words.
The paper fails to be convincing or
clear because no idea is developed;
it is a series of judgments—or repetitions of one judgment.*]

Revision (*Cont.*)

auditorium, no office space for publications or other activities.

[*The addition of some facts
makes the judgments more plausible.*]

EXERCISE 6

A. Which of the following statements are mainly fact and which mainly
judgment? Some may be considered relatively more or less factual,
depending upon the circumstances. For instance, if an entomologist
says, "That is a golden-eyed fly," he may be identifying a tabanid of
the genus Chrysopa, but if a five-year-old child makes the same remark he may be implying much less fact.

1. Water freezes at 32 degrees Fahrenheit.
2. The early bird catches the worm.
3. The road was a ribbon of moonlight across the purple moor.
4. Patriotism is the last refuge of a scoundrel.
5. If a man in some one else's house calls another a perjurer or
   accosts him insultingly with scandalous words, he shall pay 1*s.*
   to the householder, 6*s.* to the man whom he insulted, and 12*s.* to
   the king.
   —Anglo-Saxon Law, 685-86 A.D.
6. In the seventeenth century, although three hundred crimes in
   English law were punishable by death, the Massachusetts Body
   of Liberties listed only ten, and in some of the other states there
   were fewer.
7. Being in a ship is being in a jail—with the chance of being
   drowned.
8. We cannot continue to support the nations of Europe forever.
9. Parallel lines will never meet, no matter how far extended.
10. William James, elder brother of Henry James and one of Amer-
    ica's most significant philosophers, was born in 1842 and died in
    1910.

B. Study the following student theme and determine which statements
are primarily judgment and which primarily fact. Then select two of
the judgments which interest you, rewrite them as generalizations limited enough to permit illustration, and make a list of facts which you
might use in a paragraph illustrating each of your generalizations.

A good campus newspaper can be a great asset to any college or
university. However, it must be truly a campus paper, and it should
be very outstanding. Many campus papers are more concerned about

[65

national or international news than about the affairs right on the campus. They are ill-advised. It is much more desirable for a campus paper to concentrate its efforts on local matters and leave major news stories to larger papers, which have the advantages of a huge staff and expensive news services.

Local news is just as important as the events that make the headlines in the large dailies. Students are often more interested in the campus prom queen election than in the election of a representative to Congress. Interest in local affairs is highly desirable. Everyone should be interested in what goes on in his immediate surroundings.

A paper which is primarily concerned with campus events also provides better training for budding journalists. This country, and every country in the world today, has need for good journalists. Journalism has much to do with the formation of public opinion, and in a democracy public opinion is very important. It is therefore of the greatest significance for a country like ours that papers should train the best type of journalist.

A local paper is also more interesting because it does not pretend to be something more important than it is. Any pretension is always unpleasant. We can, however, really be interested in a campus paper which tells us the things we want to hear about.

For these reasons I believe that a campus newspaper should be concentrated on reporting campus news.

C. The following selections concern change in language. Which contain broad judgments? Which judgments are buttressed by fact?

1. The worst vulgarism in English speech is a habit of prefixing a neutral vowel . . . to all the vowels and diphthongs. . . . When I pass an elementary school and hear the children repeating the alphabet in unison, and chanting unrebuked "Ah-yee, Be-yee, Ce-yee, De-yee," I am restrained from going in and shooting the teacher only by the fact that I do not carry a gun and by my fear of the police.

   —GEORGE BERNARD SHAW, *The Miraculous Birth of Language*

2. A happier expedient than the use of discarded meanings by modern writers would appear to be functional shift, which also figures largely in the creation of words and has been a source of fine poetic effects in the work of our greatest poets, including Shakespeare and Keats. Since poetry may frequently be called "double talk," that is, saying one thing in terms of another, a poetic image, the change in word usage which is called functional shift would appear to have its merits.

   —MARGARET BRYANT, *Modern English and Its Heritage*

3. All languages being imperfect, it does not follow that one should change them. One must adhere absolutely to the manner in which

the good authors have spoken them; and when one has a sufficient number of approved authors, a language is fixed.

—VOLTAIRE, *Philosophical Dictionary*

4. As used in the title of this work, "Americanism" means a word
or expression that originated in the United States. The term includes: outright coinages, as *appendicitis, hydrant, tularemia;* such
words as *adobe, campus, gorilla,* which first became English in the
United States; and terms such as *faculty, fraternity, refrigerator,*
when used in senses first given them in American usage.

—MITFORD M. MATHEWS, *A Dictionary of Americanisms*

5. The mechanism of the English language would also be improved
by the adoption or invention of some indefinite pronoun other than
one to correspond in meaning and usage to French *on,* deriving
from Latin *homo, hominem* "man," and to German *man,* which
is readily distinguishable from *der Mann* both in speech (because,
like *man* in the Scandinavian languages and like *men* in Dutch, it
is pronounced with weaker stress and with reduced vowel) and in
writing (since it has one final *n* and no initial capital).

—SIMEON POTTER, *Our Language*

D. Jeremiah, 17:5-13 contains several statements of the sort called *sentences* in Hebrew literature. Compare them with Isaiah, 7:1-9. Which
passage contains more material presented as fact? Which contains
more unsubstantiated judgments (even though evidence could be presented to support the judgments)?

7. SPECIFIC DETAILS

[For Guide to Revision, see page 70]

Good writing develops generalizations with specific details.

A general term or statement refers to the whole or a class, a type, a group. A specific term or statement refers to a particular. Practically, however, any term is relative, either more or less specific than another. For instance, *man* is more specific than *living being; American citizen* is more specific than *man; John Jones* is more specific than *American citizen.* Or compare the following:

College activities are bad.

Extracurricular activities in college are harmful to the student.

Extracurricular activities in college prevent good academic work.

Bill Jones failed chemistry because he spent too much time in dramatics.

Clearly each statement is more specific than the one preceding it.

7-1 General and specific terms in writing

Both general and specific terms are, of course, essential in communication. Imagine, for example, a family isolated on an oasis which is shaded by what the family refers to as the palm, the willow, and the cottonwood. These parts of the landscape are important to the family; their specific names are used constantly and are adequate while the family remains isolated. But one day the father of the family comes upon a grove of objects which are like the palm, the willow, and the cottonwood in most ways but differ enough so that none of these names will fit. When he tries to tell about his discovery, he needs a new term, a more general one like *tree.* In order to show the relationships between ideas he needs to generalize. He could go on, if he needed, to show other kinds of relationships, to develop terms like *timber* or *plant;* or, if he began using the trees commercially, he could refer to them by still more general terms such as *natural resources* or *wealth.*

The good writer pushes as far as he can toward the specific, but he also generalizes enough to show how the more specific statements are related. Consider the following paragraph, which develops by moving from the general to the specific:

> Like most of the American Indians, except those of the Southwest pueblos, the tribes of the Northwest Coast were Dionysian. In their religious ceremonies the final thing they strove for was ecstasy. The chief dancer, at least at the high point of his performance, should lose normal control of himself and be rapt into another state of existence. He should froth at the mouth, tremble violently and abnormally, do deeds which would be terrible in a normal state. . . .
>
>   —RUTH BENEDICT. *Patterns of Culture*

The paragraph begins with a general statement. The second sentence explains the first, and the term *Dionysian,* with a statement a little more specific. The third illustrates the second and the meaning of *ecstasy.* The fourth becomes more specific still in illustrating the third. The writing becomes more vivid as it becomes more specific.

7-2 Symbolization

Specific terms are especially important in writing because they can serve as symbols for more general ideas. In conversation we rely on symbolic associations even though the symbols have become trite. We use *whistle-stop* instead of describing abstractly a provincial town; we characterize a girl by saying that she wears bobby sox and blue jeans; we classify a restaurant by referring to its red-checked tablecloths. We speak of a person who would kick small dogs or poison wells. Often, of course, such specific comments are accompanied by more general ones, but the well-selected specific detail is likely to give the desired impression more vividly and convincingly— perhaps even more accurately—than the general description. Katherine Brush, for example, in introducing a character mentions two specific details but makes no general statement about the person:

> Miss Levin was the checkroom girl. She had dark-at-the-roots blonde hair and slender hips, upon which, in moments of leisure she wore her hands, like buckles of ivory loosely attached.
>
>   —*Night Club*

Somerset Maugham makes a general comment about a room he is describing, then illustrates with two specific details which become symbols:

> It was a room designed not to live in but for purposes of prestige, and it had a musty, melancholy air. A suite of stamped plush was arranged neatly round the walls, and from the middle of the ceiling, protected from the flies by yellow tissue paper, hung a gilt chandelier.
>
> *—Rain*

7 Specific details   Spec

GUIDE TO REVISION:

Substitute specific details for general statements.

Specific details are essential to good writing. They illustrate, explain, symbolize, substantiate. Without them writing is dull and unconvincing. Specific writing demands work, but successful writing requires the effort needed to think of specific details.

General	*Specific*
There were men of many nationalities and many creeds and many occupations, in all sorts of costumes making a generally cosmopolitan appearance. [*The passage is accurate, and it gives an impression. But it is less vivid and less convincing than it would be if specific examples replaced the general summary.*]	There were American sailors from the ships in port, enlisted men off the gunboats, sombrely drunk, and soldiers from the regiments, white and black, quartered on the island; there were Japanese, walking in twos and threes; Hawaiians, Chinese in long robes, and Filipinos in preposterous hats. —SOMERSET MAUGHAM, *Rain*
As soon as the usual activities of tea had been finished, they all found themselves sitting in complete silence, not knowing what to do or what to say. The silence was oppressive and embarrassing. Everyone at the table seemed upset by it and showed how uncomfortable he really was. It was a very unpleasant experience for them and	Now when everybody was served with mussels, cockles, tea, and toast, and Mr. Povey had been persuaded to cut the crust off his toast, and Constance had, quite unnecessarily, warned Sophia against the deadly green stuff in the mussels, and Constance had further pointed out that the evenings were getting longer, and Mr. Povey had agreed

General (Cont.)

made them seem awkward and childish rather than grown up. It was not a very happy seeming group that sat around the table.

[The paragraph summarizes in general terms, but it does not develop effectively. It could be improved if the writer substituted facts for judgments and specific details for general statements. Notice that in Arnold Bennett's paragraph even silence can be expressed in specific terms. And the development leads to an interesting generalization in the final sentence.]

He was obviously the kind of man who would have found a ready place for himself among his fellow businessmen in any large or small city. He would have felt completely at home at a meeting of one of the businessmen's clubs. He would have had the mannerisms the others had, agreed with the sentiments expressed there, entered into all the humorous activities and approved the kinds of practical jokes he observed there.

[The description is correct enough grammatically, but it lacks the kind of vigor that specific details confer. General terms like large or small city, businessmen's clubs, or humorous activities are less effective than specific details which illustrate or symbolize.]

Specific (Cont.)

that they were, there remained nothing to say. An irksome silence fell on them all, and no one could lift it off. Tiny clashes of shell and crockery sounded with the terrible clearness of noises heard in the night. Each person avoided the eyes of the others. And both Constance and Sophia kept straightening their bodices at intervals, and expanding their chests, and then looking at their plates; occasionally a prim cough was discharged. It was a sad example of the difference between young women's dreams of social brilliance and the reality of life.

—ARNOLD BENNETT, *The Old Wives' Tale*

He was obviously the kind of man who would have found an instant and congenial place for himself among his fellow businessmen in Chicago, Detroit, Cleveland, St. Louis, or Kalamazoo. He would have felt completely at home at one of the weekly luncheons of the Rotary Club. He would have chewed his cigar with the best of them, wagged his head approvingly as the president spoke of some member as having "both feet on the ground," entered gleefully into all the horseplay, the heavy-handed kind of humor known as "kidding," and joined in the roars of laughter that greeted such strokes of wit as collecting all the straw hats in the cloak room, bringing them in, throwing them on the floor, and gleefully stamping them to pieces.

—THOMAS WOLFE, *You Can't Go Home Again*

[71]

EXERCISE 7

A. For each of the following words list three words, any one of which could be substituted for the term to make it more specific:

EXAMPLE: *Walk*—lurch, waddle, stride, amble, stroll.

1. flower	4. burn	7. sharp
2. see	5. dark	8. animal
3. storm	6. red	9. automobile

B. List three adjectives which could be used to discriminate between degrees or kinds of each of the following:

EXAMPLE: *Cold*—frigid, icy, chilly, cool, raw, bitter, nipping, arctic.

1. smell	4. speed	7. happiness
2. sound	5. roughness	8. brightness
3. heat	6. tiredness	9. darkness

C. Rewrite each of the following in specific terms, inventing specific details to develop the general statements:

EXAMPLE: Later Milly and her mother were sitting outside looking as usual at the flowers.

> After lunch Milly and her mother were sitting as usual on the balcony beyond the salon, admiring for the five-hundredth time the stocks, the roses, the small, bright grass beneath the palm, and the oranges against a wavy line of blue.
>
> —KATHERINE MANSFIELD, *The Dove's Nest*

1. When we rose in the morning we could see all over the streets the signs of the storm of the night.

2. Mary was always doing the kind of thing which gave her the reputation of being a girl you could not trust.

3. The shelves were packed with books of a great many kinds and varieties.

4. The pond was bordered by very beautiful patches of lovely flowers and shrubs.

5. The kitchen was well equipped with all the modern conveniences.

6. The white tablecloth was almost invisible because it was so thoroughly covered with so many good things to eat.

7. The children came to the Halloween party in the many kinds of costumes customary to such celebrations of an old holiday.

8. The desk was piled in high confusion with numerous evidences of Wendy's varied interests.

9. When Sue sat down to study, she always found her thoughts wandering off to many unrelated subjects.

10. Before he started in college, Phil had not realized that he would

constantly be needing money for a variety of incidental and miscellaneous expenses.

D. For each of the following gaps supply a highly specific modifier which might be appropriate:

1. the ——————— new house
2. some ripe ——————— pears
3. a ——————— railroad car
4. a bleak ——————— hillside
5. this ——————— labor legislation
6. a ——————— social call
7. that ——————— young lawyer
8. a few ——————— oysters
9. a ——————— frowsy brunette
10. some ——————— dripping golfers
11. our ——————— old bus
12. any ——————— disappointed office seeker
13. two ——————— young lovers
14. a ——————— new calf
15. a ——————— freshman engineer

8. ILLUSTRATION

[For Guide to Revision, see page 76]

To communicate ideas clearly, develop them with illustrations, instances, examples, comparisons.

There are many ways in which the writer can illustrate or explain his main idea; the techniques discussed here are among them.

8-1 Citing particulars

We can describe a man or a house or a scene by giving the reader particulars which will add up to a clear idea. The following paragraph lists a selection of details to set a scene and establish a mood:

> It was early evening of a day in the late fall and the Winesburg County Fair had brought crowds of country people into town. The day had been clear and the night came on warm and pleasant. On the Trunion Pike, where the road after it left town stretched away between berry fields now covered with dry brown leaves, the dust from passing wagons arose in clouds. Children, curled into little balls, slept on the straw scattered on wagon beds. Their hair was full of dust and their fingers black and sticky. The dust rolled away over the fields and the departing sun set it ablaze with colors.
> —SHERWOOD ANDERSON, *Winesburg, Ohio*

8-2 Examples or instances

"Give me an example," is a common request of anyone wanting to understand. The writer who wants to be understood complies; he clarifies with examples or specific instances. Consider the following paragraphs.

> Many naturalists are of opinion that the animals which we commonly consider as mute have the power of imparting their thoughts to one another. That they can express general sensations is very certain; every being that can utter sounds has a different voice for pleasure and for pain. The hound informs his fellows when he scents

ILLUSTRATION   8

his game; the hen calls her chickens to their food by her cluck, and drives them from danger by her scream.

Birds have the greatest variety of notes; . . .

—SAMUEL JOHNSON, *The Idler*

Johnson works toward specific instances—the hound, the hen, birds —in order to illustrate his general statement. The following paragraph develops in a similar way.

But, indeed, the dictum that truth always triumphs over persecution is one of those pleasant falsehoods which men repeat after one another till they pass into commonplaces, but which all experience refutes. History teems with instances of truth put down by persecutions. If not suppressed forever, it may be thrown back for centuries. To speak only of religious opinions: the Reformation broke out at least twenty times before Luther, and was put down. Arnold of Brescia was put down. Fra Dolcino was put down. Savonarola was put down. The Lollards were put down. The Hussites were put down.

—JOHN STUART MILL, *On Liberty*

The paragraph progresses from general statements toward specific instances or examples.

8-3 Incident

Sometimes a writer can illustrate most effectively by telling a story to show what he means. Ruth Benedict, wishing to say that the social customs of a people are fundamental to their happiness, begins her book *Patterns of Culture* by recounting her conversations with a chief of the Digger Indians of California. The old man expresses his despair as he sees a way of life disappear; his comments illustrate the writer's point vividly and feelingly.

In the following passage the historian James Anthony Froude uses a story to illustrate a point and incidentally reveals something of the differences between money values in the 1870's and now:

Will you have an example of what may be done by an ordinary man with no special talents or opportunity? A Yorkshireman, an agricultural labourer, that I knew, went to Natal twelve years ago. I suppose at first he had to work for wages; and I will tell you what the wages are in that country. I stayed myself with a settler on the borders there. He had two labourers with him, an Irishman and an Englishman. They lived in his house; they fed at his own table. To the Irishman, who knew something of farming, he was paying fourteen pounds a month; to the Englishman he was paying ten; and every penny of this they were able to save.

With such wages as these, a year or two of work will bring money enough to buy a handsome property. My Yorkshireman purchased two hundred and fifty acres of wild land outside Maritzburg. He enclosed it; he carried water over it. He planted his fences with the fast-growing eucalyptus, the Australian gum-tree. In that soil and in that climate, everything will flourish, from pineapples to strawberries, from the coffee-plant and the olive to wheat and Indian corn, from oranges and bananas to figs, apples, peaches, and apricots. Now at the end of ten years the mere gum-trees which I saw on that man's land could be sold for two thousand pounds, and he is making a rapid fortune by supplying fruit and vegetables to the market at Maritzburg.

—On the Uses of a Landed Gentry

8-4 Analogy

To explain or illustrate the unfamiliar to the reader, a writer can speak in similar but more familiar terms. That is, he can develop ideas by analogy. The device is familiar; to explain the rotation of the earth to a child, we are likely to speak in terms of a rubber ball or a top. Victor Hugo describes the Battle of Waterloo as a giant letter *A*. Thomas Henry Huxley in a famous analogy says that life is like a game of chess. Sir James Jeans describes the structure of the atom in terms of the solar system.

Rutherford supposed the atom to be constructed like the solar system, the heavy central nucleus playing the part of the sun and the electrons acting the parts of the planets.

—The Universe Around Us

8 Illustration   **Illus**

GUIDE TO REVISION:

Rewrite with specific illustrations or explanations which will clarify general ideas.

8a Adequate illustration   **Illus a**

Inexperienced writers often err in assuming that what is apparent to them is apparent to the reader. They fail to help the reader with illustrations. Or they have thoughts which are relatively vague, and they put them down without thinking of examples or instances or parallels which will help both writer and reader.

Original

Obviously, the theater was everything that a university theater should be. It had all the qualities that one wants to find in a campus playhouse. In size and equipment it was almost perfect. It is no wonder that drama was so popular on the campus and that plays were so well attended. We should attempt to get something like it for our university. And the responsibility for action rests in part with the students themselves.

[*Like most examples of inadequate development, this passage from a student theme is general rather than specific; it repeats judgments; it includes in one short paragraph material which could be developed into a long theme. The writer gets into trouble at the very beginning by failing to illustrate what he means. The writer may be willing to make his obvious statement on the basis of his knowledge, but the reader does not have enough information to accept it.*]

More than one American statesman has revealed aptitude in fields quite unrelated to politics and diplomacy. It is possible to find men in our history who were capable of all sorts of tasks, ranging from manual labor to technical science. Many men were not only skillful in political affairs but really achieved a great deal in such occupations as printing, medicine, science, agriculture, finance. Among the men with broad interests in addition to their interests in affairs of state were Washington, Jefferson, Franklin, and others. Many such men were always doing things not di-

Revision

The theater was everything that a university theater should be. It was small and intimate, holding only about 250, and you could hear and see from every seat. The seats were comfortable but not new, and an occasional rip in the leather gave the place an atmosphere of permanence; it did not have the kind of polish that makes you expect to smell fresh paint when you walk in. There was no revolving stage or other complex machinery, but the stage was large and there was plenty of room to get around backstage. There was enough equipment to make possible all kinds of experiments— good and bad—but there was not enough to keep the stage crew from using ingenuity.

[*The first sentence of the original can be developed into a paragraph. If the other general statements of the original are to remain, they need similar illustration.*]

More than one American statesman has revealed aptitude in fields quite unrelated to politics and diplomacy. There was Jefferson, for example. An astute politician, he was also an important political philosopher, developing in his writing his theories that government should rest in the hands of the producing class. His interest in science was practical as well as theoretical; he is credited with a mathematical formula that still governs the shape of plowshares, with the invention of the swivel chair, and with the design of a leather buggy top. He contributed

Original (Cont.)

rectly connected with national or foreign affairs.

[*The paragraph begins to develop at times, but it remains general and repetitious. Even a single well-developed example would illustrate better than do these general statements.*]

Revision (Cont.)

to the University of Virginia not only his knowledge as an educator but also the plans for the campus, one of the most beautifully arranged in America. He studied language, and was one of the first Americans to learn Anglo-Saxon. His was the kind of inquisitive mind that found interest and new ideas in many subjects.

8b Valid illustration   Illus b

The writer should take care that his illustrations concern the subject he has in hand, not something related to it, however closely.

Original

Very few commercial photographers have any conception of the artistic possibilities of photography. Most of them are interested only in making money, which they try to do by flattering their sitters. For instance, a photographer on 125th Street is always distracted by his wife. As soon as he has a subject posed his wife comes in to ask him whether he wants chops for dinner or those flounders they get at the corner. Then she shouts from the kitchen that the new cat isn't housebroken yet, and what is he going to do about it? After that she has mislaid her keys to the car, and where are his? Result: the photographer takes a thoroughly routine portrait.

[*This material might be worked up into an engaging sketch of a portrait photographer, but the illustration has nothing to do with the photographer's conception of the artistic possibilities of his job.*]

Revision

Very few commercial photographers have any conception of the artistic possibilities of photography. Most of them are interested only in making money, which they try to do by flattering their sitters. For instance, last week I took my grandmother to have her picture taken. I explained to the photographer that Grandmother knew she was no beauty, but we wanted a picture which would show what an honest, shrewd, and lovable old woman she is, and that was what she wanted, too. The photographer pretended to understand, but when we got the proofs he had fixed her up into a beaming, middle-aged matron, bleached-blonde and blushing. He had retouched the character out of her face and replaced it with Elizabeth Arden on her skin.

[*The new illustration suggests that at least one photographer was unable or unwilling to seize an opportunity to do an artistic portrait.*]

EXERCISE 8

A. List fifteen specific details which you might use in describing any three of the list below. Make the details concrete; prefer "the soiled brown chair with protruding springs" to "the furniture in the room."

1. A college room
2. A favorite restaurant
3. A teacher I know
4. A classroom
5. The lake front
6. A campus politician

B. List specific details which you might use to illustrate each of the following statements:

1. A university provides wide opportunities for wasting time.
2. Drugstores have become more than places that sell drugs.
3. The modern automobile has developed with concern for the comfort of driver and passengers.
4. Members of theater audiences are guilty of a variety of discourtesies.
5. Comic books are not designed exclusively for children.

C. Describe a specific instance which might be used to illustrate any five of the following statements:

1. Abraham Lincoln had great respect for the feelings of others.
2. Incidents of childhood may have profound effects on human beings.
3. The most beautiful places in America have not all been discovered by tourists.
4. Athletes are not necessarily poor students.
5. Proverbs are not always applicable.
6. Pets can be nuisances.
7. Emergency measures sometimes become permanent parts of a social system.
8. Economy does not always pay.
9. Newspaper columnists are not always right in their prophecies.
10. Individuals may profit from a war.

D. The selection below from a student theme is weak because general statements have not been illustrated and clarified. Select any two sentences from the theme and develop each into an individual paragraph, using the devices for illustration described above.

University education today is not what is should be. The programs of our colleges could be improved in many ways. Liberal arts programs are not truly liberal. Curricula should be revised to include the kinds of courses that give a student a genuine cultural background. Individual courses should be reorganized so that their approach is less specialized and more suited to the needs of the average citizen.

There should also be more courses which prepare students directly for the problems they will face in life—in marriage and parenthood and business. Professional courses should be changed so that they prepare students better for the kind of work they will have to do. The college program should be correlated more accurately with modern society.

E. If you wish to discuss the fact that the lever action of a typewriter forces the typewriter key to travel at considerable speed, you might make your meaning clear by giving the ratio of the lever action in a specific typewriter and estimating the speed a key might attain under normal touch. That is, you might give an example. Or you might try to explain the lever action and its effect by comparing the typewriter key assembly to the human forearm. That is, you might use an analogy. For each of the following statements supply (a) a possible example, and (b) a possible analogy.

1. As modern furniture becomes more popular, prices are likely to drop.
2. A rocket attains its great speed through the propulsive powers of discharging gas.
3. The central portion of the United States is a great, shallow bowl.
4. An end run can be a deceptive play.
5. A personnel manager should have training as well as experience.
6. Animals can be taught more with kindness than with whipping.
7. Race prejudice should be discouraged in the public schools.
8. This year's automobiles are designed more to sell cars than to improve transportation.

9. DEFINITION

[For Guide to Revision, see page 84]

Definition clarifies terms and develops ideas.

All of us have seen disagreement disappear when terms have been defined. Good definition promotes clear writing, but definition may also be a writing device, a means of development. For example, an interesting and revealing essay might develop as a definition of skin diving.

9-1 Methods of definition

Adequate definition is not easy. Logicians do not agree on definitions, even of *definition.* Of the various means of defining, the following are especially useful.

(1) *Definition by analysis.* This method, specified by logicians since Aristotle, places a term in a general class and distinguishes it from others within the class. Man can be classified as an animal, and distinguished from other animals by his reason.

> Man is a rational animal. A triangle is a plane figure with three sides. Materialism is a philosophical theory which holds that the existence and nature of matter sufficiently account for the universe.

This is the most precise type of definition, but not always the most readily understood.

(2) *Definition by synthesis or description.* Some terms can be defined by relating them to other known things: telling what something does, or where it is, or how it is used. Often this sort of definition is less conclusive than analytic definition because it does not distinguish a term from all others in its class. "Red is the usual color for firetrucks" might help someone to understand *red,* but it does not define adequately. Other synthetic definitions are more precise:

[81

A circle is the figure covered by a line fixed at one end and moving in a plane.

(3) *Definition by example.* Often examples help to clarify, and hence to define. Children learn meanings of words by repeated examples, but the method does not usually provide a complete definition.

Epics are poems like *The Iliad, Beowulf,* and *The Song of Roland.*

(4) *Definition by synonyms.* Some terms can be defined with synonyms, that is, with other words which have similar meanings.

Hund in German means *dog* in English. Osculation is kissing. To define is to distinguish.

All methods of definition are useful, but each has its limitations. A writer may be inaccurate if he thinks he has defined when he has only described.

9-2 Pitfalls in definition

Definition is an exacting process, and definitions can be inadequate or fallacious. The following are among the most frequent causes of difficulty:

(1) *Circular definition* (see also 11c). An analytic definition is inadequate if it defines by using the term to be defined; it takes the reader in a circle. "A washing machine is a machine that washes" does not inform the reader.

(2) *Misleading synthesis.* Definition by synthesis often lacks the thoroughness of analysis. It may describe but not define, and it can be misleading. An old definition of gold as "the most precious metal" is no longer adequate.

(3) *Metaphorical definition.* Analogy and metaphor (see 35-5) sometimes help in a synthetic definition; Aristotle's definition of matter—matter is to substance what the bronze is to the statue—uses metaphor successfully. But often metaphor which appears to be definition is only description (see 8-4). The definition of slang as "language that takes off its coat, spits on its hands, and goes to work" amuses but does not define.

(4) *Inadequate synonyms.* Definition by synonyms works only if synonyms clarify the original. "Democracy refers to the American

way of life as we all conceive it" merely substitutes one confusion for another.

9-3 Definition as development

Definition is also a useful device in development. When Cardinal Newman became rector of the new Dublin University, he needed a statement of purpose under which he, his faculty, and his students could work together. His answer was to prepare a series of lectures, now called *The Idea of a University Defined,* in which he tried to decide what a university should do by asking himself what education is. His answer is not the only possible one, but like many other people, he found that he could best explain and even persuade by defining.

Occasionally a writer or speaker will feel he must use definition and nothing but definition as a means of development. A lecturer in Anthropology 1 may define his subject, and then distinguish ethnology from cultural history and comparative anatomy from paleontology. More frequently, a writer uses definition as one device of development, as Gilbert Highet does in the following passage:

> Within climax there is one symmetrical device which is so natural and adaptable that it can be used on almost every level of speech without seeming artificial. And yet it was invented by Greek teachers of rhetoric; not all the Romans adopted it or managed it with confidence; but Cicero above all others made it his own, and, although it is not native to the modern European languages, it has now, without leaving the realm of artistic prose, entered the ordinary speech of western nations. This is the tricolon. Tricolon means a unit made up of three parts. The third part in a tricolon used in oratory is usually more emphatic and conclusive than the others. This is the chief device used in Lincoln's Gettysburg Address, and is doubled at its conclusion:
>
> > "But in a larger sense, we cannot dedicate—we cannot consecrate—we cannot hallow this ground.
> > "We here highly resolve that these dead shall not have died in vain—that this nation, under God, shall have a new birth of freedom—and that government of the people, by the people, for the people, shall not perish from the earth."
>
> *—The Classical Tradition*

Professor Highet is not here mainly concerned with defining the tricolon. He is mainly concerned to show how classical traditions have influenced the modern world, but in so doing he finds that defining a term becomes an integral part of showing how Greek rhetoric influenced modern expression.

9 Definition   **Def**

> *Supply or revise definitions to clarify unfamiliar terms and terms given special meanings; consider the possibility of further development through definition.*

Writing can be vague, confusing, or inadequate because a writer has not defined his terms or taken advantage of an opportunity to develop by definition. A statement, for example, like "The United States is not a democracy," can be intelligently discussed only when all those concerned accept one meaning for *democracy* and understand it.

Original

In the true sense of the word, a conservative is the person who really keeps our society from disaster. He is the man we should honor as the preserver of our traditions, not vilify as a foe to progress. . . .

[*The opening sentence appears to define, but does not. The remainder of the paper suffers because the reader does not understand a key term in the writer's special sense.*]

College football is no longer a sport. Coaches are hired for their ability to win games. Players are hired from whatever coal mines develop the biggest muscles, and stadiums are built or not built depending upon whether or not they will "pay off." Rooters go to the games as they would go to the movies, to see a hired actor put on a

Revision

If we consider a conservative as the person who is reluctant to change until he is convinced that the new is better than the old, we can see that the conservative keeps our society from disaster. He is . . .

[*A definition, distinguishing the term conservative as a type of person, clarifies the remainder of the discussion. The reader may not agree, but he at least understands.*]

College football is no longer a sport, at least not in the sense that a sport is an activity engaged in for the fun of the activity. Coaches are hired for their ability to win games. Players are hired. . . .

[*The original paragraph is unclear; most of what it says would apply, for instance, to professional baseball, which is usually called a*

Original (Cont.)

show. And collegiate sport promotes school spirit, but commercialized athletics does not.

Revision (Cont.)

sport. The addition of a definition, specifying the particular sense in which the word sport *is used, makes the paragraph clearer.*]

We may define luxury commodities as those commodities which are not necessary. Necessary commodities are those which are not luxuries.

[*The definition is circular, attempting to define with the terms to be defined.*]

We may define luxury commodities as those articles of commerce which are unnecessary to life and health.

[*An analytic definition helps the reader to understand an essential term.*]

EXERCISE 9

A. Indicate which of the methods of definition described above (9-1) are used in each of the following statements:

1. Rhetoric is speech designed to persuade.

2. Persuasion involves choice, will; it is directed to a man only insofar as he is *free*.

    —KENNETH BURKE

3. A narcotic is a drug which in moderate doses allays sensibility, relieves pain, and produces profound sleep, but in poisonous doses produces stupor, coma, or convulsions.

4. A chocolate éclair is like a cream puff stretched oblong and frosted or glazed with chocolate.

5. A concierge is a doorkeeper.

6. Religion is what is involved in Buddhism, Mohammedanism, and Christianity.

7. A hammer is what you use to drive nails or break rocks or beat smooth the dented fender of a car.

8. In a democratic government, the citizens, or their representatives, act freely and according to established forms to appoint or recall officers and to enact or revoke the laws by which the society is to be governed.

9. An example of a palindrome is *Able was I ere I saw Elba.*

10. In other words, education is the instruction of the intellect in the laws of Nature, under which name I include not merely things and their forces, but men and their ways; and the fashioning of the affections and of the will into an earnest and loving desire to move in harmony with those laws.

    —THOMAS HENRY HUXLEY

B. Consider the adequacy as definitions of the statements below. Describe any fault you find in them.

1. A tie rack is a rack for holding ties.

2. A fallacious argument is an argument used by somebody else to prove a conclusion you do not agree with.

3. Life is but an empty dream.

4. A good book is the precious lifeblood of a master spirit embalmed and treasured up on purpose to a life beyond life.

5. *Brillig* means four o'clock in the afternoon—the time when you begin broiling things for dinner.

6. *Toves* are something like badgers—they're something like lizards —and they're something like corkscrews.

7. A straight line is the shortest distance between two points.

8. Network: anything reticulated or decussated at equal intervals, with interstices between the intersections.

9. Liberty is the right to do anything which does not interfere with the liberty of others.

10. A man's house is his castle.

11. History is the lengthened shadow of one man.

12. History is philosophy teaching by examples.

13. A clank is a sharp, brief, ringing sound, duller than a clang and deeper and stronger than a clink.

14. Knowledge is power.

15. A genealogist is one who traces your family back as far as your money will go.

C. Define each of the following terms by putting it into a class and then adding characteristics which differentiate it from other members of the class.

1. river	4. revolver	7. botany
2. basketball	5. sonnet	8. rectangle
3. pan	6. asphalt	9. chuckle

D. Most common words are used in several senses. For each of the words below, think of as many usages as you can. Try to define each of these. Then check your definitions against those in two good dictionaries, noticing which usages you may have missed and comparing your definitions with those in the dictionaries for comprehensiveness and accuracy. Notice, also, whether the dictionaries agree with each other.

1. grief	4. man	7. knowledge
2. tap	5. run	8. point
3. home	6. stop	9. ideal

10. EVIDENCE; INDUCTIVE REASONING

[For Guide to Revision, see page 90]

Support generalizations with sound, adequate, appropriate evidence, or avoid the generalizations.

Often the writer must do more than organize and illustrate; he must make his statements plausible by showing how they are supported by sufficient evidence or how they follow from logical reasoning. The writer, in other words, must often use and record the kinds of thinking employed constantly in life—by the doctor diagnosing an illness and prescribing a possible cure, by the lawyer preparing and arguing a case, by the scientist generalizing from experiments and then applying his generalization to particular instances. This process of thinking can be considered in two parts: induction, the process of generalizing from specific data, and deduction (see 11), the process of applying generalizations, like those produced by induction, to particular instances.

10-1 Induction

A city council in the Midwest recently considered continuing government controls on rents. Representatives of landlords protested that they could not meet their bills and asserted that there was no real housing shortage. A hastily organized committee of renters appeared at the next meeting declaring that renters could not meet their bills either and asserting that there was a severe housing shortage in the area. The council, understandably, was puzzled. Finally an astute newspaperman took a list of all the apartments, real estate offices, and rental agencies in the city and started telephoning, pretending he had just arrived in the city and needed a place to live. After three hours he located only two available apartments, both at rents well above prescribed limits. His story was instrumental in the council's decision to continue rent controls. It was convincing; it was "logical"; it was based on evidence.

The newspaperman's process was inductive. He collected data which led to a generalization. He proceeded from specific instances to a general conclusion.

10-2 Generalization and hypothesis

We use induction every day; it may lead to generalizations, or it may provide hypotheses, useful mainly for further investigation.

For example, a man goes out in the yard on a cool morning in spring wondering whether a frost the night before has killed the cherries. He examines a dozen blossoms in different parts of his tree and finds black spots in the center of each where the fruit should be forming. A neighbor's tree shows similar black spots. He believes that he has found enough specific instances to warrant the generalization that there has been a killing frost. He has noticed a number of unharmed cherries on a small tree partially protected by an overhanging porch roof, but he rejects these because they are not typical instances. A generalization is reliable if it is induced from a sufficient number of typical instances. But some generalizations are more reliable than others. A generalization that all cows are black and white made by a city boy after his first visit to a farm specializing in Holstein-Frisian cattle is not reliable; it is based on too few instances. Obviously, the writer and reader need to know the extent of the evidence behind a generalization in order to estimate its reliability.

Or, a girl comes into her dormitory room late at night and finds her roommate's clothes spread about. She sees an empty flower box on the dresser. She finds a new bottle of perfume open. She remembers that is the night of a formal dance. She discovers that her roommate's new gown is missing from the closet. She forms a hypothesis to explain the facts she has observed: that her roommate received a last-minute invitation and has gone to the dance. A hypothesis is usable if it is a better explanation for all known facts than any alternative; but it is only a tentative explanation, requiring verification from the observation of more data.

10-3 Induction in writing

Writing, whether it be a sentence or a book, is often essentially an inductive process. For example, Ruth Benedict, in her book *Patterns of Culture,* suggests that among cultures there is wide diversity in social habits and attitudes, but she does not leave the statement as an unsubstantiated judgment. She examines various cultures in terms of customs concerning adulthood, warfare, and marriage. The facts gathered lead to conclusions which lead in turn to a main idea. The whole structure might be described as a pyramid, a pyramid which is solid and convincing because its foundation is factual.

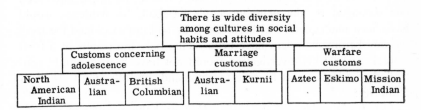

Each general statement is supported by a group of more specific details. And the analysis can be carried down to even smaller units of composition. The lower left block of the pyramid above, for example, is the following paragraph.

> Adulthood in central North America means warfare. Honour in it is the great goal of all men. The constantly recurring theme of the youth's coming-of-age, as also of preparation for the warpath at any age, is a magic ritual for success in war. They torture not one another, but themselves; they cut strips of skin from their arms and legs, they strike off their fingers, they drag heavy weights pinned to their chests or leg muscles. Their reward is enhanced prowess in deeds of warfare.

The paragraph also resembles a pyramid, with details supporting statements which support another more general statement.

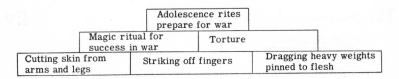

In the scheme of the whole chapter, however, as shown above, the apex of this pyramid is only another statement which the writer uses to document further conclusions.

10-4 Tests of evidence

If inductions are to be reliable they must derive from evidence which is actual—not details only resembling evidence—which is typical, and which is adequate. If the man examining his cherry trees had been nearsighted, he might have mistaken a dead bee for a frozen blossom. His observation would have been unreliable. If he had looked at only the tree protected from frost, he would not have seen a typical instance. If he had looked at only one blossom, he might have seen one damaged by the neighbor boy's baseball; his evidence would have been inadequate. Furthermore, if he had not examined the trees the day before, he might have been seeing only the results of a frost a week earlier; his investigation would not have been carefully controlled. Evidence must be able to withstand the following tests of its authority:

(1) *Is the evidence unprejudiced?* A probable partner in crime is not a reliable character witness for an alleged criminal. A biography commissioned by a political party as part of the campaign of its candidate for office is suspect.

(2) *Is the evidence up to date?* Facts about America in 1785 reveal American democracy only historically. The Battle of Bull Run does not necessarily provide evidence for current military strategy.

(3) *Has the evidence been provided by a competent observer?* If a nine-year-old boy reports that his neighbor is a political spy, his evidence must be discounted because of his limited knowledge and experience. A city businessman who has never seen a cow is not a likely source of information on the relative merits of the Hereford and Aberdeen Angus breeds. A baseball fan in the right-field bleachers probably has less reliable information than the umpire about whether or not the last pitch was over the plate.

10 *Evidence; inductive reasoning* Ev

GUIDE TO REVISION:

Supply adequate evidence for generalizations or modify the generalizations.

When a writer uses details to prove a generalization, he should be sure that the evidence is pertinent, reliable, and sufficient. The writer who says that Swedes are stubborn, or policemen have big feet, or coyotes are cowardly, and then assumes that he can *prove* such statements by citing one incident from his experience, is not likely to convince anyone whose mind is working. Generalizations are always dangerous (see 6), and unsupported generalizations are unconvincing.

10a Generalization Ev a

Human beings readily forsake the paths of logic by jumping to conclusions. A mother, quite innocently, indulges in what is known as "wishful thinking" to select only a small part of the evidence and conclude that her child has been grossly wronged by a teacher. Reporters from newspapers of rival political parties, perhaps not innocently, make different generalizations based on the same facts in their report of a mass meeting. Scholars, making every effort to be objective, may reach different conclusions from the same historical facts. Even statistics, if not interpreted carefully, easily lead to false conceptions. A campus newspaper once reported, quite accurately, that during the year 50 per cent of the women in one college of the university had married their instructors. Hasty but vociferous conclusions, based on the accurate figure but still on inadequate evidence, had to be withdrawn when it was revealed that the college was the engineering college and the total number of women students for that year was two. Generalizations which do not follow from adequate evidence should be modified or abandoned.

Original	Revision
Purebred dogs are essentially stupid. When I was a child, I had a fine pedigreed Dalmation. I tried for months to teach him to shake hands. I succeeded only in encouraging him to jump up and wipe his front feet on anyone who came in sight. An expensive spaniel which succeeded him was no better. I tried to teach him to bring in the newspaper; he learned only to chew the paper to bits.	I never expect to own another purebred dog; my experiences have prejudiced me thoroughly in favor of curs. When I was a child. . . . [*The sweeping pronouncement about dogs in the original is unjustified and also unnecessary. With an opening like that in the revision, the writer can use his details as illustrations, avoid the problem of proof, and write a convincing paragraph.*]
Statistics show that everyone in the office is making enough money to live comfortably. The average	Although the average salary for workers in the office last year was more than $6,000, many employees

[91

Original (Cont.)

salary, computed on certified figures for last year, was a little more than $6,000 per year per employee.

[*The statistics cited do not substantiate the first statement. Additional facts might reverse the conclusion, as the revision suggests.*]

Revision (Cont.)

were not making a living wage. Only three salaries, those of executives at $30,000, were as high as the average figure; whereas two clerks received $1800 per year and three others $1950.

[*Completed statistics require a different generalization.*]

10b Adequate evidence   Ev b

Even though a generalization may be tenable, it is not convincing in writing unless adequate evidence justifies it. If the evidence is inadequate, the generalization must be qualified or dropped.

Original

Laws will not stop gambling. Investigations of Senate committees showed that gambling flourishes in spite of strict laws against it. Everybody instinctively has an urge to gamble, and you cannot keep him from it. It is useless to try to stop people from gambling.

[*Except for the second sentence, the paragraph is a string of judgments, none of which is supported by adequate evidence. The last two sentences are not evidence at all, but are further judgments. The first judgment, which presumably is the proposition to be proved, needs to be supported with further facts.*]

Revision

Laws will not stop gambling. Recent investigations of Senate committees disclosed that gambling flourished openly in cities of the Middle West like Detroit and Chicago, in spite of strict laws against it. Investigations in New York and Los Angeles revealed that law enforcement officers not only condoned but participated in gambling activities. That illegal gambling exists in Florida is common knowledge. Apparently enough people want to gamble to make illegal gambling possible and profitable.

[*If a generalization seems useful, it can be qualified as in the last sentence above so that it is logically defensible.*]

10c Causation   Ev c

A person dealing with causes is especially tempted to generalize quickly, or to admit as evidence material which is not properly evidence at all. He sits in a draft Monday night, wakes up with a cold Tuesday morning, and concludes, too readily, that the draft "caused" the cold. It may, of course, have caused it or helped to cause it, but a little reflection shows that the evidence does not warrant the conclusion. He plays with a toad on Monday and discovers a wart on his finger on Friday. He finds a horseshoe at ten o'clock, throws it over his left shoulder at 10:02, and finds a $10 bill at noon. If he concludes that playing with the toad caused his wart or that finding the horseshoe was responsible for his good luck, he is making the error known as the *post hoc ergo propter hoc* fallacy, "after this therefore because of this." It is not a sound method of determining cause. Day comes after night, but night does not cause day. The fact that banks failed after the election of Herbert Hoover does not prove that Hoover caused the depression.

Original	*Revision*
Governor Jones was elected two years ago. Since that time constant examples of corruption and subversion in government have been unearthed. It is time we got rid of the man responsible for this kind of corrupt government.	Governor Jones was elected two years ago. Since that time frequent examples of corruption and subversion in government have been unearthed. It is time to see whether a new administration can clean up the government.
[*The assumption that Governor Jones caused corruption in government exemplifies the* post hoc *fallacy.*]	[*The revision is equally sweeping in its assertions, but it avoids the illogical causal conclusion.*]

10d *Reliability of evidence*   **Ev d**

To be reliable, evidence must be based on facts. Hearsay, legend, opinion, or speculation is not sufficient to support a generalization.

Original	*Revision*
Some of the most important discoveries of modern times have been the result of accidents. For instance, according to the story, the great strike at Goldfield, which uncovered more than three billion dollars in gold and silver, resulted from the random kick of a bad-tempered jackass. Old Jim, while he was prospecting the area, had made camp, and was boiling his nightly coffee. The coffee pot tipped over, and splashed some boiling water on the jackass, which kicked at the pot,	In spite of the great advance in science, individual curiosity and even pure luck still play a part in important discoveries. As a matter of course the so-called "miracle drugs" have in the main resulted from careful planning, deliberate search, and vast technical knowledge. But even here, chance observations have helped make pharmaceutical history and save lives. Consider, for instance, penicillin. . . .
	[*To substantiate his serious gen-*

[93

Original (*Cont.*)

missed, but hit a ledge of rock instead. Old Jim stood staring, and with good reason. The sharp little hoof of the jackass had knocked loose a chunk of high-grade gold ore.

[*The writer admits that his story, improbable on the face of it, has no reliable authority; yet he proceeds to use it as evidence.*]

Revision (*Cont.*)

eralization about important discoveries, the writer needs a more reliable instance than the kind of folk legend which can be given no more authority than "according to the story." If he knows the interesting story of the development of penicillin, he can proceed to write a convincing paper, with authoritative support for his generalization.]

10e *Analogy*   Ev e

Evidence should not be confused with analogy. Evidence is specific information which supports a generalization. An analogy, on the other hand, is a comparison of two objects which are essentially different but which have at least one quality in common. An analogy can never be used as proof. It is not even an example, though it may be useful as a device in explanation. A writer trying to explain the breeds of horses to city children might wish to say that just as racing automobiles have light wheels and chassis, and trucks have very heavy running gear, racing horses are relatively light and draft horses very heavy. This is an analogy. But a horse is not a machine, and an automobile is not an organism, even though the two have common use and some common qualities. The writer cannot prove anything about a horse by evidence from an automobile, but he may be able to promote understanding of the structure of the horse by noting similarities. An analogy can be a useful device, but it should not be misused.

Original

The modern corporate businessman, in his use of ingenuity, is like the Indians of western Canada. Needing light during their foggy winters, they discovered a new use for the candlefish, which had long been a staple of their diets. This fish is so fat when it swims inland to spawn in the spring that the Indian has only to stick a rush into the fish's back and light it. The fish

Revision

The modern businessman, in his use of American natural resources, has often shown ingenuity, comparable to that of the Indians of western Canada. The Indians had long included in their diet a fatty smelt called the candlefish. Finding that they had too little light through the foggy winter, they discovered that they could stick rushes in the backs of the oily fish and burn them

Original (Cont.)

will then burn like a candle. It is evident, therefore, that modern business owes its success to the ability of Americans to take advantage of their natural resources.

[*The comparison of the ingenuity of the businessman with that of the Indian may make a useful analogy, but it does not warrant the conclusion of the final sentence. The analogy could be used for explanation but not as evidence.*]

Revision (Cont.)

like candles. Similarly the great oil companies have found more uses for oil than to furnish fuel for power and heat. From petroleum they have developed many kinds of synthetic rubbers, and plastics by the hundred.

[*Used as an analogy, not as a proof, the story of the candlefish aids explanation.*]

EXERCISE 10

A. The passages given below contain generalizations which are illustrated or supported by evidence. Comment on the reliability of each generalization, indicating whether it is merely illustrated or is supported by evidence and pointing out especially instances of inadequate or unreliable evidence, of misused analogies, or of faulty causation. Examine each passage in light of the requirements listed in 10-4.

1. During the past month living costs in America have risen 3.4 per cent. This figure is based on statistics compiled by governmental bureaus through sampling prices of selected commodities, and on rents in important areas throughout the United States. It does not take any account of changes in federal or state taxes.

2. A woman preaching is like a dog's walking on his hind legs. It is not done well, but you are surprised to find it done at all.

3. There is no doubt that the students at State University want football to be continued. The campus newspaper in a recent issue invited letters showing why the present sports program should be continued, and more than 200 students replied. Every letter favored retention of football.

4. The enclosed manuscript contains about 22,000 words. In order to arrive at this figure I counted the words on ten typical pages, computed from this total the average number of words per page, and multiplied this average by the number of pages.

5. If the Jews are legally or morally entitled to Palestine, then Mussolini would have been entitled to claim Britain as a colony of the ancient Roman Empire.

6. Although there are more than a hundred quadrillion stars, space is less crowded with stars than the air of Europe would be if it were populated by three wasps.

7. On every occasion in which major tests of atomic bombs have

been made, serious storms have been reported in various parts of the United States. It is evident that these tests must be stopped unless we wish to change the entire weather pattern of our country.

8. Some people think there is nothing in spiritualism, but they have never seen any of the proofs. I was convinced last year when a friend of mine told me what he had actually seen. He had been to a meeting where a woman went into a trance, and then pretty soon people all over the room started trying to talk with spirits out of the other world. It couldn't have been faked, because the spirits knew the people they were talking to and could remember things that happened a long time ago. And a couple of the spirits even materialized and floated around the room. They didn't look much like the real people, of course, because they were spirits, but you could see them so plainly there was no doubt about them.

9. The newspapers are full of nothing but stories about sex and crime. In last night's paper, for instance, there were five crime stories on the first page.

10. The learned man will say, for instance, "The natives of Mumbo-jumbo Land believe that the dead man can eat and will require food upon his journey to the other world. This is attested by the fact that they place food in the grave, and that any family not complying with this rite is the object of the anger of the priests and the tribe." To anyone acquainted with humanity this way of talking is topsy-turvy. It is like saying, "The English in the twentieth century believed that a dead man could smell. This is attested by the fact that they always covered his grave with lilies, violets, or other flowers."

—G. K. CHESTERTON, *Heretics*

11. Clearly Mr. B cannot be guilty of using his business offices to disguise the headquarters of a world-wide syndicate distributing illegal drugs. Two of his business partners testify without reservation to his honesty and good character.

12. The Roman Empire collapsed when Rome became too prosperous. We should be sure to avoid too much prosperity for the United States.

13. "There's more evidence to come yet, please your Majesty," said the White Rabbit, jumping up in a great hurry; "this paper has just been picked up."

"What's in it?" said the Queen.

"I haven't opened it yet," said the White Rabbit, "but it seems to be a letter, written by the prisoner to—to somebody." . . . He unfolded the paper as he spoke, and added, "It isn't a letter after all: it's a set of verses."

"Are they in the prisoner's handwriting?" asked another of the jurymen.

"No, they're not," said the White Rabbit, "and that's the queer-
est thing about it." (The jury all looked puzzled.)

"He must have imitated somebody else's hand," said the King.
(The jury all brightened up again.)

"Please, your Majesty," said the Knave, "I didn't write it, and
they can't prove I did: there's no name signed at the end."

"If you didn't sign it," said the King, "that only makes the
matter worse. You *must* have meant some mischief, or else you'd
have signed your name like an honest man. . . ."

"That *proves* his guilt," said the Queen.

—LEWIS CARROLL, *Alice in Wonderland*

14. The Japanese people are completely in accord with American
democratic principles. This is the conclusion of Mr. J who has
just returned after spending a week in Tokyo visiting his son who
has been in Japan for some time as the American representative
of a large corporation. Mr. J reports that in spite of his handicap
in not knowing the Japanese language he was able to collect
many favorable opinions about this country in his conversations.

15. "People of discrimination smoke Foggs," says beautiful debu-
tante Debbie Dune, "because scientific tests have proved that they
are easier on the throat."

B. Select any three of the following generalizations and list various sorts
of evidence which might be used in support of each:

1. Extracurricular activities in college require a great deal of the
student's time.

2. Fraternities and sororities are valuable parts of college life.

3. Fraternities and sororities foster snobbishness.

4. Radio advertising is often misleading.

5. Lobbies may discourage honest legislation.

6. Convenience does not dictate fashions.

7. Comic books encourage juvenile delinquency.

8. Television is a handicap to education.

C.

Cities		Percentage of Increase, 1940–1950		
			Central	Outside Cen-
	Total	Total	City	tral City
New York	12,831,914	10.0	4.7	22.6
Chicago	5,475,535	13.5	6.2	30.8
Los Angeles	4,339,225	48.8	30.1	68.6
Philadelphia	3,660,676	14.4	6.9	25.8
Detroit	2,973,019	25.1	13.2	50.5
Boston	2,354,457	8.1	2.6	11.1
San Francisco-Oakland ..	2,214,249	51.5	21.8	104.3
Pittsburgh	2,205,544	5.9	0.3	8.6
St. Louis	1,673,467	16.9	4.5	33.2
Washington	1,457,601	50.6	20.3	116.4

The table above gives the population of the ten largest metropolitan areas in the United States according to the census of 1950, the percentage of increase since the census of 1940 for the whole city, the percentage of increase of the population within what is called the "central city," and the percentage outside the central city. Using inductive reasoning, draft three generalizations based upon the table.

D. What evidence would be required to establish the following assertions?

1. Taxes are high because of corruption in government.
2. Lanolin makes the skin softer and smoother.
3. Interpretive dancing has a great future on television.
4. Knute Rockne was the greatest football coach of all time.
5. The Mississippi and Missouri Rivers drain the largest river basin in the world.
6. International treaties can be relied upon.
7. Lemmings march by hordes to drown themselves in the sea.
8. The airplane was invented, not by the Wright Brothers, but by Samuel P. Langley.
9. The Dodgers will win the next world championship.
10. There are 5,280 feet in a mile.

11. LOGIC; DEDUCTIVE REASONING

[For Guide to Revision, see page 107]

If writing pretends to develop an idea logically, be sure that the reasoning is sound.

"To begin with," said the Cat, "a dog's not mad. You grant that?"
"I suppose so," said Alice.
"Well, then," the Cat went on, "you see a dog growls when it's angry, and wags its tail when it's pleased. Now *I* growl when I'm pleased, and wag my tail when I'm angry. Therefore, I'm mad."

The logic of the Cheshire Cat could hardly be expected to fool anyone outside Wonderland. The absurdity more than the validity of his argument suggests his madness. But consider this:

Nobody would accuse American industry of communistic tendencies. American business traditionally supports the Republican party and the interests of investors. On the other hand, labor traditionally supports the Democratic party and seeks the welfare of the worker rather than the prosperity of the investor. Naturally, therefore labor tends toward communism.

The paragraph is not obviously silly. Some persons reading it might agree with the final controversial statement. But they could not have formed their opinion on the basis of the argument presented in the paragraph. The information does no more to establish that labor tends toward communism than the argument above does to prove that the Cheshire Cat is mad. The illogicalness in both examples involves the same sort of faulty deduction.

11-1 Induction and deduction

Thinking almost always combines more than one process. For example, the man described in 10-2 recognizing a frost in the blossoms of his cherry tree could not have reached his conclusion by induction alone. He could observe that the blossoms had turned black in the

[99

center, but he could interpret this change in color only with the aid of another process. He had to call on his experience or his knowledge to give him inductively a generalization; that blossoms which have turned black in the center may have been frozen. Then he could apply this generalization to the facts he saw on his trees and reach the hypothesis that the blossoms he had examined had been frozen. Testing this hypothesis by his knowledge of recent weather and his further investigation, he could generalize that there had been a killing frost. The process by which he interpreted the meaning of the blackened blossoms is deduction, carrying understanding farther by applying generalizations to specific cases in order to learn more about the specific cases.

Thinking, in other words, progresses by chain reaction, in which induction and deduction constantly work together. By induction we examine specific instances until we are justified in making a generalization. Then we can apply this generalization to specific instances and understand the instances more fully. By induction we learn that all students in the college of arts and sciences must enroll for a course in basic science; we discover that Bill Jones is enrolled in the college of arts and sciences. By deduction, applying our general principle to the case of Bill Jones, we know that Bill Jones is enrolled for a science.

A lawyer building a case to prove that Elbridge Dangerfield is guilty of murder uses inductive reasoning to collect evidence which will lead to a generalization. He reasons inductively: a victim was shot through the heart; Mr. Dangerfield was found in the victim's room just after the shooting with a smoking revolver in his hand; the bullet taken from the victim's body was fired from the gun Mr. Dangerfield was holding; the victim had been blackmailing Mr. Dangerfield; therefore Mr. Dangerfield is probably guilty of murder. But an insurance agent sitting in the courtroom as the jury announces its verdict uses deduction to conclude that Elbridge Dangerfield is a bad insurance risk.

11-2 Deduction

Fully understood, deduction is a complicated process, but viewed simply it consists in putting two and two together. It applies generalizations—the results of induction, or general principles, or laws, or even definitions—to specific cases. The reasoning of the insurance agent making a professional estimate of Mr. Dangerfield might be formalized as follows, in a series of patterns known as syllogisms.

MAJOR PREMISE: Any man judged guilty of murder has an excellent chance of hanging.

MINOR PREMISE: Elbridge Dangerfield has been judged guilty of murder.

CONCLUSION: Elbridge Dangerfield has an excellent chance of hanging.

MAJOR PREMISE: Any man who has an excellent chance of hanging is a bad insurance risk.

MINOR PREMISE: Elbridge Dangerfield has an excellent chance of hanging.

CONCLUSION: Elbridge Dangerfield is a bad insurance risk.

The insurance man has seen the relationship between generalizations he knows about and has been able to reach a valid conclusion.

Deduction operates by putting together ideas or statements with a common term, called in logic *the middle term.* In the first group of statements above the element common to each premise is *has been judged guilty of murder;* in the second group each premise is concerned with *has an excellent chance of hanging.* Oversimplified, then, deduction is sometimes like the algebraic formula: if *a* equals *b* and *b* equals *c,* then *a* equals *c.* Two terms *a* and *c* can be related on the basis of the common term *b.* If John is the same age as Bill and Bill is the same age as George, then John is the same age as George. Or, we know that Sir Philip Sidney was killed in the Battle of Zutphen, and we know that the Battle of Zutphen occurred in 1586. We know the date of Sidney's death. We know that all students who do not have medical excuses must take physical education. We know that John Atlas is a student and does not have a medical excuse. We know that he must take physical education. Or we know that no student with a medical excuse needs to take physical education. We know that Wilfred Atlas is a student who has a medical excuse. We know that he does not have to take physical education.

We can look at deduction in another way by thinking of it as a process of relating groups or classes. The statement *Daisy, as she is a cow, is a ruminant,* involves three elements or terms, which might be represented by three circles varying in size according to the relative sizes of the classes they name.

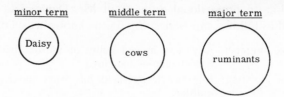

The minor term indicates the small class, the major term the large class, and the middle term the class somewhere between the other two in size. When the statement about the terms is put into its logical steps, it reads:

> MAJOR PREMISE: All cows are ruminants.
> MINOR PREMISE: Daisy is a cow.
> CONCLUSION: Daisy is a ruminant.

The statements say something about how the terms are related or, if we think of the terms as circles, about which term includes the others. By the authority of the major premise, the middle circle can go into the larger one; but the minor premise puts the small circle into the middle one. Necessarily, therefore, the small circle must also be included in the large one.

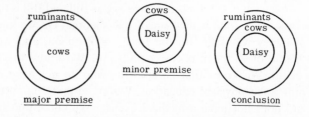

Clearly Daisy belongs among the class of ruminants; the conclusion is *valid* because it follows logically from the premises stated. It is *true* if the premises are true.

11-3 Controlling the middle term

Reasoning turns about a middle term; if conclusions are to be valid, the middle term must be clear and stable. It must have the same meaning each time it appears. *Cow,* the middle term of the statements above, refers to the same thing in both the major and the minor premise. But consider the following:

> All acts which threaten the American way of life are treasonable.
> The new bill on socialized medicine threatens the American way of life.
> The new bill on socialized medicine is treasonable.

The common element, *threatens the American way of life,* is vague to begin with, and its meaning changes from one sentence to the next. When Mark Twain says, "It is easy to give up smoking. I have done it thousands of times," he is shifting the meaning of *give up.* The effect is humorous but not logical.

The middle term must also be "distributed" at least once in any valid logical statement. A term which is distributed includes or excludes all members of the class it denotes; *all cows* or *no cows* is a distributed term. In any logical pattern, then, one premise must say something about all members of a class. The following is valid, though not necessarily true.

> All communists read Karl Marx.
> Mr. Jones is a communist.
> Mr. Jones reads Karl Marx.

The middle term, *communists,* is distributed in the first statement. Or *reads Karl Marx* could be distributed once and used at the middle term.

> Anyone who reads Karl Marx is a communist.
> Mr. Jones reads Karl Marx.
> Mr. Jones is a communist.

Reads Karl Marx, the middle term, is distributed in the major premise. The conclusion is valid, though untrue; but it would not be valid if the middle term were undistributed.

> All communists read Karl Marx.
> Mr. Jones reads Karl Marx.
> Mr. Jones is a communist.

One term, *all communists,* is distributed, but it is not the middle term. The middle term, *read(s) Karl Marx,* is not distributed, and the conclusion is not valid. Although arguments like the above are often accepted—especially when there are emotional reasons for liking the conclusion—they are no more valid than the following:

[103

All chickens have feathers.
This canary has feathers.
This canary is a chicken.

11-4 Using deductive reasoning

Most of us do not spend our time consciously forming major and minor premises, but we use deduction constantly, usually without knowing that we do so. No thinking of any sort from constructing a formula for relativity to deciding to drink a milk shake is possible without deductive logic, though the process is so familiar to us that we perform deduction without ever considering that we are doing anything so formal as thinking logically. We perform deductions so naturally that we even hop over several pairs of premises at once.

For instance, a student is aware of an unpleasant feeling in his stomach only a few minutes before his next class. He turns to the soda-fountain attendant and says, "Chocolate shake." He is probably unaware that he has thought at all. If you were to ask him why he ordered the chocolate milk shake he would probably say that he "felt like one." Actually, his reasoning is much more complex and is mainly deductive. It may have gone something like the following: I feel a little strange inside; previously, when I have felt this way I have been hungry (major and minor premise reversed); therefore, I must be hungry. Anybody who is hungry should get something to eat; I am hungry; therefore, I should get something to eat. Anyone who must get something to eat in a hurry should get something which can be prepared and eaten quickly; therefore, a chocolate milk shake is a good thing for me to order if I am in a hurry. Anyone who should be in class in seven minutes is in a hurry; I am due at Economics 106 in seven minutes; therefore, I am in a hurry. Chocolate milk shakes are available at soda fountains; this is a soda fountain; therefore, chocolate milk shakes are available here. Chocolate milk shakes can be purchased if the purchaser has the money; I have the money; therefore, I can buy a chocolate milk shake. And so on, and on, and on. The process of buying a milk shake, considered with any care, becomes such an elaborate chain of deductive patterns that any student who started to analyze his thoughts probably would never be on time at Economics 106, to say nothing of drinking his milk shake. We are all familiar with deduction as a simple process. Only when it becomes

104]

complicated, as it often does in writing, does deduction lead to faulty reasoning.

11-5 Development by deduction

If every statement in writing had to be analyzed into logical patterns like those above, writing would be both wordy and dull. Deductive patterns, however, are basic to writing, even though they are not labeled premises and conclusions. The following sentences, for example, develop mainly by deductive reasoning.

> As enemy territory becomes more thoroughly protected by fighter planes during daylight hours, it becomes increasingly difficult to take the desired reconnaissance photographs each day. Therefore, the trend is toward more night photography, when darkness lends to planes increased safety from antiaircraft fire and aerial pursuit.
>
> —GEORGE RUSSELL HARRISON, *Atoms in Action*

The logic behind the development of the passage might be put as follows:

MAJOR PREMISE: Pictures cannot be safely taken over areas protected by fighter planes.
MINOR PREMISE: In daylight, areas are protected by fighter planes.
CONCLUSION: Pictures cannot be safely taken in daylight.
MAJOR PREMISE: The trend is toward photography in periods of increased safety.
MINOR PREMISE: Darkness is a period of increased safety.
CONCLUSION: The trend is toward photography in darkness.

The reasoning could be described in other ways and broken down more completely, but clearly the paragraph develops as a series of syllogisms.

11-6 Assumptions; major premises

These syllogisms, however, are not formally expressed. In fact, the major premises are not stated at all. They are assumed by the writer, and if the reader is to accept the ideas of the paragraph he must accept these assumed premises. In actual practice—in development in writing or in everyday thinking (see 11-4)—deduction usually works in this way. Assumptions which are not formally expressed are used as the major premises of the reasoning. Both the writer and the reader, therefore, need to be able to distinguish assumptions from the discussion based on them.

[105

Assumptions lie back of almost everything we do or say. We plan tomorrow and next week on the assumption that the sun will continue to rise, that there will be a tomorrow, that the earth will not burst into a shower of meteorites. This is a tolerably safe assumption. Students go to class on the assumption that the instructor will be there. This assumption is somewhat less certain, and is more or less reliable depending upon a number of conditions, including the instructor's health. Formerly, everybody assumed that if a line looked straight it was, for all practical purposes, straight. Then Einstein demonstrated that all lines curve. Now we have two assumptions. Philosophically we assume that all lines curve. Meanwhile, carpenters work on the assumption that a plumb bob or a square will provide a straight line.

Often assumptions in writing are as reliable and acceptable as that of the carpenter. An editorial writer states: "Police records prove that the old pool hall on Jones Street is encouraging juvenile delinquency; it should be closed." He is assuming, as a major premise, that anything that encourages juvenile delinquency is bad. Probably most readers will accept his assumption and therefore his argument. Or a writer states: "The sight-seeing tour into the mountains should begin at five so that it can be completed before dark." His assumption that sight-seeing is better in daylight than darkness will probably not meet serious opposition.

Suppose, however, that a student writes a theme recommending geology as a liberal arts subject because it promotes an understanding of the world in which we live. He is making many assumptions, among them that knowing about the physical world is so good that it is helpful to everybody. A reader says, "Yes, but geology casts doubt on the truth of Genesis, and anyone who does not believe every word of the Bible will be damned. Saving our souls is the only purpose in life, and thus geology does more harm than good." The reader has not accepted the assumption. The discussion proposed by the theme is not adequate for this reader, and if discussion with him is to continue, the earlier assumption—that knowledge of the physical world is absolutely good—must become not the assumption but the subject for discussion. Or a writer comments, "The man had been on relief for three years; he was obviously lazy." His assumption, the major premise of his argument, that only lazy men are on relief, is questionable, and therefore his argument is questionable.

Clearly, the writer needs to be aware of the assumptions on which he is basing his statements. He needs to change his argument if the assumed major premise is untenable. Or sometimes he needs to state his assumption so that the reader can judge its acceptability. By 1946, a writer on military tactics could assume, perhaps without comment, that the *blitzkrieg* would be part of any subsequent war; but if he was to assume, also, that atomic weapons would determine strategy, he had to say so in order to make the basis of his discussion clear. By 1956, the writer could assume silently that subsequent weapons would be atomic; but if he assumed that an aggressor nation would attack from a space platform, he would need to state his assumption. Sometimes a writer may even adopt an unreal assumption for the sake of discussion. A writer on child psychology, for instance, might begin an article: "Let us assume that you are only three months old."

Stated or not, however, assumptions are the basis of deduction, and therefore of much of our thinking and writing. Both writer and reader need to be aware of them, to distinguish the assumptions from the discussion based on them.

11 *Logic; deductive reasoning*   **Log**

GUIDE TO REVISION:

> *Writing should be logical in its whole plan and in its parts.*

Even though a writer may not employ the formal terminology of logic, his work should be logical. Since writing is always complicated, being logical in expression involves many reasoning processes, but much of logic can be comprised within the general process of deduction. Some of the troublesome aspects of deduction are considered here.

11a Consistency   **Log a**

If a writer states in the first paragraph of a paper that freedom of speech is a basic tenet of our democracy and must be preserved and then in the fourth paragraph insists that an opposition newspaper must stop criticizing the administration, he is obviously inconsistent.

[107

He is applying principles only when they suit his convenience. Statements are logically incompatible when one implies that the other is false. If a writer believes that all criminals are stupid, he cannot logically believe that one criminal he knows is clever and intelligent. He must modify one of his beliefs to preserve logical consistency.

Original	*Revision*
Democracy can succeed only with an educated citizenry. It is of the greatest importance that our schools be as good as possible and that teachers' salaries be high enough to attract our best citizens.	Democracy can succeed only with an educated citizenry. Our schools must be as good as possible and teachers' salaries must be high enough to attract our best citizens.
The city of B has always been proud of its schools, which have stood high in comparison with those of other communities. The city has also been proud of its financial record, its freedom from debt and its willingness to live within its means. It is regrettable, therefore, that the school board in its meeting last night should have seen fit to authorize a bond issue for the sake of expanding our school system and increasing salary scales. . . .	The city of B has always been proud of its schools, but the city has also been proud of its financial record, its freedom from debt and its willingness to live within its means. The school board, therefore, should not have authorized a bond issue in its meeting last night but should have found ways to meet the educational needs of the city through taxation and more efficient use of funds. We must expand our school system and increase salary scales, but we must pay for it as we go.
[*The writer of the editorial is trying to support two incompatible propositions at the same time; he cannot logically do it. He cannot at once support the extension of education and object to the extension of education.*]	[*The revision shifts the ground of the argument in a manner which the original writer would probably not accept, but if he is to be logical, he must change one of his basic attitudes or shift the basis of his complaint.*]

11b Use of middle term   **Log b**

A logical conclusion is invalid if it results from statements in which the middle term is vague or shifting or undistributed (see 11-3). Mishandling of the middle term is at the bottom of much twisted logic, especially attempts to prove "guilt by association": Communists oppose anti-strike legislation; Mr. M opposes anti-strike legislation; therefore, Mr. M is a communist.

Original

The things which have real educational value should obviously be the core of a college curriculum. Nobody who has ever tried to get a job will deny that typing is valuable. Certainly, then, all students should be required to take typing.

[*The terms, especially the middle term* value, *shift and slide. The statements can be set into a logical pattern:*

Courses of value should be required.

Typing has value.

Typing should be required.

But the term value, *as it is used in the passage, changes from a vague general idea to a more specific practical idea.*]

Great poetry becomes richer on successive reading. This must be a great poem, since it has revealed so much more to me on each reading.

[*The passage exhibits the fallacy of the undistributed middle:*

Great poetry becomes richer on successive readings.

This poem becomes richer on successive readings.

This poem is a great poem.

The statement does not exclude the possibility that bad poems also become richer on successive readings and that this is a bad poem.]

Revision

I think that typing, because of its practical value, should be a required course in the college curriculum.

[*There is probably no way in which the writer can make his conclusions both true and valid. Revised so that the middle term is tied down, the statement is logical:*

All courses with practical value should be required.

Typing has practical value.

Typing should be required.

But the major premise—and thus the truth of the conclusion—is now in doubt. Few college curricula could find room for every subject having practical value.]

Only great poetry becomes richer on successive reading. This must be a great poem because it has revealed more to me on each reading.

[*The addition of* only *distributes the middle term in the major premise and makes the conclusion valid. There is, of course, a question about the truth of the major premise and therefore of the conclu·· sion.*]

11c *Arguing in a circle*   Log c

A circular argument assumes or implies whatever it purports to prove. The reader remains no wiser than he was at the beginning, except in his knowledge of the unreliability of the writer.

Original

There is a kind of basic sense or voice within everyone which tells him to be careful and resist when a possible act is wrong. Cheating is that kind of act. Therefore cheating is wrong, because our consciences tell us so.

[*The statement purports to be an argument, but merely turns in a circle, going no place.*]

Revision

Cheating is one of the acts which our consciences tell us are wrong.

[*There was no material for a logical conclusion in the original, but with a general statement which says what he wishes to say, the writer can then try to substantiate his main idea with other facts or arguments.*]

11d Including steps in the argument   Log d

Writers sometimes fail to carry the reader with them through all the steps of their argument, either because the argument is confused in their own minds or because they forget the need for showing the reader their reasoning processes.

Original

When clarinets are not playing, a band sounds dull, because the notes of the clarinet are so high and shrill.

[*The sentence makes no sense as it stands, although the reader can guess that the writer had some kind of logical notion in mind. But the statement makes so big a jump that the reader cannot see how highness and shrillness prevent the band from being dull.*]

Revision

The high and shrill tones of the clarinets are needed in a band to give it life and color. Therefore, when the clarinets are not playing, a band sounds dull.

[*With all the steps of the argument stated, the conclusion is valid, although many readers might reject the premise, and hence the conclusion.*]

Apparently the *Titanic* had been built very well, for the crew did not know the lifeboat assignments.

[*The ignorance of the crew about lifeboat assignments is not conceivably a reason for believing that the ship had been well built. The writer has jumped so many steps that his thinking seems confused.*]

Everyone on the ship considered the *Titanic* so well built that she was unsinkable. Members of the crew were so confident of the ship's safety that they had not even learned their lifeboat assignments.

[*With steps in the thinking filled in, the relationship between the building of the ship and the lifeboat assignments appears.*]

110]

11e Assumptions   Log e

Since reasoning seldom appears in the neat formal patterns of the syllogism, assumptions behind statements are not always apparent. The methods of deduction can be used to reveal and test assumptions. Consider, for instance, the following from a student theme:

> Although there have been a few highly publicized instances of serious injury, football is not really harmful to students and should be retained as part of every university program.

The statement appears in valid form, and some readers might accept it without question. When, however, the basic assumption of the statement appears as the major premise at a syllogism, the absurdity is apparent:

> Anything not harmful should be on a university program.
> Football is not harmful.
> Football should be part of every university program.

The syllogism is valid, but it is not true because it is based on an untenable major premise; even the writer probably would not maintain that anything harmless—eating a cream puff, for instance—belongs on all university programs. Consider another statement of the same type:

> It is difficult to take your eyes off this magnificent lamp since it is a hundred years old.

Faced with a bald statement of his assumption—that anything a hundred years old must be worth attention—the writer would probably be less positive. Or consider a less obvious example:

> He found himself actually enjoying the plays of Shakespeare.

The statement does not explicitly state a logical proposition, but behind it is the assumption that Shakespeare's plays are dull.

A logical statement is true only if its premises are true, and reader and writer must be aware of the assumptions on which statements depend.

Original	*Revision*
A liberal arts course is a waste of time because it trains for no profession.	1. A liberal arts course trains for no profession.
	2. A liberal arts course is a waste of time.
[*The assumption is that any course which does not train for a*	[*The two statements combined*

Original (Cont.)

profession is a waste of time, a more doubtful statement, perhaps, than the writer realized.]

Fraternities are obviously valuable parts of college life. Consider how long they have existed.

[Is the implied reason one the writer would try to maintain? Gangs of hoodlums also have a long history.]

Revision (Cont.)

in the original do not work together. The writer should select one, or perhaps drop the whole idea.]

1. Fraternities contribute to college life.
2. Fraternities have been a valuable part of college life for many years.

[The writer can find means of supporting his generalization if he restates it.]

EXERCISE 11

A. Indicate which of the sets of premises and conclusions given below are valid and which are true. Give the reasons for your decisions.

1. All cats have nine lives.
   Tabby is a cat.
   Tabby has nine lives.

2. All good citizens vote.
   Al Capone voted.
   Al Capone was a good citizen.

3. Money is the root of all evil.
   Time is money.
   Time is the root of all evil.

4. No tigers have wings.
   This creature has wings.
   This creature is not a tiger.

5. Sixty men require one-sixtieth the time required by one man.
   One man can remove an automobile tire in sixty seconds.
   Sixty men can remove the same tire in one second.

6. No cat has eight tails.
   One cat has one more tail than no cat.
   One cat has nine tails.

7. Any golfer who makes a hole in one is lucky.
   Francis made a hole in one.
   Francis was lucky.

8. Man is the only creature capable of reason.
   Mary is not a man.
   Therefore Mary is incapable of reason.

B. Discuss the logical truth and validity of the reasoning in the following passages:

1. Students, like all young people with active minds, are easily susceptible to any idea like communism, which seems to be advanced and at first glance may hold out hope for the impractical idealist. It is easy to see why our colleges should be shot through with communism.

2. People who are poor lack ambition; if they did not lack ambition they would not be poor.

3. The editorial in the last student newspaper says that only a student can understand the need for a better intramural program on the campus. Well, I am a student, and I certainly think that the program we now have is all anyone could ask for. The editorial writer should be more logical about what he says.

4. The money was taken between 11 o'clock and noon from the desk in this room. Nobody has left the room since eleven o'clock. One of the persons who have been present in the room must have taken the money. John was in the room. Obviously, he took the money.

5. All governments, for reasons of security, must deceive the public from time to time. This bulletin, therefore, issued by the government, must be false.

6. Houses with shallow foundations should be avoided at all costs; but since this house has an unusually deep, reinforced foundation, you can have no reason for rejecting it.

7. It was plain as a pikestaff. Anyone traveling on the African mail boat would be three days late. Mr. Sims was three days late. Therefore he must be on the mail boat from Africa.

8. We ought to be guided by the opinion of our ancestors, for old age is wiser than youth.

9. Of course, art is dying. The capacity of one man among ten million to create, whether in art or thought, whether in science or invention, is the hallmark of men's inequality, so that democracies which aim at equality have neither reward nor honor to offer to genius.

10. Man has so few distinct and characteristic marks which hold true of all his species, that philosophers in all ages have found it a task of infinite difficulty to give him a definition. Hence one has defined him to be a *featherless biped,* a definition which is equally applicable to an unfledged fowl: another, to be an animal *which forms opinions,* than which nothing can be more inaccurate, for a very small number of the species form opinions, and the remainder take them upon trust, without investigation or inquiry.

—THOMAS LOVE PEACOCK

[113

C. Each of the statements below assumes a major premise which is not stated. Supply the assumption behind each statement.

1. She must be intelligent if she is on the honor roll.

2. All high school students should have courses in driver education; careful driving is something they should know about.

3. The people next door go to church regularly; they will want to make a contribution to the Red Cross.

4. Many comic books are bad for children as they deal with wild and improbable adventures.

5. It is ridiculous to suppose that we can ever get rid of anything that has existed in our society as long as nationalism has.

6. He cannot be expected to be in sympathy with American ideas of democracy; he was born in Europe.

7. It should be a good dress; it cost more than any dress in the store.

8. You could tell she was a gossip because she criticized some of the most important clubwomen in town.

9. General B is certain to make a good university president; look how successful he was during the war.

10. Socialists really support the American system of government, for they believe in government by the people.

D. In this selection from *Macbeth,* Lady Macbeth is berating her husband because, having proposed murdering the king, he now prefers not to do so. Upon what general assumptions (major premises) is Lady Macbeth relying, even though she does not express all of them, but assumes their truth?

Lady M. Was the hope drunk
Wherein you dressed yourself? and hath it slept since?
And wakes it now, to look so green and pale
At what it did so freely? From this time
Such I account thy love. Art thou afeard
To be the same in thine own act and valour
As thou art in desire? Wouldst thou have that
Which thou esteems the ornament of life,
And live a coward in thine own esteem,
Letting "I dare not" wait upon "I would,"
Like the poor cat i' the adage?

Macb. Prithee, peace:
I dare do all that may become a man;
Who dares do more is none.

Lady M. What beast was't then,
That made you break this enterprise to me?

When you durst do it, then you were a man;
And, to be more than what you were, you would
Be so much more the man.

E. Find as many assumed generalizations as you can in the passage below. You should be able to find at least a dozen.

The steel industry is the backbone of the nation. Without steel, our armies could not advance in the field; the other great American industries could not continue their steady advance, becoming ever larger and more efficient; the manufacturers of consumer goods could not continue to create time and leisure by increasing the bulk and excellence of labor-saving devices. Without the modern American steel industry planes could not fly at ever greater speeds, bombs could not be devised for ever-widening purposes, skyscrapers could not soar to ever greater heights—in short, society could not advance in the civilized world, and civilization could not penetrate ever farther into the dark places of the world. In the good world of today and the better world of tomorrow, not only industry, but also government, education, science, and society itself advance upon the rails of steel.

12. RELEVANCE

[For Guide to Revision, see page 119]

In clear writing, every element is relevant to the final purpose of the writer.

Juliet. Is thy news good, or bad? Answer to that . . .

Nurse. Well, you have made a simple choice; you know not how to choose a man: Romeo! no, not he; though his face be better than any man's, yet his leg excels all men's; and for a hand, and a foot, and a body, though they be not to be talked on, yet they are past compare. He is not the flower of courtesy, but I'll warrant him, as gentle as a lamb. Go thy ways, wench; serve God. What! have you dined at home?

Juliet. No, no; but all this did I know before. What says he of our marriage? what of that?

Juliet has good reason to be impatient. The Nurse has failed to keep to the point of the conversation, presumably because she is a bit of a tease. She pretends to assume that Juliet wants to discuss Romeo's personal merits, and thus everything she says is irrelevant.

12-1 Keeping to the point

The Nurse's style is appropriate enough for a humorous character in a play; it is not effective in ordinary composition. Similar irrelevance, however, often mars student writing; the following sounds very much like the verbal meandering of Juliet's Nurse.

The natives along the coast seemed completely civilized. Missionaries had brought civilization to the island late in the eighteenth century. Different groups of missionaries soon followed. They represented different sects and did not agree on all points of doctrine. Sometimes they disagreed violently about plans for work on the island. It does not seem to me proper for missionaries to quarrel as they apparently did. Something, however, seems to have developed the civilization of these natives. For example, they live in quite modern houses. This is remarkable, because building materials are quite expensive. Most materials have to be imported. . . .

By this time the reader is as impatient as Juliet, waiting for the writer to decide what he is talking about. He establishes a topic in the opening sentence but strays off in pursuit of eighteenth-century missionaries. When he finally returns to the subject he has apparently planned to discuss, he remains for only two sentences. The mention of modern houses suggests another side path, and the writer rambles again. He fails to keep to a subject (see 2), to reject irrelevant material.

Clear writing keeps constantly to the purpose. Every word, sentence, or paragraph furthers the discussion. Theoretically, a writer should be able to explain to himself why he has used any expression in his paper, why it is relevant. If he cannot justify a passage, it is suspect. It is probably irrelevant or is not expressed in a manner which makes its relevance easily yet unobtrusively apparent.

12-2 Relevant development

Development is clear only if illustrations, evidence, and logical discussion clearly pertain to the writer's purpose. In writing like the following, every element can be shown to have some relevance to the purposes of the whole.

(1) So, Mr. M'Choakumchild began in his best manner. (2) He and some one hundred and forty other schoolmasters had been lately turned out at the same time, in the same factory, on the same principles, like so many pianoforte legs. (3) He had been put through an immense variety of paces, and had answered volumes of head-breaking questions. (4) Orthography, etymology, syntax, and prosody, biography, astronomy, geography, and general cosmography, the sciences of compound proportion, algebra, land-surveying and levelling, vocal music, and drawing from models, were all at the ends of his ten chilled fingers. (5) He had worked his stony way into Her Majesty's Most Honourable Privy Council's Schedule B, and had

[(*1*) *introduces the character, carrying on what has preceded.* (*2*) *makes a general statement which is to limit what follows, to determine the kind of details to be selected.*]

[(*3*) *illustrates* (*2*) *in fairly general terms, but it turns the description in a definite direction, to the man's training.* (*4*) *begins specific illustrations of training, illustrations which will combine to give an impression of one aspect of the man.*]

[(*5*) *presents further specific illustrations, presented in language which shows the writer's attitude toward the character.*]

[117

taken the bloom off the higher branches of mathematics and physical science, French, German, Latin, and Greek. (6) He knew all about all the Water Sheds of all the world (whatever they are), and all the histories of all the peoples, and all the names of all the rivers and mountains, and all the productions, manners, and customs of all the countries, and all their boundaries and bearings on the two and thirty points of the compass. (7) Ah, rather overdone, M'Choakumchild. (8) If he had only learnt a little less, how infinitely better he might have taught much more.

—CHARLES DICKENS, *Hard Times*

[*(6) is another illustration, a further example of the mass of insignificant facts the man has learned.*]

[*(7) summarizes the attitude toward this training which has been implied all along. (8) goes farther than the indication of an attitude in (7) and draws a conclusion from the details that have appeared.*]

The paragraph is effective because details fill a specific purpose, to give a particular impression of Mr. M'Choakumchild. Dickens has avoided mentioning his character's virtues, of which there must have been a few; he has restricted his paragraph to details which illustrate the ponderousness and extent of Mr. M'Choakumchild's learning. Even within this class of details, he has further restricted himself to details which illustrate the extent of Mr. M'Choakumchild's learning but which can also be presented so that they will make that learning seem insignificant or stuffy or oppressive—a disadvantage to Mr. M'Choakumchild rather than an advantage. Even the choice of words emphasizes this attitude—"at the ends of his ten chilled fingers" or "had taken the bloom off the higher branches of mathematics."

Even when the pattern is less obvious, the details in good writing are relevant.

(1) Two things happen when you look at a tree. (2) First, you have the picture of the tree reflected upon the brain through the medium of sight—that is to say, a little card picture, a little photograph of the tree. (3) But even if you wanted to paint this image with words, you could not do it; and if you could do it, the result

[*(1) sets a subject for discussion; tells the reader what to expect. (2) specifies one of the "things" promised by (1), clarifying it by comparing it to more concrete objects, "card pictures," "photograph." (3) continues the description of the first "thing" by describing what would be an irrelevant characteristic in many cir-*

would not be worth talking about. (4) But almost as quickly, you receive a second impression, very different from the first. (5) You observe that the tree gives you a peculiar feeling of some kind. (6) The tree has a certain character, and this perception of the character of the tree is the feeling or the emotion of the tree. (7) That is what the artist looks for; and that is what the poet looks for.

—LAFCADIO HEARN, *Life and Literature*

cumstances; here, as the final sentence shows, it is highly relevant. (4) brings in the second "thing" of (1). (5) specifies more clearly the second "thing." (6) again specifies and summarizes the second impression of the tree, doing it in such a way that the reader is led to (7); that is, (6) puts the idea into the terms needed to make (7) clear. (7) concludes; it ties the preceding information together, and relates the paragraph to the whole composition.]

This paragraph does more than list details illustrating a single, central idea; it selects relevant material and presents it in a way which shows its relevance. The writer must select intelligently, and show why he has selected. Each element of a piece of writing must be so presented that it shows the reader how it is related to the whole.

12 Relevance   **Rel**

GUIDE TO REVISION:

Include only material clearly relevant, or revise to clarify the relevance of material.

12a Relevant details   **Rel a**

Original

(1) Early in the morning they began chanting prayers and dancing around a large fire in the clearing. (2) The monotonous beat of the drum and the rhythm of the voices were punctuated by loud whoops. (3) The sound of the women beating sticks together, keeping time with the drums, blended with the barking of the dogs and the yelling of the children. (4) *This celebration is carried on much as it was centuries*

Revision

Early in the morning they began chanting prayers and dancing around a large fire in the clearing. The monotonous beat of the drums and the rhythm of the voices were punctuated by loud whoops. The sound of the women beating sticks together, keeping time with the drums, blended with the barking of the dogs and the yelling of the children. The bright feathers of the war-bonnets made weird shadows on the trees.

[119

Original (Cont.)

ago. (5) *They dance from morning until late at night.* (6) The bright feathers of the war-bonnets made weird shadows on the trees.

Revision (Cont.)

[*Sentences (4) and (5) are irrelevant and have been omitted, perhaps to be worked in somewhere else in the composition.*]

12b Showing relevance

Original

(1) The trend in feeding cattle in days past was to hold them in feeding lots and on range land for eighteen to twenty-four months. (2) *Today we find this situation remarkably changed.* (3) In Wyoming, Montana, and New Mexico vast areas had to be used for the grazing of large numbers of beef cattle. (4) Ranchers find they are able to raise as many cattle today on only one half the amount of land they previously needed. (5) *Modern feed for beef cattle consists of timothy, oats, wheat, and alfalfa.* (6) *Roughage of corn is used with molasses for a winter feed.* (7) *These feeds are being fed beef cattle with completely satisfactory results.* (8) Thus irrigated pastures and formulated food in the diet of the beef herd have brought about conservation of land and resources.

[*Sentences (2) and (5-7) seem unrelated to the main idea of the paragraph, not because they are irrelevant but because their relevance is not shown.*]

Rel b

Revision

The trend in feeding cattle in days past was to hold them in feeding lots and on range land for eighteen to twenty-four months. In Wyoming, Montana, and New Mexico vast areas were used for grazing large numbers of beef cattle. Today feeding methods are remarkably different. Ranchers find they are able to raise as many cattle today on only half the amount of land they previously needed. Using irrigated pastures and feed such as timothy, oats, wheat and alfalfa, supplemented in winter with roughage of corn used with molasses, ranchers can conserve land and resources.

[*The same details can be made relevant when they are rearranged and rewritten; (2) becomes clear when it is moved to a more logical position after (3). The material in (5-7) is relevant when it is worked into the paragraph in parts of other sentences.*]

EXERCISE 12

A. The paragraphs below from student themes contain elements which either are irrelevant or are not written so that their relevance is clear. Rewrite the paragraphs so that all details are clearly relevant.

1. Human beings are far different from the three-toed sloth, but the sloth has many advantages in his way of life. The definition of the sloth as found in the dictionary is "a South American

arboreal quadruped which hangs from branches, back down, and feeds on leaves and fruits." No human being can spend his days curled up in a ball in a tree, so indistinguishable from his surroundings that no one could find him to injure him or set him to work. None of the emotional problems of the human being bothers the sloth. A mother sloth, for example, never seems to worry about her offspring. If the young sloth moves too far away, he is simply abandoned. And the sloth's daily bread is a simple matter. He simply reaches in his extraordinarily leisurely way for a leaf or two and never seems to crave variety in his diet.

2. Finally, I plan to study law because I believe that lawyers are in a position to do a great deal of good for humanity. Abraham Lincoln and many other famous men were lawyers. The lawyer is responsible for making legislation work. He therefore can work to see justice done, whether by saving an innocent person from unjust punishment or by helping to protect society from the dangers of unrestricted violation of the law. One man I know was almost found guilty of embezzlement because of a mistake in his records at the bank where he was teller—a mistake made by someone else. The lawyer also can help protect the property rights and civil liberties of individuals. His legal knowledge makes him able to forestall the attempts of the unscrupulous to infringe upon the rights of others. He even helps to develop legislation by revealing the inadequacies of existing statutes and suggesting revisions.

3. The main reason for housing shortages in the United States today is the wide gap between the costs of producing housing and the ability to pay of those who need it. It has been estimated that we need 3,000,000 dwelling units in the United States today. According to the 1955 census report, 26.8% had no tub or shower; 49.6% had no central heating. New housing is being built, but almost no rental units are being constructed which can be rented for less than $60 or $65 a month. And very few new houses are being built to sell at less than $6,000 or $7,000; in fact, most new houses are nearer $10,000. Rents have increased since the 1945 census, but at that time more than three-fourths of renters were paying less than $40 a month, and houses occupied by their owners were worth about $3,000 each. The people needing the new housing are not in a position to pay more. In 1950 the index of new house construction rose to a peak of 172.6% of the 1947-49 average index, 1935–1939, but it has since declined. A recent War Department survey showed that of veterans needing housing less than a fourth could pay more than $50 a month for rent or for payments if they were buying. Some kind of low-cost housing is needed to bridge the gap that separates supply and demand. Remodeling of obsolete structures has also declined.

B. Using the notes on the passage from Dickens's *Hard Times* (pages 117-118) as a model, analyze two paragraphs from one of your themes, describing the relevance of each sentence, telling what it does or how it contributes to the whole.

C. Assume that you are to write an essay on each of the following subjects: (a) "Television Supplants Radio," (b) "Radio Around the World," (c) "An American Is a Man with a Receiving Set," (d) "Radio-Television: Big Business," (e) "Two Decades of Radio." Which of the following facts would be relevant to which essays?

1. Radio sets in the U.S.S.R., 1950—8,000,000.

2. Value of radio and television tubes manufactured in the United States, 1930—$50,000,000.

3. Radio and television sets in Europe, 1950—61,500,000.

4. Sets manufactured in the United States, 1947—radio, 17,000,000; television, 210,000.

5. Frequency modulation stations in the United States, 1950—760.

6. States having the largest number of broadcasting stations—Texas, 222; California, 219.

7. In 1950 Transjordania, Northern Rhodesia, and French Somaliland each had only a few hundred receiving sets.

8. Value of radio and television tubes manufactured, 1950— $550,000,000.

9. Radio and television sets in Asia, 1950—12,000,000.

10. Sets manufactured in the United States, 1950—radio, 14,000,000; television, 6,500,000.

11. Television broadcast stations, 1950—New York, 13; Ohio, 12; California, 11.

12. Total sets of all kinds in the United States, 1950—103,000,000.

13. Replacement tubes in the United States, 1950—100,000,000; value, $160,000,000.

14. In 1930 practically no auto sets were in use; by 1950 Americans were using 17,000,000 sets.

15. Total sets of all kinds outside the United States, 1950—92,500,000.

16. By 1950, radio and television sets in Italy numbered 2,204,580; in Spain, 557,794.

17. Television sets in use in the United States—close of 1949, 3,250,-000; close of 1950, 9,800,000.

18. By 1950, the annual bill of the United States for radio and television had passed $4,450,000,000.

19. Retail value of sets manufactured in the United States, 1950— radio, $650,000,000; television, $2,000,000,000.

20. Frequency modulation resulted in part from the discoveries of Dr. E. H. Armstrong.

21. In 1950 in the United States there were radios in 45,000,000 homes; 27,000,000 of these homes had secondary sets, and 8,000,-000 of these homes had television sets; cars driven by residents in these homes had 14,000,000 radios.

22. By 1950, there were 1,500 radio, television, and record manufacturers in the United States, doing an annual gross business of $1,500,000,000, and unnumbered distributors doing an annual gross business of $2,500,000,000.

13. POINT OF VIEW; TONE

[For Guide to Revision, see page 129]

Point of view refers to the position in space and time from which a writer views his material; tone refers to the attitude the writer adopts toward his material and his reader.

Following are passages from two student themes, written on the same topic and about the same central idea—that some types of advertising should be discontinued.

> The general public has great faith in the printed word. People tend to believe what they read in supposedly reputable newspapers and magazines. Advertising, therefore, which makes false claims about the values of a product or the consequences of failing to use it may cause real hardship and may eventually even harm the standing of the company.

> In the living room I found my mother in tears; she had been snubbed by the Tuesday Afternoon Bridge Club. Sadly I watched her fingering the white blouse in which tattle-tale gray persisted in spite of the new soap. My sister was revising the second paragraph of her suicide note; she had not had a date for a week in spite of using all the proper soaps and toothpastes and mouthwashes. She faced the question why romance had passed her by, and there were no more answers in the advertisements.

The two writers attempt to make essentially the same point, but they differ widely. The first theme is serious and objective, an attempt to make a reasoned, logical statement; the second is ironic, exaggerated; it employs ridicule, reducing to absurdity the kind of advertising its author resents. The themes differ in *tone*—that is, in the attitude the writer takes toward his material and toward his reader.

Or compare two professional writers describing the same scene from the reign of terror that followed the French Revolution.

The call to plunder was received with enthusiasm, and in the morning of the 25th of February a troop of women marched to the Seine and, after boarding the vessels that contained cargoes of soap, helped themselves liberally to all they required at a price fixed by themselves, that is to say, for almost nothing. Since no notice was taken of these proceedings, a far larger crowd collected at dawn of the following day and set forth on a marauding expedition to the shops. From no less than 1200 grocers the people carried off everything on which they could lay their hands—oil, sugar, candles, coffee, brandy—at first without paying, then, overcome with remorse, at the price they themselves thought proper.

—NESTA H. WEBSTER, *The French Revolution*

And now from six o'clock, this Monday morning, one perceives the Bakers' Queues unusually expanded, angrily agitating themselves. Not the Baker alone, but two Section Commissioners to help him, manage with difficulty the daily distribution of loaves. Soft-spoken, assiduous, in the early candle-light, are Baker and Commissioners: and yet the pale chill February sunrise discloses an unpromising scene. Indignant Female Patriots, partly supplied with bread, rush now to the shops, declaring they will have groceries. Groceries enough: sugar-barrels, rolled forth into the street, Patriot Citoyennes weighing it out at a just rate of elevenpence a pound; likewise coffee-chests, soap-chests, nay cinnamon and clove-chests, with *aqua-vitae* and other forms of alcohol,—at a just rate, which some do not pay; the pale-faced Grocer silently wringing his hands!

—THOMAS CARLYLE, *The French Revolution*

These passages differ in tone, but they differ most notably in *point of view*—that is, in the position in space and time from which the writer looks at his subject. The first writer assumes that she is looking back on events of the past, describing them objectively. The second asks the reader to imagine himself on the scene and describes events as if they were occurring as he writes.

13-1 Varieties of tone

Tone reflects the attitude of the writer toward his material and his expected reader. Tone, therefore, depends upon the abilities and purposes of the writer, the nature of his material, the education, interests, and prejudices of the reader, and the circumstances which have called forth the composition. Obviously, tone can be almost infinitely varied. The writer may approach his material and his audience seriously, or he may adopt a joking or whimsical manner toward both. He may promote confidence with a judicial calm, or he may stimulate action with exaggerated enthusiasm. He may be objective, formal, informal, ironic, jovial, confidential, flattering, wheedling, belligerent, conciliating, or what not. The following are only a few of the more obvious approaches which may affect the tone of a composition:

(1) *Objective*. A telephone directory or a compilation of statutes reveals little of the opinions or prejudices of its writer, but it has tone; that is, it assumes an objective, noncommittal attitude toward its material and its readers. Many other types of writing approach a similar tone, offering material as impartially as possible. Scientific works, textbooks, histories, newspaper accounts, factual magazine articles, or informative bulletins are likely to be primarily objective in tone.

(2) *Formal*. Serious writing often, though not always, promotes a formal author-reader relationship, the writing acquiring a dignity and decorum dictated more by literary tradition than by the habits of ordinary speech. Consider the following selection from Emerson's essay, *Self-Reliance:*

> Trust thyself: every heart vibrates to that iron string. Accept the place the divine providence has found for you, the society of your contemporaries, the connection of events. Great men have always done so, and confided themselves childlike to the genius of their age, betraying their perception that the absolutely trustworthy was seated at their heart, working through their hands, predominating all their being.

The tone of planned, formal expression appears in the vocabulary, in the patterned, balanced rhythm, in the elevated manner. The tone suits Emerson's subject and purposes; a similar manner would be embarrassingly inappropriate for a student theme pleading for softer seats in the gymnasium.

(3) *Informal*. Much modern writing gains the allegiance of the reader by an intimate, genial manner. Charles Lamb's essay, *Old China,* establishes an informal tone at once:

> I have an almost feminine partiality for old china. When I go to see a great house, I inquire for the china-closet and next for the picture-gallery. I cannot defend the order of preference, but by saying that we have all some taste or other, of too ancient a date to admit of our remembering distinctly that it was an acquired one.

Lamb chats with his reader, observing neither forms nor ceremony. His essay may have a serious purpose, but it remains friendly, informal.

(4) *Emphatic, enthusiastic.* Especially in fiction, writers may heighten style and overstate for emphasis. Observe an emotional scene in Charles Dickens' *Bleak House:*

> I saw before me, lying on the step, the mother of the dead child. She lay there, with one arm creeping round a bar of the iron gate, and seeming to embrace it. She lay there, who had so lately spoken to my mother. She lay there, a distressed, a sheltered, senseless creature.

The context may justify the highly rhetorical, figurative style, although out of context the passage sounds inflated. Such a tone conveys emotion, but unjustified, it rings false. Outside a context which warrants overstatement, an exaggerated manner becomes stupid pomposity or sentimentality, a cheap attempt to stimulate undue emotion.

(5) *Ironical.* Compare with the above excerpt from Dickens another passage by the same writer, this from *Pickwick Papers:*

> Rising rage and extreme bewilderment had swelled the noble breast of Mr. Pickwick, almost to the bursting of his waistcoat, during the delivery of the above defiance. He stood transfixed to the spot, gazing on vacancy. The closing of the door recalled him to himself. He rushed forward with fury in his looks, and fire in his eye.

The two passages by Dickens differ in tone. In *Bleak House* the tone is dramatic and tense, in keeping with the narrator's discovery of his dead mother. In *Pickwick* the scene shows a humorous character reacting to a belligerent little doctor who has just said, "I would have pulled your nose, sir." The incident is dramatic but not tragic, and the tone is ironic. That is, the reader understands from the context that he is not to interpret words literally—that the breast of Mr. Pickwick is more "noble" in size than in courage, that the "fury" in Mr. Pickwick's look or the "fire in his eye" is more ludicrous than frightening. Irony may vary from this sort of tolerably subtle whimsy to bitter sarcasm. It may be the tone of a sentence like a young man's "Aren't you afraid we'll be early?" to a girl who has kept him waiting in the dormitory hall until the play is half over. It may be the tone of an entire essay like Swift's famous *A Modest Proposal,* suggesting that if Irish children are to be starved they had as well be butchered. Writing may be ironic whenever a statement in its context suggests a sense different from—often opposite to—its literal meaning.

The possible variations on these or other approaches are infinite; good writing requires a tone which is appropriate to the writer, his material, and the reader. Usually what seems most "natural" to the writer works best, but once the tone is established it should be maintained.

13-2 Consistency in person

There is a story that Harold Ross, long editor of *The New Yorker*, had a favorite criticism of a cartoon: "Who's talking?" He would often demand that the artist open the speaker's mouth wider or otherwise indicate who was responsible for the words in the caption. The writer has less trouble than the cartoonist in showing who's talking, but he has to do it. Usually the writer uses the third-person approach for objectivity: *Student government requires . . . The new teacher entered . . .* He may want to assume a more personal relationship and describe events or facts in the first person as he saw them: *I observed student government . . . My new teacher saw me . . .* He may, although it is out of fashion except in some newspapers, avoid *I* by using the editorial *we,* a device for shifting the responsibility for a statement by suggesting that the entire newspaper accepts it: *We believe that student government requires . . .* In a slightly different sense, *we* is often used—as it is in passages in this text—to indicate people in general: *We use pronouns to stand for nouns.* In a narrative the writer may speak objectively but recount events from the point of view of a main character: *George soon discovered that student government . . .* The possibilities are numerous; the writer should be consistent enough to keep the reader from confusion.

13-3 Consistency in space

Often the position of a writer in space is not important; we need not, for example, know the location of a writer discussing philosophy. In a description, however, and in some other expository compositions, location may be very important. The writer must assume that he is located in some relation to his material, and if he moves about without letting the reader know, the reader is confused.

13-4 Consistency in time

The writer assumes a position in time in relation to his subject; he must let the reader know his position, and he must not shift without warning. In a narration he probably will assume that he is looking back from the present, as in the first paragraph on the French Revolution on page 125; or he may pretend to record events as they occur, as in the second paragraph. A term paper on Shakespeare may involve a variety of times which the writer needs to distinguish.

1. Shakespeare *was* thirty-eight years old when the first edition of *Hamlet* appeared in London.
2. He *had earned* a reputation as one of the leading dramatists of his day.
3. *Hamlet has been discussed* and *criticized* more than any of the other plays.
4. It *is* a favorite on the modern stage.
5. In the play Hamlet *is faced* with a decision which he *cannot* make.
6. Ironically the only course consistent with Hamlet's character and satisfactory to the audience *leads* to disaster.

The sentences illustrate only a few of the kinds of time (see 30-3 to 30-5). The first indicates the basic attitude of the writer; he is in the present writing of events in the past. The second mentions what has occurred *before* the past time of the first. The third concerns what has occurred continuously and indefinitely in the past. And the last three treat the play as it exists at the time the writer is discussing it.

13 Point of View; Tone   PV; Tone

GUIDE TO REVISION:

> *Revise the composition to make it appropriate and consistent in tone and point of view.*

A composition requires various materials and therefore varies in tone, person, place, and time. A writer may even take a position in the present looking back and then shift for a paragraph or two to pretend he is at the scene of a past event: *Let us imagine ourselves looking at the eight towers of the Bastille on July 14, 1789. Before us is the high central gate. . . .* But the writer must not make such shifts in point of view without reason and without showing the reader what is happening.

13a Appropriateness and consistency in tone   PV a; Tone

An appropriate tone fits its subject matter and its reader. A student who writes in sober ecstasy of the world-shaking importance of a home-run he hit to win a junior-league baseball game is likely to create more unintentional humor than genuine respect for his batting eye. The lecturer who takes a tone of patronizing condescension to a group of college students misjudges his audience by treating them as children and annoys more than he informs. The writer who offers commonplace or trivial ideas in a formal, rhetorical manner is likely to appear more pompous than wise. An appropriate tone should be established and maintained.

Original

Graduation from high school is a very important event, often shaping much of a person's future career in life. It is a time of commencement, not of ending. But it also is a time when a person realizes the importance of the hard struggle that has carried him successfully through four years of heartbreaks and triumphs. When those wonderful words of congratulation ring out after the awarding of diplomas, every graduate knows a thrill which he will never forget. It is truly a wonderful moment.

[*The tone of overstatement and high seriousness is not justified by the occasion, and the passage does more to reveal the immaturity of the writer than to convince a reader.*]

. . . Tying flies requires patience, practice, and skill, but there is a kind of special thrill in hooking a trout with a fly you have made yourself.

And now if you are not completely bored by my lesson on how to tie a fly, let us go on, dear reader, to what the flies are to be used for. Fly-fishing. . . .

[*After a straightforward discussion, the writer shifts to what is perhaps an attempt at mild humor or "lightening" the paper.*]

Revision

To the high school graduate, commencement may seem the most important event in life. The parade in white dresses and blue suits or caps and gowns, the music with all the ringing discords of which a nervous school orchestra is capable, the grim, freshly-scrubbed faces, the earnest platitudes of the student orations, all convince the graduate that this is the real turning point of his life. He leaves certain that he will never forget a moment of what has occurred, and a year later he may actually remember something of it.

[*A lighter tone, with factual details replacing the overstatement, leads to a less naïve paragraph. Other approaches, of course, would have been possible.*]

. . . Tying flies requires patience, practice, and skill, but there is a kind of special thrill in hooking a trout with a fly you have made yourself.

Catching a trout, however, requires not only a well-made lure but a good deal of skill in using it. Fly-fishing. . . .

[*A more direct transition introduces the new topic equally well and avoids the awkward shift in tone.*]

13b Consistency in person   **PV b**

See also 28j.

Original

If you want your campfire to be both safe and useful, you have to build it carefully. You have to begin by selecting a good place for the fire. One should be sure that there are no trees within ten feet of the site and that all leaves and brush have been cleared away.

[*The writer begins with* you *as his subject but shifts in the third sentence to* one, *for no apparent reason.*]

Revision

If you want your campfire to be both safe and useful, you must build it carefully. Begin by selecting a good place for the fire. You should be sure that there are no trees within ten feet of the site and that all leaves and brush have been cleared away.

[*Changing* one *to* you *keeps the point of view consistent. The writer might, of course, have used* one *and* he *instead of* you *with equal consistency.*]

I looked out over the pines toward the tiny lake a thousand feet below us. You could hardly see the cabin where we had spent the night.

I looked out over the pines toward the tiny lake a thousand feet below us. I could hardly see the cabin where we had spent the night.

After the textbook had been mastered, he had no trouble with chemistry.

[*The impersonal passive construction shifts awkwardly to the active with the subject* he.]

After he had mastered the textbook, he had no trouble with chemistry.

Germany has developed new attitudes toward government, but they preserve some of the ideas which allowed a dictatorship to flourish.

[*In the same sentence, the writer shifts his point of view, thinking first of the nation in general and then of the people in it. See also 24.*]

1. The Germans have developed new attitudes toward government, but they preserve some of the ideas which allowed a dictatorship to flourish.

2. Germany has developed new attitudes toward government but preserves some of the ideas which allowed a dictatorship to flourish.

13c Consistency in place   **PV c**

Original

From my corner I could see the long platform of the subway stretch-

Revision

From my corner I could see the long platform of the subway station

Original (Cont.)

ing dimly beside the tracks. A girl clicked through the turnstile and sat at once on the bench beyond the change booth. The street was empty and quiet. For a moment there was no rumble of trains, no sound of voices—a frightening silence.

[*The third sentence shifts the point of view by making the reader change the position he has assumed to imagine the scene.*]

Revision (Cont.)

stretching dimly beside the tracks. A girl clicked through the turnstile and sat immediately on the bench beyond the change booth. For a moment there was no rumble of trains, no sound from the street above, no voice—a frightening silence.

[*The revision retains the detail of the original, but presents it from the point of view already established.*]

13d Consistency in time

PV d

For shift of time within the sentence see 30a to 30e.

Original

The old house was set back in a grove of oaks. As we come nearer we can see the broken shutters and the tumble-down porch. The only sound is the rustling of leaves.

[*The writer assumes at first that he is looking back from the present, but after one sentence some kind of time-machine translates him to the scene itself. The reader cannot be sure where he is.*]

Revision

The old house was set back in a grove of oaks. As we came nearer, we could see the broken shutters and the tumble-down porch. The only sound was the rustling of leaves.

[*The revision preserves the point of view established in the beginning.*]

The play begins with a scene on the castle walls of Elsinore. Horatio, a friend of Hamlet, met the soldiers who were on watch and learned from them about the ghost that had appeared. Then as the soldiers were talking, the ghost, dressed in full armor, appeared again.

[*The writer, as he proceeds, perhaps begins to think of his experience in reading or seeing the play rather than the play itself. After one sentence he writes as if he were describing actual events.*]

The play begins with a scene on the castle walls of Elsinore. Horatio, a friend of Hamlet, meets the soldiers who are on watch and learns from them about the ghost that has appeared. Then as the soldiers are talking, the ghost, dressed in full armor, appears again.

[*The revision considers consistently the play as a piece of literature still in existence which can therefore be referred to in present time.*]

Original (Cont.)

After we had waited about twenty minutes, I saw a pair of antlers pushing up from behind the hill. Another followed. Now the whole herd began to appear, moving down toward the water hole.

[*The writer forgets his point of view momentarily, and the* now *shifts it.*]

Revision (Cont.)

After we had waited about twenty minutes, I saw a pair of antlers pushing up from behind the hill. Another followed. Then the whole herd began to appear, moving down toward the water hole.

EXERCISE 13

A. Following are selections from varied types of prose, taken from their contexts. Describe what seems to you to be the tone of each selection and point out how the tone is revealed. You may wish to look at the whole compositions from which some of the selections have been taken in order to check your judgments.

1. Although I had been baffled in my attempts to learn the origin of the Feast of Calabashes, yet it seemed very plain to me that it was principally, if not wholly, of a religious nature. As a religious solemnity, however, it had not at all corresponded with the horrible descriptions of Polynesian worship which we have received in some published narratives, and especially in those accounts of the evangelized islands with which the missionaries have favoured us. Did not the sacred character of these persons render the purity of their intentions unquestionable, I should certainly be led to suppose that they had exaggerated the evils of Paganism, in order to enhance the merits of their own disinterested labours.

          —HERMAN MELVILLE, *Typee*, Chapter XXIV

2. In taking up the clue of an inquiry, not intermitted for nearly ten years, it may be well to do as a traveller would, who had to recommence an interrupted journey in a guideless country; and, ascending, as it were, some little hill beside our road, note how far we have already advanced, and what pleasantest ways we may choose for further progress.

          —JOHN RUSKIN, *Modern Painters*

3. Of recent years there has been a noticeable decline of swearing and foul language in England; and this, except at centres of industrial depression, shows every sign of continuing indefinitely, until a new shock to our national nervous system—such as war, pestilence, revolution, fire from Heaven, or whatever you please—revives the habit of swearing, together with that of praying. Taking advantage of the lull, I propose to make a short enquiry into the nature and necessity of foul language: a difficult theme and one seldom treated with detachment.

          —ROBERT GRAVES, *Lars Porsena*

4. "And who is this? Is this my old nurse?" said the child, regarding with a radiant smile a figure coming in.

Yes, yes. No other stranger would have shed those tears at sight of him, and called him her dear boy, her pretty boy, her own poor blighted child. No other woman would have stooped down by his bed, and taken up his wasted hand, and put it to her lips and breast, as one who had some right to fondle it. No other woman would have so forgotten everybody there but him and Floy, and been so full of tenderness and pity.

—CHARLES DICKENS, *Dombey and Son,* Chapter XVI

5. THE KING? There he was. Beefeaters were before the august box; the Marquis of Steyne (Lord of the Powder Closet) and other great officers of state were behind the chair on which he sate. *He* sate—florid of face, portly of person, covered with orders, and in a rich curling head of hair. How we sang, God save him! How the house rocked and shouted with that magnificent music. How they cheered, and cried, and waved handkerchiefs. Ladies wept; mothers clasped their children; some fainted with emotion. People were suffocated in the pit, shrieks and groans rising up amidst the writhing and shouting mass there of his people who were, and indeed showed themselves almost to be, ready to die for him. Yes we saw him. Fate cannot deprive us of *that* . . . that we saw George the Good, the Magnificent, the Great.

—WILLIAM MAKEPEACE THACKERAY, *Vanity Fair,* Chapter XLVIII

6. I suppose you could call it a frame. But it wasn't like no frame that was ever pulled before. They's been plenty where one guy was paid to lay down. This is the first I heard of where a guy had to be bribed to win. And it's the first where a bird was bribed and didn't know it.

—RING LARDNER, *A Frame-up*

7. John B. Smith takes the stand.

Q. Mr. Smith, are you familiar with the clichés used in football?

A. Naturally, as a football fan. . . .

Q. Mr. Smith, as an expert, what lesson do you draw from the game of football?

A. Life is a game of football, Mr. Sullivan, and we the players. Some of us are elusive quarterbacks, some of us are only cheer leaders. Some of us are coaches and some of us are old grads, slightly the worse for wear, up in the stands. Some of us thump the people in front of us on the head in our excitement, some of us are the people who always get thumped. But the important thing to remember is—Play the game!

Q. How true!

—FRANK SULLIVAN, *Football is King*

8. Animals talk to each other, of course. There can be no question about that; but I suppose there are very few people who can understand them. I never knew but one man who could. I knew he could, however, because he told me so himself. He was a middle-aged, simple-hearted miner who had lived in a lonely corner of California, among the woods and mountains, a good many years, and had studied the ways of his only neighbors, the beasts and the birds, until he believed he could accurately translate any remark which they made.

—MARK TWAIN, *Jim Baker's Blue-Jay Yarn*

9. It is true to nature, although it be expressed in a figurative form, that a mother is both the morning and the evening star of life. The light of her eye is always the first to rise, and often the last to set upon man's day of trial. She wields a power more decisive far than syllogisms in argument, or courts of last appeal in authority. Nay, in cases not a few, where there has been no fear of God before the eyes of the young—where His love has been unfelt and His law outraged, a mother's affection or her tremulous tenderness has held transgressors by the heart-strings, and been the means of leading them back to virtue and to God.

—T. L. HAINES and L. W. YAGGY, *The Royal Path of Life*

B. Revise the following passages so that the point of view is consistent:

1. Unless the pine trees could become tall and reach for the sun, how could they survive against their many rivals in the forest? As the pine tree grew, it began to branch out.

2. As soon as we finished packing, we hurry to the station.

3. At the beginning of the play Romeo was very much in love with Rosalind. He seemed almost amusing as a lovesick youth. Then he meets Juliet, and at once he is madly in love with her. The sudden change was not convincing to me.

4. No matter how carefully one plans, you can always count on forgetting something.

5. The six main streets of the town spread out like spokes of a huge wheel, whose hub was the courthouse circle where I walked. As I crossed Central Avenue, I could see traffic lights blinking off to the north for eight or ten blocks. A dozen girls in blue jeans and bright shirts giggled by me, bound for the first show at the Circle Theater. The theater was garish in the bright lights of the orchestra as a small crowd waited for the picture to begin. I walked on past the theater entrance, past a bookstore whose window display suggested that it specialized in office equipment rather than books, and then I turned up Grand Avenue to the northwest.

6. After Binny had reported on his investigation and they had weighed the chances of getting caught against the possibilities for a substantial haul, it was decided to go home and make the attempt some other time.

[135

7. When I first read the story I thought Hemingway was interested mostly in the two killers who come into the restaurant and inquire about Ole. They are revealed through their clipped speech and their attempts to bully the boys in the diner. Most of the story seems to concern them. Nick did not speak very often.

8. If you expect people to take you seriously, you must take time to think about what you say. It is not enough to speak with conviction or pound the table with enthusiasm. One must know what he is trying to do and have a plan for doing it.

9. The dough should be kneaded every hour for three hours, and you should keep it in a warm place so that it will rise.

10. Mexico has a wide variety of climates and beautiful scenery, and they manufacture fine leather goods.

11. After he ate the soup and finished the huge salad, he began to regain his cheerfulness.

12. Fish began jumping all around me. I quickly threw my line out. And now the rain began.

13. *Huckleberry Finn* is more than a children's book. Huck, of course, is interesting to children. He was always doing something exciting. I can remember still how interested I was when I first read the book. But the novel has ideas in it that appeal also to an adult mind.

14. After the mowing of the lawn had been accomplished, he was free to go to the movies.

15. A person who wants to get something out of his classes must do more than simply the required work. You can often get a degree by doing just the minimum, but you cannot get an education that way.

C. Biblical scholars recognize that the Old Testament we know is made up of several older versions edited into one by breaking up the earlier accounts and running them together. Two of these versions are called *P* and *JE, P* standing for a version which we suppose to have been the Priests' Code, and *JE* for a more popular account which combined two versions, in one of which the Lord is called Javeh, and in the other Elohim. Thus, whatever the reason for the Bible's appearing in this form, many of the Old Testament stories are told twice, and naturally the tone differs in the two versions. Just where the versions begin and stop is a matter for some argument, and slightly varying estimates will be found in the various Bible dictionaries and encyclopedias. The following is a relatively acceptable division of these chapters between the two accounts: Genesis 5:1-28 (P); 5:29 (JE); 5:30-32 (P); 6:1-8 (JE); 6:9-22 (P); 7:1-5 (JE); 7:6 (P); 7:7-24 (JE); 8:1-5 (P); 8:6-12 (JE); 8:13-20 (P); 8:21-22 (JE); 9:1-17 (P); 9:18-27 (JE); 9:28-29, 10:1-7 (P); 10:8-19 (JE); 10:20 (P); 10:21 (JE); 10:22-23 (P); 10:24-30 (JE); 10:31-32 (P). The numbering of the verses is that of the King James version; in some versions the numbering differs slightly. Now read through Chapters 5-10, reading all the P verses and then all the JE verses. Then try to characterize the tone of each version. Is the subject matter different? Is there a difference in the manners of the writers, or in their apparent purpose?

D. In the 19th century, two contemporaries wrote philosophies of clothes. One, ecstatic, philosophical, and violent, was the work of Thomas Carlyle. The other, moral, pedantic, doctrinaire, was an editorial by Louis A. Godey, editor of *Godey's Lady's Book*. The "paragraph" below has been made by mixing selections from these two accounts. Naturally, the tones of the two are quite different. Judging by the tone, try to sort out the sentences so that you get two consistent accounts. The sentences occur in the same order they had in the original versions. The following might be used as a topic sentence for the matter from Carlyle: "Man's earthly interests are all hooked and buttoned together, and held up, by Clothes." The following would serve as a topic sentence for the passages from Godey: "The Bible, as our readers well know, is the standard of authority by which we test the right or the wrong of ideas and usages; nor can we comprehend the full import of clothing or its advantages unless we look at the evil results that follow neglect of or disobedience to this law of necessity for the human race, ever since 'the Lord God clothed' the first man and woman before sending them out of Eden."

(1) Clothing has nine distinct phases of teaching the philosophy of its usefulness. (2) It gives covering, comfort, comeliness; it marks custom, condition, character, and civilization; it symbolizes Redemption through Christ, and the holiness of the saints in Heaven. (3) Society sails through the Infinitude on cloth, as on a Faust's mantle. (4) Strange enough, it strikes me, is this same fact of there being Tailors and tailored. (5) The Horse I ride has his own whole fell; the noble creature is his own sempster, and weaver, and spinner. (6) A clothing of rags symbolizes wretchedness, wickedness, ignorance, imposture, or imbecility. (7) While I—good Heaven—have thatched myself over with the dead fleeces of sheep, the bark of vegetables, the entrails of worms, the hides of oxen and seals, the felt of furred beasts. (8) Nakedness is savagery, or shameless sin, or extreme misery. (9) Heathenism has no darker shadow on its God-forsaken horizon than the half nude millions on millions of its worshipers; until these people are clothed, neither China nor India can become Christian countries. (10) Day after Day I must thatch myself anew; day after day this despicable thatch must lose some film of its thickness, till by degree the whole has been brushed thither, and I, the dust-making, patent Rag-grinder, get new material to grind on. O subter-brutish! vile! most vile! (11) Wherever Christian civilization prevails, as in Europe and America, dirt and disorder in a household or in dress are proofs of ill-conditioned or ill-trained people. (12) For have not I too a compact all-enclosing Skin, whiter or dingier? Am

I a botched mass of tailors' and cobblers' shreds, then; or a tightly-articulated, homogeneous little Figure, automatic, alive? (13) The dress must be decent before we can have confidence in the character of any person. (14) For my own part, these considerations, of our Clothes-thatch, and how, reaching inwards even to our heart of hearts, it tailorizes and demoralizes us, fill me with a certain horror at myself, and mankind. (15) We feel and judge thus intuitively, because the instincts of humanity tell us that without decent clothing there cannot be real delicacy of feeling or true dignity of mind, unless the 'miserable' suffers from the sins of others. (16) And this does not weaken the force of our moral of dress—that there is or has been wrong doing wherever we see people badly or indecently clothed. (17) There is something great in the moment when a man first strips himself of adventitious wrappages; and sees indeed that he is naked, and, as Swift has it, 'a forked straddling animal with bandy legs'; yet also a Spirit and unutterable Mystery of Mysteries.

III. Paragraphs and Continuity

Order is Heaven's first law.—ALEXANDER POPE.

We have seen that a writer or speaker must have something to say, must organize his thoughts and develop them so that he produces something interesting or informative or persuasive, a creation of his own. He must, however, also know how to construct the basic unit of organization in writing, the paragraph, how to use paragraphs to make his thoughts move smoothly from point to point, and how to insure continuity and coherence within his paragraphs.

A reader can be compared to a person following a trail through a strange land, and the writer is the guide who must show where the trail leads. If the trail is long, the guide must break the journey into stages, so that those who follow the trail do not become exhausted, but have places to stop for rest or food. If there are obstacles in the trail, the guide must provide methods for coping with them—with rivers, mountains, or swamps. There must be a plan in the whole route, and a plan in the parts. Similarly, the writer must give adequate instructions at the start and must give warning every time there is a turn in the trail. He should even give occasional assurance that the reader is still on the trail, just as the markers of highways occasionally put up a sign, *U.S. 30,* even though there has been little opportunity to get off the road.

The divisions of a composition, the stages in the journey, are called paragraphs. They vary in length and in pattern according to the material and the purposes of the writer as the stages in a journey vary according to the terrain and the traveler's desires. Paragraphs are brief compositions in themselves, and need individual organization and pattern. They need also to be fitted into the whole. The writer must provide directions which will lead the reader easily and understandingly through each paragraph and from one paragraph to the next.

Devices for guiding the reader, for marking the trail, give writing *continuity* and *coherence*. They show how the thought continues from one element to another and how the parts *cohere,* stick together. Inevitably, all writing having continuity is writing in paragraphs, and hence everything that has been said in the first two main sections of this book applies to the paragraph. It applies, however, in some special ways. This third section will consider how these fundamental devices in writing are useful in building and relating paragraphs. It will consider standard patterns for paragraph structure, then devices for getting continuity and coherence in the whole composition and within paragraphs, and finally two parts of the composition especially important in knitting the paragraphs together—the introduction and the conclusion.

14. THE STANDARD PARAGRAPH

[For Guide to Revision, see page 149]

*Construct paragraphs as units; do not merely divide
a composition into paragraphs.*

A few years ago, at a Midwestern university, funds were appropriated for a new gymnasium which was to include four handball courts in the basement. Construction costs rose, and the plans had to be changed. The architect suggested, as one economy, that two of the handball courts be omitted. The superintendent of buildings was reluctant; his specifications called for four courts. He thought of a compromise, and the building was constructed with four handball courts —each half size and each useless.

14-1 Paragraphs as brief compositions

Paragraph division in some student themes is about as useful as a half-size handball court, because it is made without reason. A paragraph, except in newspapers, is not a mechanical device for breaking up a page. It is not a specific number of words or sentences. It is a unit in the organization of the composition, an organized discussion of one topic or one part of the topic. The indentation which marks it helps the reader to understand the plan of the entire paper.

Paragraphs are essentially brief compositions, and they should follow principles of organization and development discussed in I and II. They vary in content and length, depending upon the needs of the writer. In narration, paragraphs may show relatively little organization and require little transition from one paragraph to the next, since the flow of the story, the chronology of events, may provide most of the organization. But in most informative or argumentative prose, clarity requires that there be order as well as development within the paragraph, and that there be evidence of this order that the reader can readily recognize.

Paragraphs are infinitely varied, but, in general, expository paragraphs are of two sorts: they may provide guides for the reader, transitions, introductions, or conclusions; or they may mainly present the information and the argument of the writing. In the present section we shall be concerned with the second of these, the paragraphs that provide details, present evidence, offer examples, elaborate ideas. This kind of paragraph is so useful and so universally used in good nonfictional writing that it might be considered *the standard expository paragraph.*

14-2 The standard expository paragraph

The standard paragraph, which might even be called the "workhorse paragraph," has a simple but flexible construction. It goes something like the following:

(1) Topic sentence (including transition, or preceded by transition)
(2) Indication of main divisions of paragraph
(3) Development of first main division of paragraph
(4) Subtopic sentence
(5) Development of second main division
(This is continued so long as necessary, although usually a paragraph has relatively few main divisions.)
(6) Conclusion (sometimes with transition to the next paragraph)

Obviously this sort of paragraph is essentially like most compositions considered as wholes, which usually start with a statement of the subject, develop the subject in an orderly way, and reach a conclusion. Similarly, the standard paragraph suggests the standard English sentence, which starts with a subject, and continues with a statement about that subject. Consider the following:

I try each year to disbelieve what my senses tell me, and to look at the harvest moon in a cold and astronomical light. I know that it is a small cold sphere of rock, airless, jagged and without activity. But the harvest moon is not an astronomical fact. It is a knowing thing, lifting its ruddy head above the rim of the world. Even to the thoroughly civilized mind, where caution for the future is supposed to rule all impulse, the orange moon of autumn invites the senses to some saturnalia, yet no festival

TOPIC SENTENCE

FIRST SUBDIVISION

CONCLUSION
SUBTOPIC SENTENCE

DEVELOPMENT

of merriment. The harvest moon has no inno-   FURTHER DEVELOPMENT
cence, like the slim quarter moon of a spring
twilight, nor has it the silver penny brilliance
of the moon that looks down upon the resorts
of summertime. Wise, ripe, and portly, like an   CONCLUSION
old Bacchus, it waxes night after night.

—DONALD CULROSS PEATTIE, *An Almanac for Moderns*

Not every paragraph is so regular as this. Peattie, for instance, often omits the conclusion, and embodies it in a separate paragraph which is also a transition to the next. Many paragraphs have no subtopic sentence; others have a topic sentence which is actually the introduction for a whole sequence of paragraphs, the first paragraph having a subtopic sentence which follows immediately after the more general topic sentence. But with minor variations, a paragraph roughly like this does most of the work for most writers.

14-3 The topic sentence

Just as a statement of the main idea of a composition guides its planning (see 2, 5), a statement of the main idea of a paragraph controls its structure. This statement, the *topic sentence,* tells the reader what to expect. It introduces an idea, a facet of the subject, the next step in the reader's progression. Ideally it relates this part of the discussion to what has gone before (see 15-2), distinguishes this section of discussion from all others, and starts the reader on this particular segment. It may appear at various places in the paragraph —at the end, for instance—but usually it begins the standard expository paragraph, as it does the following:

> Nineteenth-century writers admired this culture for two chief reasons: because it was beautiful, and because it was not Christian. They saw their own civilization as squalid and greedy; they praised the Greeks and Romans as noble and spiritual. They felt contemporary Christianity to be mean, ugly, and repressive; they admired the cults of antiquity as free, strong, and graceful. Looking at the soot-laden sky, pierced by factory chimneys and neo-Gothic steeples, they exclaimed
>
> Great God! I'd rather be
> A Pagan suckled in a creed outworn.

The paragraph is part of Professor Highet's discussion of the impact of Greek and Roman culture on the life and thought of the nineteenth century. The topic sentence opens a new stage in the discussion and also relates the paragraph to what has preceded. It ties the new material to previous paragraphs with the words *this culture*. It also announces the new topic, the admiration of nineteenth-century writers for this culture.

Good topic sentences have recognizable characteristics. For instance, Professor Highet might have written:

> In this connection it is interesting to note that earlier periods exerted a certain charm over many of the more sensitive spirits of the nineteenth century and that among the reasons for this charm were the differences between theirs and an earlier day.

As a topic sentence this could have been worse. It would have permitted the writer to go ahead, saying almost anything he pleased; but it is clearly a worse topic sentence than Professor Highet's, partly because it is less exact, less precise. It tells the reader too little of what he should know; it does not restrict the paragraph to just that material which is to be its content.

Similarly, Professor Highet might have begun his paragraph in this manner:

> Nineteenth-century writers resented living under a soot-laden sky. They resented the growing ugliness of an industrial society. They disliked the factory chimneys that thrust up everywhere, and not only the factories but the neo-Gothic spires, which suggested that the Christianity of the day, like the industry, was ugly. . . .

Again, he did not, and the reason is obvious. He would have been starting with material so specific that it provides no proper introduction to the whole. Instead, he lets us know, clearly and briefly, what are to be the subjects of the paragraph. He will talk about "nineteenth-century writers" and he will say of them that they turned to classical culture because (1) "it was beautiful" and (2) "it was not Christian."

These are the marks of a good topic sentence: that it is interesting in itself, that it ties the paragraph to previous and sometimes to subsequent paragraphs, that it is general enough to account for the paragraph to come, and that it is specific enough so that the reader knows what to expect.

14-4 Patterns of paragraph development

Paragraphs can be developed in many ways, and an experienced writer may use various techniques in a paragraph quite unconsciously.

144]

Even the writer consciously constructing the kind of standard expository paragraph described above will find that his purposes and materials dictate varied approaches. He will begin by settling on a topic sentence to announce his subject. Then he may use any combination of the techniques discussed in II to develop this topic: citing facts, illustrating with examples or analogies, analyzing, defining, reasoning, presenting evidence. Paragraphs discussed in the remainder of this section illustrate only some of the common methods for developing a topic sentence. But they are standard methods and they will work.

14-5 Statement and particulars

Make a statement and then cite particular instances which illustrate or support it (see also 8-1).

Consider the following:

His folks talked like other folks in the neighborhood. They called themselves "pore" people. A man learned in books was "eddicated." What was certain was "sartin." The syllables came through the nose; "joints" were "j'ints"; fruit "spiled" instead of spoiling; in corn-planting time they "drapped" the seeds. They went on errands and "brung" things back. Their dogs "follered" the coons. Flannel was "flannen," a bandanna a "banddanner," a chimney a "chimbly," a shadow a "shadder," and mosquitoes plain "skeeters." They "gethered" crops. A creek was a "crick," a cover a "kiver."

—CARL SANDBURG, *Abe Lincoln: The Prairie Years*

The first sentence makes a statement. The remainder of the paragraph lists particular instances, more or less at random. The first sentence ties the particulars together; the particulars illustrate and clarify the first sentence.

The following paragraph has the same pattern:

Proud of his wonderful achievemen⁺s, civilized man looks down upon the humbler members of mankind. He has conquered the forces of nature and compelled them to serve him. He has transformed inhospitable forests into fertile fields. The mountain fastnesses are yielding their treasures to his demands. The fierce animals which are obstructing his progress are being exterminated, while others which are useful to him are made to increase a thousand-fold. The waves of the ocean carry him from land to land, and towering mountain-ranges set him no bounds. His genius has moulded inert matter into powerful machines which await a touch of his hand to serve his manifold demands.

—FRANZ BOAS, *The Mind of Primitive Men*

[145

The first sentence makes a general statement about man; each sentence which follows describes some particular accomplishment of man which justifies the opening assertion.

14-6 Statement and example or illustration

Make a statement and then describe an example which clarifies it (see also 8-2).

Consider the following:

> As a matter of fact, we are all of us original in our expression until our wings are clipped. I know a three-year-old boy who calls an automobile a "cadeúga." It is, both to him and in point of fact, an excellently descriptive term, based, like many a word in the pristine days of speech, on the sound the thing makes. But you can't go to the telephone and ask for a "cadeúga" with any valid hope of seeing it appear. And since the world with which the young adventurer must communicate prefers to call the affair a motor, or a car, or a machine (incomparably less exact and fitting terms), he will infallibly drop his own fresh and vivid coinage, and conform. The tangential energy of the individual beats its wings in vain against the centripetal force of the community, and every infant anarchist in speech yields at last to the usage of that world by which, if he is to live, he must be understood.
>
> —JOHN LIVINGSTON LOWES, *Convention and Revolt in Poetry*

The paragraph begins with a general statement which is illustrated by a story. Then the example is interpreted as it relates to the opening statement, and a final sentence can carry the main idea a little further.

14-7 Comparison and contrast

Illustrate or clarify a statement by comparing it or contrasting it with something simpler or more familiar.

Comparison shows likeness; contrast shows difference. Although they are devices for illustration, not proof (see 8-4, 10e), both are useful in developing a paragraph. A writer clarifies his view of the behavior of the tubercle bacillus by describing it as a warrior of old, in a coat of mail, using military tactics against humanity. Another discusses "feeding the mind" by contrasting it with feeding the body. To make a point about the achievements of modern man, a writer contrasts the building of Grand Coulee Dam with the building of the Great Pyramids. In a famous comparison, Edward Bellamy explains his view of the social structure of the 1880's in terms of a stage coach:

By way of attempting to give the reader some general impression of the way people lived together in those days, and especially of the relation of the rich and the poor to one another, perhaps I cannot do better than to compare society as it then was to a prodigious coach which the masses of humanity were harnessed to and dragged toilsomely along a very hilly and sandy road. The driver was hunger, and permitted no lagging, though the pace was necessarily very slow. . . .

—*Looking Backward*

The paragraph continues describing the passengers on the coach, the hazards in the road, the dangers of overturning the coach, and so on. Wallace Stegner uses comparison for a brief, pointed concluding paragraph:

That will do for a final word on the teaching of writing. Learning to write is like learning to fly. Watch the old birds in midsummer kicking the protesting young out of the nest.

—WALLACE STEGNER, *Writing as Graduate Study*

14-8 Statement and reasons

Make a statement and then cite reasons for its validity (see also 10, 11).

The pattern "This is so because . . . because . . . and because . . ." is perhaps a special variation of the formula in which particulars support a main topic.

The Yellow or Silver Pine is more frequently overturned than any other tree on the Sierra, because its leaves and branches form the largest mass in proportion to its height, while in many places it is planted sparsely, leaving long, open lanes, through which storms may enter with full force. Furthermore, because it is distributed along the lower portion of the range, which was the first to be left bare on the breaking up of the ice-sheet at the close of the glacial winter, the soil it is growing upon has been longer exposed to post-glacial weathering, and consequently is in a more crumbling, decayed condition than the fresher soils farther up the range, and therefore offers a less secure anchorage for the roots.

—JOHN MUIR, *The Passes of the Sierra*

The opening clause is justified by succeeding reasons or explanations.

14-9 Progression of ideas

Connect logically related statements to develop the desired general idea.

[147

Often the writer does not wish a pattern as formal as those described above. He can, however, move from one statement to another that logically follows it, progressing from one concept or attitude to another.

> If you subtract from this book the personality of H. L. Mencken, if you attempt to restate his ideas in simple unexcited prose, there remains only a collection of trite and somewhat confused ideas. To discuss it as one might discuss the ideas of first rate thinkers like Russell, Dewey, Whitehead, or Santayana would be to destroy the book and to miss its importance. Though it purports to be the outline of a social philosophy, it is really the highly rhetorical expression of a mood which has often in the past and may again in the future be translated into thought. In the best sense of the word the book is sub-rational: it is addressed to those vital preferences which lie deeper than coherent thinking.
>
> —WALTER LIPPMANN, *Men of Destiny*

Each sentence moves the reader logically nearer the final statement. And now consider the following:

> It was easy in those days to be hopeful, to prophesy, if not a renaissance, at least an efflorescence of native genius such as had never before occurred in the Western Hemisphere. But since that memorable uprising of 1913 something has happened. The sensational issues are dead and buried; the lust for battle has dwindled into an ignoble truce with the Academy; the creative stream has run dry; and Modernists, at home and abroad, are wearily sifting and resifting its barren deposits. Let us look into the matter.
>
> —THOMAS CRAVEN, *Men of Art*

Here the paragraph progresses so far from the first statement that the body of the paragraph becomes a denial of what was suggested in the first sentence.

14-10 Chronological and spatial patterns

Record incidents in the order in which they occurred in space and time.

When events are to be narrated, paragraphs usually become episodes in the action, scenes in the drama.

> After a full minute, something of memory stirred in his brain, and he again reared and looked back at me. To heave eight hundred pounds about on its pivot a second time was too much even to consider, so he simply bent back and back until his head almost touched his hind flippers, and gazed with uncomprehending wistfulness full

into my face. Whether I appeared more attractive or less fearsome wrongway up, or whether—well, just whether—his head slowly sank down again on the sand. With a gargantuan sigh he cleaned out a deep hollow and erased me from his memory. Again my sea-elephant slept.

WILLIAM BEEBE, *Book of Bays*

For other examples of patterns in time and space, see 5.

14-11 Related details

Combine related details.

Details may be related because they are all characteristics of a person or parts of a scene or aspects of the same problem. If their connection with one another is obvious, they can be collected as a paragraph.

> Five miles below the foot of Moraine Lake, just where the lateral moraines lose themselves in the plain, there was a field of wild rye, growing in magnificent waving bunches six to eight feet high, bearing heads from six to twelve inches long. Rubbing out some of the grains, I found them about five-eighths of an inch long, dark-colored and deliciously sweet. Indian women were gathering it in baskets, bending down large handfuls, beating it out, and fanning it in the wind. They were quite picturesque, coming through the rye, as one caught glimpses of them here and there, in winding lanes and openings, with splendid tufts arching above their heads, while their incessant chat and laughter showed their heedless joy.
>
> —JOHN MUIR, *The Passes of the Sierra*

14 *The standard paragraph* ¶; no ¶

GUIDE TO REVISION:

Revise so that each paragraph is a unit in the thought of the composition.

Usually, faulty paragraphing reveals some more fundamental difficulty (see especially 2, 5, II). A series of short, choppy paragraphs suggests that ideas are not organized in units according to their relationships with one another. Lack of paragraph division suggests that ideas have not been classified, that some elements have not been subordinated to others. Weaknesses of paragraphing, therefore, can seldom be corrected simply by removing or adding indentations. Rebuilding paragraphs about a clear topic sentence, perhaps according to the patterns suggested above, leads the writer to improve not only the paragraphing but many other aspects of composition.

14a *Plan in the paragraph*   ¶ a

A paragraph should be built upon a conscious plan, and this plan should be apparent to the reader. There are many methods of making a plan clear; the most common employ a topic sentence, supplemented with other transitional material at various points through the paragraph.

Original

Gail McDermott is likely to win the election as president of the Associated Students. He is both a quarterback and an actor, and has support from organizations all over the campus. Meanwhile, some candidates for offices are running unopposed or are opposed by candidates who have little support. The widest interest in the election is being drawn by the races for the three vacant seats in the Student Senate. Many campaigners believe that the election of so many as one candidate for the Senate supported by the Associated Resident Halls Party, known as The Barbs, will assure the decline or abolishment of football at State University. The reasons for this belief are complicated and will later require some analysis. Meanwhile, Nancy Jenkins and Dorothy Cochran are leading a lively field of candidates for the presidency of AWS. That race is attracting no attention off the campus, and very little on the campus, though the question of who is to be elected to the Student Senate has become a statewide issue. The other contests, except for the race for the Student Senate, are side-

Revision

Interest in the State University student elections this year centers in the race for the three vacant seats in the Student Senate. The other contests are likely to be sideshows. Gail McDermott, known as both an actor and a quarterback, has support from so many organizations that his election as president of the Associated Students is practically conceded. Some of the class officers are running unopposed, and other races are attracting little attention. None of the freshman candidates, for instance, is well known or widely supported. For the presidency of AWS Nancy Jenkins and Dorothy Cochran are leading a lively field of candidates, but the race is attracting no attention off the campus, and relatively little on the campus. The election of three members to the Senate, on the other hand, has become a question of interest throughout the state and has led to so much electioneering that placards are plastered all the way from the President's gate to the back door of the Aggie Greenhouse. The issue, of course, is the future of football at State University, and many cam-

Original (Cont.)

shows. None of the freshman candidates, for instance, is well known or widely supported. But the Senate race has raised questions of such interest and has stimulated so much electioneering that billboard space is getting scarce on the campus, with placards plastered all the way from the President's gate to the back door of the Aggie Greenhouse.

[*Much of the effect of this paper is lost because there is no apparent plan. Furthermore, since this is the first paragraph of a theme, it should lead naturally to the next paragraph, which it does not.*]

Revision (Cont.)

paigners believe that the election of so many as one candidate from the Associated Resident Halls Party, known as The Barbs, will assure the decline or the abolishment of football at State University. The reasons for this belief are complicated, and will require some analysis.

[*The paragraph now has a clear plan. The topic sentence announces the purpose. A subtopic sentence introduces the campaigns of minor interest. The discussion of candidates is tied together by synonyms. The second half of the paragraph is introduced by "The election of three members to the Senate, on the other hand. . . ." It leads to a conclusion and a transition to the succeeding paragraph.*]

Failure to state the proposition may weaken any unit of composition (see 2). Not all paragraphs have topic sentences, but the paragraph built about a statement of its main proposition is one of the easiest to construct and one of the most effective. Frequently a writer can best pull together a shakily built paragraph by tying other sentences to a topic sentence.

Original

A teacher must be interested in his subject. A teacher must also be able to understand his pupils and reach them on their own level. I had a number of teachers who could do this. I did not consider them stupid or below a mental age of fifteen. They were intelligent and well-educated people. My mathematics teacher in junior high school had a Master's degree from a good university. He knew mathematics. He was vitally interested in his subject. He could also relate

Revision

A teacher need not have a mental age below fifteen in order to reach pupils on their own level. I had a number of teachers who were intelligent and well-educated and who could sense my interests and abilities. My mathematics teacher in junior high school, for example, had a Master's degree from a good university and a vital interest in his subject, but he could relate mathematics to what I understood. He could show me how to use mathematics in building a

Original (*Cont.*)

mathematics to what I was interested in. He could show us how we could use mathematics in building our cars for the soap-box derby or in keeping our allowances straight. I think that it was partly because he was intelligent that he could approach us on our own level.

[*The paragraph is repetitious, badly organized, and choppy, but a central weakness is its lack of a main idea.*]

Revision (*Cont.*)

car for the soap-box derby or keeping my allowance straight. I think that it was partly because he was intelligent that he could approach pupils at their own level.

[*The sentence structure has been improved, and by opening with a topic sentence, the writer has some basis for organizing the material, selecting the details which are relevant, and centering attention on a main point.*]

14c Journalistic paragraphs   ¶ c

For reasons unrelated to the logical development of a paragraph—reasons of appearance and quick readability—newspaper writers customarily start a new paragraph every few lines, often at the end of every sentence. In writing which does not follow the special forms of journalism, however, choppy paragraphing is usually a symptom of poor organization or a lack of continuity. Indentations every sentence or two do no more to help the reader than the period that ends each sentence.

Original

(1) In the suburbs and on the highways of many large American cities, young men are killing themselves by the thousands.

(2) Many of the accidents could be avoided if a little common sense were used. When a boy gets behind the steering wheel of a car, the first thing he thinks of is how fast he can go.

(3) Speed is the reason for so many deaths. The teen-ager does not seem to realize that his car is dangerous if it is not used sensibly.

(4) There is another reason for a large number of teen-age automobile accidents.

Revision

On the highways in and around many large American cities, young men are killing themselves by the thousands in automobile accidents which could be avoided by the use of a little common sense. First, young drivers must learn to be sensible about speed. When a boy gets behind a steering wheel, the first thing he thinks of is how fast he can go. He does not seem to realize that his car is dangerous if it is not used sensibly. Second, young drivers must learn some sense about the senseless games played with cars which kill hundreds of teen-agers each year.

Original (*Cont.*)

(5) This is the playing of games with cars. These senseless games kill hundreds of teen-agers every year.

(6) The most popular game is "Ditch 'Em." Two or more cars. . . .

[*The theme proceeds with a series of paragraphs, each discussing a different game, the first five introductory to the main subject. The indentations here do nothing to help the reader see the plan of the paper, to help him group ideas in units, and the random division is accompanied by related weaknesses—lack of continuity between sentences, lack of subordination.*]

Revision (*Cont.*)

The most popular game is "Ditch 'Em." Two or more cars. . . .

[*The first five paragraphs have been combined into a single introductory paragraph, but the revision has involved more than removing the indentations. For example, the first two sentences have become a single sentence, with elements subordinated. The three sentences of paragraphs 4 and 5 have become a single sentence. Sentences have been reworked to provide continuity between them, and the remark of the original about common sense has been exploited as a device to provide unity.*]

14d Dialogue paragraphs ¶ d

In order to help the reader identify speakers, writers of dialogue have adopted the convention of beginning a new paragraph whenever the speaker changes, as indicated in the version on the right below.

"Good evening. It's a cold night," said Holmes. The salesman nodded, and shot a questioning glance at my companion. "Sold out of geese, I see," continued Holmes, pointing at the bare slabs of marble. "Let you have 500 tomorrow morning." "That's no good."

"Good evening. It's a cold night," said Holmes.

The salesman nodded, and shot a questioning glance at my companion.

"Sold out of geese, I see," continued Holmes, pointing at the bare slabs of marble.

"Let you have 500 tomorrow morning."

"That's no good."

EXERCISE 14

A. Discuss each of the following as a topic sentence for a paragraph in context. Assume that the paragraph will contain approximately 150 words.

1. There are many things about the university which I do not like.

2. In consideration of these factors, there are several aspects in the case which seem to be basic for a fundamental understanding of the circumstances.

3. In spite of my many objections to fraternity life, I found that I enjoyed my days in Upsilon Delta, mainly because I liked the easy camaraderie among the men.

4. I also recall my great-grandfather, partly because of the intense, blinking way he had when he looked at me over his spectacles.

5. In selecting the brick with which to line the fireplace, you should consider color, size and shape, and resistance to heat.

6. The most important thing for a girl to consider in college is the preparation for her future life.

7. Basketball is an excellent sport because it can be enjoyed by players and spectators alike, comes at a season when there are few outdoor sports, and can be played by a few players, making it suitable for the small high school.

8. Weaving as though driven by a drunken driver, a red convertible roared down the highway toward me, traveling at least ninety miles an hour.

9. Now, I want to tell you all about it.

10. So then I thought it all over, and that is something I often do, thinking things all over.

B. Consider the following topic sentences:

1. Mrs. Jones was even stingier than her daughter.

2. Mrs. Jones was the stingiest woman I ever knew.

3. Mrs. Jones's name was a synonym for *stingy* in our town, and everybody had some anecdote to tell about her.

Each of these sentences might serve as a topic sentence, but each implies a different paragraph. The first implies that the daughter's stinginess has been discussed in a previous paragraph. The second seems to imply that Mrs. Jones is to be compared with all other stingy women the writer has known; probably he has no such intention, and the reader would probably assume that these words mean no more than "Mrs. Jones was very stingy," but the writer would do well to say what he means. The last sentence could suitably introduce a paragraph of tales told about Mrs. Jones. Now examine the following groups of possible topic sentences and distinguish the implications of each.

1. a. Janet is the most tiresome salesgirl I ever dealt with in my whole life.

   b. I do not like Janet as a salesgirl.

   c. Obviously, Janet is a poor salesgirl.

   d. Janet is a poor salesgirl because she wants to do all the talking.

   e. Janet is a poor salesgirl because she has never learned to let the customer do a little healthy griping.

f. Janet is the worst salesgirl in the store.

g. Janet would be a better salesgirl if she would cultivate a little interest in her customers.

h. Janet would be a better salesgirl if she were a kind and sympathetic person who could take a natural interest in her customer's wishes.

i. Janet might be a better salesgirl if she would read a book on selling.

j. Janet would not be such a bad salesgirl if she would remember what she was told in her course in salesmanship.

2. a. The French attitude toward South Asian affairs is wholly wrong.

   b. The French attitude toward South Asian affairs seems to me wrong.

   c. The French attitude toward South Asian affairs seems to me unrealistic.

   d. The French attitude toward South Asian affairs seems to me shrewd but dangerous.

   e. The French do not understand the Pakistan problem.

   f. If the French understand the Pakistan problem, their recent moves do not reveal the fact.

   g. The French may or may not understand Pakistan problems, but they are endeavoring to give the impression of knowledge, not to say clairvoyance.

   h. The French cannot be expected to reveal their Pakistan proposals until they have studied the reactions of London and Washington.

   i. The French attitude toward Pakistan is uncertain and probably unimportant.

   j. Barring unexpected developments in the French attitude toward Pakistan, at least one trend in South Asian affairs would seem certain.

3. a. All that I can now remember learning in high school I gained from playing basketball.

   b. Until I started playing basketball, I had no interest in high school.

   c. Chemistry is now my major interest, but I got started in chemistry only through my high school basketball coach.

   d. For me, basketball was a bridge between bumming around town and studying chemistry.

   e. If I ever become a chemical engineer, one reason is to be sought in a tricky backhand shot I have, which brought me to the coach's attention.

    f. I think basketball should be a required course for every student.

    g. Basketball is an American invention, and the more people live in cities where there is no room for baseball diamonds the more basketball becomes our national sport, and that was my experience, that it changed my life.

    h. The lessons learned on the basketball court are the factors which make for success in the classroom and in the world of today.

    i. For all-around fun and character building, give me basketball.

    j. Basketball, so called because the first games were played with a peach basket with the bottom knocked out, provided a turning point in my life.

C. The paragraphs below lack unity because they have inadequate statements of their main ideas; that is, they lack topic sentences. Revise the paragraphs, beginning each with a clear topic sentence.

    1. There are many dictionaries on the market, and some of these are reprints of older dictionaries. Some are good and some are bad. Some of these reprints reproduce books which were badly prepared when they were new, and some of them are reprints of books which were once good, but are now out of date. Many of them carry the name *Webster* on the title page. In fact, more than 140 dictionaries have that name on the cover, and the word *Webster* has been declared by the Supreme Court as part of eminent domain. Thus anyone can now use the word if he wants to, although anyone who uses it must be able to show that it follows principles laid down by Noah Webster. This, however, is not hard, and thus the word *Webster* does not tell much about what is inside a dictionary.

    2. Although it is far from the largest museum in New York, the Cloisters is one of the most interesting for its size in the city, well arranged and well managed. It provides ready and revealing insight into the Middle Ages. Here, within a few miles of the greatest industrial concentration in the world, is a little bit of the Middle Ages. A thirteenth-century French cloister, with its ancient stonework from corbels to statues, has been taken down stone by stone and re-erected here.

    3. The electric saw is certainly one invention which has helped the modern carpenter. With an electric saw a carpenter can cut the frame for a small house in a few hours. Or with an electric drill an electrician can drill the frame for wiring in a short time. In the old days cutting framing timbers by hand was a long and tedious job, in spite of a sharp saw. Today few people are alive who know how to sharpen a saw properly. And drilling was always a long and hard job. In the same manner the sanding and finishing of hardwood floors has been simplified by electrical tools.

D. The following paragraph—minus its topic sentence—is taken from a letter from an officer in the Second Iowa Regiment describing what he saw and heard of the Battle of Shiloh, April 6, 1862. Endeavor to construct topic and closing sentences which taken together will give the paragraph unity.

"What was the plan of the battle, General?" asked Gen. Buell of Acting Brig. Gen. Tuttle. "By God, sir, I don't know!" he replied. Gen. Sweeney on our right said he gave all his orders on his own hook, and so of many others. The army was scattered over about twenty miles. The greenest regiments were on the outposts, and not a shovel full of dirt thrown up to protect them until they could be reinforced from the interior of the camp. As a natural consequence, they were panic stricken and retreated in, reporting their regiments "all cut to pieces." Col. Peabody's brigade, on the left, had none but green regiments, viz.: the 12th Michigan, 16th Wisconsin, and the 23d and 25th Missouri. They lost both their batteries, which soon were turned upon us. Sherman's regiments on the right and Prentiss in the centre had few troops that had ever seen a fight.

E. The paragraphs below, with the sentences numbered for reference, are to be studied especially for their organization and development. Consider each paragraph and answer the following questions: a. What is the general pattern of the paragraph's development? b. What is the relationship of each sentence to the other sentences and to the plan of the whole?

1. (1) The banks of the Hudson are generally high and precipitous, and in some places they are mountainous. (2) No flats worthy of being mentioned occur until Albany is approached; nor are those which lie south of that town of any great extent compared with the size of the stream. (3) In this particular the Mohawk is a very different river, having extensive flats that, I have been told, resemble those of the Rhine in miniature. (4) As for the Hudson, it is generally esteemed in the colony as a very pleasing river; and I remember to have heard intelligent people from home admit that even the majestic Thames itself is scarcely more worthy to be visited, or that it better rewards the trouble and curiosity of the enlightened traveler.

—JAMES FENIMORE COOPER, *Satanstoe*

2. (1) Conscience, Elizabeth never wearied of proclaiming, was unmolested; every English subject might think what he pleased. (2) No Inquisition examined into the secrets of opinion; and before the rebellion no questions were asked as to what worship or what teaching might be heard within the walls of private houses. (3) The Protestant fanatics, who had from time to time attempted prosecutions, were always checked and discouraged; and unless the laws were ostentatiously violated, the Government was wilfully blind.

[157

(4) Toleration was the universal practice in the widest sense which the nature of the experiment permitted; and if it was now found necessary to draw the cords more tightly, the fault was not with Elizabeth or her ministers, but with the singular and uncontrollable frenzy of theology, which regards the exclusive supremacy of a peculiar doctrine as of more importance than the Decalogue.

—JAMES ANTHONY FROUDE, *History of England*

3. (1) The development of language is the history of the gradual accumulation and elaboration of verbal symbols. (2) By means of this phenomenon, man's whole behavior-pattern has undergone an immense change from the simple biological scheme, and his mentality has expanded to such a degree that it is no longer comparable to the minds of animals. (3) Instead of a direct transmitter of coded signals, we have a system that has sometimes been likened to a telephone-exchange, wherein messages may be relayed, stored up if a line is busy, answered by proxy, perhaps sent over a line that did not exist when they were first given, *noted down and kept* if the desired number gives no answer. (4) Words are the plugs in this super-switchboard; they connect impressions and let them function together; sometimes they cause lines to become crossed in funny or disastrous ways.

—SUSANNE K. LANGER, *Philosophy in a New Key*

4. (1) Among medieval and modern philosophers, anxious to establish the religious significance of God, an unfortunate habit has prevailed of paying to Him metaphysical compliments. (2) He has been conceived as the foundation of the metaphysical situation with its ultimate activity. (3) If this conception be adhered to, there can be no alternative except to discern in Him the origin of all evil as well as of all good. (4) He is then the supreme author of the play, and to Him must therefore be ascribed its shortcomings as well as its success. (5) If He be conceived as the supreme ground for limitation, it stands in His very nature to divide the Good from the Evil, and to establish Reason "within her domination supreme."

—A. N. WHITEHEAD, *Science and the Modern World*

F. Select three of the possible topic sentences given below and develop each into a paragraph. Then write an analysis of each of your paragraphs, describing the general pattern used and pointing out the relation of each sentence to the whole.

1. Students have developed a variety of techniques to conceal inadequate study from their teachers.

2. The educational value of college social life is greatly overrated.

3. A campus newspaper reflects the interests of the student body.

4. If there were no God, it would be necessary to invent one.

5. For me registration day was only a series of confusions.

6. The campus was unified about the main quadrangle.

7. A little learning is a dangerous thing.

8. There are certain qualities which a student expects to find in a good classroom lecture.

9. A student union building should serve students.

10. Human beings do not always seem wiser than animals.

G. Select one of the topics in F, above, and write three different paragraphs on this same subject, using the same topic sentence for each, but developing each by a different method (statement and particulars, related details, sequence of ideas, statement and reasons, cause and effect, comparison and contrast, statement and example).

H. A rather ignorant and illogical woman visited the Comstock Lode during the mining boom and wrote a description of the mines. It reads in part as follows:

In many of the mines the miners cannot strike the pick more than three blows before they have to go to the cooling station and stay double the time they are at work.

The cooling stations are where they have a free circulation of air. These stations are on every level. They have large tanks or reservoirs to hold the water that is pumped from one level to another. These vats are often full of boiling water. In many of the mines the water is so hot that if a person slips into one of these tanks, he is generally scalded to death before he can be rescued.

If he is rescued alive, it is only to linger a few days, suffering the most intense agony, till death relieves him of his sufferings. He is often so completely cooked in the scalding vats that the flesh drops from the bones while taking him out. His suffering and agony are terrible to witness.

The heat of the mines is very great. In some mines it is almost unendurable. In such mines it is almost impossible to work, while in others they can work without such excessive heat.

Miners are brought to the surface almost daily from overheat.

There is scarcely a day in the year that there is not from one to two funerals among the miners; and I have known of there being five in one day.

There are a great many different causes of death. Sometimes death is caused by the caving in of rock, or by falling into the scalding tanks, or by a misstep, by falling hundreds of feet down the shafts or inclines.

—MRS. M. M. MATHEWS, *Ten Years in Nevada,*
or Life on the Pacific Coast

This writing is not without promise. It contains concrete observation and some significant generalization, but the whole is jotted down in a scatter-brained way. Try to make a good paragraph of this material, expressing a central idea in a topic sentence, developing the paragraph in accordance with some orderly plan, and omitting extraneous matter.

I. Below are paragraphs from student themes which are faulty because they lack plan, fail to turn about a topic sentence, include irrelevant material, or lack continuity. Criticize each paragraph; then supply a plausible topic sentence for each and rewrite it into a coherent unit.

1. In his story *The Devil and Daniel Webster,* Stephen Vincent Benét uses the Devil, or Mr. Scratch, to stand for evil. There is entirely too much evil in this world of ours. Mainly the story teaches a very important rule, that evil can win over almost anything but not over goodness. This appears at the end of the story. Daniel Webster has been losing almost all the time in the trial, because he is not dealing with a fair judge or a fair opponent. In the beginning of the trial a legal battle is fought between Mr. Scratch and Daniel Webster, with Webster trying to argue fine legal points with the Devil. Finally Daniel Webster realized that he could not fight his opponents with their own weapons. You cannot win fighting evil with evil. The tactics of Daniel Webster were changed, and a long speech about the good things in the world was the next order of business. "The simple things that everybody's known and felt" were what he talked about. The rule has been taught to society in many ways, but this method of teaching it through fiction is one of the most effective. Evil cannot conquer goodness is the rule which is the main theme of the story.

2. For one thing, cotton had to be picked by hand in the eighteenth century. The pickers had to spend long hours working with the cotton if they were to get anywhere. Cotton is an example of how the Industrial Revolution developed in the eighteenth century. From the fields the cotton went to the home. Here seeds were removed from the cotton by hand. This job required a considerable amount of time and patience. Then the cotton was spun into thread and woven into cloth. Men finally became tired of slow and tedious manual labor, and they began to seek new methods of producing cotton textiles. It was about the middle of the century when a number of inventions appeared which tended to shift the cotton industry from the home to the factory. Hundreds of workers could be replaced by the new machinery. Factories were built in order to house this machinery.

3. She has native aptitude as a literary critic, or at least as a critic of current magazines. Unless restrained, she literally devours *The Atlantic,* concentrating on the front and back covers, if she can

stuff them into her mouth. My young brother attributes this preference for *The Atlantic* to the whisky advertisements on the back page, but I am convinced she genuinely has taste for a good thing, something solid enough so that she can get her teeth into it. This theory of mine gains support from her other tastes. She prefers the woodpulp of *The New York Times* to that of the local paper, and I confess that I prefer the *Times,* also, to read as well as to swat flies. She will have none of the sleazy magazine digests. She throws them on the floor with a squawk of disgust. The *Saturday Evening Post* and Mother's home-building magazine intrigue her for short periods—she likes to chew the square binding at the back, for there is a certain four-square practicality in Barbara—but not for long. I gather she finds them jargonic and repetitious, lacking in the sort of body required by a young woman with three teeth. *The New Yorker* she toys with, but never consumes. I suspect that it is too brittle for her taste, caviar to the nursery. Mother, I am happy to report, encourages Barbara in her literary leanings; Mother approves of *The Atlantic,* partly because the covers are so tough that Barbara can seldom chew anything loose. Think what might happen to her taste and her stomach if she were some day to swallow a chunk of the *Reader's Digest.*

15. CONTINUITY AND COHERENCE

[For Guide to Revision, see page 168]

The writer must guide his reader from point to point through the composition.

Even though paragraphs are well planned and developed, writing will not be clear unless the reader is helped to move easily from one paragraph to the next and from one idea to another within the paragraphs. That is, the writing must have continuity and coherence. Important guides for the reader usually appear in the introduction and conclusion (discussed in 16), but various devices for establishing continuity are useful throughout a composition.

15-1 Revealing the main outline

A writer should give the reader signposts or indications of the main plan of the composition. Without relying on the overformal "firstly, secondly, and thirdly," he can naturally and directly keep the reader aware of where the discourse is headed. Following, for example, are guides included by Sir Arthur Keith in an essay on studying the human body.

In all the medical schools of London a notice is posted over the door leading to the dissecting room forbidding strangers to enter. I propose, however, to push the door open and ask the reader to accompany me within. . . . We propose to watch them [the students] at work. Each student is at his allotted part, and if we observe them in turn we shall, in an hour or less, obtain an idea of the main tissues and structures which enter into the composition of the human body.

[*These passages appear in the opening paragraph and show the reader the over-all purpose of the essay and the writer's plan for achieving it—by observing the students as they dissect.*]

By good fortune a dissection is in progress in front of the wrist, which displays, amongst other structures, the radial artery. . . .

Lying side by side with the sinews of the wrist there is another cord. . . . It is the median nerve. . . .

We propose to observe the dissector as he traces the radial artery to the heart. . . .

Before leaving the dissection we have been surveying it will be well to see one of those marvelously contrived structures known as a joint. . . .

We have surveyed the anatomy at the wrist in some detail and with a very distinct purpose. . . .

We now propose to transfer our attention for a short time to two students who are uncovering the parts in front of the neck between the chin and breastbone or sternum. . . .

Our time with the students in the dissection room has almost expired; there remains only a moment to glance at a dissection which is exposing the important organs which are enclosed within the thorax and abdomen. . . .

Our cursory visit to the dissecting room has not been in vain if the reader has realized how complex the structure of the human body really is, and how necessary it is that those who have to cure its disorders should try to understand the intricacy of its mechanism. . . .

—*Man: A History of the Human Body*

[*The second paragraph locates the reader near the first student.*]

[*The third paragraph tells the reader that the essay is turning to another aspect of the wrist dissection.*]
[*The reader is guided to a further observation.*]

[*The reader is led to another aspect of this dissection and is also warned of a change to come.*]

[*A summary marks the end of this episode; the reader is led to a turn in the trail.*]
[*The writer indicates a major shift to a new dissection.*]

[*The writer marks another turn and also prepares the reader for the end of the trail.*]

[*The conclusion reminds the reader of the purpose of the discussion.*]

The essay includes even more guides to its general pattern than have been excerpted here, but these samples, most of them opening sentences of paragraphs, illustrate the importance of such aids. These passages outline the complete essay:

> TOPIC STATEMENT: A visit to the dissecting room reveals the complexity of the human body and the importance of studying it.
> I. The anatomy at the wrist: the first dissection
>   A. The radial artery
>   B. The median nerve
>   C. Tracing the radial artery to the heart
>   D. The joint
> II. The parts in front of the neck
> III. Organs within the thorax and abdomen

The reader can follow clearly and easily because the writer has revealed his outline step by step.

15-2 Topic sentences as transitions

As the selections above indicate, the topic sentence (see 14-3) is the most useful guide from paragraph to paragraph. It introduces the topic of its own paragraph, but it can also link its paragraph with preceding material, providing a transition. Consider, for example, the following three topic sentences, taken at random from a discussion of the formation of a national government in America:

> This solution was achieved under the Articles of Confederation, a formal agreement which had loosely unified the colonies since 1781. . . .
> Thus a new colonial policy based upon the principle of equality was inaugurated. . . .
> Unfortunately, however, in the solution of other problems the Articles of Confederation proved disappointing.

In the first of the topic sentences, *This solution* refers directly to what has preceded; then the sentence goes on to introduce the Articles of Confederation as the topic of its paragraph. The second sentence refers with the word *Thus,* but it provides continuity also because it summarizes the entire preceding paragraph, putting the material into new terms which emphasize the new aspect of the topic to be considered, the use of equality as a basis of the policy. The third provides a transition in two ways, by echoing the word *solution* from the first sentence and by referring to previous material with *other problems.*

Frequently, in order to clarify a transition, a writer uses two sentences, making his transition in the first sentence of the paragraph and stating his topic in the second. For example, DeWitt H. Parker moves to a new section of an essay on aesthetics as follows:

> In our discussion thus far, we have been assuming the possibility of aesthetic theory. But what shall we say in answer to the mystic who tells us that beauty is indefinable? . . .

The first sentence summarizes what has preceded. The second introduces the topic of the paragraph, which goes on to discuss the possibilities of defining beauty.

15-3 Transitional paragraphs

For most student papers, well-written topic sentences can supply all the transitional material necessary. Longer compositions, however, sometimes are broken into large divisions containing several paragraphs, and transitions are important enough to require a brief transitional paragraph. Thomas Henry Huxley needs an entire paragraph for a relatively formal transition in an essay on the method of scientific investigation. He moves from a series of examples of how we behave "scientifically" in everyday life to a more serious discussion of causal relationships.

> So much, then, by way of proof that the method of establishing laws in science is exactly the same as that pursued in common life. Let us now turn to another matter (though really it is but another phase of the same question), and that is, the method by which, from the relations of certain phenomena, we prove that some stand in the position of causes toward the others.
>
> —*Darwiniana*

The paragraph has the qualities of a good topic sentence used transitionally, although it is developed more fully. Its first sentence summarizes what has preceded; the second tells us precisely and directly what is to follow.

15-4 Words of transition

Transitions from sentence to sentence usually do not require a sentence or paragraph and can be handled by word order and sometimes by transitional words. English includes a large number of words which function primarily to indicate a relationship and to provide continuity. For some of the most common of these words, see 33-4 to 33-5.

[165

    a. To mark an addition: *and, furthermore, next, moreover, in addition, again, also, likewise, similarly, finally, second*

    b. To introduce or emphasize a contrast or alternative: *but, or, nor, still, however, nevertheless, on the contrary, on the other hand, conversely*

    c. To mark a conclusion: *therefore, thus, then, in conclusion, consequently, as a result, in other words, accordingly*

    d. To introduce an illustration or example: *thus, for example, for instance, that is, namely*

Others indicate shifts of time or introduce clauses; almost all connectives can provide transitions. Overuse of transitional expressions makes stiff prose; careful use of them helps make clear prose.

15-5 Repetition of words and ideas

Almost every sentence in clear prose is linked with the sentences around it by direct or implied references. Sometimes pronouns in one sentence refer to words in the sentence before. Sometimes an idea of one sentence is briefly rephrased in another. Repeated references to the central idea of the paragraph may serve to bind sentences together. These central ideas echoing through the composition, along with transitional expressions, make the parts of the writing cohere and draw the reader effortlessly along the trail of the writer's thoughts. The following passage indicates how parts of clear writing are linked together.

    A driver doesn't have to look at his road map once he starts on a highway, as long as he doesn't come to any intersections. He doesn't have to worry about which way to go if he has no choice about it. But when he comes to a crossroads, with signs pointing in various directions— then he can't just let the road decide where he is to go; he has to make up his mind. He has to stop and think.

                             —MONROE C. BEARDSLEY, *Thinking Straight*

The passage carries through a single subject, *driver,* designated by the pronoun *he* after the first mention. Sentences cohere, also, by the repetition of patterns like *doesn't have to* and *has to, intersections* and *crossroads;* the connective *but* holds the two main parts of the paragraph together, marking the contrast between them.

    Another passage relies on different echoes of meaning and pattern.

In time of peace in the modern world, if one is thoughtful and careful, it is rather more difficult to be killed or maimed in the outland places of the globe than it is in the streets of our great cities, but the atavistic urge toward danger persists and its satisfaction is called adventure. However, your adventurer feels no gratification in crossing Market Street in San Francisco against the traffic. Instead he will go to a good deal of trouble and expense to get himself killed in the South Seas. (In reputedly rough water, he will go in a canoe; he will expose his tolerant and uninoculated blood to strange viruses.) This is adventure. It is possible that his ancestor, wearying of the humdrum attacks of the saber-tooth, longed for the good old days of pterodactyl and triceratops.

> —JOHN STEINBECK and EDWARD F. RICKETTS, *Sea of Cortez*

A pronoun subject, standing for *adventurer,* carries through, but references to adventure and danger also hold the paragraph together. *However* and *instead* mark shifts in the thought.

15-6 Continuity and word order

Most of the devices mentioned above succeed because they rely upon the word order in the sentence (see 19-6).

Repetitions of sentence patterns emphasize parallels or contrasts in ideas and help the reader to move smoothly from paragraph to paragraph, from sentence to sentence. In both the paragraphs above, the sentence subjects link one sentence to the next mainly because each sentence repeats the order of the preceding one. The following two sentences are linked, even though the subjects differ, because the subjects appear in the same relative place in each:

> An old man stood in front of the monkey cage excitedly throwing peanuts at a score of begging arms. A small boy only a few feet away sat with his face buried in a comic book.

The repetition of sentence order sharpens the contrast between the two main actions, and the contrast helps link the sentences. On the other hand, variations from usual word order may provide bridges, carrying special emphasis from one sentence to another.

> In front of the monkey cage stood an old man, excitedly throwing peanuts at a score of begging arms. Only a few feet away sat a small boy with his face buried in a comic book.

[167

The shift in order throws emphasis on the location, heightens the contrast in the actions by stressing the nearness of the two persons, and helps link the sentences through the repetition of the reversed pattern. There is some loss of continuity when the word order pattern is not repeated.

> In front of the monkey cage stood an old man, excitedly throwing peanuts at a score of begging arms. A small boy only a few feet away sat with his face buried in a comic book.

15 Continuity and coherence   **Con**

GUIDE TO REVISION:

> *Revise sentences or supply transitions so that each*
> *step in the composition leads clearly to the next.*

Writing must have continuity and coherence. Each word or sentence or paragraph must lead clearly to the next, and the parts of a composition must stick together—must cohere. When they do not, there may be basic weaknesses in the organization (see 5), or there may be irrelevancies which break the movement (see 12). Often, however, the paper can be improved by clearing the trail between ideas.

15a Revealing the main plan   **Con a**

A clear plan in the writer's mind or in his outline is not enough. The plan must be revealed in the paper, so that the reader knows where he is going.

Original

What State University needs is an all-college, Saturday night dance. . . .

Some freshmen know plenty of students of the opposite sex, mostly high school friends who came down to State about the time they did. . . .

The dance could be held in the gym, and a nominal fee would pay for a good orchestra. . . .

[*These sentences, which begin*

Revision

State University needs an all-college Saturday night dance. . . .

Newcomers have few friends; we should pity the lonely freshman, and give him one all-college dance a week. . . .

Even the older student could afford to widen his acquaintance. . . .

The finances and management of the proposed dance could easily be provided for. . . .

Original (Cont.)

major sections and seem to be topic sentences, do not reveal the organization of the composition.]

Revision (Cont.)

[*Orderly statement of what each paragraph is to contain makes the organization clear.*]

15b Transitions   Con b; Tran

Failure to provide adequate transitions breaks the continuity of the thought and obscures the main plan of the writing.

Original

The modern automobile is so far advanced in comfort and power that drivers have a false sense of security at high speeds. New cars and roads may be safer, but speed cannot be increased beyond the ability of the person behind the steering wheel of the auto.

Fast driving has a definite effect on the number of accidents that occur in the United States. In a survey. . . .

The severity of accidents is also affected by fast driving. . . .

[*The introductory paragraph is not clearly linked to the following ones, even though the relationship may be quite clear in the writer's mind. A transition is needed to show the reader the main outline of the composition and to link the two paragraphs.*]

Thus the pursuit of folklore motifs has become one of the most fascinating sports in modern scholarship.

The Widow of Ephesus is the story of the woman who mutilates the body of her first husband in order to promote her marriage to a second. . . .

[*Transitional material is needed*

Revision

The modern automobile is so far advanced in comfort and power that drivers have a false sense of security at high speeds. New cars and roads may be safer, but speed cannot be increased beyond the ability of the person behind the steering wheel of the auto. Since drivers are imperfect, speed contributes significantly to both the frequency and the severity of accidents in the United States.

The correlation between the frequency of accidents and speed can be demonstrated statistically. . . .

[*A transitional sentence tells the reader that the essay will discuss the effect of fast driving on (1) frequency and (2) severity of accidents. It shows the reader the outline. The second paragraph can then open with an echo of the first,* frequency of accidents, *which links the paragraphs.*]

Thus the pursuit of folklore motifs has become one of the most fascinating sports in modern scholarship.

For instance, in a common tale known to folklorists as *The Widow of Ephesus,* a woman mutilates the body of her first husband in order to promote her marriage to a second. . . .

[169

Original (*Cont.*)

to show the relationship of the second paragraph to the first.]

I thought, "That woman is just plain mean."
When I came to know my new teacher. . . .
[*A new idea has begun in the second paragraph, but the reader has not been prepared for it.*]

Revision (*Cont.*)

[*The addition of a few phrases makes clear that we are now to be given a specific example of the general statement with which the preceding paragraph ended.*]

I thought, "That woman is just plain mean."
But I was wrong. When I came to know my new teacher. . . .
[*A brief sentence of transition prepares the reader for the new paragraph.*]

15c Coherence through words and constructions   Con c

Especially within paragraphs, the repetition of words, of ideas through synonyms, and of grammatical structures promotes coherence.

Original

(1) A fraternity pledge finds life during the week preceding his initiation complex and not very pleasant. (2) This week is commonly known as hell week, and there are many good reasons for the name. (3) The pledge cannot speak to any person without first begging for permission in a long and difficult set oration. (4) Any member can make the pledge do his bidding. (5) He can make him shine anybody's shoes, and the pledge must sing, dance, and generally entertain at all meals and sleep under the dining room tables at night. (6) An infraction of any of the rules brings any number of swats from the members' paddles. (7) The swats are not administered gently and are by no means soothing to the receiver. (8) Why it is called hell week is a question never asked by any pledge. (9) Since it is the last test and marks

170]

Revision

(1) For a week preceding his initiation a fraternity pledge finds life complex and not very pleasant. (2) The week is commonly known as hell week, and there are good reasons for the name. (3) For seven days the pledge cannot speak to any person without first begging for permission in a long and difficult set oration. (4) He must do the bidding of any member; shine the shoes of anybody a member designates; sing, dance, and generally entertain at all meals; and sleep under the dining room tables at night. (5) An infraction of any of these rules brings swats from the members' paddles, not administered gently and by no means

Original (Cont.)

the end of months of trial, most freshmen look forward to it.

[*Some of the weaknesses of this paragraph result from failure to subordinate secondary ideas (see 4c); (6) and (7), for instance, might be combined. The choppiness, however, is evidence that sentences are not arranged and linked so that continuity is smooth.*]

Revision (Cont.)

soothing to the receiver. (6) No pledge ever asks why the week is called hell week. (7) Nevertheless, most pledges look forward to it as their last test and the end of months of trial.

[*Here (1) has been revised, and a transition has been prefixed to (3) so that* week *holds the three sentences together; (4) and (5) are combined and rearranged to have the same subject as (3). These rules in (5) refers to the two preceding sentences. A necessary transition introduces (7), and the sentence is re-ordered to carry through the subject of earlier sentences.*]

Clumsy repetition produces awkward, wordy writing. Useless repetition of the same idea produces only redundancy (see 36a). Skillful repetition, however, particularly skillful use of synonyms, will give the small units of writing a coherence which can be obtained in no other way.

Original

Modern scholars now agree that the ancestor of the Romance languages is not now much taught in our schools. It was Vulgar Latin, which is usually taught today only in the graduate schools. The kind of language that was written by Virgil and Cicero is the kind that is usually taught both in high school and in college, but that is not the kind from which French or any other language of that sort has come. In English we have words from the language of the Romans, and some of those words did come from the language written by the

Revision

The modern Romance languages descended from Latin, but not from the Latin usually taught in the schools. There are several Latins, notably Classical Latin, Church Latin, and Vulgar Latin. Of these three divisions of the Latin language, Classical Latin is taught almost exclusively. Church Latin is still spoken but is seldom taught to undergraduates. Vulgar Latin is taught only in a few graduate schools. Yet Vulgar Latin is the ancestor of all modern Romance languages—Italian, French, Spanish, Portuguese, and Romanic. Clas-

Original (Cont.)

famous Romans. However, what are called Romance languages did not. The working men were the ones who determined the language in the various countries which had been conquered by Caesar and the other classical generals. Church Latin is still spoken but is not much taught. Vulgar Latin is made up of words spoken by the common people, or *vulgus.*

[*This paragraph is confused, partly because the order of material is faulty, but partly also because sentences are not linked by synonyms and repeated words. Three ideas run parallel in the paragraph: the kinds of Latin, the descent of the Romance languages, the teaching of Latin in the schools. These ideas should be distinct, but should also be tied together.*]

Revision (Cont.)

sical Latin has accounted for words borrowed into these languages, as it accounted for words borrowed into English, but all scholars now agree that the Romance languages did not come from the classical speech of Virgil and Cicero. French and Italian and Spanish came from the Latin speakers who were working in France and Italy and Spain, the soldiers, the merchants, the laboring men, that is, the *vulgus* whose speech is known as Vulgar Latin.

[*The three ideas are carried through the paragraph by repetition of words like* Latin, *and the generous use of synonyms and partial synonyms like* Vulgar Latin *and the classical speech of Virgil and Cicero.*]

Similar constructions in consecutive sentences help to tie a paragraph together.

Original

Most co-eds at State University did not come here to get married, though the president did make a joke something like that. We didn't come to get dates, either, at least not mainly, though the Dean kind of hinted that. And I suppose the profs think we are just being nice to them to get good grades without working.

[*This paragraph is not completely incoherent, but the reader is given little help in moving through it.*]

Revision

Whatever the administration may imply, the co-eds at State University have not come here mainly to get married. Whatever the Dean of Women may say, they have not come mainly to get dates. And whatever the faculty may think, they have not come mainly to get good grades by flashing their smiles at professors.

[*With sentences having similar constructions and similar or contrasting words, the paragraph moves to a cumulative effect.*]

Especially within a paragraph, material can be cemented together by a subject continued throughout the paragraph, kept as the subject of consecutive sentences.

Original

I can remember when tires were quite different from what they are today. Twenty to thirty thousand miles is not now considered unusual tire mileage, provided tires are kept at proper inflation and are not run at excessive speeds. Also, anybody can change a tire with ease now. The modern tire is a marvel and a joy. A good tire, when it is new, will turn most nails and almost any old tire ought to zip through broken glass from milk bottles without a scratch. You can buy tires in nonskid, high-speed, and antisnow types.

[*The reader is needlessly confused because the subject shifts from sentence to sentence, though ostensibly the paragraph has only one subject, modern tires.*]

Revision

To anyone who knew touring in the old days, the modern automobile tire is a marvel and a joy. It will run, with proper care, twenty to thirty thousand miles. It will zip through smashed milk bottles without a scratch. When new, it will turn most tacks and nails. At reasonable speeds and with proper pressure, it is almost blowout-proof. It is available in nonskid, high-speed, and antisnow types. Best of all, it can be changed in a few minutes.

The ancestor of the modern tire, however, was quite different. . . .

[*The paragraph gains coherence because the subject of discussion has become the grammatical subject of the individual sentences.*]

EXERCISE 15

A. Describe the methods used in the following paragraphs to gain continuity, and point out specific examples of each method:

1. The doctrine of energy has to do with the notion of quantitative permanence underlying change. The doctrine of evolution has to do with the emergence of novel organisms as the outcome of chance. The theory of energy lies in the province of physics. The theory of evolution lies mainly in the province of biology, although it had previously been touched upon by Kant and LaPlace in connection with the formation of suns and planets.

—A. N. WHITEHEAD, *Science and the Modern World*

2. I have already given you a summary account of the manner in which young misses are educated in this country. They are all sent early to school; where they are taught to spell, and read, and write. From parochial schools, many of them are transferred to boarding-schools and academies. Here they learn to understand arithmetic, which indeed is usually taught them in parochial schools, and study English grammar, geography, history to some extent, criticism, and composition. In a few instances they are taught moral science, and in some ascend to higher branches of mathematics, the Latin and French languages. To these are added embroidery, drawing, and music.

—TIMOTHY DWIGHT, *Travels in New England and New York*

3. Twenty-four hours have elapsed since writing the foregoing. I have just returned from the haymow, charged more and more with love and admiration of Hawthorne. For I have just been gleaning through the Mosses, picking up many things here and there that had previously escaped me. And I found that but to glean after this man, is better than to be at the harvest of others. To be frank (though, perhaps, rather foolish) notwithstanding what I wrote yesterday of these Mosses, I had not then culled them all; but had, nevertheless, been sufficiently sensible of the subtle essence in them, as to write as I did. To what infinite height of loving wonder and admiration I may yet be borne, when by repeatedly banqueting on these Mosses I shall have thoroughly incorporated their whole stuff into my being,—that, I cannot tell. But already I feel that this Hawthorne has dropped germinous seeds into my soul. He expands and deepens down, the more I contemplate him; and further and further, shoots his strong New England roots into the hot soil of my Southern soul.

—HERMAN MELVILLE, *Hawthorne and His Mosses*

B. Of the following sentences, assume that *a* is the concluding sentence of one paragraph and that *b* is the topic sentence of the next paragraph. Consider the following pair:

   a. Thus a thunder shower saved us from losing the first baseball game of the season, and gave us another week in which to tighten our team play.

   b. A week later our pitchers were in better condition.

This is not a good transition. The opening of the second sentence, *a week later,* does something by setting the time; but the end of the preceding paragraph had seemed to promise some account of the practice during the week to develop team work, and sentence *b* does not fulfill the promise. Something like the following would be better:

   c. Next Monday afternoon the coach started a series of drills intended to show us how to work together.

Now consider the following sequences of sentences. Which provide good transitions? Which are inadequate, and why?

1. a. The poll to assess student sentiment showed overwhelming enthusiasm for the proposed Student Union Association.

   b. They decided I should be chairman of the membership drive committee.

2. a. Here with a view of the mountains on three sides and the tiny creek near the center of the area was a perfect site for the new school.

   b. The site was nearly fifty miles from a sizable town. Supplies and help would be a problem. Building costs would be high.

3. a. Everybody had left by midnight, and we went to bed.

   b. I put the coffee on and started to mix batter for pancakes.

4. a. Interpreting local news, therefore, is perhaps the most important single function of the college newspaper.

   b. National affairs should be of interest to college students and college journalists.

5. a. In such ways are college traditions useful as laws or regulations which help students to live together.

   b. The tradition of fraternity hazing does not, it seems to me, have any reason for continued existence.

6. a. Late that afternoon we arrived at Quahog Beach, ready for two glorious weeks of sun, sand, and sea.

   b. After the storm and the big waves of the previous week, there was nothing left of the cottage but the piling, sticking up through the rock-strewn shore.

7. a. Thus for a century or two, the natives of southeast Asia have associated extortion, brutality, and bad manners with white men.

   b. They are making white men pay—all white men, from whatever country they come and whatever their previous connection with Asia—for the mistakes and crimes of a few.

C. The following topic sentences of paragraphs selected from various essays provide transitions. Study each one and try to determine what has preceded the sentence and what is to follow. Some reveal more than others.

1. The distribution of the three techniques between the three departments of study is, however, less watertight than might be supposed. . . .

2. What is true of Heinrich Hertz working quietly and unnoticed in a corner of Helmholtz's laboratory in the later years of the nineteenth century may be said of scientists and mathematicians the world over for several centuries past.

3. The impact of such lawless novelties upon the more staid English of the motherland is terrific.

4. This knowledge of nature reacted on the conception of human life.

5. Meantime, there occurred an equally notable expansion of the time frame of reference.

D. Rewrite the following paragraphs from student themes, attempting to improve the continuity from sentence to sentence:

1. The mythology and folkways of a primitive people are the basis of their society. Wise men and priests explain the mysteries of the universe. Folkways are learned by the young by imitation and under the pressure of authority. Traditions of a different society are sometimes imposed on a primitive group, and then the old

folkways are submerged and covered by superficial acquired habits. The dress and language of the new society are adopted. You have to probe beneath the surface to find the old beliefs persisting.

2. What to wear was a very important problem to me. Blue was the color which my mother considered most flattering to me, but I liked red. I was only in the seventh grade. It was very hard for me to find a formal that fit me. Dress designers apparently did not take sufficient account of the special problems of seventh-graders. Many dresses, both blue and red, were presented. I did not seem to have curves in the right places. When I did find a suitable dress, the alterations turned out to be more complicated than making the dress could have been.

E. Consider an essay designated by your instructor or select an essay from one of the following magazines: *The Atlantic, The Reporter, Harpers, Yale Review, Pacific Spectator,* or *The Sewanee Review.* Read the article carefully, and then record the following: (a) the theme sentence, statement of main idea, or indication of what the article is about; (b) indication of the main portions of the article, by pages and paragraphs; (c) the words, phrases, sentences, or paragraphs which indicate to the reader where each of these main sections begins and ends; (d) the most important indications within each of these main sections which guide the reader through them.

F. Select a paragraph from a theme you have written. Using the paragraphs in 15-5 as models, draw lines tracing the continuity from key word to key word. Then revise the paragraph, attempting to improve its continuity, and draw lines on the revision to test whether more ideas carry from sentence to sentence.

16. INTRODUCTION AND CONCLUSION

[For Guide to Revision, see page 183]

The introduction should interest the reader, lead him to the main thought of the paper, and show him how to follow the plan of the composition. The conclusion should conclude, reinforcing the important ideas of the paper.

"I think," Anton Chekhov is reported as saying, "that when one has finished writing a short story one should delete the beginning and the end. That's where we fiction writers mostly go wrong." Student themes also are often weighed down by heavy, obscure introductions or conclusions, but all compositions must start and stop. Beginnings and endings are important.

16-1 Functions of the introduction

Introductions vary. A long paper usually requires more introduction than a short one. Special circumstances demand that the introduction do special jobs, but, in general, introductions do the following:

(1) The introduction must introduce. It must lead directly into the paper.

(2) Usually, the introduction must tell, directly and simply, what the paper is to be about. That is, it usually states the main idea of the composition. If not, a statement of purpose should usually follow the introduction, as a sort of second introduction.

(3) It may provide necessary preliminary information.

(4) It may provide background concerning the writing of the paper, the validity of the material, and the like.

(5) It may be used to attract the reader's attention.

(6) It usually sets the tone of the paper.

A good introduction is likely to do several of these at once. The most important, of course, are the first two. Whatever else it does, the introduction must tell the reader what the paper is about and lead him gracefully into the body of the discussion. It must not be so long that it is out of proportion to the rest of the paper; usually a student theme requires only two or three sentences. There are no recipes for introductions; various approaches may serve well. Furthermore, the writer may change his introduction half a dozen times before he finishes the final draft. He may prepare a very formal introduction which he knows he will discard, go on to complete the writing, and then return to work out a final introduction. Or he may hit upon a telling idea for an introduction as he is doing his first thinking on the subject.

16-2 Stating the problem or the purpose

Many beginnings say directly what the paper concerns; they start the reader properly and indicate the subsequent plan. Beginnings should not be as formal as: "In this paper I am going to show. . . ." or "These pages are intended to prove. . . ." Still, they should leave the reader in no doubt as to the subject.

FORCE AND FREEDOM

Can there be a moral basis for freedom in a world of force? This is one of the ugly questions which disturb many intelligent people at this moment. Can we reconcile the doctrine of military force—the idea of killing men in war—with a moral purpose? As a matter of history, freedom has often emerged from the successful use of force; yet we abominate war as intensely as we love freedom. How are we to resolve this paradox?

—JAMES BRYANT CONANT

[*The opening paragraph uses a series of questions to lead to the basic problem of the paper: the relationship between force and freedom. The first question is the main question the writer will try to answer. This type of introduction is often effective, although the use of questions can be made to seem overoratorical and affected by an unskilled writer.*]

An introduction by direct statement may be more formal; for instance, it may analyze the subject:

178]

Juvenile delinquency is one of the most pressing problems in the city of C, and it can be solved only after more careful study than the heated and usually uninformed letters that have been appearing in the newspapers or the irate and accusing speeches in recent P.T.A. meetings. A first step is careful examination of at least three related matters: the adequacy of recreational facilities in the city, the methods of the police in dealing with juvenile delinquency, and the question of the relations between juvenile delinquency and problems of home life.

[*A paper like the student investigative paper from which this introduction is taken often profits from an introduction which maps out the course to be followed. The introduction here summarizes the analysis which is to be developed.*]

An effective variation upon this standard beginning opens with a statement the writer expects to oppose. He describes a popular opinion which he believes is erroneous; he comments on earlier writing with which he expects to disagree; he mentions a person with whom he differs. By this device the writer can gain the interest that always attaches to an argument, and at the same time define his own stand by its opposite.

ROOSEVELT AND THE FAR EAST

Even the most friendly of the many Roosevelt biographers have a tendency to imply that the President gave little thought to foreign affairs before 1939. The impression created is far from accurate.

—SUMNER WELLES

[*The introduction moves the writer—and the reader—quickly into the main matter of the essay: a discussion of Roosevelt's understanding of foreign policy, which the writer wishes to defend.*]

16-3 Establishing background and authority

A writer may work logically into his subject by summarizing events or attitudes on which his new comments are based. Historical or political commentaries frequently follow this pattern, leading to discussions of current situations by brief outlines of what is behind them. Such discussions can take a dramatic form.

THE PITTSBURGH STORY

Six years ago, insiders were wondering if Pittsburgh was a used-up community. For a variety of reasons, the oldest, biggest, and most powerful center of heavy industry, the leading steel-maker for all the world, was shriveling away. . . . Then, suddenly, something happened.

[The essay describing the plan on which a city is being developed begins by describing the situation which stimulated development of the new plan.]

—KARL SCHRIFTGIESSER

Subjects sometimes require that the writer make clear what right he has to discuss particular material. He may have been an eye-witness to an important event; he may have done exhaustive research; he may have conducted controlled experiments. Research papers often require some statement of this sort so that the reader may judge the validity of the material presented.

THOMAS COUTURE

My first meeting with Couture, who became one of my best and dearest friends, was odd and characteristic. It was in 1834; I was not yet one and twenty, and had just arrived from the United States, well provided for in the way of courage and determination, with a stock of youthful illusions, and very little besides.

[The introduction has the easy grace of familiar narration, but it also lets the reader know that the writer is speaking on the basis of long and intimate acquaintance with his subject.]

—GEORGE P. A. HEALY

16-4 Attracting the reader's attention

In order to gain the attention of readers, modern writers often begin with a sample of their most striking illustrations, with pertinent facts that are dramatized into conversation, with a record of an event that demonstrates the importance or interest of the views to be presented in the discussion. The following examples illustrate some of the many possible variations of this general method:

THERE IS NO AVERAGE BOY

Sam had only just passed his fourteenth birthday but he weighed 150 pounds, was 5 feet 10 inches

[The introduction continues with a description of Billy, another boy who is quite different, and then

tall, and might well have shaved every day. His ninth-grade teachers complained that he seemed listless and uninterested and did not show the maturity which they felt a boy as big and as apparently grown-up should have. "You'd think he'd be a leader, but he has no sense of responsibility and he's always doing childish, silly things."

—J. ROSWELL GALLAGHER

leads into the main idea, that there is no average boy, a thesis illustrated by the opening instances.]

CAN FRANCE COME BACK?

Some time ago Monsieur Schuman, French Foreign Minister, was taking an early morning walk in the gardens of his official residence on the Quai d'Orsay. In the course of it he met an elderly gardener at work upon a flower bed. "Be off with you," said the gardener, "the public are not allowed in these gardens." "But I am the Minister." The gardener gazed distastefully at Monsieur Schuman. "Oh, well," he said at last, "if you're the Minister . . ." and turning his back, went on with his work.

Such an attitude may betoken. . . .

—HILARY ST. GEORGE SAUNDERS

[*An amusing anecdote which illustrates an attitude important to the theme catches the interest of the reader. Note that the second paragraph proceeds at once to explain the significance of the incident for the purposes of the essay and to lead the reader from it into the main matter to be discussed.*]

16-5 Functions of the conclusion

Since the final position is emphatic, the conclusion offers an opportunity for the writer to press whatever points he wishes his reader to remember most. In a short paper, the writer may need no formal conclusion, but he will still choose carefully the idea with which he closes. Whether a full summary or a brief final statement, a conclusion has the following functions:

(1) The conclusion must close the paper, and make the reader feel that the writer stopped because he completed what he had to say—not because a bell rang or he came to the bottom of a page.

(2) The conclusion must recall the *whole* composition, the central idea. It should help the reader see what the paper has accomplished.

(3) The conclusion offers an opportunity for any final suggestion or warning the writer wants to add.

16-6 Statement of main point

Probably the most common type of ending in essays in current magazines is a statement—usually a restatement—of the main idea, of what the writer wants the reader to remember. It may be brief. One essay on the development of the city of Pittsburgh ends with a three-word paragraph: "Meanwhile, Pittsburgh booms." It may be a fully developed conclusion.

CAN FRANCE COME BACK?

France has been in as bad a plight before and has survived to become strong and powerful again. She has done so because of the love of thrift and the will to work in the tillers of her soil.

—HILARY ST. GEORGE SAUNDERS

[The final brief paragraph answers the question in the title; at the end, the answer gains emphasis.]

WHO WILL DO THE DIRTY WORK?

"When two men ride a horse, one must go in the front," said Thomas Hobbes. The time has come when Americans must consider whether their countrymen will be long content to ride on the mare's rump.

—DAVID L. COHN

[The essay enlarges on the main idea that the United States is developing a national discontent because most people "must content themselves with becoming, at best, skilled workers." The final two sentences restate the main idea.]

16-7 The dramatic conclusion

To emphasize the theme, the writer may close with a dramatic incident, a striking example or illustration, or a telling quotation. The method has the advantage of making a point objectively and strongly, and it is often used, especially in an essay that has been largely a record of facts or incidents.

THE PRIVATE EYES

As one professional private detective, admitting a personal fondness for whodunits, put it recently, "I read that stuff just to get my mind off my work."

—WILLIAM S. FAIRFIELD and CHARLES CLIFT

[The exposé of private detectives is composed of four sections, each of which ends with a dramatic incident or telling quotation. This section concerns the ruthless but pedestrian competence of some private detectives.]

182]

16-8 Request for action or for an attitude

Often the writer concludes by adding to his main idea a plea for action. He suggests that the reader do something specific, that he heed a warning, that he accept a point of view.

MOONLIGHT AND POISON IVY

Better marriage relations in this country await an extensive revaluation of our attitude towards life and living. If our values are shabby and our attitudes adolescent, how can American marriage, made in our image, be anything but a monumental failure?

[An essay on the weaknesses of our attitudes toward marriage ends by suggesting that we change and by pointing out the necessity for change.]

—DAVID L. COHN

The conclusion, then, is designed chiefly to make sure that the reader leaves the essay with its main point clearly in mind. It helps the reader recall the pattern of relationships which the essay has followed; sometimes it makes a final effort to show him the special significance of those relationships. Any method which will accomplish these purposes is acceptable.

16 *Introduction and conclusion*   **Intro; Conc**

GUIDE TO REVISION:

Rewrite the introduction or conclusion so that it contributes to the interest and coherence of the writing as a whole.

Introductory and concluding paragraphs, which have as their main purpose contributing to the coherence of the whole composition, should usually be direct, brief, and, if possible, striking. Introductions should introduce; that is, they should direct the reader toward the subject and start him on it. Conclusions should conclude; that is, they should bring a composition to an appropriate close and enforce the basic idea.

16a Introduction that introduces   **Intro a**

Perhaps the most common weakness of beginnings in student papers is that they fail to show the reader what the paper is to be about—

they do not introduce. The introduction should present the subject. Sometimes the opening paragraph can best be omitted.

Original

PROPER FEEDING OF CATTLE

I have always been interested in cattle, and I have noticed the growing importance of the cattle industry in all parts of the country. Not only has the quality of American beef improved in recent years, but the raising of beef cattle has spread throughout the nation.

The first requirement of proper feeding for beef cattle is. . . .

[*The main idea of the paper is that scientific feeding of cattle has improved the entire beef industry. The introduction does not prepare the reader for it.*]

Revision

PROPER FEEDING OF CATTLE

The American beef industry has shown important developments in recent years. Not only has cattle raising been introduced in areas formerly thought unsuitable; at the same time the quality of beef has improved. The progress is due primarily to the introduction of scientific feeding.

The first requirement of. . . .

[*The revised introduction omits superfluous, confusing material and tells the reader what the paper is to be about; it introduces the subject.*]

Often an introduction fails because the writer does not show how it is related to the main body of the discussion. The writer sees the connection, but he forgets that the reader may not see it unless he is shown how to see it.

Original

COLLEGE HUMOR

Last week four mechanical engineering students dismantled a Model-T Ford, carried the parts quietly up the back stairs of the dormitory one night, and reassembled the car in the third-floor hall. It was an interesting example of college humor, of the practical variety, as it exists in colleges today.

[*The incident attracts the reader's attention and makes an effective opening. But the second sentence does not relate it to the main idea of the paper, that practical joking in college has remained about the same for many years.*]

Revision

COLLEGE HUMOR

Last week four mechanical engineering students dismantled a Model-T Ford, carried the parts quietly up the back stairs of the dormitory one night, and reassembled the car in the third-floor hall. Undergraduates admired, janitors were puzzled, and the incident made the national news reports, but it was only a repetition of a pattern that has characterized practical jokes in college for many years.

[*The new transitional sentence interprets the introduction in terms of the main idea of the paper.*]

16b *Introduction independent of title*   **Intro b**

The introduction should be independent of the title, partly because the title may be changed or may be dropped from a paper submitted for publication. Especially, a pronoun or adjective like *this* or *these* referring to the title should not begin the paper.

Original

Revision

FREEDOM OF SPEECH

This subject is basic to the survival of democracy in America.

[*The reference to the title weakens the introduction by destroying its independence and betrays the writer into using imprecise diction. Strictly,* freedom, *not the* subject, *is* basic.]

FREEDOM OF SPEECH

Freedom of speech is basic to the survival of democracy in America.

[*Repetition of the title makes the introduction independent, and also more accurate.*]

HOW TO MAKE FISH CHOWDER

First, you should get some potatoes, carrots, celery, onions, herbs. Most of all, you need fresh fish.

[*The introduction does not refer directly to the title but depends on it.*]

HOW TO MAKE FISH CHOWDER

To make fish chowder you need potatoes, carrots, celery, onions, herbs. Most of all, you need fresh fish.

16c *The adequate conclusion*   **Conc c**

The paper that seems to stop in the middle of things is usually less effective than one that stops because the writer has completed his job. Usually a single sentence is enough to conclude a theme.

Original

Revision

. . . All too frequently scholastic standards have been subordinated to football. I know of one instance in which an important player was allowed to take a final examination over twice, for no reason except that it took him that long to pass it. All of us have heard of exceptions to entrance requirements made for athletes.

[*The paper is attempting to show that football is a business in this*

I may be condemned for lack of school spirit or for idealism or for something worse, but I cannot help hoping that some day football in State University may become a sport instead of a business.

[*The addition of a concluding paragraph which returns to the central topic rounds out the composition. It suggests that the writer has concluded, not just stopped. The conclusion here presents the point*

[185

Original (*Cont.*)

student's university. *The final sentences concern only one aspect of this theme; they do not bring the reader back to the main idea.*]

Revision (*Cont.*)

of view which the writer has explained by the evidence already submitted.]

A conclusion is illogical if it makes a statement not justified by the body of the paper. The trouble may lie in the paper itself; difficulty in finding a logical conclusion suggests that the writer has not proved his case.

Original

[*The body of the paper presents reasons to justify the heavy expenditures on modern college football.*]

On Saturday afternoon in the crowded stadium twenty-two young men are fighting for the kinds of ideals that have made this country great. May the best team win!

[*The conclusion is a string of stock statements that happen to fit football, but it has no intimate relationship with the point of the paper.*]

[*The body of the theme enumerates various improvements in automobiles in recent years.*]

Some control of speed must be introduced, or accidents and loss of life are going to increase. Translating plans into action is the only way to curb speeding and stop accidents.

[*Perhaps misled by some notion that a conclusion ought to involve a lesson or an exhortation, the writer has finished with a statement that may be true but is not illustrated by his theme.*]

Revision

Football may have become big business, but it is a business worth preserving because its aims are the aims of education.

[*When the writer starts thinking about what he has said—not just vaguely putting together sentences that happen to get associated in his mind with the subject of football—he finds that he can make a general statement that sums up his main argument and effectively concludes his theme.*]

In the past twenty-five years the automobile has developed from a temperamental, often makeshift experiment to a highly complicated piece of precision machinery.

[*The revised conclusion omits the unsubstantiated moral and summarizes the material of the theme.*]

The conclusion should concern itself with the main idea of the *whole* composition and with illustrations of this main idea. Details that do not apply to the whole theme distract the reader and reveal bad organization.

Original	*Revision*
Sitting there, waiting for a big one to come swimming into view, always gives me a special fever of anticipation. You keep the decoy moving in large circles. When the fish approaches, he stops for a second or two. The spear should strike the fish as near the neck as possible. It is a real thrill to be one of the fellows in a fish house. [*The paper tells how to spear fish. The conclusion is confusing because it brings in at the end details which belonged in the body of the theme.*]	Sitting there, waiting for a big one to come swimming into view, always gives me a special fever of anticipation. To wait in a fish house, with poised spear, is a real thrill. [*With the misplaced details omitted, the conclusion ends the paper with an indication of the writer's purpose and also the importance of the subject. The omitted details should be dropped or put into the theme in a more appropriate place.*]

16d Proportion in introduction or conclusion   Intro d; Conc d

Most student themes are so short that they require little introduction or conclusion; the writer is wise to start what he wants to say as quickly as he can and to stop when he is finished. An introduction that uses, say, 200 words of a 500-word paper is obviously out of proportion (see 5b); often it merely multiplies judgments or generalities (see 6) and postpones development of the writer's ideas. A rambling, repetitious ending is no better.

Original	*Revision*
DECORATING A LIVING ROOM	DECORATING A LIVING ROOM
As a hobby, I draw house plans, one of which I hope to have blueprinted and built in the near future. I have been working on various plans for many years, and I find the hobby fascinating. It is instructive as well as pleasant, and I have learned many things from my experiments. My first plans were amateurish and impractical. The plans I draw now are more detailed and more concerned with functional requirements. I have been especially interested in plans for decorating living rooms because actually the living room sets the theme for the rest of the house.	Decorating the living room is the most important step in decorating a house, since the living room sets the theme for all the other rooms. . . . [*The introduction was obviously too long for a paper of 300 words. The solution, as usually, is to omit material not relevant to the main purpose of the paper. The omission makes the paper more direct as well as better proportioned. The student might appropriately write, on another occasion, a paper detailing his experiences as an amateur architect, but the material is not appropriate here.*]

Original (*Cont.*)

[*More than a hundred words
separate the reader from the subject,
decorating a living room.*]

16e Apologetic introduction or conclusion   Intro e; Conc e

Out of what may be commendable motives of modesty, a writer is sometimes tempted to begin or conclude by protesting his own inability to deal with his topic or by apologizing for the topic itself. Such apologies should be avoided. The reader sees that if the apologetic writer means what he says, he should have kept his pen in his pocket. If he does not mean it, and is being falsely modest, the reader sees the deception.

Original

ILLEGAL GAMBLING

I have no first-hand knowledge of illegal gambling, and perhaps I should not write about it. But I do have some opinions . . .

[*One suspects that the writer's first impulse was right; he should have changed his topic.*]

Revision of introduction

ILLEGAL GAMBLING

Illegal gambling is dangerous to our society mainly because of the other crimes which accompany it.

[*The writer has thought of the "opinion," which is what he planned to discuss and has used it to start the paper.*]

Revision of conclusion

The only hope for peace in our time lies in world federation.

Although this is a brief and inadequate treatment of so complex a subject, it perhaps serves to give some idea of my feelings.

[*The qualification may be honest and may even be useful elsewhere, but it should not weaken the beginning or ending of the theme.*]

The only hope for peace in our time lies in world federation.

[*Omission of the final apology, or inclusion of a shortened form of it somewhere in the body of the theme, concludes the paper with a strong and pertinent statement.*]

16f Interest in introduction or conclusion   Intro f; Conc f

Better be dull than confusing or misleading. A reader will usually forgive dullness in an introduction or a conclusion if the writing is clear and direct, especially in very practical writing, but a skillful writer can be at once interesting and exact. In many kinds of writing an interesting introduction is imperative. Many an article is made or ruined by the introduction. An introduction can prepare the reader to go on with a zestful sense of anticipation, or it can make him toss the article away. Similarly, an interesting conclusion can enforce a discussion at its most crucial point.

Original	_Revision_
I am going to tell you what happened the last time I went out with our truck. It was quite a rainy day, and we live quite a ways out in the country, and I had a big load of hogs to haul.	It was stuck, hub down in the black gumbo, a great hulking five-ton truck, loaded with a couple of dozen grunting, squealing sows. I was alone. I was still weak from influenza. And I had lost a chain, somewhere back in the sea of mud.
[_After a fashion this introduces, though not very exactly. We do not yet know that anything interesting is to happen, and the wordy way in which the passage is written leads us to believe it will not._]	[_The introduction has become dramatic, and we know that the driver, in a very unpleasant situation, must somehow try to get out of it._]

EXERCISE 16

A. Below are beginning paragraphs, with the sentences that follow them, taken from papers discussing the general subject of fraternities and sororities in college. Comment specifically on the effectiveness of each as an introduction.

1.   College fraternities obviously fail in a number of ways, but I believe that they are essentially valuable to our educational system because they contribute to the social development of the individual student.
     First of all, they help the student learn how to get along with other human beings. . . .

2.   Fraternities have long been an essential part of the educational system of the United States. Most major colleges and universities now have many chapters on their campuses.
     The first reason that they should be retained is that they provide living quarters for many students. . . .

3.   When Bill Jones came to college he was one of my closest friends, the kind of person everybody liked. Then he joined a fraternity. Now he hardly speaks to his old friends.
     This is just one of the reasons for abolishing fraternities and sororities. . . .

4.   Birds of a feather flock together. In the same way those who want to join sororities join, and those who do not stay out.
     It is obvious, therefore, that there is no reason for changing the sorority system on our campuses. . . .

5. Not being a member of a fraternity, this is a subject about which I have little information. I will write about it as well as I can, however.

   I am sure, however, that there needs to be a drastic change in the way fraternities operate on this campus. . . .

6. I have been a pledge to a national sorority for nearly three months, and I am sure that most of the criticisms that one hears about sororities are not true. These criticisms that sororities are snobbish and that they do not encourage study certainly do not apply to my sorority.

   The first advantage of sororities which I want to consider is . . .

7. When I first proudly attached my fraternity pledge pin to my lapel, I dreamed happily of the days the rushing chairman had described for me—days of scholarly companionship, of good food and superior lodging, of brotherly love, of the cultural benefits of sophisticated social life. After three months of waxing floors and reaching for my toes my dreams are the same, but they are no longer connected with the fraternity.

   I dream, for instance, of the scholarly companionship, but I have not found it. . . .

8. In this theme I shall consider fraternities and sororities.

   There are both disadvantages and advantages to fraternities and sororities. . . .

B. Below are concluding paragraphs taken from papers discussing the general subject of fraternities and sororities in college. Comment specifically on the effectiveness of each as a conclusion.

1. [*The paper cites instances from the writer's experience which seem to him to show disadvantages of living in a fraternity.*]

   It took me only three months as a pledge to learn that there is a wide difference between the stories pledges hear during rush week and the realities of life in a fraternity house.

2. [*The paper cites evidence intended to show that living in a sorority is really no more expensive than living in a dormitory and that one gets more for her money in the sorority.*]

   Sororities, therefore, should be encouraged on our campuses in America. They give a girl the kind of college life which prepares her for real-life situations.

3. [*The paper maintains that sororities aid education because they provide necessary supplements to academic work.*]

   My sorority includes the nicest group of girls I have ever known. It is a pleasure and an honor to be associated with them.

4. [*The paper maintains that fraternities are undemocratic in their methods of selecting members and should therefore be banned from campuses of state institutions.*]

Instances like those I have presented could be multiplied to show that fraternities discriminate against certain races and religions. I believe that such organizations should not be recognized by colleges and universities in a democratic country.

5. [*The paper presents a logical argument to establish the idea that democracy is based on individual freedom and that any organization should be given freedom to choose its members as it pleases.*]

Of course, there may be other arguments, and this is a big subject which requires further investigation, but I see no reason for discriminating against fraternities.

C. Select one of your previous themes and rewrite the beginning and the ending in three ways. Try to use a different approach for each pair. For instance, if you used a direct statement of purpose in your original theme, you might try to phrase this statement more briefly and picturesquely; you might begin with a question or series of questions, or you might make use of an incident or a quotation.

D. Read all the nonfiction articles in one issue of *The Atlantic, Harper's, The Reporter,* or a similar periodical designated by your instructor. Notice any inadequacies in introductions and conclusions. Select two articles in which you feel that the introductions and conclusions are unusually apt, and give specific reasons for your choice.

E. Read Psalms 8, 9, 15, 19, 22, and 27 (in the numbering used in the King James version of the Bible). Which have effective introductions? Which have telling conclusions? What comment can you make on the purposes of the introductions and conclusions?

IV. The Basic Sentence Pattern

*The congruent and harmonious fitting of parts in a
sentence hath almost the fastning and force of knitting and connexion: As in stones well squar'd, which
will rise strong a great way without mortar.*

——BEN JONSON

Writing communicates partly because words are signs of meaning; that is, they convey to a reader the writer's thought about a thing or
a quality or an action (see 35). The word *girl* is a sign which conveys an idea of a particular kind of creature; *love* is a sign for a particular action or way of feeling; *farmer* "means" a man of a particular
group. But the words alone are not enough to communicate; *farmer
girl love* does not say anything clearly. The reader needs to know not
only what the words mean but how they are related, and consequently
how the ideas which the words represent are related.

The relationships among words in a language are the grammar of
a language, and devices of grammar are those which reveal or specify
these relationships. To understand, then, the reader must have not
only signs of meaning but signs of grammar.

The signs of grammar differ in different languages. Some languages
rely primarily on inflectional endings or changes in the forms of words
to reveal grammar. Latin, for example, indicates which word is the
subject and which the complement in a sentence by the endings of
the words. *Puella agricolam amat* says that the girl loves the farmer.
A simple change in endings alters meaning considerably. *Puellam
agricola amat* says that the farmer loves the girl. Changing the order
would have no effect on the meaning; changing the endings changes
the grammatical relationships. A grammar which is revealed mainly in
this way is called an *inflectional* or *synthetic* grammar. Classical Greek

and Latin had primarily inflectional grammars; like them, Anglo-Saxon, the ancestor of modern English, was strongly inflected.

English, however, has now a different kind of grammar. We could use endings with a group of three words like *farmer girl love*. We could, for example, put an *s* on *love* and make it *loves*. But we would still not know who loved whom, and we have no endings for *farmer* or *girl* which would tell us. We could tell, however, if we put the words into a different order: *farmer love girl*. We do not have a conventional sentence, but the words make a kind of pidgin-English sense, at least. The essential relationships, who does the acting and what he does, are clear. English, in other words, expresses most grammatical ideas not by inflection but by word order.

A grammar depending mainly on word order is called a *distributive* or *analytic* grammar. Of great modern languages only English and Chinese are characteristically distributive, although many European languages are becoming more distributive.

The following sections of this book, therefore, consider the distributive grammar of English with emphasis on word order as a grammatical device. Sections IV and V discuss how word order and the meanings of words work together to express relationships among ideas: (1) The basic sentence relationship, the working together of subject, verb, and complement, is discussed in IV; (2) Co-ordination and subordination, secondary relationships, are discussed in V.

The two grammatical devices which supplement word order in English, inflectional changes and function words, are considered in VI.

17. THE COMPLETE SENTENCE; THE FRAGMENT

[For Guide to Revision, see page 202]

A complete sentence says something about something.

Consider the following simple sentence:

The dog bites the man.

We understand the sentence because, in the first place, we know what the words mean, that *dog* conveys a concept of a particular kind of four-legged creature with good teeth. But we understand it also because we sense a particular relationship between the words. Knowing the meanings of individual words is not enough. Look at the same group of words again:

The man bites the dog.

Without changing a single word, we have altered completely the meaning of the simple sentence—made news, according to the bromide. We have changed the relationships between the ideas expressed because we have changed the order of the words. We have made a grammatical change. Now change the sentence in any other way:

Man the dog the bites.
Man dog bites the the.

The sentence has become nonsense.

Or consider the following words, arranged in alphabetical order: *aid, all, come, for, good, is, men, now, of, party, the, the, the, time, to, to.* So arranged, the words make no sense, with or without commas. Rearranged, they become the familiar practice sentence:

Now is the time for all good men to come to the aid of the party.

Nonsense has been turned into sense by changing the order of the words. And no word in the sentence can be moved without either changing the meaning of the sentence or rendering the whole into nonsense.

[195

17-1 Grammatical devices in English

Thus, the most important statement that can be made about our grammar might be phrased: *In English, word order expresses most grammatical relationships.* That is, words are related, and hence gain much of their meaning, through their positions in the sentence. Anyone who thinks he "never can learn grammar" should be encouraged; he has already learned the bulk of it from his experience in putting words in order.

He has also learned to use a second grammatical device which supplements word order. If we look again at the sentence

Now is the time for all good men to come to the aid of the party

we notice several words which have little meaning but are essential to it. What is the meaning of *for* or *to* or *of?* They have no independent "meaning" as words like *aid* or *time* or *come* have meaning. They show how other words are related. *Of,* for instance, determines the relationship between *aid* and *party*—or rather *of* contributes to determining this relationship, for even here order is essential, and *aid* must come before *party* with *of* and *the* between them. Words of this sort, which primarily show relationships between other words, may be referred to as *function words* (see 33) or *relationship words,* or usually *connectives.* A second important statement about English grammar, then, might be: *If the relationships between words are not made clear by order, order is most frequently supplemented by function words.*

These two devices, word order and function words, express most of the grammatical relationships in English, but a third device survives from an earlier period in the history of the language. In Anglo-Saxon the grammatical relationships in a sentence like *The dog bites the man* were shown by the forms of the words themselves rather than by their order. One ending for the word would indicate that the word designated the actor, another that the word designated what was affected by the action. The sentence above might have been written in Anglo-Saxon as *Thone monnan biteth se hund.* The reader would have understood the relationships among the words not by their order but by their forms. Both *thone* and *se* are forms of the same word, comparable with *the* in the modern sentence, but the form *se* indicates who did the biting, and *thone,* along with the ending on *man,* indicates that the man rather than the dog needs a bandage. Most of

196]

these form changes have dropped out of English, but enough of them remain to warrant a third statement about grammar: *Form changes have survived in English to express grammatical relationships in a few situations.* Since users of English have come to depend so constantly on word order and function words to express grammatical ideas, this third device is often troublesome; it is discussed in detail in VI.

17-2 The basic pattern for the complete sentence

We make ourselves understood in English mainly because we learn to put words into patterns which indicate certain relationships to the reader. The basic pattern is the sentence.

A single word can symbolize, can name. The word *Plato* stands for something, but it is not a complete sentence. It must be completed by something understood from its context (see 17-6) or by other words, so that it says something about Plato. *Plato studies* is a complete sentence. It says something about Plato, that he did something. *Plato studying* is not a complete sentence, even though it joins two ideas. *Flying time* or *the flight of time* only names or points out. *Time flies* is a complete sentence.

To be complete, a sentence must have these basic elements: a subject and a word telling what it does. Often the basic pattern also includes the object or receiver of the action: *Plato studies philosophy* or *Plato admired Socrates.* Sometimes it includes a subject complement which identifies the subject: *Plato was a philosopher* or *Plato was studious.*

17-3 Subject, verb, complement

Simple structures like those in 17-2 are the framework of every sentence, no matter how complex it may be. English sentences take this form, and writers using English think in this form. When we think, we choose a subject and think something about that subject; and when we express our thoughts in words, we follow the same process. The subject of the sentence usually is what we are thinking about and propose to talk about. The verb tells something about this subject; that is, it asserts, postulates, or declares about this subject. To use a grammatical term, it predicates; the verb, and all the words which go along with it, are accordingly called the *predicate.* This is the core of our thinking and writing: a subject, which names what is to be discussed, and a predicate, which makes an assertion or a predication about the subject. In adult thinking, however, assertions or predications are usually complicated. They require more than a verb and are completed by one or more constructions which are called complements and modifiers.

The main parts of a sentence, then, may be identified as follows:

The *subject* governs the verb grammatically, names whatever acts through the verb. Usually it names whatever the sentence is about—a person, a thing, a concept, condition.

> *Taffy* stole a bone.
> *Knowledge* is power.
> *Girls* like new clothes.

In a few formalized sentence patterns or variations from usual patterns (see 19) the real subject of discussion is not the same as the grammatical subject of the sentence.

> One seldom finds rattlesnakes in this area.

The sentence is about either rattlesnakes or this area, but the grammatical subject is *one*. Usually sentences are stronger when the real subject and the grammatical subject are the same.

The *verb* predicates; that is, it shows that the subject exists, acts, has a certain characteristic, or is linked with another subject or quality. It indicates that the subject is or does something.

> Fish *swim*.
> The mirror *broke*.
> The ferry *was about to leave*.

In one type of construction the verb directs its predication toward the subject.

> All the passengers *were killed*.
> The villagers *ought to have been warned*.

The *complement* elaborates, limits, or otherwise completes the predication begun in the verb, provided the verb is not complete in itself.

> Boy meets *girl*.
> The girl may be *good looking*.
> She may give *the boy a piece of her mind*.

17-4 Kinds of complements

These complements are of several kinds, but they can all be divided into two main categories, subject complements and object complements.

The *subject complement* completes the verb but elaborates or modifies the idea expressed in the subject. It may give another name for the subject, mention a class which includes the subject, or include the subject in a group and sharpen our understanding of it.

> Tam O'Shanter was a *Scotsman.*
> He was an old *soak.*

The student may already be familiar with this type of complement under the name *predicate noun* or *predicate nominative,* since it is the name of something and it appears in the predicate. The subject complement may also give a characteristic or quality of the subject.

> Tam seemed *thirsty.*
> He was *drunk* every Saturday night.

The student may know this type of complement under such names as *predicate adjective, predicate attribute,* or *attribute complement.*

The *object complement* completes the verb by introducing the name of something which is not the subject and which receives the predication of the verb.

> Tam saw a *witch.*
> He admired her short *skirt.*
> The devil was going to roast *him.*
> His wife was nursing her *wrath* to keep it warm.

These object complements are highly varied, and a complete analysis of them is not easy. For instance, in the sentences *Mary made a cake* and *The cake made Jimmie sick,* the cake, clearly, did not make Jimmie in the same sense that Mary made the cake. Fortunately, however, the student need not be able to distinguish all the different sorts of object complements in order to understand fundamental English sentence structure, or to write correct and vigorous sentences. He may already have learned to recognize object complements like those above under the name *direct object.* Two other types of object may be worth identifying. One is called the *indirect object* and is most frequently encountered in sentences declaring that something (the direct object) is given to something or somebody else (the indirect object).

> Tam gave his *nag* (indirect object) a *dig* (direct object) in the ribs.
> Tam's wife gave *him* (indirect object) a *scolding* (direct object).
> She told *him* (indirect object) the *truth* (direct object).

If in doubt the student can identify an indirect object by recasting the sentence so that the indirect object appears in a phrase introduced by *to*: *Tam's wife gave a scolding to him.* Without the *to,* the indirect object comes before the direct object; with the *to* it follows the direct object.

A similar complement is sometimes called an *objective complement,* since it provides another name for the object or otherwise completes the statement as it affects the object. It comes after the direct object.

> Tam's wife called *him* (direct object) a *blithering blellum* (objective complement).
> The devil wanted to make Tam's *wife* (direct object) a *widow* (objective complement).

17-5 Parts of the basic pattern

These are the main parts of the basic sentence; along with two others discussed in the following pages, they constitute the five parts of any sentence: subjects, verbs, complements, connectives, modifiers. No matter how these five parts are used or how elaborately they may be developed, they constitute a basic pattern in which

Something	does			something.
Subject	*Verb*			*Complement*
		Indirect Object	*Direct Object*	*Objective Complement*
Blue	fades.			
Tam	sang		a sonnet.	
The voters	made		Hoover	an ex-president.
Jack	threw	Evelyn	the orchid.	

OR

Something	is (or) is like	something.
Subject	*Verb*	*Subject Complement*
Life	is	real.
The moon	was	a ship.
The coat	felt	good.

200]

This actor-action-goal pattern is the core of our thinking and the means of our speaking and writing. Most of all that we think or say in any coherent and communicable way takes this pattern, and the pattern is so important that any divergence from it, or omission of any part of it, may damage what we are trying to say. For this reason most good sentences in English have the actual subject of discussion named as the subject of the sentence. For this reason, also, most good paragraphs have the subject of discussion as the subject of sentence after sentence.

17-6 The incomplete sentence

Often in conversation, and sometimes in writing, basic sentence parts are not expressed; they are understood from the context. They are incomplete in form, but they can stand independently in their contexts and are punctuated as sentences. Among the most common are exclamations, like *Oh, wonderful!* or *Incredible!* or *Good morning,* and replies to questions, like *No, Yes,* or *Of course.* Also used in both speaking and writing is the command, in which no subject is expressed: *Go wash the dishes* or *Let sleeping dogs lie.* Our feeling for usual word order is so firm, moreover, that other types of incomplete sentences can make complete statements in context. *How old are you?* might be answered by the complete sentence *I am twenty years old,* but the incomplete sentence *Twenty* is more likely. *Years old* can be omitted because we habitually state ages in years (we would specify *two decades*), and *I am* can be omitted because it is so obvious a part of the regular word order that the question implies it. The following from Dickens's *Pickwick Papers* concludes with a properly independent incomplete sentence:

> But bless our editorial heart, what a long chapter we have been betrayed into. We had quite forgotten all such petty restrictions as chapters, we solemnly declare. So here goes, to give the goblin a fair start in a new one. A clear stage, and no favour for the goblins, ladies and gentlemen, if you please.

A paragraph from Wolfe's *Of Time and the River* illustrates a modern writer's use of the incomplete sentence, punctuated like a complete sentence and making a statement.

> The coming on of the great earth, the new lands, the enchanted city, the approach, so smoky, blind and stifled, to the ancient web, the old grimed thrilling barricades of Boston. The streets and build-

[201

ings that slid past that day with such a haunting strange familiarity, the mighty engine steaming to its halt, and the great trainshed dense with smoke and acrid with its smell and full of the slow pantings of a dozen engines, now passive as great cats, the mighty station with the ceaseless throngings of its illimitable life, and all of the murmurous, remote and mighty sounds of time forever held there in the station, together with a tart and nasal voice, a hand'sbreath off that said: "There's hahdly time, but try it if you want."

Such sentences are incomplete as grammatical units because they omit one of the essential elements, subject or verb. They are often successful, as they are above, because basic word order has become standard in English. We anticipate missing elements, and in successful incomplete sentences we automatically supply them. The writer establishes a pattern in his style which helps the reader perceive unexpressed thoughts. The incomplete sentences in the Wolfe paragraph above are subjects; the reader can understand what the writer means to say about these subjects—that they were observed or were part of his experience. Most writers, however, use the incomplete sentence sparingly, except in reports of conversation. It is a special device, to be used for special effects. In the hands of anyone but an expert, it is usually unsuccessful because basic patterns have not been established, and missing ideas cannot be supplied.

Quite different are the incomplete sentences which result from carelessness or ignorance of the English sentence pattern. For instance, the writer who intends to write an independent complete sentence confuses his reader if he begins with a word which signals that the subsequent material is subordinate to something else (see 17c). *We were eating dinner* is a complete and independent sentence, but *When we were eating dinner* is not. Such unsuccessful incomplete sentences, *sentence fragments,* are common and serious errors.

17 *The complete sentence; the fragment*   **Frag**

GUIDE TO REVISION:

Complete an incomplete sentence mistakenly used as complete, or join it to another sentence.

Incomplete sentences are useful in English, especially in spoken English. The student writer may need them for reporting conversation or, occasionally, for other special types of writing. But for most student prose the only safe rule is: *Be sure that every group of words punctuated as a sentence contains at least one independent basic sentence pattern with a subject and verb.* Almost all standard writing is done in sentences, and the fragment is a serious error, resulting from carelessness or from confusion about the very basis of English communication, the sentence pattern. Usually, in fact, the fragment is a symptom of a more fundamental weakness in writing, failure to relate ideas logically (see 22). As in the examples below, most fragments should not be corrected simply by supplying missing elements; they need to be combined with other sentences to show how ideas work together.

17a Fragments with incomplete verb   Frag a

The English verb is often made up of a series of words (see 30-2), centering about one key verb; *was going, was planning to begin, should have been preparing.* These combinations do the work of the verb only when they are complete; omission of a part of them is omission of a crucial part of the sentence. A form customarily used only as part of a verb ceases to function as a verb when it is used by itself; it takes the character of a subject or complement (see 27-3) or modifier (see 32-2).

Original

A communistic government attempts to distribute the products of industry equally. It often restricts individual liberty, however. The system requiring careful control of the means of production.

[*The final group of words contains no verb.* Requiring *could work as part of a combination of verbs,* is requiring *or* had been requiring, *but alone it is not a verb. Here it seems only a modifier of* system. *The final group of words is only a name; it does not say something about the system. The error can be corrected, as the revisions show, by making the fragment a dependent clause* (1); *changing*

Revision

(1) A communistic government attempts to distribute the products of industry equally, but since the system requires careful state control of the means of production, it often restricts individual liberty.

[*Usually this method of revision is best, since it clarifies relationships of ideas.*]

(2) The system requires careful control of the means of production.

(3) It often restricts individual liberty, however, requiring careful state control of the means of production.

Original (*Cont.*)	*Revision* (*Cont.*)
the part of a verb to a verb (*2*); *making the fragment a modifying phrase* (*3*).]	
The actor had to strap his ankle to his thigh. In this manner giving the impression that he had only one leg.	The actor had to strap his ankle to his thigh in order to give the impression that he had only one leg.

17b Fragments lacking subject and verb   Frag b

Original	*Revision*
He failed the course in physics. Either because of laziness or because of stupidity. [*The final group of words fills no basic sentence pattern. The writer probably only mispunctuated, having meant something like* (*1*). *He could revise also by adding a verb* (*2*) *or by making the subordination clearer* (*3*), *which is often preferable.*]	(1) He failed the course in physics, either because of laziness or because of stupidity. (2) He failed the course in physics. Either laziness or stupidity was his trouble. (3) Because of either laziness or stupidity, he failed the course in physics.
With the knowledge that, although the documents have been stolen, they have not yet been seen by a foreign agent. [*The group of words can add information to something else, but it cannot stand alone as a sentence.*]	We know that, although the documents have been stolen, they have not yet been seen by a foreign agent. [*The revision adds a subject and verb to make the fragment a sentence.*]

17c Fragments with subordinating word   Frag c

Original	*Revision*
In the morning Thoreau was released from jail. Although he still refused to pay the tax. [*Although labels the second group of words as dependent, incapable of standing as an independent sentence* (see 18-1). *The fragment can be joined to the independent clause it depends upon* (*1*); *or it can be made independent by removing* although (*2*).]	(1) Although he still refused to pay the tax, Thoreau was released from jail in the morning. (2) In the morning Thoreau was released from jail, but he still refused to pay the tax. [*The second revision alters the meaning, but the meaning of the fragment itself is uncertain—just because it is a fragment.*]

204]

Original (*Cont.*)

We learned about the spring from an old prospector. Who had drawn a rough map of the area.

Revision (*Cont.*)

We learned about the spring from an old prospector who had drawn a rough map of the area.

17d Names used as sentences   **Frag d**

Original

Looking out toward the horizon, she saw only the old cabin in which Mary had been born. A single cottonwood that had escaped the drought. The apparently boundless expanse of sunburned prairie.

[*The last two groups are actually additional objects of* saw; *they name and do not tell anything* about *what they name. They are not complete. They can be placed in the usual word order as complements* (1), *or they can be made sentences by supplying verbs* (2).]

In my home town there are only two important social groups. The Ladies' Aid Society, which attracts most of the women in town to meetings twice a month. The Saturday Poker Club, which meets on any night except Saturday above Barker's garage.

[*The last two expressions name societies but say nothing about them. They lack verbs; they are not complete. They can become parts of the first sentence as modifiers* (1), *or the fragments can become sentences with subjects and verbs* (2).]

Revision

(1) Looking out toward the horizon, she saw only the old cabin in which Mary had been born, a single cottonwood that had escaped the drought, and the apparently boundless expanse of sunburned prairie.

(2) Looking out toward the horizon, she saw only the old cabin in which Mary had been born. A single cottonwood that had escaped the drought stood near it. The apparently boundless expanse of sunburned prairie spread into the distance.

(1) In my home town there are only two important social groups: the Ladies' Aid Society, which attracts most of the women in town to meetings twice a month, and the Saturday Poker Club, which meets on any night except Saturday above Barker's garage.

(2) In my home town there are only two important social groups. The Ladies' Aid Society attracts most of the women in town to meetings twice a month. The Saturday Poker Club meets on any night except Saturday above Barker's garage.

EXERCISE 17

A. Choose at random any passage of English prose 200-300 words long. Select it from one of your texts or any other book easily available. Analyze the structure of the sentences, pointing out the subjects, verbs, and complements in each. Observe the word order and copy

[205

any sentences which deviate from the usual actor-action pattern. Can you see reasons for the deviation?

B. Analyze a theme you have written, underlining subjects, verbs, and complements in each sentence. Mark any sentences which deviate from usual word order; revise these sentences so that they fit the actor-action pattern, and judge whether the new or old version is more effective.

C. Point out subjects, verbs, and complements in the sentences in the following paragraph:

We have another neighbor, whose name is Bates; he keeps cows. This year our gate has been fixed; but my young peach trees near the fence are accessible from the road; and Bates's cows walk along that road morning and evening. The sound of a cow-bell is pleasant in the twilight. Sometimes, after dark, we hear the mysterious curfew tolling along the road, and then with a louder peal it stops before our fence and again tolls itself off in the distance. The result is my peach trees are as bare as bean-poles.

—FREDERICK S. COZZENS, *Living in the Country*

D. The passage below contains a number of fragments used as sentences. Revise the passage, using methods outlined above, to make the fragments complete sentences or combine them with other sentences.

(1) Catherine II, called Catherine the Great, came to the throne of Russia in 1762. (2) Her reign being the most notable of those which followed the long rule of Peter the Great. (3) Although she was actually not a Russian by birth, Catherine remained on the Russian throne for thirty-four years. (4) Since she was a German princess whose marriage to Peter III had been arranged by Frederick the Great. (5) Peter III being half-insane when he took the throne. (6) Catherine, a despot who wished to be regarded as an "enlightened" despot like Frederick II of Prussia, more concerned actually with maintaining prestige than spreading culture through her country. (7) She continued some of the work of Peter the Great, ruling the country firmly, and strengthening the central authority by administrative reorganization. (8) Divisions of the government under appointed governors and vice-governors, all responsible to the tsarina. (9) A church dependent for its property and power on the desires of the central authority. (10) By maintaining a strong foreign policy and striking her rivals when they were weak, she established the international position of the Russian empire. (11) A war against the Ottoman Empire, 1768-1774, was highly successful. (12) Which led to navigation rights for Russian ships and added considerably to Russian territory. (13) Poland, weakened by internal strife, and easily preyed upon by surrounding empires. (14) By 1795 Poland had virtually ceased to exist as an independent state.

(15) Her territory partitioned among Austria, Prussia, and Russia. (16) With Catherine getting the lion's share.

(17) Catherine's internal policies did bring about a number of reforms. (18) The establishment, for example, of schools and academies. (19) Reform, however, being carefully regulated. (20) In order to prevent genuine enlightenment of the masses which might weaken the position of the aristocracy.

E. In the passages below, identify fragments (a) which do not have subjects, (b) those which do not have predicates, and (c) those which have neither subjects nor predicates. Revise the passage so that all fragments necessary to the composition become parts of sentences.

(1) Aunt Agnes, who was one of the gentlest women I have ever known, although that was not the reason she was my favorite aunt. (2) She being quite a nuisance to her husband at times, Uncle Joe, who was kind enough but did not believe in carrying things too far. (3) Just one of those things. (4) Uncle Joe being a very good shot, and there being a turkey shoot that year at the factory where Uncle Joe worked, where, in fact, he was the oldest workman in point of service. (5) Down by the levee, just north of the railroad tracks. (6) Uncle Joe brought home a turkey, a fine big gobbler, and chained up in the back yard to get fat for Thanksgiving. (7) Aunt Agnes, who had the notion that turkeys ate only wild rice, and that got pretty expensive, considering what wild rice costs. (8) She doted on that turkey. (9) Got it to eat out of her hand, and would stand by the half hour looking at it. (10) Called it pet names, Little Turkey-urkey, and the like. (11) And occasionally, as though she were joking—and especially when Uncle Joe had just eaten a big dinner and was feeling good—as though she did not really mean that they should not eat Little Turkey-urkey, but that was what she suggested. (12) Nonsense. (13) Uncle Joe said.

(14) Then it was the day before Thanksgiving, and Uncle Joe brought home a hand axe from the shop in the factory. (15) Aunt Agnes, meeting him at the door, telling him he must not kill the turkey, and she would not cook it if he did, and she would gag on it if she tried to take a bite. (16) Please, she begged, could they not buy a turkey? And buy one they did. (17) Aunt Agnes all this time very grateful to Uncle Joe for being so understanding, and promising that they would keep the turkey just a little while. (18) Before Christmas, trade it for another turkey, and then she would not mind the turkey they traded for being killed.

(19) Then the day after Thanksgiving, and Aunt Agnes feeding Little Turkey-urkey, thinking surely he looked sad, sad enough to die. (20) She was sure he was getting thinner. (21) Thinner every day. (22) Obviously being lonesome, and why would he not be lonesome without any woman turkey? (23) Accordingly, the next day,

which was of course Saturday. (24) Uncle Joe had to drive out to a turkey farm and buy a turkey hen. (25) Christmas came and passed. (26) Then New Year's. (27) And Turkey-urkey and his hen sitting peaceful in Aunt Agnes' back yard, getting fatter and fatter. (28) Eating wild rice at two dollars a pound. (29) In those days wild rice being only two dollars a pound. (30) Never did eat those turkeys and both drowned in a flood the next spring.

18. COMBINING CLAUSES; RUN-ON

[For Guide to Revision, see page 212]

Clauses are actor-action-goal patterns which function as major parts of complicated sentences.

"I see the kitty" is a sentence, and within its uses nothing is wrong with it, but few writers who have progressed beyond kindergarten are likely to have much use for it. Modern life is sophisticated and complicated, and communication must be, also. Even relatively simple situations usually require a somewhat varied use of the basic sentence pattern.

18-1 Clauses

Consider the following:

> The sun had set. A cool breeze was blowing across the lake. The tiny cabin was still too warm to be comfortable.

Here are three sentences; each can be considered a complete idea. One concerns the sun, one the breeze, and one the cabin. But more revealingly, there is only one idea here, that in spite of certain cooling agents the cabin was still too hot. Obviously, the three sentences had better become one, somewhat as follows:

> Although the sun had set and a cool breeze was blowing across the lake, the tiny cabin was still too warm to be comfortable.

The actor-action-goal patterns of the three short sentences are preserved here, but the patterns work together to make a single sentence with a larger purpose than any of the sentences had separately. These groups of words which complete the sentence pattern but which are themselves parts of a sentence are called *clauses*. A clause is any section of a sentence which contains a subject and verb.

[209

18-2 Varieties of clauses

English sentences have complex structures, and, accordingly, clauses appear in a bewildering variety, even though they have the common basic structure, actor-action-goal. They are commonly divided into two main groups, called *independent clauses* and *dependent clauses*. Consider the following:

> Marriage and hanging go by destiny. Matches are made in heaven.
> Marriage and hanging go by destiny; matches are made in heaven.
> Marriage and hanging go by destiny, but matches are made in heaven.

In the first version, the two ideas stand as independent sentences, although they are obviously to be taken together. In the second version the ideas are still independent—neither relies on the other—but their inter-relation is emphasized by their being joined into one sentence with a semicolon between them. What were formerly sentences have become independent clauses. Robert Burton understandably preferred the idea in this form. The third version also contains two independent clauses, with the contrast between them emphasized by the signal word *but*.

Now consider the following witticism by Fred Allen:

> He is so narrow-minded that, if he fell on a pin, it would blind him in both eyes.

Obviously, Mr. Allen could not have obtained the effect he wanted without constructions something like these. These groups of words follow the actor-action-goal pattern, but at least some of them could not serve as independent sentences. The word *if* at the beginning of the clause "if he fell on a pin" warns us that these words have their meaning only when taken with some other clause. Such groups of words are called *dependent* or *subordinate clauses* because they depend on something else in the sentence.

18-3 Distinguishing clauses

The distinction between independent and dependent clauses is not exact, for clauses are probably too varied to fit into sharp divisions, but the distinction has enough validity to be useful. Consider the following sentences:

> I drink to Joe Doakes, for he is a jolly good fellow.
> I drink to Joe Doakes, because he is a jolly good fellow.
> He is a jolly good fellow, which nobody can deny.
> He is a jolly good fellow; that, nobody can deny.

Each of these sentences is composed of two clauses, and in each the first clause is clearly independent. The situation is not so clear in the second clause, which would be conventionally called independent in the first and last sentences, dependent in the second and third. Yet "for he is a jolly good fellow" would seem to be roughly equivalent to "because he is a jolly good fellow"; each provides the reason for the first clause. Similarly, consider the remark by Mr. Allen above. "If he fell on a pin" is obviously dependent. "That it would blind him in both eyes" also presumes something else in the sentence. Conventionally, "He is narrow-minded," with *so* acting as part of the introduction to the following clause, is independent. It could stand as it is, but if so it has a meaning which is not the meaning of the complete sentence. The more one examines this sentence the more one feels that the three clauses in it are rather like a tripod, each pole unable to stand in this position without the other two. Even a clause introduced by *but,* though it can confidently be called independent, presumes that something else has gone before, and does not have its full meaning without what has gone before.

Perhaps one can say no more than this with confidence. Some clauses are clearly independent (*I say it's spinach, and I say to heck with it*). Some are clearly dependent (*My grandfather,* who always took candy away from babies, *was the meanest man in town*). Most clauses are not quite one or the other, although they are usually dominantly dependent or independent, and if we do not insist on rigidity of terms, the distinction is often revealing. The following observations help. If an independent clause appears first in a sentence, it commonly is preceded by no signal word (*He is a jolly good fellow, which nobody can deny*). If it appears after another clause, it may be indicated by no signal word, but by a mark of punctuation, usually a semicolon if the preceding clause is independent (*Marriage and hanging go by destiny; matches are made in heaven*). Independent clauses may be joined by the signal words *and, but, for, or, nor* or conjunctive adverbs (see 33-5) (*Marriages and hanging go by destiny, but matches are made in heaven*).

Dependent or subordinate clauses are usually identified by one of a rather large number of signal words, which include *who, that, which, where, when, how, why, although, if, since, because, after,* and the like (see 33-4). In some sentence patterns, dependent clauses require no signal word. Robert Ingersoll wrote, "Give to every human being every right that you claim yourself," but the sentence would also have been clear if he had left out *that*.

18 Combining clauses; run-on   **Run-on**

GUIDE TO REVISION:

> *Combine major sentence elements to reveal their relationships, usually by joining independent clauses with appropriate punctuation and signal words, or by making independent clauses dependent.*

When clauses, basic sentence patterns, are combined, the relationships between them must be clarified. Sentences in which independent clauses are combined without sufficient punctuation or appropriate function words to distinguish them are called "run-on" or "fused." Current usage shows considerable variation in what constitutes adequate punctuation between independent clauses, but the student writer can make sure he is writing clearly if he separates independent clauses by

(1) a semicolon:

> We always like those who admire us; we do not always like those whom we admire.
> Man is certainly stark mad; he cannot make a worm, and yet he will be making gods by dozens.

(2) a comma, when the second clause is introduced by *and, or, nor, but, for:*

> Statesmen are not only liable to give an account of what they say or do in public, *but* there is a busy inquiry made into their very meals, beds, marriages, and every other sportive or serious action.

Notice, however, that *and, or, nor, but, for* do not have commas before them when they join two words or phrases or dependent clauses. Compare:

> The blue canoe slipped quietly away from the others, *and* I saw that it was making for the sandy beach where we were hiding.
> The blue canoe slipped quietly away from the others *and* made for the sandy beach where we were hiding.

The first sentence requires the comma because *and* introduces a new clause.

Short, closely related clauses or short clauses in a series may be joined with only commas between them.

> The camera rolls back, the boom moves out, the water ripples gently, and the only one now to make a move outside the lighted circle is the man with the little fog can and the fan.

Between short clauses, also, the comma may be omitted before *and*.

> The winds came and the rain beat on the house.

The comma can seldom be omitted before *or* or *but*.

> The winds blew, but the house stood.

The run-on sentence, however, is not merely an error in punctuation; it is a symptom of faulty thinking. Sometimes it indicates that the writer is trying to combine ideas which should form separate sentences.

> The barn stood on a little hill behind the house, the old cow was patiently waiting just inside the door.

As the sentence stands, there is no apparent relationship which warrants combining the two main parts. There should be a period after *house* and a capital *T* to start the new sentence. On the other hand, a preceding sentence may point to a relationship between the two clauses and make joining them logical. If the sentence before the one above were

> Jim drove the wagon out the Turkey Creek road looking for his uncle's huge barn and the one old cow that remained in his herd.

then the relationship between the clauses of the sentence would be clear. With a semicolon to replace the inadequate comma, the clauses can be joined.

> Jim drove the wagon out the Turkey Creek road looking for his uncle's huge barn and the one old cow that remained in his herd. The barn stood on a little hill behind the house; the old cow was patiently waiting just inside the door.

Usually the run-on sentence indicates that the writer is not showing the relationship between his ideas clearly enough, and his revision should show which ideas depend on others.

> The old cow was patiently waiting just inside the door of the barn, which stood on a little hill behind the house.

[213

18a *Sentences joined without function words*   Run-on a

Original

The children tore the stuffed stockings from the mantel then they crept quickly back to bed.

[*The two statements are related closely enough to be joined in a single sentence, but they are not so closely related that they can be fused without some sign to mark the point of separation. The clauses can be made separate sentences, or separated with a semicolon (1); one clause can be subordinated (2); or one subject can be removed and the verb in the clause made part of a compound verb (3).*]

The hawk circled gracefully for a moment it seemed unaware of the scurrying chicks below.

Revision

(1) The children tore the stuffed stockings from the mantel; then they crept quickly back to bed.

(2) After the children had torn the stuffed stockings from the mantel, they crept quickly back to bed.

(3) The children tore the stuffed stockings from the mantel and then crept quickly back to bed.

The hawk circled gracefully; for a moment it seemed unaware of the scurrying chicks below.

18b *Sentences joined by* and, or, nor, but, for   Run-on b

Original

Jack had been brought up on golf and tennis held no interest for him.

[*Until he reaches* held, *the reader is not aware that a new clause begins with* tennis; *he assumes as he reads that Jack was brought up on both games.*]

Men have sworn at one another from earliest times, according to a Chinese classic on profanity, and to abstain from this natural exercise of the tongue is unhealthful but since elaborate swearing requires high intellectual ability, the ordinary swearer is cautioned to consider moderation.

[*Complicated clauses, containing commas within them, are joined here without punctuation.*]

Revision

(1) Jack had been brought up on golf, and tennis held no interest for him.

[*Supply the comma.*]

(2) Since Jack had been brought up on golf, tennis held no interest for him.

[*Make one clause dependent.*]

Men have sworn at one another from earliest times, according to a Chinese classic on profanity, and to abstain from this natural exercise of the tongue is unhealthful; but since elaborate swearing requires high intellectual ability, the ordinary swearer is cautioned to consider moderation.

[*A semicolon is needed to point out the major division of the sentence.*]

18c Sentences joined with a comma and no co-ordinating conjunction; the comma fault or comma splice

Original

The two boys cleared away the brush, then they pitched their tent and spread out their blankets.

[*The comma, since it ordinarily sets apart dependent elements, does not indicate a large enough break to signal the beginning of a new statement. The sentence can be revised by supplying a semicolon (1), by making one element dependent (2), or by constructing a single clause (3).*]

Talking is like playing on the harp, there is as much in laying the hand on the strings to stop their vibration as in twanging them to bring out their music.

He had been, he said, a most unconscionable time dying, however he hoped they would excuse it.

[*A conjunctive adverb* (however, moreover, therefore, then, hence) *is a modifier and does not change the requirement that a semicolon separate the clauses.*]

Revision

(1) The two boys cleared away the brush; then they pitched their tent and spread out their blankets.

(2) After they had cleared away the brush, the two boys pitched their tent and spread out their blankets.

(3) The two boys cleared away the brush, pitched their tent, and spread out their blankets.

Talking is like playing on the harp; there is as much in laying the hand on the strings to stop their vibrations as in twanging them to bring out their music.

(1) He had been, he said, a most unconscionable time dying; however he hoped that they would excuse it.

(2) He had been, he said, a most unconscionable time dying; he hoped, however, that they would excuse it.

[*For position of the conjunctive adverb see 23f.*]

EXERCISE 18

A. In the paragraph below, put parentheses around each independent clause and brackets around each dependent clause. Then underline subjects, verbs, and complements in all the clauses.

The village stands far inland, and the streams that trot through the soft green valleys all about have as little knowledge of the sea as the three-years' child of the storms and passions of manhood. The surrounding country is smooth and green, full of undulations; and pleasant country roads strike through it in every direction, bound for distant towns and villages, yet in no hurry to reach them. On these roads the lark in summer is continually heard; nests are plentiful in the hedges and dry ditches; and on the grassy banks, and at the feet of the bowed dikes, the blue-eyed speedwell smiles its benison on the passing wayfarer. On these roads you may walk for a year and encounter nothing more remarkable than the country cart, troops of tawny children from the woods, laden with primroses, and at long intervals—for people in this district live to a ripe age—a black funeral creeping in from some remote hamlet; and to this last the people reverently doff their hats and stand aside. Death does not walk about here often, but when it does, he receives as much respect as the squire himself.

—ALEXANDER SMITH, *Dreamthorp*

B. Combine each of the following pairs of sentences into a single sentence supplying appropriate connectives and punctuation when necessary:

1. Quadrille, she often told me, was her first love. Whist engaged her maturer esteem.

2. I looked to the weather side. The summer had departed.

3. I am ready to give up the dialogues in Heaven, where, as Pope justly observes, "God the Father turns a school-divine." Nor do I consider the battle of the angels as the climax of sublimity, or the most successful effort of Milton's pen.

4. Useful knowledge then, I grant, has done its work. Liberal knowledge as certainly has not done its work.

5. His health beginning to fail at the expiration of that time, the surgeon recommended that he should work occasionally in the garden. And as he liked the notion very much, he went about his new occupation with great cheerfulness.

6. No open window was within view. No window at all was within view, sufficiently near the ground to have enabled their old legs to descend from it.

7. To fancy all men found out and punished is bad enough. Imagine all women found out in the distinguished social circle in which you and I have the honor to move.

8. To be sweet, a thing must have a taster. It is sweet only while it is being tasted.

9. For what is wanted is the reality and not the mere name of a liberal education. This college must steadily set before itself the ambition to be able to give that education sooner or later.

10. Literature is not upon the college program. I hope some day to see it there.

C. Revise the following run-on sentences by reducing one of the independent clauses to a dependent expression:

(1) In the sixteenth century Nicholas Copernicus announced certain theories about the universe and those theories were to have

profound effect on the later course of human affairs. (2) His theories concerned the relation of the earth and the sun, they denied the Ptolemaic theory of a geocentric universe. (3) His theories were inspired by ancient Greek views of a moving earth and they proposed the view that the earth revolves around the sun. (4) Before the views of Copernicus could be accepted, however, there had to be rejection of Ptolemy's theories and Ptolemy's theories had been accepted for nearly fourteen centuries. (5) Furthermore, the old system had the support of the Roman Catholic church, it also was supported by the Protestants. (6) The old system placed the earth in the center of the universe, therefore it bolstered man's faith in his own significance. (7) Planets, sun, moon, and stars moved about the earth and as a result man could believe that the universe was regulated for his benefit. (8) Man was situated in the center of the universe and he could easily believe that the universe was created to fill his needs. (9) He was moved by the Copernican theories to a subordinate planet and the universe seemed less obviously a creation for the convenience of humanity. (10) The heliocentric system is by now a commonplace of everyday knowledge but it is easy to see why there was opposition to it in the sixteenth century.

D. The passage below includes run-on sentences, fragments, and a few grammatically correct sentences. Revise fragments or run-on sentences according to the most appropriate of the methods described above.

(1) In Shakespeare's day there was no system of copyright as it exists today and authors did not receive royalties from their books. (2) Normally a work being sold outright to a publisher for a lump sum. (3) Early regulation of the book trade was not designed to protect the rights of authors, it was rather intended to prevent the publication of "seditious books," and the spreading of "great and detestable heresies." (4) No real recognition of author's rights was established until after the Copyright Act of 1709 and the numerous legal contests which clarified it during the 18th century.

(5) There was, however, regulation of the book trade in Elizabethan England and it was established in 1557 by the creation of the Company of Stationers. (6) The company, or guild, was granted power to restrict printing to its qualified members and was authorized to seize or destroy prohibited books or to imprison anyone printing contrary to its orders. (7) The Company, through its officers, enforced rules by levying fines, in extreme cases it destroyed a press entirely. (8) Also requiring that books should be registered with the Stationers' Company before publication. (9) Such registration established the copies as the property of certain members and book pirates who ignored these priorities were subject to the punishment of Company officers. (10) The written registers of the Stationers' Company

survive and they are among the most valuable of the sources of information about early printing and publishing.

(11) These regulations were designed to protect the publisher and to make censorship easy, therefore they were of little benefit to authors. (12) Their plays enjoyed considerable popularity in printed as well as dramatic form but writers like Shakespeare or Marlowe probably realized only small initial payments from publication. (13) Censorship continued to be the main purpose of such regulation, in fact, Milton protested against the attitude in *Areopagitica.* (14) He objected to the licensing of all books but spoke of the "just retaining of each man his several copy, which God forbid should be gainsaid." (15) The desire for protection of author's rights was growing but the protection was not to come for many years.

E. The run-on sentences below could be corrected by supplying adequate punctuation, but most of them would be improved by revision. Correct each by changing punctuation; then revise each by making one of the independent clauses dependent and compare the results.

1. It was cold and rainy outside, however, the house was warm and dry.

2. I was in the hospital and during the time I was there I fell in love with the head nurse.

3. I finished washing all the dinner dishes and then Mary said she thought we might mop and wax the kitchen floor.

4. I never learned the multiplication tables and for this reason I have always been slow at mathematics.

5. The clerk opened the bank door and at the time he did so the three robbers pushed their way into the bank.

6. The team lost the final game of the tournament, for this reason June cried herself to sleep that night.

7. The music stopped, all the girls ran for the chairs around the dance floor.

8. My sister was beautiful and talented but she did not win a trip to Atlantic City.

19. EMPHASIS; VARIATIONS OF THE BASIC SENTENCE PATTERN

[For Guide to Revision, see page 226]

Prefer the standard subject-verb-complement word order except for special meaning or emphasis.

Most pages of English prose contain few variations from the actor-action patterns described above. Deviations from usual word order produce special meaning, or special emphasis, or special weakness. Commenting on the style of *Time, The New Yorker* quips, "Backward ran the sentences until reeled the mind."

Some variations are like counterpoint or variations on a theme in music, which depend for their effect on recollections of the original or basic pattern. Other deviations are emphatic; a word shifted from its usual position gains emphasis, as a man in a bathing suit would gain attention at a formal dinner party. Still other deviations are mistakes; proverbially carts do not work well before horses, and in English grammar, some words do not work well in front of some others.

19-1 Variations for emphasis

Logically, from what we have seen of word order, the usual subject position, before the verb, is the place of greatest prominence or emphasis. Most of the common variations listed below give prominence to elements other than the subject by putting them in the subject position. They vary from the usual by following definite patterns for specific purposes. Used for these purposes, appropriate variations are indispensable, but some variations are easily misused—even frequently misused—and writers should handle them with caution. They are a little like high-powered rifles, which are good to hunt deer with, but if carelessly used, dangerous for the hunter and his neighbors.

19-2 Inversion to emphasize complement or modifier

A complement or modifier can gain emphasis through variations in word order, even by the overused device of reversing the complement and the subject. Orators often use the construction, and often would speak better if they did not.

> *Dead* are the brave *men* who began this task.
> *A weary and dejected group* were the *travelers* who stumbled into the room.

An object may acquire emphasis ahead of the subject.

> The *soup* we placed on the table at once.
> The *old man* the children decided to spare.

Reversing subject and verb can emphasize a modifier.

> *In Shakespeare* were all the qualities of literary greatness.
> *Never before* were human beings so happy.

19-3 The postponed subject

The words *it* and *there* can introduce a sentence so that the subject is postponed. These introductory words are signals, reminders to the reader that a subject is coming in an unusual position. Usually the construction combines with some form of the verb *is* to assert only the existence of the subject; and since the subject with its modifiers is the core of the sentence, unusual word order provides appropriate emphasis.

Introductory Word	*Verb*	*Subject*	*Modifier*
There	are	two reasons	for doubting his word.
There	will be	time	for a hundred questions.

Notice that in these examples we would never use usual word order and say *Two reasons for doubting his word are* or *Time for a hundred questions will be* (although we might say *Two reasons for doubting his word exist*). Often, however, usual word order would be possible but would change emphasis.

> There are two men in the boat. (Compare *Two men are in the boat.*)
> It was heavy artillery which finally stopped us. (Compare *The heavy artillery finally stopped us.*)
> It is John who should be blamed. (Compare *John should be blamed.*)

220]

Often normal word order would put a long or heavily modified subject at the beginning of the sentence and would weaken the complement. The complement gains emphasis when a long subject is postponed.

Subject	Verb	Complement	Subject with Modifiers
It	is	impossible	to believe that nobody would contribute to the campaign.

Frequently, however, constructions with postponed subjects result from no careful planning. They are blundered into, and the writer would do well to recast his sentence:

Obviously, some contributors will support the campaign.

19-4 The substitute subject with linking verb

In the typical English sentence, the grammatical subject names what the sentence is about, usually the actor. Sometimes, however, to provide a transition from preceding sentences or to give a word special emphasis in the subject position, the writer prefers a framework with the verb *to be,* the linking verb (see 29-2). For example, in the usual pattern one might write

John studied only his algebra course that year.

The sentence is about John; John is the actor. In some contexts, however, *algebra* might require special emphasis:

Algebra was the only course John studied that year.

The goal of the basic pattern, *algebra,* becomes the grammatical subject with the verb *was,* and the actor has a secondary position in a dependent clause. A subject displaces the actor so that it gains special prominence. Compare:

He could remember only the sound of her voice.
The sound of her voice was all he could remember.
He saw no course open to him but bankruptcy.
Bankruptcy seemed the only course open to him.
He chiefly regretted this quarrel with his son.
This quarrel with his son was his chief regret.

Although they are often stylistically useful, such constructions with substitute subjects are less direct than actor-action-goal patterns and often lead to wordiness and circumlocution.

19-5 The passive

Usually the agent or actor needs to be mentioned first in a sentence, so that we know what we are talking about. But sometimes the agent or actor is less important than the action or the result; sometimes the actor is unknown, or should not be mentioned. By changing the form of the verb (see 30-3 to 30-5) and varying word order, we can shift emphasis away from the actor. The actor is either omitted or relegated to a subordinate position in the sentence. The verb is made passive. The goal or receiver of the action—which would be a complement in a sentence following standard order—becomes the grammatical subject.

Compare the following:

> In June somebody completed the new road.
> The new road was completed in June.

The first sentence follows the actor-action pattern, but forces the indefinite *somebody* into the subject position. The second sentence omits mention of the actor and uses the complement of the first as its subject. The device may be considered a variation of word order, which provides a subject-verb-complement pattern to take care of instances in which the actor or agent is not appropriate as the subject.

Passive constructions are frequently misused, but they have good uses. Sometimes the actor is unimportant. Suppose, for example, we wish to mention the publication of a book in 1623, but we have no reason to name the publisher. We want the publishing to be the main action, but if we use the usual actor-action pattern, we are faced with something like this:

> A person or persons whom we do not wish to mention just now published the book in 1623.

In this sentence, the receiver of the action, *book,* is more important than the missing actor. We therefore solve the problem by putting *book* into the subject position and using a passive form of the verb.

> The book was published in 1623.

For a statement as simple as this, however, a passive sentence is usually inappropriate; the writer might better reduce the idea embodied in this sentence to a modifier and go on to another idea.

222]

The book, *published in 1623,* has provided the basis for all subsequent editions of Shakespeare's works.

Sometimes circumstances make the passive construction convenient, or even imperative. The actor may be known, but there may be reasons for not mentioning him. A newspaper reporter might be telling the truth if he were to write:

> John A. Scrogum murdered Joseph Meek at 7:45 this morning in the Hot Spot Lunch.

This statement is libelous; the reporter, and the newspaper which publishes the sentence, can be sued for accusing a man of murder who has not been legally convicted. Accordingly, the reporter would probably write something like the following:

> Joseph Meek was shot and killed at 7:45 this morning in the Hot Spot Lunch.

The actor has now been removed, and the statement is legally publishable.

Or the actor or agent may not be known. A historian writes:

> The world of St. Paul was steeped in guilt and wretchedness.

He does not know who steeped it; the agent, even if it could be determined, would be much too complicated for expression in a single sentence. Or consider:

> Nations which have lost their moral self-respect are easily conquered.

This sentence is a generalization which does not depend at all on who conquers these nations; no one actor could be specified.

Occasionally, a passive construction is desirable for stylistic reasons; for instance, a writer may wish to avoid inserting complicated material between the subject and verb.

> The hearing was opened by the chairman of the committee, who was known for his ruthlessness in smirching the reputation of innocent witnesses and for his cleverness in beclouding the issue by his own witticisms and innuendoes.

> The chairman of the committee, who was known for his ruthlessness in smirching the reputations of innocent witnesses and for his cleverness in beclouding the issue by his own witticisms and innuendoes, opened the hearing.

The first version, although it employs the passive, has the advantage of keeping subject and verb together.

[223

The passive, then, has very definite uses. It is properly used when

(1) The subject is not known;

(2) The subject is known, but for some good reason cannot, or had better not, be mentioned;

(3) The receiver of the action is so much more important than the actor that emphasis properly belongs on the receiver.

(4) One of the elements of the actor-action pattern must be moved from its normal position for stylistic reasons.

Except in these special situations, the passive usually weakens English prose. Consider the following passage, in which most of the verbs are passive:

> Zoroaster's spirit was rapidly caught by the Persians. A voice which was recognized by them as speaking truth was responded to eagerly by a people uncorrupted by luxury. They have been called the Puritans of the Old World. Never, it is said, was idolatry hated by any people as it was by them, and for the simple reason that lies were hated by them.

Compare this passage with the following written by James Anthony Froude.

> The Persians caught rapidly Zoroaster's spirit. Uncorrupted by luxury, they responded eagerly to a voice which they recognized as speaking truth to them. They have been called the Puritans of the Old World. Never any people, it is said, hated idolatry as they hated it, and for the simple reason that they hated lies.

Froude's version keeps the actor-action pattern everywhere but in the third sentence and the parenthetical *it is said* of the fourth—in which the actual subjects of the action are unknown. Obviously, his paragraph is more direct, more economical, and more effective.

19-6 Contexts and variations in word order

Since the patterns described above are variations, their use implies an unusual situation, and they should be used with caution. Situations warranting variations in word order sometimes develop out of the pattern of the paragraph or the whole composition (see 15-5, 15-6). The context in which a sentence appears—the other sentences before and after it—often dictates word order. Standing alone, for example, the following sentence seems unnecessarily backward:

> This heifer they sold in despair.

When the sentence is put into its context, however, the reasons for the irregular order are clear.

> One heifer refused to stay in the farm close. This heifer they sold in despair.

Or consider the following, which at first seems an unjustifiable inversion:

> The ashes Daniel spread over the floor.

Compare the sentence in its context:

> The servant brought a gleaming torch and a sack of ashes. He set the torch in a bracket on the wall. The ashes Daniel spread over the floor.

One sentence, or group of sentences, suggests by its meaning and its emphasis the principal idea of the subsequent sentence.

19-7 Repetition of word-order patterns

Consider the uses of variation to stress parallel ideas:

> By foreign hands thy dying eyes were clos'd,
> By foreign hands thy decent limbs compos'd,
> By foreign hands thy humble grave adorn'd,
> By strangers honoured, and by strangers mourn'd!

Usual order is changed in each clause in a curious way so that each involves a kind of double inversion. The usual pattern would be:

> *Subject*   *Verb*   *Complement*
> Foreign hands   closed   thy dying eyes.

The poet, Alexander Pope, has followed two procedures for varying word order. He has reversed subject and object, making the verb passive:

> Thy dying eyes were closed by foreign hands.

Then he has gone a step further and moved the modifier, which would have been the subject of the action in a conventional sentence, into the position of emphasis at the beginning. The result is stress on the initiator of the action, *foreign hands*—even more stress than normal word order would provide.

Repetitions of this pattern throughout the clauses multiply the stress. The first three clauses build on the importance of *by foreign hands* so that the meaning of *by strangers* is sharp and and clear. The result is that the reader remembers most vividly, even in the presence of death itself, the circumstance that only strangers were present at the death.

Less spectacularly, but equally importantly, repetitions in word order affect meaning and emphasis in ordinary prose. Repetition of the standard actor-action pattern to introduce each of the following sentences reinforces the parallel in the ideas presented:

> *Dr. Woods looked* his *creed* more decidedly, perhaps, than any of the professors. *He* had the firm *fibre* of a theological athlete, and *lived* to be old without ever mellowing, I think, into a kind of half-heterodoxy, as old ministers of stern creed are said to do now and then,—just as old doctors grow to be sparing of the more exasperating drugs in their later days. *He had manipulated* the *mysteries* of the Infinite so long and so exhaustively that he would have seemed more at home among the mediaeval schoolmen than amidst the working clergy of our own time.
>
> —OLIVER WENDEL HOLMES, *The Autocrat of the Breakfast Table*

This paragraph is more typical of writing in English than is the passage of poetry above. In it the pattern of the ideas forces the sentences into the actor-action order. Continuity of thought in a paragraph usually demands this normal order. The writer should be sure, therefore, that the context of his sentences justifies a variation before he deviates from standard order.

19 *Emphasis; variations of the basic sentence pattern*   **Em**

GUIDE TO REVISION:

> *Revise word order or omit words in order to clarify meaning and make emphasis appropriate to the sentence in its context.*

19a *Inverted sentences*   **Em a**

Shifting subject, verb, or complement from its usual position can achieve special effects, but unless these effects are justified, normal word order should remain. Inverted sentences not required by the context or warranted by special intentions of the writer make writing confusing, falsely rhetorical, or affected.

Original

We were never happy about the climate in New York. Cold were the winters; hot were the summers.
[*This inversion, unless the writer is attempting some kind of half-humorous exaggeration, sounds absurd.*]

We camped beside the stream that night. Many were the hardships we were to face before the dawn.
[*The inversion in the second sentence creates a melodramatic effect, weakens continuity, and overemphasizes the modifier* many.]

I was only a child, inexperienced and trusting. Little did I know what was in store for me.
[*The second sentence is trite, but the staleness is obvious because the inversion is unwarranted. The unusual word order makes the sentence overdramatic.*]

Revision

We were never happy about the climate in New York. The winters were cold, the summers hot.
[*Usual order is more direct, and there is no artificially induced special emphasis.*]

We camped beside the stream that night. We were to face many hardships before morning.
[*The revision avoids the trite echoes of fifth-rate novels and avoids the false emphasis of unjustified inversion.*]

I was only an inexperienced and trusting child, unaware of what was in store for me.
[*Restoration of usual word order removes most of the affectation from the sentences, although the reader is still suspicious of the significance attached to the facts.*]

19b Postponed subjects   Em b

We need the reverse gears of an automobile in order to back into a parking place; but we do not, after we have discovered how to shift into reverse, go backward down the highway just because the reverse gears are available. We need the construction with *it* and *there* in English to delay expression of the subject in certain special situations, but we should not use the device just because it exists. Overuse of the postponed subject is one of the sins of student writing. The construction is by its nature roundabout; often it is wordy, and it obscures the parts of the sentence which are potentially strongest, the subject and the main verb. Many a page of weak writing is weak because sentence after sentence, which should begin with the name of some concrete thing, begins with *it* or *there*. Consider the following:

It is a fact that it is hard to get people to see that there is a lot of sport in skiing.

[227

Several weaknesses mar this sentence, but the needlessly postponed subjects cause most of them. The writer might better have said

> Skiing can be a good sport, though few people know it.

A writer who finds himself beginning many sentences with *it* or *there* can appropriately ask himself: have I any good reason for not beginning this sentence with its logical subject?

Original

It was after a long argument that we decided to push on. It was soon agreed among us, however, that we had made a mistake. Within an hour there were two sharp attacks which scattered our rear guard. It was obvious that we should have stayed at the fort.
[*Postponed subjects become troublesome when successive sentences are needlessly inverted. One inverted sentence may add variety; a dozen make writing indirect and wordy.*]

It is true that the parkway is crowded by thousands of commuters, but it is not impossible for it to be patrolled by an adequate police force.
[*The sentence is wordy and roundabout.*]

His escape set England again on fire. There were Llewelyn wasting the border, the Cinque Ports holding the sea, the garrison of Kenilworth pushing their raids as far as Oxford.
[*Postponement of the subject weakens the second sentence and blocks the continuity of ideas from one sentence to the next.*]

There were two solemn confirmations of the Charter which failed to bring about any compliance with its provisions.

Revision

After a long argument we decided to push on. Soon, however, we agreed that we had made a mistake. Within an hour two sharp attacks scattered our rear guard. Obviously, we should have stayed at the fort.
[*Normal order strengthens and shortens the passage. For variety some writers might prefer to leave the last sentence:* It was obvious that we should have stayed at the fort.]

Although the parkway is crowded with thousands of commuters, an adequate police force could patrol it.
[*Normal word order in the main clause makes the first clause dependent and brings the important actor-action elements of the sentence into focus.*]

His escape set England again on fire. Llewelyn wasted the border; the Cinque Ports held the sea; the garrison of Kenilworth pushed their raids as far as Oxford.
[*With normal order restored, the reader can see that the second sentence develops the general idea of the first; parallel patterns clarify further relationships.*]

Two solemn confirmations of the Charter failed to bring about any compliance with its provisions.

19c Substitute subjects with linking verb   Em c

Unless there are stylistic reasons for variation, sentences are strongest in the actor-action-goal pattern. Unjustified use of a framework with a linking verb and with a subject other than the name of the actor often leads to awkward, roundabout writing.

Original	*Revision*
The way in which Mary wore her clothes was with an air of sophistication.	Mary wore her clothes with an air of sophistication.
[*The actor in the sentence is Mary, but* way *is used as the subject.*]	[*The framework is useless; the actor-action-goal sentence is clearer, more direct.*]
Every morning in his eight-o'clock English class is the time Harry studies his French.	Harry studies his French every morning in his eight-o'clock English class.
The reason Alice wants a new dress is because there is a dance Friday that is to be her first formal.	Alice wants a new dress for her first formal dance Friday.

19d Passive sentences   Em d; Pass

Usually a statement tells who or what acts (the subject) and what it does (the verb). Inversion through use of the passive verb throws stress on the receiver of the action and draws attention away from the actor-action pattern. It makes the receiver of the action the subject and the center of attention. This type of inversion, therefore, is justified only in the special circumstances described above (see 19-5). Used indiscriminately it weakens writing much as does the unnecessarily postponed subject (see 19b), diverting attention from the main ideas of the sentence. A sentence like the following is painfully awkward.

> The lake where the meetings of our gang are held is reached by an old road that was found by me when I was hidden out there by the kidnappers.

Less cluttered sentences may be equally harmful to direct communication, especially when they occur frequently and do not provide special emphasis warranted by the context. Needless passive constructions weaken a writing style.

A student writer, therefore, can find few better ways to improve his style than to practice using active instead of passive verbs, to hesitate every time he finds himself using a passive form, to ask himself whether the passive form is justified, and if not, to try recasting the sentence in actor-action order.

Original

That there were many difficulties whereby women were unable to use the new union lounge was the attitude which was stated by the first speaker. It was her contention that women were resented in the lounge by the men students and that this resentment was clearly made known by the men in their actions. A different point of view was introduced by the second speaker, by whom it was stated that the reason for the inability of the women to make full use of the lounge was caused by the attitude of the women themselves. The views which were expressed by this speaker were the objects of sharp criticism from the other members of the panel.

Revision

The first speaker insisted that women were unable to use the new union lounge because men students resented having women there and made their resentment clearly known. The second speaker introduced a new point of view, that women were unable to make full use of the lounge because of their own attitude. The other members of the panel sharply criticized the views of this speaker.

[*The original has many weaknesses, but basic to most of its difficulties is overuse of unwarranted passive sentences. The revision still needs development, but it makes the passage clearer and more economical, mainly by recasting sentences in the actor-action pattern.*]

The trouble was caused by John's insistence that he begin.

[*Nothing here warrants departing from normal order. The actor-action elements are present and important; they should appear in normal order.*]

(1) John's insistence that he begin caused the trouble.

(2) John caused the trouble by insisting that he begin.

[*More thorough revision, reducing part of the subject to a modifier, clarifies the sentence.*]

Hoping to shut out a flood of foreign ideas and movements, overfastidious literary tastes were encouraged by the schools.

[*Note that the ill-advised passive is partly responsible for a dangling modifier.*]

Hoping to shut out a flood of foreign ideas and movements, the schools encouraged overfastidious literary tastes.

The new type of synthetic rubber was originated in government laboratories.

The new type of synthetic rubber originated in government laboratories.

230]

Original (Cont.)

[*Sometimes, from bad habit, a passive form slips in when the real subject is expressed and the active form of the same verb would work.*]

19e Minor words in emphatic positions   Em e

Original	*Revision*
This nation must return to the ideas which inspired its founding. *Yes,* we must re-examine our goals.	This nation must return to the ideals which inspired its founding. We must re-examine our goals.
[*The frequent insertion of words like* Yes, indeed, well, now, *borrowed from speech, can emphasize insignificant parts of the sentence.*]	[*Even with the* yes *omitted, the sentence is oratorical enough in its tone.*]
Well, first I thought I ought to see what was in the cave. *Now* I was not really afraid to look, but I decided there was no hurry.	(1) First I thought I ought to see what was in the cave. I was not really afraid to look, but I thought there was no hurry.
[*The italicized words would be useful only if the writer was trying to reproduce the effect of some kind of speaking.*]	[*Omission of the introductory words removes the false emphasis, but weakens the connection between the sentences.*]
	(2) I thought I should first see what was in the cave, but, although I was not really afraid to look, I decided there was no hurry.

19f Rhetorical questions   Em f

The rhetorical question is an inversion of regular sentence order for the sake of emphasis, a statement in question form. Sometimes the answer is assumed to be so obvious that the reader will supply it automatically and will be convinced of the entire implied statement. Sometimes the writer supplies the answer. In either instance the device—another favorite in oratory—provides strong emphasis and should be used only when the situation warrants unusual stress.

Original	*Revision*
There are five reasons for joining a sorority in college. *What are those reasons?* The first is . . .	There are five reasons for joining a sorority in college, of which the first is . . .

Original (*Cont.*)	*Revision* (*Cont.*)
[*The question dramatizes a prosaic statement, which should be clear enough without repetition in inverted order.*]	[*Omission of the rhetorical question makes the emphasis more appropriate to the meaning.*]

EXERCISE 19

A. Write a paragraph in which you avoid all use of the passive verb and do not postpone subjects with *it* or *there*.

B. Mark every sentence in one of your themes in which you vary from usual word order. Then revise these sentences to the actor-action pattern and judge whether or not the change improves the theme.

C. The sentences below vary word order by having the receiver of the action at the beginning and by using a passive verb. Revise the sentences so that they follow usual word order with active verbs.

1. A small shop was opened on Fifth Avenue by two of my classmates where clothes could be designed by them to suit both the figure and the purse of the average girl working in an office.

2. A very rigid censorship was imposed by the commanding officer on war news.

3. For the first time officeholders could be criticized by the people.

4. By using a spectroscope it is possible for many metals to be identified by a laboratory technician.

5. The man in the street is granted by the Constitution the right to say what he pleases without fear of prosecution.

6. A moral is conveyed to the reader by many kinds of stories.

7. Important information about military matters should not be revealed by the newspapers.

8. After working for fifteen minutes, the ground was finally cleared and leveled by the men enough for the sleeping bags.

9. Provisional governments were set up by the military forces as soon as an area had been conquered.

10. Citizens of the United States were guaranteed freedom of speech by the first ten amendments to the Constitution.

11. If the petition is signed by enough people, it will be considered by the assembly.

12. Drifting down the river out of control, a series of dangerous rapids was approached by the boat.

13. The enemy was driven into the sea by our reinforcements.

14. Although still eager to write a great epic, many prose pamphlets had to be turned out by Milton.

15. The ball was thrown accurately by the first baseman, but it was

missed by the catcher, and the runner was waved home by the third-base coach.

16. Blue taffeta dresses were worn by all the girls in the class.

17. The introduction of the speaker was made by the past president of the club.

18. Undeterred by the stories in the papers, a trip around the lake after midnight was contemplated by Jane and her roommate.

19. At the end of the passage our progress was arrested by a pile of huge boulders.

20. Tickets were bought by Mr. Sims from a scalper for twice their value.

D. Revise the following sentences by making more extensive use of the actor-action pattern:

1. There were two chaperons in attendance at the dance, but still the uninvited guests soon outnumbered the invited ones.

2. It was because so many students had forgotten to register for the examination that there were new rules passed by the academic council.

3. There was a tall white stallion standing all alone at the edge of the cliff.

4. It is obvious that there should be more courses in fine arts taken by the average student.

5. There were two points of basic disagreement which prevented successful negotiation.

6. It is in his book *The Diary of a Writer* that Dostoevsky describes how a mother hen defended her chickens from a brutal and sadistic boy.

7. If there is the desire to help, there are always lots of ways for a father to be saved money by the student.

8. It was when I was waiting in a registration line and I was talking with a graduate student that the realization came to me of how complicated a university is.

9. That was the time when there was an opportunity for me to buy my first colony of bees.

10. There was quite a lot of commotion because of there being a live mole in my roommate's bed.

E. Revise for emphasis and clarify the faulty sentences in the following student theme; often sentences can appropriately be combined.

(1) When our Constitution was written, the thing foremost in the people's mind was to have freedom of speech. (2) People were tired of listening to the government tell them what to say and what not to say. (3) They had come over here to escape from a society where

[233

there were always government agents, and the people could be perse-
cuted by them. (4) Town meetings were broken up unless the speakers
were told by a government official exactly what to say.

(5) After the Constitution took effect, freedom of speech began to
be used by the people in its true meaning. (6) Opinions could be
voiced by anyone on any subject. (7) No longer did a person have
to be afraid of landing in jail or getting deported from the United
States. (8) Often there were soap-box speakers, and they stood on
boxes in the streets or in the city squares and gave speeches. (9) Sometimes public officials were attacked by these speeches. (10) These
speeches were finished without punishment by the speakers.

(11) It seems that nowadays nothing can be said by a citizen, or
he will be in danger of being thrown in jail by the government. (12)
If a person talks against our government or any high official in it,
he may be labelled a Communist. (13) I wish a different system
could be found by the Government to enforce its laws. (14) Yes,
what people say should not be used as evidence against them. (15) If
it were not, there would be for us more of the kind of freedom of
speech we used to have.

20. PREDICATION; MEANING AND SENTENCE PATTERNS

[For Guide to Revision, see page 237]

As a first principle of clear sentence structure, the writer must preserve and present clearly his basic subject-verb-complement pattern.

The subject-verb-complement pattern in English is so standard that we can understand the grammatical relationships involved in even nonsense like the following:

The grimp wocks the rinch.

We know that a *grimp* acted and that a *rinch* was affected, but we do not know what happened because we do not know what a *grimp* or a *rinch* may be, nor do we know anything about *wocking*.

20-1 Making the sense fit the pattern

Even when ordinary words are used, the sense must fit the pattern in which the words appear. The following sentence is as uncommunicative as the nonsense above:

Any person would have meant the failure.

We know the meanings of the words and can see how they are related grammatically, but the ideas for which the words stand do not make sense when put into this pattern. Now observe the sentence from which the above basic pattern was taken:

Any person ill on the day of that first performance would have meant the failure of the entire summer theater.

Some kind of meaning can be extracted, but the sentence seems obscure and confused because the basic subject-verb-complement pattern is the nonsense sentence quoted above. The reader can guess what the writer meant to say, but, strictly, the writer produced only

[235

nonsense. Specifically, the writer did not express as his subject the threat he wanted to talk about, illness. He probably meant:

> The illness of any member of the cast on the day of that first performance would have caused the failure of the entire summer theater.

As a first essential to clear communication, then, the writer must be sure that the parts of his basic sentence, subject-verb-complement, work logically together, that the meanings of the words make sense in the grammatical positions in which they appear. In other words, the sentence must make a logical predication. The writer must exercise special care when he is using abstract or general terms.

20-2 To be and complements

The problems of predication become especially complex in sentences in which subject and complement are linked by some form of the verb *to be*. The verb *to be* is perhaps the most useful one in the language. It can do any of the following: imply definition or classification (*Music is an art*), supply a name (*This is John*), connect a subject with a modifier (*The apple is ripe*), act as part of another verb (*The picture* is being made *now*), merely assert a kind of present existence (*It is time to go*); and it has a variety of other uses. Used with a complement, however, the verb *to be* almost always implies some kind of identity between subject and complement.

Compare the following sentences:

> Two and two *are* four.
> My sister *is* a trained nurse.
> Alcoholism *is* the root of his trouble.
> Life *is* a dream.
> Beauty *is* truth.

The closeness of the relation between subject and complement varies widely, but in each sentence *to be* suggests some connection.

This flexibility, however, leads to one of the most common abuses of the language in writing, illogical equations with the verb *to be*. The writer carelessly links a subject and complement which do not plausibly work together, do not have enough in common to permit identification with each other.

20 Predication; meaning and sentence patterns   **Pred**

Examine the subject, verb, and complement basic to the sentence and revise so that their meanings work together to make sense.

20a Subjects and predication   **Pred a**

The meaning of the subject must fit logically with the verb and the complement. Often when sentences are not clear, the writer has not chosen the subject he intends to talk about or has buried the real subject in a modifier.

Original

My mother being unable to resist installment buying meant the difference between a comfortable existence and constant fear of poverty.
[Mother *makes no sense as a subject for* meant. *The subject probably intended is buried as a modifier.*]

The cowboy's job seems about to be replaced in many areas by helicopters and jeeps.
[*Not the job but the cowboy is being replaced.*]

The setting of this picturesque little town was filled with a colorful history.
[*The setting was not filled. The writer should pick an appropriate subject and start over.*]

The lack of a proper diet and work as heavy as lumbering demanded a man with a strong body.
[*The second part of the compound subject fits logically with the verb, but the first does not.*]

Revision

My mother's inability to resist installment buying meant the difference between a comfortable existence and constant fear of poverty.
[*Not mother, but mother's weakness was probably intended as the subject.*]

The cowboy seems about to be replaced in many areas by helicopters and jeeps.

This picturesque little town had a colorful history.
[*The writer may have meant this or something else, but the revision at least makes sense.*]

Work as heavy as lumbering, carried on without a proper diet, demanded a man with a strong body.
[*The main subject is selected and the inappropriate idea becomes a modifier.*]

[237

Original (*Cont.*)

Roads covered with gravel or ice double stopping distance.

The parrot can be stroked on the chest, but anywhere else usually costs the admirer a sore finger.
[*The subject of the second clause must be inferred.*]

Revision (*Cont.*)

Gravel or ice on the road doubles stopping distance.

The parrot can be stroked on the chest, but petting anywhere else usually costs the admirer a sore finger.

20b Verbs and predication   Pred b

The verb must not stand for some action which the subject is logically incapable of performing. Errors of this sort may result from careless diction (see 35a).

Original

They should not have allowed such tragedies to exist in their community.
[*Tragedies do not exist.*]

Revision

(1) They should not have allowed conditions in their community which further such tragedies.
(2) They should not have allowed such tragedies to occur in their community.

Mr. Johnson's disagreement with Wilde was apparently done after a good deal of thought.
[*A disagreement is not* done. *The writer should be careful of the verb,* to do, *which is often misused.*]

(1) Mr. Johnson's disagreement with Wilde was apparently entered into after a good deal of thought.
(2) Apparently, Mr. Johnson broke with Wilde only after a good deal of thought.

The central idea of the poem shows how in youth all is beautiful.

The central idea of the poem is that in youth all is beautiful.

Especially when verbs refer to subjects in another clause, the writer must be careful that they do not represent actions inappropriate for the remainder of the sentence.

Original

Perhaps there are omissions which should have been included.
[*Even though the verb should have been included is in a subordinate clause, it must make sense with* omissions, *represented by* which. *As it stands, the sentence is absurd;*

Revision

(1) Perhaps there are omissions which should have been remedied.
(2) Perhaps material has been omitted which should have been included.
[*The second revision is more thorough and clearer.*]

Original (Cont.)

even if an omission were included there would still be an omission.]

Here are the remains of an era that gripped the United States ten years ago.
[*Can an era grip?*]

Revision (Cont.)

Here are the remains of an era through which the United States passed ten years ago.

20c Equations with verb to be   **Pred c; Eq**

When the verb *to be* links a subject and complement, the ideas connected must have enough in common to make the connection plausible. Sometimes the verb *to be* should be replaced by a verb carrying more of the action of the sentence (see 19, 29b). Sometimes the subject or the complement should be changed.

Original

The only knowledge I have had about horses is living on a farm and raising them.
[Knowledge *is not* living.]

Revision

The only knowledge I have of horses comes from living on a farm and raising them.
[*Changing the verb makes the sentence logical.*]

Perhaps the most important action regarding the teacher's technique of adjusting behavior problems in the classroom is her attitude toward the problem child.
[*An* action *is not an* attitude, *and the sentence is further complicated by other inexact constructions.*]

(1) Perhaps the most important decisions for the teacher facing problems of classroom behavior grow out of her attitude toward the problem child.
(2) The teacher who wishes to solve her problems of classroom behavior should be careful of the attitude she adopts toward the problem child.

When a sentence is so constructed that a form of *to be* seems to be leading to a complement, the complement must appear and must be in some way equal to the subject or must be a quality of the subject. Often the substitution of another verb for *to be* improves the sentence.

Original

The only uniform I have been issued was in camp last August.
[*The sentence is unclear because*

Revision

(1) The only uniform I have been issued is the one I received in camp last August.

[239

Original (Cont.)

was *links no complement with* uniform. *Either supply a complement (1) or change the verb (2).*]

The most dominating characteristic of Spanish architecture is in the element of contrast.
[*The sentence lacks a complement and is wordy.*]

The process of cutting hay in the early days was by means of the scythe, which was manipulated by hand.

Revision (Cont.)

(2) I have been issued only one uniform, which I received in camp last August.

Contrast is the dominating characteristic of Spanish architecture.
[*The sentence does contain a plausible equation when the extra words are cleared away.*]

(1) In the early days hay was cut by hand with a scythe.
(2) Pioneers mowed with a scythe.

Sentences are usually awkward if they contain plural and singular expressions carelessly equated.

Original

The trouble was the many difficulties which complicated the sending of the invitations.
[Trouble *is singular and* difficulties *plural. As a result the meaning is not precise.*]

One thing I like about the room is the two big closets.
[*Two closets are not one thing.*]

Another almost constant hardship was the debts which seemed to keep him from having peace of mind.

Revision

(1) The trouble was that many difficulties complicated the sending of the invitations.
(2) The trouble grew out of complications in sending the invitations.

(1) One thing I like about the room is that it has two big closets.
(2) I like the two big closets in the room.

Another almost constant hardship arose from his debts, which robbed him of peace of mind.

20d Choice of complements   **Pred d**

A complement must have a meaning which makes it logically capable of receiving the action of the verb.

Original

He managed during his life to defy all the traditional qualities of an outstanding politician.

Revision

He managed during his life to defy all the traditions associated with success in politics.

Original (Cont.)

[To defy qualities *makes no sense. The basic sentence is not logical.*]

Economists are still piecing together the over-all situation.

[*One cannot piece together a situation. If the writer insists on the trite metaphor, he must carry it through.*]

Revision (Cont.)

(1) Economists are still piecing together a picture of the period.

(2) Economists do not yet understand all that occurred.

20e Shifts in structure   **Pred e**

Sometimes the writer disturbs the subject-verb-complement pattern by carelessly changing the structure of the sentence as he develops it.

Original

For information concerning almost any happening which is too minor to be found in periodical articles may be located through *The New York Times Index.*

[*The writer starts with one construction and shifts to another; thus the "sentence" never acquires a subject.*]

Revision

(1) For information concerning almost any happening which is too minor to be found in periodical articles the research worker may use *The New York Times Index.*

(2) *The New York Times Index* will serve to locate information concerning almost any happening too minor to be reported in periodical articles.

Any passage that pleased him he tried to write something in the same style.

[*What promises to be the subject,* passage, *is replaced by a new subject,* he.]

(1) Any passage which pleased him was likely to become the model for a passage in the same style.

(2) He would imitate any passage which pleased him.

EXERCISE 20

A. The sentences below contain faulty predication: that is, the basic sentence in each is illogical. Analyze subject-verb-complement relationships, and revise each sentence so that the subject, verb, and complement make sense together.

    1. Her mental attitude is disturbed and may not return for several hours.

    2. Abraham learned that necessities come by dint of hard labor.

    3. For a person to not obey the Duke's wishes would mean the person's death.

4. For a rifle team to become a success, many points must be accomplished.
5. The amount of money lost by both the strikers and the employers took a matter of years in order to regain them.
6. The main idea of Donne's *Song* seems to be about a man who has been jilted by his mistress.
7. Before we can criticize the essay, fundamentalists in the sense they were used in the essay must be explained.
8. These are basic traits of character which I hope to attain.
9. The setting of the play takes place in Athens.
10. I realized that the child's new parents caused many new angles.
11. Many citizens practiced an anti-Christian cult during the period.
12. It does not seem plausible that God makes him victorious as much as the confidence the man has in himself.
13. Constant experimentation with different techniques of painting increased her versatility and incidentally her composition.
14. Any person that annoyed him he tried to make the person uncomfortable by sarcastic remarks.
15. In two years in the club she managed to break every situation required by the rules.
16. As soon as they are corrected these disadvantages will improve the club a great deal.
17. The theme of the *Tempest* is set in two places.
18. A people needing food and insecure in their jobs ultimately causes revolution.
19. Pineridge is my grandmother's house in which so many happy days took place.
20. The fenders spattered with road oil made the car very hard to wash.
21. I should like to apply for the vacancy in the mailing department.
22. The manager of the team did not approve of the situation which had taken place in his absence.
23. The new taxes were unjust in many cases, which should be rectified.
24. Childhood for me is filled with many happy memories, which I hope someday to achieve again.
25. A person of so little experience in charge means that nobody will be able to do his work properly.
26. The friends that you make often result from your manners.
27. A girl may have some classes after lunch, but if there isn't she may study.
28. All the people in the novel seemed to have a very good evaluation of themselves.
29. This method took as long as three days to plant three hundred acres.
30. Poor people are often impressed by the material evidences which they see which can be purchased with money.

B. The sentences below contain inaccurate equations linked by forms of the verb *to be*. Identify subjects and complements in each sentence. Then revise each sentence, either by using a more expressive verb than *to be* or by changing subject or complement so that they work together. Make any other necessary alterations.

1. The plans of a log cabin should be very compact and not too roomy.
2. The value of this book, in my opinion, was in the fact that it showed more than one cause of juvenile delinquency.
3. The story is where a group of men find themselves the sole survivors of a civilization destroyed by war.
4. The reason I was nervous is because I used to stutter.
5. A fireplace planned from a diagram is the best clue to a comfortable living room.
6. A person's education is a very important task and one that may decide his whole future.
7. The purpose of a Geiger counter is with it you can find uranium.
8. The subject of *The Washerwoman's Day* is about the situation in which a girl finds herself.
9. One other example of Shakespeare's humor being portrayed in his characters was Bottom.
10. A basic method of binding books is the use of cords to which each signature is stitched.
11. Using acquired good taste is an advantage in any social situation.
12. The primary purpose of colleges was intended to be an institution of higher learning.
13. The most outstanding of their rivalries were over a woman.
14. A follower and a leader are both qualities he must possess to enable him to achieve his goals.
15. Journalism is not a romantic life as some books play it up to be, and as some people believe; it is a hard job for anyone to undertake.
16. It can clearly be seen from the story that the desire to return Cassio to her husband's favor was because she honestly felt that it was best for him.
17. The most important reason for the growth of the Diesel locomotive is its many advantages over steam locomotives.
18. The source of my material is from two books.
19. A logical grammar for modern Americans would be to teach them the present system that we now have.
20. He thought that government was the only path to follow.
21. Liberalism has always been a pleasing connotation to Americans.
22. College spirit is an experience long remembered after school is over.
23. The only halt for undemocratic ideas is through the education of the masses.

24. In the play, the weavers' situation, which in broad terms is a people born into a society where they must struggle to develop in all ways, is a basic problem of humanity.
25. Participating in extracurricular activities is the basic factor in the college life of many students.
26. A profit-making organization coming to the campus is poor relations with the public.
27. Some people believe the smaller kernels and no husks to be a blessing.
28. The most important part of any student girl's life is the acquaintances she makes.
29. His reputation was the best miner in the country.
30. One thing pleasant about the university is small classes.

C. Identify subjects of the sentences in the passage below. Then, substitute for each subject some other word in the passage, or another word of your own which is not a synonym for the subject, and change the construction to make sense. Which version is briefer, yours or Hardy's? Which is more effective?

The lamb, revived by the warmth, began to bleat, and the sound entered Gabriel's ears and brain with an instant meaning, as expected sounds will. Passing from the profoundest sleep to the most alert wakefulness with the same ease that had accompanied the reverse operation, he looked at his watch, found that the hour hand had shifted again, put on his hat, took the lamb in his arms, and carried it into the darkness. After placing the little creature with its mother, he stood and carefully examined the sky, to ascertain the time of night from the altitudes of the stars.

The Dog-star and Aldebaran, pointing to the restless Pleiades, were half way up the Southern sky, and between them hung Orion, which gorgeous constellation never burnt more vividly than now, as it swung itself forth above the rim of the landscape. Castor and Pollux with their quiet shine were on the meridian; the barren and gloomy Square of Pegasus was creeping round to the north-west; far away through the plantation, Vega sparkled like a lamp suspended amid the leafless trees, and Cassiopeia's chair stood daintily poised on the uppermost boughs.

"One o'clock" said Gabriel.

—THOMAS HARDY, *Far from the Madding Crowd*

D. In a local newspaper find twenty sentences which are clumsy because the subject of the sentence is not the actual subject or because the verb is followed by an inappropriate complement.

E. Select three passages of 100 to 150 words each, one from a current novel, one from a current magazine, and one from a textbook. If possible, change all of the verbs to some form of the verb *to be* and add any words that may be necessary to restore the original sense. Compare the effectiveness of your version with the original.

F. Select four passages 100 to 150 words in length, one from a current newspaper, one from a current novel, one from a magazine like *Harper's,* the *Atlantic Monthly,* or *The Reporter,* and one from a textbook. Count the number of forms of the verb *to be* in each, and the number of verbs not forms of *to be.* Study the styles of the four works, and make any observations you can as to the effectiveness of the four writers, as writers, and what effect their use of the verb *to be* has upon their writing. Report your findings in a written statement, giving the facts and your conclusions.

V. Co-ordination and Subordi-nation

The turn of a sentence has decided the fate of many a friendship, and for aught we know, the fate of many a kingdom.—JEREMY BENTHAM

A small boy, developing his feeling for sentence structure more rapidly than his knowledge of natural history, heard someone remark that "he was hungry as a bear." The pattern was attractive, and for some months the child was regularly "tired as a bear, sleepy as a bear, cold as a bear, happy as a bear, scared as a bear." Even though the meanings of the words were not especially appropriate, the intention of the child was clear, because his word-order pattern is standard in English.

For complex communication, however, the boy's method was inadequate. He could sense the basic structural patterns of the sentence, the skeletons which support the flesh and sinew of meaning, but he needed more knowledge and experience before he could use the patterns well. English uses special sentence patterns, like the small boy's formula for comparisons, which are so firmly established that they continue to carry their meaning, even though they carry an unwanted meaning. For example, the New York newspaperman who wrote the following knew the basic device of parallel structure:

> Among the items in the collection are the only known document bearing the signatures of Queen Elizabeth and Sir Walter Raleigh and a cigar-store Indian.

By fitting his words inappropriately into the pattern, however, the writer attributed more skill to the Indian than he probably intended.

The examples above illustrate some of the patterns which appear when the sentence is developed beyond the basic pattern discussed with its variations in IV. The subject-verb-complement pattern is the core of the sentence and also of the divisions of complex sentences, that is, of clauses. But subjects, verbs, and complements themselves are not simple. In a complicated world requiring complicated expressions, they are often expanded to reveal relationships more precise than those expressed by the basic actor-action pattern. In general, these relationships can be considered as co-ordination and subordination.

Co-ordination, the grouping together of like ideas and constructions, and subordination, which clarifies the inter-reliance of unlike ideas and constructions, allow the writer to develop sentences beyond the basic pattern. Compare the following:

Knowledge is repetition.

All the knowledge, skill, art, and science that we use and revere, up to Einstein's formulas about the stars, is a mere repetition and extension of the initial feat of learning to walk.

The sentences turn about the same core, the same subject-verb-complement relationship, but Jacques Barzun has needed more than the simple pattern of the first to express more complicated relationships. He has used co-ordination to expand two of the main parts of the sentence: the subject becomes *knowledge, skill, art, and science;* the complement becomes *repetition and extension.* And to each of these parts he has subordinated other expressions which modify them, make them more specific.

This section discusses some of the procedures and problems of relating co-ordinate and subordinate elements in sentences.

21. CO-ORDINATION OR PARALLELISM

[For Guide to Revision, see page 252]

For economy and clarity, group like ideas in like forms and constructions.

Sorting like things together is one of the natural ways in which we use the mind; we notice that two objects are alike in at least certain respects, and group them (see 4). We group men and women as human beings, red and blue as primary colors. In composition, this process is called co-ordination if we approach the process on the basis of meaning, parallelism if we approach it as form. Since we recognize that like ideas should receive like treatment, the words *co-ordination* and *parallelism* are, in effect, synonyms.

21-1 Co-ordination

We have already encountered co-ordination in the discussion of clauses. We recognized that the sentences *Marriage and hanging go by destiny* and *Matches are made in heaven* are parts of one idea, that they are co-ordinate in sense and parallel in form (see 18-2). We recognized them as equal parts of a compound sentence. We must now notice that the same device which we have used to co-ordinate clauses can be at least as useful in co-ordinating the parts of clauses, that co-ordinating minor sentence elements can remove the need for many clauses. Consider the following sentences:

> In the Indian Parliament a member may call his colleague a simian.
> In the Indian Parliament a member may not call his colleague a baboon.

Obviously, the sentences are alike except for one part of the complement. The whole can be said with one sentence having a co-ordinate complement:

> In the Indian Parliament a member may call his colleague a simian, but not a baboon.

Buffon was using a similar sort of co-ordination, although he co-ordinated more parallel complements, when he wrote:

> The human race excepted, the elephant is the most respected of animals. . . . We allow him the judgment of the beaver, the dexterity of the monkey, the sentiment of the dog, and the advantages of strength, size, and longevity.

Using a sentence for each of the elephant's virtues would expand the statement to a paragraph. In these sentences, only the complements are co-ordinated, but most elements of a sentence can be used co-ordinately, and most sentences of any complexity have more than one sort of co-ordination. For instance, H. L. Mencken recorded his disapproval of zoos as follows, without, of course, italicizing his co-ordinate elements:

> The sort of man who likes to spend his time watching *a cage of monkeys chase one another,* or *a lion gnaw its tail,* or *a lizard catch flies,* is precisely the sort of man whose mental weakness should be *combated* at the public expense, not *fostered.*

21-2 Co-ordination and parallel structure

Co-ordination can be more or less elaborate. When a zoo keeper remarked that "We need good, strong cages to protect the animals from the public," he was using co-ordination very simply to join the words *good* and *strong.* On the other hand, the same device can be used to knit together extremely complicated structures; for instance, in the sixteenth century, balanced and contrasted constructions became a fad, and when John Lyly wrote the following he was gaining a number of effects, along with having fun with language:

> This young gallant, of more wit than wealth, and yet of more wealth than wisdom, seeing himself inferior to none in pleasant conceits, thought himself superior to all in honest conditions, insomuch that he deemed himself so apt to all things that he gave himself almost to nothing but practicing of those things commonly which are incident to these sharp wits, fine phrases, smooth quipping, merry taunting, using jesting without mean, and abusing mirth without measure.
>
> —*Euphues*

The style is exaggerated, but the passage illustrates how intricately words, phrases, and clauses can be balanced against one another in writing.

However complicated or simple the co-ordination may be, the

pattern of the sentence should be clear; that is, the co-ordinated elements should be sufficiently parallel so that their relationship is certain. As a minimum, the co-ordinated elements should be alike grammatically. In the phrase *good, strong cages,* only the most common grammatical devices are required. *Good* and *strong* are words of similar type; they both describe the cage. They have the order of words in a series; that is, they stand side by side. The comma between them indicates that they are a series. No more parallelism is needed to assure us of their co-ordinate meaning.

More complicated co-ordinate ideas may require more complicated structures. In the quotation from Mencken, for example, the first series of clauses is made coherent by the repetition of *or.* In the quotation from Lyly this device is carried further. Lyly might have written *of more wit than wealth, and yet more wealth than wisdom.* These phrases would be understandable, but the reader might hesitate as to which of the elements the word *and* co-ordinates. As Lyly did write the sentence, repeating the word *of,* misunderstanding is scarcely possible. Such use of signal words supplements grammatical parallelism.

Word order also helps to support co-ordination. Signal words especially need to be placed carefully. Compare:

> You are either *late* or *early.*
> Either *you are late* or *I am early.*
> You are either *late* or *I am early.*

The first two sentences are clear because the signal words *either* and *or* appear just before the two expressions to be co-ordinated. The third is not clear because *either* is out of position. The following howler from a student paper illustrates a similar danger.

> To be polite he first poured some of the wine into his glass so that he would get the cork and not the lady.

The intention of the writer is clear enough; in speech he could have made himself understood by emphasis. In writing he would need to put the parts of his compound subject together.

> To be polite he first poured some of the wine into his glass so that he, and not the lady, would get the cork.

The requirements of handling co-ordinate material may be summarized as follows:

[25]

(1) Co-ordinate elements must usually be in parallel grammatical form, independent clauses with independent clauses, subjects with subjects, complements with like complements.

(2) Co-ordinate elements must appear in the proper order, usually in series, with appropriate punctuation.

(3) Co-ordinate elements should often be joined with signal words indicating co-ordination: *and, but, or, nor, yet,* and some correlative groups like *either . . . or, neither . . . nor.* The signal words need to be placed so that the elements to be parallel are clearly distinguished.

(4) If necessary to indicate co-ordination, other kinds of signal words (*of, the, in, to,* for instance) should be repeated in parallel structures.

21-3 Comparison as co-ordination

Like things are sometimes grouped in special patterns in which one is compared with another. Comparison is a special sort of co-ordination, and the patterns of comparison are similar to those of parallelism.

> The *joke* was as old as the *hills.*
> *George* looked like his *mother.*
> *My cousin* was older than *any other freshman.*
> It is easier *for a camel to go through the eye of a needle* than *for a rich man to enter into the kingdom of God.*

In each sentence, the italicized expressions are put into parallel forms and are comparable in meaning. These sentence patterns work in English so long as expressions in parallel positions have parallel form and compatible meanings.

21 *Co-ordination or parallelism*   **Paral**

GUIDE TO REVISION:

> *Revise to make appropriate use of co-ordination or to put co-ordinate elements in parallel form.*

Co-ordination—especially within sentences—can strengthen, enliven, and clarify prose, giving it at once economy and order. Beginning writers, especially, often make too little use of co-ordination, writing consecutive simple sentences or clauses which could be combined as co-ordinated subjects, verbs, complements, or modifiers (see 21-1).

21a Parallelism in Co-ordination   Paral a

Parallelism is effective only when the balanced expressions correspond in form. When two or more words are joined by *and, or, nor, but,* or *for,* or are in a series, they should, in general, all be the same parts of speech or words of the same class (for grammatical forms, see VI). Balanced phrases or clauses should correspond in structure.

Original	*Revision*
Today a secretary has to be *attractive* in appearance and a high *intelligence.* [Attractive *is here a modifier,* intelligence *a noun. Revise by making both modifiers* (1) *or both nouns* (2).]	(1) Today a secretary must be *attractive* and *intelligent.* (2) Today a secretary must have an attractive *appearance* and high *intelligence.*
Buffalo Bill could *ride like the wind* and *who shot a bottle cap thrown into the air.*	Buffalo Bill could *ride like the wind* and *shoot a bottle cap thrown into the air.*
A ward attendant is responsible for his ward *in matters of cleanliness* and a *large number of patients to look after.*	A ward attendant is responsible for *keeping his ward clean* and *looking after a large number of patients.*
The laboratory was not equipped *for careful work* or *to accommodate a great many students.*	The laboratory was not equipped *for careful work* or *for the accommodation of a great many students.*

When items occupy parallel positions in a series, they should have consistent forms, even though the series is long.

Original	*Revision*
Mary enrolled for *painting, harmony, music appreciation,* and *to study art history.* [*The final item of the series is not parallel.*]	Mary enrolled for *painting, harmony, music appreciation,* and *art history.* [*The final item appears as the name of a course, like the others.*]

[253

Original (Cont.)

My sister was *pretty, intelligent, generous,* and *every characteristic of a likable person.*
[*The writer has apparently forgotten how he began.*]

Revision (Cont.)

My sister was *pretty, intelligent, generous,* and *likable.*
[*The revision is parallel, clearer, and more concise.*]

21b Repetition of signals in parallelism   Paral b

Often parallelism will be apparent if similar structures are placed side by side, but in more complicated sentences words which signal similarities should be repeated. A student wrote the following excellent sentence:

> Bacon's "idols" dwell in the minds of men, but their temples are in London, in Moscow, and in Washington, for in these world capitals clouded thinking is condoned, perpetuated, and to some extent originated.

The writer wisely repeated the signal *in* to make the parallelism certain.

Original

I told him that he should have an agreement about his situation at home, he needed a room to himself with a good light, and specified hours when he could depend upon being free to study.
[*Failure to repeat the signal word* that *leaves the sentence confused. The reader starts to read* he needed *without understanding that he has begun the second of three things which* I told him.]

Revision

I told him that he should have an agreement about his situation at home, that he needed a room to himself with a good light, and that he should be allotted specified hours when he could depend upon being free to study.
[*The three clauses which follow* I told him *are now marked off by the repeated signal word* that.]

A girl ought to become well acquainted with a number of boys; only by doing so can she learn to distinguish between the flatterers and the polite people, know when a boy is trying to mistreat her, and how to handle boys who become too intimate.

A girl ought to become well acquainted with a number of boys; only by doing so can she learn to distinguish between the flatterers and the polite people, to know when a boy is trying to mistreat her, and to know how to handle boys who become too intimate.
[*The repetition of* to *makes the parallelism clear.*]

Original (Cont.)

The only enemies of the sloth are *the eagles, jaguars,* and *the large boas.*
[*Inconsistency in the use of articles in a series is not always confusing, but it breaks the rhythm of the sentence and destroys the parallel structure.*]

The parakeet can be found in *a* green, pale blue, or *a* chartreuse color.

Revision (Cont.)

(1) The only enemies of the sloth are *the* eagles, jaguars, and large boas.
[*The first* the *is understood for all items of the series.*]
(2) The only enemies of the sloth are *the* eagles, *the* jaguars, and *the* large boas.

The parakeet may be green, pale blue, or chartreuse.

21c Misleading parallelism   Paral c

Expressions not parallel in sense should not appear in a pattern suggesting parallel structure. Difficulty arises especially when parallel passages are woven together in a sentence and the writer fails to keep his strands separate.

Original

On the first day we visited the *Metropolitan Museum,* the *Planetarium,* and *rode* the ferry to Staten Island.
[*Museum, Planetarium, and* rode *are not parallel in meaning, and should not appear in parallel form. The first two are logically parallel, but* rode *should parallel* visited.]

Penicillin was found to cure most diseases *more quickly, effectively,* and *less dangerously* than did the sulfa drugs.
[*Again the series is not a series as it stands. The sentence can be revised either to avoid the illogical series or to make it logical.*]

He escaped to the United States, a coward and afraid to die for liberty.

Revision

On the first day we *visited* the *Metropolitan Museum* and the *Planetarium* and *rode* the ferry to Staten Island.
[*Insertion of* and *in place of the first comma breaks up the illogical series and makes the parallels clear.*]

(1) Penicillin was found to cure most diseases *more quickly* and *effectively* and *less dangerously* than did the sulfa drugs.
(2) Penicillin was found to cure most diseases *more quickly, more effectively,* and *less dangerously* than did the sulfa drugs.

He escaped to the United States, a coward afraid to die for liberty.
[*There are no parallel ideas in*

[255

Original (Cont.)

[Coward *and* afraid *are treated as parallels, but one is used as a noun and the other as a modifier.*]

Two men were *on the edge* of the dock and *fishing* in the river.

New Orleans is exciting, surprising, and which I should like to visit again.

Revision (Cont.)

the sentence, and the revision removes the illogical and. With little loss, a coward might be omitted.]

Two men were on the edge of the dock fishing in the river.

New Orleans is exciting and surprising, and I should like to visit it again.

21d Parallelism in comparisons   Paral d; Comp

Like other parallel structures, comparisons require parallel forms and word order. Furthermore, comparisons make sense only if the expressions in parallel positions stand for comparable ideas. We can logically compare teaching with stenography but not with a secretary; that is we can say:

Teaching is more exacting work than stenography.

We cannot say:

Teaching is a duller profession than a secretary.

Original

During the war the *value* of the Negro troops was found to be on a par with white service *forces.*
[*The sentence compares* value *and* forces, *which are not logically comparable. The writer probably intended to compare the value of one force with the value of the other, or to compare the two* forces.]

The foreman insisted that his job was harder than a common laborer.
[Job *and* laborer *are not comparable.*]

His ears were longer than a jack rabbit.

Revision

(1) During the war the Negro *troops* were found to be on a par with white service *forces.*
(2) During the war the Negro *troops* were as valuable as the white *forces.*
[Troops *and* forces *can be logically compared. The idea of value can be retained by making it the basis for comparison.*]

(1) The foreman insisted that his job was harder than a common laborer's.
(2) The foreman insisted that his job was harder than that of a common laborer.

His ears were longer than a jack rabbit's.

Original (Cont.)

The lecturer compared his life with a medieval peasant.

Wordsworth's *Prelude* was written, not like Rousseau wrote his *Confessions,* to reveal himself, but for the happiness and moral betterment of man.

But the *battle* against eating umpkin seeds in school continued, as *gum chewing* does in most American schools.
[*The words put into parallel positions,* battle *and* gum chewing, *are not comparable.*]

Cyrano is more popular than *any* of Rostand's plays.
[Cyrano *cannot be more popular than itself, and* any of Rostand's plays *includes* Cyrano.]

Because cars are so well built, the driver drives much faster than he can safely handle the car.

Revision (Cont.)

The lecturer compared his life with that of a medieval peasant.

Wordsworth wrote his *Prelude* not as Rousseau wrote his *Confessions,* to reveal himself, but to make man happier and morally better.

(1) But the *battle* against eating pumpkin seeds in school continued, as does the *battle* against gum chewing in most American schools.
(2) But the eating of pumpkin seeds in school continued, as gum chewing does in most American schools.

Cyrano is more popular than any *other* of Rostand's plays.
[Cyrano *can logically be compared with the* other *plays of Rostand.*]

Because cars are so well built, the driver drives at speeds much faster than those at which he can safely handle the car.

EXERCISE 21

A. Each of the sentences below violates parallelism. Recast the sentences so that ideas and forms are parallel, or remove unwarranted parallel structure.

1. To survive without a guide in the north woods one has to be well trained as a woodsman as well as excellent physical condition.

2. *Hamlet* has been more criticized than any of Shakespeare's plays.

3. She told her mother she wanted either a wedding in a church with flower girls, organ music, long trains, or a quick elopement to a justice of the peace.

4. I much prefer listening to concerts on the radio rather than to sit in the heat and discomfort of our auditorium.

5. We found worms in the corn, tomatoes, and the broccoli.

6. His career was more brilliant than any musician who graduated in his class.

7. His career, unlike most people who played a musical instrument, ended when he left school.

8. His job consisted mostly of planning and constructing roads, bridges, and various forms of surveying.

9. From the air the stream looked languid, twisted, and flowed on its course like some giant caterpillar en route to its cocoon.

10. The vampire leered at the little girl showing teeth as white and sharp as a wolf.

11. She dreamed that she had gone to the concert wearing a scarlet bathrobe, black riding boots, and carrying a silver fox muff.

12. He accused the senator of being a fool and too stupid to know the real issues.

13. The professional players were more skillful, accurate, but less enthusiastic than their amateur opponents.

14. The dean told Alice that she should find a better place to study, she needed to spend less time at the movies, and ought to attend class more frequently.

15. She seemed pretty, clever, perceptive, and the courtesy required of an airline hostess.

16. We found the two gamblers in the dressing room and talking to the captain of the team.

17. Elaine, the first girl elected president of the student council, was attractive, popular, capable, but placed in a position of special difficulty.

18. June much preferred making her own clothes rather than to buy them in the shops.

19. In the test the ability of the freshman was found to be equal to the seniors in most subjects.

20. She liked Picasso better than any artist.

B. Combine the materials of each of the following groups of sentences into a single sentence using parallel structure.

1. A course of study in music may prepare a student for concert performances. It may also provide preparation for a career in teaching. And many students gain preparation for occasional recreational activity through their entire lives.

2. Upon the chair hung a neatly folded suit. Over it was a crumpled red tie. A crushed gardenia was also on the chair.

3. Every person in the tournament knew bridge thoroughly. Each one was intelligent in his playing. A firm determination to win was in every player.

4. The battle proved the courage of the recruits. They behaved just as courageously as the seasoned veterans.

5. Seated on the steps were a tan spaniel and brindle boxer. Angela, the Manx cat, was also there.

6. A good nurse possesses a willingness to do more than her required tasks. She is also constantly alert to guess her patient's wishes.

7. The brown pup seemed to possess intelligence. None of the other dogs in the litter seemed so intelligent.

8. A nationalistic rather than a sectionalistic attitude developed in the West. This was partly because the West needed a national government to protect it from the Indians. It also looked toward the national government to provide aid in the development of transportation facilities. Furthermore, foreign affairs could be handled by a strong national government.

9. Without the mariner's compass, Columbus could not have discovered America. Neither could Vasco da Gama's trip to find a sea route to India have occurred. Magellan's sailing around the world would not have taken place without it, either.

10. Jean spent an hour with the tea committee. After it she knew that she had never before known how intricate planning a tea could be. She did not believe that the event was worth the trouble it took. She would never be on another tea committee, she was sure.

22. SUBORDINATION

[For Guide to Revision, see page 263]

To show relationships, dependent ideas should be subordinated to main ones.

Whenever we make one idea primary in a paragraph or theme, or one idea a subject and another a modifier in a sentence, we decide to make one idea subordinate. Most of these decisions are automatic; if we had to stop to think about each word, communication would be slow work. But often the writer can profit by careful consideration of subordination, for it provides an excellent pattern with which to relate ideas.

22-1 Subordination and style

The writer addicted to choppy composition can reduce some sentences to subordinate parts of others, adding clarity to his writing as well as variety to his style. Notice, for example, the obvious immaturity of writing like the following:

> Beechwood is a park. It is in my home town and is a cool, shady park. I knew it as a child. Then I went on many picnics there.

The repetitions indicate that all four sentences would combine into one.

> When I was a child, I went on many picnics to Beechwood, a cool, shady park in my home town.

The final sentence becomes the basis of the new sentence, and all the other sentences are subordinated as short modifiers. Or consider the following roundabout sentence:

> Sometimes a person is assigned the writing of a research paper, and then he has to know how to gain knowledge about it, and so he must go first of all to the library and there find out how to locate material and thereby gain the knowledge he needs.

Much of the difficulty stems from careless repetition, but the confusion can best be removed by choosing a central subject-verb-complement pattern and subordinating other ideas to it.

> To write a research paper, one must first learn how to locate material in a library.

Reduction of lengthy clauses to short, subordinate modifiers clarifies and strengthens the sentence.

22-2 Subordination to show relationships

As in larger units of composition (see 4-2), subordination shows relationships in the sentence. A writer might, for example, have the following ideas in his mind:

> We are offered a penny for our thoughts.
> We consider what we have been thinking.
> Many things have been in our minds.
> From these many things we can select a few.
> The things we select do not compromise us too nakedly.

These ideas could be set down as separate sentences, as they are above, or they could be strung together with *and* into a rambling co-ordinate sentence. But the skillful writer would subordinate some of the ideas, picking out the idea he wanted to stress and subordinating the others to it. He might end with something like the following sentence, from which the above ideas were taken:

> When we are offered a penny for our thoughts we always find that we have recently had so many things in mind that we can easily make a selection which will not compromise us too nakedly.
>
> —JAMES HARVEY ROBINSON, *Mind in the Making*

22-3 Subordination and emphasis

Like many devices of sentence structure, subordination allows the writer to show relationships and to shift emphasis. The purposes of the writer determine which ideas are subordinated and the manner of their subordination. Consider, for example, various ways of combining the following relatively simple ideas:

> I was twelve years old.
> I got my first long pants.
> I took the girl next door to the movies.

Most obviously, perhaps the first idea might be subordinated to the others as an indication of the time; the last two ideas share equally the stress of the sentence.

> When I was twelve years old, I got my first long pants and took the girl next door to the movies.

A change in the subordinating word (see 33-4), however, would vary the meaning and emphasis considerably.

> Although I was only twelve years old, I got my first long pants and took the girl next door to the movies.

Or both the first two ideas might be subordinated.

> When I was twelve years old and in my first long pants, I took the girl next door to the movies.

The trip to the movies becomes the event which the writer wants primarily to talk about, and the acquisition of the pants drops out.

22-4 Subordination and contexts

Subordination should vary with the sentences which precede and follow. The last version above, for example, might be appropriate in a paragraph narrating a story about the friendship of a boy and girl. The context might suggest even wider variations in the pattern of subordination. Consider:

> When I had my first long pants and had taken the girl next door to the movies, I was twelve years old.

This unusual emphasis might be logical if the preceding sentence had read:

> The actual date of my twelfth birthday meant nothing to me.

Or a different preceding sentence might suggest the wisdom of a parallel pattern of subordination following it.

> At the age of eleven, I tore my knickers trying to catch a toad with which I hoped to frighten the girls at the Sunday School picnic. At twelve, I wore my first long pants to take the girl next door to the movies.

The second sentence fits the pattern of the first, draws the contrast between the events, and enforces the continuity (see 15-6).

22 Subordination   **Sub**

GUIDE TO REVISION:

Subordinate elements which require less emphasis to those which require more emphasis.

Adequate subordination requires clear classification (see 4) and the use of subordinating patterns to make clear such relationships as cause, result, and modification. Inadequate subordination characterizes the kind of writing sometimes called "primer English" because it suggests a schoolboy's reader. Strings of short sentences, excessive use of *and* and *so* to join clauses, and repeated use of *this* and *that* as subjects are usually symptoms of inadequate subordination.

Original

I reported the next morning. I was then assigned to Guided Missiles. This is a very large department, and so it hires hundreds of employees.

Margot Macomber must have been a very beautiful woman. She had everything except wealth. When she married Francis Macomber she acquired this wealth. Although she was married to Francis, she was very untrue to him.
One day they went on a hunting expedition to Africa. They took a white man as a guide. His name was Wilson. Of course, Margot had to have his attention, and she did. Francis felt very sorry for himself. He knew that she would never leave him because of his wealth. He would never divorce her because of her beauty.
One day Francis and Wilson went out hunting lions. They came upon one and wounded it. It ran

Revision

On reporting the next morning, I was assigned to Guided Missiles, a very large department hiring hundreds of employees.
[*Subordination promotes economy and clarity.*]

Margot Macomber was a very beautiful woman who had everything except wealth. When she married Francis Macomber, she acquired that. Although she married Francis, she was untrue to him, and during a hunting expedition to Africa, she sought the attention of their white guide, Wilson. Although Francis felt very sorry for himself, he knew his wealth would keep Margot from leaving him and that her beauty would keep him from divorcing her.
One day while Francis and Wilson were out hunting, they wounded a lion and let it get away to hide in the brush. They moved into the brush after him, although getting him out was dangerous.

[263

Original (Cont.)

into the brush and hid. Getting the lion out would be a very dangerous job. Wilson and Francis began moving into the brush looking for the lion. All of a sudden, the lion jumped out of the brush. Macomber became frightened. He turned and ran. Wilson stood his ground and shot the lion, killing it. Francis knew that he would be the laughing stock of the party.

Some time later, they went on a buffalo hunt. They came upon a herd of buffalo. A buffalo was wounded and ran into the brush. Previous incidents seemed to be repeating themselves. Francis saw a chance to redeem himself. He ·began going through the brush. All this time, his wife had been watching him from a distance. All of a sudden, the buffalo jumped up and charged Francis. Francis held his ground and aimed at the animal's nose. In the meantime, Margot saw the animal charge too. She brought a heavy rifle to her shoulder. Then there was the sound of two shots. Francis and the buffalo both toppled to the ground dead. When she saw that Francis was dead, she became hysterical. She began to realize that Francis was really the man she loved.

[*The theme above deserved the F it received—in spite of its lack of grammatical errors. The style is that of a small child telling the story of Red Riding Hood in his own words.*]

Revision (Cont.)

Suddenly the lion jumped out. Macomber, frightened, turned and ran. Wilson stood his ground and killed the lion. Francis knew he would be the laughing stock of the party.

Some time later they went after buffalo, found a herd, and wounded one, losing him in the brush. As the earlier situation re-occurred, Francis saw a chance to redeem himself and began to go into the brush. Suddenly the buffalo jumped up and charged Francis. He held his ground and aimed at the buffalo's nose. Margot, who had been watching from a distance, saw the charge, too, and raised a heavy rifle to her shoulder. Two shots sounded. Francis and the buffalo both toppled to the ground dead. When Margot saw that Francis was dead, she became hysterical, realizing that Francis was really the man she loved.

[*The theme purported to be a character sketch of Margot Macomber, but turned out to be merely a plot sketch revealing some curious misinterpretations of Hemingway's story. The revision is still a naïve misreading of the story, but it illustrates how much the style can be improved and clarified simply by subordinating some elements to others. For the most part the revision does nothing beyond reducing independent sentences to dependent clauses, phrases, or single words.*]

22a Repeated subjects and subordination   Sub a

Perhaps the most frequent sign of inadequate subordination is the repeated subject, especially the word *this* needlessly and often vaguely carrying on as the subject of a new sentence (see 24a). Usually the two sentences should be joined.

Original	*Revision*
When Lord Byron was at Cambridge, he published *Hours of Idleness*. This was in 1807. The volume was Byron's first book of poems. [*The repetition of subjects—this and volume—suggests inadequate subordination.*]	In 1807, when Lord Byron was at Cambridge, he published his first book of poems, *Hours of Idleness*. [*The combination says everything in the original more clearly and more economically.*]
Dramatics develops assurance. This is very valuable.	Dramatics develops valuable assurance.
The river was only a tiny creek. It was a victim of the new irrigation projects. This river was the one I had learned to swim in.	The river, in which I had learned to swim, was only a tiny creek, a victim of the new irrigation projects.

Some sentences wind on and on, held together by connectives like *so* and *and*. Almost always they can be improved by selecting one part of the sentence as a main clause and subordinating other elements to it.

Original	*Revision*
Louise was tired of listening to the concert and it was dark enough that her grandmother could not see her and so she slipped out into the lobby. [*The relationships between the three clauses are not accurately marked for the reader by linking them with and and so.*]	Since Louise was tired of listening to the concert, she slipped past her grandmother in the dark into the lobby. [*With ideas subordinated to a main subject-verb framework—she slipped—the sentence is clearer and more economical.*]
There was a garage just around the corner and nobody wanted to be responsible for the keys so we took out our luggage and put the car in the garage.	Since nobody wanted to be responsible for the keys, we removed our luggage and put the car in a garage just around the corner.

22b Illogical or upside-down subordination   Sub b

Making the wrong element dependent obscures relationships; the secondary idea becomes the core of the sentence with the main idea subordinate to it. A shift in the subordination improves such a sentence.

Original

Joe pulled the rug out from under her, when she fell down.
[*The sentence is upside down. The fall should surely constitute the main action.*]

She walked back and forth over the beach for an hour, finally finding her lost watch.

Revision

When Joe pulled the rug out from under her, she fell down.
[*The subordinate idea has been subordinated.*]

After walking back and forth over the beach for an hour, she finally found her lost watch.

EXERCISE 22

A. Combine each of the following groups of sentences into a single sentence:

1. Henry Purcell was a composer. He was English. He lived in the seventeenth century.

2. Many of the new dance steps are difficult. Anyone can learn them, however. That is, anyone can learn them if he has a good sense of rhythm.

3. I am not a very good swimmer. This is because I have always been afraid of the water. I have spent many hours on the beach, however.

4. In *Jane Eyre* Charlotte Brontë describes abuses of education. These were in a real school. Miss Brontë had once attended the school, and it was at Cowan Bridge.

5. The oboe is a difficult instrument. This is because it has a double reed. This is hard to blow.

6. First all the girls in the camp had to take exercises. Then all the girls had breakfast and had to clean up the bunks. Then all the girls of the camp reported for swimming. I liked swimming better than any other activity.

7. In 1864 Atlanta was one of the most important cities of the South. This was so for the reason that the Confederacy had developed it as an important railroad center. It was also developed as a manufacturing center. This was done in the belief that it was far from the center of military activity. It would therefore be safe.

8. I grew up in a small town. It was in the South. I have not visited this town for many years. To be exact, I have not been there for eight years. It is still, however, the place I think of as home.

9. *Charley's Aunt* is still a popular play. It was first presented, however, in 1892. And it is implausible and farcical.

10. Many flowers come out in the spring. They include violets, anemones, blood root, and trilliums. This is in the Middle West. These flowers appear about May. They cover the ground in woods and parks.

B. Revise any sentences among the following in which the wrong element is subordinated:

1. Although we had been warned against hiking over the rocky slope in the dark, we started before daylight. The sun peeped over the horizon just as I fell and sprained my ankle.

2. After three months of haunting casting offices and leaving her phone number with producers, Jane decided to go back to St. Louis. The telephone rang when she was almost too disgusted with New York to answer it.

3. Jack was seven years old, although he had never seen grass growing. He had never been outside the area about four blocks square which surrounded the dingy apartment house.

4. When he finally decided to work, he had no trouble finding a job. But when he had trouble keeping it was after he had taken a job.

5. By midnight all of us in the car were sure that we could get to Santa Fe in time for the plane. Then we just rounded a curve and saw the lights of the city when a tire blew out.

6. The man who was peeping in the window and who was immediately noticed by me, was on the outside.

7. Abraham Lincoln was the man that was the leader of the Union cause and Jefferson Davis was the president of the Confederate states, although there are reasons to think of Robert E. Lee as the true leader of the South, and there were generals in the Northern armies, of whom one was to become famous as General Ulysses S. Grant.

8. Since I am majoring in automotive design, I am interested in aeroplane motors, especially jet propulsion units.

9. We moved from Charleston to Durham, North Carolina, in which I found the customs about having dates were very different.

10. I was still very young, although I thought it was getting to be time for me to make up my mind about whether I wanted to be a teacher or a librarian or an airline stewardess.

C. Rewrite the following selection from a student theme, improving its style in any way you can and paying particular attention to opportunities for clarifying relations between ideas by subordination:

On the night of the flood four of us drove across the river away from home to see what damage had been done. We drove around on the other side for about an hour and a half. We finally decided to start home. We came back to the bridge. There was about three feet of water over the road. We had to get across for classes the next day, so we had to find some way to cross to the other side. After considerable debate we decided to drive across. We had gone about a fourth of the way and the ignition got wet. The car stalled in about two feet of water. The water started pouring in under the doors. The heat of the engine dried the ignition, and the car started again. We went about half way and stalled again. This time we were in about three feet of water. The water poured in. We talked about pushing the car across. The three boys got out and pushed. I steered. The water was deep, and so they could not push the car. They got back in. I thought maybe the water would get deeper. It was very exciting. The water was swift. Finally a large truck came in behind us. He pushed us across. We still could not start the car, and so we had to leave it. The water was still rising. We came back the next day. The car was still there and the water had not come to it again. We tried to start it. It would not start. We pushed the car for three or four blocks. It did not fire at all. We pushed it to a garage, and the mechanic said the carburetor was full of mud. The river water was very muddy in the flood. We left the car at the garage to be cleaned.

23. MODIFIERS; METHODS IN SUBORDINATION

[For Guide to Revision, see page 275]

Words, phrases, or clauses which describe, qualify, limit, emphasize, or point to other parts of the sentence are modifiers.

A child, with two or three strokes of a crayon, can draw a recognizable picture of a man, but his creation is not a finished portrait. It does not, for example, present a particular impression of a particular person. It distinguishes a man from a horse, but it does not distinguish one man from other men. As the child grows older, he may make more complicated drawings: the lines for the hat brim may lengthen, and the picture represents a cowboy; or the head enlarges to a globe-like helmet, and the picture represents a space man. The skillful portrait painter does more than the child with his few lines. He makes his outline more accurately; he adds details which distinguish his sitter from others, and he alters the general outline to convey a specific impression.

The method whereby the artist relates his details to one another is so obvious and so fundamental that we do not stop to think about it, but what he does is to relate his details by position. He selects certain details to draw, but he also puts them in specific places. The same line might be an eyebrow in one place but a mustache in another. Modern artists like Picasso have even experimented with special effects of emphasis or exaggeration by altering usual patterns, putting an eye in the middle of the forehead or a nose on the side of the face.

23-1 Modifying expressions

The writer thinking his ideas onto paper follows a similar method. He discovers that he can alter or qualify the meaning of the subject or verb or complement of a sentence by putting appropriate words near them. The process is modification, putting words into the normal sentence order in places where they describe, limit, qualify, emphasize, or point to other parts of the sentence, and thus reveal the manner in which certain parts of the sentence are subordinate to other parts. Compare:

> Man
> The man
> The old man
> The old man in the gray suit
> The old man in the gray suit who was getting off the train

Each additional modifier shows a little more particularly which man is being named. *Man* applies to an entire class of creatures; *the old man in the gray suit who was getting off the train* singles out an individual.

23-2 Subordination and modification

Consider the following sentences:

> Calling a spouse vile names is grounds for divorce, *and this is true if the names are put into language composed only of signs.*
> Calling a spouse vile names *which are couched in the language of signs* is grounds for divorce.
> Calling a spouse vile names *by using the language of signs* is grounds for divorce.
> Calling a spouse vile names *in sign language* is grounds for divorce.

Notice what has happened to the idea of using signs for marital epithets. In the first sentence, this idea requires all the words after the function word *and;* that is, it is an independent clause and a rather complicated one. In the second sentence the idea has been reduced to the italicized dependent clause. In the third sentence this idea has been subordinated still further to the italicized group of words introduced by *by*. In the last sentence the idea has become *in sign language*. The groups of words which express this idea in the last three sentences can all be thought of as modifiers; they all show subordination, but the subordination is progressive. Naturally, the Spokane court which made this ruling preferred the last sentence, in which the modifiers show the greatest evidence of subordination.

270]

In sentences, expressions which are grammatically subordinated usually modify. Instead of acting as main sentence parts, they become subordinate parts of what might be called the "complete" subject, verb, or complement. Compare:

> I bought a dress. It is chartreuse.
> I bought a chartreuse dress.

Sometimes, of course, subordinated material does not modify but acts as a main sentence part. Compare:

> Mary knew something about Jack. He had been married twice before.
> Mary knew *that Jack had been married twice before.*

The italicized clause in the second sentence is a complement, even though its idea has been subordinated. This sort of reduction of sentence elements is important for economy and directness. Most subordinate sentence elements, however, are modifiers.

23-3 Types of modifiers

In general, modifiers fall into three groups:

(1) *Dependent clauses.* Many of the dependent clauses mentioned above (see 18-3) are modifiers (*The man* who takes candy away from babies. . . .)

(2) *Phrases.* Groups of words which do not fit the actor-action pattern may be modifiers. They may involve a verbal (see 30-6; Stunned by his wife's death *and* enraged by the defection of his followers, *Macbeth still tried to defend his castle*). They may be groups in which a preposition (see 27-1, 33-6) relates a noun to some other part of the sentence (*of him, to the theatre, without a thought*). These are conventionally called *prepositional phrases.*

(3) *Single words.* These are conventionally distinguished in form as *adjectives* and *adverbs* (see 32).

Most complicated sentences have modifiers of all these sorts. Consider the following sentence, which uses various types of modifiers:

> The various forms of intellectual activity, which together make up the culture of an age, move for the most part from different starting points and by unconnected roads.

The simple statement of the sentence is *forms move,* but twenty-five other words tell what forms move in what ways.

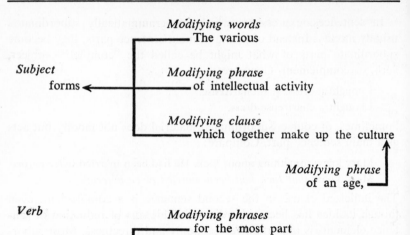

23-4 Word order of modifiers

Like other parts of the sentence, modifiers assume their meaning in the sentence and their grammatical relationship to it because of their position. In a sentence like

> The maid guided the old gentleman through the dark hall, turning suddenly at the end of the passage to a heavy door.

we know that the gentleman, not the maid, is old, because of the positions of the words. We know that it was the turning which was sudden and the hall which was dark. When the order of words changes, the application and meaning of the modifiers changes.

> The old maid suddenly guided the heavy dark gentleman through the hall, turning at the end of the passage to a door.

In general, modifiers are understood to modify the eligible expressions nearest them. Modifiers, however, are extremely adaptable, and the language has developed numerous arrangements for them which seem to follow these general principles:

(1) Modifiers which apply clearly and specifically to particular expressions in the sentence are in fixed positions, usually immediately before or after the expressions they modify.

(2) Modifiers which do not apply to particular expressions but modify more generally may occupy different positions.

(3) Variations in the positions of modifiers produce variations in meaning and emphasis.

23-5 Fixed modifiers

Modifiers of specific expressions, especially of noun expressions, normally appear in fixed positions according to the following word-order patterns:

(1) Single-word modifiers of noun expression usually precede the expressions they modify.

The *bright red* convertible pulled into *the filling* station.

Since this word order is standard, variations from it turn special emphasis on the modifier and are useful devices in writing and speaking. Sometimes single-word adjectives are given prominence in a position immediately after the expression they modify.

The convertible, *bright red,* looked like a fire engine.

Appositive modifiers, which repeat in different words the expressions they modify, conventionally follow what they modify.

My brother, a former private *detective,* took charge of the investigation.

In this shifted position, single-word modifiers are usually set off by commas, which mark the change from normal word order. Or consider the changes in meaning and emphasis in the following:

They found the *deserted* village.
They found the village *deserted.*

The sentences have different meanings, imply different contexts.

(2) Modifiers used as complements take the complement position after the verb.

Grass is *green.*

Reversals of the order gives special emphasis to the modifier.

Gay were our hearts.

(3) Normally, phrases and clauses immediately follow the expressions they modify.

He walked *with a slight limp.*
The captain *of the ship* set out to find the boat *which had broken from its moorings.*
I was the first person *the board interviewed.*

(4) Modifiers of other modifiers immediately precede the expressions they modify.

They supplied *too* little *too* late.

Very quickly we were *thoroughly* disgusted.

(5) Certain limiting modifiers (*only, nearly, just, almost, merely, ever, hardly, scarcely, quite*) usually modify most clearly when placed immediately before the expressions they modify. Compare:

> *Only* Williams could hope to win the hundred dollars.
> Williams could *only* hope to win the hundred dollars.
> Williams could hope to win *only* the hundred dollars.

(6) Modifiers of verbs may appear in any of several positions, sometimes without much shift in meaning or emphasis. They occur most frequently directly after the verb (*He drove* slowly *down the street*). They may appear within complex verbs (*She was* always *losing her gloves*). Many one-word modifiers can occur immediately before the verb (*I* soon *recovered;* but not, *I* into the street *fell*). Some modifiers, especially those of direction, regularly appear after the verb but either before or after the complement (*Take* back *what you said;* but usually *Take that* back). Sometimes one position is obligatory, or almost so (*Set the clock* ahead; but usually not *Set* ahead *the clock*).

Many modifiers have become so closely associated with verbs that they are best thought of as parts of verbs (see 29-4). They usually appear before or after the complement, often with little difference in meaning or emphasis (*Turn* off *the light;* or *Turn the light* off).

23-6 Sentence and clause modifiers

Fitted into such word-order patterns, modifiers tend to limit specific expressions. Some modifiers, however, are not intended to modify a single word; they modify all of an actor-action pattern and do not function in fixed positions. They are best considered as sentence modifiers.

> *Before lunch,* he read two novels.
> He, *before lunch,* read two novels.
> He read, *before lunch,* two novels.
> He read two novels *before lunch.*

Since it modifies the entire action of the sentence, *before lunch* can occur in various positions, although it is least awkward at the begin-

274]

ning or end. Such sentence or clause modifiers are movable, relating to the entire sentence pattern and not to individual words.

Sentence modifiers, however, are movable only within limits. Consider the following:

> *Walking in the park* the man found a mushroom.
> The man *walking in the park* found a mushroom.
> The man found a mushroom *walking in the park*.

In the first sentence, *walking in the park* modifies the action of the entire sentence. In the second, however, the phrase identifies the man. In the third, it has moved into the position of a fixed modifier of *mushroom* and causes either awkwardness or absurdity. Sentence or clause modifiers do not usually occupy fixed positions, but there are relatively few points at which they can appear without ruining or altering the sentence. Often they work best at the beginning of the sentence, where they do not interrupt the subject-verb-complement pattern or fall into fixed positions for modifiers of specific expressions.

23 Modifiers; methods in subordination   Mod

GUIDE TO REVISION:

> *Place fixed modifiers in their appropriate restricted
> positions and sentence modifiers so that they give the
> desired emphasis.*

A manufacturer uses the following slogan: "Our aspirin is the world's largest seller at ten cents." Is the aspirin the world's largest seller, which incidentally costs only ten cents? Or is it the largest seller only among aspirins that sell for a dime, not among those that sell for eleven cents or twenty-nine cents? Both the selection of the modifier itself and its position obscure the meaning. Such modification is useful only if the speaker deliberately wants to be vague; if he wants his ideas sharp and precise, he must order his modifiers carefully.

> Our aspirin, at ten cents, is the world's largest seller.
> Our aspirin is the world's largest-selling ten-cent aspirin.

The errors that result from misplacing modifiers vary from false shading of meaning to complete monstrosities. The following is a good rule:

The meaning is more readily clear to the writer than to the reader; avoid any construction that can be misunderstood.

23a Position of fixed modifiers   **Mod a**

Usually, fixed modifiers can appear in only one position for a given purpose. In any other position they have a different meaning or become ludicrous.

Original

He gave the book to his father *that was bound in leather.*

[*The final clause should modify* the book, *but it does not appear in the usual fixed position immediately after the expression it modifies. Moreover, the word* father *intervenes, and thus the man rather than the book seems to have the leather binding. The word order can be changed (1, 2), or the sentence revised (3, 4). Usually misplaced modifiers are symptoms of wordiness; the cure is cutting and revising.*]

In order to understand the importance of the magazines, it is necessary to investigate *their* sources of popularity.

[*The sense of the sentence suggests that* their *was probably intended to modify* popularity.]

The youngest girl only thought of new clothes.

[*The context might make the sentence clear, but a reader could be temporarily misled to take* only *as a modifier of* thought—*suggesting that the girl* only *thought* of *clothes, did not, for instance, buy any.*]

My sister only read the newest novels.

Revision

(1) He gave the book *that was bound in leather* to his father.
(2) He gave his father the book *that was bound in leather.*
(3) He gave the *leather-bound* book to his father.
(4) He gave his father the *leather-bound* book.

[*The sentence is revised; modifiers are reduced so that they can be more easily applied. Obviously the last two revisions are preferable to the longer versions above.*]

In order to understand the importance of the magazines, it is necessary to investigate the sources of *their* popularity.

[*The single adjective is placed in its fixed position before the word it modifies.*]

The youngest girl thought only of new clothes.

[*In some colloquial idioms* only *appears before the verb even though it modifies the complement:* He only paid me a quarter. *Here the sentence is clearer with the modifier in its usual position.*]

My sister read only the newest novels.

Original (Cont.)

[*The order may suggest that she did not, for example, study them; she only* read *them.*]

She *nearly* saved half her allowance.

Revision (Cont.)

[*With* only *in its usual position, immediately before what it modifies, the sentence is clearer.*]

She saved *nearly* half her allowance.

23b "Squinting" modifiers   Mod b

Shifting adverbial modifiers can be so misplaced that they apply with equal ease in more than one way. They "squint," seeming to look in more than one direction at once. The difficulty arises when an adverbial modifier follows a word which it would normally modify but also precedes another word which it can modify.

Original

The person who lies frequently gets caught.

[Frequently *can be taken to modify either what precedes it or what follows it; it "squints." The writer may have intended the word to modify the whole sentence. If* frequently *modifies the whole sentence, it should precede it (1). Sentences (2) and (3) are possible if they convey the writer's meaning. The sentence might well be recast (4).*]

She told me *as soon as the dance was over* she would marry me.

Revision

(1) *Frequently,* the person who lies gets caught.
(2) The person who lies gets caught *frequently.*
(3) The person who *frequently* lies gets caught.
(4) Anybody who lies *frequently* is likely to get caught.

(1) *As soon as the dance was over,* she told me she would marry me.
(2) She told me she would marry me *as soon as the dance was over.*

23c "Dangling" introductory modifiers   Mod c; DM

Some sentence modifiers, especially verbal phrases, do not contain subjects in themselves. Even though they modify the sentence as a whole and appear at the beginning or end, they tend to depend on the subject or on the noun nearest them in the main sentence to clarify their meaning. Compare:

> *Eating lunch on the lawn,* the children were amused by the speeding cars.
>
> *Eating lunch on the lawn,* the speeding cars amused the children.

The first is clear, but the second is ludicrous because the subject, *speeding cars,* cannot logically supply the sense of a subject for the verbal *eating*—cannot tell what was eating. Similarly, the modifier that opens the following sentence dangles:

> *Sitting on the bridge,* the huge steeple looked like part of a toy village.

The subject, *steeple,* seems to govern *sitting,* but the huge steeple could scarcely be sitting on the bridge. The sentence can be revised by using as a subject whatever was sitting on the bridge (*Sitting on the bridge,* we *could see . . .*). The sentence can be revised, also, by providing the modifier with a subject of its own (*As* we *sat on the bridge, the huge steeple . . .*), or by changing the modifier in some other way so that it does not rely on anything in the main clause (*From our position on the bridge, the huge steeple . . .*).

Since introductory modifiers readily refer to the subject, confusion may result if the subject is postponed or the sentence is passive (see 19). Notice the following:

> *Finding something important,* there are complete details to be recorded by the secretary.
>
> *When finding something important,* complete details were recorded by the secretary.

The modifiers make sense only if the reader can tell who was doing the finding. Usually the name of the actor used as the subject of the sentence, in the position just after the modifier, supplies this information. In sentences like the above, therefore, in which the actor is not the subject, the modifiers dangle. Compare:

> *When the staff found something important,* the secretary recorded complete details.
>
> *When they found something important,* the staff dictated complete details to the secretary.

Such sentences can often be best revised by naming the actor in the normal position in the actor-action pattern. In English the feeling for this pattern is sufficiently strong so that it will work even though the subject is only implied, as in a command:

To avoid a cold, wear a piece of red flannel around your neck.

If normal order is not followed, the modifier dangles:

To avoid a cold, a piece of red flannel may be worn around the neck.

The initial modifying phrase is so common in the pattern of the English sentence that an introductory modifier without its own subject may still seem relatively clear in itself and be useful because it is economical.

Talking with students, the same questions arise time after time.

Since *talking* is so nearly complete in its meaning—like *fishing* or *swimming*—that it relies but little on the subject, *question,* the sentence is reasonably clear. Or consider:

When lunching at the Union, conversation must be sacrificed for speed.

The conversation is not lunching, of course, but the sentence is not confusing, and the use of an impersonal *one* or *a person* would not improve it.

Original	Revision
Having rotted in the damp cellar, my brother was unable to sell any of the potatoes.	(1) Having rotted in the damp cellar, my brothers' potatoes were unfit for sale.
[*The modifier applies automatically to the main action as it is expressed, to the subject-verb of the sentence. The result is the absurdly unsanitary state of the decomposing brother. The modifier should apply to an actor-action pattern of which* potatoes *is the subject, but* potatoes *is not in the subject position.*]	[*Word order is changed so that the subject referred to by the modifier becomes the subject of the sentence.*] (2) Since the potatoes had rotted in the damp cellar, my brother was unable to sell any of them. [*The modifier is changed to a clause, which can include its subject,* potatoes.]
Convinced that people of the state were not well-informed about the university, pamphlets were printed describing the postwar educational program.	(1) Convinced that people of the state were not well-informed about the university, the committee published pamphlets describing the postwar educational program.
[*The sentence is not obviously absurd, but it is unclear because the reader needs to know who was con-*	(2) Since the committee was convinced that people of the state were not well-informed about the uni-

Original (Cont.)

vinced, and pamphlets *does not tell him accurately. A subject to complete* convinced *may be supplied in the sentence (1) or in the modifier (2).*]

On entering the room, only the huge portrait seemed visible.
[*Probably the sentence would not confuse a reader, but the possible absurdity of a walking portrait makes revision preferable.*]

At the age of ten, cowboys and Indians were my main interest.
[*The modifier concerns the writer, not the age of a group of youthful cowboys and Indians; the sentence is imprecise.*]

Brought up among many advantages, it was only natural that Florence should show distaste for a life of poverty.
[*The reader can see easily the application of the modifier to Florence, but he could understand more easily if* Florence *were the subject of the main clause, not a dependent clause. The real problem is the unnecessary postponement of the logical subject,* Florence.]

Bemused by the smoke, the fireman was mistaken by my uncle for a pillar in the hallway.
[*Confusion is especially easy when the sentence concerns more than one person.*]

Revision (Cont.)

versity, it published pamphlets describing the postwar educational program.

(1) On entering the room, we could see only the huge portrait.
(2) When we entered the room, only the huge portrait seemed visible.

(1) When I was ten, cowboys and Indians were my main interest.
(2) At the age of ten, I was interested mainly in cowboys and Indians.

(1) Brought up among many advantages, Florence naturally showed distaste for a life of poverty.
[*With* Florence *as subject of the main clause, modification is clearer, and the sentence is more concise.*]
(2) Since Florence had been brought up among many advantages, it was only natural that she should show distaste for a life of poverty.

(1) *Bemused by the smoke,* my uncle mistook the fireman for a pillar in the hallway.
(2) To my uncle, who was bemused by the smoke, the fireman looked like a pillar in the hallway.

23d "Dangling" concluding verbal phrases   Mod d; DM

Concluding verbal phrases, like introductory ones, often depend on the main sentence, usually on the name of the actor, to complete their meaning. If the word to be understood as a subject for the verbal is not expressed or is obscured in a passive construction, the modifier dangles.

Original

The grain fields had been burned by the invaders, *thus causing suffering in the valley.*

[*The sentence seems to say that the fields caused the suffering; the intention obviously was to say that the burning of the fields, not expressed in the sentence, caused it.* Invaders *cannot complete the meaning of* causing *because it is put into a dependent position in the passive sentence. The sentence is logically unbalanced; the main idea is subordinated in the modifier.*]

Revision

(1) Because the invaders had burned the grain fields, there was suffering in the valley.

[*The dangling expression, since it is really the most important idea of the sentence, is made the main clause.*]

(2) By burning the grain fields, the invaders caused suffering in the valley.

(3) The invaders burned the grain fields and caused suffering in the valley.

(4) The inhabitants of the valley suffered because the invaders had burned the grain fields.

I worked overtime all summer, *thereby giving me enough money to finish school.*

[*The modifier has nothing to clarify its meaning.*]

(1) By working overtime all summer, I earned enough money to finish school.

(2) After working overtime all summer, I had enough money to finish school.

He hit a home run in the eighth inning, *resulting in the winning of the game.*

[*The modifier has nothing to modify, but the confusion arises from obscuring the predication* He won the game *in the modifier.*]

(1) His home run in the eighth inning won the game.

(2) By hitting a home run in the eighth inning, he won the game.

(3) He won the game with a home run in the eighth inning.

23e "Split" constructions   **Mod e**

Normally modifiers should not be allowed to split constructions by separating closely related sentence elements, particularly if the separating element is long or complicated, although sometimes separation is unavoidable or is desirable for special effects. Subject and verb, parts of the verb, verb and complement, parts of a verbal, or elements of a series should be separated only with caution.

We may, if the weather clears, go to Birmingham.

Separation of parts of the verb *may go* is clumsy and throws the modifier into an unusual position where it has unwarranted emphasis.

Usually the subject opens a sentence and the verb follows it; subject and verb should not be separated without good reason.

> The *driver,* confused by the snow balling upon his windshield wiper and the tires skidding on the ice and his wife yanking at his elbow, *yelled.*

Similarly, verb and complement or parts of the complement should not be needlessly separated.

> I *asked* the *conductor,* because at home we have breakfast in bed and I always get a headache unless I have some coffee before I do another thing, *if there was a diner on the train.*

Such separation may be useful for emphasis.

> The more obnoxious of my cousins, after insulting all the guests and breaking three cocktail glasses, finally made me lose my temper— he tried to borrow ten dollars.

The separation of subject and verb is not troublesome, partly because the modifier is brief and unified enough so that we do not lose sight of the sentence pattern, and partly because the sentence gains rhetorically by building up to a climax. Like all sentences which deviate from usual order, however, this type of sentence should be attempted only with caution.

Original	*Revision*
I, every Saturday afternoon I got the chance, would take the subway to Coney Island. [*Subject and verb are needlessly separated.*]	Every Saturday afternoon I got the chance, I would take the subway to Coney Island.
He expected that they would *in the shortest possible time* agree to our terms. [*The long modifier obscures the main word order pattern of the sentence by separating words that logically belong together.*]	He expected that they would agree to our terms *in the shortest possible time.* [*The modifier should be placed where it does not interrupt the main sentence movement.*]
When the baskets had all been opened, she called us to dinner, *as*	*When the baskets had all been opened and the food had been*

Original (Cont.)

soon as the food had been arranged on the rough table.

[*Two clauses modify the main sentence, but they are awkwardly and uneconomically placed at the beginning and the end.*]

Revision (Cont.)

arranged on the rough table, she called us to dinner.

[*The parallel modifiers of the expression should be combined, for the sake of both clarity and economy.*]

Similarly, separation of *to* from the remainder of an infinitive usually not only weakens the sentence by separating closely connected elements but also by falsifying emphasis.

He promised to *firmly* hold our position.

The meaning is clear, but the sentence is weak because the infinitive construction is split—perhaps because the writer sensed that he would have similar difficulty if he placed the modifier immediately after the infinitive. The solution, of course, is to put it after the complement where it can modify the whole construction.

He promised to hold our position *firmly*.

On the other hand, a split infinitive sometimes becomes almost a necessity. The modifier cannot be placed in its usual positions without destroying meaning. The officers of the bank that exposed the following notice were using an infinitive which was justifiably split:

Depositors are asked to *kindly* fill out their own slips.

Kindly, if moved anywhere else, either changes the meaning or "squints." Similarly a desire to put the emphasis of unusual word order on a modifier sometimes justifies a split infinitive.

I told him to *please* get out of the way.

Herman Melville in *The Confidence Man* prefers to split an infinitive for the sake of clarity in modification.

The sick man seemed to have *just* made an impatiently querulous answer.

Placed either before *to* or after *made* the modifier *just* would change meaning, carrying something of the sense of *only*. Usually, however, the split infinitive should be regarded as a deviation from normal word order, warranted only by special circumstances.

Original	Revision
I expected to *quickly* remove my incomplete, and to *never again for any cause whatever* get another. [*Revision of the first split infinitive is advisable and revision of the second is imperative.*]	I expect to remove my incomplete *quickly* and *never again* to get another *for any cause whatever.* [*Revision of both split infinitives tightens the sentence structure and promotes ready comprehension.*]
He promised to *carefully and painlessly* extract my tooth.	He promised to extract my tooth *carefully and painlessly.*

23f Position of modifier-connectives   Mod f

Modifying words which serve also as connectives [*however, therefore, moreover, consequently,* sometimes called *conjunctive adverbs* (see 33-5)], appear at the beginning of a clause when they modify its entire action; placed within a clause they throw stress on the words they follow. Preceding clauses or sentences usually indicate which sentence parts need emphasis and therefore indicate where conjunctive modifiers should be placed.

> John was afraid to look at me; *however* he was eager to look at Alice.
> John was afraid to look at me; he was eager, *however,* to look at Alice.

The position of *however* in the second sentence stresses *eager* and accents the contrast between *eager* and *afraid.* The following sentences illustrate a related problem in emphasis:

> I had no desire to listen to another hour of boasting; *therefore* I determined to try to slip out of the lecture.
> I had no desire to listen to another hour of boasting; I determined, *therefore,* to try to slip out of the lecture.

Even though *determined* requires no emphasis, the second sentence would usually be preferable because it avoids special stress on an unimportant modifier like *therefore.* In the first version, *therefore* gains undue accent at the beginning of the second clause.

Original	Revision
He ate baseball, slept baseball, and dreamed baseball; and when he thought he thought baseball.	He ate baseball, slept baseball, and dreamed baseball; and when he thought he thought baseball.

Original (*Cont.*)	*Revision* (*Cont.*)
Therefore, a mere football game could hardly make him blink an eye.	A mere football game, *therefore,* could hardly make him blink an eye.
[*Therefore* *has stress at the beginning of the sentence, which it probably does not deserve, and in its present position, it fails to emphasize a significant contrast.*]	[*Placed as it is here,* therefore *emphasizes* football game *and the contrast between football and baseball which is crucial for the sentence.*]

23g *Sentence modifiers in fixed positions*   Mod g

Since the same words or groups of words can be used as either fixed or movable modifiers, the reader must depend on word order to see how they apply and what they mean. He interprets according to his expectations of word order patterns. From the sentence

The man *in the boat* was a tyrant

the reader understands automatically that *in the boat,* in a fixed position, is a modifier specifically locating the man. If the phrase is moved, the reader interprets it as a movable modifier which applies to the entire sentence, and he understands the sentence differently.

In the boat, the man was a tyrant.

The first sentence makes clear that the man was a tyrant, presumably all the time. The second preserves a little respect for him, limiting his tyranny to the time during which he was in the boat. So long as the sentence modifier is kept out of a fixed position, it may be moved, with changes in emphasis but no alteration of essential meaning.

In the boat, the man was a tyrant.
The man was a tyrant *in the boat.*

The writer must be sure that modifiers intended to apply generally are not put where they apply to a specific word. Compare:

At first he thought that the detective would believe him.
He thought that the detective would believe him *at first.*

In the first version, the modifier does not attach clearly to any particular expression and applies to the entire action. In the second, *at first* becomes part of the dependent clause rather than the entire sentence and modifies its action; the meaning of the sentence changes.

Negative sentences especially cause trouble. Compare:

[285

> Nobody was ever punished *because the camp was run so carelessly.*
> *Because the camp was run so carelessly,* nobody was ever punished.

With the clause at the end, the sentence is ambiguous; it can mean either what the second version says or that the careless management of the camp brought no punishment.

Original	Revision
He fired three shots at the lion *with a smile of triumph on his face.*	*With a smile of triumph on his face,* he fired three shots at the lion.
[*Often a sentence modifier may appear at either the beginning or the end, but at the end it may fall into a fixed position. In this sentence the reader has trouble locating the smile.*]	[*The modifier is moved so that it applies to the action of the sentence and does not seem to be a fixed modifier describing the lion.*]
I didn't know whether the planes would find me *on the first day.*	*On the first day,* I didn't know whether the planes would find me.
[*The writer probably intended the modifier to apply to the main action; in this position it becomes part of the dependent clause and seems to modify find.*]	[*The modifier is shifted from the end of the sentence so that it clearly modifies the entire predication.*]
Closed accounts are not to be deleted in order that numerical sequence will be preserved.	So that numerical sequence will be preserved, all closed accounts are to be retained.
[*The reader cannot be sure whether deleting or keeping the closed accounts will preserve numerical sequence.*]	[*Changing the negative sentence to positive clarifies at least one possible meaning.*]
Charles was not killed because he was a king.	(1) Because he was a king, Charles was not killed.
[*At the end of the sentence, the clause can be taken to modify either the whole sentence or the negative verb; the reader is not sure whether Charles died or not. He may have been killed, but for reasons other than his position.*]	[*If it is intended to modify the whole sentence, the clause is clearer at the beginning.*] (2) Charles was spared because he was a king. [*The clause can be made to modify the verb clearly.*]

286]

EXERCISE 23

A. Point out each modifier in the following paragraph and then describe
what and how it modifies:

> To every one of us the world was once as fresh and new as to
> Adam. And then, long before we were susceptible of any other mode
> of instruction, Nature took us in hand, and every minute of waking
> life brought its educational influence, shaping our actions into rough
> accordance with Nature's laws, so that we might not be ended un-
> timely by too gross disobedience. Nor shall I speak of this process
> of education as past, for any one, be he as old as he may. For every
> man the world is as fresh as it was at the first day, and as full of
> untold novelties for him who has the eyes to see them. And Nature
> is still continuing her patient education of us in that great university,
> the universe, of which we are all members—Nature having no Test-
> Acts.
>
> —THOMAS HENRY HUXLEY, *A Liberal Education*

B. Below are groups of slightly varied sentences. Comment on distinctions in emphasis or meaning you can discern among the versions in
each group.

1. a. The past, at least, is secure.
   b. The past is secure, at least.
   c. At least the past is secure.

2. a. The Duke still lives that Henry shall depose.
   b. The Duke still lives that shall depose Henry.
   c. The Duke that Henry shall depose still lives.

3. a. Hope springs eternal in the human breast.
   b. Hope springs eternally in the human breast.
   c. Eternal hope springs in the human breast.

4. a. The law smiles in your face while it picks your pocket.
   b. While it picks your pocket, the law smiles in your face.
   c. While the law smiles in your face, it picks your pocket.

5. a. In the long run, we are sure to lose.
   b. We are sure to lose in the long run.
   c. We are, in the long run, sure to lose.

6. a. This was a better way of making a living.
   b. This was a way of making a better living.
   c. This was a way of making a living better.

7. a. Just before noon we decided that the program was too long.
   b. We decided that the program was too long just before noon.
   c. We decided that the program just before noon was too long.

8. a. Although he hated everyone there, John stayed at the party.
   b. John stayed at the party, although he hated everyone there.

9. a. With the field glasses the girl found the dog.
   b. The girl with the field glasses found the dog.
   c. The girl found the dog with the field glasses.
10. a. Suddenly the clown jumped up and slapped the acrobat.
    b. The clown suddenly jumped up and slapped the acrobat.
    c. The clown jumped up and suddenly slapped the acrobat.

C. Revise each of the sentences below, moving the italicized modifier to a different position. Then explain any changes in meaning or emphasis effected by the shift in word order.

1. I decided I would get up *when my roommate threw a glass of water on me.*
2. The room looked filthier than any stable I had ever seen *by daylight.*
3. He decided that working was a way of making a *better* living.
4. He decided to fight *because he disliked the color of Bill's hair.*
5. He guessed that *only* about half the new troops were fully equipped.
6. The boy *climbing the rope* threw his knife at the old sailor.
7. *Wishing he had never heard of sloe gin,* he opened the door and saw his uncle.
8. *For two days* I wondered what my brother had been doing.
9. Tennyson looked like a lion *with his mane parted in the middle.*
10. I am certain the Smiths can come; I am not sure, *however,* about the Joneses.
11. The girl *with the broken arm* grabbed the new doll.
12. The children promised to *carefully* chew every bite.
13. She *nearly* threw away all her diamonds.
14. *In complete confusion* the speaker finally found his audience.
15. *Happily* the old man watched the children singing.
16. One girl *I know* is in love with you.
17. The hill is not really pretty *because of the big rocks on it.*
18. We found the girl *breaking into the back room.*
19. He ordered them *at once* to dump the ammunition into the sea.
20. *In a few minutes* the new bridge was built.

D. The sentences below probably do not say what their writer intended. Revise them, paying particular attention to modification.

1. The nurse brought in Robert, Jr., to see his father in his bassinet.
2. I do not believe that the pterodactyl was able to catch fish for several reasons.
3. The truck's bumper was bent and twisted when it struck several logs enroute to San Francisco.

4. The player who breaks the rules in the end hurts his own team.

5. No one is allowed to dump anything along this road except a city official.

6. *The Secret Life of Walter Mitty* by James Thurber is the typical story of a daydreamer.

7. A person in the assembly line only worked eight hours a day five days a week except for foremen.

8. After two days in an open boat we began to get frightened with only a little water and a few biscuits.

9. He knew that the boat had been sunk because he had seen the battle.

10. My home is a good place for a boy who likes horses to grow up in the United States.

11. The old man was not arrested because he had befriended the natives.

12. Explain and demonstrate the various positions of the foot on which words of command are given, first in slow time, then in quick time.

13. Clarity was their basis of effectiveness.

14. Joan decided that she would not marry him at the last possible moment.

15. They should not move the old road so that the trees will shade travelers.

E. Revise the following sentences so that modification is clear and logical:

1. Being very dark, we were unable to find our way about the cellar.

2. Knowing that the whole future of the club was at stake, the investigation found us reluctant to say a word.

3. At the age of nine my father's interest in languages was already developing.

4. Every promise had been broken by the new governor, causing widespread dissatisfaction.

5. On approaching the village the gold spire was the only evidence of civilization that we could see.

6. Although only pretending to shoot, the gun suddenly went off with a loud roar.

7. Having had no sleep for two nights, the dirty haystack actually seemed inviting.

8. Being afraid of his own shadow, we were not much disturbed by his threats.

9. Trying to climb in the dormitory window at night, the Dean of Women caught her and recommended her suspension.

    10. When hardly more than a baby, a gang of older boys threw me into the creek and told me to sink or swim.

F. Revise the following sentences by reducing italicized expressions to shorter modifiers, by making clauses into phrases or phrases into shorter phrases or single words:

    1. The will, *which can never be conquered,* sustains the rebel.

    2. He was not merely a chip *which had been cut from the old block,* but the old block itself.

    3. *When twelve o'clock had rolled around,* I was ready to eat.

    4. *When I was a child,* I learned to respect nature.

    5. *Since the potatoes had rotted in the damp cellar,* my brother was unable to sell any of them.

    6. They looked at the cow *whose horn had been crumpled.*

    7. *When breakfast had been finished,* the boys got out their fishing tackle.

    8. The children's voices rang out *in loud tones.*

    9. She was *the kind of girl that is a blonde type.*

    10. She specializes in answers *that are in the negative.*

    11. *Smoking when a person is in bed* is prohibited.

    12. He avoided tall girls *because of the fact that he was only five feet two in height.*

    13. He did not believe *in the factor of hereditary influences.*

    14. Hybrids are formed by crossing two species *which are pure before they are crossed.*

    15. I confess *in a spirit of freedom and willingness.*

G. Combine the sentences below with the *introductory modifier* suggested for each, leaving the modifiers as they are but revising the sentences so that the combinations are clear and logical. Notice that the sentences as they now stand have passive verbs. Most of the sentences join logically with the modifiers if you make the verb active.

    1. After walking for an hour. The old cabin was finally seen by our leader.

    2. After watching for an hour. The rare birds were finally seen by us.

    3. Unable to get materials. A new product was put on the market by my father's company.

    4. Playing the last ten minutes with a broken finger. The game was finally won by Jack with a free throw.

    5. While flying a kite in a storm. Information about electricity was discovered by Benjamin Franklin.

    6. While raking the yard. Her left knee was twisted.

7. To prove that there were no hard feelings. A dinner was given for us by the winning team.
8. Working without rest for two afternoons. The cabin was finally cleaned by the Boy Scouts.
9. While trailing his line carelessly beside the boat. A five-pound bass was caught by Jim.
10. Having turned off the light. Ominous shadows were seen by Marie lurking in every corner.

24. REFERENCE

[For Guide to Revision, see page 295]

Whenever words are ordered so that they refer to one another grammatically, their meanings and forms must be compatible with the grammatical relationship.

The patterns of co-ordination and subordination which have been discussed in this section almost all concern the ways in which one word refers to another as a sentence proceeds. The patterns are often possible only because by meaning and position words in English, especially pronouns, can be used to repeat or summarize or develop other words.

24-1 Meaning and word reference

Whenever one word repeats or develops the idea of another, relationships of meanings are important. Consider the following sentence:

> He annoyed many people by his smugness and intolerance, attitudes which developed from his early training.

Attitudes can be said to refer to *smugness* and *intolerance*. It restates them in order to develop the sentence. To observe the importance of selecting words so that such reference is clear, consider the following:

> He annoyed many people by being smug and intolerant, attitudes which developed from his early training.

No attitudes have been described in this sentence, and as a result the word reference is faulty. Or consider another sentence:

> People in America believe that everyone should share the good and the bad, but this principle does not apply here.

The sentence turns on the reference of the word *principle* to the clause *that everyone should share the good and the bad*. The sentence is clear. But compare the sentence from a student theme from which the above was revised:

Our country's democracy believes in everyone's sharing the good and the bad, and in this case the assumption would not hold true.

The words mean something as individual words, but they do not combine to make a clear sentence. Part of the trouble is that subjects, verbs, and complements do not work sensibly together, but further trouble arises from the key word, *assumption,* which does not logically refer to any previous idea—no assumption has been made.

24-2 Signals of reference; pronouns

Some words, most of them pronouns, by their very nature are always reference words (see 28); that is, they restate an antecedent, usually a noun expression. Consider:

The people do not want John to break *their* idols, as *he* has threatened.

The italicized words are reference words, substitutes which have their meaning only in relation to their antecedents. *Their* and *he* are pronouns referring to their antecedents, *people* and *John.* The use of the reference words avoids awkward repetitions. Compare:

The people do not want John to break the people's idols, as John has threatened.

Since a pronoun carries little meaning in itself, the reader must be able to understand its antecedent immediately. To keep the relationship between a pronoun and its antecedent clear, a writer in English must be concerned with both word order and forms.

In languages which depend mainly upon form changes to indicate grammatical relationships, an ending indicates the connection between a reference word and its antecedent. Because modern English grammar relies on word order, clear reference in English follows mainly from clear order. The situation is complicated because the pronoun retains considerable remnants of earlier form changes. Thus both form and position are important in establishing clear reference between pronouns and their antecedents.

In complicated prose, of course, there are many patterns of reference, but clear reference can be insured by observance of one rule:

Be sure that every reference word has a clear antecedent, and be sure that the form of the reference word and the order of words in the sentence make the reference immediately certain.

To select the proper forms to clarify reference, the writer need only

[293

be sure that his pronouns agree in person, number, and gender with their antecedents. Often choice of proper forms, along with attention to meaning, is enough to establish reference. The following sentence, for example, is clear:

John showed *his* sister *his* copy of the book which *she* had written.

Since *she* is feminine in form it must refer to sister; the authorship is clear.

Notice, however, the difference if John had met his brother.

John showed *his* brother *his* copy of the book which *he* had written.

Because of meaning and order we could probably guess whose copy is involved, but we cannot even guess who wrote the book. Form distinctions are not enough to establish reference.

24-3 Patterns of reference

Often we must rely on word order to establish reference relationships, and the patterns of reference in English sentences are variable enough to make vague and inaccurate references a hazard for the writer. There is no simple, universally applicable rule, but in general the following principles apply:

(1) The subject, as the most important noun or pronoun in a clause, and especially the subject of a main clause, tends to become an antecedent of a personal pronoun. Consider:

Shakespeare was two months younger than Marlowe; a record of his baptism April 26, 1564, has been preserved.

Even though *his* could apply sensibly to either *Shakespeare* or *Marlowe,* and even though *Marlowe* is much nearer *his* in the sentence, the reader knows that *Shakespeare,* the subject, is the antecedent of *his.*

(2) If the subject is obviously impossible as the antecedent of a personal pronoun, a complement tends to be the next choice.

She took the rooster out of the sack and put a rock in *its* place.

Its cannot refer to the subject, but it does refer to *rooster.* Notice that while the meaning helps clarify reference, the order is essential here. We could change the fate of the rooster by transposing *rock* and *rooster.*

(3) The less important the position of the word in a sentence, the

greater is the difficulty of making the word an antecedent. Modifiers and other words in subordinate uses, however, often work as antecedents of pronouns used in parallel ways.

> I visited the library and spent an hour looking through the book. I found nothing in *it.*

It refers to *book;* pronoun and antecedent have parallel uses and positions.

(4) A noun expression immediately before a relative pronoun tends to be its antecedent. Notice what happens when a relative pronoun is used in the sentence above.

> Shakespeare was two months younger than Marlowe, a record of whose baptism in February, 1564, has been preserved.

The relative pronoun *whose* refers to *Marlowe,* and the date has to be changed to keep the sentence accurate.

24 Reference   **Ref**

GUIDE TO REVISION:

Select and arrange all reference words so that they refer clearly and logically to antecedents.

The head of a department in a university recently received a letter beginning, "I should like to apply for the position of instructorship in your department." The applicant was not using words so that their form and meaning fitted the modification pattern of the sentence. *Instructorship* names the position; the writer of the letter could not logically use *of* and connect *instructorship* as a modifier of *position.* He could apply for an instructorship or for the position of instructor. The applicant did not get the job.

24a Reference to general ideas   **Ref a**

Pronouns like *this, that, it,* and *which* are sometimes used, especially colloquially, to refer to a general idea.

> I had thrown a loaf of bread at the Marquis, which hit him on the cheek, and *that* made me feel good.
>
> —ROBERT GRAVES

[295

No particular noun can be labeled as the antecedent of *that,* but the meaning is clear, with *that* referring to the entire action which is described in the first part of the sentence. This use of the pronoun, however is subject to considerable abuse, especially in student writing. Too often the construction disguises sloppy thinking; the pronoun is used to stand for an idea which the writer assumes the reader understands, but which he has not made clear to the reader and may not have made clear to himself. Too often, also, the device is a symptom of failure to subordinate (see 22a). Before using a pronoun to refer to a general idea, the writer must be sure that the reference is not vague and that the sentence would not be clearer with a different construction.

Original	*Revision*
Some critics have accused Chaucer of Frenchifying English, which has been disproved. [Which *has no certain antecedent.*]	Some critics have accused Chaucer of Frenchifying English, but the accusation has been disproved. [*Now no antecedent is necessary.*]
The tone must be soft and sweet, and metal mouthpieces can not do this.	The tone must be soft and sweet, and metal mouthpieces can not produce this effect.
The constant reminder of Norway and home made Beret become nostalgic, which was one of the causes of her insanity. [*The antecedent is only implied; the sentence would be clearer with an expressed antecedent.*]	(1) The constant reminder of Norway and home made Beret become nostalgic, and her nostalgia provided one cause of her insanity. (2) The constant reminder of Norway and home caused Beret's nostalgia, which promoted her insanity.

Sentences sometimes begin with a dependent clause followed by a pronoun referring to a noun in the clause.

If this article makes a few people take democracy seriously, it will have served its purpose.

It is a clear restatement of *article.* This construction has perhaps led to the colloquial popularity of a similar pattern in which the pronoun lacks an antecedent and in which the vague reference handicaps the reader. Compare:

If this article makes a few people take democracy seriously, it means that some progress has been made.

It has no clear antecedent. The sentence is weak because the main clause has no clear subject.

Original	*Revision*
If they are taken into the army, it means they will not graduate.	If they are taken into the army, they will not be graduated.
[*It lacks an antecedent. Even the loose idea which the reader might supply for* it, *their induction into the army, does not make a good subject for the main clause.*]	[*Usually, as here, vague reference is a symptom of roundabout writing. The vague pronoun usurps the position of the real subject of the sentence,* they.]
If there were some way to get all people to use the same dialect, it would be much simpler.	If there were some way to get all people to use the same dialect, communication would be much simpler.
[*Not even a vague idea can be supplied as an antecedent for* it.]	[*Revision supplies a subject to replace the vague* it.]

24b Reference and position of antecedents   Ref b

Unless pronoun forms clarify reference, a pronoun usually refers clearly only to a noun expression in an important position in the sentence or in a use parallel to its own. If the word order does not clarify the reference, the sentence must be revised or an antecedent provided.

Original	*Revision*
I should like to find out how authors were affected during the depression and how it changed their styles of writing.	(1) I should like to find out how authors were affected during the depression years, and how the depression changed their styles of writing.
[*Presumably* depression *is the antecedent of* it, *but this relationship is not at once apparent, because* depression *is not the subject, does not occur immediately before the pronoun, and is not in parallel structure.*]	(2) I should like to find out how the depression affected authors, and how it changed their styles of writing.
	[*In (1),* it *has been removed in favor of a noun; in (2) it* refers to depression *because that word has become the subject of a preceding clause.*]

Original (Cont.)

The evaluation of art presents a very difficult problem, since the effect it produces is not the same on various people.

[It *should have* art *as its antecedent, but cannot readily do so, since the reader has the subject,* evaluation, *in mind.*]

In Hemingway's book *For Whom the Bell Tolls,* he tells about an American teacher in the Spanish Civil War.

[*Reference is more difficult than it need be because the pronoun* he *refers to a noun in a subordinate and unparallel position.*]

Novelists gave biographers help. They set the example by showing them the value of records of life.

[*Since* novelists *is the subject and* biographers *comes shortly before* they, *the reader must hesitate before he is sure who is helping whom.*]

American women are thought more of than just being slaves and are treated as such.

[*Since* such *has no certain antecedent, we do not know whether American women are treated like slaves or not.*]

Revision (Cont.)

Artistic evaluation is very difficult, since art produces various effects on various people.

[*The sentence has been recast to avoid the awkward reference.*]

In his book *For Whom the Bell Tolls,* Hemingway tells about an American teacher in the Spanish Civil War.

[*With the pronoun in the dependent position and the noun,* Hemingway, *as the subject, the reference of* his *is clear.*]

Novelists helped biographers by showing them the value of records of life.

[*They has been removed, and* them *is sufficiently near to being parallel with* biographers *so that the relationship is clear.*]

American women are not thought of as slaves and are not treated like slaves.

24c General pronoun reference   Ref c

Colloquially *they* and *it* are used as indefinite pronouns to refer generally to "people" or "society." Except in reference to weather (*It is cold today*), this indefinite use is often indirect and vague and is inappropriate in serious writing.

Original

In the paper it says the weather will change.

Revision

The paper says that the weather will change.

Original (Cont.)
[*Nobody knows who it is.*]

Revision (Cont.)
[*Omission of the vague pronoun often is the solution.*]

When we went to the house, *they* told us John had left.

At the house we learned that John had left.

While she was in the hospital her hair turned white, and now *they* say she dyes it.

While she was in the hospital, her hair turned white, and now, apparently, she dyes it.

24d Reference with impersonal constructions   Ref d

Impersonal constructions become ambiguous when the sign of the impersonal construction can be mistaken for a personal pronoun. *It,* used for either purpose, readily becomes ambiguous.

Original

My Chevrolet has a Mercury motor which makes it hard to shift gears.
[*The second* it *should be impersonal, but it appears at first to be a personal pronoun with* Chevrolet *as its antecedent.*]

Revision

(1) My Chevrolet has a Mercury motor; with this combination I have trouble shifting gears.
(2) I have trouble shifting gears because my Chevrolet has a Mercury motor.

The building of the Mississippi River jetties should be a good research topic, but it is going to be hard to find the technical details of construction.
[*It* is impersonal, but seems to refer to building.]

The building of the Mississippi River jetties should be a good research topic, but I expect trouble when I try to find the technical details of construction.

24e Word reference in restatements   Ref e

Word reference may become inaccurate when specific terms are restated by a general word or when general terms are broken into more specific parts. The writer, as he moves forward in the sentence, becomes careless of the exact terms he has used and refers to them by a word that applies only inexactly. Consider, for instance, the following sentence from a student theme.

I don't know just what I was expecting, but the faces were friendly, self-confident, individual, and interesting, not the featureless automatons I had read about.

By the time the writer wants to refer to the faces of the early part of the sentence, he has forgotten the words he used; and thinking of the people who have the faces, he refers to *faces* as *automatons*. Whenever ideas are repeated or referred to more than once in the progress of a sentence, the writer must be sure that he uses terms which can logically work together.

Original	*Revision*
The field of interior decorating holds vast opportunities for the women who want to apply themselves to the task.	(1) Interior decorating holds vast opportunities for women who want to apply themselves.
[*A* field *is not a* task, *and the repetition helps make the sentence ambiguous.*]	(2) Women who become interior decorators have vast opportunities.
	[*Here, as often, confusion can best be cured by deletion.*]
A good teacher must be patient, and I do not fall into that category.	A good teacher must be patient, but I am not.
[Category *cannot logically refer to* patient *or to anything else in the sentence.*]	
Of all the regulations for women, I hated most being in by nine o'clock.	I hated most the regulation for women requiring us to be in by nine o'clock.
[Being in *is not a regulation; the general term does not logically include the specific one.*]	[*The restatement is avoided.*]
One of the most important things in any girl's life, including myself, is her first date.	(1) One of the most important things in any girl's life, including my own, is her first date.
[Life *cannot logically be repeated as* myself.]	(2) One of the most important things to any girl—and I am no exception—is her first date.
Like other professions, the clergy eked out their income by teaching.	Like members of other professions, clergymen eked out their income by teaching.

24f Reference with modifiers   Ref f

Modifiers and the words to which they refer must be compatible in meaning. When they are not, the modifier should be changed or a more appropriate word supplied for it to modify.

Original

   He started out as a senior economist, very difficult for a person without much experience.
[*The writer probably did not mean to say that the economist was difficult, but that his work was.*]

Revision

   He started out as a senior economist, doing work very difficult for a person without much experience.
[Work *provides a plausible idea for* difficult *to modify.*]

   When she applied the next time, she was appointed head dietician, vacated only the day before by a sudden resignation.
[Vacated *requires something to modify;* dietician *will not serve. The position, not the dietician, was vacated.*]

(1) When she applied the next time, she was appointed to the position of head dietician, vacated only the day before by a sudden resignation.
(2) When she applied the next time, she was appointed head dietician, filling a position vacated only the day before by a sudden resignation.

   Appositive modifiers must refer logically to the terms they restate. For words in apposition, see 32-3.

Original

   Bowling Green, the name of my home town, is in the southern part of Kentucky.
[Bowling Green *can be either a name or a town, but the town, not the name, is in Kentucky.*]

Revision

   Bowling Green, my home town, is in the southern part of Kentucky.

   Football teaches students to accept success with modesty, a valuable lesson to be used later in life.
[*The sentence contains nothing which* lesson *can logically restate.*]

   Football teaches students to accept success with modesty, a valuable quality to be used later in life.
[*To accept success with modesty can be considered a quality.*]

   Some modifiers resemble pronouns in that they refer to an antecedent at the same time that they serve their own grammatical function. Words of this sort include *the* and *such, there, here, other, another, this, that, these,* and *those,* when they are used as modifiers.

Original

   He meant no harm by his pranks, but this result did not always come

Revision

   He meant no harm; his pranks were only mischievous, but they

[301

Original (*Cont.*)

of his mischief. Such result came from one affair.

[*Both* this *and* such *require antecedents but do not have them.*]

China's unceasing wars are just one symptom of her decadence. In such a country corruption is common.

I feel that harbor dredging will be a very interesting subject. Since I have lived there for fifteen years, I am well acquainted with it.

[There *has no antecedent.*]

We saw a little adobe house and rode over. The man and his wife greeted us pleasantly.

[The *suggests a man who has been mentioned before, but presumably he has not.*]

Revision (*Cont.*)

sometimes ended unhappily.

[*The sentence has been recast and the awkward construction removed by simplified word order.*]

China's unceasing wars are only one symptom of her decadence, and in a decadent country corruption is common.

I feel that harbor dredging will be a very interesting subject, and I am well acquainted with it, since for fifteen years I have lived where I could observe operations.

We saw a little adobe house and rode over. A man and his wife greeted us pleasantly.

[A *indicates that the man is being introduced; the false reference disappears.*]

24g Shifts of meaning

Faulty reference sometimes involves a careless shift in the meaning or the point of view of the writer, which is revealed in illogical word relationships.

Original

Unless a writer is careful, he will carry a man or woman from a high moral character to an immoral person.

[A character, *in this sense, can not become a person.*]

One of the greatest changes in my life came when I transferred from the familiar world of high school to the unknown life of college.

[*The writer moving from* world *to* life *probably goes further than he intended.*]

Revision

Unless a writer is careful, he may change a moral character into an immoral one.

One of the greatest changes in my life came when I transferred from the familiar world of high school to the unknown world of college.

A singular word cannot clearly refer to a plural word or idea.

Original

 Hundreds of soldiers threw their gun into the river and ran.

 Women are treated as an equal, however, when they work in the fields.
[*Several women can scarcely be treated as one equal.*]

 The men wear long robes, which somewhat resemble a dress.

Revision

 Hundreds of soldiers threw their guns into the river and ran.

 Women are treated as equals, however, when they work in the fields.

 The men wear long robes which somewhat resemble dresses.

24h *Reference of substitute verb forms*   **Ref h**

 A substitute verb or verbal (see 25), usually some combination with *to do,* must refer clearly and logically to another verb.

Original

 He expresses the revolt against bondage and the desire to be free. His argument centers around the possibility to do so.
[*There is no verb in the first sentence which could work as an antecedent for* to do so *except* expresses, *and reference to it does not make sense.*]

 If he has any time for fooling around after class, he will do so.
[*He cannot* do *fooling around.*]

Revision

 He speaks of revolting against bondage and being free. His argument assumes the possibility of doing so.
[*The original is so unclear that accurate revision is difficult, but the rearrangement provides parallel antecedents in* revolting *and* being.]

 If he has any time to fool around after class, he will.
[*With the form changed, no substitute is necessary.*]

EXERCISE 24

A. Revise the following sentences, correcting any examples of illogical word reference:

  1. Since all of my friends play bridge, I am glad that I come under that class.

  2. They are taught to be agreeable and sociable with their companions, an advancement toward friendly relations.

  3. Gordo, the name of my dog, chased the rabbit into the woodpile.

[303

4. The church objected to an occupation such as physicians because they interfered with miraculous cures.

5. Of all the arrangements for the convention, I was most impressed by my room to myself in the dormitory.

6. His long punts and accurate passes, qualities which made him feared by all opponents, helped us to win the championship.

7. He was always boasting about his conquests in love, and I have never admired this characteristic.

8. He applied for the position of office manager, much too ambitious for a beginner.

9. Swimming is good exercise for anyone who approaches the matter seriously.

10. The girls decided to restrict membership in the club to members of sororities, an attitude which seemed to me undemocratic.

11. Girls who are friendly lead happy lives, and I am glad I share this quality.

12. After refreshments all of us sat around and talked, an event which I enjoyed.

13. Of all the people in our neighborhood, the sadness of one case affected me most.

14. The field of chemistry is exciting for anyone who undertakes this great adventure into science.

15. All the men were looked on as a brother in the camp.

16. An important part of a student's life, especially a man, is activity in student government.

17. College, the word dreamed about by so many high school students, was not what I had expected it to be.

18. The other secretaries all conspired to give me the most unpleasant jobs, aspects I had not anticipated.

19. Many opportunities are available for the person with ability, and the methods of salesmanship are among the most interesting.

20. Several incidents occurred while I was learning to operate a switchboard, but I remember best my many conversations with the chief operator.

21. I believe that Hoover Dam, which is the topic for my paper, is one of the greatest sources of power in the world.

22. On inspecting the engineering field you will find that not only are improvements made but inventions are brought forth by these gallant young explorers.

23. Although there are many faults in the unicameral system of legislation, there are not enough to make it an unprofitable change.

24. If the state chose to give money to public and parochial schools alike, nobody could criticize it for this affair.

25. Some feel that they do not have the ability to study, and others feel that they have better things to do. The latter include marriage, traveling, or work.

B. Correct the faulty references in the following passage:

Our outfit, which was among the toughest men in the infantry, had several Texans on its roll call. Not all Texans I have known are the boaster type, but one of these men thought Texas had the biggest of everything. I suppose he even thought they had bigger modesty than anybody else, but he certainly was not in that category. We called him Fort Worth, because that town was always in his mouth. Our sergeant, who came from Pennsylvania—a pretty capable collection of boasters, too—did not like Fort Worth, I suppose because they were both too much of a boaster. Fort Worth would get the better of the sergeant boasting, and the sergeant would get even with Fort Worth by putting him on latrine duty or giving him some other menial task. This went on and on, with the enlisted men siding with Fort Worth so often that the sergeant even threatened to charge him with insubordination, a condition which is a very serious offense in the army. Finally, the German lines gave way a little, a movement that is very hard to follow in rough mountains, but we surged forward to a ridge, and from being there we could see Vesuvius over to our left, rolling up smoke, and at night a dull red glow.

"Hey, Fort Worth," the sergeant called, indicating the spectacle which every school child knows is practically a synonym for *marvel,* "you got any a' them volcanoes hotter 'n that one in Texas?"

The Texan looked at the fiery mountain as though he were trying to recall himself from the scenes of battle to the details of Texas terrain, and then he said, "No, we ain't. But in Fort Worth we sure got a fire department could put her out."

C. Most faulty sentences can be improved with any of several means of strengthening structure. Most of the sentences in Exercise 20B can be most readily improved by substituting a more expressive verb for *to be,* but many of them could be strengthened in other ways. Try to revise each sentence in 20B by keeping a form of the verb *to be* but clarifying word reference. For which of the sentences do you consider the revision satisfactory?

D. Revise the following sentences so that all pronouns or other reference words refer clearly to logical antecedents:

1. Macbeth fears that Banquo knows that he has killed Duncan, the king, and this necessitated his death.

2. When you add all this evidence together, it looks like arson.

3. If clear, unemotional words were used by people in the government, it would benefit the world greatly.

4. While dialects do not help the standards of speech, they do not hinder it too greatly.

5. Charles lacked refinements, which annoyed her.

6. Before the depression people might have gone on vacations or patronized community amusements, but now this was impossible.

7. Lady Macbeth could see what the affair was doing to her husband, and no doubt this had as much to do with her madness as did the thoughts of the murder itself.

8. Television requires little mental activity, and in my opinion this is what we need.

9. When Admetis discovered that the veiled woman was his wife, it certainly had a significant effect on his thoughts.

10. Some of Cortez's horses were so outstanding in battle that it caused the Indians to consider them gods.

11. We spent the entire day under the blistering sun, swerving around on aquaplanes, and this made my head ache.

12. In the pterodactyl the hind legs were poorly developed, and thus we do not see any of them walking or crawling around on land.

13. If anything wrong has been done, I hope they put them in jail.

14. In Los Angeles where my parents live they do not have a very extensive system of public transportation.

15. Nowadays practically all the people we meet we do so in some group.

16. In the time of Shakespeare there existed much anti-Jewish prejudice and their religion set them apart from the rest of the people.

17. The chest had been her mother's, and she remembered the sorrow she had felt when she left for America.

18. The only used trailers we found for sale had been lived in by families with children which had been all scratched up.

19. At the club they said that all matches had been postponed.

20. The children had scattered small pieces of bread among the ducks which they had been eating all afternoon.

21. Later several experimenters added more keys to the clarinet to give it range, and this is why its popularity increased.

22. Glass-making flourished in very early times; it was made and used by the Egyptians before 1400 B.C.

23. In the first chapter of Miss Langer's book she talks about symbols.

24. Too often people make the mistake of thinking that education is not as valuable as experience, and that is why I am in school.

25. If the minister can really influence people with his sermons, it will do a lot more good.

E. Notice carefully the occurrences of *this* in the paragraph below, and revise so as to remove any vague reference.

Acetylene is usually only mildly poisonous and it is commonly available; this makes it a handy way of getting rid of vermin. It has other properties aside from being poisonous and convenient, and this is not always remembered. A Swedish garage owner recently provided an example of this. While he was driving to work, he became aware that a rat was chewing the cushion of the rear seat of his car, and hearing this, he stopped to kill the rat. This did not help much, because the rat scrambled under the back of the seat, which could not be removed although the seat could have been. Knowing this, the garage owner drove to his place of business, determined to poison or to smoke out the rat. This was sensible, and the garage owner got out his acetylene welding kit with a good fresh tank of gas, thinking this would kill the rat or get him out. It got him out. Shortly after the car was filled with gas, the garage owner saw his roof flying seventy-five feet into the air, this presumably being due to a short circuit in the automobile which had ignited the acetylene. Along with the roof went much of the owner's automobile, and parts of five others. This was not the only damage the owner saw around him. Six men had to be hospitalized because this was so unexpected that people stood still in the street staring while pieces of garage fell on them. The rat has not been seen since. Neither has the cushion. In spite of this, the garage owner is not taking out a patent on his rat exterminator.

F. Use the facts given below for a brief composition. Subordinate as many of the details as the material warrants, using reference words and being sure your reference words have clear antecedents. If the present phrasing does not supply these antecedents, insert them.

Alice Marriott wrote an article.
The article is called "Beowulf in South Dakota."
Alice Marriott is an ethnologist.
Alice Marriott studies American Indian tales.
The New Yorker published the article.
The New Yorker is a sophisticated magazine.
The author was collecting stories from an old Indian.
The Indian lived in South Dakota.
One day the old Indian was bored and restless.
The Indian looked as though he did not want to tell more stories.
The Indian asked a question.
The Indian wanted to know why the white people wanted his stories.
The Indian wanted to know if the white people had no stories of their own.

The author said she wanted to compare the stories of the Indians with the stories of the white people.

The old Indian became interested.

He acted pleased.

The Indian said that the author's idea was a good idea.

The Indian said he wanted the author to tell him one of the white people's stories.

The author retold the story of *Beowulf*.

The author used Indian terms and Indian concepts.

The author made Beowulf a great war chief.

Beowulf gathered the young men of the tribe around him.

Beowulf and the young men went on a war party.

Beowulf and the young men attacked the Witch of the Water and her son.

The Witch of the Water lived under a great stone in a rushing, dangerous river.

A great fight took place under the water.

There was blood welling up through the water.

The water was as red as the sun rising.

Beowulf killed the Witch of the Water and her son.

The Indian liked the story.

The author had to tell it over and over.

The Indian told it to his friends and the friends talked about it.

The Indians talked about Beowulf.

The Indians sounded like a seminar in literature.

The Indian did not tell any more stories that day.

The author had to go home and wait until the Indians recovered from *Beowulf*.

The old man told the author many stories.

The storytelling continued for weeks.

Another ethnologist was trying to get the old Indian to tell him stories.

Ethnologists have methods of working and standardized ethical practices.

An ethnologist who tries to use another ethnologist's information is unethical.

Two ethnologists are likely to confuse an informant.

A confused informant gives unsatisfactory evidence to both scientists.

The old Indian said he liked the author.

The author was the friend of the old Indian.

The Indian offered not to tell the other ethnologist Indian stories.

The author went back to her university.

The author heard that the other ethnologist wanted to question the old Indian.

Two or three years passed.

The author was reading a learned journal.

The author found an article signed by the other ethnologist.

The article was called "Occurrence of a Beowulf-like Myth among
    North American Indians."
The author wondered whether or not she should tell what she knew.

(If you want to see what Alice Marriott did with the story, you will
find the reference in 46-13.)

25. INCOMPLETE CONSTRUCTIONS AND SENTENCE PATTERNS

[For Guide to Revision, see page 311]

Excessive repetition can be avoided by using sentence patterns.

Consistency in patterns like parallel structure or the *to be* equation is necessary because the reader gets some of the meaning, the relationships of the ideas, from the pattern itself. In fact, the reader is so accustomed to following standard patterns that he can often supply expressions which the writer omits.

The writer, therefore, can economize on words. He can leave out passages which would repeat meanings, allowing the reader to fill in missing elements from what has preceded. Even so common a device as using co-ordinate sentence parts (see 21) saves words by combining two simple sentences into one.

He knew the rules and (*he knew the*) regulations.

The italicized repetition is understood easily and need not be expressed.

The pressure of word order allows many such short cuts. For example, verbs or parts of them can often be omitted in parallel sentences.

We knew that we would soon have to stop using paper plates and (*we knew that we would soon have to*) start washing dishes.

The opening words automatically carry over to their position in the parallel structure. Or, in a comparison, we do not write:

Plants grow more rapidly in California than (*plants grow rapidly*) in New York.

We sometimes substitute shorter expressions whose meaning is clear because they occupy the same relative positions as the words they stand for (see 24h).

Plants grow more rapidly in California than *they do* in New York.

Or we omit the repeated expressions and allow the pressure of word order to carry the meaning.

Plants grow more rapidly in California than in New York.

She was treated more politely than he (*was treated*).

Connectives can sometimes be omitted from parallel structures and subordinate expressions.

He was afraid of no man and (*of*) no rule.

Philo knew (*that*) he was being followed.

Word order is sufficient to indicate relationships without the help of the connectives.

Even when a repeated idea is not expressed in the required form, it can sometimes be omitted. Sentences like the following are common, especially in informal English:

He ran as fast as he could (*run*).

Usually, however, such omissions are clear only if other words in the sentence give the reader the exact information needed to fill in missing parts of the patterns. Whenever the "understood" expressions cannot repeat exactly a previously expressed construction, there is danger of obscurity.

25 Incomplete constructions and sentence patterns **Inc**

GUIDE TO REVISION:

Supply missing sentence elements or revise sentences so that omissions do not obscure meaning.

25a Economy with verbs **Inc a**

Original

The liquor was confiscated and the barrels dumped in the sea.

[*The reader is expected to be able to supply a verb between* bar-rels *and* dumped, *but the verb suggested by word order is* was, *which does not fit the plural* barrels.]

Revision

The liquor was confiscated, and the barrels *were* dumped in the sea.

[*The construction requires a plural verb to agree with* barrels. *Note that the omission would have been clear in* The liquor was con-

[311

Original (*Cont.*)

Revision (*Cont.*)
fiscated and the bootlegger arrested.]

Many of the soldiers saw only what hundreds of tourists always had and always will be seeing.

Many of the soldiers saw only what hundreds of tourists always had *seen* and always will be seeing.

Mary will go if you are.

(1) Mary will go if you *are going.*
(2) Mary will *go* if you go.

The water cask was nearly empty by noon and drained for evening rations.
[Drained *must be preceded by* was *understood, but the* was *after* cask *is a complete verb; it cannot be understood as part of the verb* was drained.]

(1) The water cask was nearly empty by noon and was drained for evening rations.
(2) The water cask was nearly empty by noon; we drained it for evening rations.

He spoke as only a fool can.
[*Meaning is clear enough, but formal style would require re-expressing the verb in its proper form.*]

He spoke as only a fool can *speak.*

25b Omission of prepositions   Inc b

The preposition can be omitted in parallel passages only when the expressed preposition fits logically into the place where it is to be understood (see also 21b). The preposition should not be carelessly omitted from clauses in which it is separated from the verb.

Original

Revision

D'Artagnan was interested and skillful at fencing.
[*No connective follows* interested; at, *which does not make sense, is the only word available.*]

(1) D'Artagnan was interested *in* and skillful at fencing.
(2) D'Artagnan was interested in fencing and skillful at it.

He was helpful and considerate of his friends.

He was helpful to his friends and considerate of them.

Original (Cont.)	*Revision (Cont.)*
[Of *will not work with* helpful.]	
My mother objected to the people which I associated.	My mother objected to the people with whom I associated.
[*The writer has forgotten the preposition needed to supplement the meaning of* associated.]	

25c Omission of subordinating words   Inc c

Word order often makes subordination clear without the use of introductory words like *that, who,* or *which*.

Everybody knew (*that*) he had failed.
None of the books (*which*) I had studied clarified the question.

Before a dependent clause used as a subject, object, or complement, however, omission of the connective is often confusing.

Original	*Revision*
Mr. Chamberlain forgot the umbrella had been torn.	Mr. Chamberlain forgot *that* the umbrella had been torn.
[*The reader is momentarily misled into interpreting* the umbrella *as the object of* forgot *rather than the beginning of a clause.*]	[*The connective is supplied, and the reader can no longer suppose that Mr. Chamberlain left the umbrella behind.*]
The trouble was the janitor had forgotten to lock the doors.	The trouble was *that* the janitor had forgotten to lock the doors.
[*A clause used as a subjective complement is seldom clear without the connective.*]	
In the introduction the author proposed nothing happens.	In the introduction *which* the author proposed, nothing happens.

25d Omissions in comparisons   Inc d; Inc Comp

Comparisons frequently fit a word-order pattern so well fixed that parallel elements need not be completely repeated, and when a shorter construction becomes established, it, too, provides a pattern and the basis for further economy. Consider the following:

> It was easier to take a cab *than it was easy to take* the bus.
> It was easier to take a cab *than to take* the bus.
> It was easier to take a cab *than* the bus.

One idiomatic pattern in English involves a special problem. Sentences like the following are common colloquially:

> That night the team was as good if not better *than* any other team in the league.

But the connective *than* cannot be logically understood after *good*, where *as* is required. Standard English, therefore, requires some kind of completion of comparisons of this sort.

In another colloquial pattern which sometimes causes trouble in writing, expressions like *so beautiful, most wonderful, biggest, finest, prettiest* appear as vague indications of enthusiasm.

> It was *such* a lovely party.
> He was the *nicest* man.

These expressions begin a comparison, and in standard written English either the comparison should be finished or modifiers should be used which do not imply a comparison.

Original	*Revision*
I knew her better than Mary. [*With parts of the comparison omitted, two meanings are possible.*]	(1) I knew her better than Mary did. (2) I knew her better than I knew Mary.
The people had been as kind if not kinder than my own family. [Than *cannot serve both comparisons. Revision* (2) *is accurate, though stiff;* (1) *lacks logical connectives, but follows a familiar pattern.*]	(1) The people had been as kind as my own family, if not kinder. (2) The people had been as kind as, if not kinder than, my own family.
The heroine was so charming. [*The sentence begins a comparison; the reader expects further information about the heroine's charm. The writer probably did not intend a comparison but added*	(1) The heroine was charming. (2) The heroine was so charming that I paid no attention to the other characters. [*If the writer has a comparison in mind, he should complete it.*]

Original (*Cont.*)

the intensifier under the false impression that it made his statement more convincing.]

It was the best dinner.

Revision (*Cont.*)

(1) It was an excellent dinner.
(2) It was the best dinner I had ever eaten.

EXERCISE 25

A. In the sentences below, supply any words needed for clarity. The meaning of some sentences is immediately and certainly clear; indicate that these sentences are correct as they stand.

1. Drama is the poetry of conduct, romance the poetry of circumstance.

2. He did not consider the team would be able to take a united stand.

3. He learned respect and obedience to the new officers.

4. She soon became aware living with her husband was impossible.

5. I don't believe that churches are increasing people's belief and trust in God. They are changing from the way they used to.

6. People say that reading a book a week increases your vocabulary and your manner of speaking.

7. The girls found the cabin so beautiful, and Aubrey was such a handsome man.

8. Her gray hair adds rather than detracts from her appearance.

9. There were great scientific advances, but precious little chance to use them until government regulations had been removed.

10. Some cruelties still pass for service done in her honor: no thumbscrew is used, no iron boot, no scorching of flesh; but plenty of controversial bruising, laceration, and even lifelong maiming.

11. I have and will continue to be a defender of liberty.

12. She looked as old or older than Methuselah.

13. After an hour of this conversation, I decided that I disliked Mary's cousin as much as Mary.

14. At the same time he was afraid and fascinated by the eyes of the tiger.

15. He promised the people food and medical supplies would be flown into all the flood areas.

16. It is one of the cruxes of history, the Celts having captured Rome, did not keep it.

17. Her insistence her son should become a doctor ruined his health.

18. Chiffon is as hard to sew on a sewing machine or harder than burlap.

19. The Bunkville Police Force today captured the six juvenile delinquents who have been terrorizing local filling stations. Picture above shows Patrolman Clarence Jones and Peggy (Little Moll) Watkins, 17, when the police cordon flushed them out of the bushes.

20. When I looked into the cell I disliked Dandy Jack as much as the police officer.

B. From current magazines select three articles which you consider represent good modern prose. Choose a passage of about a thousand words from each and another thousand words of writing of your own, as represented in themes returned to you. Count the number of occurrences in each passage, including your own material, of the following reference words: *which, who, whose, whom,* and *that.* Now count the number of times each writer has used some economical subordination for which you could substitute a clause beginning with one of these words. For instance, "She is the only soprano I can endure," is a more economical equivalent of "She is the only soprano whom I can endure." Next, study your results and observe whether or not the writers who manage to write with economical subordination increase the vigor and clarity of their prose. Finally, try to find out how the writer who is most skillful in his subordination gets his results. What sort of subordination does he use most? How does he keep his meaning clear even though he omits words?

Now write a 300-word report of your findings.

C. As English grammar has become more distributive and the patterns of sentences have become stronger, users of the language feel less and less use for connectives, relying upon sentence patterns to make meaning clear. Many translations of the Bible in current use were prepared more than three hundred years ago, and hence reflect an earlier stage of the language. For instance, Genesis 31:16 (King James numbering) reads in the King James version as follows:

For all the riches which God hath taken from our father, that is ours, and our children's: now then, whatsoever God hath said unto thee, do.

If you were to modernize this passage, you would probably change words like *hath* and *whatsoever,* but you might also feel you could omit a number of connectives, and come out with something like the following:

All the wealth God has taken from our father is ours and our children's; accordingly, whatever God has told you to do, do it.

Notice that the revision omits *for, which,* and *that.* Picking up with the next verse, continue through the remainer of Chapter 31, noting any connectives which you would omit if you were modernizing the translation. You may use either the King James or the Douay version.

VI. Selection of Forms; Function Words

The textbooks mostly used for grammar are six-pennyworth of horror calculated to make a lad loathe his own tongue.—J. RUNCIMAN

The notion of grammar as an instrument of torture has grown mainly from misconceptions about the importance of the forms of words in modern English. Relatively speaking, forms are no longer important in English grammar, but the rules which most students have been taught in the name of grammar rest on the assumption that forms are all-important. The schoolboy, impatient with grammatical concepts which seem not to help much when he tries to understand or to make himself understood emerges with a large share of justice on his side. This is not to say that grammar is unimportant, but the grammar which most of us have learned does not describe the English language either adequately or accurately.

Three devices enunciate most of the grammatical relationships in English (see IV, 17). Of these, IV and V consider mainly word order; VI discusses the remaining devices, changes in form or inflectional changes and function words. Of the three, word order is certainly the most important, for, as we have seen, modern English grammar is mainly distributive. In this type of grammar, word order makes many relationships clear, but when it does not, words which have relatively little independent meaning complete the indication of relationship. In this book, such terms are called *function words,* since they show how other words function.

To see how function words work, consider three meaningful units, *Bill Sikes, dangled,* and *a rope.* In this order they make sense, but if they are to describe a familiar scene in *Oliver Twist,* something must be added to change the relationships, as in *Bill Sikes dangled from a rope.* In a distributive grammar, relationship words like *from* supplement word order.

English, however, has not always been a distributive language. Like most European languages, it descended from a very early language known as Indo-European, which relied upon a third device, *inflection.* That is, Indo-European indicated relationships mainly by changing the forms of words. This device was still prevalent in Anglo-Saxon, the ancestor of English, and in 17-1 we saw that by inflecting the Anglo-Saxon words for *man* and *dog* we could change the actor to the goal, the biter to the bitten, without changing the order of the words. We must now observe that function words can take over other relationships within the sentence, which in an inflectional grammar are handled by changes in form.

These relationships are many and varied. An Anglo-Saxon chronicler, for instance, when he believed that the Lord had intervened on behalf of his people, could write *Godes thonkes,* putting our words *God* and *thank* into the genitive case. We would say something like *by the grace of God,* using three function words instead of two endings. According to a poem inserted in the *Chronicle,* King Athelstan and his brother gained fame *sweorda ecgum.* Here *ecgum* is the word *ecg* (our *edge*) with the ending *-um,* which indicates that the word is a plural in the instrumental case, that is, it is a means of doing something. *Sweorda* is our word *sword* with a genitive plural ending, and the two words with these endings mean "with the edges of their swords."

Most Anglo-Saxon endings, including *-um,* were useless in a distributive grammar, and have disappeared. A few endings survived, including *-s* for the plural and a genitive form, now spelled *-'s,* for the possessive. Even here, however, we have constructions requiring function words, *a hundred boys* but *dozens of people, my father's head* but *the head of the house.*

In modern English, both function words and inflectional devices offer special problems. The function words carry so much of the grammar of the sentence that they must be chosen carefully, and they are themselves so seemingly minor that they sometimes receive insufficient attention. As for inflection, speakers of English have become so accustomed to distributive grammatical devices that they have little feeling for inflection. This section, then, concerns function words and inflection, and the difficulties they present.

26. PARTS OF SPEECH

[For Guide to Revision, see page 324]

Changes in form to reveal grammar are still important and require unusual attention because they are rare.

In grammar, "Whatever is, is right," provided it *is* long enough and in the minds of enough people. For instance, the meaning of the previous sentence requires that *the* precede *minds* because everybody uses the words in that order, but if everyone reversed the words, the sense would require *minds the*. Words acquire their meaning and grammatical devices develop their force because users of the language agree at least roughly as to usage. The importance of usage in word choice will be discussed 37-1 to 37-8; here we must notice that usage determines what is "right" and "wrong" in grammar. Usage determines order or pattern as well as form, but since native speakers of English handle order easily, questions of right and wrong in grammar usually concern form and the selection of words, especially of function words.

26-1 Form changes in English grammar

Usage has always been the basis on which grammar grew, but it has not always been the basis of arguments about grammar. Teachers of composition and authors of books on writing formerly endeavored to police English by citing rules, and these rules were not always applicable to English because they were mostly the rules of Latin. This situation had a historical background. Latin and Greek were long the basis of British education, and were accepted as the best of all possible languages. Accordingly, when Britons tried to describe their language in grammatical terms, they turned to Latin and Greek. They assumed that the classical rules were not merely the rules of the clas-

[321]

sical languages, but were grammar per se, and British and American grammarians applied these rules wherever possible.

Applying these rules was not always possible. As we have seen, classical Latin grammar relies mainly on inflections; English retains relatively few inflections and relies mainly on order and function words. But when the rules would not apply, the grammarians assumed that the English language, not the grammatical statement, was at fault. This so-called grammar persisted in the schools—and remains there today—but the English language has not changed to conform to it. English has gone on growing, as a language must, in accordance with usage. As a result, much of what is commonly taught as grammar is irrelevant or inadequate, and the schoolboy who objects to applying Latin grammar to English is perhaps being more logical than he realizes.

On the other hand, English makes some use of form changes to show grammatical relationships, and these changes are troublesome, mainly because the language tends to do without them and to rely on word order instead. Changes in the form of the verb to designate the subjunctive mood, for example, are seemingly disappearing, especially from spoken English. Even when changes in form persist, confusion develops because of the pressure of word order, a device so prevalent that the ordinary user of the language automatically gives it preference. Personal pronouns, for example, retain form changes which indicate their use; *I* is used as a subject, *me* as an object. The tradition of form changes requires the subjective form in the sentence *It is I* because *I* is a subject complement and therefore should be in the subjective form. But according to the principles of word order, the pronoun is in the position usually occupied by the object. As a result *It is me* is becoming more and more common, at least in spoken English.

Form changes as grammatical devices, then, must be given special attention, not because they are prevalent in English grammar but because they are exceptional. Furthermore, the writer of standard English must often preserve even distinctions which are disappearing from speech. Language changes constantly, and change is healthy in language. By changing, language fills our changing needs, but if language changes so rapidly that users of the language have difficulty understanding one another, or the language of one user seems markedly strange and out of place to other users, both language and communication suffer. Thus the makers of dictionaries and handbooks of usage, and the teachers who endeavor to apply these books, very properly discourage rapid change in grammatical usage, as they discourage rapid change in word usage (see 37). Our grammar has undergone a revolution; our language is probably the better for the change, but only because the revolution proceeded through many hundreds of years. Grammatical devices, whether sentence patterns or forms of words, can function only because they have currency, and currency is destroyed by rapid change.

26-2 Parts of the sentence; parts of speech

The five basic parts of the sentence have been described: subject, verb, complement, modifier, function word (see 17-3, 17-5). Individual words or word groups in sentences can be classified on the basis of their use as one or more of these sentence parts. Further classification is useful in discussing forms because some words or forms traditionally function as one part of speech but not as others.

The classification is not easy. English, being a distributive language, does not readily fit into the classifications of parts of speech which have been borrowed from Latin grammar. Some names for parts of speech, however, we must have, and discussion will be easier if we use familiar terms in so far as they describe English.

The classification into parts of speech is based on the *use* of words or word groups in particular sentences. That is, a noun is not a noun for any mystical reasons, but because it is *used* as a noun in the sentence under discussion. In English, most common words can be used as more than one part of speech, although many words appear more often as one part of speech than as any other. *Cow,* for example, is usually used as a noun. But consider the following:

> The principal thought he could *cow* the rebellious students.
> The road to the old mine was little more than a *cow* path.

In the first sentence *cow* is a verb, in the second a modifier. Or the word *fast* can be thought of as any of several parts of speech.

> He ran *fast.*
> It was a *fast* trip.
> We *fast* during Lent.
> They broke their *fast* on Easter Sunday.

Classification, therefore, does not justify our saying categorically that any word *is* any part of speech. We cannot say *cow* is always a noun. We can say that in the sentence

> The *cow* was chewing her cud

cow is a noun. Or we can say *cow* may be used as a noun or verb or modifier.

The parts of speech, therefore, as they are here described, are to be identified on the basis of the functions of words in specific sentences. Distinctions are not always sharp; some forms serve more than one purpose at one time, but most words can be classified within the four main categories discussed in the pages that follow as the four basic parts of speech: noun expressions, verbs, modifiers, function words.

26 *Parts of speech*   **PS**

GUIDE TO REVISION:

> *Substitute a word which in standard usage is appropriately used as the part of speech required.*

Although many English words are used as more than one part of speech, usage dictates which functions are appropriate for which words. *Telephone,* for example, functions readily as a noun or a verb or a modifier, whereas *television* works only as a noun or modifier and *televise* has developed as a verb. Conversion, however, is common and easy; that is, we readily convert words restricted to use as nouns into verbs, verbs into modifiers, nouns into modifiers. When we invent a radio, the noun soon becomes a modifier so that we can refer to *radio waves,* and *radio* has become a verb even though we have the verb *broadcast.*

Conversion is characteristic of a distributive language and is becoming constantly more common in American speech. In writing, however, conversions are accepted more reluctantly, and circumstances of usage (see 37) are particularly pertinent in determining the suitability of a converted expression. Many conversions are appropriate for speech or informal writing—newspaper columns or advertising, for example—which would not be accepted in more formal prose and might alienate some readers. Furthermore, many such expressions develop as language fads, and their sudden overuse very quickly makes them trite (see 35e).

Original	*Revision*
Philosophy is a *must* in a liberal arts course.	Philosophy is necessary in a liberal arts course.
[*Now recorded in current dictionaries, the use of* must *as a noun has only recently been popularized, particularly in advertising.*]	[*Since the noun* must *retains the associations of its sudden rise to popularity, it seems in serious writing a naïve—and trite—attempt at cleverness.*]
The secretary was ordered to *contact* all chapters in the state.	The secretary was ordered to write all chapters in the state.
[*The sudden overuse of* contact *as a verb with a new meaning— especially in business—has caused many writers to object to it as trite and affected.*]	[*Traditionally used as a noun or a verb implying actual physical contact,* contact *in its converted use is often less precise than more conventional diction.*]
I *suspicioned* her.	I suspected her.
[*As a verb,* suspicion *is characteristic of dialectical or colloquial English.*]	
I *officed* with the superintendent.	I shared an office with the superintendent.

Words usually used as nouns are readily adapted as modifiers. Since, however, a reader tends to think of them first as nouns, excessive use of them is confusing.

Original	*Revision*
We took a character trait identification test.	We took a test intended to identify traits of character.
[*Three consecutive words usually used as nouns cannot modify one another without confusion.*]	
He was referred to the price stabilization committee office.	He was referred to the office of the committee for price stabilization.

EXERCISE 26

A. Identify the words of the following paragraph as noun expressions, verbs, modifiers, or function words:

I hastened to prepare my pack, and tackle the steep ascent that lay before me; but I had something on my mind. It was only a fancy; yet a fancy will sometimes be importunate. I had been most hospitably received and punctually served in my green caravanserai. The room was airy, the water excellent, and the dawn had called me to a moment. I say nothing of the tapestries or the inimitable ceiling, nor yet of the view which I commanded from the windows; but I felt I was in some one's debt for all this liberal entertainment. And so it pleased me, in a half-laughing way, to leave pieces of money on the turf as I went along, until I had left enough for my night's lodging. I trust they did not fall to some rich and churlish drover.

—ROBERT LOUIS STEVENSON, *Travels with a Donkey*

B. Correct the questionable uses in the following:

1. Our new Sun-Brown leg make-up is a must for every smart young woman.

2. The columnist reports that Veronica Viem is summering in Miami and expects to middle-aisle in August.

3. I suspicioned him as soon as I saw how shifty-eyed he was.

4. And of course just when I planned on a week end of fishing, I had to help Father Celotex the rumpus room.

5. Any boy who was not a good dancer could not quite rate with us.

6. I will contact him by phone and find out how wholesale his prices are.

7. Mother stated that she did not like the sort of boys I was dating.

8. Until I became important enough to rate a desk of my own, I officed with our contact man.

9. As soon as I moved in, I suspicioned that there was something crazy about the setup.

10. We partied until after midnight.

27. NOUN EXPRESSIONS

[For Guide to Revision, see page 329]

Noun expressions are parts of the sentence which are used as subjects, complements, or objects of prepositions.

Noun expressions may be single words or word groups; for pronouns see 28. Except for pronouns and a few other exceptional forms, these noun expressions are related grammatically to the sentence primarily through word order. Although an elaborate system of endings distinguished nouns in Anglo-Saxon, only two endings are used with nouns in modern English: *-s* (or *-es*) to indicate the plural, and *-'s* (or *-s'*) to indicate the possessive. These forms are easily identified and are considered below as problems in spelling (see 42a, 42c). For the possessive form used with the gerund, see 32f.

27-1 Uses of noun expressions

Noun expressions include all words or word groups used as subjects or complements, except modifiers used as complements (see 32b). They name what is being talked about or what is receiving the action.

The *boy* speared the *fish*.
They knew *what they wanted.*
Chatterton was a *poet.*

Noun expressions may be linked to the sentence by a type of function word, a preposition (see 33-6). The noun is then referred to as the object of the preposition.

Most *of the passengers* were staring *out the window.*

The preposition *of* relates *passengers* to *most* so that *passengers* completes the idea of the subject, modifying it and functioning as part of it. Similarly, *out* links *window* to the verb, so that *window* completes the idea carried forward through *were staring.* Thus a noun can become a modifier by means of a preposition, by being what is called the object of the preposition.

27-2 Types of noun expressions

Proper nouns name particular places, persons, things, or ideas and are distinguished by capital letters (see 41a).

> *Ambrose Bierce* was born in *Ohio,* but he spent much of his life in the *West* and finally disappeared in *Mexico,* where he had gone to join the staff of *General Villa.*

Collective nouns name groups rather than individuals. They include words like *squad, committee, flock, swarm, family, group, herd.* For the use of collective nouns as subjects see 31h.

Noun clauses are dependent clauses (see 18-2) used as subjects, complements, or objects of prepositions. They are usually introduced by certain function words, the most common of which are *that, which, who, whose, whoever, what, whatever, how, whether, if.*

> We wondered *whether we would ever reach the top of the hill.*
> *How to break the news to the children* was our first problem.
> *Whoever ate the pie* ought to confess.
> He found out *that he could get through the course without working.*

27-3 Verbal nouns

English retains some multiple-purpose forms, among which are the verbals, so called because they come from verbs and like verbs can take a subject or complement, but function also as nouns or modifiers (see 30-6). They include verbal nouns, which function not as complete verbs but as noun expressions.

> The Joneses always *go* to the moving pictures.   (*verb*)
> The Joneses *are going* to the moving pictures.   (*verb*)
> *Going* to the moving pictures amuses them.   (*verbal*)
> His ambition was *to go* to the moving pictures.   (*verbal*)

The verbs *go* and *are going,* with their accompanying subject, complements, and modifiers, make complete assertions. The verbals *going* and *to go* do not make complete assertions.

Two types of verbals are used as nouns: the *infinitive,* usually characterized by its sign, *to,* preceding it (*to see, to be lost, to have found*), and the *gerund,* identifiable because some part of it always ends in *-ing* (*seeing, being seen, having found*).

328]

Verbal nouns are useful because they can name an action for which no regular name exists in the language. Even when a noun for the action exists, the verbal noun sometimes allows special distinctions in meaning. Compare:

> The mad hatter liked *conversation* at the tea table.
> The mad hatter liked *to converse* at the tea table.
> The mad hatter liked *conversing* at the tea table.

Verbal nouns may have any of the usual functions of noun expressions:

> *Infinitive as subject: To understand* his decision was impossible.
> *Gerund as subject: Knowing* German got him a new job.
> *Infinitive as postponed subject:* It was impossible *to understand* his decision.
> *Gerund as subject and subject complement: Seeing* is *believing.*
> *Infinitive as object of verb:* He tried *to bribe* the clerk.
> *Gerund as object of preposition:* He replied by *hitting* George in the left eye.

27 *Noun expressions*   **Noun**

GUIDE TO REVISION:

Revise to avoid excessive use of nouns.

Noun expressions are, of course, essential to writing, but a sure way to make a passage lumber laboriously toward its meaning is to rely too heavily on nouns, especially on abstractions (see 35-3). A "noun style" often sounds affected, often is vague or unclear; overuse of nouns is the trade-mark of so-called "officialese." The solution is to use nouns which are as concrete and specific as possible and to revise the passage so that ideas move on a carriage of active verbs.

Most errors in the form of noun expressions concern number and the possessive, considered as spelling problems (see 42a, 42c). For the possessive noun with the gerund see 32f.

Original	*Revision*
Because of the great increase in activity producing a requirement of special ledger accounts, the imple-	Because more special ledger accounts are now necessary, we shall have to begin using a special code

Original (*Cont.*)

mentation of a special code system has been made a necessity for the clear definition of each account.

[*The sentence of "officialese" relies too heavily on nouns and becomes wordy and obscure.*]

In reply to your communication of July 14 inquiring about the shipment of your order of plastic materials, filling of the order can now be completed as materials are again in stock and delivery will be effected this week.

I always took pleasure in going to the moving pictures.

[*Constructions with the gerund are sometimes roundabout.*]

Revision (*Cont.*)

system to define each account clearly.

[*With more of the meaning carried by verbs and verbals, the sentence is shorter and clearer.*]

The plastics you inquire about in your letter of July 14 are now in stock and will be delivered to you this week.

I always liked to go to the moving pictures.

EXERCISE 27

A. Identify the noun expressions in the following passage:

Then came the question—horrid thought!—as to who was the partner of Ellen's guilt? Was it, could it be, her own son, her darling Ernest? Ernest was getting a big boy now. She could excuse any young woman for taking a fancy to him; as for himself, why she was sure he was behind no young man of his age in appreciation of the charms of a nice-looking young woman. So long as he was innocent she did not mind this, but oh, if he were guilty!

She could not bear to think of it, and yet it would be mere cowardice not to look such a matter in the face—her hope was in the Lord, and she was ready to bear cheerfully and make the best of any suffering he might think fit to lay upon her. That the baby must be either a boy or a girl—this much, at any rate, was clear. No less clear was it that the child, if a boy, would resemble Theobald, and if a girl, herself. Resemblance, whether of body or mind, generally leaped over a generation. The guilt of the parents must not be shared by the innocent offspring of shame—oh, no—and such a child as this would be . . . She was off in one of her reveries at once.

The child was in the act of being consecrated Archbishop of Canterbury when Theobald came in from a visit in the parish, and was told the shocking discovery.

—SAMUEL BUTLER, *The Way of All Flesh*

B. Revise the following passage to make it more direct, expressing the action in verbs rather than nouns whenever possible.

Recent exhaustive observations have unfortunately revealed that a condition is rapidly developing in the lawn situated at the east end of City Park which is causing considerable apprehension, and in the absence of urgent and positive action grave possibilities threaten of the permanent unsuitability of this lawn for use and the consequent loss of this aspect of the city's investment.

This is attributed to the several trees on City land in very close proximity to the park's eastern boundary which cause a shaded condition to remain for several hours of the early morning, with consequent loss of the benefit of the sun which is so vital to the life of the turf and the progressive development of the Park property.

As the present serious position can be arrested only by action which presumably falls within your jurisdiction, I am soliciting your co-operation in maintaining our assets by your arrangement for the trimming of all offending trees to a height of about ten feet from ground level.

28. PRONOUNS

[For Guide to Revision, see page 336]

> *Pronouns, which include several sorts of highly flexible*
> *noun expressions, serve as function words and also*
> *as noun forms. They have special forms that show:*
> *(1) case; (2) number, person, and gender.*

Pronouns give unusual trouble in modern English, because they have preserved more of the Anglo-Saxon declension than has any other group of words.

28-1 Pronoun forms; antecedents

A *pronoun's case* (*that is, the subjective, objective, or possessive form*) *derives from its use as a noun expression in its own clause.*

A *pronoun conforms in number, person, and gender with its antecedent.*

The antecedent is the noun expression to which the pronoun refers (see 24). Consider the following sentence:

> Jean asked the florist whether *he* had made up the corsage of faded carnations *which* Jack had sent *her.*

He, which, and *her* are pronouns, each with a different antecedent. *He* refers to its antecedent, *florist; which* to *corsage,* and *her* to *Jean.* The selection of each pronoun depends upon its use and its antecedent. *He,* for example, is the subjective form because it is used as the subject of its clause; it is masculine and singular to conform with its antecedent. *Her* is the objective form because it is the indirect object of the verb *sent;* it is feminine and singular because it refers to *Jean.* Pronouns of the various classes discussed below can be selected on this basis.

28-2 Personal pronouns

Personal pronouns distinguish the speaker (first person), the person spoken to (second person), and the person spoken of (third person). They are preserved in three cases, as follows:

SUBJECTIVE (NOMINATIVE)

	First Person	Second Person	Third Person
Singular	I	you, thou	he, she, it
Plural	we	you	they

These forms are used for subjects of clauses and sentences and for subject complements after linking verbs.

OBJECTIVE (ACCUSATIVE)

Singular	me	you, thee	him, her, it
Plural	us	you	them

These forms are used for all objects and complements, except subject complements, both of verbs and prepositions, and for the subjects of infinitives.

POSSESSIVE (GENITIVE): FORMS USED AS MODIFIERS

Singular	my	your, thy	his, her, its
Plural	our	your	their

These forms are used as modifiers to show possession (see 32-3).

Your nose has *its* own shape.

They also indicate a wide variety of intimate relationships which cannot be classified as indicating possession. Consider the following sentence:

Our representative in *your* territory will be glad to call at *your* office.

The word *our* does not indicate possession; the company hires this representative but does not own him. Nor does the first *your* indicate possession; the prospect merely does business in the territory. Whether it be New York City or the state of Louisiana, he does not own it. The third *your* may indicate possession; the prospect may own his office, but it is more likely that he rents it or that it has been assigned him by his employer. For possessive forms with the gerund, see 32f.

POSSESSIVE (GENITIVE): FORMS USED AS SUBJECTS OR COMPLEMENTS

Singular	mine	yours, thine	his, hers, its
Plural	ours	yours	theirs

These forms are used as subjects or objects, but most frequently as subject complements.

> The book is *mine.*   My daughter is *yours.*   *Yours* is *mine.*

The alternate forms given here for the second personal singular are no longer in use, except for special purposes, notably in addresses to the deity, in the speech of certain sects, and for archaic diction.

28-3 Relative pronouns

Relative pronouns are function words which join a dependent clause to the remainder of the sentence, but they act also as noun expressions within the clause.

> Grandmother, *who* wore spit curls to her dying day, arrived sprouting curlicues like a squid.

Who relates the clause to the main predication but serves also as the subject of the dependent clause, *who wore spit curls to her dying day.* The relative pronouns *who* and *whoever* are declined as follows: *who, whoever* (subjective); *whom, whomever* (objective); *whose, whosever* (possessive). These forms are used for persons. *Which, whichever, what, whatever* are used for inanimate objects, and usually for animals. The forms for persons are also sometimes used for animals. *That* is used for either persons or things. Relative pronouns other than *who* and *whoever* are not declined; the other relative pronouns use the same form for the subjective and objective, and *whose* for the possessive. Some writers prefer *that* for a restrictive clause, *which* and *who* for a nonrestrictive. For punctuation of restrictive and nonrestrictive clauses, see 39d.

The relative pronoun can be readily confused with the relative or subordinating conjunction, the more because some of the forms are the same. A relative pronoun can be distinguished because it serves as a noun in the grammar of its clause. The relative conjunction has no grammatical function within the clause. In

> I tried to buy Fido, *who* had just swallowed a twenty-dollar bill.

who is the subject of a clause and is thus a pronoun. In

> I tried to buy *whichever puppy* had swallowed the twenty-dollar bill.

puppy is the subject of the clause, and *whichever* does not function as a noun. It is a modifying relative conjunction (see 33-4).

334]

28-4 Interrogative pronouns

Interrogative pronouns signal a question and act as noun expressions.

> *Who* is he? *What* is he doing?

Most of the words and forms which serve as relative pronouns can serve also as interrogative pronouns.

28-5 Indefinite pronouns

Indefinite pronouns refer to unspecified persons or things.

> In our house, *anyone* can have *anything* he wants.

Words like *anyone, everyone, anybody, everybody, anything, everything, each, any,* and *all* can serve as indefinite pronouns if they fill the function of noun expressions. Words like *each, any,* and *all* can serve also as modifiers.

28-6 Intensive pronouns

Intensive pronouns give emphasis; they thus resemble nouns in apposition.

> I will cut the rope *myself.*

Forms of the intensive pronoun are developed from the personal pronoun; they are: *myself, yourself, himself* (*not* hisself), *herself, itself, ourselves, yourselves, themselves* (*not* theirselves).

28-7 Reflexive pronouns

Reflexive pronouns redirect the action or predication of the verb to the subject.

> I cut *myself.*

The forms of the reflexive pronoun are identical with those of the intensive pronoun.

28-8 Demonstrative pronouns

Demonstrative pronouns point out; they can be distinguished from demonstrative adjectives because they function as noun expressions.

> *That* is the man I saw through the window. (Demonstrative pronoun)
>
> *That* man was outside my window. (Demonstrative adjective)

[335

28 Pronouns

Pron

GUIDE TO REVISION:

Select the form of the pronoun which is determined by its use as a noun expression in its clause and which agrees in person, number, and gender with its antecedent.

28a Pronoun agreement with indefinite pronouns · Pron a; Agr a

Indefinite pronouns like *everybody, anybody, everyone, each, somebody* are traditionally considered singular, as specifying one of a group. They have been used so often, however, with a plural sense—to mean "all people," for example—that colloquially they have long been considered plural. Even in formal writing, *none* is used as either singular or plural, depending on the sense intended, and words like *everybody* are occasionally considered plural when they clearly have a plural sense. Generally, however, in serious writing such pronouns are considered singular, and pronouns referring to them should be singular. The singular pronoun is particularly necessary when the meaning is clearly singular or when a singular verb form follows the subject (see also 31d).

Original

When *everybody* has given *their* opinions, the committee can decide.
[Everybody *has a singular meaning here and is used with a singular verb. The pronoun referring to it should be singular.*]

Anybody knows it is to *their* advantage to have a college degree.

Everybody has their price.

Revision

When *everybody* has given *his* opinion, the committee can decide.
[*The singular* his *has replaced the plural* their.]

Anybody knows it is to *his* advantage to have a college degree.

Everybody has his price.

28b Pronouns with alternative subjects   Pron b; Agr b

Alternative subjects, usually separated by *or* or *nor,* are logically singular and require a singular pronoun, unless the alternatives are themselves plural as in *Either the Republicans or the Democrats see* their *candidate defeated* (see 31b).

| *Original* | *Revision* |

Neither Columbus nor Henry Hudson achieved *their* ambitions.
[*The subject, being alternative, is singular.*]

Neither Columbus nor Henry Hudson achieved *his* ambition.
[*The singular* his *has replaced the plural* their.]

28c Number after collective nouns   Pron c; Agr c

In written English, a collective noun is treated as singular unless the meaning clearly shows that the parts in the collection, not the collection as a whole, are being considered. If the collective noun is singular and takes a singular verb, a pronoun referring to it should, to be consistent, have singular form. Colloquially, however, plural pronouns are common even when the sense of the collective noun is singular.

| *Original* | *Revision* |

The *company* moves forward to *their* position in the line.
[*The company, thought of as a unit, is singular.*]

The *company* moves forward to *its* position in the line.
[*The singular pronoun* its *has replaced the plural* their.]

The company considers John one of *their* best men.
[*Their* can be replaced with the singular form (1), or it can be given an antecedent (2).]

(1) The company considers John one of *its* best men.
(2) The managers of the company consider John one of *their* best men.

The sixth grade pawed in *its* desks for *its* geographies.
[*The subject is plural because the sentence refers to individuals.*]

The sixth grade pawed in *their* desks for *their* geographies.
[*The plural* their *has replaced the singular* its.]

28d Personal pronoun subjects   Pron d

The subjective form should be used as the subject of a sentence or a clause, regardless of the use of the pronoun's antecedent.

| *Original* | *Revision* |

Jim and *me* made the first team as forwards.

Jim and *I* made the first team as forwards.

Original (*Cont.*)

Since I was not hungry, I told them that *him* and Mary could divide the lunch.

[*Though they follow the main verb* told, *the words* him and Mary *comprise the subject of* could divide the lunch.]

Revision (*Cont.*)

Since I was not hungry, I told them that *he* and Mary could divide the lunch.

[*The objective form* him *has been changed to the subjective form* he.]

28e Personal pronouns after linking verbs   Pron e

If we follow the practices of inflected grammar, a linking verb (see 29-2) should be followed by the subjective form, since the verb links a following complement to the subject. The subject-verb-object sentence pattern is so prevalent, however, that users of English tend to use the objective form whenever it appears after the verb.

There is a legend that the late Professor George Lyman Kittredge, one of the world authorities on language, was working late in his office one night when an alert student janitor became suspicious that robbers might be ransacking the professor's office.

"Hey, who's in there?" the student yelled.

"It's all right," Professor Kittredge replied. "It's me. Kittredge."

"The devil it is," the student retorted. "Kittredge'd say, 'It is I.' "

Whether or not this story is apocryphal, there is a growing tendency to use the objective form after *it is,* especially in colloquial speech— *It's me, It's her.* Careful speakers still preserve logic under formal circumstances, however, and say *It is I, It is she.* If, for instance, the student janitor had gone down the hall and telephoned, Professor Kittredge might have said, "It is I."

Original

"May I speak to Dr. Jordan, please?"
"This is *him*."

Revision

"May I speak to Dr. Jordan, please?"
"This is *he*."

28f Objective form of personal pronouns   Pron f

Use the objective case for an object complement (direct or indirect object), for the principal word of a prepositional phrase (object of a preposition), or for the subject or object of an infinitive (see 27-3).

Original

We never liked the Broadnicks, neither *she* nor her husband.
[*She is in apposition to Broadnicks and is thus part of the object complement.*]

It was impossible for Mary and *I* to hand in our papers Friday.
[*The subject of an infinitive has the objective form.*]

Just between *you* and *I*, no hair ever got that color naturally.

The manager promised my wife and *I* the new apartment.

Revision

We never liked the Broadnicks, neither *her* nor her husband.
[*The objective* her *has replaced the subjective* she.]

It was impossible for Mary and *me* to hand in our papers Friday.
[*The objective* me *replaces the subjective* I.]

Just between *you* and *me,* no hair ever got that color naturally.

The manager promised my wife and *me* the new apartment.

28g *Relative or interrogative pronoun*   **Pron g**

Like other pronouns, a relative or interrogative pronoun takes its number and gender from its antecedent, and takes its form from its function in its clause. This duality causes some difficulty. Since interrogative and relative pronouns are function words, they must be placed so that they show relationships within the sentence. As pronouns, they are often either subjects or complements; but since they acquire their position as function words, the normal order of actor-action-complement may be disturbed. The result is pressure to choose a pronoun form which would fit the order, not the logic of the sentence.

I asked him *who* he thought he was hitting.
I asked him *whom* he thought he was hitting.

In these sentences *who* and *whom* function as object complements of *was hitting*. Logically, the correct form is *whom*. The word is the first word in its clause, however, and since it occupies the subject position, speakers naturally say *who*. The English language seems here to be in transition, *whom* preserving a detail of our declined grammar, *who* being natural to a distributive grammar. Many careful writers would still insist upon *whom* in this example, but more liberal authorities would sanction *who,* especially in colloquial use. Similarly, the pressure of word order has made sentences like *I knew* who *you wanted* common colloquially, even though the logic of inflection requires *I*

[339

knew whom *you wanted.* Interrogative pronouns particularly, since they always appear at the beginning of the sentence in the subject position, tend to have the subjective form in all but the most formal situations (Who *do you mean?* Who *did Tom invite?*). Occasionally writers who have been corrected for using *who* in sentences of this sort become fearful and use *whom* whenever they are in doubt, even in sentences like *Whom does he think he is?*, which can scarcely be justified on any ground.

Original	*Revision*
I asked him *whom* he was. [Whom *is not the object of asked, but the subject complement of* was.]	I asked him *who* he was. [*The subjective form has been substituted.*]
I met the girl *whom,* everyone said, was going to win the beauty contest. [Whom *is not the object of said, but the subject of* was.]	I met the girl *who,* everyone said, was going to win the beauty contest. [*The subjective form has been substituted.*]
She will ask *whoever* she can find. [Whoever *is the object complement of* can find.]	She will ask *whomever* she can find. [*The objective form,* whomever, *has been substituted.*]
Who are you calling? [*Common in most situations.*]	*Whom* are you calling? [*Appropriate formally.*]
We wondered *who* he would take to the party.	We wondered *whom* he would take to the party.

English no longer has a possessive form to correspond to *which.* Most writers now use *whose* freely for this purpose, but some authorities object to using a form of *who* to refer to inanimate objects. The usage can be avoided by a change in structure.

Original	*Revision*
I do not like a ring whose setting reminds me of Grandmother's day. [*Usually acceptable and more economical than the revision.*]	(1) I do not like a ring with a setting which reminds me of Grandmother's day. (2) I do not like a ring the setting of which reminds me of Grandmother's day.

28h *Reflexive pronouns used for personal pronouns*   Pron h

Perhaps in a mistaken effort to avoid the choice between *I* or *me,* writers sometimes use the reflexive or intensive form of the pronoun in constructions calling for a personal pronoun. The usual personal pronoun is the preferred form for such constructions.

Original	*Revision*
Henry and *myself* started to make a "hot-rod" car. [Myself *is part of the subject.*]	Henry and *I* started to make a "hot-rod" car. [*The subjective form has been substituted.*]
They invited Anne and *myself* to the Sigma Nu formal dance.	They invited Anne and *me* to the Sigma Nu formal dance.

28i *First person in series*   Pron i

As a courtesy, *I* and *we* usually are last in a sequence; other pronouns usually appear first.

Original	*Revision*
I and Evelyn won the doubles.	Evelyn and I won the doubles.

28j *Consistency in pronouns*   Pron j

Avoid unnecessary shifting from one person to another (see 13b). This problem presents some difficulties in English, since modern English has no good impersonal construction. Constructions like *we find, they say,* and *you go* are common, but ambiguous. The indefinite *one* is less ambiguous but can become very awkward, especially when the possessive *one's* is required. For all but the most formal writing, however, *one* can be combined with *he* and *his.*

Original	*Revision*
When *one* is abroad, you will almost always find somebody who can speak *your* language. [*The shift from* one *to* you *is a shift of person.*]	When *one* is abroad, *he* will almost always find somebody who can speak *his* language. [*The third person forms,* he *and* his, *are consistent with* one.]
I think everybody should be careful of *one's* grammar.	I think everybody should be careful of *his* grammar.

28k Distinction between that and what   **Pron k**

What is used for the archaic *that which* and in this usage should not be confused with *that*.

Original   *Revision*

   That you have learned will be useful someday.

   What you have learned will be useful someday.

EXERCISE 28

A. Identify the various kinds of pronouns in the following sentences:

  1. Whoever says that places himself in a suspicious position.
  2. The dean, himself, wanted to know what you have been doing.
  3. That is the man who told me that amazing story about myself.
  4. I asked him what he thought you could expect from anybody like that.
  5. Everyone must be his own judge of questions of conscience.
  6. Anyone will grab at any means of survival.
  7. Just between us, nobody can do that or be that good.
  8. I told him that he ought to try to catch whoever did it.
  9. He must be a quack, because he said that he, himself, had psychoanalyzed himself.
  10. You might call me when you find out who has the answer.

B. In the following sentences choose the correct pronoun to agree in number with the collective noun which is its antecedent:

  1. The herd of wild burros follows (its, their) path up the canyon.
  2. The gang held (its, their) regular meeting Wednesday after school.
  3. The Chamber of Commerce cast (its, their) ballots for various candidates for beauty queen.
  4. The team took (its, their) positions about the field.
  5. The Security Council will endeavor to reach (its, their) decision today.
  6. The convention of nurses kept busy brushing (its, their) respective teeth.
  7. A handful of small boys searched vainly in (its, their) pockets.
  8. The fraternity bowling team has just won (its, their) first victory.
  9. The cordon of policemen tightened (its, their) net around the hideout.
  10. The committee approved the minutes of (its, their) last meeting.

C. Choose the correct pronoun form in the following sentences, and give the reason for your choice:

1. The recording secretary? That is (she, her) at the table.
2. Everybody said Uncle Adrian was stingy, but he left (we, us) girls a beautiful house.
3. None of the committee had brought (his, their) minutes of the last meeting.
4. When she had the ingredients jumbled in the pan, she stood staring as though she did not dare ask what (we, us) girls would have done.
5. Ask the patrolman (who, whom) he thinks he is arresting.
6. The quarrel between my sister and (I, me, myself) began when I was a child.
7. Everybody grabbed for (his, their) weapons.
8. I cannot help wondering (who, whom) he thinks he is.
9. Aunt Amy asked Ethel and (I, me, myself) out for the weekend.
10. If one is in a national park (you, he, they) can find drinking water if (you, he, they) will ask a ranger.
11. We heard voices coming over the water, and we knew it was (they, them).
12. We sorted out the mittens to the children, each according to (his, their) age.
13. Neither Martha nor Emily had ever seen (her, their) escort before.
14. You may nominate (whoever, whomever) you please.
15. Harry kept complaining about the rain, but after a while we agreed that (he, him) and (I, me) would start out.
16. When Father cooks, nobody feels sorry for (he, his, him) sweating over a hot stove.
17. He stabbed in the dark, without knowing (who, whom) he might hit.
18. The janitor was always nice to (we, us) girls.
19. Anybody who tries, whether from the Golden Rule, the *Analects* of Confucius, or Kant's categorical imperative, can discover what is (your, their, his) duty.
20. Either the president of the sorority or the treasurer must put (her, their) signature on the note.

29. CHOICE OF VERBS

[For Guide to Revision, see page 347]

*Verbs may be classified, according to their uses, on
the basis of their relationships with complements.*

Compare the following sentences:

INTRANSITIVE: The tide turned.
INTRANSITIVE: The car turned over.
LINKING: The milk turned sour.
LINKING: The book turned up missing.
TRANSITIVE: The car turned the corner.
TRANSITIVE: The cook turned on the gas.

The same verb appears in each sentence, but its meaning alters in
its three different uses: (1) as an *intransitive* verb, which completes a
predication without a complement but may be modified; (2) as a
linking verb, which links a subject and a subject complement; or (3)
as a *transitive* verb, which is completed by an object complement.
Furthermore, meanings alter within each use as verbs combine with
suffixes (*over, up, on*). Verbs can be classified according to these uses.

29-1 Intransitive verbs

When a verb has no complement it is called *intransitive*. That is, it
does not *transfer* or *transmit* meaning to a complement. In sentences
like *She lives, She sings, She used to sing, She was singing,* all the
words except the pronoun subject *she* are intransitive verbs or parts
of intransitive verbs. Or an intransitive verb may be the core of a
long sentence.

In spite of her incipient laryngitis, the drafty old barn in which she
was asked to perform, and the handicap of a foreign audience, she
sang very well, reaching high C with scarcely a suggestion of a
squeak.

The subject is *she* and the verb is *sang,* used intransitively, without a complement. Some verbs in English are appropriate in only intransitive uses (*exist, occur, belong, subside, faint, depart,* for example), but many verbs, like *turned* above, fit more than one use.

29-2 Linking verbs or copulas

Linking verbs seldom have much meaning and serve mainly to link a subject with a subject complement (see also 20-2).

> Life *is* real, life *is* earnest.   Life *is* a shadow.

Is links the subject *life* with words which describe it, *real* and *earnest,* or it links *life* with another noun, *shadow,* which tells something about the subject by restating it in different terms. Forms of *to be* (*am, is, are, was, were*) are the most common linking verbs and seldom appear except as linking verbs or function words. Other verbs which are frequently used transitively or intransitively may become linking verbs with special meanings when used with a subject complement. Among the most common of them are *seem, appear, look, get, become, feel, taste, smell,* and *sound.* Compare:

> You look tired.   You look at the apple.
> The rose smelled good. He smelled the rose. The dog smelled.
> The task proved impossible. The exception proves the rule.

In the first of each group, a verb is used with a subject complement as a linking verb; in the other uses each verb has different meanings. Note that the last sentence is ambiguous; *proves* can be interpreted as either a linking verb or a transitive verb, to mean either *becomes* or *tests.* For questions of pronouns and modifiers with linking verbs see 28e, 32b.

29-3 Transitive verbs

When it takes a complement which does not merely describe or repeat some aspect of the subject, a verb is called *transitive.* The relationships in meaning between verb and complement vary. Consider the following sentences:

> God made a green apple.
> Johnny saw the apple.
> Johnny wanted the apple.
> Johnny ate the apple.
> Thereafter Johnny disliked green apples.

In each sentence, *apple* is the object complement, but its relationship with the rest of the sentence varies. It does not always "receive action" from the verb, but it does complete the meaning of the verb. If, for example, the object were dropped from the fourth sentence, the meaning would change.

29-4 Verbs and separable suffixes

The variety of verbs in English is constantly growing as users of the language combine words to function as verbs. Consider the following sentences:

> Johnny looked at the apple.
> Johnny picked up the apple.
> Johnny broke off the stem.

Superficially, these sentences look different from those in 29-3. It is possible to say that in the first sentence *looked* is the verb and that this verb is modified by *at the apple*. This does not, however, make very good sense. Johnny did not just *look,* his look being modified by the direction of his looking, *at the apple.* He was scrutinizing the apple, deciding what to do next, as becomes clear in the following sentences:

Subject	Verb	Complement
Johnny	examined	the apple.
Johnny	looked at	the apple.

Clearly *examined* is the grammatical equivalent of *looked at,* and *apple* is most logically thought of as the complement of both verbs. Similar analysis is needed to explain the other sentences, especially the third, where it is clear that Johnny did not *break* in any particular way, but that he *broke off* something.

Similarly, words are combined to function as intransitive verbs.

> The airplane blew up.

What does *up* mean here? Obviously not *up* in the sense of away from the earth. The plane, or what was left of it, came down. Nor does *blew* in this sentence mean *blew.* The two words, *blew up,* mean *exploded.* That is, two words have lost their original meanings and have become a new word with a meaning of its own. There are many such, as in *hold up a train, get up a subject, call up a girl. Up* is not the only word so used; hundreds of combinations employ *at, by, in, on, of, off, out, to,* and the like. Constructions of this sort are often called *verb-adverb combinations,* since the element which was not a verb was probably formerly an adverbial modifier.

These verbs are peculiar in that the second element must often be separated from the verb and placed after the complement or at the end of the clause or sentence.

> You can *count* me *out.*
> How are we going to *find* that *out?*

In some sentences the second element can be separated, or need not be.

> *Look* these words *up.*
> *Look up* these words.

These combination verbs are multiplying rapidly in the language, and many have developed so recently that they lack currency or have been accepted only as colloquial or vulgate.

29 Choice of verbs   VC

GUIDE TO REVISION:

> *Select verbs which, according to standard usage, have*
> *the meaning required by the sentence.*

29a Distinction between similar verbs   VC a

Three pairs of similar verbs have been so thoroughly confused in dialect and vulgate usage that many people have trouble distinguishing between them in meaning and spelling, particularly in their uses with separable suffixes.

 Lie (lay, lain), intransitive, but usually modified or combined with a suffix like *down,* indicates that the subject occupies a position.

> The book *lies* on the table.
> The book *lay* on the table yesterday.
> The book *has lain* on the table in the past.

Lay (laid, laid), transitive except for a few special uses (*The hens lay well. Lay on, Macduff*), means *place* or *put* and now appears mainly in a variety of special contexts (see dictionary).

> He *lays* brick in his spare time.
> The men *laid* their plans carefully.
> The soldiers *have laid* down their arms.

Sit (sat, sat), intransitive except for a few uses, especially with suffixes like *out* or *with* (*She sat out the dance. She sits a horse gracefully.*), indicates that the subject occupies a place or seat or is in a sitting position.

> He *sits* by the window.
> He *sat* by the window last week.
> He *has sat* there for a year.

Set (set, set), transitive except for a few uses (*The sun sets in the west. The hens are setting.*), means *place* or *put*, often varied in combinations with words like *off, up, by*.

> He *sets* the lamp on the table.
> They *set up* the new organization yesterday.
> Finally they *have set out* on their journey.

Rise (rose, risen), intransitive, often combined with suffixes like *up*, indicates that the subject moves.

> He *rises* before dawn.
> He *rose* before dawn yesterday.
> He *has never risen* before dawn in his life.

Raise (raised, raised), usually transitive (but *John opened the betting, and Tom raised.*), indicates that the subject acts on something, making it rise or appear.

> He *raises* his hand when he wants to talk.
> The committee *raised* a new issue.
> His salary *has* not *been raised* for a year.

Original	*Revision*
Her clothes were *laying* on the bed.	Her clothes were *lying* on the bed.
[*A mistaken notion that* lie *refers only to animate things sometimes leads to this error.* Lay *needs an object to complete it.*]	[To lie *indicates that the subject occupies a position.*]
We decided just to *lay* around on the beach.	We decided just to *lie* around on the beach.
[To lay on *means* to place another object upon.]	[To lie on *means* to place oneself upon.]
He *laid* on the sofa.	He *lay* on the sofa.
[*This sentence—if the feat were*	[*In verbs meaning to place one-*

348]

Original (*Cont.*)

possible—would mean that he laid an egg on the sofa.]

Revision (*Cont.*)

self or rest, lie *appears as* lie, lies *in the present,* lay *in the past, and* lain *in the past participle. In verbs meaning to place another object,* lay *appears as* lay *or* lays *in the present, and* laid *in the past and past participle.*]

When the preacher *raised* his hands, and we all *raised* up, Ma just *set.*

[Raised *is a transitive form; the first use is therefore correct, the second incorrect.* Set *is a transitive verb except in the meaning "to endeavor to hatch eggs."* The sun sets *is an exception sanctioned by usage.*]

When the preacher *raised* his hands, and we all *rose,* Ma just *sat.*

[*The intransitive* rose, *the past form of* rise, *has replaced the incorrect use of* raise. Sat, *the past form of* sit, *has replaced* set.]

29b Linking verbs   VC b

Sometimes linking verbs can be very effective.

Although he *looks* gentle, he *is* the notorious hatchet murderer.

Part of the impact of the sentence depends on the slight difference in meaning between *looks* and *is*. Usually, however, the linking verb has little meaning; and since the verb in good prose carries much of the meaning, a writer who uses excessive linking verbs dilutes his prose and introduces needless, childish predications. Usually excessive use of linking verbs, especially of forms of *to be,* betrays the writer's lazy thinking or faulty structure. The overuse of *to be* often reveals inadequate subordination (see 22) or illogical relationships between ideas (see 19c), or excessive use of nouns (see 27). Often linking verbs usurp places better filled by more vigorous verbs.

Original

The conversion of the pottery craft into what is now a highly ramified industry is due to a long series of improvements, as well as to the methods which are now in use in distribution and marketing. The first step toward the better

Revision

A series of improvements in manufacturing, distributing, and marketing turned the craft of pottery making into a highly ramified modern industry. Salt provided the first improvement. Cast into the furnace when the earthenware

Original (Cont.)

manufacture of pottery was the use of common salt. When the pot was red hot in the oven, the attendant was ready to pour salt through the top of the furnace. This method was the factor which put a smooth, colorless glaze on the earthenware. It was one hundred years later when Enoch Booth was the introducer of the double-firing process to improve glazes. . . .

[*The paragraph is cumbersome because misused forms of the verb* to be *require awkward, roundabout sentences.*]

Revision (Cont.)

glowed red hot, it fused to form a colorless glaze. A hundred years later, Enoch Booth improved glazes with a method of double firing which permitted the use of colors. . . .

[*Removing the inappropriate linking verbs shortens and strengthens the paragraph.*]

29c Use of separable verbs   VC c

Some separable verbs are branded in the older handbooks as "incorrect," on the theory that the separable part of the verb is a preposition, that the word *preposition* means *before something,* and that these separable elements should therefore not appear at the end of a sentence, where they cannot be before anything. This would not be very good logic, even if the words were prepositions. Some parts of separable verbs must be put at the end of the sentence, and others may be. These verbs offer difficulties, however. Verb forms with separable suffixes are developing rapidly, more rapidly than they are being accepted into standard usage. Sometimes verbs are formed which persist in colloquial usage without being accepted as suitable for more formal prose. Sometimes, on the analogy of standard verbs with separable suffixes, forms are concocted which have no separate meaning, no excuse for existence, and no place even in colloquial usage.

Original

If they don't like it, they ought to get out.

[Get out *may become standard, but it can not now be considered suitable for formal writing.*]

Revision

If they don't like it, they should leave.

Original (*Cont.*)

The student council should have an eye out for ways to raise money.

After reading the letter, she was all set up again.
[*The slang is difficult to translate; its vagueness is part of its weakness.*]

I could not see where it was at.
[At *here adds nothing.*]

Revision (*Cont.*)

The student council should be alert to new means of raising money.

After reading the letter she felt happy again.

(1) I could not see where it was.
(2) I could not see it.

EXERCISE 29

A. In the following passage identify the active and passive verbs, the linking verbs, the intransitive verbs, and the transitive verbs:

1. Then the Lord said unto Moses, Go in unto Pharaoh, and tell him, Thus saith the Lord God of the Hebrews, Let my people go, that they may serve me.

2. For if thou refuse to let them go, and wilt hold them still,

3. Behold, the hand of the Lord is upon thy cattle which is in the field, upon the horses, upon the asses, upon the camels, upon the oxen, and upon the sheep: there shall be a very grievous murrain.

4. And the Lord shall sever between the cattle of Israel and the cattle of Egypt: and there shall nothing die of all that is the children's of Israel.

5. And the Lord appointed a set time, saying, Tomorrow the Lord shall do this thing in the land.

6. And the Lord did that thing on the morrow: but of the cattle of the children of Israel died not one.

7. And Pharaoh sent, and behold, there was not one of the cattle of the Israelites dead. And the heart of Pharaoh was hardened, and he did not let the people go.

8. And the Lord said unto Moses and unto Aaron, Take to you handfuls of ashes of the furnace, and let Moses sprinkle it toward the heaven in the sight of Pharaoh.

9. And it shall become small dust in all the land of Egypt, and shall be a boil breaking forth with blains upon man, upon beast, throughout all the land of Egypt.

10. And they took ashes of the furnace, and stood before Pharaoh;

and Moses sprinkled it up toward heaven; and it became a boil breaking forth with blains upon man, and upon beast.

—Exodus

B. In the following sentences select for each blank an appropriate form of one of the verbs in parentheses preceding each blank.

1. While I (*lie, lay*) _____ hidden behind the sofa, the other members of the family filed into the dining room and (*sit, set*) _____ down to dinner.

2. He had been (*lie, lay*) _____ on his back for three weeks, and he was so weak that he could not (*rise, raise*) _____ his hand.

3. The coat still (*lie, lay*) _____ where we had left it in the morning.

4. When the peasants finally (*rise, raise*) _____ in rebellion, issues which had (*lie, lay*) _____ dormant for years assumed new importance.

5. The sun (*rise, raise*) _____ at 6:30 a.m. and (*sit, set*) _____ at 5:50 p.m.

6. After I had eaten, I (*lie, lay*) _____ down on the couch and (*sit, set*) _____ the book on the stand in front of me.

7. All the children were (*lie, lay*) _____ in the tall grass watching the ducks (*rise, raise*) _____ into the air and head south.

8. The pitcher should be (*sit, set*) _____ wherever you (*sit, set*) _____ it this morning.

9. He decided to (*lie, lay*) _____ the difficult problems aside.

10. They let the injured man (*lie, lay*) _____ in the middle of the highway until the ambulance arrived.

11. (*Lie, lay*) _____ the slices of eggplant in a dish, (*lie, lay*) _____ a weight on them, and allow them to (*sit, set*) _____ there overnight.

12. He (*lie, lay*) _____ the canceled check in the drawer, and presumably it (*lie, lay*) _____ there yet.

13. I have (*lie, lay*) _____ in bed all morning, and now you say I must (*lie, lay*) _____ here all afternoon.

14. He had (*lie, lay*) _____ emphasis on this fact, that the land (*lie, lay*) _____ adjacent to the river.

15. He (*lie, lay*) _____ a wager that the billfold would be found (*lie, lay*) _____ on the dresser.

C. Distinguish between types and meanings of verbs in the following groups of sentences.

1. a. Her nose turned up at the end.

   b. The book turned up under the bed.

   c. The car turned up the hill.

2. a. I ran into my brother after the dance.
   b. The car ran into a tree.
3. a. Some witnesses lie in court.
   b. The clothes lie in the basket.
4. a. The party broke up in the early morning.
   b. The axle broke up in the mountains.
5. a. After the quarrel the children made up.
   b. Mary made up for the play in five minutes.
   c. Bill made up for lost time.
   d. Louise made up the entire story.
   e. Progress was being made up on the hill.
   f. The costumes were made up in New York.

30. FORMS OF VERBS

[For Guide to Revision, see page 363]

The verb combines with the subject to become the core of good writing. The English verb is so varied that it promotes both vigor and exactness.

The English verb, and especially the American verb, is so intricate, delicate, and varied that very few people not native to the language ever master it. Having said so much, one can add that the difficult parts of the verb cause native speakers little trouble. Natives learn verbs naturally and are usually unaware that they are doing something difficult with great ease. Most of our elaborate verbs rely upon order, and we handle order in grammar easily. The conjugated forms, however, give us trouble. Fortunately, they are relatively few and not difficult to master.

To see how our verbs work, consider the following sentences:

I should have liked to be with you.
I should have liked to be able to be with you.
I should have liked to have been able to be with you.
I should have liked to have been able to have been with you.

All of these verbs are complicated, and they carry delicate gradations of meaning. But many an American who could handle these four verbs and think nothing of the feat would be uncertain whether to write *lie* or *lay*. We can appropriately give particular attention to the relatively few conjugated forms which survive in modern verbs.

30-1 Principal parts of verbs

For convenience in keeping verbs in order, we recognize principal parts, from which other forms can be inferred. To use verbs accurately, the writer should know their principal parts. The task is easier than it sounds, since the principal parts of most verbs follow a rule. Most of the others fall into recognizable patterns.

We use three principal parts, as follows: (1) the infinitive, which (except for *to be* with *I am*) is the same as the present form used with *I* (*go, see, jump, mimeograph*); (2) the past form (*went, saw, jumped, mimeographed*); (3) the past participle (*gone, seen, jumped, mimeographed*). For most verbs, these three forms are reduced to two. Every verb now being made and every verb made during the last thousand years have had two principal parts, the infinitive, and the infinitive plus -*d* or -*ed,* which serves for both past and past participle (*sew, sewed; dance, danced*). Verbs of this type, for no good reason, are called *weak verbs.* In a very early ancestor of English verbs had principal parts which expressed a change of sound (and accordingly a change of spelling) within the verb itself. Most of these old verbs have disappeared from the language or have become weak verbs, but some have preserved their early forms and are usually called *strong verbs.* They often seem irregular, although usually they are not. There were once many classes of these verbs, each with a different sequence of changes, and since only a few verbs have survived from each class, strong verbs now seem irregular. Patterns can be observed, however, in verbs like the following: *sing, sang, sung; ring, rang, rung; ride, rode, ridden; write, wrote, written.* Past participles formerly ended in -*n,* and some still do.

Many of these old verbs are among the most common and important in the language. Thus they require special attention. The list below of principal parts includes the verbs which most commonly give trouble. A writer should be sure he knows them.

Infinitive	*Past*	*Participle*
awake	awaked, awoke	awaked
be	was, were	been
bear	bore	borne
begin	began	begun
blow	blew	blown
break	broke	broken
burst	burst	burst
catch	caught	caught
choose	chose	chosen
cling	clung	clung
come	came	come
dive	dived, dove	dived

Infinitive	Past	Participle
do	did	done
drag	dragged	dragged
draw	drew	drawn
drink	drank	drunk
eat	ate	eaten
fall	fell	fallen
give	gave	given
go	went	gone
grow	grew	grown
have	had	had
know	knew	known
lay	laid	laid
lead	led	led
lend	lent	lent
lie	lay	lain
lose	lost	lost
pay	paid	paid
prove	proved	proved, proven
put	put	put
ride	rode	ridden
rise	rose	risen
run	ran	run
see	saw	seen
set	set	set
shine	shone	shone
sit	sat	sat
speak	spoke	spoken
steal	stole	stolen
swim	swam	swum
swing	swung	swung
take	took	taken
teach	taught	taught
throw	threw	thrown
wake	woke, waked	waked
wear	wore	worn

30-2 Composition of verb forms

We use two devices to make verbs: (1) we change the form of a single word (*I am, he is; I go, he goes; I speak, I spoke*); or (2) we put several words together to make a verb (*I expect to be able to go; I should have liked to go*). Many verbs combine these devices. The result is that modern English affords a richness and accuracy in verb choice which has quite possibly never been paralleled in any other

356]

language. Our verb is an extremely exact and useful tool; but anything complicated requires some discretion in its use, and the verb is no exception.

On the whole, changes in individual words come down to us from an earlier stage of the language; verbs made by placing words side by side are of more recent development. On the whole, also, native speakers have little trouble with verbs which are constructed by placing words side by side—that kind of grammar, apparently, Americans find easy. Fortunately, most of our verbs are of this sort. On the other hand, Americans often have difficulty with the single words which change in form, perhaps just because there are so few of them that we do not learn them as part of our familiar speech pattern. They require special attention.

The modern verb is too complicated to permit giving a synopsis of it here. The groups of forms below include only the most common, and those most likely to give trouble. Verbs can be variously classified. They may be *active* or *passive* (see 19-5). They may indicate the speaker's concept of the sentence, that is, the *mood.* Common moods include the following: the *indicative,* which presents material as fact; the *conditional,* which provides conditions; the *subjunctive,* which indicates varying degrees of doubt, desire, uncertainty; the *interrogative,* which asks a question; and the *imperative,* which gives a command. Verbs may represent the *aspect* from which the action is viewed; for instance, *I go to school* implies that the action is customary; *I keep making that same mistake* implies that an action repeats itself; *I am about to start payments* implies that an action is to begin.

Verbs can represent *person* and *number.* English formerly had an elaborate inflectional system to designate these, but only a few endings remain. In general, *-s* or *-es* is added to the infinitive or first-person form in the third person present singular. Other forms have no ending. (The second person singular, which adds *-t, -st, -est* is now almost unused.) For the agreement of subject and verb in person and number, see 31. The verb *to be,* since it preserves forms from four old verbs, is irregular; for its forms, see the lists below. *Have* has the third person singular *has.* Verbs can be divided, also, on the basis of the time to which they refer, that is, on the basis of *tense: I will go, I am going, I have gone, I had gone.*

30-3 Present tense

Simple present
I prove
> *I prove the theorem this way.*
> *I go to class at eight.*

Often called the simple present, but not usually used for this purpose. Used most commonly to indicate a customary action.

> *Familiarity breeds contempt.*
> *Antonio is a good man.*

Often used for generalizations.

> *He cudgels his brains, fills reams of paper with strange marks, and proves the binomial theorem.*

Used sometimes as the so-called historical present.

Progressive or continuous
I am proving
> *I am trying to help you.*
> *I am living in Eastwood.*

Uncommon in English until the eighteenth century, progressive verbs are now probably the most common for expressing the simple present.

> *What are you doing now? I am going to college.*

Particularly suited to actions begun in the past and continuing into the present.

Emphatic
I do prove
> *I am proving it.*

Do, characteristically used in interrogative forms, also makes an emphatic form.

Interrogative
Do I prove?
> *Do you find the city pleasant?*
> *Are you happy here?*

Inversion can make almost any form interrogative, but *do* makes an interrogative form of the simple present.

Passive
It is proved
> *Examinations are given on Tuesdays.*
> *Nothing can be done about it.*

To be is used as an auxiliary in verbs which allow the receiver of the action to take the place of the subject.

Variations in mood and aspect
> *Life can be difficult.*
> *I may be staying all night.*
> *I keep remembering her face.*
> *I should be working now.*
> *I must try to improve.*
> *This must be the place.*
> *He would sing if he were able to.*
> *Would this watch be yours?*

Through the use of various function words, the English verb expresses a remarkable variety of ideas such as hope, wish, probability, obligation, conceivability, and the like.

30-4 Past tense

Simple past
I proved
> *We won the first set easily.*

More limited than other past tense verbs, almost always refers to action completed in past.

> *He returned Tuesday.*
> *Just then the storm began.*

Usually used with modifiers which specify the time.

> *We played tennis every day.*

Can indicate continuous action completed in past.

Present perfect
I have proved
> *I have finished my lessons.*
> *Someone has broken the gate.*
> *We have all eaten breakfast.*

Probably most common of past forms, usually indicates action carried out before the present, with emphasis on fact that it is completed or "perfected" at the present.

> *I have always hated turnips.*

Can indicate action begun in past and continuing in present.

> *I have just spent my last dollar.*

Can, with modifiers, indicate past action without emphasis on present state.

Past perfect or pluperfect
I had proved
> *By Wednesday we had finished.*
> *Before the guests came, John had prepared lunch.*

Related to past time as present perfect to present; that is, it indicates action as completed by some past time which is usually specified in the sentence.

Progressive or continuous
I was proving
I have been proving
I had been proving
> *At six o'clock the sun was shining.*
> *We have been talking about you.*
> *He had been smiling while I talked.*

Widely used in all past tenses, especially for action continuing at specified times in the past; can be used for past actions which continue into the present.

Emphatic
I did prove

Interrogative
Did I prove?

[359

Passive
It was proved
It has been proved
It had been proved

Used in all past tenses, with *to be* as function word.

Variations in mood and aspect
We used to skip rope after school.
Then we would usually go swimming.
He must have seen her.
It could have happened.
He may have told his father.
He might have told his mother.
He should have telephoned.
Had it been possible, he would have come.

Function words vary mood and aspect widely when used with the above tense forms. They can suggest completion or continuation of action, habitual action, doubt, uncertainty, possibility, obligation, and various other modal ideas.

30-5 Future tense

Shall-will future
I shall (will) prove
He will make up the test tomorrow.
Nobody will understand.

Shall or *will* is used in what is traditionally called the "simple" future, although the form carries a sense of modality and other forms frequently express simple futurity. For distinctions between *shall* and *will*, see 30g.

I'll prove

Contracted form.

I prove
He makes up the test tomorrow.
I go to Chicago next week and I get home on the first.

The same form used for the present often serves for the simple future when modifiers specify the future time.

I am to prove
I am to arrive at the airport in two hours.

Can be used for most future situations.

Immediate future
I am going to prove
Are you going to invite the teacher?
Who is going to be first?
He is going to make up the test soon.

Currently the most common future form, especially colloquially.

Future perfect
I shall have proved
By Monday he will have learned his lines.

Refers to an action which is imagined as completed at some indicated time in the future.

360]

Progressive or continuous
I shall be proving
I am proving
   They will be driving by in a
   minute.
   I am taking the next train.

With *will* and *be* as function words or with the usual present tense form, progressive verbs are useful to express the future.

Passive
It will be proved
It is going to be proved
It will have been proved

Passive versions of the forms above use *to be* as a function word.

Variations in mood and aspect.
   When you arrive, call me.
   He could finish if he would try.
   I must see you at once.
   I should write some letters.
   I can meet you at nine.
   I have to be ready in an hour.
   I could meet you at the library.
   Let us try again next week.
   You may go when you have
   finished.
   It would be fun to go.

Since the future is always uncertain, almost all future verbs are to a degree conditional, some more than others. English is uncommonly rich in ways of expressing in verbs various degrees of such uncertainty. The sentences here represent only a few of the more common variations in mood and aspect in verbs suggesting future time.

30-6 Verbals

Two types of verb forms may have special uses, retaining enough of their characteristics as verbs to take subjects and objects but functioning generally as nouns or modifiers. The two types are those usually characterized by the separable prefix *to* and those with the endings *-ing* or *-d* or *-ed*. They appear frequently in the lists above in combination with function words; such combinations predicate as complete verbs. Outside these combinations, however, these forms are not complete verbs and are called *verbals.* Compare:

   Verb: They *are going to prove* the theorem.
   Verbal: We asked the students *to prove* the theorem.
   Verb: Somebody *has been proving* the theorem.
   Verbal: Proving the theorem was their assignment.

The first of these forms is the *infinitive,* one of the principal parts of the verb and usually distinguishable by its sign, *to,* and it may be used as a verbal noun (see 27-3) or sometimes as a verbal modifier (see 32-2). The following six forms are relatively common in modern English:

	Active	*Passive*	*Progressive active*
Present	to lose	to be lost	to be losing
Past	to have lost	to have been lost	to have been losing

The second type of verbal is called a *gerund* when it is used as a verbal noun (see 27-3) and a *participle* when it is a verbal modifier (see 32-2). The most common forms of this verbal are:

	Active	*Passive*
Present	proving	being proved
Past	proved, having proved	having been proved

The simple past form *proved* is common for the participle but is not used for the gerund.

The form of a verbal is determined by the relationship of the time of the action of the verbal to the time of the action of the main verb. The present verbal is most common and is used when the verbal and the main verb refer to action at the same time.

> We expected him *to burn* the papers.

Both verb and verbal refer to the past; the verbal is therefore present in form.

> *Smiling* at his discomfort, she looks at the photographs.

Verb and verbal both refer to the present and both forms are present. The present form is also used sometimes with a function word like *after* to suggest action preceding that of the main verb.

> After *smiling* at his discomfort, she closed the photograph album.

The past forms regularly indicate action previous to the time of the main verb.

> We expected him *to have burned* the papers.
> *Having smiled* at his discomfort, she closed the photograph album.

The burning and the smiling preceded the expecting and the closing. The simple past participle often describes a state of affairs caused previously but existing at the same time as that of the main action.

> *Reconciled,* he continued to praise the photographs.

30 Forms of verbs   **Vb**

GUIDE TO REVISION:

*Supply the verb form appropriate to the voice, mood,
and tense the sentence requires.*

In English many verb forms can be used in a variety of situations.
Tense forms can often be used interchangeably, but the flexibility of
the verb also breeds carelessness. The writer must choose a verb form
which will do what he wants done.

30a Consistency in a tense   **Vb a; Tense a**

A shift in tense shifts the point of view of the writing (see 13).

Original	*Revision*
Finally Mr. B abducts Pamela and keeps her prisoner at a country estate. Mrs. Jewkes guards her day and night. Pamela made only one attempt to escape, and it failed.	Finally Mr. B abducts Pamela and keeps her a prisoner at a country estate. Mrs. Jewkes guards her day and night. Pamela makes only one attempt to escape, and it fails.
[*The writer shifts, in the third sentence, from present to past forms.*]	[*When* makes *and* fails *replace the past forms, the passage is consistent. The writer might have made all verbs past.*]

30b Sequence of tenses   **Vb b; Tense b**

When the sense requires it, tenses should be changed (see 13-4).
Particularly, when two or more times are distinguished within the
sentence, the forms of the verbs should indicate which events come
before and which after. Partly because many English verb forms can
serve several functions, these distinctions require attention. In general, the relationships of the tenses can be suggested by a formula
like the following:

The pluperfect forms   are to   the other past forms
    as the past forms   are to   the present forms
  as the present forms⎫
        and   ⎬ are to   the other future forms.
the future perfect forms⎭

This works out somewhat as follows:

When the boss *had come* (pluperfect form) I *received* (past form) my pay.

At noon, if the boss *has come* (past form) I *receive* (customary present form) my pay.

By noon, the boss *will have come* (future perfect form), and I *shall receive* (future form) my pay.

By noon, if the boss *comes* (present form), I *shall receive* (future form) my pay.

Original

She *broke* the doll her mother *gave* her for her birthday.

[*The doll had been given before it was broken.*]

When he *wrapped* and *addressed* the package, he *took* it to the post office.

[*He did not do the wrapping on the way.*]

When you *wrap* the package, be sure you *sealed* the ends.

[*The actions are to be simultaneous, and the tenses should be the same.*]

He was sad, because he *thought* his wife was faithful to him.

[*The writer, by failing to use a tense to show a completed action in the earlier past, says what he does not mean.*]

Revision

She *broke* the doll her mother *had given* her for her birthday.

[*The pluperfect, had given, makes the sequence of time clear.*]

When he *had wrapped* and *addressed* the package, he *took* it to the post office.

[Wrapped *has been changed to* had wrapped.]

When you *wrap* the package, be sure you *seal* the ends.

He was sad, because he *had thought* his wife was faithful to him.

[*Use of the pluperfect form establishes that the sadness follows the acquisition of knowledge.*]

30c Tense in indirect quotations   **Vb c; Tense c**

When a direct quotation is made into an indirect quotation, the tense is pushed back. That is, a past form becomes the pluperfect form, a present form becomes a past form, and a future form becomes a present or conditional form.

Original

DIRECT DISCOURSE: "I don't want that junky old car parked in front of my house," the old lady yelled at me.

Revision

DIRECT DISCOURSE: "I don't want that junky old car parked in front of my house," the old lady yelled at me.

Original (Cont.)

INDIRECT DISCOURSE: The old lady yelled at me that she *does* not want my junky old car parked in front of her house.

[*The verb has been changed from first to third person, but the time has not been changed.*]

DIRECT DISCOURSE: "You were wrong," he said.

INDIRECT DISCOURSE: He said I *was* wrong.

Revision (Cont.)

INDIRECT DISCOURSE: The old lady yelled at me that she *did* not want my junky old car parked in front of her house.

[*The present form* don't want *of the direct discourse has become the past form* did not want.]

DIRECT DISCOURSE: "You were wrong," he said.

INDIRECT DISCOURSE: He said I *had been* wrong.

30d *Tense of verbals*   **Vb d; Tense d**

A verbal usually has a present form when it and the main verb refer to the same time. It takes a past form when it refers to a time before that of the main verb (see 30-6).

Original

I was pleased to have received your note.

[*This sentence implies that he became pleased some time after he had received the note.*]

Hamlet found Claudius about to have prayed and spared him.

Now I am in college I know I am lucky to have a good teacher in high school.

Revision

I was pleased to receive your note.

[*The pleasure is now simultaneous with the receiving of the note.*]

Hamlet found Claudius about to pray and spared him.

Now I am in college I know I am lucky to have had a good teacher in high school.

30e *Principal parts of verbs*   **Vb e; Prin**

Proper principal parts, especially of strong verbs, must be used in the formation of verbs (see the list in 30-1).

Original

I must have broke my glasses in the fall.

[*The third principal part, the participle, is required in the perfect form of the verb.*]

Revision

I must have broken my glasses in the fall.

[Broken, *not* broke, *is the participle form.*]

Original (*Cont.*)

By noon we had finished the dig-ging and began to pour the con-crete.

[Began *is parallel with* finished, *with* had *understood.*]

Revision (*Cont.*)

By noon we had finished the dig-ging and begun to pour the con-crete.

[Begun *is the proper principal part to be used in forming the pluperfect tense.*]

30f Moods   **Vb f; Mood**

The writer should choose a form representing proper mood: the indicative to state a fact, the interrogative to ask a question, the im-perative to issue a command, the conditional for conditions, and the subjunctive for situations involving uncertainty, suppositions, or de-sire. Of these moods, the subjunctive occasions the greatest difficulty because a few uses requiring special forms survive, and these are disappearing except in formal usage.

The main situations in which the special forms are still used are: (1) in main clauses to express a wish (*The Lord be with you*); (2) in *if*-clauses expressing a so-called "condition contrary to fact," that is, a supposition that is impossible or thought to be improbable (*If I were he, I would quit*); (3) in *that*-clauses expressing a wish, com-mand, or request (*The major ordered that the prisoners be held for interrogation*). In formal uses the present subjunctive is sometimes used in if-clauses which are not contrary to fact (*If these data be verifiable, the hypothesis becomes untenable*).

The special forms for the subjunctive which survive are two: (1) the third person present subjunctive singular does not have the ending -*s* or -*es* (indicative, *he proves;* subjunctive, *if he prove*); (2) for the verb *to be,* the present singular subjunctive form is *be,* the past sin-gular subjunctive form *were.*

Original

If my brother *was* here, you would behave differently.

[*The clause states a condition contrary to fact but uses an in-dicative verb form according to mmon colloquial practice.*]

If I *was* you, I would tell him what I think of him.

Revision

If my brother *were* here, you would behave differently.

[*Formally, the subjunctive form still appears in such clauses; the subjunctive* were *replaces indicative* was.]

If I *were* you, I would tell him what I think of him.

Original (Cont.)

[*Even colloquially the subjunctive is usual in this particular expression;* if I was you *is more characteristic of dialect or vulgate usage.*]

The President will refuse if the Senate demands that he discharges his secretary.
[*The* that-*clause expresses a command.*]

Is he live, or *is* he dead,
I'll grind his bones to make my bread.
[*In archaic, very formal or oratorical practice, the subjunctive is often used in conditional clauses.*]

Revision (Cont.)

[*The subjunctive form has been substituted in the* if-*clause.*]

The President will refuse if the Senate demands that he *discharge* his secretary.
[*The subjunctive has been used in the* that-*clause.*]

Be he live, or *be* he dead,
I'll grind his bones to make my bread.

30g Shall *and* will   **Vb g**

The verbs *shall* and *will* are troublesome because they have a troubled background. In Anglo-Saxon *shall* and *will* were not signs of the future; the word for *shall* meant *ought to* and the word for *will* meant *willing to, to be about to.* These meanings have been preserved in *should,* which implies obligation, and *would* which implies willingness. But *shall* and *will* became indications of the future, just as words with the same meaning today (*I am about to go; I have to go*) are becoming future forms. For hundreds of years little effort was made to distinguish between *shall* and *will* as auxiliaries, and users of English apparently never have had any deep-rooted feeling for a distinction between them—a fact which may account for the distinction's being difficult.

In the eighteenth century, a popular grammarian laid down rules for the use of *shall* and *will,* and most handbooks of usage since then have repeated his rules—though a few have turned them exactly backwards. At present, most people, especially in America, pay little attention to these rules. Partly because contractions (*I'll, we'll*) are so common in speech, *will* is used in all persons in most informal situations. A few people, however, attach great importance to the arbitrary distinction between the words, and the following rule is still observed in some formal English.

In the first person, use shall *to denote simple futurity,* will *to denote determination and purpose; in the second and third persons, use* will *to denote simple futurity,* shall *to denote determination and purpose.* In general, *should* and *would* also follow this rule, except when the use would interfere with the basic meaning of these two words, *should* implying duty, *would* implying willingness.

Original

I *will* consider each of the arguments of my colleague.

[*Presumably the verb implies only simple futurity; the form* will *is common informally, but is often not accepted in formal English.*]

I predict that the people *shall* rise up in indignation.

[*Consciousness of a distinction sometimes leads writers to a mistaken preference for* shall *as an affectation of "correctness."*]

Revision

I *shall* consider each of the arguments of my colleague.

[*According to rule,* shall *is used with the first person to indicate simple futurity,* will *with the second and third persons.*]

I predict that the people *will* rise up in indignation.

[*There is no need for the unusual form of the original; the verb is not expressing determination.*]

EXERCISE 30

A. For each blank in the following sentences select an appropriate form of the verb in parentheses:

1. If you are going fishing with me you _____ (be) quiet.
2. When I _____ (eat) my lunch, I took a short nap.
3. If you want to stay out after hours, you _____ (ask) permission.
4. While I was looking in the closet for my windbreaker, part of the ceiling _____ (fall) down.
5. Since you say you can see in the dark so well, why _____ you _____ (stumble)?
6. While I _____ (set) the table, you might put some water to boil.
7. Before you screw down the lid, be sure you _____ (check) the safety valve.
8. You _____ (prove) the theorem before you could have proved the corallary.
9. Mother told me that strange men _____ (be) not to be trusted.
10. When Uncle Joe came to dinner he always _____ (bring) us oranges.

B. For each blank in the following sentences select an appropriate form of the verb in parentheses:

1. If I _____ (be) you, I would take it back and get my money.

2. If it _____ (be) noon, I would go right now.

3. If the plant _____ (be) sitting on the piano, it must have left a mark in the dust.

4. If only Father _____ (be) here!

5. If anybody _____ (save) him, Dr. Worley would be the man.

6. If your father _____ (be) not carrying a gun, I would think him a religious man.

7. Mary, I often wish you _____ (be) smarter than you are.

8. John, I often wish you _____ (act) smarter than you do.

9. Children, _____ (can) you not keep from squabbling if you would try?

10. If those children _____ (can) keep from squabbling, I would let them play together.

C. Supply the verb forms missing in the following table:

Present form used with I	Past form	Past participle
1. pay	. . . .	. . . .
2.	caught	. . . .
3. run	. . . .	. . . .
4.	. . . .	chosen
5. drag	. . . .	. . . .
6. swing	. . . .	. . . .
7. swim	. . . .	, . . .
8.	. . . .	done
9.	. . . . '	set
10. see	. . . .	. . . .
11. lay	. . . .	. . . .
12.	lay	. . . .
13. wear	. . . .	. . . .
14. wake	. . . .	. . . .
15. sit	. . . .	. . . .
16. steal	. . . .	. . . .

D. In the following sentences, select the appropriate forms of the verbal and explain the reason for your choice:

1. I was glad (to receive, to have received) your invitation.

2. It was the largest audience ever (to convene, to have convened) in Severing Hall.

3. When you get into the boat be sure (to fasten, to have fastened) your life belt.

4. The stairs are steep; be sure (to hold, to have held) the guard rail.

5. Father came along just when I was about (to be lost, to have been lost).

6. I was ashamed (to lose, to be losing, to have been losing) the game for our team.

7. If they were not doing their algebra, they ought (to be doing, to have been doing) it.

8. Those who were about (to die, to have died) took a last glance at each other.

9. She was frightened (to undergo, to have undergone) the operation.

10. He expected (to be, to have been) elected house manager.

31. AGREEMENT OF SUBJECT AND VERB

[For Guide to Revision, see page 372]

Subject and verb agree in number and person.

Agreement is a fundamental principle of an inflected grammar, but it has only limited use in a distributive grammar like English. Nevertheless, a few form distinctions for verbs survive in English (*-s* to mark third-person singular present, and forms like *am, is, was, were, have, has, do, does*) and are used to agree in number and person with their subjects.

In most sentences agreement between subject and verb causes difficulty only to the most inexperienced writers (*he goes, they go*), but some constructions cause trouble because the subject is not readily recognizable as either singular or plural (*the committee votes* or *vote*), and in some sentences the actor-action pattern is so obscured that the subject is not readily recognized.

> The dancer, with her ballet company, her orchestra, her stage crew, and her managers and directors, occupies the sixth floor.

Dancer, although separated from the verb by modifiers that are plural, is singular, and *occupies* is singular to agree.

For these special problems no single rule suffices, but surviving inflections give the writer an opportunity to specify number more exactly. He therefore selects verb forms according to the meaning intended for the subject, singular if the subject has a singular sense, plural if the meaning of the subject is plural.

31 Agreement of subject and verb **SV**

GUIDE TO REVISION:

Change either the subject or the verb, usually the verb, so that the two agree in number and person.

Errors of agreement usually occur because the writer fails to identify the subject, confuses the subject with its modifiers, does not know proper verb forms, or mistakes the number of the subject (see 28a-c). Meaning determines the number of the subject.

Two *hours* of his last twelve *were gone.*
Two *hours is* a long time.

In the first sentence *hours* is plural, according to the sense of the sentence, but in the second sentence, in spite of its plural form, *two hours* specifies a singular unit of time and is therefore in agreement with a singular verb. Usually form and meaning are the same, and often when a subject plural in form is used in a singular sense it is imprecise. Consider

Late *hours was* responsible for his illness.

The sense of the subject is singular, but revision would make the meaning more exact.

Keeping late hours *brought on* his illness.

Original	*Revision*
The officers *was* the only students at the meeting.	The officers *were* the only students at the meeting.
I did not know you *was* afraid.	I did not know you *were* afraid.

31a Agreement with compound subjects **SV a**

A compound subject usually is plural, even though its parts are singular. *Corn and lettuce* combine into a subject as clearly plural as a plural form like *vegetables.* The meaning of the subject, however, usually determines its number, and occasionally compound subjects join to form a noun expression whose sense is singular. Compare:

Ham and eggs are among his most profitable products.
Ham and eggs is a good dish.

372]

The compound is plural in the first sentence, but in the second it names a single item for a menu.

Original	Revision
Adrian and Harry *rides* the trolley to school and *walks* home.	Adrian and Harry *ride* the trolley to school and *walk* home.
[*The compound subject is plural, even though the part of it near the verb is singular.*]	[*The plural verbs* ride *and* walk *replace the singular so that subject and verbs agree.*]
A horde of little Mexicans and one lone donkey *was* trooping down the road.	A horde of little Mexicans and one lone donkey *were* trooping down the road.
[Donkey *is singular, but the subject is compound and thus plural.*]	[Were *agrees with* horde *and* donkey.]

31b Agreement with alternative subjects   **SV b**

Either, neither, or, nor usually separate alternatives and do not combine elements as compounds. Logically alternative subjects govern verbs individually: *Misery or death was* (not *were*) *his only prospect.* Colloquially, such subjects are not always regarded individually, and competent writers sometimes feel that the sense of alternative subjects is plural: *Neither of them were afraid.* Formally, the singular is preferred when alternative subjects are singular. When they differ in number the plural is usual, although writing is clearer when alternative subjects of differing number are avoided.

Original	Revision
Either French dressing or mayonnaise *go* well with tomatoes.	Either French dressing or mayonnaise *goes* well with tomatoes.
[*The subject is singular,* dressing *or* mayonnaise, *not both.*]	[*The singular* goes *has replaced the plural* go.]
Neither the captain nor the radar men *was* aware of the approaching bomber.	Neither the captain nor the radar men *were* aware of the approaching bomber.
Neither processes of education nor force is likely to succeed.	Neither education nor force is likely to succeed.

31c Agreement with modified subjects   **SV c**

When a subject is modified, a writer may carelessly mistake the modifier for part of a compound subject or may make the verb agree with the modifier rather than the subject. Colloquially, however, a subject modified by a prepositional phrase is sometimes used as a compound: *The captain with most of the crew were standing on deck.*

Original

Orrie, with his little sister, were squatting in the middle of the puppy pen.
[Orrie *is a singular subject, modified by* with his little sister.]

Jim, as well as his brothers, *plan* to enter the university.

The employer of all sorts of people, highly trained scientists, ignorant laborers, callow youths and lovesick stenographers, *have* to have wide understanding of human nature.
[*The subject,* employer, *requires a singular verb.*]

Revision

Orrie, with his little sister, *was* squatting in the middle of the puppy pen.
[*The singular* was *has replaced the plural* were.]

Jim, as well as his brothers, *plans* to enter the university.

The employer of all sorts of people, highly trained scientists, ignorant laborers, callow youths and lovesick stenographers, *has* to have wide understanding of human nature.
[*The singular* has *has replaced the plural* have.]

31d Agreement with indefinite pronouns   **SV d**

Indefinite pronouns often indicate one of many, and if so, they are logically singular. Some indefinite pronouns, especially *everyone* and *everybody,* are popularly thought of as plural, probably because they contain the word *every,* which suggests a plural number. Accordingly, sentences like *Everybody in the room have taken their hats and gone* are common colloquially and are sometimes considered acceptable in writing. Careful writers, however, treat *everybody* and *everyone* as singular. The sentence above could be revised to retain the plural (*They have all taken their hats and gone*). *None* can be singular or plural, depending on the meaning intended (*None of you is to blame. None but the brave deserve the fair*).

Original

Each of the umpires *have* to have *their* eyes examined.
[Each *refers to only one of the* umpires *at a time; the plural* umpires *should not be allowed to obscure the singular* each.]

Revision

(1) Each of the umpires *has* to have *his* eyes examined.
(2) The umpires ought to have their eyes examined.

31e Agreement with subordinate clauses   SV e

A clause or phrase as subject is treated as singular.

Original

What you are looking for *are* in the closet.

To know birth and death *are* to know life.
[*The subject is* To know birth and death, *a phrase, which is singular.*]

Revision

What you are looking for *is* in the closet.

To know birth and death *is* to know life.
[*The singular* is *has replaced the plural* are.]

31f Agreement in subordinate clauses   SV f

A verb in a subordinate clause agrees with the subject of the clause. When the subject is a relative pronoun, the verb agrees with it and reflects the number of its antecedent. In a few types of sentences, therefore, the number of the verb form chosen may reflect different meanings in different contexts. Compare:

> The court is concerned mainly with the group of delinquent children responsible for the vandalism. John is one of those children, who *seems* unaffected by punishment.
> The courts have to deal with many different types of children. John is one of those children who *seem* unaffected by punishment.

The writer must be sure that the verb form reflects the intended meaning.

Original

My father was one of the many businessmen who *was ruined* by the depression.
[*The subject of* was ruined *is* who, *which almost certainly is intended to refer to* businessmen *and thus is plural.*]

Revision

My father was one of the many businessmen who *were ruined* by the depression.
[*The plural form* were *replaces the singular* was; *only in an unusual context would* one *be the antecedent of* who.]

31g Agreement when subjects follow verbs   SV g

Subject-verb-complement order is so well-established in English that speakers often have trouble recognizing a subject that follows the verb and fail to make the verb agree with it. Colloquially, an introductory *there* or *it* is frequently taken for a singular subject and followed by a singular verb, even when the real subject is plural. In standard writing, however, the verb takes the number of its subject, even though the subject may follow it.

Original

There *was* left only one seat in the balcony and one behind a post. [*The subject is compound and thus plural.*]

Revision

There *were* left only one seat in the balcony and one behind a post. [*The plural* were *has replaced the singular* was.]

Behind the tree *was* two squirrels. [Squirrels *is the subject.*]

Behind the tree *were* two squirrels.

When the subject and complement of a linking verb differ in number, the linking verb agrees with whichever precedes it.

Original

The *answer* to our problems *are* well-trained soldiers. [*The verb should agree with* answer. *This sentence will be awkward unless the linking verb is replaced* (*see* 29b).]

Revision

(1) The *answer* to our problems *is* well-trained soldiers.
(2) We need well-trained soldiers.

31h Agreement with collective nouns   SV h

In American idiom, a collective noun is treated as singular unless the sense of the sentence clearly indicates that the subject represents the parts of the collection, not the collection as a whole.

Original

The committee *have* voted to lay the motion on the table. [*The committee acted as a body and is singular in meaning.*]

Revision

The committee *has* voted to lay the motion on the table. [*The singular* has *replaces the plural* have.]

The committee *differs,* some supporting the motion, some opposing it, and some calling the proposal irrelevant. [*Here the various members of the committee are the subject, not the committee as a unit.*]

The committee *differ,* some supporting the motion, some opposing it, and some calling it irrelevant. [*The plural* differ *indicates the plural sense of the committee.*]

376]

EXERCISE 31

In the following sentences select for each blank the appropriate form of the verb in parentheses:

1. A sales lot full of old cars, some with battered fenders and bashed grills, some badly needing paint, and some with broken glass and missing chrome, _____ (*resemble*) a portable junk yard.

2. Neither Darwin nor his critics today _____ (*understand*) the full implication of the theory of evolution.

3. In the United States, everyone who _____ (*want*) an education can have it.

4. Clarence is one of those men who never _____ (*do*) tomorrow what can be put off until next week.

5. Clark, with all his little brothers and sisters, _____ (*be*) trying to squeeze through the closing subway door.

6. A sundae, loaded with syrups, marshmallow and whipped cream toppings, nuts, and all the fixings _____ (*be*) always too much for Elaine's diet.

7. Each of them, in spite of the most stubborn resistance to education, _____ (*find*) that he cannot entirely escape learning something.

8. If either of you _____ (*like*) the sweater, you can have it.

9. If either Helen or Judy _____ (*like*) the sweater, I will give it up.

10. A parade, made up of a few children and a few horses, all the dogs in the neighborhood, and a home-talent rodeo, _____ (*be*) our annual Fourth of July celebration.

11. He was one of those lucky soldiers who _____ (*seem*) always to be where there is no battle.

12. There _____ (*be*), after all is said and done and your life has mostly run away, only two rewards which make life worth living.

13. The chairman of the committee, even the chairman of several committees, in spite of reams of advice and all the promises of help from committee members, usually _____ (*have*) to do most of the work.

14. To know death in all its various forms around you on the battlefield _____ (*be*) to know the value of life and peace.

15. What you are searching for and longing for _____ (*be*) not to be found in books.

16. "All for one and one for all" _____ (*have*) been the motto of many a fighting group.

17. Marjorie is one of those women who never _____ (*stop*) chattering.

18. I can see the planes, like a flock of great birds which had studied formation flying and was now following its leader _____ (*bank*) and _____ (*turn*) abruptly south.

19. There _____ (*be*) only one old Chevrolet and a foreign car on the lot.

20. The Seminole chief, with quite a following of the older men of the tribe, _____ (*be*) waiting to smoke the pipe of peace with Zachary Taylor.

21. They grew up on hamburgers, but neither Ellen nor Avery _____ (*like*) hamburgers now.

22. Either the major or one of the colonels _____ (*have*) taken over the divisional headquarters.

23. Boardman's accurate shooting and our tight four-man defense _____ (*be*) keeping our little Class-B team within a few points of the champions.

24. The state senate _____ (*have*) acted like so many ward politicians, each one promoting his own petty interests.

25. The faculty _____ (*have*) approved your petition.

32. FORMS OF MODIFIERS

[For Guiae to Revision, see page 382]

The few distinctions among the forms of modifiers should be carefully observed.

In many languages the forms of modifiers are extremely difficult; elaborate systems of endings relate modifiers with expressions they modify. In English, word order indicates grammatical relationships of modifiers (see 23), and English modifiers have lost most of their endings. *Red* can modify a girl's hair or a man's shirt, and if the red hair as subject is resting on the red shirt as object, the same form, *red* serves all purposes. The only surviving important form changes for modifiers serve to distinguish adverbs and adjectives and to indicate the degree of modification.

32-1 Adjective and adverb

Many modifiers can be distinguished either as adjectives, which modify noun expressions, or as adverbs, which modify other parts of the sentence. The distinction is important for single-word modifiers because certain words and forms are restricted by usage to function only as either adjective or adverb. *Satisfactory,* for example, can be used as an adjective to modify a noun expression, but not as an adverb; *satisfactorily* can be used as an adverb, but not as an adjective. The following statements describe certain characteristics of forms of modifiers:

(1) *Most single-word adverbs end in* -ly. Not all adverbs can be so distinguished, but most adverbs were formed by the addition of the word *like* to some other word, usually an adjective. When combinations such as *stormy-like* or *handsome-like* were shortened, they became *stormily* or *handsomely.* We now make adverbs by adding *-ly* to almost any modifier. A few adjectives have been formed by adding *-ly* to a noun (*homely, leisurely*).

(2) Some adverbs existed in Anglo-Saxon and have survived in their early form; thus the ending -ly was not necessary to make adverbs of them (*well, however, down, ahead*).

(3) A few words function as either adverbs or adjectives (*better, early, fast, much, more, late*).

(4) A few words function informally or colloquially as either adverbs or adjectives, even though -ly adverb forms exist and are usually preferred in formal writing or speaking (*cheap* or *cheaply, close* or *closely, deep* or *deeply, even* or *evenly, loud* or *loudly, slow* or *slowly, tight* or *tightly*). Compare:

It was a *slow* train.

Go *slow* in this zone.

You should proceed *slowly* with the reorganization.

(5) A few words are frequently confused because of similarities in spelling and meaning.

Adjectives	*Adverbs*
good (kind, agreeable, satisfactory)	*well* (satisfactorily, in a pleasing or desirable manner)
well (fortunate, fitting or proper, in good health)	
real (authentic, genuine)	*really* (actually, in a real manner)
sure (firm, secure, dependable)	*surely* (certainly)
some (in an indefinite amount)	*somewhat* (to a certain extent or degree)

32-2 Verbal modifiers

Verbals (see 30-6) may be used as modifiers as well as nouns (see 27-3). Like other verbals, verbal modifiers cannot serve as the complete verb in a clause (see 17a), but they can take a complement. Both infinitives and participles serve as verbal modifiers, functioning either in fixed positions or as movable modifiers.

INFINITIVE AS SENTENCE MODIFIER: *To insure* delivery he sent the letter by registered air mail.

PARTICIPLE AS SENTENCE MODIFIER: *Relying* on our compass, we tried to keep a constant course through the underbrush.

PARTICIPLE MODIFYING NOUN: It was a *trying* experience.

PARTICIPLE AS MODIFYING SUBJECT COMPLEMENT: The experience was *trying*.

Notice that constructions with verbal modifiers are often much like constructions with complex verbs which use verbal forms in combination with function words.

VERB: He *was trying to forget* the experience.

32-3 Other types of modifiers

A few other types of modifiers need to be distinguished.

(1) *Appositive modifiers* usually follow noun expressions (see 23-5), repeating an idea with a slightly different emphasis.

My *mother,* a very strong-minded *woman,* believed that a human back should never touch a chair back.

Woman, a word which usually works as a noun, is here called an appositive or said to be in apposition with *mother.*

(2) *Demonstrative adjectives* are function words which "point out" a noun expression: *these, those, this,* and *that* are most common. They are like pronouns in form (see 28-8) and like pronouns emphasize the reference between words in the sentence (see 24f).

(3) *Articles, a, an,* and *the,* are special function words which introduce noun expressions (see 33-7).

(4) *Possessive modifiers,* the possessive forms of nouns (see 42a) and pronouns (see 28-2), act as modifiers.

He put *his* head in the *lion's* mouth.

32-4 Comparison of adverbs and adjectives

We recognize three degrees of modifiers, as follows: Positive, implying no comparison (*fast car, beautifully landscaped*); comparative, implying that one exceeds another (*The boulevard is a faster street than the highway and more beautifully landscaped*); and the superlative, which implies the highest degree, at least within certain limitations (*The boulevard is the fastest road out of town, and the most beautifully landscaped*).

Modifiers are compared in two ways.

	Positive	*Comparative*	*Superlative*
Short adjec- tives	red	redder	reddest
	short	shorter	shortest
	greedy	greedier	greediest
	homely	homelier	homeliest

	Positive	*Comparative*	*Superlative*
Long adjec- tives	beautiful superficial	more beautiful more superficial	most beautiful most superficial
Adverbs	slow rapidly beautifully superficially	slower more rapidly more beautifully more superficially	slowest most rapidly most beautifully most superficially

Short adjectives (all adjectives of one syllable and most adjectives of two syllables) and a few adverbs (especially those not ending in -*ly*) are compared by adding -*er* in the comparative and -*est* in the superlative. All long adjectives and most adverbs are compared by preceding the positive form with *more* and *most*. Adjectives of two syllables can be compared either way, and the distinctions are too subtle to be described by rule. The same person might say

> He is *stupider* than an ox

but write

> I never saw a *more stupid* boy.

A few modifiers retain irregular forms.

Positive	*Comparative*	*Superlative*
good	better	best
well	better	best
bad	worse	worst
little	less	least
much	more	most
many	more	most
far	farther	farthest

32 *Forms of modifiers*   **Adj; Adv**

GUIDE TO REVISION:

> *Substitute a form of the modifier appropriate in standard English for its use in the sentence.*

Usage requires that some single-word modifiers be either adjectives or adverbs, and form changes enforce the distinction. Other form changes distinguish the degree of modifiers. Confusion of these forms is not acceptable in standard English.

32a Adjectives and adverbs
Adj a; Adv a

Some words (see 32-1) are used as either adjective or adverb, but only colloquially as adverbs; others are restricted to only one of these uses.

Original

Jack can *sure* sing.
[Sure *has developed a special meaning in this colloquial use.*]

When I called, they came *quick*.

She played her piece *real good*.

None of the work was done *satisfactory*.

Revision

Jack can sing very well.
[*More formal expressions do not translate the original exactly.*]

When I called, they came *quickly*.

She played her piece *very well*.

None of the work was done *satisfactorily*.

32b Modifiers after linking verbs
Adj b; Adv b

A modifier used as a subject complement after a linking verb should be an adjective, not an adverb. As a subject complement it modifies the subject, which is always a noun expression. Errors develop whenever the writer has trouble recognizing a linking verb, especially with a verb which can be either transitive or linking. *Tastes,* for example, can be a transitive verb (*He tastes wine*) or a linking verb (*The wine tastes good*). *Good,* in the second sentence, is an adjective modifying *wine.* To say *The wine tastes well* would be nonsense. We cannot speak of the skill of wine in tasting. We could say *He tastes well* or *He tastes the wine well,* a compliment for a professional wine-taster. To say *He tastes good* implies cannibalism. As a kind of rough test, the writer can sometimes substitute a form of *to be* for the verb. If *to be* can be substituted without creating nonsense, the original verb is a linking verb and should be followed by a subject complement, not an adverb.

Original

The dog smelled *badly*.
[*Unless the writer intends a reflection against the dog's ability as a bloodhound, he needs the adjective as a subject complement.*]

Tweed feels *roughly*.

Revision

The dog smelled *bad*.
[*Since* is *could be substituted for the verb without making nonsense,* smelled *is probably a linking verb.*]

Tweed feels *rough*.

[**383**

Original (Cont.)

He looked *timidly* standing all alone before the judge.
[COMPARE: He looked timidly about the room, *in which the adverbial form is properly used.*]

Revision (Cont.)

He looked *timid* standing all alone before the judge.

32c Comparative and superlative   Adj c; Adv c

Although colloquial usage has never supported the distinction, formal practice restricts use of the superlative to comparisons among not fewer than three.

Original

Between the flatboat and the sponson canoe, I should say that the flatboat offers the *best* chance of shooting the rapids.

Revision

Between the flatboat and the sponson canoe, I should say that the flatboat offers the *better* chance of shooting the rapids.

32d The superlative   Adj d; Adv d

Extravagant superlatives may trap a writer into making statements he cannot substantiate and ultimately make his writing less strong and less convincing than more soberly qualified prose. Often overuse of superlatives leads to incomplete constructions (see 25d).

Original

Washington was the *greatest* American president.
[*Perhaps he was, but greatness is an uncertain term, and several other candidates might plausibly be supported. An unsupported superlative like this does more discredit to the writer than credit to Washington.*]

The Mount Rushmore Memorial represents Gutzon Borglum's *most* artistic achievement.
[*A judgment of this sort can be no more than an opinion and is likely to impress the reader as an unreliable opinion.*]

The Byington Parkway is the *most modern* highway in all the world.

Revision

Washington was *one of the greatest American* presidents.
[*The statement has been sufficiently qualified so that it is within the realm of probability. The reader is likely now to be impressed by the writer's desire to make only carefully considered statements.*]

(1) *Some critics consider* the Mount Rushmore Memorial Gutzon Borglum's *most artistic* work.
(2) The Mount Rushmore Memorial is impressive in its mass and artistic in its conception.

The Byington Parkway embodies *many of the most recent developments* in highway construction.

384]

32e Modifiers not subject to comparison   Adj e; Adv e

Some modifiers have meanings which are not logically subject to comparison (*opposite, final, dead*—in the sense of deceased, *opposite, waterproof, entirely, diametric,* for example). Strictly speaking, *fatal* cannot be thought of in degrees; a wound is fatal or not fatal. Colloquially, however, the function words indicating comparison (*most* and *more*) are often used to mean *more nearly* or *very* and are used with such words. Furthermore, colloquially many such words are losing their traditional meanings and assuming meanings which are comparable. Many of these new meanings have not been accepted for standard usage.

Original

The new turbo-jet is a *most unique* advance in aeronautical science.
[Unique *originally meant single or* sole, *but it has come colloquially to be a rather vague—and overused —modifier meaning* extraordinary.]

He was the *most outstanding* scholar in the school.
[*Although* outstanding *has developed a meaning like "excellent" or "distinguished," it often seems redundant when compared.*]

The waitress is slow, but she is *more better* than she used to be.
[Better *is already a comparative form.*]

Revision

(1) The new turbo-jet is *unique.*
(2) The new turbo-jet represents a radical departure in engine design, since it relies upon a newly discovered principle of fuel consumption.

He was the *outstanding* scholar in the school.
[*Without* most, *the modifier is more economical and more forceful.*]

The waitress is slow, but she is *better* than she used to be.

32f Possessives before gerunds   Adj f; Adv f

When nouns or pronouns are intended to modify gerunds (see 27-3), modifying forms (that is, possessive forms) can make meaning more precise. Since these forms often make no substantial difference in meaning, they are not regularly used colloquially.

Original

The principal was not amused by *them* playing poker in class.

Revision

The principal was not amused by *their* playing poker in class.

Original (*Cont.*)

[*Probably because it follows the preposition* by, *the writer has used the objective form* them. *But* playing, *not* them, *is the word related to the sentence by* by.]

I was always surprised by my *father* believing in ghosts.

[Father *seems intended to modify* believing, *but it is not possessive.*]

Revision (*Cont.*)

[*With the possessive form, the meaning of the sentence is clear; the* playing *failed to amuse the principal.*]

I was always surprised by my *father's* believing in ghosts.

[*The possessive form makes it clear that* believing, *not* father, *is the object.*]

EXERCISE 32

A. In the following passage identify the verbal modifiers or participles and parts of verbs which are identical in form with participles; indicate which are present and which past:

I called the dog off; turning back into the thicket to hunt the other two [panthers], I heard him again running in full cry. I pursued them, and found by their tracks that he was pursuing the old one, which ran down a terribly steep hill toward the Savage River, and into a thicket of laurel, when the dog came to bay. I went to him, and found him looking up a tree; but there was nothing on it. I examined, and found the scratches of her nails where she had climbed the tree; but as she was not there, I concluded that she had jumped off the tree before the dog had come in sight, and had run off. I looked around to see in what direction she had gone, but I could find no tracks in the snow. I then took a wider circle, and closed in; but still finding no track, I sat down on a log, and considered how it could be that she was gone, and no track left in the snow.

I reasoned with myself, that as she could not fly, she must have got on another tree, but there was no tree within her reach, though there were two large laurels standing in such a position that she could jump to them, and close by there were other laurels, so thick and strong that she might clamber on them. That was the last place I could see on which she could go without coming to the ground. But on looking down the hill, I observed, about twenty feet below, a leaning birch, which was so crooked that the top came within ten or fifteen feet, while the middle of it was perhaps twenty feet, from the ground. It had been so long crooked that two or three sprouts, about as thick as my thigh, had grown up from the main trunk; and between two of these sprouts lay the panther, lengthwise on the tree, with her long tail passed around one sprout, and crooked so as to lie on the trunk beyond the sprout next to her. I had passed directly under her, in circling around to find her tracks, and she was not more than fifteen or twenty feet above my head.

—Slightly adapted from MESHAK BROWNING,
Forty-Four Years of the Life of a Hunter

B. Supply for the blanks in the following sentences appropriate modifiers; some sentences may require modifiers of more than one word:

1. When the doctor arrived, the patient was looking very _____.
2. Both the tires are old, but put on the _____ of the two.
3. Neither cup is full, but yours is _____ than mine.
4. Alice's dress is unique, but mine is more _____ than hers.
5. He may not be simple-minded, but he always acts _____.
6. She came to our pledge party, but we decided that she was too _____ for us.
7. Walter Johnson was one of the _____ baseball pitchers this country ever produced.
8. The apartment was old and in a poor part of town, but it looked _____.
9. I watched both girls and decided the _____ one was probably a snob.
10. I ran to the window and looked _____ down into the street.

C. In the sentences below, decide whether each italicized modifier is appropriate or inappropriate. If it is inappropriate, select a better form.

1. Our "open-house" was the *most unique* party I can remember.
2. Your collie may be smart, but she looks *mean*.
3. The cougar clawed, and looked *meanly* from between the bars of its cage.
4. Before we were halfway down into the Grand Canyon my mule became *lame*.
5. The dog yipped, looked around as though for some protection, and ran *lame* toward his kennel.
6. Janice and Lorry lived in houses across the street from ours, but Janice's house was *more opposite* ours than Lorry's was.
7. Of the two sets, I should say that the *smallest* one has the *highest* fidelity.
8. When I was young I thought "The Song of the Lark" was the *beautifullest* picture I had ever seen.
9. When I saw that the cow moose had a calf with her I scrambled *lively* down the hill.

[**387**

10. If I had had a shell in my gun, I could have shot that squirrel *easy*.
11. Mother was always an *easy* mark for any clever salesman.
12. Our old car did not have much power, but it rode *easy*.
13. The chair was deep, soft, and pitched back, so that it looked very *easily*.
14. Daniel Webster was the *most eloquent* orator whose voice ever rang through the halls of the Senate.
15. The old square in New Orleans is a *most unique* sight.

33. FUNCTION WORDS

[For Guide to Revision, see page 395]

English grammar gains flexibility through function words.

English, as has already been observed (see 26-1, and the introductions to IV and VI), has developed a grammar which is primarily distributive. Its characteristics distinguish it from inflected languages; they appear in a comparison of three versions of the following passage from Boethius's *Consolation of Philosophy:*

Latin of Boethius:

Tandem,	"Vincimur,"	arbiter
At length	*"We are overcome,"*	*the judge*
Umbrarum	miserans	ait
Of Hades,	*pitying,*	*said;*
"Donamus	comitem	viro
"Let us give	*his consort*	*to the man;*
Emptam	carmine	conjugem."
He has bought	*with his song*	*his wife."*

Anglo-Saxon of King Alfred:

Tha cleopode se hellwara cyning,	ond cwæth	"Wuton
Then spoke the of Hell king	*and said:*	*"We ought*
agifan	thæm esne	his wif,	for thæm he hi hæfth
to give back	*to the husband*	*his wife,*	*because he her has*
gearnad mid his hearpunga.		
earned with his harping.		

Middle English of Chaucer:

At the laste the lord and juge of soules was moevid to misericordes, and cryeded: "We been overcomen," quod he; "yeve we to Orpheus his wif to beren him compaignye; he hath wel y-bought hire by his faire song and his ditee."

[389

A number of differences are apparent among the passages beyond those in vocabulary. Word order has replaced the endings of the Latin to reveal the actor-action grammatical pattern. The number of words has notably increased, twelve for Latin, twenty-two for Anglo-Saxon, and forty-two for Chaucer. Translation into modern English would require a few more words: *we been overcomen* would be *we have been overcome,* and *yeve we* would be *let us give.* The comparison illustrates a second characteristic of distributive grammar, that it sorts out and separates the signs of grammatical function from the signs of meaning. Whereas an inflected grammar, like that of Latin, puts the two kinds of signs into a single word, a distributive grammar, like that of modern English, tends to use one word to signal a grammatical relationship and another word to convey meaning.

Modern English, then, uses words in two ways, as signs of meaning and as signs of grammatical function. That is, the words in sentences can be roughly distinguished as *content words* and what we have called *function words.*

33-1 Function words and content words

Partly because English is still in process of becoming a language with a distributive grammar, words cannot be sharply classified as either content words or function words, and such classification is not necessary. Distinction between the two kinds of uses, however, is possible. Compare the following groups of sentences:

> I *have* two apples.
> I *have* eaten two apples.
> The apple is *pretty*.
> The apple is *pretty* good.
> *Up* is the right direction.
> The balloon blew *up*.
> He blew *up* the balloon.
> The wind blew the balloon *up* the road.
> What he says is not *so*.
> The truth was not *so* easy to discover.
> He left *so* that we could speak freely.

In the first sentence, *have* is clearly a content word, a sign of meaning; but in the second it is a function word, a sign of the tense of the verb. In the second group, *pretty* is a content word in the first sentence, but a function word in the second. In the third group, *up* ap-

390]

pears in a variety of uses: first as a content word naming a direction, second as a part of a verb *blow up* which works as a sign of meaning, third as a part of the same verb representing a different meaning in its transitive use, and fourth as a function word joining *road* to the sentence. In the final example, *so* appears first as a content word and then as two different kinds of function word. Since most function words formerly had other uses, they are now multiple-purpose words which did not lose entirely their old uses when they began to fill new functions required by our changing language.

33-2 Variety of function words

Function words have developed remarkable variety and adaptability. Charles Carpenter Fries distinguishes fifteen groups of function words and points out that function words constitute a third of the bulk of the extensive materials he has examined.[1] In the following sentence, nearly half the words, those in italics, act as function words.

> *Although the* room contained many women *who would have* died unhesitatingly *for their* children, *when a* mouse appeared, courageous mothers *who had been* sitting *on* chairs found *themselves* standing *on the* tops *of* piano benches *or* clinging *to* strange men *for* protection.

Although relates the words before the first comma to the rest of the sentence, but it also suggests that the clause it introduces presents a seeming contrast to the main assertion. *The* warns us that we are concerned with a specific room. *Who* relates the following words to the rest of the sentence, especially to *women,* and implies that the idea involved in *women* will serve as the subject of a dependent clause. *Would have* has little meaning but specifies the form of the verb. *For* is best thought of as part of the verb, but it shows the relationship of *children* to the remainder of the sentence. To see how hard it is to reduce some function words to a meaning, try to find a definition which will fit this *for* and the *for* toward the end of the sentence. *When* warns us that a dependent clause is coming and that the action in the clause determines the time of an event expressed elsewhere in the sentence. *A* introduces one particular mouse, but with the understanding that this mouse might as well have been any mouse. *In, of, on,* and *to,* like *for,* may be parts of the verb, but they also show how

---

[1] Charles Carpenter Fries, *The Structure of English* (New York: Harcourt, Brace & Company, Inc., 1952), pp. 87-109.

words like *tops, tables,* and *piano benches* are related to other parts of the sentence. *In* and *on* have meanings of their own; they modify our conceptions of space relationships. But what is the meaning of *of? And* and *or* join other words; *and* suggests that two words are to be taken together, *or* that there is an alternative between the ideas expressed in two words. And so on.

Function words, most of which we use without difficulty, specify grammatical ideas which cannot be observed from word order. For example, we can often know that we are dealing with a question only because certain words signal a question. Compare:

> Jack spoke.
> *Who* spoke?

Word order does not show that the second is a question; we must recognize *who* as a sign of a question. Similarly, function words identify the variation from the actor-action pattern in passive sentences (see 19-5). Compare:

> Jack *has* told a lie.
> Jack *was* told a lie.

Only the difference in the function words specifies whether Jack was actor or receiver. Accuracy in the use of function words as connectives is especially important: failure to understand the subordinating function of some connectives is frequently responsible for fragmentary sentences (see 17c). Certain groups of function words are therefore considered in detail.

33-3 Classes of function words

Function words are so shifting in their combination of meaning and grammatical function, and so varied in the functions they perform for complex modern sentence structures, that definitions and classifications are not exact. Many function words tell something about the meaning and application of another expression. *Have* or *shall* or *may* joined with a verb signals something about the use of the verb. *More* or *most* before an adverb or adjective indicates the degree of modification. Such function words are usually considered in this book in discussions of the expressions with which they are allied. Other function words have quite distinctive uses. *It* or *there,* for example, may be used to postpone a subject. Most commonly, perhaps, function words are used as connectives, relating various elements in the sentence. Considered here are four groups of function words, three of them of connectives, not considered elsewhere.

33-4 Conjunctions

Conjunctions join sentence elements and have no other grammatical function. Authorities conventionally recognize co-ordinating conjunctions, subordinating conjunctions, and correlative conjunctions, although the distinction among them is not so sharp as most dictionaries and handbooks suggest. Theoretically, a *co-ordinating conjunction* joins like and equal elements, a *subordinating* (*relative, dependent*) *conjunction* joins a dependent element to an independent element. *And, but, for, or,* and *nor* are conventionally recognized as co-ordinating conjunctions; they may join independent clauses or other sentence elements in parallel construction.

> I jumped into the car without trouble, *but* Mary slammed the door on her fingers.
> Although it was Sunday *and* although I knew I ought to get up for church, I turned over to take another nap.
> The pavement was icy *and* treacherous from a night of raining *and* freezing.

Subordinating conjunctions join dependent clauses to other sentence elements (see 18-3).

> *When* his watch disappeared, he immediately suspected me.
> He said *that* he did not know who took his watch.

The italicized words are subordinating conjunctions; the word *who* in the last sentence is a relative pronoun, not a conjunction, since it serves as subject of a clause (see 28-3).

The distinction between co-ordinating and subordinating conjunctions is not always sharp.

I struggled hard;	I could not get loose.
I struggled hard, but	I could not get loose.
Although I struggled hard,	I could not get loose.
I struggled hard; however,	I could not get loose.
I struggled hard, even though	I could not get loose.

By conventional statement *but* is a co-ordinating conjunction, and the two clauses in the second sentence are independent. *Although* is a subordinating conjunction, and the first clause in the third sentence is subordinate. *However* is a conjunctive adverb (see 33-5), and accordingly in the fourth sentence both clauses are independent. *Even though* is a subordinating conjunction, and accordingly the second clause in the fifth sentence is dependent. These differences in classification may seem too varied to account for the changes in the sentences, but the differences are the basis of our standardized punctuation of sentences of this sort, and accordingly the writer should know them.

Correlative conjunctions combine to show a relationship between sentence elements and are separated by one of these elements.

> *Either* you stop complaining, *or* I leave.
> *Neither* Mary *nor* Ruth knew what he was talking about.
> *If* six is one factor, *then* the other factor must be five.

33-5 Conjunctive adverbs

Conjunctive adverbs join clauses and act as modifiers within their own clauses.

> I wanted one of the then fashionable dirndls; *however,* I got Jinny's old plaid skirt.
> She was in no mood to take advice. I was angry, *however,* and I told her what I thought of her leaving the party.

The second *however* links the sentence to a preceding sentence. Other conjunctive adverbs include the following: *thus, then, nevertheless, nonetheless, moreover, likewise, similarly, also, furthermore, consequently, therefore, hence,* and *besides.* (See also 33-4).

33-6 Prepositions

Prepositions show the relationship between noun expressions and other sentence elements.

> My uncle, a man *of* few ideas, built the company *by* patient industry.

Of permits *ideas,* a noun expression, to modify *man. By* relates *industry* to the rest of the sentence. The preposition is conventionally thought of as the first word of a prepositional phrase (see 23-3).

33-7 Articles

The *articles* are sometimes classified as modifiers, sometimes as function words; like many function words they serve far more than one use. *The,* called the *definite article,* often refers to something previously mentioned.

394]

One evening Father remarked casually that we might soon go to see Niagara Falls. Thereafter, for days, all conversations led inevitably to a discussion of what we would do when we went to see *the* Falls.

The often identifies a particular object from others in its class. Compare:

He lost his eye in *an* accident.
He lost his eye in *the* accident I was telling you about.

The can replace a personal pronoun referring to part of the body.

Take the bow in *your* left hand and the bowstring in *your* right.
Take the bow in *the* left hand and the bowstring in *the* right.

The *indefinite articles a* and *an* have developed from the numeral *one* and retain some of their earlier meaning. Usually they have the force of *any. An* is used before words beginning with a vowel; *a* before words beginning with a consonant (*an* officer, *an* enlisted man, *a* private). Since speech usually determines language, words beginning with a vowel sound may require *an* even though the word is spelled with an initial consonant (an hour), and, conversely, a word beginning with a consonant sound may require *a* before a vowel (a European, a unit).

Many noun expressions require no article. Plural nouns including all members of a class usually require no article.

On the whole, *Americans* like *dogs, cats,* and *children.*

Abstract and general nouns usually require no article.

The history of your town is part of the study of *history.*
Evening came down and soon we could see thousands of *stars. The night* was clear and bright.

33 *Function words* FW

GUIDE TO REVISION:

Consider the exact implication of a function word, and choose carefully; if necessary consult a good dictionary or synonym book to be sure the word does just what you want it to.

Function words are pivotal words; one function word can change the whole tenor of a sentence.

Because I love you I must leave you.
Although I love you I must leave you.

Accordingly, function words should be chosen with unusual care.

33a Co-ordinating conjunctions   FW a; Conj a

Be sure to use the most meaningful co-ordinating conjunction. *And* joins like elements of thought or adds a similar element; *but* emphasizes a contrast; *or* offers a choice.

Original	*Revision*
The sea was like glass, *and* that was the last calm day we had at the beach. [*Clearly, a contrast is intended.*]	The sea was like glass, *but* that was the last calm day we had at the beach.
You can play all sorts of games, *and* if you want to, you can spend the afternoon under a tree reading a book. [*Obviously, a choice is intended.*]	You can play all sorts of games, *or* if you want to you can spend the afternoon under a tree reading a book.

Avoid running together with *and* clauses which are not properly co-ordinate and which become boring and undifferentiated when strung together. Usually, excessive co-ordination is a symptom of more basic weaknesses (see 22).

Original	*Revision*
The lights were out, *and* I did not know where the fuse box was, *and* I thought I had better find the fuse box *and* put in a new fuse, *and* all this time Aunt Agnes was complaining, *and* she and my cousins could not finish their game of canasta. [*Clauses of varying importance have been jumbled together and joined by inappropriate* and's.]	The lights were out, and I knew I should replace a fuse, but since I did not know where the fuse box was, I was at a loss what to do, while Aunt Agnes kept complaining that she and my cousins could not finish their game of canasta. [*The sentence has been strengthened by subordinating some material, and by choosing more accurate function words.*]

In order to avoid lengthy sentences modern writers sometimes put co-ordinate ideas in separate sentences, beginning the second sentence with a co-ordinating conjunction.

The wolf is today what he was when he was hunted by Nimrod. But, while men are born with many of the characteristics of wolves, man is a wolf domesticated, who both transmits the arts by which he has been partially tamed and improves upon them.

—R. H. TAWNEY, *Religion and the Rise of Capitalism*

Although the sentences might have been combined, the separation sharpens the contrast between ideas, because *but,* the sign of the contrast, is in the position of emphasis at the beginning of the sentence. This device, however, is easily overworked. It is useful only when the writer needs the special emphasis given to the co-ordinating conjunction by the initial position.

Original

At first I thought I would decorate the table with flowers. But I found that the roses had gone to seed.

[*Opening the second sentence,* but *is unduly emphatic.*]

The adviser suggested mathematics. But I had failed algebra in high school. And I did not like physics. And chemistry and biology smell bad.

[*As frequently, co-ordinating conjunctions opening sentences are symptoms of inadequate thinking.*]

Revision

At first I thought I would decorate the table with flowers, but I found that the roses had gone to seed.

[*As a conjunction within a compound sentence,* but *is appropriately inconspicuous.*]

[*Sentences of this sort must be rethought and then recast. Some material should be subordinated; some can probably be co-ordinated, but probably not by beginning sentences with conjunctions.*]

33b Subordinating conjunctions   **FW b; Conj b**

Subordinating conjunctions do more than indicate that one part of a sentence is dependent; they also specify the particular way in which it is dependent. Compare:

Although she was his wife, she stayed at a hotel.
Because she was his wife, she stayed at a hotel.
Before she was his wife, she stayed at a hotel.
Until she was his wife, she stayed at a hotel.
After she was his wife, she stayed at a hotel.
While she was his wife, she stayed at a hotel.
Whenever she was his wife, she stayed at a hotel.

[397

In each sentence, the conjunction indicates a different kind of relationship between the ideas in the two clauses and gives the sentence a different meaning. Subordinating conjunctions need to be chosen with care to define relationships precisely.

Original

While Father did not approve of alcoholic beverages, he always had some in the house for guests.

[While *is loosely used as an equivalent of* although *or* because. *Strictly used it means that one event takes place at the same time as another. That is, this sentence suggests that Father eventually approved of alcoholic beverages and thereafter illogically refused liquor to his guests.*]

I came in one door, *and* she went out the other.

[*The colorless* and *leaves the relationships between the clauses obscure.*]

Since my mother was a little girl, she was not allowed to sit at the table.

[Since, *strictly, refers to time, but it has come also to be used in the sense of* because. *Here there is confusion.*]

I did not know *but what* she was afraid to come in.

He had heard *as how* anyone could make a living panning gold.

Marilyn preferred long hair which swept below her shoulders, *while* Louise liked to be able to run a comb through her short haircut and be ready for breakfast.

Revision

Although Father did not approve of alcoholic beverages, he always had some in the house for guests.

[*The subordinate clause mentions a concession, and the concessive conjunction,* although, *has accordingly replaced* while, *which properly concerns simultaneous times.*]

(1) *While* I came in one door, she went out the other.
(2) *Because* I came in one door, she went out the other.

Because she was only a little girl, my mother was not allowed to sit at the table.

I did not know *but that* she was afraid to come in.

He had heard *that* anyone could make a living panning gold.

Marilyn preferred long hair which swept below her shoulders; *whereas* Louise liked to be able to run a comb through her short haircut and be ready for breakfast.

Original (*Cont.*)

I washed my face *so as* I would be allowed to go in for dinner.

Revision (*Cont.*)

I washed my face *so that* I would be allowed to go in for dinner.

I arrived on time *so* I could leave early.

I arrived on time *so that* I could leave early.

33c Like *and* as   FW c; Conj c

In standard English *like* is used only as a preposition (*He ran like a deer.*) and *as* and *as if* are conjunctions (*He ran as if he had seen a ghost.*) *As* is not used instead of *that* to introduce a noun clause. Colloquially, however, *like* is frequently used as a conjunction, and students, perhaps overcautious in avoiding errors with *like* in their writing, sometimes misuse *as* as a preposition. Notice the differences in meaning between *He slipped into the house as a thief* and *He slipped into the house like a thief,* or between *He cried as a baby* and *He cried like a baby.*

Original

He cried *like* his heart would break.

Revision

He cried *as if* his heart would break.

I do not know *as* I believe you.

I am not sure *that* I believe you.

A person *as* my mother never forgets.

A person *like* my mother never forgets.

33d Is-because, is-when, is-where *clauses*   FW d; Conj d

A clause used as a subject complement after the verb *to be* is conceived to repeat or identify the subject (see 20-2). *Because, when,* and *where* do not logically introduce such clauses; they rather introduce clauses which the reader takes to modify the predicate.

Radicalism is *when* you jump to conclusions and go off half-cocked.

The *when*-clause does not repeat the subject or define it, and it can hardly be taken to modify the verb. Presumably the writer does not mean to say that radicalism exists at a certain time; he has not thought out his definition precisely enough. He needs to rethink it so that he can either use a predicate which his clause can modify (*Radicalism is dangerous when . . .*), or use a logical complement (*Radi-*

[399

calism is a political attitude which . . .), or recast the sentence (*Radicals incline to hasty conclusions*).

Original	*Revision*
A syllogism *is where* you use a major and minor premise to get a logical answer. [*A syllogism is not a place.*]	In a syllogism, you use a major and minor premise to obtain a logical answer.
The reason I do not like herring *is because* they taste so fishy. [*A reason is not because.*]	I do not like herring because they taste fishy. [*The revision makes clear the causal relationship between the reason and the taste of the fish.*]
Probation *is when* you are not eligible for competition.	On probation you are not eligible for competition.

33e Correlative Conjunctions   FW e; Conj e

A correlative conjunction should be completed with the proper word to fill the sentence pattern.

Original	*Revision*
Neither the socket wrench *or* my patented ratchet would reach the rear connecting rod bolt.	*Neither* the socket wrench *nor* my patented ratchet would reach the rear connecting rod bolt.

33f Prepositions   FW f; Prep

Prepositions determine many intimate relationships within the sentence; the writer should know the meaning of prepositions and should choose them with care. In addition, the use of certain prepositions with certain words and for particular usages has grown with custom; our usage of prepositions is not always based on apparent logic. It is what is often called *idiomatic*, but it is no less exact for that.

Original	*Revision*
He went *in* the house and stopped *at* the mirror.	He went *into* the house and stopped *before* the mirror.
I had never heard *about* him or *of* his famous rescue.	I had never heard *of* him or *about* his famous rescue.

Some prepositions must be composed of more than one word, but involved prepositions are to be avoided if a simpler construction will suffice.

Original

I found the keys *in back of* the water pitcher.

He spoke *in regards to* the paving *of* the alleys.

Revision

I found the keys *behind* the water pitcher.

(1) He spoke *about* paving the alleys.
(2) He discussed paving the alleys.

33g Conjunctive adverbs   FW g; Conj Adv

Conjunctive adverbs are unusually useful to show relationships, but they must be chosen carefully and should not be used to excess. At the beginning or end of a sentence a conjunctive adverb is usually falsely emphatic (see 23f).

Original

Clubs for girls can fill useful social functions. However, they should not take up all of a girl's time. Then, they merely interfere with a girl's achieving social maturity. Nevertheless, there is a time in a girl's life when a club can be helpful, and even exciting. [*A collection of childish sentences like these cannot be cured by removing excessive adverbial conjunctions, though several of them can well be dropped.*]

Revision

If a girl allows her clubs to consume all her time, they may only interfere with her achieving social maturity. Nevertheless, there is a period in a girl's life when a club can be helpful, even exciting. [*The structure has been made simpler and more direct, and with the change several conjunctive adverbs have been dropped.*]

33h Articles and demonstrative adjectives   FW h; Art

The articles and demonstrative adjectives (see 32-3) carry little meaning as modifiers, but they cannot be used interchangeably. Failure to use articles which make the desired distinctions between the words they modify (see 33-7) makes unclear writing. Especially troublesome is the *generic singular,* in which a singular noun combines with *the* to imply all or most of the members of a class (*the man in the street, the average car buyer*). The generic singular should be used consistently, not interspersed with plurals.

Original

When we first entered the park, it seemed almost deserted. *The* man was sitting alone on a bench, and a pigeon pecked at a paper cup. I saw no other signs of life.

[*Unless some missing part of the context has introduced* the man, *he is probably appearing here for the first time and should not be singled out by* the.]

On our way home from Sunday School, *this* man came up to me and took my hand, and then *this* fellow said. . . .

[This *is sometimes overused, especially in narratives told by children, without any reference to what has preceded.*]

A good student keeps abreast of world affairs. Good students are always informed about current events.

[*The article appears in one of its common uses, to specify a singular as the type of a whole group, but in the next sentence the writer changes his device.*]

Revision

When we first entered the park, it seemed almost deserted. *A* man was sitting alone on a bench, and a pigeon pecked at a paper cup. I saw no other signs of life.

[*The more indefinite* a *serves to introduce the man.*]

On our way home from Sunday School, a man came up to me and took my hand, and then he said. . . .

[A *is preferable, since* this *is not designating any specific person but is acting only as a kind of vague and misleading intensive.*]

The good student keeps abreast of world affairs. He is always informed about current events.

[*The use of the article to specify an example of a group is common; compare the use of* the writer *in this book. But the device should be used consistently and not allowed to shift point of view.*]

EXERCISE 33

A. With each of the two pairs of clauses below make five sentences with five different meanings or shades of meaning by varying the conjunctions or conjunctive adverbs. You may change the order of the clauses if you wish.

1. I slid down the eaves spout   I heard somebody scream upstairs
2. It is election day   I go fishing
3. I have fast reaction time   I like sports
4. I have to ride the subway to school   I study the advertising on the car cards
5. The boat heeled over   He worked at the sails

B. The sentences below contain some faulty usage in the italicized function words. If the function word is inappropriate, choose a better form, or revise the sentence.

1. *While* I do not like to complain about my guests, I do object to anybody who comes in with his shoes dripping mud.

2. I had expected to love Venice, *and* when I got there I could not stand the smell of the canals.

3. The weight-lifter came on the stage, *and* Jim would square his shoulders.

4. Extra-curricular activities is *where* you learn to make friends.

5. Mother always said that childhood is *when* you have the best time.

6. *While* I don't usually eat green onions, I sometimes do.

7. *While* I was trying to get the hook out of the pickerel, I jabbed it into my own thumb.

8. The reason I do not approve of federal aid for education is *because* we must protect our liberties.

9. We spent our vacation in the Big Smokies, *and* we knew it would be cool there.

10. The ore boats cannot come to Gary, *and afterward* the ice goes out.

C. Strengthen the following paragraph by adding and improving conjunctions and conjunctive adverbs; you may change the form of the verbs and the order of the clauses if necessary.

Time is very interesting. Our lives are made of time. Nobody knows what time is. You go in one direction and you gain time. You go in the other direction and you lose time. Airplanes now fly so fast that time stands still. A plane can fly as fast as the earth revolves past the sun. A baby born in a plane flying in the right direction could theoretically live its whole life of many years without living through one day. It would have a long birthday. Its whole life would be its birthday. Suppose the plane should fly faster. The baby would soon be minus-one day old. The plane flies still faster. The baby would be minus an old man. There is one place in the United States, and there time is different in every direction. The time belt follows the Snake River. The river makes an ox-bow bend. From within the ox-bow you shoot a long-range rifle north, east, south, or west. The bullet will land almost an hour before it was fired. The ox-bow is completely surrounded by another time belt. Time is all anyone has in the world. It is fluid. Nobody has ever found a good way of measuring it.

VII. Words

Old fellow, how would you render that field of wheat?

—JOSEPH CONRAD

When Ford Madox Ford heard of the death of Joseph Conrad, his long-time friend and collaborator, he tells us that he saw again in his mind the two of them driving past "a ramshackle, commonplace farm building in an undistinguished country over slight hills on a flinty bye-road and heard Joseph Conrad saying to him, 'Well, Ford, *mon vieux,* how would you render that field of wheat?'" He goes on to recount that they had spent many hours through many years in that way, jolting through "a country of commonplace downlands," asking themselves how they would describe a field of wheat under the particular conditions of the moment. Should one say, "Fields of wheat that small winds ruffled into cat's paws"? No, that was too literary. But what ideas and what words should one use? Then there was that "ten-acre patch of blue-purple cabbage." What should one do about that?

Here we have the picture of two of the distinguished writers of our time, spending great chunks of their lives asking each other what words to use to describe a field of wheat or a patch of cabbages. Quite surely they were good writers partly because they were students of words and the power of words.

Conrad said that his purpose was "above all things to make you see." But he understood that before he could make anyone else see, he had to see. Unless a writer sees sharply, he cannot make others see sharply. Unless he hears vividly, he cannot make others hear vividly. How does snow look when it falls in large flakes, widely spaced, in no wind? How do the brakes of a car sound when the driver jams them on suddenly to avoid a crash? What is the difference between the smell of roasting turkey and roasting goose? If one goes to his wardrobe in the dark and finds the particular garment he wants by feel, what is there about the texture of the cloth that makes him know it? What is the taste of Roquefort cheese?

A writer who will ask himself questions like these is likely to find that his writing improves because he has more to say. Granted that he has something to say, he needs words with which to say it; he needs vocabulary. The Anglo-Saxons had a revealing term for vocabulary; they called it a "word hoard," a treasury of words that each man owned and on which he could draw at any time he wanted to speak. They seem to have understood that if a man is to be rich intellectually, he needs a great store of words; the more words he has the richer he is. Modern psychologists agree with the Anglo-Saxons about this. They have found more direct relationship between the size and accuracy of vocabulary in one test, and general intelligence in another, than between general intelligence and anything else.

Certainly words are important, because they are the tools with which one speaks and writes. To express himself well, a writer must have a large number of words in his word hoard and must be able to select just the right word for each purpose. Let us postpone the question of selection and ask first how the writer can develop a rich treasury of words. The writer can learn words by many means, but perhaps most easily by listening to intelligent conversation and reading intelligent writing. Most people who have large vocabularies have learned the greater part of their words by reading, particularly by reading carefully and using a good dictionary. In the long run, nothing can help a student so much as the habit of reading widely and critically. If he does not have the habit, he can acquire it. But building a cultural background, if it is the only genuinely good way to build a vocabulary, is also slow. Anyone who determines tonight to read more will not have improved his vocabulary much by tomorrow.

Fortunately, there are quicker ways to build a vocabulary. They require a little attention, but they can be fun, too, and properly used they will produce noticeable results more quickly than one might expect.

34. VOCABULARY; THE DICTIONARY

[For Guide to Revision, see page 477]

We can write only with words. Every successful writer must have an adequate vocabulary.

Almost everyone has at least four basic vocabularies. First, he uses a relatively small number of words which we may call the *speaking vocabulary*. It includes words which will come to the speaker's tongue without his thinking much about them. A dull person is likely to use only a few hundred words in this way; even a moderately articulate speaker uses only a few thousand.

Every literate person has a second vocabulary, a *writing vocabulary*. It includes the words in the speaking vocabulary, plus other words which he can call up for use if he has time to think and revise. A good writer may employ a vocabulary of ten thousand, twenty-five thousand, perhaps fifty thousand words. A poor writer, on the other hand, is likely to have a writing vocabulary not much larger than his speaking vocabulary.

Every literate person has also a *reading vocabulary,* made up of words which he would not speak in conversation or use when he writes but which he knows when he sees them written. For most people the reading vocabulary is much larger than either the speaking or writing vocabulary—fifty thousand, seventy-five thousand, a hundred thousand words, perhaps more.

Then there is a fourth sort of vocabulary, the largest of all, which we may call the *acquaintance vocabulary*. It includes the other three, but it includes, also, a considerable number of words which the owner of this vocabulary has seen or heard before but does not know much about. He knows he has seen these words; he even remembers enough about them so that he can usually guess their meaning in context. He has a nodding acquaintance with the words, not much more. Vocabularies of this sort, of course, can be very large, for most people much larger than the reading vocabulary.

From the description of these four vocabularies, the student has probably guessed at least one way to improve his oral and written expression. Since speaking and writing vocabularies are relatively small and reading and acquaintance vocabularies are relatively large, he has only to move words from his reading and acquaintance vocabularies into his speaking and writing vocabularies. This operation requires work, but it is by no means impossible, and there are sensible ways of handling the job.

34-1 Word hoards and dictionaries

In any deliberate attempt to improve vocabulary, the most useful aid is usually a good dictionary. At this writing, three desk dictionaries are much the best in their class. They are *Webster's New World Dictionary of the American Language* published by the World Publishing Company, *The American College Dictionary,* published in a trade edition by Random House and in a text edition by Harper & Brothers, and *Webster's New Collegiate Dictionary,* published by the G. & C. Merriam Company. No one serious about his writing should be content with an inferior book, even though it is cheap. Of course there is no substitute for the bigger dictionaries, and students should know all the important ones. Of the so-called "unabridged" dictionaries, the *Webster's New International,* published by the G. & C. Merriam Company, is the best one widely used in this country. Two British dictionaries of about the same size are excellent in various ways: the H. C. Wyld *Universal Dictionary* and the *Shorter Oxford.* In many ways the most interesting American dictionary is the *Century Dictionary and Cyclopedia,* which runs to ten volumes. It is old but still a mine of valuable material. The great dictionary of the language, of course, is the *New English Dictionary on Historical Principles,* usually called the *Oxford English Dictionary.* For Americans it should be supplemented with the *Dictionary of American English,* and the more recent *Dictionary of Americanisms.*

No student should be content with meager dictionaries. Why starve when we have the Lord's plenty? A writer will remember words longer and use them more accurately the more he knows about them. Furthermore, using a book like the *Oxford English Dictionary* can be downright exciting.

34-2 Using a dictionary

Any user of a dictionary should learn how much information he has available. He should examine the table of contents and preface and learn where to find foreign words and phrases, new words, proper names, and other special subjects. He should learn the pronunciation system and find the list of abbreviations used in the book. A good desk dictionary should be adequate for at least the following uses:

(1) *Spelling.* Dictionaries record preferred current spellings for words. Since a student can usually guess the first letters of a word from its sound, he can use the dictionary whenever he is in doubt. The dictionary indicates where words can be divided between syllables and whether compounds are usually written as single words or with a hyphen.

(2) *Pronunciation.* Dictionaries reprint each word with special marks to indicate the location of accents and the sounds of individual letters. The marks, called diacritical marks, are explained in the introduction, and usually examples appear at the bottom of each page of the text.

(3) *Word origins.* Every dictionary adequate for student use describes, using abbreviations explained in its introduction, the origins of words. Knowledge of derivations can be extremely useful in learning and remembering words. It gives the student a feeling for the limitations and possibilities of the word's uses, and familiarity with word roots is a constant aid to building a vocabulary.

(4) *Grammatical information.* The dictionary indicates, with abbreviations, the grammatical uses for which a word is considered suitable.

(5) *Usage.* Dictionaries endeavor to distinguish words which have general use from those which have not by indicating that certain words or certain usages of the word have limited currency. A word no longer used is marked *obsolete,* usually abbreviated to *obs.* Words restricted to a certain occupational group may be marked *cant.* Other words or usages may be labeled *colloquial* (*colloq.*), *dialectal* (*dial.*), or *slang.* For levels of usage see 37.

(6) *Definition.* Most important of all, a dictionary endeavors to define words. A good desk dictionary should define most meanings of all but rare and highly specialized words. Some of the problems of meaning are discussed in 35.

[409

34-3 Increasing a writing vocabulary

A student familiar with his dictionary is prepared to observe the following simple procedures which will help him to increase his vocabulary.

(1) *Learn words which you will use.* You may be able to baffle your friends if you know the meaning of *ento-ectad,* but words completely strange to you are hard to learn, and unless you use them you are likely to forget them. Learn words which you encounter and recognize but cannot define or use.

(2) *When you learn a word, learn enough about it to make it yours.* Notice its various usages. Try to find out details about the origin and history of the word, where it came from and what has happened to it in English and American speech. For this, the *Oxford English Dictionary* is excellent; the *Century* and the others mentioned above are also good.

(3) *Learn words by groups.* If you will learn related words together, you can learn several words, sometimes a dozen, as easily as you can learn one, often more easily. Suppose you were to look up the word *pictograph.* You would find that it is related to the words *picture* and *graph,* both of which you probably know, though you may have to find out what the Greek root *graph* means here. Any good dictionary ought to have twenty or thirty more words related to *picture* in adjacent columns; make out a list and learn them all as a group. In learning words by groups, knowing foreign languages helps. Latin and Greek are especially useful. Even if you do not know these languages, you can learn a few Latin and Greek prefixes; a list of common ones will be found in Exercise 34c.

(4) *Once you have learned a word, use it.* Many a good student, presented with a word he does not know, will look it up and immediately forget it. Do something deliberate to keep your words. Find a way to use them in conversation or in your next theme. Make up a list of words, put the list in your purse or pocket, and glance over it at some odd time every day for a week. Stick the list in the corner of your mirror.

34 *Vocabulary; the dictionary* **Dict**

GUIDE TO REVISION:

Use the dictionary to develop a usable and meaningful vocabulary.

The dictionary can serve many purposes. Writing which suffers from poverty of words can be improved by better use of the dictionary. The writer should become well acquainted with his dictionary, its marks and abbreviations, and the arrangement of its materials. He can then make the book his basic tool for improving diction.

EXERCISE 34

A. On pages 412-414 are reproductions from *Webster's New World Dictionary of the American Language,* College Edition, the *American College Dictionary,* and *Webster's New Collegiate Dictionary.* Try to learn what you can about the contents of a good dictionary by comparing these pages in detail, beginning with *gab* and ending with *Gaboriau.* Notice several sorts of information.

(1) *Word-list.* Does one dictionary include entry words not in another? Does one dictionary have phrases not in another?

(2) *Pronunciation.* Do the dictionaries agree in pronunciation? Are alternate pronunciations in the same order?

(3) *Etymologies.* Which book tells you the most about the origin and growth of a word? Which puts this technical information most clearly? Do the dictionaries include any Indo-European bases? (Indo-European, abbreviated IE., was the ancient ancestor of English). For this question you will need a few uncommon abbreviations, AS. (Anglo-Saxon), ME. (Middle English), Ar. (Arabic), L. (Latin), MD. (Middle Dutch), MHG. (Middle High German), OFr. (Old French), ON. (Old Norse), and abbreviations for modern languages like It. (Italian).

(4) *Meanings.* How do the meanings compare? Are the meanings in one more understandable than in another? More exact? Does one book treat certain sorts of words, such as obsolete words or technical words, better than another?

(5) *Uses.* All the dictionaries recognize several uses of the more common words. Does any omit important uses?

(6) *Encyclopedic material.* Dictionaries vary as to the amount of encyclopedic material they include. What seem to be the policies of these dictionaries? (One of them has two supplements at the end, one for biographical names, one a gazetteer.)

[411

gab (gab), *v.i.* [GABBED (gabd), GABBING], [ME. *gabben;* prob. < ON. *gabba,* to mock, reinforced by OFr. *gaber,* to boast, deride; the base occurs in AS. *gaffetung,* a scoffing, mocking & *gaf-spræc,* foolish speech; IE. base *ĝhabh- < *ĝhei,* etc., to yawn, have the mouth open], [Colloq.], to talk much or idly; chatter; gabble. *n.* [Colloq.], chatter; talkativeness.

  gift of (the) gab, [Colloq.], the ability to speak fluently; eloquence; glibness.

gab·ar·dine (gab′ẽr-dēn′, gab′ẽr-dēn′), *n.* [var. of *gaberdine*], 1. a woolen, cotton, or rayon cloth twilled on one side and having a fine, diagonal weave, used for suits, coats, dresses, etc. 2. a gaberdine.

gab·ber (gab′ẽr), *n.* [Colloq.], a person who gabs.

gab·ble (gab′'l), *v.i.* [GABBLED (-'ld), GABBLING], [< *gab* + *-le,* freq. suffix; ? suggested by MD. *gabbeln,* to chatter], 1. to talk rapidly and incoherently; jabber; chatter. 2. to utter rapid, meaningless sounds, as a goose. *v.t.* to utter rapidly and incoherently. *n.* rapid, incoherent talk or meaningless utterance.

gab·bler (gab′lẽr), *n.* a person who gabbles.

gab·bro (gab′rō), *n.* [It. < L. *glaber,* bare, smooth], any of a group of dark, heavy igneous rocks, composed chiefly of pyroxene and feldspar.

gab·by (gab′i), *adj.* [see GAB], [Colloq.], talkative; inclined to chatter.

ga·belle (gə-bel′), *n.* [Fr.; It. *gabella;* Ar. *gabālah*], a tax levied in certain countries; especially, a tax on salt, levied in France before the Revolution of 1789.

gab·er·dine (gab′ẽr-dēn′, gab′ẽr-dēn′), *n.* [earlier *gawbardyne;* OFr. *gauvardine, galvardine* < MHG. *walvart,* pilgrimage < *wallen,* to wander about + *vart* a trip < *varen,* to travel], 1. a loose coat or cloak made of coarse cloth, worn in the Middle Ages, especially by Jews. 2. gabardine.

gab·er·lun·zie (gab′ẽr-lun′zi; Scot. gȧb′ẽr-lün′yi), *n.* [Scot.; printing form of *gaberlunyie* (with printed z for *y* as in pers. name *Menzies*); earlier also *gaberloonie;* prob. < Scot. Gaelic], a wandering beggar.

ga·bi·on (gā′bi-ən), *n.* [Fr.; It. *gabbione,* large cage < *gabbia,* cage, coop < L. *cavea,* cave, cage], 1. a cylinder of wicker filled with earth or stones, formerly used in building fortifications. 2. a similar cylinder of metal, used in building dams, foundations, etc.

ga·bi·on·ade (gā′bi-ən-ād′), *n.* [Fr. *gabionnade*], a defensive embankment or structure made of gabions.

ga·ble (gā′b'l), *n.* [ME.; OFr.; prob. < ON. *gafl,* gable; basic sense, "forked twig" seen in G. *gabel,* a fork], 1. *a)* the triangular wall enclosed by the sloping ends of a ridged roof. *b)* popularly, the whole section, including wall, roof, and space enclosed. 2. the end wall of a building, the upper part of which is a gable. 3. a triangular decorative feature in architecture, such as that over a door or window. *v.t.* [GABLED (-b'ld), GABLING], to put a gable or gables on. *v.i.* to be in the form of, or end in, a gable.

GABLE

From *Webster's New World Dictionary of the American Language, College Edition,* copyright, 1956, by The World Publishing Company.

GABLE (sense 3)

gable roof, a ridged roof forming a gable at one end or both ends.

gable window, 1. a window in a gable (sense 2). 2. a window with a gable (sense 3) over it.

Ga·bon (gȧ′bōn′), *n.* a French colony in French Equatorial Africa, on the Gulf of Guinea: area, 92,218 sq. mi.; pop., 382,000 (1946); capital, Libreville: also **Gabun.**

Ga·bo·riau, É·mile (ā′mēl′ gȧ′bô′ryō′), 1835–1873; French writer of detective stories.

gab (găb), *v.*, **gabbed, gabbing,** *n. Colloq.* —*v.i.* **1.** to talk idly; chatter. —*n.* **2.** idle talk; chatter. **3.** glib speech: *the gift of gab.* [var. of *gob* mouth, t. Gaelic or Irish]

gab·ar·dine (găb/ər dēn/, găb/ər dēn/), *n.* **1.** firm, woven fabric of worsted, cotton, or spun rayon, with steep twill. **2.** a man's long, loose cloak or frock, worn in the Middle Ages. Also, **gab/er·dine/.** [t. Sp.: m. *gabardina,* ult. der. MHG *wallevart* pilgrimage]

gab·ble (găb/əl), *v.*, **-bled, -bling,** *n.* —*v.i.* **1.** to talk rapidly and unintelligibly; jabber. **2.** (of geese, etc.) to cackle. —*v.t.* **3.** to utter rapidly and unintelligibly. —*n.* **4.** rapid, unintelligible talk. [freq. of GAB] —**gab/·bler,** *n.*

gab·bro (găb/rō), *n.*, *pl.* **-bros.** *Petrog.* a granular igneous rock composed essentially of labradorite and augite. [t. It.]

gab·by (găb/ĭ), *adj.*, **-bier, -biest.** loquacious.

ga·belle (gə bĕl/), *n.* **1.** a tax; an excise. **2.** (in France before 1790) a tax on salt. [t. F, t. Pr.: m. *gabela,* t. It.: m. *gàbella* tax, t. Ar.: m. *(al-)qabāla* the impost]

Ga·bès (gä/bĕs), *n.* **Gulf of,** a gulf of the Mediterranean on the E coast of Tunisia.

ga·bi·on (gā/bĭ ən), *n.* **1.** a cylinder of wickerwork filled with earth, used as a military defense. **2.** a cylinder filled with stones and sunk in water, used in laying the foundations of a dam or jetty. [t. F, t. It.: m. *gabbione,* aug. of *gabbia,* g. L *cavea* cage]

ga·bi·on·ade (gā/bĭ ə nād/), *n.* **1.** a work formed of or with gabions. **2.** a row of gabions sunk in a stream to control the current. [t. F: m. *gabionnade.* See GABION]

ga·ble (gā/bəl), *n.*, *v.*, **-bled, -bling.** *Archit.* —*n.* **1.** the end of a ridged roof cut off at its extremity in a vertical plane, together with the triangular expanse of wall from the level of the eaves to the apex of the roof. **2.** a similar end, as of a gambrel roof, not triangular. **3.** an architectural member resembling the triangular end of a roof. **4.** an end wall. —*v.t.* **5.** to build with a gable or gables; form as a gable (chiefly in **gabled,** *pp.*). [ME, prob. t. Scand.; cf. Icel. *gafl.* Cf. also OHG *gabala,* G *gabel* fork] —**ga/ble·like/,** *adj.*

Gables (def. 1 and 2)

gable end, (in a gabled building) the triangular wall space between the eaves level and the ridge, or the decorative wall carried up past the ends of a gable roof, and sloped, stepped, or scrolled to follow at a higher level its approximate shape.

gable roof, a ridged roof terminating at one or both ends in a gable.

gable window, **1.** a window in or under a gable. **2.** a window having its upper part shaped like a gable.

Ga·bon (gà bôn/), *n.* **1.** a colony in the SW part of French Equatorial Africa. 410,000 pop. (1936); 91,506 sq. mi. *Cap.*: Libreville. **2.** an estuary in this colony. Also, **Ga·bun** (gà bōōn/).

Ga·bo·riau (gà bô ryō/), *n.* Émile (ĕ mēl/), 1833 or 1835–73, French novelist.

Ga·bri·el (gā/brĭ əl), *n.* one of the archangels, appearing usually as a divine messenger. Dan. 8:16, 9:21. Luke, 1: 19, 26. [t. Heb.: m. *Gabrī'ēl* the man of God]

Ga·bri·lo·witsch (gä/brĭ lŭv/ĭch; *Russ.* gä/vrĭ lŏ/vĭch), *n.* **Ossip** (ŏ/sĭp), 1878–1936, Russian pianist and conductor, in America.

ga·by (gā/bĭ), *n.*, *pl.* **-bies.** *Colloq.* a fool. [orig. uncert.]

gad[1] (găd), *v.*, **gadded, gadding,** *n.* —*v.i.* **1.** to move restlessly or idly about. —*n.* **2.** act of gadding. [? special use of GAD[2]] —**gad/der,** *n.*

gad[2] (găd), *n.*, *v.*, **gadded, gadding.** —*n.* **1.** a goad for driving cattle. **2.** a pointed mining tool for breaking up rock, coal, etc. —*v.t.* **3.** to break up with a mining gad. [ME, t. Scand.; cf. Icel. *gaddr* spike]

Gad (găd), *n.*, *interj.* *Archaic.* a euphemistic form of *God* used as a mild oath. Also, **gad.**

Gad (găd), *n.* **1.** son of Jacob by Zilpah. Gen. 30:11, etc. **2.** a Hebrew prophet and chronicler ot the court of David. 2 Sam. 24:11–19. **3.** one of the twelve tribes of Israel. **4.** its territory east of the Jordan.

gad·a·bout (găd/ə bout/), *n.* *Colloq.* one who gads, esp. for curiosity or gossip.

gad·fly (găd/flī/), *n.*, *pl.* **-flies.** any fly that goads or stings domestic animals, as many voracious, blood-sucking flies of the dipterous family *Tabanidae.* [f. GAD[2] + FLY]

gadg·et (găj/ĭt), *n.* *Colloq.* a mechanical contrivance or device; any ingenious article. [orig. uncert. Cf. F *gâchette*]

Ga·dhel·ic (gə dĕl/ĭk, -dē/lĭk), *adj.*, *n.* Goidelic.

Gadfly,
*Tabanus
ruficornis*
(Ab. 1½ in.
long)

From *The American College Dictionary,* text edition, copyright, 1948, by Harper & Brothers.

gab (găb; *Scot.* gàb), *n.* *Scot.* The mouth.

gab (găb), *v. i. & n.* *Colloq.* Chatter; gabble.

gab'ar·dine' (găb'ẽr·dēn'; găb'ẽr·dēn), *n.* **1.** = GABERDINE. **2.** A woolen fabric closely resembling serge, but twilled on one side only; also, a similar fabric of cotton or rayon.

gab'bard (găb'ẽrd), **gab'bart** (-ẽrt), *n.* [F. *gabare, gabarot.*] *Obs. exc. Scot.* A lighter, barge, or similar vessel.

gab'ble (găb'ʼl), *v. i. & t.;* GAB'BLED (-ʼld); GAB'BLING (-lǐng). **1.** To jabber; chatter. **2.** To utter inarticulate sounds rapidly, as fowls. — **gab'ble,** *n.* — **gab'bler** (-lẽr), *n.*

gab'bro (găb'rō), *n.* [It., fr. L. *glaber* bare, smooth.] *Petrog.* Any of a family of granular, igneous rocks essentially of plagioclase with a, ferromagnesian mineral and accessory iron ore, etc.

gab'broid (-roid), *adj.* *Petrog.* Resembling gabbro.

gab'by (găb'ǐ), *adj.* *Colloq.* Loquacious; talkative.

ga·belle' (gȧ·bĕl'), *n.* [F., through Pr. & It., fr. Ar. *qabālah.*] A tax; specif., an impost on salt, levied in France for several centuries prior to 1790, and in use down to the present day in China.

gab'er·dine' (găb'ẽr·dēn'; găb'ẽr·dēn), *n.* [Sp. *gabardina.*] **1.** A coarse loose frock or coat; — chiefly of medieval costume. **2.** The medieval Jewish gown or mantle. **3.** Var. of GABARDINE.

gab'er·lun'zie (găb'ẽr·lŭn'zǐ; *Scot.* găb'ẽr·lün'yǐ, -lōon'yǐ, -lōon'ǐ), *n.* *Scot.* A wandering beggar.

ga'bi·on (gā'bǐ·ŭn; 58), *n.* [F., fr. It. *gabbione* a large cage, fr. *gabbia* cage, fr. L. *cavea.*] A hollow cylinder of wickerwork, iron, or the like. Gabions are filled with earth and used in building fieldworks, mining, etc.

ga'bi·on·ade' (gā'bǐ·ŭn·ād'), *n.* [F. *gavionnade.*] A work made with gabions.

ga'ble (gā'b'l), *n.* [OF., fr. ON. *gafl.*] *Arch.* **a** The vertical triangular portion of the end of a building, from the level of the cornice or eaves to the ridge of the roof. Also, a similar end when not triangular in shape, as of a gambrel roof. Hence: **b** The end wall of a building, as distinguished from the front or rear side. **c** A decorative member having the shape of a triangular gable, such as that above a Gothic arch in a doorway. — *v. t. & i.;* GA'BLED (-b'ld); GA'BLING (-blǐng). To furnish with gables; to terminate in a gable; as, a *gabled* roof.

gable roof. A roof which forms a gable at each end.

gable window. A window in a gable, or one with a gable.

Gable a.

Ga'bri·el (gā'brǐ·ĕl), *n.* [Heb. *Gabhrī'ēl.*] An angel of comfort to man (*Dan.* viii and ix), a herald declaring the coming of the Messiah. In Jewish and Christian tradition, he is one of the seven archangels. He is believed by Mohammedans to have dictated the Koran to their prophet.

ga'by (gā'bǐ; *dial. also* gô'bǐ), *n.* *Colloq.* A simpleton.

gad (găd), *n.* [ON. *gaddr* a sting, spike.] **1.** A goad; as, upon the *gad*, that is, suddenly, as if goaded. **2.** *Mining, etc.* A pointed iron or steel bar for loosening ore, etc.

gad (găd), *v. i.;* GAD'DED (-ĕd; -ǐd); GAD'DING. To wander about idly. — *n.* *Colloq.* A gadding, or rambling; — only in *on,* or *upon, the gad.*

Gad (găd), *n.* A softened form of *God,* used as a mild oath, as in **Gads'bod'i·kins** (gădz'bŏd'ǐ·kǐnz), **Gads'woons'** (-wōonz'), **Gad'zooks'** (găd'zōoks'), etc.

Gad (găd), *n.* *Bib.* See JACOB.

gad'a·bout' (găd'ȧ·bout'), *adj.* Gadding; roving. — *n.* *Colloq.* One who gads about.

gad'bee' (găd'bē'), *n.* A gadfly.

gad'der (găd'ẽr), *n.* One who roves about idly; a gadabout.

gad'fly' (găd'flī'), *n.; pl.* -FLIES (-flīz'). [1st *gad* + *fly.*] A fly that bites cattle; a horsefly.

gadg'et (găj'ĕt; -ĭt), *n.* *Slang.* A contrivance, object, or device for doing something; esp., a part of machinery.

Ga·dhel'ic (gȧ·dĕl'ĭk; -dē'lĭk; găd'ĕ·lĭk). Var. of GOIDELIC.

ga'did (gā'dǐd), *n* [See GADOID.] A fish of the cod family (Gadidae). — **ga'did,** *adj.*

ga'doid (-doid), *adj.* [NL. *gadus* cod + *-oid.*] Like or pertaining to the cod family (Gadidae), a large family of soft-finned, chiefly marine food fishes, including the cod and haddock, having a rather elongated body and a large mouth. — *n.* A fish of the cod family or of a group (Anacanthini) of teleost fishes that comprises the codfishes, hakes, and their allies.

gad'o·lin·ite (găd'ô·lǐn·īt), *n.* [After J. *Gadolin* (1760–1852), Finnish chemist.] A black or brown vitreous silicate of iron, beryllium, yttrium, cerium, erbium, etc. H., 6.5–7. Sp. gr., 4–4.5. It is a source of rare earths.

gad'o·lin'i·um (-lǐn'ǐ·ŭm; 58), *n.* [NL.] *Chem.* A metallic element, one of the rare-earth metals, found in combination in gadolinite and certain other minerals. Symbol, *Gd*; at. no., 64; at. wt., 156.9.

By permission from *Webster's New Collegiate Dictionary,* copyright, 1949, 1951, by G. & C. Merriam Co.

Now write an account of your findings, 300-500 words long, citing specific evidence.

B. Your instructor will assign one of the following words to each member of the class:

above, *prep.*	lake, *n.*	sail, *v.*
appreciate, *v.*	legal, *adj.*	sick, *adj.*
apron, *n.*	make, *v.*	sun, *n.*
bedlam, *n.*	manufacture, *v.*	street, *n.*
bully, *n.*	noun, *n.*	tap, *n.*
cotton, *n.*	nobody, *p.*	tender, *adj.*
dead, *adj.*	over, *prep.*	tool, *n.*
find, *v.*	paper, *n.*	up, *adv.*
goose, *n.*	paternal, *adj.*	up, *prep.*
head, *n.*	quick, *adj.*	veal, *n.*
idle, *adj.*	read, *v.*	water, *n.*
judge, *v.*	red, *adj.*	wiggle, *v.*
kick, *v.*	road, *n.*	yank, *v.*

Look up your word in each of the following dictionaries: *A New English Dictionary on Historical Principles* (*Oxford English Dictionary*), *Dictionary of American English, Dictionary of Americanisms,* Wyld's *Universal Dictionary of the English Language, Century Dictionary and Cyclopedia, New International Dictionary of the English Language,* and *New Standard Dictionary of the English Language* (these last two are the so-called "unabridged" dictionaries published by the Merriam Company and by Funk and Wagnalls respectively). Use the questions in A of this exercise, and add to them the following:

Which dictionaries give examples of the use of the word? Which dictionaries give such systematic lists of examples that they constitute a history of the word in English or American speech?

Using your notes, prepare an oral report on your word, or write a 300-500 word paper, as your instructor directs.

C. The following are some of the more common prefixes from Latin and Greek used in modern English:

ab- (abs-)	cata-	hyper-
ad- (ac-, af-,	circum-	in- (il-, im-, ir-)
ag-, al-, an-,	com- (co-, col-),	inter-
ap-, ar-, as-,	con-, cor-)	intra-
at-)	contra-	intro-
ambi- (ambo-)	de-	mal-
ante-	di- (dis-)	multi-
anti- (ant-)	ex- (e-, ef-)	neo-
arch-	ex- (ec-)	non-
bi-	extra-	ob- (oc-, of-, op-)

para-	pseudo-	super-
per-	re-	supra-
peri-	retro-	syn- (sy-, syl-, sym-)
post-	se-	trans-
pre-	semi-	tri-
pro-	sub- (suc-, suf-, sug-,	uni-
proto-	sum-, sup-, sur-,	vice-
	sus-)	

Be sure you know the use and meaning of each prefix, verifying in a good dictionary those about which you may be uncertain. Then choose five prefixes, and find at least ten words in which each of these occurs.

For more extensive lists of prefixes and suffixes, see Arthur Garfield Kennedy, *Current English* (Boston, 1935), pp. 337-345.

D. Select two or three of the dictionaries listed in Exercise 34B, preferring those which you have already found useful for etymological study. Then look up the following words, and write a brief paragraph about each, summarizing the most interesting facts you have discovered about the history of the word. Be sure to use at least one book which provides Indo-European bases.

atlas	explode	pants
canary	futhark	piano
change	infantry	pool
corollary	melancholy	quick
defense	mercury	stable
dollar	neighbor	travel

35. WORD CHOICE

[For Guide to Revision, see page 424]

Select words which precisely fit their contexts in meaning, attitude, and suggestiveness.

Selection of the right word for each job is not easy. Knowledge of dictionary meanings is fundamental, but often is not enough. The choice usually is not a simple one between two words, one wrong, the other right. Words are more or less expressive, more or less precise, more or less instinct with the power to make the reader see, hear, feel, or understand. Words should be chosen for many qualifications—their sound, their associations, their currency, their meaning, and many others. But meaning is of first importance.

35-1 The "meaning of meaning"

Strictly speaking, no word has meaning as a physical object can have length. The bars of metal in the Bureau of Standards, for instance, which determine our inches and feet, keep the same length at a given temperature, no matter who measures them, so long as the measuring is accurately done, but no words are kept at a controlled temperature in the Bureau of Standards. Words exist only in people's minds, and all minds are different. No word has a "meaning" which it inevitably calls up in everyone.

Theoretically, then, Humpty Dumpty is justified in telling Alice, "When *I* use a word, it means just what I choose it to mean—neither more nor less." No authority can keep him from using the word *glory,* as he does, to mean *there's a nice knock-down argument for you.* Practically, however, Humpty is not communicating much. Words have no mystical connection with a particular "meaning," but communication is possible because at any time in history by common agreement people associate certain words with certain thoughts. We

[417

can communicate because we agree, closely enough for practical purposes, to let certain words symbolize certain ideas.

35-2 Referent, thought, word

People can agree about meaning because words relate to things in
the real world and are, relatively speaking, common and enduring.
But the use and choice of words is complex because words are related
to things by human beings through minds, which are not all the same.
A word is a symbol which a human being uses to reveal an idea he
has about something.

Referent   Thought   Word

                                                       daisy

Daisy is a symbol which a writer or speaker can use to express his
thought about a thing, a particular flower growing in a meadow, a
referent. Speakers of English, by general agreement, use this symbol
when they think of this particular kind of flower. The symbol would
not work if the writer were thinking of a four-footed animal that
brays or of a carved representation of George Washington. Neither
would it work if he were writing in French or German. Conversely,
any users of the language, readers or listeners, could interpret this
symbol into similar thoughts about the same kind of referent.

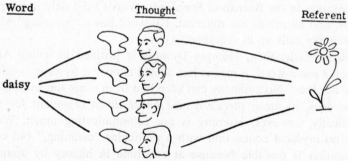

Word   Thought   Referent

daisy

Word choice, however, is not always so simple as this. A writer may have various thoughts about a referent he sees growing in a meadow, and he may choose a word quite different from *daisy*.

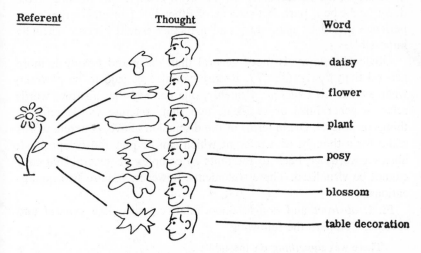

Referent	Thought	Word
		daisy
		flower
		plant
		posy
		blossom
		table decoration

Each of these words—and many others that might be thought of—has the same referent, but each conveys a slightly different thought about the referent. *Plant* indicates that the writer is distinguishing the referent less precisely than does *flower; posy* suggests something about the attitude of the writer; *blossom* and *table decoration* indicate special attitudes toward the referent.

These differences illustrate some of the distinctions involved in effective word choice, distinctions between concrete and abstract words, between denotation and connotation, between different meanings in different contexts. They may even represent differences in the same person from day to day or minute to minute as his mood changes.

35-3 Abstract and concrete

Drawing a picture of the referent of the word *daisy* is relatively easy, and the resulting picture may also portray the referent of the word *flower*. But a picture of the referent behind the "full" meaning of the word *flower* would be more difficult. It would have to include not only daisies but also irises and begonias and violets and the blooms on thistles, in fact everything in the writer's experience which made up the idea he was expressing by the word. Or consider drawing a picture of the referent behind the word *beauty*. The picture of the daisy might be a part, but dozens of other bits from the writer's experience would be necessary, and a picture would become virtually impossible.

Obviously, *flower* is more general than *daisy* and *beauty* is more general than *flower* (see 7). *Beauty* can also be said to be *abstract,* whereas *daisy* is *concrete*. Roughly, one can say that abstract words refer to generalities or to ideas, and that concrete words refer to things or objects. Or, in terms of the discussion above, concrete words stand for a thought of a referent which can be pictured or specified; abstract words go back to referents so complex or general that they cannot be visualized. These statements, however, require two qualifications.

First, *abstract* and *concrete* are relative terms, like *general* and *specific*. Compare the following:

> There was *something* on the table.
> There was *food* on the table.
> There was a *bowl of fruit* on the table.

Food is more concrete than *something, bowl of fruit* more concrete than *food*. The ideas become more specific; the words become more concrete and increase in exactness and suggestiveness as they do so.

Second, just as the general develops out of the specific, abstract expressions grow from more concrete ones. *Color* stands for a thought which would be hard to express if we had only more concrete terms like *red, yellow, blue, green*.

Consider the following sentence proposed by George Orwell to illustrate how some writers might translate a passage of the Bible:

> Objective consideration of contemporary phenomena compels the conclusion that success or failure in competitive activities exhibits no tendency to be commensurate with innate capacity, but that a considerable element of the unpredictable must invariably be taken into account.

The sentence exaggerates, but it suggests how abstractions piled upon abstractions can obscure ideas. Compare the passage from Ecclesiastes which Orwell has "translated."

420]

I returned, and saw under the sun, that the race is not to the swift, nor the battle to the strong, neither yet bread to the wise, nor yet riches to men of understanding, nor yet favour to men of skill; but time and chance happeneth to them all.

Instead of one general statement, the original uses five specific examples; instead of abstractions like *consideration, phenomena, conclusion, success,* and *failure,* the original uses more concrete words like *race, battle, bread,* and *riches.* Almost always, clear and accurate writing uses concrete words whenever possible.

35-4 Denotation and connotation

Roughly speaking, a word's communication of a thought about a referent is the word's denotation, what is sometimes called its "dictionary meaning." *Daisy* and *flower* and *table decoration,* therefore, have different denotations; *flower* and *posy* can hardly be distinguished in denotation. Still, no botanist today would write that the "begonia bears monecius posies"; he would feel that the word *posy* is unsuited to scientific description. On the other hand, one might wish to suggest that certain wallpaper was old-fashioned by saying, "It was all cluttered up with pink posies." That is, each of these words can do something more than point to a particular thought. This power of a word to do more than designate, to make emotional and interpretive suggestions, is the word's *connotation.* Connotation is an essential part of the meaning of a word, to be distinguished from denotation only in analysis.

The connotation of a word always has an individual basis. To a garden lover, the word *flower* may suggest hours of pleasure in the sunshine, a sense of pervading joy, or even ecstasy. To someone else it may suggest Georgia O'Keefe's paintings, or if one has been ill from mimosa, it may even suggest nausea. But to a considerable degree, even though the basis of connotation is personal, most people share much of the connotative power of a word, for most of us have somewhat similar heritages and experiences. The word *home* connotes something different for each of us, but most people share feelings about the word, and would distinguish them from other feelings associated with *house.* Thus, to a degree, the emotional qualities of words can be used for communication, and the connotative power of words is so great that most good writers make conscious use of connotation.

[421

35-5 Applications of connotation

In general, the connotations of words serve to emphasize certain characteristics of a referent or to reveal certain attitudes toward it. *Statesman* and *politician* may describe the same person, refer to the same referent.

Referent	Thought	Word
		statesman
		politician

The thoughts expressed by the words differ, however; the words have become associated with emotional suggestions so that *statesman* emphasizes wisdom, dignity, vision, and integrity, and *politician* suggests intrigue, time-serving, and self-seeking. Through their connotations, the words present different views of the referent. Connotational meanings, therefore, are exploited especially in any writing or speaking which seeks to persuade, to move, or to stimulate emotion.

Slanting. Concern for propaganda and analysis of propaganda have made our society particularly aware of the emotional qualities of words, especially as used in politics or advertising. Compare the following statements, which describe the same incident:

> Senator A ranted interminably this afternoon in a bigoted attack on the new budget.
>
> Senator A delivered a full and detailed address this afternoon in a spirited criticism of the new budget.

Through their connotations, the words in the first are clearly "slanted" or "loaded" against the senator; words in the second seek to move the reader to approve the speech. To suggest that "emotional" words should not be used is absurd, but the writer needs to be aware of their limitations and their weaknesses. The trouble with both the statements above is that the reader does not know what Senator A did. The connotations of the words outweigh their denotations. Many similar words in English, especially words like *freedom, communist, authority, glamorous,* or *sensational,* have developed such varied connotations that they can be used only with care and skill if the writer is to avoid

422]

distortion. Furthermore, misleading use of the emotional power of words is as false as any other kind of verbal lie because the connotations of a word are part of it. The writer who intentionally distorts the truth through his choice of "loaded" or "slanted" words should be challenged on his integrity rather than his skill with language.

Figurative language; metaphor. Irresponsible exploitation of connotations of words can distort truth, but skillful management of emotional meanings can make language more precise, more interesting, more intense. The importance of connotations can be seen especially in figurative language, in a device like the metaphor. Metaphor, or comparison in language, is more than embellishment; it is part of language itself. We use metaphors constantly in conversation (*He ran like a deer. He was a pig at the table*). Words develop through metaphors; we speak of the *hands* of the clock, the *foot* of the bed, the *head* of the household, the *legs* of a chair. Sails *belly,* and crowds *thunder* applause as the *shell shoots* across the *line.* We no longer think of the italicized words as figures of speech, but they developed as metaphors, and words are developing in this manner all the time (*foxhole, brass hat, pump-priming, underground*). Metaphor, then, is a device by which connotations of words provide precise and vivid meanings. Consider the following relatively elaborate comparison from *Romeo and Juliet,* which uses one of the words considered above.

> This bud of love, by summer's ripening breath,
> May prove a beauteous flower when next we meet.

The metaphor is complex, but essentially it is using the word *flower* to express the referent usually expressed by *love.*

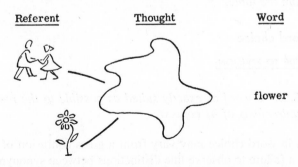

Referent	Thought	Word
		flower

By using the word *flower* rather than the word *love,* Shakespeare emphasizes parts of both the connotational and denotational meanings of love. He makes us think of the "flowerlike" significance of love, its ability to grow, its beauty, its relation with time. The metaphor, in its context, allows the writer to exploit the emotional meanings of the words.

35-6 Words in their contexts

The writer, then, needs to choose his words with care, selecting so that in both denotation and connotation they are appropriate in their contexts. Words affect, and are affected by, the words with which they are used. Consider, for example, the following sentences:

> My *love* is like a red, red rose.
> The *love* of money is the root of all evil.
> Greater *love* hath no man than this, that a man lay down his life for his friends.
> Friendship is *Love* without his wings.
> The score was forty-*love*.
> God is *love*.

The word *love* appears in each sentence, but the meanings differ. The context, the company the word keeps, indicates its meaning.

The writer must choose his words with their contexts in mind. The lists of discriminative synonyms in dictionaries suggest how words fit different contexts (look up, for example, *joke, wit,* or *wise*). Even synonyms cannot be changed at random. For example, dictionaries list *exonerate* as a synonym for *clear*. Substituting *exonerate* would sharpen meaning in a sentence like *The attorney hoped to clear the ex-convict.* It would not serve in a sentence like *Mary cleared the dishes from the table.*

35 *Word choice*   **W**

GUIDE TO REVISION:

> *Select a word as exactly suited as possible to the requirements of its context.*

Errors in word choice may vary from a gross confusion of difficult words to a failure to observe fine distinctions between synonyms. (For word choice involving forms, see 26, 29b, 30, 32.) Mrs. Malaprop, a character in Sheridan's *The Rivals,* made herself famous and added the word *malapropism* to the language by misusing words she did not understand. When she complimented herself on a "nice derangement of epitaphs" and said that someone was "headstrong as an allegory on the banks of the Nile," she certainly did not mean to say *derangement, epitaphs,* or *allegory.* Slips in word choice may be as ludicrous as Mrs. Malaprop's, but less easily observed. They may result from ignoring connotations of a word, from failure to utilize concrete terms, or from failure to distinguish synonyms like *splash, slop,* and *spatter* which may be equally concrete but differ in meaning.

Original	*Revision*
The capture of the ridge had seemed an *inhuman* feat.	The capture of the ridge had seemed impossible.
[*Probably some kind of mental confusion with* humanly impossible *or* superhuman *accounts for the inaccuracy.*]	[*It is difficult to guess precisely what the writer had in mind.*]
The inheritance brought them only *transitive* pleasure.	The inheritance brought them only *transitory* pleasure.
The Argentine government *interred* the cruiser.	The Argentine government *interned* the cruiser.
Dr. Brinkley ran *a fowl* with other regulations concerning his practice.	Dr. Brinkley ran *afoul* of regulations concerning his practice.
Indians of all sorts had rattles. Some Indians made odd-shaped rattles from the skins of animals, and some of the Indian children could use parts of plants for rattles just as they grew. There were primitive metal rattles, too, and clay dishes so constructed that they would make a noise.	The Indians, adults and children, loved rattles. Many tribes devised loop-shaped rattles from dried buffalo tails, and Pueblo children found a natural rattle provided for them in the rattlebox plant. In the Southwest, children shook copper tinklers, and adults used ceramic vessels with hollow heads, from which clay pellets would give forth a dull click.
[*This paragraph does not contain words as clearly "wrong" as those in the examples above, but the lack of precision weakens the writing.*]	[*Terms are more precise, sometimes partly because they are more concrete.*]

Words similar in spelling or meaning are easily confused; distinctions between many common words must be learned. See Glossary and 42-9.

Original	*Revision*
The critic's statement *inferred* that he had plagiarized.	The critic's statement *implied* that he had plagiarized.
Every *affect* has a cause.	Every *effect* has a cause.
Most everybody was going to the party.	*Almost* everybody was going to the party.
There were *less* women than men in the class.	There were *fewer* woman than men in the class.
Brigham found the *sight* for a new city.	Brigham found the *site* for a new city.
She tried to *leave* her brother go first.	She tried to *let* her brother go first.
He did not understand the *illusions* to mythology.	He did not understand the *allusions* to mythology.
When he entered her face turned a *livid* red.	When he entered, her face turned a *vivid* red.

35a "Direction" in words　　　　　　　　　　W a

Words sometimes have meanings which will make sense in only one "direction." That is, if you mean that Irene likes jewels, you can say *Jewels have an attraction for Irene.* You cannot say *Irene has an attraction for jewels* without meaning something quite different, without using *have an attraction* with what might be called "false direction." Confusions of this sort are varied and usually develop from careless thinking and the kinds of basic errors considered in 20 and 24e-24g.

Original	*Revision*
The Elizabethan audience had a great *fascination* for wars and duels.	Wars and duels *fascinated* the Elizabethan audience.
I have a very *inadequate* feeling when I think of writing about this book.	I feel *inadequate* when I think of writing about this book.

426]

Original (Cont.)

Nor does an enemy of the prairie dog ever manage to approach the "town" *unawares.*

Of course I am not *in reference* to the everyday loafer who comes and goes as he pleases.

Once action is put forth the problems become disintegrated; therefore, let us *build up our weaknesses.*

Necessary financial reimbursements sent to the above address will receive my prompt attention.

Revision (Cont.)

No enemy of the prairie dog can approach the "town" *undetected.*

Of course I am not *referring* to the common loafer who comes and goes as he pleases.

Prompt action will solve many problems; therefore let us *overcome our weaknesses.*

I shall promptly pay any bills sent to the same address.

35b Concrete and abstract words   W b

Some words are more concrete than others. They refer to real things, even to particular objects. A blow is more specific than an insult, a right hook to the ear more specific than a blow. Chanel No. 5 is more specific than perfume. General and abstract words have their uses, but on the whole, vigorous writing is specific, concrete writing. Many a dull writer has only to substitute concrete words for his more abstract words to become interesting. See also 7.

Abstract

When we were in some fighting it was hard to know what was going on because so many things were happening that usually you did not know much about it until after it was over. You were excited, and though maybe you would know the things which were occurring, it was hard afterward to know just what had happened, especially around you.—*Student theme.*

More Specific

Who know the conflicts, hand to hand—the many conflicts in the dark, those shadowy-tangled, flashing moonbeamed woods, the writhing groups and squads, the cries, the din, the cracking guns and pistols, the distant cannon, the cheers and calls and threats and awful music of the oaths, the indescribable mix; the officers' orders, persuasions, encouragements; the devils fully roused in human hearts; the strong shout, *Charge, men, charge;* the flash of the naked sword, and rolling flame and smoke?—Walt Whitman's diary, slightly repunctuated.

[427

Original

I always used to like to go out camping when I was younger because Father was always doing funny things, and that always made us have a lot of fun. Father was always a funny man and he would do things you would not expect your father to be doing, and usually his things didn't work.

Revision

Camping with Father was always fun, because he was sure to come lugging some contraption he had just invented, a chipmunk-repeller, which was supposed to keep chipmunks from devouring the soap—and did not—or an electrically driven decoy duck, which would get short-circuited halfway across the lake.

Abstract words are sometimes used as if they had no meaning at all, as blankets to cover meaning in the vicinity of the writer's idea. Such words go in and out of fashion, but the following are among those currently popular: *angle, aspect, claim* (verb), *contact* (verb), *point, factor, setup, situation, deal, phase, basic, regard, fundamental, force, rate* (verb), *worth-while, unique,* and *outstanding.* Blanket words are closely related to jargon (see 36c) and often appear in roundabout and wordy sentences (see 36).

Original

The question in this regard is directly related to the basic circumstances of the situation.

The abnormal condition within Hamlet's mind is a governing factor which is the foremost force in molding his character traits.

The coach stated that Jerry never rated very high with him because he never really came through in our particular setup.

He has familiarity with the medieval language picture and is an authority within the areas of that field.

Revision

The question is basic.

The turmoil in Hamlet's mind altered his character.
[*This may not be true, but it is apparently about what the student meant to say.*]

The coach said that Jerry never adapted himself to our style of play.

He is an authority on medieval languages.

35c Colored, "slanted," or prejudicial words W c

In an oration once popular in high-school contests, Regulus addressing the Carthaginians referred to "the slimy ooze that stagnates in your veins," contrasting it unfavorably to the blood of the Romans. Obviously Regulus was not trying to be objective in his typing of Carthaginian blood. Similarly, when a mother says, "Now take your nice medicine," she is not necessarily describing her own impression of the medicine objectively. As they are here used *slimy, ooze, stagnates, nice* are colored, calculated to influence feelings, not to communicate truth. The connotations of words always influence their effect. Usually colored words are combined with ideas calculated to appeal to fears and prejudice. Notice the following:

> Rush me airmail without cost or obligation to me all the exciting facts about your amazing new "Pay-Check Protective System" that pays me $300.00 a month for life with other valuable benefits. I understand that the remarkable dividends of this plan will give me money to help pay bills, keep me out of debt, and take care of my family's needs.

At times a writer may wish to play upon the emotions and the prejudices of others, but most writing is the better for being objective. Often, slanted words are so obvious in their intent that they fail to make even a convincing emotional appeal.

Original	*Revision*
In high school there were some radicals who always stabbed any new worth-while project in the back just because they were rats at heart.	There was one faction in our high school which tried to block any change that my group instituted.
[*The writer probably does not know the meaning of the word* radical, *nor care how he uses the word* rat. *Apparently, he is trying to discredit by calling names, but he is mainly discrediting himself.*]	[*The attitude of the writer has changed, and relatively objective words have replaced colored words.*]
My mother is a perfect angel with a saintly face and the most perfect disposition in the world.	Mother is seldom cross, never angry without good reason, and always helpful; years of smiling have left little wrinkles at the corners of her mouth.
[*Words like* angel *and* saintly *have some emotional force, but are vague enough to be unconvincing.*]	[*Concrete terms clarify the passage and strengthen the appeal.*]
He had an unwholesome mouth that was disturbing to look at.	He had chalky teeth which looked as though they were decaying.

[**429**

35d Metaphorical writing   **W d**

Comparisons and figures of speech often make language brighter, more specific, and more precise. Many words have the meanings they do because they are old metaphors which are no longer recognized. *Outskirts* comes to us from the days when women wore more skirts than most women do now, and the "outskirts" were of course on the circumference. Much of the most vigorous, charming writing is metaphorical writing.

Prosaic	*Metaphorical*
Falstaff is so big and fat that he sweats a great deal when he walks too fast.	Falstaff sweats to death And lards the lean earth as he walks along. —SHAKESPEARE, *Henry IV,* Pt. 1
My roommate has a funny-looking face because his nose is short and kind of flattened.	My roommate's nose looks as though he always has it smudged up against a window pane.
The long mountains came down to the abrupt coast, and you could see them rather mixed up, running every which way. Some were angular, and some were rounded, and they all looked sad and depressing. Back from the shore where they were high the peaks were all snow-covered, and even nearer there were patches of snow and glaciers on them.	These long mountains . . . lie, one after another, like corpses, with their toes up, and you pass by them, . . . and see their noses, tipped by cloud or snow, high in behind, with one corpse occasionally lying on another, and a skull or a thigh-bone chucked about, and hundreds of glaciers and snow-patches hanging to them, as though it was a winter battlefield. —WORTHINGTON C. FORD, *Letters of Henry Adams*

A metaphor can be a useful instrument. So can a stick of dynamite. Either can be dangerous. Avoid mixed metaphors, and avoid shifting metaphors so quickly that your reader is thinking about one figure of speech when you have gone on to another.

Original	*Revision*
A creative person who has no political crystallization, not merely cuts the production end of his work, but loses a vital gut that is part of the social continuum.	A creative artist who ignores contemporary politics limits himself as a creator and to a degree cuts himself off from society. [*This is prosaic, perhaps, but*

Original (Cont.)

[*Doubtless the man who published this to advertise an obscure magazine thought he was both profound and witty, but we only laugh at the poor artist, whacking off his production while slowly disemboweling himself, and all because he has not undergone crystallization.*]

Since then the snowball of knowledge has swept relentlessly on, stamping with each year another rivet of reliability and craftsmanship into the name of the House of Melarkey.—London trade advertisement.

Revision (Cont.)

understandable, and at the worst, not silly.]

The House of Melarkey has advanced with the times, in experience, in craftsmanship, in reliability.

Some mixed figures, like those above, result from a misguided striving to write well. Much worse are the mixed metaphors caused by careless use of language.

Original

Relying on the circumstances of the case, it seemed best to take the bull by the horns, even if I shuffled off this mortal coil.

We keep clipping the wool off the goose that lays the golden eggs, and instead of getting on the beam we pump her dry.

Revision

I had to do something.

Taking excessive profits inevitably destroys the source of those profits.

35e *Trite or hackneyed expressions; clichés*   W e; Trite

Many expressions in English can not stand popularity. Idioms, of course, and standard expressions appear over and over without losing their effectiveness, but slang or other attempts at cleverness or vividness emerge after overuse with as little vigor as any other stale joke. Metaphors which do not enter the language as new words often become trite. The writer who first referred to a wife as a *ball and chain* may have been amusing on the comic-strip level; the thousandth person who imitated him was not amusing on any level. Expressions

[431

which have been so tarnished by time that their charm, and often even their meaning, is gone are called trite or hackneyed expressions or clichés. Trite expressions are dangerous partly because they paralyze the mind. As ready-made channels for thought they invite the ideas of the writer, who can then cease thinking. An editorial writer commented in a discussion of academic freedom in a university:

> Any teacher who disagrees with his dean's academic views is not playing on the team and should turn in his suit.

The "team" metaphor was worn out long ago, but the writer fell into the set pattern so easily that he failed to analyze his own remarks. The convenience of the trite expression led him into an argument by false analogy (see 10e).

Original	*Revision*
When war first reared its ugly head, John Q. Public took it in his stride and played ball.	Faced with war, we did what had to be done.
In our day and age, in this great country of ours, progress has taken place by leaps and bounds.	America has progressed.
Back in the old home town and under the paternal roof, Jim found that, having struck it rich out in the great open spaces, the fatted calf was now prepared for the prodigal son.	Back home from the West, wealthy, Jim found that he had become suddenly popular.
We found that fraternity initiations were not what they were cracked up to be. As a matter of fact the general consensus of opinion was that they were like something the cat brought in.	We disliked the initiation from the time we had to scrabble among the rosebushes looking for a rabbit's foot that was supposedly buried there, until we were all lined up in the chapter room, shivering in our shorts.

EXERCISE 35

A. In the sentences below some words have been mistaken for other words, and some have been misunderstood. Make the necessary corrections.

    1. I became so completely dissolved in our card game that I forgot all about the dog.

2. Falstaff finally realized that he had been the brunt of a joke.

3. I am fighting because I want to make life better and happier for myself and my posteriority.

4. I decided that in regards to my future, my first duty was to go to college.

5. Their propaganda pictures showed our captured soldiers being treated with the upmost kindness.

6. His house looked like a mid-evil estate.

7. In *The Bishop Orders His Tomb;* Browning is satyrizing a Renaissance bishop.

8. In spite of my long slide down the glacier, my camera was in tact.

9. The marine biologist asked for a leave to investigate the debts of the sea, and his request was granite.

10. He announced his presence in a loud voice, and stood in the middle of the room until I asked what he meant by his frontery.

B. Correct the false direction of words in the following sentences:

1. Physical exercise can achieve rest of the mind.

2. He was afraid of how the discriminated groups might react.

3. Many results may be obtained which make their scientific value skeptical.

4. Shirley instilled an unreasonable fear of spiders as a small child.

5. You never know what your weaknesses are until you are applied to them.

6. When a point is trying to be made, a reader must watch the evidence.

7. The people who want more rigid rules for the girls in the dormitories are attributed to the older generation.

8. I entered the state music festival, where every contestant was competed with by music from all over the state.

9. Jake yielded a very profitable income from these products crossing his bridge.

10. They were inculcated with the idea that they were well informed.

11. The education of the teacher of youth must be developed, and more important, it must never be allowed to become relaxed or neglected.

12. Sewage disposal in that rural area has always been carried out by the use of septic tanks and cesspools.

13. Fishing was once regarded as anything but a skillful art.

14. Enterprising publishers have now started bringing out a dearth of older detective stories.

[433

15. The purpose of college sports is to instill students with courage and vigor.

16. Her abrupt, exaggerated movements gave the impression of being a small child.

17. Today, as never before, the church should have an unsurpassable bearing on modern civilization.

18. The modern supermarket brings grocery buying to the highest convenience.

19. Artichokes are among the vegetable improvements which could help better the condition of the southern truck gardener.

20. Massachusetts was one of the first states which was instigated by higher education for women.

21. She lost her self-respect as a result of her drink-fogged brain.

22. From their difficult work teamsters derived the name "bull-skinners."

23. If you ask the average person what a hot rod is, he will picture a broken-down wreck with a bad driver.

24. The first sight of a person coming up the hill is a ramshackle old barn.

25. Students are required to take some courses because it is known that the course will be profited by the students.

C. Each of the sentences below is followed by words which can be synonyms for the italicized words in the sentence. Indicate which could be substituted in the sentence and explain changes in meaning that would result.

1. Mary felt no *fear* as she faced the microphone. (*dismay, alarm, horror, anxiety, dread*)

2. The president did not have enough *power* to enforce the rules. (*potency, puissance, strength, energy, force*)

3. Her *pride* would not allow her to dress as the other girls in the house did. (*vanity, haughtiness, superciliousness, egotism, vainglory*)

4. *Examination* of the evidence showed that the jury had been wrong. (*inquiry, inquisition, scrutiny, investigation, proposition*)

5. The judge had no *sympathy* for law-breakers. (*pity, commiseration, condolence, tenderness, agreement*)

6. His devices were so *transparent* that nobody was deceived. (*translucent, lucid, diaphanous, limpid, luminous*)

7. The entire *company* joined in the song. (*group, throng, assemblage, flock, circle*)

8. Her dyed hair and *gaudy* clothes shocked the congregation. (*ostentatious, pretentious, tawdry, garish, flashy*)

9. Many members of the audience were *moved* to tears. (*incited, prompted, impelled, instigated, actuated*)

10. The general was not willing to pay the *price* of victory. (*value, charge, cost, expense, worth*)

D. For each of the following words think of five more specific equivalents:

1. eating place	6. boat
2. recompense	7. something said
3. hill	8. book
4. local officeholder	9. dance
5. cloth	10. ceremony

E. The metaphors and similes in the following sentences vary in complexity and effectiveness. Study each one in terms of the referent-thought-word relationship discussed above (35-5). Then decide as specifically as you can which parts of the referent are emphasized or changed by using words metaphorically.

1. The moon was a ghostly galleon. . . . —Alfred Noyes

2. This man was hunting about the hotel lobby like a starved dog that has forgotten where he has buried a bone.—O. Henry

3. A wit's a feather, and a chief a rod;
An honest man's the noblest work of God.—Alexander Pope

4. An honest God is the noblest work of man.—Samuel Butler

5. A pun is not bound by the laws which limit nice wit. It is a pistol let off at the ear; not a feather to tickle the intellect.—Charles Lamb

6. Like our shadows,
Our wishes lengthen as our sun declines.—Alexander Pope

7. I wonder why anybody wanted to wing an old woman in the leg.—Hilda Lawrence

8. More than a catbird hates a cat,
Or a criminal hates a clue,
Or the Axis hates the United States
That's how much I love you.—Ogden Nash

9. So 'tis not her the bee devours,
It is a pretty maze of flowers;
It is the rose that bleeds when he
Nibbles his nice phlebotomy.—John Cleveland

10. Let us go then, you and I,
When the evening is spread out against the sky
Like a patient etherized upon a table.—T. S. Eliot.

11. All of Stratford, in fact, suggests powdered history—add hot water and stir and you have a delicious, nourishing Shakespeare.
—Margaret Halsey

[435

12. Our two souls, therefore, which are one,
    Though I must go, endure not yet
    A breach, but an expansion
    Like gold to airy thinness beat.—John Donne

F. Revise the following passage by replacing the italicized words with other words which make us see, hear, taste, smell, or feel:

When I *entered* the *enclosure,* the *affair* was *going on.* I *found a place,* and was *feeling pretty good* if a *little uncomfortable* because of *the circumstances,* when I saw a *person* approaching me. She was a *female,* and *seemed to be in an agitated condition.* Her face looked *kind of funny,* and she *moved in a peculiar way.* She started *saying things* in an *odd kind of voice,* and I *realized* that she was in *an intoxicated condition.* Her *way of standing* was *unusual.* Then some *other persons approached,* including a *man,* who seemed to think he *was important around there.* He *spoke to me.* I also, was *in an agitated state* by now, so that I was *not sensitive to all that was transpiring,* but I heard *certain sounds from various people.* Somebody with a *repulsive face* was *admonishing* me. *One individual inquired* if I *was not aware* that I was an *improper person* to be *in these surroundings.* He *had a threatening attitude.* I *replied* that I *was unaware of the circumstances,* but that I would *accede to their wishes and retire.* As I *took my departure* I heard them *expatiating upon me.*

G. The following advertisement appeared in a metropolitan newspaper:

4 EXQUISITE LIFE-LIKE PLASTIC ROSES IN A GLAMOROUS GLASS BRICK!
When you fill your Rosaquarium with water no one will believe that these lovely red roses, expertly reproduced in life-like plastic, aren't real! An incredibly beautiful decorative piece for table, mantel, or TV set.

Obviously, this is not an objective description; it is full of colored words. To see that the words are colored, one need only replace some of them with words colored in the opposite direction.

4 LIVID GHASTLY PLASTIC ROSES IN A DUST-CATCHING GLASS BRICK!
When you fill your Rosaquarium with water, everyone will know that these hideous, cerise imitations, caricatures in gaudy plastic, are phony. An incredible piece of junk to clutter up table, mantel, or TV set.

Find ten advertisements in which colored or "slanted" words are used to influence sales, not to describe a product.

H. Look up each of the following words in a good desk dictionary and study the discriminative synonyms listed. For each word and each of its listed synonyms write a sentence putting the word in a suitable context.

1. anger	8. law	15. relevant
2. beg	9. lift	16. see
3. change	10. material	17. smell
4. copy	11. object	18. stick
5. crowd	12. power	19. think
6. debase	13. proud	20. weaken
7. guide	14. rebellion	

I. Substitute fresher, more expressive terms for the trite expressions in the sentences below. You may find that you must use more revealing words than those in the original, since trite expressions often become very nearly meaningless.

1. I slept like a log, and woke up at the crack of dawn, fresh as a daisy.

2. With her hair a sable cloud about her face, her peaches-and-cream complexion, her ruby lips, and her eyes like stars, she was as pretty as a picture.

3. Martha was a perfect baby, as happy as the day is long.

4. The wily southpaw zipped a fast one over the corner, and the old speed king had done it again. You can't hit 'em if you can't see 'em.

5. The last examination had put me out like a light, and accordingly, although I was down in the dumps—it was blue Monday for me—I determined to burn the midnight oil.

6. Crime never pays and true Americanism requires that we stamp it out, each and every time a crime wave raises its ugly head in this great and glorious land of ours.

7. And last but not least, in advertising you have to sell yourself; that is, to make it short and sweet, you have to hit the market smack on the nose.

8. We would willingly point with pride at the progress onward and upward in this land of the free; we have no inclination to drag a red herring across the trail to becloud the issue; but any lover of government of the people, by the people, for the people must view with alarm the state of the nation in this day and age, and unless we go back to the principles of the founding fathers, we are in grave danger of having our cherished liberties gone with the wind.

9. He took the unwelcome news like a man. He became sober as a judge, but I knew he was true as steel, all wool and a yard wide, and that he would snap out of it.

10. He was tall, dark, and handsome, with lean flanks and piercing eyes, always smelling faintly of good English tobacco and well-oiled leather, every inch a man's man.

36. ECONOMY IN WORDS

[For Guide to Revision, see page 441]

Good writing is economical writing.

People in dreadful need of communication can usually make themselves understood in few words. "Help!" "Fire!" "Murder!" say more than "I am in need of assistance," "There is a conflagration," and "A person is being illegally dispatched." Of course complicated ideas and fine distinctions require elaborate treatment; they cannot be considered in few words, but the fewer the better, so long as the expression is adequate. Good writing results from a plenitude of ideas and an economy of words, not from a desert of ideas and a flood of vocabulary. Most writers, especially most beginning writers, should throw out words.

36-1 Economy through development and structure

Good writing leads a reader by a minimum of words to clear understanding. Wordiness, offensive in itself, usually implies a more fundamental lack in writing. Consider, for instance, the following paragraph from a student theme.

> The world is full of rare oddities, like the warm water discovered at the North Pole. This is quite an unusual discovery, since the temperatures deep into the arctic circle are so low that you would not expect to find warm water there, but that is what happened. The water was found to be very warm near the North Pole, and was warm enough so that it was not frozen, although you would expect everything to be frozen so far north.

The paragraph is wordy because the writer has not developed the idea in his topic sentence, but by restating has ballooned a sentence into a paragraph. To cure his wordiness he needs to think, to get facts, to illustrate, to provide examples.

Similarly, awkward sentence structure makes the following wordy:

438]

The reason why I have come to college is because there are requirements for being a mortician in this state, and that is why I matriculated here, certain credits being necessary to pass the state requirements, and I have been promised that I can enter my father's business.

Ruthless pruning would improve the sentence, but only reconstruction using a direct pattern would make the sentence clear and economical (see 19).

36-2 Economy with words

Even well-constructed sentences, however, can often be improved by removing nonessential or redundant words, substituting more direct sentence patterns for roundabout ones, and economizing on modifiers.

Cutting deadwood. Almost a sure way to improve composition is to resolutely cut out the words doing no work. Notice the italicized words in the following sentences:

> *It happened that* she was elected *to the position of* secretary *and this was* [of] the oldest club *that existed* in the city.
>
> Although he had always considered his sister *to be of the* awkward *type,* he found her *to be* a good dancer.

With the italicized words omitted, the sentences are clearer and sharper.

Direct expressions. Often shorter, more direct routes to meaning can be discovered. Notice, for example, the substitutions suggested in brackets for the italicized words in the following sentences.

> Mary's tears *had the effect of making* [made] Jim regret *the accusation which he had made hastily* [his hasty accusation].
>
> *By the time the end of the month rolled around* [By the end of the month] *it seemed to us a certainty* [we knew] that our first business venture would *be a success* [succeed].

A well-chosen verb or adjective may say as much as a wordy clause.

Economy in modifiers. Every modifier added to a sentence decreases the impact of the others. Words like *very, really, surely, actually, merely, simply, great,* and *real* tend to accumulate in careless composition. Consider whether the modifiers italicized in the following sentence should be omitted.

> As I crept *hesitantly* out of the *dark,* dingy, *grimy* hotel and felt the *blazing,* withering sun on my back I was *very* sure I did not *really* want to spend a month in the city.

Often the effect of modifiers can be embodied in telling nouns or verbs. *Liar,* for most purposes, says everything in *a person given by nature or habit to disseminating untruths; canter* or *gallop* says more than *ride at a rapid pace.*

36-3 Word economy and adequacy

Brief writing is not necessarily good writing; expression in a complicated world must usually be detailed, and details require words, many of them. Even publishers, who have to pay printing bills, often advise writers to "write it out," but granted that the writer uses words enough to express himself, the fewer words the better. Notice the following:

> Spring comes to the land with pale, green shoots and swelling buds; it brings to the sea a great increase in the number of simple, one-celled plants of microscopic size, the diatoms. Perhaps the currents bring down to the mackerel some awareness of the flourishing vegetation of the upper waters, of the rich pasturage for hordes of crustaceans that browse in the diatom meadows and in their turn fill the waters with clouds of their goblin-headed young. Soon fishes of many kinds will be moving through the spring sea, to feed on the teeming life of the surface and to bring forth their own young.
>
> —Rachel L. Carson, *Under the Sea Wind*

This is good writing, not because it is brief, but because it is economical. Miss Carson is saying something more than that the mackerel, after hibernating off the continental shelf, mysteriously wake up every spring; she is fitting the annual migration of the mackerel into the impelling cycle of the seasons; explanation requires detail, and details require words. The student might try going through this passage, endeavoring to remove one word without damaging the effect. In the last line, for instance, *teeming life* could be reduced to *life,* but the account would suffer. Note how much is implied in a passage like "hordes of crustaceans that browse in the diatom meadows." Word economy is not sparing words; it is putting them to work.

36 *Economy in words*   # **Wordy**

GUIDE TO REVISION:

*Remove needless words, substitute expressive words
for vague words, or recast, using briefer and more
vigorous structure.*

Wordy writing is seldom wordy in only one way. Often a writer
can revise a wordy passage best by thinking it through again from the
beginning and trying to express the idea as simply and directly as
possible. Good thinking, expressed in simple structures with carefully
chosen words, will automatically remove wordiness.

Wordy

Although the story is in the
supernatural class, Hawthorne
manages to put over his point and
show the effects on a person when
he is confronted with the fact that
everyone contains a certain amount
of evil in their physical make-up.

When someone is dead in a house
it can always be seen that there
is a change comes over you, there
being so much to be done because
of the death and the funeral and
it is so sad. There is always quite
a lot to do about the house, and
then there is the adjustment factor
because all of you have to get used
to the situation of being without
the dear one who was loved and
is now gone forevermore.

But if you get right down to the
facts in the case, we cannot reorient
this tract of real estate, nor can we
determine what disposition is fated
to be made in the future of this
acreage fresh from God's hand,
and last but not least we cannot

Concise

Hawthorne uses the supernatural
to suggest that there is some evil
in everyone.
[*The original version was cluttered; with the verbiage cleared
away, the writer can make the sentence direct and precise.*]

The bustle in a house
The morning after death
Is solemnest of industries
Enacted upon earth,—

The sweeping up the heart
And putting love away
We shall not want to use again
Until eternity.
                        —EMILY DICKINSON

But in a larger sense, we cannot
dedicate, we cannot consecrate, we
cannot hallow this ground.
—ABRAHAM LINCOLN, "Gettysburg
                                Address"

Wordy (Cont.)

render a decision as to whether or not this section of the earth's surface is to be employed for purposes other than those of the divine.

36a Repetition   Wordy a; Rep

Repetition is often an effective device for emphasis, and it is often necessary. Repetition of a key word, for example, is preferable to the use of ostentatious synonyms. A paper on Shakespeare is bound to repeat words like *drama* or *play* or *Shakespeare,* and to avoid repeating the author's name with clichés like *the Bard* or *the Swan of Avon* is more obvious than the repetition. Careless repetition, however, particularly of easily noticed expressions, makes writing wordy and amateurish.

Original	*Revision*
Goldwyn added a little more spice by putting the beautiful girl in Walter's dreams. The girl made the play a little more interesting. He made the story move by adding comedy, and the people were a little more satisfied when they left the theatre.	Goldwyn added spice and interest to the play by putting the beautiful girl in Walter's dreams. He made the story move by adding comedy, and the people were a little more satisfied when they left the theatre.
[*Repetition of* a little *in three successive sentences suggests language poverty.*]	[*The qualification in* a little *probably is not needed at all. Certainly its first two uses can be dropped, and sentences can be combined for economy.*]
Users of the library often use little care in handling books.	Users of the library often **are** careless in handling books.
He announced that if anyone wanted to argue that he should wait until the next meeting.	He announced that if any**one** wanted to argue he should **wait** until the next meeting.

36b Redundancy   Wordy b; Red

Excess words, especially those which double the meaning of neighboring words, are called redundant, and are usually the results of careless repetition or of inadequate knowledge of the full meanings of the words used. *Repeat again, continue on, return back, refer back* are common examples of redundancy.

Original

He was the first originator of the theory that we all now unanimously accept that understanding should be substituted in the place of punishment.

Revision

He originated the theory, now unanimously accepted, that understanding should replace punishment.
[*The following of the original are redundant:* first, originator, all, unanimously, substituted, in the place of.]

In this modern day and age of the present, one can never return back to the old methods of home industry of earlier times.

One cannot return to old methods of home industry.

That night the Badgers won their fourteenth straight victory without a defeat.

That night the Badgers won their fourteenth straight victory.

To these early, primeval inventors like Lenoir and Gurney we owe our modern, high-powered cars of today.

We owe the modern automobile to early inventors like Lenoir and Gurney.

36c *Jargon, journalese*

Jargon is vague writing using blanket terms (see 35b), but it is notable in that the writer of jargon uses more words than he needs, apparently pleased with himself because the large, pompous words fill so many pages. He is not concerned with making the words say much. The writer of jargon says *the field of mathematics* rather than *mathematics, difficult in character or nature* rather than *difficult, in an intoxicated condition* rather than *drunk*. Favorite words of the jargon fancier include *case, factor, character, circumstances, conditions, situation, picture, line, persuasion, level, variety, degree, type, outstanding, worth-while*.

Original

In the case of Jim, it was apparent that his illness was of a serious nature.

Revision

Jim was seriously ill.

For reasons of safety, and in view of the circumstances which are unavoidably associated with the

For safety, no child under ten will be admitted without a parent or authorized guardian.

[**443**

Original (Cont.)

factors involved in a manufacturing enterprise, no young persons will be permitted within these premises if unaccompanied.

There were several instances where Hamlet could have put the quietus on the King, but he failed to come through because the situations were not applicable to the circumstances in his case.

Any attempt to enter the straits would have endangered the situation even more than its present status.

Revision (Cont.)

[*The words of the original say very little; they do not even proscribe two infants toddling in together. In the revision the words mean what they say.*]

On several occasions Hamlet could have taken revenge, but he wanted to kill Claudius in some act which would assure the King's going to hell.

Entering the straits would have been hazardous.

A particular sort of jargonic writing has long been known as journalese because it reveals the flamboyant, careless superficiality which is characteristic of cheap journalism, though not of good newspaper writing. Avoid it by refusing to use words just to make an impression, by thinking clearly, and by endeavoring to say exactly what you think.

Original

A new edition of State University hoopsters is slated to make its debut Saturday night to lift the curtain on the current hardwood season.

[*The trite substitutes for ordinary English do more to obscure than to brighten the passage.*]

Four weary underground explorers dumbfounded their rain-stymied would-be rescuers last night by walking unheralded and unharmed out of the sub-Alpine "Hell's Hole" caverns where high water had trapped them for nine and one-half days.

Revision

State University's basketball team will play its first game of the season Saturday night.

[*The revision may be flat sports writing, but the kind of journalese in the original does not give it life.*]

Four explorers, trapped in Alpine caverns by high water for nine and one-half days, reached safety unaided last night. Rain had prevented surface attempts at rescue.

36d Wordiness and humor   Wordy d

Like almost anything else, wordiness can be turned to humor. The American pioneer was amused by a word he devised, *segastuate,* by which he meant walk. In place of *someone had jimmied the kitchen window,* the following might conceivably be amusing: *It became apparent a party or parties unknown had gained entrance to the culinary regions by means of that instrument of ingress commonly known as a "jimmy."* Usually, however, the use of circumlocutions in the hope that overblown words will be funny leads only to boredom. A writer should use the device only with the greatest caution.

Wordy

The tuneful canine when you hear him yodeling his native woodnotes wild in the dead of night, reminds one of the gentlemen of the press; to put it mildly they can sound like the last trumpet on the day of judgment.

Concise

Dogs are born journalists; their voices are like extras of dismay.
—CHRISTOPHER MORLEY

EXERCISE 36

A. Remove redundant words and phrases from the following:

1. It was the consensus of opinion that the statements were directly antithetical.
2. Her rendition was absolutely perfect.
3. While the nations work against one another, the presence of war is constantly at hand.
4. We hold diametrically opposite views on most questions.
5. My mother, she thought I ought to go to the cheaper college, but the differences in cost were infinitesimally small.
6. The way this story was written made it seem to make me feel that it could really have actually happened to me.
7. A girl should be able to make a living in her special particular line.
8. In spite of all the illegal crimes he had committed, the leader of the gang went entirely scot-free.
9. It is the one and only unique sacred white Burmese camel in the United States.
10. Formerly in the olden days the girls of the parish had to crawl

through a small stone window to prove they had behaved themselves.

B. The passages below are wordy, many of them because they contain
jargon. Rewrite them, making the sense clear in good English, if the
passage suggests any sense. Some sentences may mean almost nothing,
for blanket terms characteristically fill space with words, not with
meaning. If a sentence has no discoverable meaning, write a sentence
which says what you imagine the writer may have intended to say.

1. Full benefits of radio, magazine, and newspapers could not be
   derived if a person is incapable of comprehending on those
   particular levels.

2. Though the evidence in the case seems to be that the crisis has
   passed and the Giants are over the hump of the slump that
   cost them great gobs of ground in the pennant chase, the Giant
   high command did not permit the chinks in the Giant armor
   turned up by the losing skid to go unnoticed. Quietly, behind
   the scenes, they are attempting to mend their fences, and you
   may be sure they will leave no stone unturned in their effort to
   batten down the hatches.

3. Another advantage of the cow is her ability to relax, and humans
   would be better off if they had this fundamental feature.

4. In this day and age the problem of drinking intoxicating beverages has had a much freer scope in recent years than was the case
   at an earlier period in time.

5. The person in search of worth-while science fiction material can
   find the basic circumstances at every facet of modern literature.

6. Some critics commented on his lecture to the highest degree.

7. Everybody should be capable of practicing in some line of work.
   Being able to support yourself is very important in this respect.

8. Although this may not be the over-all case, it does include the
   majority of advertisements, and the factors in the movement are
   to the extreme.

9. If such a case occurs, the gangster takes account of the principal
   factors in the circumstances and takes a few weeks off.

10. Reading—the anesthetic of a tired mind; the broadening of one's
    educational frame of reference; the opening of new and unfound
    fields of thought; a must in everyone's life.

11. There are only two aspects in the wide scope of life in college.

12. The big day rolled around, but Hamlet, who had the inclination
    for abruptness of action, curbed his burning desires, and there-
    fore slowness of action resulted.

13. The picture is identical with the fundamental German emotional
    make-up that allowed the last war.

14. In our particular setup, people are inclined to use trite expressions, and since they make no effort to better the circumstances in the case, they remain in a constant rut.

15. I told her that if she wouldn't get on the beam and stop blowing up the insignificant factors in the case she had better get out of the picture.

37. GOOD USAGE

[For Guide to Revision, see page 455]

> *They're cur'ous talkers i' this country, sir; the gentry's
> hard work to hunderstand 'em. I was brought up
> among the gentry, sir, an' got the turn o' their tongue
> when I was a bye. Why, what do you think the folks
> about here say for 'heven't you?' the gentry, you know,
> says 'heven't you'—well, the people about here says
> 'hanna yey.' It's what they call the 'dileck' as is spoke
> hereabout, sir. That's what I've heard Squire Donni-
> thorne say many a time; 'it's the dileck,' says he."*
>
> —GEORGE ELIOT, *Adam Bede*

What is "correct" English? The answer is not easy. Perhaps the best answer is that it is many things, or that the term is not very meaningful. But the practical problem of choosing among expressions is with us; and since the eighteenth century at least, English speaking people have been trying to solve it.

37-1 Usage and language

In general, they have looked at the question from two points of view. Some have assumed that language is an entity, mystically or otherwise created, which either fits or should be made to fit logical patterns. What is right therefore turns out to be what reason can fit into a pattern or a "system." Usually, this view points toward a language controlled by authority. A second view, now accepted by students of the language, observes that language is a complex, sometimes haphazard, development of human habits.

In an earlier chapter (26) we observed that grammar exists and functions because speakers of a language use words in a way that other speakers recognize and can interpret. Similarly, words have meaning only because they are used and are understood by human beings—who do not always behave logically about language. In the end, only usage is behind what is "right" or "wrong" in speech or writing. This second view, of course, is scientifically sound and is generally accepted today—although popularly the notion persists that grammarians or school teachers or other "authorities" determine "correctness" and could, if they would only agree, tell everyone what to say.

Usage is behind "correctness," but it does not offer a simple answer to all language problems. That is, we do not decide what to say by counting noses. We cannot say that an expression is correct because most people use it, or even because the "best" people use it. We can say that "correct" English is that English *which does what we want it to do.* In other words, a scientific understanding of language shows us that the question of "correctness" in the usual sense—in the sense of rules of conduct—is not an issue at all. We do not try to use good English *because* other people do or *because* someone has made a rule, any more than a carpenter cuts a board with a saw because other carpenters do or because someone has made a rule about saws. The carpenter uses the saw because it cuts better than a breadknife.

All problems of language, then, involve usage, not because usage makes rules but because usage determines what a word or expression does, what effect it will have. The discussions in this book are attempts to describe the effects expressions will have and to point to some which will not work in serious writing. But an expression is not right or wrong according to which people use it. An expression is useful if it will do what the writer wants done; if not, it is inappropriate.

In English, the study of usage is complicated because usage itself varies. It changes historically; it varies from one English-speaking country to another, and in various parts of them; it varies among people within countries according to occupation, education, and social status. These variations are important because the situations in which an expression customarily appears become part of its total effect, of its meaning.

37-2 Usage and linguistic change

English is constantly changing, and as it changes, the effects of various expressions change. For example, the double negative, used by Chaucer and Shakespeare to intensify a negative, and still so used in French, is now regarded as illogical and a sign of ignorance. Words change meaning in a variety of ways. Meaning may narrow or specialize: *starve* has changed from meaning merely "to die," not necessarily from lack of food; *deer* in Shakespeare's time could mean "animal" generally. By an opposite process, meaning may become more general, more extensive. *Very* once was restricted to mean "true"; *bird* referred only to a young birdling. By metaphor, still wider extensions occur; *head* can be applied to a hammer, a cabbage, a business, a pin, a coin, a line in a newspaper, or the froth on beer. Words may change completely the attitude they suggest toward what they symbolize: *knave* once meant just "a boy," but *boy* had something of the sense of "rascal" that *knave* has today. Many other kinds of changes have occurred and are occurring. And, of course, words are always dropping out of use and new words are appearing. Writers need to be sure that the words they are using are sufficiently current in the intended senses to make them appropriate. They can find suggestions about historical variations in usage from dictionaries, which record changes in meaning and mark obvious restrictions with terms like *obsolete* or *archaic*.

37-3 Dialect

The English language has developed in different ways in different areas, in pronunciation, in ways of putting words together, and in meanings. A sidewalk is a pavement in England, and a footpath in Australia. If a Briton says "She lives *in* Oxford Street," he means that the person referred to has Oxford Street as an address, but in the United States anybody who lives *in* the street has no address at all. What is a sack in the Middle West of America may be a poke in the South. "Where at do you'uns go of a Sunday" might be heard in some dialects of the Middle West, but it would sound strange in New York. There is nothing "wrong" or "right" about the customs of different areas, about the differences in dialect. Often the differences reflect genuine needs, and objection to them is absurd. In the eighteenth century one British writer commented condescendingly about a city in Georgia: "It stands upon the flat of a hill; the bank of a river (which they in barbarous English call a bluff)." The writer did not notice that *bluff* says in one word what had taken him nine. But the effectiveness of expressions used only in certain areas is limited. The student must realize that any expression common only in a particular dialect will have a special effect when used, and he must use it only when he wants that special effect. The dictionary labels some terms *dialectal* or *provincial* and sometimes names areas of use.

37-4 Idiom in language

Since language lives and grows by custom, good speech rests upon the speech habits of the users of a language. These crystallized speech habits are called the *idiom of the language.* Most native speakers are entirely unconscious of the idioms which they have learned as naturally as they learned to breathe or to walk.

> I introduced him *to* my sister *at* Mary's party.
> I introduced him *at* my sister *to* Mary's party.

Any native speaker of English will know that the first of these two sentences is what we call "correct"—that is, it is idiomatic—but a foreigner who had learned English in school might find the second sentence as logical as the first. Most idioms have logic and good sense behind them. *To* and *at* differ, and in the first of the sentences above the two words are used in accordance with certain of their familiar uses. Many ideas, however, could be expressed logically in several ways, and the way sanctioned by idiom would seem to be nothing more than standardized custom. Some idioms are illogical; we say *The sun sets,* although logically we should say *The sun sits.* Logical or illogical, idiom is the language; there always has been and presumably always will be illogical idiomatic expression.

Since idioms grow from speech habits, they may change with time and place or may be characteristic only of the speech of limited groups of people. The appropriateness of some idioms, therefore, is hard to determine. Some have gained wide use in speech but are still suspected by conservative users of the language. *The teacher blamed the affair on Johnny,* for example, uses a common colloquial idiom, but the idiom might suggest to some readers that the writer was unaware of standard customs. Some would insist on *The teacher blamed Johnny for the affair.* An idiom like *I can't help but know* . . . is in wide colloquial use, but some speakers would object and prefer *I can't help knowing.* . . .

37-5 Other variations in usage

Variations and restrictions in usage develop in many ways. Workers coin terms which are easily understood among themselves but are not widely current. To printers, *pie* describes jumbled type, but to a sixteenth century divine *pie* referred to ecclesiastical rules, and to some drivers it means a truck owned by the Pacific Intermountain Express. Slang develops in groups: for instance, the rhyming slang of the underworld (*half-inch,* rhyming with *pinch,* means "steal"); the slang of jazz musicians (*gut bucket* for "bass viol"); the slang of college students (*bust* or *flunk* for "fail a course"). Some words also are barred from general use as impolite or obscene or irreligious, although society's attitude varies about specific words with changes in time and place. Most important, perhaps, some expressions, quite understandable and quite widely known, are popularly conceived to be used mainly by "ignorant" or "uneducated" or "vulgar" people. And many expressions are more or less characteristic of particular social groups in particular situations. Many such expressions may be useful or logical (*I can't hardly tell* is as clear as *I can hardly tell*), but the associations of usage attached to them make them dubious choices for serious writing. The locutions are limited and usually inappropriate for formal purposes. Dictionaries distinguish some variations by specifically naming an occupation or subject or by using terms like *professional, slang, obscene,* and the like.

37-6 Language levels

Obviously, the ordinary person trying to decide whether to say "It is I" or "It is me" cannot examine all the complex variations of usage. Thus, some broad distinctions help, and we can notice three sorts of situations which give rise to three levels of language.

Formal circumstances, important affairs, difficult subjects, and wide audiences require careful and reliable language. The Constitution of the United States has been weighed word by word for generations. Nobody would want it written in language which would rapidly change in meaning. A book on atomic power may be read anywhere in the world; it should be written in language which all speakers of English understand. An article in a good magazine will be read by all sorts of people; it should be written in language which has a common meaning for a bank president and for the freshman who talks college slang. An applicant for a position will wish to convince his prospective employer that he is a cultured, competent person; his letter of application should be written in the language of cultured people. Language of this sort is called *standard English*.

Many situations do not require the precision of standard written English. Conversation, for example, has a limited audience and can be more informal, more idiomatic, more cognizant of special information and special attitudes of the speakers. It reflects our childhoods, our occupations, the various groups with whom we associate or have associated. It is used in various types of informal writing—informal articles, fiction, newspaper stories—and is sometimes called *informal English*. It is also characteristic of conversation and is sometimes designated *colloquial English*. *Colloquial* derives from the Latin word meaning *speech*.

On a third level is the language, chiefly spoken, which is not socially acceptable for any serious use. It includes some regional dialects, some shop talk, some slang. It is often vivid and expressive, but it is limited in its use because it is conventionally associated with illiteracy and with the uneducated, and because it does not have general currency. It is referred to as *illiterate* or *vulgate English*.

37-7 Importance of language levels

These distinctions between three levels of language usage are, of course, only approximations. Obviously they overlap. Many slang expressions, for example, are classified by different persons as either vulgate or colloquial.

The writer should not, however, neglect the existence of these levels in selecting his expressions. All kinds of expressions have their uses, but all are not useful in all situations. In other words, the appropriateness of an expression to the situation in which it is being used determines part of its effect. A word like *ain't* is avoided in standard English, not because it is "wrong" in some mysterious way and not because it is unclear. It is easily understandable and fills a need in the language, but it is traditionally connected with language on the vulgate level, and it cannot be used in standard English without seeming inappropriate.

An expression or construction gains some of its "meaning" from its association, and many expressions are appropriate at only one level of usage. Part of their meaning is involved in the suggestions they invoke. In this sense, then, an "error" of usage is not just an offense against polite society or a failure to do what "the best people" do; it is a failure to select words which do the jobs for which they are intended.

37-8 Standard English

Anyone who hopes to do serious work in modern society should command the standard idiom of his native tongue, even though he must learn to do so. Language, like money, serves as a medium of exchange only if it has common currency, that is, only if it has a known and relatively stable value. If we cannot agree as to what a dollar is worth, we cannot trade much in goods, and if we cannot agree what a word is worth, we cannot trade much in ideas. Admittedly, no word has a fixed, absolute, and permanent value. Neither has the dollar, but it has been so stable and so widely accepted that business can be done with it. Similarly, some words have relatively reliable currency.

To write anything of importance, we must know what words, and what usages of these words, have sufficient currency to admit them to standard, acceptable English. The word *man* has meant an adult human male for more than a thousand years. It is standard English. Only recently has a *good guy* been an approved male; formerly, if a guy was not a piece of rope or wire it was a person who looked like a scarecrow. *Guy,* in the sense of *man,* is not acceptable standard English because its effectiveness in that sense is limited; it carries associations with nonstandard situations which are part of its meaning. In its newer, vaguer sense the word has not become part of the established body of standard English which can be relied on to maintain a relatively constant meaning.

Every student should be able to write and speak so that he will be understandable wherever his words may go, to New York or Dallas, to Cape Town or Liverpool. His writing should be understandable for longer than a few years. In this book, therefore, passages are revised whenever they are not clearly standard English, not because colloquial or vulgate writing is "wrong," but because students need to learn standard practices. They will continue to use informal speech in informal situations, but they need to be sure they know how to use more formal language when they need it.

37 Good usage   Usage

GUIDE TO REVISION:

Select appropriate words, using in serious writing only expressions characteristic of standard English.

Language gains its value by currency, by the fact that most readers and speakers of a language have roughly common values for words and constructions. Accordingly, all formal writing and speaking should conform to standards acceptable to the intelligent, cultured body of the users of the language. Careful writing and speaking should be idiomatic, but it should not be strongly colloquial, and it should avoid slang, which may be picturesque but seldom has either currency or permanence.

37a Colloquial English   Usage a; Colloq

Colloquial English is excellent for most conversation, familiar letters, and the like but should be avoided in formal composition.

Original	*Revision*
Lots of people know they better keep an eye out for opportunities.	Many people know they should look for opportunities.

Colloquial English which rests upon the usage in occupations and has never attained common currency is often called *cant*. It can be very useful, but should be used with caution in formal composition.

Confusing	*Clear*
Give the stiff the gandy.	Tamp that railroad tie.
[*If the context requires the use of a word like* gandy, *it should be put in quotation marks and explained.*]	[Stiff *is a picturesque word for a railroad tie, but most people would not know what it means, and explanations can become awkward.*]
In this groove winds the cable, as the giraffe is let down into or drawn up out of the mine.	In this groove winds the cable, as the incline-car, the "giraffe," is let down into or drawn up out of the mine.
	—DAN DE QUILLE, *The Big Bonanza*

[455

Like other colloquial locutions, contractions are suited to intimate or nonchalant relationships. They have developed because they are convenient aids to speech, easy to pronounce, but they are not appropriate to formal writing.

Original	*Revision*
We *don't* as yet have accurate relative heights for the tallest mountains, partly because mountaineers *haven't* agreed on a uniform method of measurement.	We *do not* as yet have accurate relative heights for the tallest mountains, partly because mountaineers *have not* agreed on a uniform method of measurement.

NOTE: *don't* is sometimes confused with *doesn't* as a contraction.

don't = do not	doesn't = does not

One contraction is frequently misspelled.

it's = it is	its (possessive or genitive for *of it*)

37b *Slang*   **Usage b; Sl**

Slang develops variously, notably because we like to play with words. We put old words to new uses or coin new expressions, largely for the sake of novelty or cleverness. The results vary. Occasionally a slang expression fills a genuine need, persists, and is accepted as part of the language. Often it is accepted by limited groups and remains current on the vulgate or colloquial level. Usually it has quick popularity and then disappears.

Using slang—especially if you make it up yourself—can be amusing, and the result vivid, but slang is characteristic of vulgate or colloquial language. For two reasons it is limited in its usefulness. First, it is usually known to so few people, in such a restricted group geographically or socially, and for so short a time that it can be used for only the most local and ephemeral purposes. Second, much slang is so general that it means almost nothing. The user of slang often does not know what he wishes to say, and the listener to slang does not know what, if anything, has been said.

Slang seldom has currency. At this writing, a Navy man might say, "Salts know who's four-o, and if a boot goes smokestacking, or sandbagging in stud, he gets the deep six." This is terse and vivid language, if you happen to know the language. It can be interpreted about as follows: The old-timers know a competent man when they see one, and if a beginner plays the fool, bluffing, or pretending in a game of stud poker that he is drunk so as to throw the other players off guard, they will see to it that the youngster suffers for it. Vivid or not, language like this has obvious limitations as a means of communication.

Slang tends either to disappear quickly or to become so general that it has little meaning, except as context provides a meaning.

Slang	*Standard English*
Okay, it's jake with me.	The total is correct (or) I will meet you at ten-fifteen (or) I quite agree with you (or almost anything else).
So what?	What should we do next? (or) That is true but inconsequential (or) So far as I can see there is no answer (or what you will).
The bums on Capitol Hill better not steam-roller anything through about prayer-boning and sky-piloting, or try any shenanigans to keep other dopes from blowing off steam if they've got gripes.	Congress shall make no law respecting an establishment of religion, or prohibiting the free exercise thereof; or abridging the freedom of speech or of the press; . . . .—The Constitution, Bill of Rights, Article 1. [*The framers of the Constitution studied composition more than two centuries ago, but they wrote standard English, and we still know essentially what they wanted to say.*]

37c *Idiom*   **Usage c; Id**

Idiom is the result of custom in language. Usually it is logical, though not always, and to use the language a writer must learn idioms, whether they are logical or illogical. Native speakers have learned most idioms unconsciously, but writers with poor linguistic backgrounds have trouble. Furthermore, many idioms have become common colloquially but are not appropriate in standard English; certain of these are discussed in the Glossary (see 47).

[457

Original	*Revision*
He *hadn't ought to* go.	(1) He *should not* go.
	(2) He *ought not* to go.
She told me *by* words of one syllable that the other girls had no affection *in* me.	She told me *in* words of one syllable that the other girls had no affection *for* me.

37d Coinages   Usage d

Writers struggling for rare effects sometimes endeavor to coin words and are sometimes successful when they try, but inexperienced writers usually do better to use the half million words recorded in a good dictionary.

Original	*Revision*
I would say that the second letter makes fun of the *overboardness* that the first writer went in his letter.	I would say that the second letter makes fun of the *exaggerations* in the first letter.

EXERCISE 37

A. The words listed below were once used in this country, but they were slang or colloquial and have now largely disappeared. Try to make a sentence with any you think you know. Then check your meanings against the meanings given in the *Dictionary of Americanisms*. The number after each word indicates the usage; for instance, *cutter, 2*, would refer to the second meaning of the word, "a device for checking a wagon going downhill."

1. out-Cherokee (under Cherokee, v.)
2. gorilla, 2
3. female tom
4. smoke, 3
5. rackabone (4 under *rack*)
6. muffy
7. monocrat
8. shell, 1
9. Hudson Dusters
10. bank whig, 2 (29)

Try to make up a list of similar words which you hear your companions use but which will probably not be understood in fifty years.

B. Start reading the current issue of your college newspaper, beginning with the head at the top of the left-hand column. Record the first ten words you find which your dictionary does not admit as standard English. Then count the total number of words in the columns in which these ten words occur, stopping with the last occurrence. Assuming that all of these slang and colloquial words should drop out of the language, what percentage of your college paper will not be understandable next century?

C. Discuss the suitability of the italicized expressions in the following sentences for (a) campus conversation, (b) informal composition, and (c) formal composition.

1. Those *babes really rate* with me.
2. My *girl-friend* knows so little about football she *thinks* "clipping" is charging six *bucks* for seats in the end zone.
3. A *stolid,* bald-headed gentleman was *staring* at me as though he thought he was *acquainted with* me, but was not *quite* certain.
4. *Here's* the *deal,* and you can *take it from me, it's a dilly.*
5. Whatever you want, she is *liable* to want something *diametrically opposed,* like *movieing* while you want to *shoot the breeze.*
6. *Irregardless* of my mother's warnings, I decided to *date* him.
7. I was so *enthused I figured I'd contact 'em first off.*
8. I *suggest* the *inclusion* of this *data* on the *agendas.*
9. She was *cute,* all right, but, *last but not least,* I *suspicioned* she *wasn't* the *swell dame* she was *cracked up to be.*
10. A *great number* of onlookers *blamed* the accident *on* Jim.

VIII. Mechanics

> *At this moment the King, who had been for some
> time busily writing in his note-book, called out "Si-
> lence!" and read out from his book "Rule Forty-two.
> All Persons more than a mile high to leave the court."*
>   *Everybody looked at Alice.*
>   *"I'm not a mile high," said Alice.*
>   *"You are," said the King.*
>   *"Nearly two miles high," added the Queen.*
>   *"Well, I sha'n't go, at any rate," said Alice: "be-
> sides, that's not a regular rule: you invented it just
> now."*
>   *"It's the oldest rule in the book," said the King.*
> —LEWIS CARROLL, *Alice's Adventures in Wonderland*

An oriental guest, to be polite, takes off his shoes, and after the meal, belches. An American guest takes off his hat and refrains from belching. The conventions differ.

Many of the mechanical aspects of composition are conventional, and conventional only. Many of the "rules" represent codified good sense, what Alice thought of as "regular rules." Others smack of the judicial processes of the King of Hearts, but whether or not they are now "the oldest rules in the book," they have been established by convention, and conventions are necessary for clear communication. Ignoring conventions may even be dangerous. Anyone in this country who consistently drives on the left-hand side of the road will not stay long out of jail, a hospital, or the morgue. Anyone who drives on the right-hand side in England is in similar danger. A writer who fails to follow certain conventions, though he may be physically safe is in danger of being misunderstood.

Furthermore, although the mechanical conventions surrounding writing are not the only conventions possible, sound reason stands behind each of them, and *in toto* they offer the writer useful stand-ardized devices. Typed copy is double spaced because double-spaced copy is easier to read than single-spaced copy and because it allows room for editing. Margins are preferred because a crowded page looks messy. Manuscripts are written on one side of the paper because pages which must be turned over lead to confusion and costly errors. Our conventions of capitalization are not the only possible ones; German capitalizes all nouns and Spanish capitalizes no proper adjectives, but our system has its uses. With it, one can distinguish at once an *opal* from *Opal, Hamlet* from a *hamlet.* Our system of punctuation permits the writer to make his meaning immediately and sharply clear, and he can do so because conventions are standardized and recognized. There is a difference between "The man who customarily wears a beret. . . ." and "The man, who customarily wears a beret, . . ." although the difference is made clear by nothing but commas. The conventions of writing and the mechanics which embody these conventions help a writer because they put useful tools into his hands.

Almost all publishers and many publications have style sheets which cover matters of manuscript form, punctuation, capitalization, and even spelling; they include details of style which are too specialized to be covered by general rules. For instance, a builder's manual may have a style sheet including special punctuation for unusual measurements; bibliographies often have special style sheets which permit elaborate abbreviation of the information concerning the format of a book; a chemistry-journal style sheet will include abbreviations for compounds; newspapers record details of their style in stylebooks. For details of style not covered below, *A Manual of Style,* prepared by the staff of the University of Chicago Press (Chicago, 1949), has been standard practically since the first edition appeared in 1906. John Benbow, *Manuscript and Proof* (New York, 1943), is the manual for the American Oxford University Press. Useful for technical work is the *United States Government Printing Office Style Manual* (Washington, D.C., 1953); it is frequently revised.

In general, punctuation serves two sorts of purposes: to make the structure of the sentence readily apparent, and to establish minor relationships within the sentence and identify certain forms. The period, question mark, semicolon, and colon are used mainly to reveal structure. The comma is both structural and formal; most other sorts of punctuation are used exclusively for formal or conventional purposes.

462]

38. END PUNCTUATION

[For Guide to Revision, see page 465]

Punctuation marks clarify meaning and structure.

In *A Midsummer Night's Dream,* Shakespeare introduces a play produced by some well-meaning but ignorant people, with a prologue read as though it were punctuated as follows:

> If we offend, it is with our good will.
> That you should think, we come not to offend,
> But with good will. To show our simple skill,
> That is the true beginning of our end.
> Consider then we come but in despite.
> We do not come as minding to content you,
> Our true intent is. All for your delight
> We are not here. That you should here repent you
> The actors are at hand, and by their show
> You shall know all that you are like to know.

Some of this makes no sense, and some bad sense. Certainly the actors had not come to make the audience repent their attendance. Repunctuated, the passage is more appropriate.

> If we offend, it is with our good will.
> That, you should think. We come not to offend,
> But with good will to show our simple skill.
> That is the true beginning. Of our end,
> Consider then. We come. But in despite
> We do not come. As minding to content you,
> Our true intent is all for your delight.
> We are not here that you should here repent you.
> The actors are at hand, and by their show
> You shall know all that you are like to know.

Not every passage can be changed so much as can this by mispunctuation, but good punctuation can make meaning certain and reading more rapid.

38-1 Structural punctuation

Until a century or so ago punctuation in English was primarily rhetorical; that is, marks or "points" were stage directions for speaking, indicating where pauses of greater or lesser duration should occur. In modern English, punctuation marks cannot be located in terms of the length of "pauses" which might occur if the sentence were read aloud. "Pauses" in reading and location of marks usually do coincide, it is true, but the punctuation is not located to mark the pauses. The pauses and the punctuation both accent the structure of the sentence.

Structural punctuation in modern English helps the reader to see the basic sentence pattern (see 17); it preserves the unity of the actor-action-goal core of every sentence. It depends on basic values generally assigned to the various punctuation marks: the period, question mark, and exclamation mark point to the end of a major unit, usually a sentence; the semicolon and colon mark secondary breaks; and the comma marks minor divisions in the sentence or sets off interrupting elements. Structural punctuation functions in three ways: (1) it separates sentences and clauses from one another; (2) it sets apart any sentence elements which may interrupt the flow of thought from subject to verb to complement; and (3) it separates co-ordinate elements not sufficiently separated by function words.

38-2 Styles in punctuation

Fashions in punctuation vary somewhat from writer to writer, from country to country, and from time to time. A few poets have felt that they gained particular effects by omitting punctuation or by using special punctuation, and writers of fiction often use punctuation in individual ways. Standard usage tends to require a comma before an *and* joining words in a series; informal usage often omits the comma. A few hundred years ago there were no generally accepted conventions for English punctuation, and there are still a number of situations in which opinions differ as to whether to use one mark or another or none at all. Writing being as flexible as it is, and human minds being as various and variable as they are, there will doubtless always be some wavering in punctuation practice. In spite of this variety, American punctuation of formal expository and argumentative prose is sufficiently standardized so that relatively few statements describe the majority of uses.

The following pages, therefore, do not cite rules which are never violated, but describe the most common American practices in punctuation. Other methods of punctuation are possible, but these principles offer a system which a writer can use with confidence that he will be punctuating clearly.

38 *End punctuation* **P; EP**

GUIDE TO REVISION:

> *Use appropriate end punctuation to identify sentences and major sentence elements.*

Punctuation has important structural uses by marking the ends of sentences and major sentence elements. The marks for this purpose— used as well for some conventional punctuation—are the period, question mark, exclamation mark, colon, and semicolon.

38a *Period; period fault* **EP a; ⊙**

Structurally, the period is the most important device for punctuation since it marks the end of any sentence not to be distinguished as a question or an exclamation. Misuse of the period in this situation, sometimes called the *period fault,* usually reveals faulty sentence patterns or inappropriate sentence fragments (see 17, 18).

The period is used after an indirect question, that is, after a question which is not phrased verbatim.

I asked her, "Will you go?" (*Direct question*)
I asked her if she would go. (*Indirect question*)

Original

The question was whether Morgan would attack the center or make the long detour around Old Baldy and attack on the flank?
[*The indirect question should be followed by a period. If the question were put directly, it would be followed by a question mark.*]

Revision

(1) The question was whether Morgan would attack the center or make the long detour around Old Baldy and attack on the flank.
(2) The question was this: would Morgan attack the center, or would he make the long detour around Old Baldy and attack on the flank?

[465

Three consecutive periods (. . .) make a punctuation mark known as the ellipsis, inserted in the place of material omitted from a quotation. When the omission comes after a completed sentence or completes a sentence, the period needed to mark the end of the sentence is retained. In such instances, therefore, four consecutive periods appear.

Original

Genius is the activity which repairs the decays of things, whether wholly or partly of a material and finite kind. Nature, through all her kingdoms, insures herself.

——RALPH WALDO EMERSON,
"The Poet"

Revision

Genius is the activity which repairs the decays of things. . . . Nature . . . insures herself.

——RALPH WALDO EMERSON
"The Poet"

The period is used, also, after most abbreviations: p.m., Mr., pp., Ave., St., U. S. A., *ibid.,* A. D. Any good dictionary will include abbreviations in the word list or in a special section.

EXCEPTION: The period is not used after letters standing for recently created government bureaus: NLRB, CAP, ANZUS; after letters which represent scholarly or technical journals: PMLA, CA, MLR; after letters of radio stations: KLRB, WUISB, KATO; after MS (plural, MSS) for *manuscript;* certain unions and associations: WAA, AEF, CIO.

38b Question mark   **PE b; ?**

The question mark (interrogation point) is placed after a direct question. It is not used after an indirect question (see 38a).

Original

By Sunday I could stand no more, and I said, "Aren't you ever going to leave."

Perhaps I was not very polite, but what, under the circumstances, could I do.

Revision

By Sunday I could stand no more, and I said, "Aren't you ever going to leave?"

Perhaps I was not very polite, but what, under the circumstances, could I do?

The question mark is occasionally used after inserted interrogative material.

Anyone who loves his country—and who does not?—will answer a call to duty.

The question mark is used, sometimes in parentheses, to indicate that a fact is approximate or questionable, especially a date.

> The Play of the Weather (1533?) continues the convention. John Heywood, 1497(?)-1580(?), wrote the play.

Used as an attempted witticism or to mark sarcasm, the question mark is out of fashion and likely to appear amateurish.

> The next motion showed how wise (?) [*better omitted*] the committee really was.

A request or command which for politeness is phrased as a question may conclude with either a question mark or a period.

> Will you please sign and return the enclosed voucher? *or* . . . voucher.

38c Exclamation mark   P c; !

The exclamation mark may be used at the end of a complete or incomplete sentence to indicate violent emotion or very strong feelings. It is seldom used except in reporting conversation, particularly after interjections like *Ouch! Murder!* Some beginning writers endeavor to make their composition more exciting by liberal use of exclamation marks. This device seldom works. Any prose which is so feeble that it must be propped up with punctuation had best be revised. Modern practice is to use the exclamation mark sparingly.

Original	*Revision*
"Help," she screamed. "My dress, in the cogs."	"Help!" she screamed. "My dress! In the cogs!"
[*If the girl finds herself being dragged into power machinery, she may well be excited enough to warrant a few exclamation marks.*]	[*The revision does not bolster weak prose; it makes clear at once the drama of the sentences.*]
And then! Just think! Out of the cocoon came a pale green luna moth! And still damp!!!	And then, out of the cocoon came a pale green luna moth, still damp.
[*This is overblown. It may please children, but scarcely adults.*]	[*The use of two or three exclamation marks together is best confined to comic books.*]

38d Colon   P d; ⊙

Modern practice is to use the colon sparingly. It resembles in its force the sign of equality in mathematics ($=$); that is, whatever

[467

comes before the sign is in at least one sense equal to what comes after it. It is most frequently used to precede a series which has already been introduced by a completed statement, often containing the word *following*.

> The common silk dress goods are the following: raw silk, taffeta, crepe de Chine, shantung, pongee, silk chiffon, silk organdy, satin, and silk velvet.

> I found that there were four kinds of girls in college: those that came to get married, those that came to get an education, those that came because their parents made them, and those that came because they did not know what else to do.

The colon is not needed, however, when the series immediately follows the verb as a group of complements.

Original	*Revision*
The common silk dress goods are: raw silk, taffeta, crepe de Chine, shantung, pongee, silk chiffon, silk organdy, satin, and silk velvet.	The common silk dress goods are raw silk, taffeta, crepe de Chine, shantung, pongee, silk chiffon, silk organdy, satin, and silk velvet.
[*The list is a complement and should not be separated from the verb it completes.*]	[*The colon which breaks the continuity of the subject-verb-complement pattern is omitted.*]
In high school I competed in the principal girls' sports, that is: in hockey, swimming, and basketball.	In high school I competed in the principal girls' sports, that is, in hockey, swimming, and basketball.
[*The colon properly introduces a formal series; here* hockey, swimming, *and* basketball *are three noun forms in apposition with* sports.]	[*The meaning is at once clear with a comma, and accordingly the lighter punctuation is preferable.*]

The colon is occasionally used between independent clauses when the second part of the sentence has been directly introduced in the first.

> Two events occurred that spring to make Marie less happy in her new home: the mangy cat that had been her best friend was hit by a car, and the low spot near the garage which became a fine mud puddle after every shower was filled and leveled.

The colon is unusual in this use, however, and is appropriate only when the second part of the sentence clearly repeats or clarifies the first.

Original

    Almost everybody tries to come to Washington: everybody complains about the weather after he gets here.
[*The construction requires the semicolon, not the colon; see 18, 38e.*]

Revision

    Almost everybody tries to come to Washington; everybody complains about the weather after he gets here.

The colon also has certain conventional uses, notably after the formal address of a letter (Dear Miss Smith:, Dear Sir:), in statements of time (8:35), and in citations from the Bible (Genesis 5:1-3 *or* Genesis V, 1-3). For other conventional uses of the colon, see *A Manual of Style* (Chicago, 1949).

38e *Semicolon*   **PE e; ⊙**

    The semicolon is used mainly to separate independent clauses not joined by a conjunction; failure to use a semicolon between clauses usually indicates misunderstanding of sentence patterns and causes run-on sentences. For a full discussion of the semicolon between clauses, see 18. Use of a comma when a semicolon is required is sometimes called a comma fault or comma splice (see 18c). The semicolon is preferred even though a conjunctive adverb separates the clauses. The semicolon is also used rather than a comma whenever clauses are long or punctuation is complex. Two independent clauses, for example, when joined by a co-ordinating conjunction need only a comma to separate them (see 18b). But if either of the clauses is long or complex or contains commas within it, then the main division between the clauses may be marked by a semicolon.

Original

    Aunt Judy, who was young in spirit, and not so old as her title suggests, was always running off to foreign countries and bringing back strange dances, teaching us, among others, the tango, rumba, bolero, and samba, but after Anne's parents had shown her the Charleston, everyone deserted the Spanish-American steps for the dances of the flapper age.

Revision

    Aunt Judy, who was young in spirit and not so old as her title suggests, was always running off to foreign countries and bringing back strange dances, teaching us, among others, the tango, rumba, bolero, and samba; but after Anne's parents had shown her the Charleston, everyone deserted the Spanish-American steps for the dances of the flapper age.

[469

Original (Cont.)

[*Since each of the independent clauses contains internal punctuation, the comma does not mark clearly the point at which they are divided.*]

Revision (Cont.)

[*The semicolon indicates the main division of the sentence.*]

The semicolon also substitutes for the comma to divide items in a series or list (see 39c) when the items are complicated and contain punctuation within them.

Original

She told me that, in view of my prejudices, my poor health, and my interests, I would never be happy as a teacher, that I would find myself, at the end of a day, exhausted from policing dozens of squirming children, and that I would find my evenings, during which I hoped to practice music, given over to school plays, the school band and orchestra, and playing command canasta with the superintendent's wife.

[*Since the sentence is long and involved, and broken only by commas, the reader has difficulty seeing at once the organization.*]

Revision

She told me that, in view of my prejudices, my poor health, and my interests, I never would be happy as a teacher; that I would find myself, at the end of the day, exhausted from policing dozens of squirming children; and that I would find my evenings, during which I hoped to practice music, given over to school plays, the school band and orchestra, and playing command canasta with the superintendent's wife.

[*The three dependent clauses, each beginning with* that, *are now separated by semicolons, which mark the main divisions of the sentence.*]

The Council included the following representatives: President John A. Rickert, administration, Professor George P. Barrows, faculty, Avery Warren, student council, and Janice Worley, W. A. A.

The Council included the following representatives: President John A. Rickert, administration; Professor George P. Barrows, faculty; Avery Warren, student council; and Janice Worley, W. A. A.

EXERCISE 38

Supply appropriate punctuation in the following sentences. The meaning of some sentences may change with various sorts of punctuation.

1. One avocado did not ripen I don't know why the other one did
2. He was the worst dean I ever heard of with the alumni his putting the whole Sigma Nu house on probation is still a favorite story

3. He was playing left end you say so you say he was playing left end is that it

4. Two times two are four four times four are fifteen no four fours are sixteen or are they or is it is

5. I want you to wash the windows tomorrow you can go to the ball game if you want to

6. I said rats if they are eating the cake I don't want any of it

7. So you think you're pretty good do you feel like taking off your glasses and settling this outside.

8. Elmer Davis said when he resigned as a radio news commentator I am not leaving on account of political pressure or economic pressure only on account of blood pressure and my own at that

9. A certain truck carries the following signs this truck stops for a red light or a red head backs up 25 feet for a blonde courtesy is our motto

10. Joseph Joubert is credited with the following some men find their sole activity in repose others their sole repose in activity

11. The following have registered thus far Alice Melarkey Los Angeles Muriel Jones St. Louis Florence O'Brien Seattle Florence Schmidt Syracuse and Helen Adney Atlanta

12. A number of changes account for the movement of beef raising into the southeast wornout cotton lands heavily cropped for years will not longer raise a high production crop successfully and meanwhile Texas ranchers finding they have insufficient pastures in this the driest year in a decade are glad to acquire additional grazing land in the eastern gulf states

For additional exercises in end punctuation see Exercises 17 and 18.

39. THE COMMA

[*For Guide to Revision, see page 474*]

The comma is a work-horse mark of punctuation to signal many sorts of relationship within the sentence.

The comma, although it has become almost the symbol of insignificance, is important enough to warrant treatment by itself. The inclusion, omission, or interpretation of certain commas has been sufficiently crucial to warrant carrying cases to the Supreme Court. Recently, days of learned argument concerned a 79-year-old statute which might read either "individual Indians, not citizens" or "individual Indians not citizens." The presence or absence of the comma would determine whether the statute applied to all Indians or only those of Mexican or Canadian extraction. But the comma is mainly useful—and troublesome—because of its frequency. It is the most used and the most variously used mark of punctuation.

39-1 Commas as structural punctuation

We have already seen that some end punctuation, the question and exclamation marks, are used exclusively to indicate sentence structure, and that periods, colons, and semicolons are mainly used structurally. Commas, also, may be used structurally, but only to mark a lesser break in thought than that which would require a period or a semicolon. Roughly speaking, a comma plus a co-ordinating conjunction may be thought of as equivalent to a semicolon or a period in separating independent statements (see 18). A comma is often sufficient to separate independent clauses if they are short and not much complicated, as in "Go west, young man, go west," which would certainly be as clear as "Go west, young man. Go west," even though slightly different in impact. Commas may also be used to separate dependent clauses from the remainder of the sentence, especially when the sen-

472]

tence might be confusing if the major divisions were left unmarked, as the sentence you are reading, for instance, would be.

Structurally, however, commas are most useful to keep punctuation from obscuring the subject-verb-complement relationships.

> Before the argument had finished the friendship between the two men was firmly established.

Until he reaches *was* the reader is developing an entirely erroneous notion about what happened to the friendship. He assumes that *friendship* is a complement in the modifying clause rather than the subject of the main clause. Punctuation makes the structure clear.

> Before the argument had finished, the friendship between the two men was firmly established.

Or consider the following:

> Mary the new president promised of course to govern democratically.

The reader is not helped to understand which words are subject, verb, and complement; he needs punctuation marks to keep the nonessential elements from intruding.

> Mary, the new president, promised, of course, to govern democratically.

Structural punctuation to separate co-ordinate elements not otherwise separated is used primarily in series.

> The class considered air conditioning internal combustion engines of all types and certain kinds of electrical appliances.

Commas are obviously needed to show where the items of the series should be separated.

> The class considered air conditioning, internal combustion engines of all types, and certain kinds of electrical appliances.

39-2 Commas as conventional or formal punctuation

The comma is the least specialized mark of punctuation, and hence will serve to indicate almost any minor break in the sentence which requires some sort of designation. As such, it has a large number of formal uses. Suppose a sentence starts as follows:

> This fall, river mass production . . .

Let us now alter the sentence as follows:

> This Fall River, Mass., production . . .

Nothing has been disturbed but the punctuation and capitalization, but the meanings of some of the words have been changed and so have most of the relationships. Punctuation of this sort does not reveal the large groups and relationships within the sentence, but it can be important for more restricted areas of both vocabulary and grammar. Conventional punctuation follows logically the value of the punctuation marks, but this logic has crystallized into rather rigidly conventional forms, which the writer should know. Particularly, as in the example above, commas are used with geographical, temporal, and metrical material. The details are somewhat complicated, and can best be considered separately (see 39j).

39 The comma   **P; Com; (,)**

GUIDE TO REVISION:

> *Clarify meaning by using commas to indicate minor junctures in the sentence or by removing excessive commas.*

39a Comma between co-ordinate clauses   **Run-on; Com a**

A comma is required to clarify meaning between clauses joined by a co-ordinating conjunction (*and, or, for, nor, but*). Omission of the comma obscures sentence structure and causes a run-on sentence (for full discussion see 18b).

39b Comma fault or comma splice   **Run-on, Cf; Cs; Com b**

Unless they are joined by a co-ordinating conjunction, complicated independent clauses must be separated by stronger punctuation than a comma. Use of a comma when a period or semicolon is needed causes an error in structure, a run-on sentence, discussed in 18c. The error is sometimes called a comma fault or comma splice.

39c Commas in a series   **Com c**

Commas are used to separate words, phrases, brief dependent clauses, and very brief independent clauses in a series of three or
474]

more (see 21a). Some newspapers do not require a comma before *and* (*lettuce, endive and celery*), but most publishers and writers of standard English prefer the comma before *and* (*lettuce, endive, and celery*) on the ground that the omission of the comma is occasionally confusing.

> Their menu includes the following: veal steak, roast beef, pork chops, ham and eggs.
> She purchased the following: veal, beef, pork, ham, and eggs.

In the first sentence the reader may be uncertain whether or not the eggs are fried with the ham.

If all the items in a series are joined by connectives, no punctuation is needed (*lettuce and endive and celery*).

Original	*Revision*
We distinguished highways, roads, trails, streets and alleys.	We distinguished highways, roads, trails, streets, and alleys.
[*Acceptable in some informal writing; usually not preferred in standard English.*]	
She planted stocks zinnias and delphiniums.	She planted stocks, zinnias, and delphiniums.

A combination like *bread and butter* within a series is treated as one element of the series.

Original	*Revision*
We considered the following subjects: criticism, science, medical, and dental surgery, education, and educators, and law, and the courts.	We considered the following subjects: criticism, science, medical and dental surgery, education and educators, and law and the courts.

Consecutive modifiers that tend to modify individually rather than to combine as a composite modifier form a series and are usually separated by commas. Compare:

> The streetcar had badly constructed, old-fashioned seats.
> The streetcar had grimy cane seats.

In the first the adjectives seem to modify *seats* independently. As a rough test, insert the word *and* between them and see if the construction still makes sense. If it does, the modifiers are probably in a series, as they seem to be here: *badly constructed and old-fashioned seats.*

In the second, however, *grimy* seems to modify all that follows it; the modifiers do not work independently in a series. *Grimy and cane seats* does not make sense.

Numerals and common adjectives of size, color, and age seldom appear in series:

Twenty-four scrawny blackbirds; two little girls; a spry old man; a pretty little girl

Original

I canned dozens of gleaming many-colored jars of fruit.
[*The modifiers are in series;* and *could sensibly be put between them.*]

Revision

I canned dozens of gleaming, many-colored jars of fruit.
[*A comma should separate the items of the series.*]

He bought a worn, old horse.
[*Worn and* old *do not modify separately.*]

He bought a worn old horse.

The only available room was a dirty, vermin-infested, sleeping porch.
[*Dirty and* vermin-infested *modify in series, but* sleeping *is not part of the series.*]

The only available room was a dirty, vermin-infested sleeping porch.
[*Only the two items in series are separated; each of them modifies* sleeping porch.]

39d Comma with nonrestrictive modifiers   Com d

Modifiers which are part of a subject, verb, or complement are called *restrictive;* they are not set off by commas. Constructions which are not essential to the subject-verb-complement combination, which supply incidental information (as this clause does), are called *nonrestrictive,* and must be set off by commas. Compare:

All the children who were in the front row received ice cream.
All the children, who were in the front row, received ice cream.

The first sentence suggests that of all of the children assembled only certain lucky ones, those in the front row, were treated; *who were in the front row,* without commas, is read as restrictive. It restricts or limits children to the group it names, specifies certain children. The second sentence says that all the children received ice cream. The clause is nonrestrictive, as the commas indicate.

Sometimes, as in the sentences above, modifiers can be interpreted as either restrictive or nonrestrictive, but usually the modifiers make sense with only one kind of punctuation. A nonrestrictive modifier can be recognized because it can be dropped out of the sentence without distortion of the main meaning.

The old house, badly out of repair, was hard to sell.

Omission of *badly out of repair* would not change the central idea of the sentence. But compare:

An old house badly out of repair is not a good bargain.

Badly out of repair is required as part of the subject; it cannot be omitted without shifting the meaning.

Punctuation on only one side of a nonrestrictive modifier is especially confusing because it serves only to separate essential parts of the main sentence pattern.

Following are some of the types of modifiers which are commonly nonrestrictive and therefore require commas:

(1) *Appositive modifiers*

My brother, chairman of the board, opposed the stock issue.

Chairman of the board adds incidental information but is not essential to the subject-verb-object pattern. Sometimes, however, an appositive does restrict the subject and is not separated.

My brother John is chairman of the board.

John specifies which brother, restricts *brother*.

(2) *Verbal modifiers*

The catcher, having played twelve innings, was glad to be taken from the game.

(3) *Adjectives following the words they modify*

The three books, dirty and charred, were all he saved from the fire.

Original	*Revision*
I bought the material, that Mother had picked out.	I bought the material that Mother had picked out.
[*The modifier identifies or defines the material; it is restrictive.*]	[*The restrictive use of the modifier is clear without punctuation.*]

[477

Original (Cont.)

That evening which has always seemed the most terrifying of my life the dining room ceiling fell on us.

[*The modifier is not essential; it adds incidental information and is nonrestrictive.*]

My grandmother, who still had a powerful voice went to the door and shouted.

[*The modifier has a comma preceding it but none following. As a result, the subject,* grandmother, *is separated from the verb, and the modifier is not set off.*]

The bodice, a severe bolero with hand embroidery reached scarcely to the waist.

The meal badly cooked and awkwardly served was a failure.

We started running for the express station which was still several blocks ahead.

[*Correct only if there are at least two express stations, and the clause identifies one station.*]

She was the aunt, who had given me the turquoise earrings.

Revision (Cont.)

That evening, which has always seemed the most terrifying of my life, the dining room ceiling fell on us.

[*The nonrestrictive modifier must be punctuated to set it apart from the main parts of the sentence.*]

My grandmother, who still had a powerful voice, went to the door and shouted.

[*Commas should appear both before and after the nonrestrictive modifier.*]

The bodice, a severe bolero with hand embroidery, reached scarcely to the waist.

The meal, badly cooked and awkwardly served, was a failure.

We started running for the express station, which was still several blocks ahead.

[*In most contexts, the clause would be nonrestrictive*]

She was the aunt who had given me the turquoise earrings.

39e Comma with parenthetical matter   Com e

Parenthetical expressions, which are usually nonrestrictive modifiers, should have punctuation before and after them to set them apart from the main movement of the sentence. General modifiers of the sentence like *of course, for example, that is, however, indeed,* and *in conclusion* need such punctuation unless they modify restrictively.

He decided, however, not to throw the pie.
The cape, as the illustration shows, reaches nearly to the ground.

When such modifiers are not set off with punctuation both before and after the modifier, the main pattern of the sentence may be obscured.

Original

Dancing slippers of course are not very useful for a tramp through the woods.
[Of course *is parenthetical.*]

Revision

Dancing slippers, of course, are not very useful for a tramp through the woods.
[*The parenthetical expression is set apart by commas.*]

Politicians, generally speaking consider the desires of their constituents.
[*The expression must have punctuation both before and after.*]

Politicians, generally speaking, consider the desires of their constituents.

The discussion is, indeed, silly.
[*The punctuation is not wrong, but it probably sets off the modifier more than necessary.*]

The discussion is indeed silly.
[*Probably the writer intends* indeed *to modify* silly *only, not to be parenthetical.*]

Parenthetical expressions which interrupt sharply or dramatically or which are not grammatically a part of the sentence are sometimes set off by dashes (see 40b), or parentheses (see 40c).

39f Comma with qualifying clauses   **Com f**

Clauses which begin with words like *although, as,* and *since,* are usually best set off with commas, unless they follow independent clauses which are not logically complete without them.

Original

Aunt Agnes dyed her hair, painted her eyelashes, and plucked her brows although she always wore shoe-length dresses.
[*The* although-*clause had best be set off with a comma.*]

Revision

Aunt Agnes dyed her hair, painted her eyelashes, and plucked her brows, although she always wore shoe-length dresses.

I went, because I had to.
[*The independent clause is not logically complete without the* because-*clause.*]

I went because I had to.
[*The comma is unnecessary.*]

39g Comma with introductory modifiers   Com g

Introductory modifying clauses and other long or complicated modifiers are set off from the rest of the sentence by commas. The punctuation is especially necessary, even with a short modifier, if the reader might otherwise have difficulty identifying the point at which the modifier stops.

Original

Revision

Before we had finished eating the salad and the fish were snatched away from us.
[*A comma after the introductory clause would prevent momentary misunderstanding.*]

Before we had finished eating, the salad and the fish were snatched away from us.
[*The comma marks the end of the modifier.*]

By daylight, we could find our way.
[*The comma could not be called wrong, but the introductory modifier is short enough to make it unnecessary.*]

By daylight we could find our way.

In the morning light filtered through the chinks in the ceiling.
[*Even though the modifier is short, the comma is needed to prevent misunderstanding.*]

In the morning, light filtered through the chinks in the ceiling.
[*The comma separates the two words which might otherwise be linked by their meanings.*]

Accordingly I resigned.
[*The introductory element is brief, but it is set off in meaning, and would be set off in reading.*]

Accordingly, I resigned.
[*The comma is preferable.*]

Discovered just after they had crawled through the barbed wire they fell flat on their faces.

Discovered just after they had crawled through the barbed wire, they fell flat on their faces.

Being without money and knowing no one in the town we slept on a park bench.

Being without money and knowing no one in the town, we slept on a park bench.

39h Comma to clarify or emphasize structure   Com h

The comma is frequently useful to separate words which might be erroneously run together, to mark omission of a word used in a double capacity, or to emphasize structure when a connective is omitted.

Original	Revision
Whatever is is right. [*The two uses of* is *are confusing without separation.*]	Whatever is, is right. [*The words are separated for clarity, even though normally one would . not separate subject and verb.*]
The next day he told me what he meant what he had intended to say.	The next day he told me what he meant, what he had intended to say.
An hour of lecture presumes two hours of preparation, an hour of laboratory none. [Presumes *is assumed between* laboratory *and* none.]	An hour of lecture presumes two hours of preparation, an hour of laboratory, none. [*The comma makes the structure clear.*]
Admission ten cents.	Admission, ten cents.

39i Comma with quotations   Com i

A direct quotation is separated from the remainder of the sentence by commas.

The first little girl said, "Let's hide the body in that trunk."
I said, "I have always hated Pomeranians."

But the comma is not used before an indirect quotation, that is, a quotation which is not verbatim.

I said that I had always hated Pomeranians.

Original	Revision
"Tomorrow," Mother said "we are washing those curtains."	"Tomorrow," Mother said, "we are washing those curtains."
Then Juliet asked "Why is your name Romeo?"	Then Juliet asked, "Why is your name Romeo?"
Then Juliet asked, why his name was Romeo. [*The quotation is indirect and should not be set off.*]	Then Juliet asked why his name was Romeo. [*The comma of the original separates verb from complement.*]

39j Comma with geographical, temporal, and metrical material   Com j

The comma has a number of conventional uses to separate parts of geographical, temporal, or metrical material, or other matter which may take a statistical form.

(1) Commas are used between all elements of a date. When a year is part of a date, it has commas both before and after it. Parts of a single element, such as the name of a month and the figure indicating the day, are not separated. With abbreviations both a period and comma are often required.

> They arrived by train at 10 A.M., Monday, January 17, 1956.
> Tuesday night, July 6, 1820, the debate began.

(2) Elements of addresses are similarly separated. When more than one element appears in an address, the last element is followed by a comma, unless the address is itself a separate unit, as in the address of a letter. Parts of elements, such as a street number and the name of the street following it, are not separated. Postal zone numbers are not separated from the cities in which they are located.

> He gave 1162 West Avenue, Cleveland 9, Ohio, as his address.

(3) Commas separate parts of measurements, divisions of a whole, and other statistical details. The last element of a series of divisions, like parts of a book, is usually separated from what follows, but the last part of a series constituting a measurement is usually not.

> He was six feet, eight inches tall.
> The sentence appears on page 11, line 28, of the new book.
> She must enter in Act III, scene 2, before the music begins.

Original	*Revision*
Mary was born January 4, 1952 in Chicago.	Mary was born January 4, 1952, in Chicago.
The play was first produced in December 1853 to a full house.	The play was first produced in December, 1853, to a full house.
He cleared the bar at six feet four inches.	He cleared the bar at six feet, four inches.
Drive to 1062, Second Avenue.	Drive to 1062 Second Avenue.

482]

McGrawHill ---January 4, 1952, ---
--- January, 1952, --- or ---January 1952 ---

39k Inappropriate commas   No Com; Com k

Commas dividing closely related elements of the sentence are unnecessary and even obscure meaning. Especially, subject and verb or verb and complement should not be separated. Commas setting off parenthetical or nonrestrictive material do not separate subject and verb so long as they appear both before and after the expression, but a comma on only one side of such an expression breaks the continuity of the sentence.

Original

Hundreds and hundreds of tattered men, came tramping back from the war.
[*There is no good reason to separate the subject,* men, *from the verb,* came tramping back.]

Mary was afraid, that someone else would wear a pirate costume.

Even Pearl, who had worn saddle shoes all her life bought a pair of high-heeled pumps.
[*The comma after* Pearl, *on only one side of the modifier, separates subject from verb.*]

My father, and John ran up the walk, and threw their arms around us.
[*Because a comma is used before* and *when it connects independent clauses, inexperienced writers sometimes use it indiscriminately before connectives.*]

Revision

Hundreds and hundreds of tattered men came tramping back from the war.

Mary was afraid that someone else would wear a pirate costume.

Even Pearl, who had worn saddle shoes all her life, bought a pair of high-heeled pumps.
[*When commas enclose the modifier, they set it apart and accentuate the subject-verb relationship.*]

My father and John ran up the walk and threw their arms around us.
[*Except when co-ordinating conjunctions join independent clauses, they do not require punctuation before them; for commas in a series see* 39c.]

EXERCISE 39

The sentences below contain nonrestrictive modifiers or parenthetical material of several sorts; identify the different sorts, and punctuate the sentences properly.

1. The tailored suit which I had brought home with me from Hadley's Bazaar a department store in New York City hung on me like a Hindu robe, but everybody admired the outfit I had made a simple

little dress I devised out of some coarse basket-weave that Aunt Lilly gave me.

2. The brook seeded with boulders and lined with brush looked exciting but hard to fish.

3. That summer I was employed as assistant to the playground director in Jordan Park the same park in which the previous summer I had refused to take part in the group games.

4. In our school Beeson County High School most of the students were interested in sports especially basketball and accordingly you did not ask whether a boy had anything in his head but only whether he was tall enough to hold his head six feet in the air.

5. Gladys who was the only daughter of a steel manufacturer used to make me angry and jealous showing off her new clothes.

6. She is the girl who won the 4-H scholarship.

7. The atoll a coral reef which barely broke the water was nothing to turn to for protection particularly in stormy weather.

8. We were told that the highway to Alaska which had just been opened the summer before was bumpy and provided little by way of accommodation gasoline meals or lodging.

9. After one hour saturate the curls with neutralizer for bleached, dyed, or overdry hair see instructions on the front of the folder.

10. The sorority which my mother favored was the only one that showed me any attention.

11. My advisers said I would have to take a science physics chemistry biology for instance and a girl who had just failed chemistry told me I had better not take that.

12. Then she started talking about a tepidarium whatever that is.

13. What we called the "coasting hill" a long grade that wound past the cemetery and down through the school yard unfortunately crossed Lake Street at the intersection by the feed and grain store a crossing which was much used by farmers on Saturday our only coasting day.

14. The pencil which was very hard a 6-H I think jabbed a hole in my left little finger.

15. Whoever tied that knot intended it to stay.

16. The bottle was what is called "desert glass" that is glass which has lain long enough in the strong sun of the desert to turn purple blue or green.

17. Jerry's aunt a little bird of a woman was dabbing with a cloth at the gravy he had spilled on his lapel.

18. The advertisement which I had seen in a cheap magazine promised great quantities of money for song writers and I was then too naive scarcely seventeen to know that such advertisements are intended only to cheat the gullible.

19. Of course we should not have taken a road like that which was obviously untraveled.

20. That summer I spent most of my free time going to and from work walking to the car line waiting for the street car and jolting along mile after mile.

40. FORMAL PUNCTUATION

[For Guide to Revision, see below]

Specialized marks of punctuation identify certain sorts of material and clarify some relatively rare relationships.

Several specialized marks of punctuation serve restricted purposes, mostly formal or conventional. Quotation marks indicate material quoted verbatim; brackets set off material introduced into a quotation. Hyphens and apostrophes are used mainly for spelling, and are discussed under 42a, 42b. Some of these specialized marks, however, can serve also as structural punctuation; parentheses and dashes can sometimes replace commas or even heavier marks of punctuation.

40 *Formal punctuation*   **P; FP**

GUIDE TO REVISION:

Clarify meaning by using one of the specialized marks of punctuation in accordance with conventional usage, or by removing unnecessary punctuation.

40a Quotation marks   **FP a; Quot**

Quotation marks enclose direct quotations, words actually said or previously written.

> "Get out," she said.
> After his service in Korea he agreed that "the paths of glory lead but to the grave."

This use is sometimes extended to include short expressions which quote speech from a special level of usage or from a particular person, or which call attention to a way of saying something.

486]

We learned that the diners at the next table were "hepcats" waiting for the "squares" to leave.

A conservative oxford was at that time called an "opera pump."

The quotation marks are used because a quotation from some other speaking group is implied. Quotation marks are not generally used any longer as indiscriminate apologies for slang or colloquial English. In most instances, the slang should be used without apology if it is appropriate and omitted if it is not.

Quotation marks are sometimes used to indicate that a word is used as a word, but italics are more common; see 41f.

The noun "boy" is the subject.

Quotation marks are used for titles of brief works, especially of an essay, article, poem, or short story which would usually be printed as part of a longer work, but italics are usual for most titles (see 41e, 43-11).

Robert Frost's "Mending Wall" appears in *Poetry of America.*

Quotation marks appear before and after the quoted material. When a quotation runs for more than one paragraph, the mark of quotation begins every paragraph but closes only the last one. Long quotations are sometimes printed in smaller type and indented; in typescript, the passage is indented and typed single-space.

An indirect quotation is not placed within quotation marks, but a few words within an indirect quotation may be quoted directly.

In his quiet way, he said that he was "excessively annoyed" with the gangsters next door.

Original	*Revision*
I am sorry, she said, but those weeds you are lying in are poison ivy.	"I am sorry," she said, "but those weeds you are lying in are poison ivy."
[*Material quoted directly should be set off by quotation marks.*]	
Shaw pretended to believe that all man's civilization is founded on his cowardice, on his abject tameness, which he calls respectability.	Shaw pretended to believe that all man's civilization "is founded on his cowardice, on his abject tameness, which he calls respectability."
[*The latter part of the sentence is quoted directly.*]	[*The quoted matter has been placed within quotation marks.*]

Original (Cont.)

I told "her she ought to stop wasting her time."

[*The quotation is not direct; the direct quotation was something like "You'd better stop wasting your time."*]

She said I was in a hassel and that I had blown my top.

[Hassel *and* blown my top *are quotations from the character's manner of speech.*]

They were doing what they called trolleyizing the old tramway.

The old garden had been taken over by heather aster, the so-called poverty weed.

[*A word to which attention is directed is usually placed within quotation marks.*]

Revision (Cont.)

I told her she ought to stop wasting her time.

[*The quotation marks have been removed, since an indirect quotation is not enclosed.*]

She said I was in a "hassel" and that I had "blown my top."

[*The characteristic words have been enclosed within quotation marks.*]

They were doing . what they called "trolleyizing" the old tramway.

The old garden had been taken over by heather aster, the so-called "poverty weed."

For a quotation within a quotation, use single quotation marks (' '), the apostrophe on the typewriter, returning to double marks for a quotation within a quotation within a quotation.

> The witness said, "I was just opening the door when I heard her scream, 'Drop that!' "

The position of the quotation mark in relation to other punctuation used with it is determined partly by logic and partly by arbitrary convention. Commas and periods are always placed inside quotation marks. All other punctuation marks are inside if they punctuate only the quoted words, outside if they punctuate an entire sentence containing a quotation.

> The rafters used a long handspike, which they called a "picaroon."
> He asked me to open the "boot"; I did not understand.
> "Are you ready?" I asked.
> Do you know who said that "life is but an empty dream"?

Original	*Revision*
An upright contraption, known as a "moon box", was used to show an artificial moon on the stage. [*The comma always goes inside the quotation.*]	An upright contraption, known as a "moon box," was used to show an artificial moon on the stage.
"Are you afraid of the dark"? the child asked. [*The question mark punctuates the quoted material and belongs inside the quotation marks.*]	"Are you afraid of the dark?" the child asked.

40b *Dash*   **FP b; Dash**

The dash (—), made with two hyphens on the typewriter, is used to mark sudden breaks in the flow of the sentence. It stops the reader abruptly, a little like a closet door bumped into in the dark. If, however, a walker in the dark discovers that his path is obstructed by a series of closet doors, he goes slowly, and even the closet doors lose their effect. Dashes are useful and versatile punctuation marks, but they should be used with care and restraint. Most commonly they have the following uses:

(1) A dash may emphasize a sharp break or change in thought, separating sentence elements or marking a break at the end.

> If he has any decency he will come and apologize—but has he any decency?
> He walked with quiet dignity up to the altar—and tripped on the first step.
> He knew the soldiers would march up in formation, aim their rifles, and then—

(2) A dash may set off parenthetical material (see 39e) when the writer desires a sharper separation than commas signify. Dashes are used to emphasize a dramatic or striking interruption; parentheses usually set off an insertion which is not grammatically part of the sentence (see 40c).

> The new queen of the senior ball—and she was fully aware of her royalty—swept into the room.
> Some of them overlooked—if they ever knew—the dangers of driving with bad brakes.

The dash is especially useful if the modifier itself has internal punctuation.

> Often had he sighed, in Africa, for its drowsy verdant opulence—those willow-fringed streamlets and grazing cattle, the smell of hay, the flowery lanes.

(3) The dash is often useful in a sentence in which a long subject is repeated by a pronoun. The dash marks the end of the subject.

> A brown, crusty turkey, fluffy mashed potatoes, jars of jam, pickles, and olives, and mince and pumpkin pies—all these and more appeared before Linda, as if she were in a dream.

(4) The dash is sometimes used between clauses when one clause introduces another, or it may introduce a list, less formally than a colon (see 38d).

> Of the thoughts that flashed through my mind one persisted—if I screamed the children would wake up.

> He bought samples of all the common silk dress goods—raw silk, taffeta, crepe de Chine, shantung, pongee, silk chiffon, silk organdy, satin, and silk velvet.

(5) The dash has various conventional uses, especially before a citation at the end of a quotation.

> "Nothing endures, nothing is precise and certain (except the mind of a pedant)."
>
>   —H. G. WELLS, *A Modern Utopia*

It is used also in various kinds of informal tabular arrangements.

> Humanities—fine arts, literature, language, philosophy.

> Social sciences—history, political science, sociology, economics.

The dash is now used with no other punctuation marks except those that can close a sentence.

Original	*Revision*
These discoveries,—evolution, relativity, and now atomic fission, —have given us a new conception of the world.	These discoveries—evolution, relativity, and now atomic fission— have given us a new conception of the world.
[*The comma is not necessary with the dash.*]	

Writers who are too indolent to decide what they wish to say, and thus how to punctuate, sometimes try to save themselves trouble by using dashes for everything, hoping that the reader will do the thinking that the writer should have done. The device seldom works. The prospective reader may well conclude that if the writer was too indifferent to decide what he wanted to say, the reader will be too indifferent to try to find out.

Original	*Revision*
Knowing only the most elementary principles of chemistry—I should never have attempted the experiment alone—However—I set up the equipment—and got out the necessary materials—not knowing how explosive they were—especially in combination—	Knowing only the most elementary principles of chemistry, I should never have attempted the experiment alone. However, I set up the equipment and got out the necessary materials, not knowing how explosive they were, especially in combination.
[*This is a jumble because the writer has not finished his job; he has not punctuated the passage.*]	[*The dashes have been replaced by standard punctuation.*]

40c Parentheses   FP c; Parens

Parentheses enclose inserted material which does not fit into the grammatical structure of the sentence and which adds incidental information. In this book, for example, parentheses punctuate cross references or examples inserted into sentences. They can also enclose sentences or passages irrelevant to the main discussion.

> The statue bears this inscription: "To our bountiful lady, Margarita Fernandez." (Señora Fernandez was an Indian woman who married a Spaniard and at his death inherited his mining wealth.) It is an outstanding example of Spanish baroque.

Parentheses have various special uses such as enclosing numbers or letters in an enumeration.

> He cited reasons as follows: (1) no students had been allowed in the building in the past; (2) furniture was not well enough built to stand student use; and (3) students had adequate facilities without new quarters.

Punctuation goes inside the parentheses when it punctuates only the parenthetical material, outside when it punctuates the whole passage. Parentheses are used only in pairs. In most contexts they are best used sparingly.

Original

He distinguished between the members of the family *Juniperus, Juniperus communis, Juniperus virginiana,* and the like, and the plants resembling juniper, such as retem, *Retama raetam.*

[*This is confusing, partly because the words separated by commas seem at first to be words in a series.*]

Revision

He distinguished between the members of the family *Juniperus* (*Juniperus communis, Juniperus virginiana,* and the like) and the plants resembling juniper, such as retem (*Retama raetam*).

[*The parentheses clarify the sentence at once.*]

Original

To write you need a sharp pencil and a quick mind (the first of which can be easily acquired).

[*Clauses within a sentence are usually sufficiently set off with commas.*]

Revision

To write you need a sharp pencil and a quick mind, the first of which can be easily acquired.

[*The comma is sufficient; if the break were more violent, a dash would be preferable to parentheses.*]

40d Brackets   **FP d**

Square brackets are used to enclose matter inserted into a direct quotation. Since standard typewriters do not have brackets, they should be inserted by hand in typed material or made with the diagonal and underlining bars.

Original

We hold these truths to be *self-evident* (the italics, of course, are mine), that all men are created equal. . . .

[*The parentheses imply that the inserted matter was part of the original and was there in parentheses.*]

Revision

We hold these truths to be *self-evident* [the italics, of course, are mine], that all men are created equal. . . .

[*The inserted matter has been enclosed within square brackets.*]

Brackets are used for parenthetical material within matter within parentheses, to avoid the confusion of parentheses within parentheses.

EXERCISE 40

A. Supply the missing punctuation in the sentences below, and correct inappropriate punctuation; where two marks of punctuation are required, be sure you put them in the proper order. Some sentences are well punctuated as they stand.

492]

1.   . . . the play's the thing
   Wherein I'll catch the *conscience* the italics are mine of the king.

2. Janice (a quiet girl who went out little) was very anxious to have dates.

3. I turned and ran toward the subway station,—or thought I did, for it was snowing so that I could not see,—then I bumped into someone.

4. If you will look up the citations I have given you Ephesians 2:6, 12, 20 you will see that Paul referred variously to his Lord.

5. Maximilian had three courses before him he could try to become a genuine ruler of the Mexicans for the Mexicans; he could take his scraps of a French army and flee; or he could go on living in indolent luxury, which would probably be ended by a firing squad.

6. Knowing what she did there was only one thing to do—give back the ring.

7. "The so-called Dixiecrats [dissident southern Democrats] hoped by this move to gain the balance of power."

8. Inside I saw: a cat, some kittens, and an old white-haired Negro.

9. Alice—the scrawniest little girl in our block—was growing up to be a beauty.

10. To distinguish the types of furniture, note the following: bamboo grows in sections and is hollow between the sections; rattan, a much stronger material, grows solid.

11. Is that what you mean by "whooping it up?"

12. They had something they called a "booby-hutch," which was defined as "a carriage body put upon sleigh runners."

13. "They the Pueblo Indians make a kind of bread called guayave which the white people call a 'hornet's nest.'

14. I decided to wear my new hat—but just as I was locking the door I noticed it was starting to rain.

15. If you want to be chigger-bitten, go: I am staying home.

B. Paragraph the following passage and supply missing punctuation:

When I was a student in the far West, I lived in a dormitory in which the principal diversion was what was called stacking a room. My roommate told me about the institution. They find some way to get in he explained by stealing your key and getting a duplicate made or something. Then they come in when you're gone, sweep everything off your desks and tables, empty the drawers on the floor, pile your beds and chairs in the middle, and leave you a note which says Pleasant dreams, Pals, or something like that. I lived in fear of having our room stacked. It was. Everybody's was, except the cubbyhole of one quiet boy who came from out in the desert. He seemed to be a natural butt for jokes, so I asked my roommate one day How come they never stack Dave's room? I wouldn't know he answered quietly—he comes from out in the desert, too. But last fall I heard some of the boys talking. One of them said Dave within three weeks I'll have stacked your room. Now, everybody knows Dave keeps a rattlesnake in his room. A rattlesnake! Oh, yes. It's a pet. I don't know how the housemother misses it when she makes inspection, or why it doesn't rattle. I've heard her say dozens of times Why can't you boys keep your rooms as neat as Dave keeps his? But doesn't it bite her I asked. I suppose she never looks at the back of his lower dresser drawer. Dave keeps a clean white shirt over him. As he says, Pete likes white shirts. Pete is the rattlesnake's name. How does Dave get the shirt when he needs it I asked. He just takes it. But he doesn't like to. He doesn't like to see Pete upset. That's the reason Dave doesn't go to parties much. He's only got the one white shirt. He washes it and irons it himself, but there's always a few hours Pete doesn't have a shirt. Pete's always kind of nervous when he doesn't have his shirt Dave will say ironing away at it. But why didn't they stack his room I asked. Oh, yeah. I forgot. Well, when this fellow said they'd stack his room, and another one spoke up and said You said you weren't going to have your room stacked, but we'll stack her, Dave just said, kind of drawly, If you stack my room I'll put my rattlesnake in your bed. Well, Dave has a way of doing what he promises, and maybe that had something to do with his room not being stacked. Could be. Yes I said it could be.

C. Insert the correct punctuation in the following:

When I was in Cuernavaca Mexico just before our entry into the second world war in May 1941 I heard a story of what became of one of Rivera's murals It seems that the proprietor of a fashionable restaurant ordered his walls decorated Since I do not wish to be libelous let us say that the restaurant was at 268 Morales Avenue which it was not The proprietor a small ingratiating excitable man considered various muralists interviewing them from the time he arose at 10 a m until he went to bed at 2 a m Finally he settled upon Rivera who was known to be fashionable with certain groups especially the foreigners The mural finished he awaited the approval of the dignified people in the town Members of the important old families who were eager to view the newest monument to local progress responded to his invitation They came in holiday mood and looked they left enraged They had seen their own faces painted upon the bodies of gangsters robbers cutthroats and quacks with small ceremony and no delay at all they rendered their artistic judgment If those pictures stayed up the most important people would stay out What to do The proprietor loved his murals for they had cost him much money he loved his business for it had brought him much money So he paced the floor which was new and only partly paid for and tore at his trim carefully waxed mustache At that he had an idea and with deft strokes painted bushy whiskers sprightly goatees and respectable muttonchops upon the faces of the abused citizens Should he not reason that whiskers that would render a mayor unrecognizable would also make him genial and as a result might he not be expected to eat the restaurant beefsteak But the device which the proprietor's mustache inspired was more ingenious than successful The outraged citizens were more outraged than ever not only had the proprietor insulted them by calling them bandits but he had further and doubly insulted them by implying that they grew bad beards As for Rivera he threatened to shoot the proprietor for desecrating art Torn between art and the artist between his patrons and their patronage the bedeviled proprietor saved at once his sanity and his business by having the whole room replastered.

41. THE MANUSCRIPT

[For Guide to Revision, see below]

Follow standard practices or a special stylebook in preparing a manuscript.

Individual publications, newspapers, or college classes have special requirements for preparation of a paper, but any manuscript, whether submitted for publication, presented as a business report, or prepared to fill a class assignment, should be neat, standard in appearance, and conventional in capitalization, syllabification, and use of italics and numbers.

41 *The manuscript* M

GUIDE TO REVISION:

Check carefully the modern requirements for acceptable manuscript.

The following rules are standard and fit the requirements of almost any publisher or reader:

(1) Typewrite or write in black or blue ink on one side only of standard size (8½ x 11-inch) paper, unruled for typing, and ruled for handwriting with standard measure ruling, not the narrow ruling sometimes used for notebook paper.

(2) Double-space between lines of a typewritten manuscript. Most editors refuse to look at unsolicited copy which is not double- or triple-spaced. Keep typewriter type clean and use a well-inked ribbon.

(3) Make handwriting legible, distinguishing clearly between capital and small letters.

496]

(4) Leave generous margins on all sides of the paper—at least an inch and a half at the top and the left and an inch at the right and the bottom.

(5) Indent about half an inch for each new paragraph—five spaces on the typewriter. In typing, leave one space after internal punctuation, two spaces after end punctuation.

Manuscripts submitted for publication usually carry a notation like the following in the upper right-hand corner of the first page:

> My Years in Jail
> John Doe
> 13 Skidrow Street
> About 92,000 words

Papers submitted for class requirements are usually folded lengthwise if they are brief, and the required information is written on what would be the front cover if the report were a book. Longer papers are left flat, and the information appears on the outside page. For class papers, a notation like the following is usually sufficient:

> Mary Edmonton
> English 101, Sec. 24
> Theme VI
> October 10, 1956
> Professor John Hancock

41a Capitalization — M a; cap; lc

English has many conventions concerning the use of capital letters, often called "upper case" because they are found in the upper case of a font of hand-set type, as distinguished from small letters, referred to as "lower case." Styles and use of these conventions vary. Most American newspapers, for example, use what is called a "down" style; that is, they capitalize only the definitive part of a proper name unless the generic portion comes first (*Hudson river,* not *Hudson River; Northwestern university,* not *Northwestern University;* but *University of Chicago*). This system is intended to avoid excessive capitalization, since newspaper accounts are, of necessity, crammed with titles and names. It is used only by practicing journalists working for newspapers; the system is described in almost any basic journalism text. The style used for most literary, social, and commercial purposes, however, is an "up" style, and it is described in the following list of some of the most common uses of capitals in English.

(1) *Proper nouns* are capitalized. Clearly, to be useful, this statement requires definition of the word *proper noun* (see 27-2). The
definition gives some trouble, not because the main distinctions involved in it are illogical, but because they are subtle enough to require
clear thinking. For instance, Mrs. Hardy has a son, whom she names
Thomas. Obviously, *Thomas Hardy* is a proper noun, the given name
of one particular individual. Thomas Hardy writes some novels set in
southwestern England near an imaginary town called Casterbridge.
Casterbridge, also, is a proper noun. But suppose that a tourist wishes
to visit the scenes of these novels, does he visit the Hardy Country or
the Hardy country? Similarly, a river is named for Henrik Hudson. Is
it the Hudson River or the Hudson river? Does it flow through the
Hudson River Valley or the Hudson River valley? There is a women's
college on the bank of this river; is the president the President of Vassar
College, since there is only one such president at a time, or the president
of Vassar College, since presidents are of common occurrence? Are the
subjects taught in this institution American literature or American
Literature, History of the Americas or history of the Americas?

The confusions arise in several ways, but partly because every
object on earth exists as an individual. Every pebble on the beach is
a separate pebble, but one of them becomes the basis of a proper noun
only if it is given a name, Plymouth Rock, for instance. On this basis
one can answer the questions in the previous paragraph. The area
described in Hardy's novels is the Hardy country, because there is no
definite, designated area which has been officially so named, as there
is an area officially named Connecticut. For the same reasons, it is
Hudson River, but Hudson River valley. The president of Vassar
College is president, not President, unless she should sign herself,
with her title, which then becomes Mary E. Smith, President of Vassar College. The subjects taught are American literature and history
of the Americas, but if these subjects become titles of specific courses,
then as titles they would be written American Literature and History
of the Americas. The question is not whether the noun is the name of
an individual object, being, sort, area, or anything else, but whether
the noun is a name given to a particular unit, not shared by other
units of its sort.

(2) Words derived from names and closely associated with them
are usually capitalized. *American* derives from the name *America,*
and although there are many Americans the word is capitalized.

(3) *Proper nouns which have become common nouns* are not capitalized.

In the early nineteenth century, sample forms for the British army were made out with the name *Thomas Atkins*. Eventually Tommy Atkins became the colloquial name for a British soldier; now *tommy* has become a common noun. Similarly, a Victrola was a trade name of an instrument manufactured by the Victor Company, but the instruments have become so common that any record player can be called a *victrola*. Salad dressing made of oil and vinegar is called French dressing, because French cooks developed and popularized it and Americans borrowed it from France, but if salads increase in popularity we may yet put french dressing on them. We use the Bible in church, but the incoming college student is expected to con the student handbook, often called the "freshman bible." Thus some words which are proper nouns become common nouns, at least in some usages. If the writer is uncertain whether a proper noun has become common, he should consult a good dictionary.

(4) *The first word of a sentence or a line of poetry* begins with a capital letter.

(5) *The pronoun I* is capitalized.

(6) *References to deity* usually begin with capital letters.

To God the Father, God the Son,
And God the Spirit, Three in One.

(7) *Initials and abbreviations* often require capitals (for details see 41b).

(8) *The first letters of principal words in titles* are capitalized (see 41e).

Original

During my Second Year in High School, I took American Literature, European History, Mathematics, french, and Home Economics, and a new course entitled social problems.

[*Words like* high school *are not proper nouns, even though the writer is thinking of only one school, nor is* literature *a proper noun, even though there is only one American literature.*]

Revision

During my second year in high school, I took American literature, European history, mathematics, French, and home economics, and a new course entitled Social Problems.

[*Social Problems* is capitalized *because it is a title given to a course, not a description of the material in the course.*]

Original (*Cont.*)

We crossed over the Mount Vernon Road and down into the Coon River Bottoms.
[*This capitalization is correct if* Mount Vernon Road *and* Coon River Bottoms *are given names.*]

Revision (*Cont.*)

We crossed over the Mount Vernon road and down into the Coon River bottoms.
[*This capitalization assumes that the road is, let us say, Highway 56a but is called the Mount Vernon road because it goes to Mount Vernon, and the Coon River bottoms are the low land along the Coon River.*]

I went to the Library and read a copy of the Library.

I went to the library and read a copy of *The Library*.
[*The revised form makes clear the nature of each* library.]

I bore down on the tiller of the lazy Susan and swung into Put-in-bay.

I bore down on the tiller of the *Lazy Susan* and swung into Put-in-Bay.

In the Autumn the ducks move South out of Canada, and hunting is good in some parts of the west.
[*Names of the seasons are not capitalized; the indication of a direction is not capitalized, but a direction as name of an area is.*]

In the autumn the ducks move south out of Canada, and hunting is good in some parts of the West.

God so loved the world that he gave his only begotten son.
[*References to deity are usually capitalized.*]

God so loved the world that He gave His only begotten Son.
[*Both the pronouns referring to sacred persons and the words naming them are capitalized.*]

41b Abbreviation   M b; Ab

In general, abbreviations are avoided in writing, except in footnotes, bibliographies, formal lists, compilations of statistics, tables, addresses, and the like. There are a few exceptions: common forms of address when used with proper names (*Mr., Mrs., Messrs., Dr., Jr., Sr., Ph.D., LL.D., D.D., S.J.;* but not *Rev., Sen., Gov., Prof.,* or *Pres.* in formal writing); *before Christ* and *Anno Domini* when used with a date (*B.C., A.D.*); a few common standard abbreviations when used in informal, technical, or business writing (*cf., e.g., no., etc.*); some government agencies (*NLRB, OPA, ICC*). Except in footnotes, bibliographies, addresses, tables, and the like, the following are spelled out: names of states and countries (*California, United States*); details of publication (*volume, page, chapter*); addresses (*street, avenue, road*); months and days of the week (*December, Sunday*); business terms (*company, manufactured*); and other words not specifically excepted (*Christmas, mountain, fort, saint*). Contractions (*don't, aren't*) are inappropriate in formal writing (see 37a).

Original	*Revision*
The pol. sci. assign. for Mon. is something about the U.N. meeting in N.Y.	The political science assignment for Monday concerns the United Nations meeting in New York.
During the Xmas vacation I got a job with a mfg. co.	During the Christmas vacation I got a job with a manufacturing company.
Rev. McIntosh will offer the prayer at the commencement ex. [*The abbreviation is used only in newspaper writing and some informal writing. Formally, the titles* Reverend *and* Honorable *are preceded by the* and *accompanied by the first name or initials of the person or by the title* Mr.]	(1) The Reverend Mr. McIntosh will offer the prayer at the commencement exercises. (2) The Reverend Ira J. McIntosh will offer the prayer at the commencement exercises.
Sen. Oldham announced a new govt. research grant to be administered by Prof. Jenkins. [*First names should identify the persons when their names are first mentioned:* Senator John J. Oldham.]	Senator Oldham announced a new government research grant to be administered by Professor Jenkins.
Rome endured from 390 b.c., when it was sacked by the Celts, until 410 a.d., when it was sacked by the Germans. [A.D. *and* B.C. *are always capitalized.*]	Rome endured from 390 B.C., when it was sacked by the Celts, until A.D. 410, when it was sacked by the Germans. [*Note that* A.D. *precedes the date and* B.C. *follows it.*]

41c Numbers   M c; Num

Numbers which can be written in two words are written out in standard writing; thus, all numbers one hundred or below are written out. *McGraw Hill write out 1-99, figures for >99 or " " if 1-2 words, " " > 2 words*

Exceptions to this rule are:

(1) If several numbers are used in a passage and some of them are large, all of them are written in figures.

> On a western highway, one passes through towns marked on the map with populations from zero up. For instance, traveling east on Highway 40, one leaves the San Francisco-Oakland metropolitan area, population 2,214,249; passes through Sacramento, 275,659; Verdi, 250; Mill City, 72; and Toy and Dad Lees, 0, since the Lees have moved.

(2) Figures are regularly used in certain standard contexts: for street and room or apartment numbers in addresses (*1238 Ralston Street, 14 West Twenty-third Street*); to designate portions of a book (*Chapter 10, page 371*); for dates (*January 10, 1838*), and for decimals and percentages when using words would become complicated (*3.1416, 57%*).

Figures are not used to begin a sentence, and numbers are not written both as figures and as words, except in legal documents.

For hyphenation in numbers see 42b.

Original	*Revision*
1938 is remembered in our valley as the snowy year. [*A figure should not begin a sentence.*]	In our valley, we remember 1938 as the snowy year. [*The sentence is re-arranged to avoid the initial figure.*]
The 4 of us moved into a little garden cottage at sixty-two Longfellow Avenue. [*Write out numbers which can be expressed in two words, except in formulas like addresses.*]	The four of us moved into a little garden cottage at 62 Longfellow Avenue.
There were 32 students in our zoology laboratory and only 27 microscopes, but after we got our first grades, 11 students dropped the course.	There were thirty-two students in our zoology laboratory and only twenty-seven microscopes; but after we got our first grades, eleven students dropped the course.

41d Division of words M d; Div

A somewhat uneven right-hand margin is preferable to numerous divided words, or words incorrectly divided. In copy to be printed, hyphenation is uncommonly inconvenient, since the printer may not be sure whether the hyphen marks only the end of a line, or the end of a line which breaks a hyphenated word. When necessary, however, words may be divided between syllables. Syllabification is complicated. In general, it follows pronunciation, and consonants attach to the vowels following them (*pa-per, re-gard*); two consonants which represent two sounds go one with each syllable (*mis-ter, har-dy;* but *soph-o-more*); but prefixes and suffixes remain syllables by themselves (*ach-ing, ex-alt*), unless modern pronunciation has obscured a suffix (*chil-dren*). Double consonants are separated unless they are the ending of a word with a suffix (*rat-tle, swim-ming,* but *miss-ing*). Words of one syllable cannot be divided. Words should not be divided so that a single letter appears on either line. There are more rules and many exceptions; unless the writer is certain he should consult a good dictionary. When a word is divided, the hyphen appears at the end of the first line, not at the beginning of the second.

41e Titles M e; Tit

The title of a brief theme or other piece of writing should be centered on the first page, separated from the body of the composition by a blank line if handwritten, and by at least four spaces if typed. Principal words, usually all except articles and prepositions, are capitalized, but a title at the head of a manuscript is not underlined or enclosed in quotation marks. Titles of long manuscripts are placed on a separate title page.

When a title of a book, magazine, newspaper, play, poem, story, or moving picture appears within a manuscript, it should have capital letters to begin all words except prepositions and articles and should be underlined to indicate that it would be printed in italics (see 41f). Mechanical limitations sometimes necessitate variations; for example, newspapers tend not to use italics because they complicate typesetting. But modern practice more and more consistently prefers italics rather than other typographical devices to distinguish titles referred to in a text.

[503

The *Times* reviewed *The Red Badge of Courage* enthusiastically.

Milton's *Lycidas* is a poem in the pastoral tradition.

The *Tribune* critic praised Audrey Hepburn's performance in *Roman Holiday.*

When a short work must be distinguished from the larger work which contains it (see 43-11, 45-3), quotation marks distinguish an article or chapter from the periodical or book in which it appears, a short story or poem from the volume in which it is printed.

"How to Build Your Own Home" is a feature in the *Herald* every Saturday.

The New York Times had a review of *Garland of Bays* called "The Robust Elizabethan Days."

"Miniver Chevy" can be found in Robinson's *Collected Works.*

41f Italics   **M f; Ital**

Italic type in printing, indicated in manuscript by single underlining of the words to be italicized, is increasing in popularity and respectability as a means of setting off certain words in the composition. It is now regularly used for titles referred to in a manuscript (see 41e). It is used for all foreign words and phrases not yet Anglicized. It is acceptable form for words used out of context and words to which special attention is called. For most of these uses, quotation marks were formerly used, and for some of them quotation marks may still be used (see 40a).

Indiscriminate use of italics to emphasize certain words is to be avoided, but italics can be used for emphasis and contrast.

I said he was drunk? No! I said he was *not* drunk.

Original

Soon, very soon, we shall start for *sunny California,* hoping to have the *time of our lives.*
[*Overuse of italics for emphasis destroys the emphasis.*]

After Professor Lovejoy's lecture, it became "de rigueur" to have read "The Road to Xanadu."
[*Italics are preferable.*]

Revision

Soon, very soon, we shall start for sunny California, hoping to have the time of our lives.

After Professor Lovejoy's lecture, it became *de rigueur* to have read *The Road to Xanadu.*

Original (*Cont.*)

Man is the subject of the sentence.

[*Italics should point to* Man, *used out of context.*]

Americans like to make new words out of old, to sleep in a motel and eat cheeseburgers.

Revision (*Cont.*)

Man is the subject of the sentence.

Americans like to make new words out of old, to sleep in a *motel* and eat *cheeseburgers.*

EXERCISE 41

A. Correct the faulty capitalization in the following:

Texas, the largest State in the Union, has never been quite sure that it is part of the United States, and texas people have their own notions and are likely to live by them. Inhabitants of the lone star state are convinced that any texan can "lick his weight in wildcats" or ten times his weight in yankees, and texans have always had their own Ways of Thinking. Consider, for instance, old judge Bean, who called himself the Law west of the Pecos, meaning, of course, the Law west of the Pecos river. But when I speak of the independence of texans, I am thinking particularly of the individuality of the Buckaroos, or as they are sometimes called, "Cowpokes," up in the Panhandle Country. That, of course, is the area around the Town of Panhandle, but the whole Northwest part of the Sovereign State of Texas is sometimes called The Panhandle. And when I think of those Panhandle Buckaroos, I am reminded especially of the way they love their horses to the exclusion of everything else.

According to the story, one of these Buckaroos who lived in the northern part of Carson county, not far from the Town of Panhandle itself, heard about the moving picture *Gone With The Wind,* and decided he wanted to see it. He had heard it was about the civil war, and his Grandfather had fought in that War. Accordingly, he saddled his Palomino pony, rode into the town of White deer, and then down to Panhandle. At the Moving Picture Theater he found there was a Double Bill, and accordingly he sat through a showing of *Roaring riders.* He liked that because there were many good Quarter Horses in it. Then he saw the ravages of the union army, the burning of plantations, and Scarlet O'Hara baring her bosom to the camera. When he got back to the Ranch, somebody asked him how he liked Scarlet.

"all right, I guess," He said. He said nothing more for some time, and then he added, "jest been wonderin' how they got them horses out past them flames."

B. Correct the errors in abbreviations, contractions, and numbers in the passage below. Note which forms would be acceptable in colloquial writing but unsuitable in formal writing.

I've just purchased in a 2nd hand book store a copy of *Appleton's Guide* to the United States for eighteen ninety-two. It's full of entrancing old things, but since for the past 8 or 10 years our family has gone every summer to the Adirondack Mts., I was particularly interested in the description of those mts. The eds. point out that this sec. 30 yrs ago "was known even by name only to a few hunters, trappers, and lumbermen," but they're now able to give a detailed description of it. They correctly locate the area between L. Champlain and L. George on the E., and the St. Lawrence R. on the w. They also identify Mt. Marcy as the tallest mt. in the area, giving the measurement as five thousand three hundred thirty-four feet. They concede that this pk. is not so high as the Black Mts. of N.C., nor the White Mts. of N. Hampshire, but they point out that they're interspersed by more than 1000 lakes, the largest of which are more than 20 mls. long. These lakes're said to be infested with trout weighing 20 lb. or more. Hunting was also A-1; for instance, the hunter could take woodcock from Sept. 1st to April thirtieth, & the fine for shooting game out of season seems to have been only $25, which by our standards wasn't very high. The publication also gave instrs. that a "lady's outfit" should include "a short walking-dress, with Turkish drawers fastened tightly with a band at the ankle." Travel in the area was apparently done by boats, built a few ft. long, carried by the guides on their shoulders from lake to lake and from river to river.

C. Correct the faulty use or omission of italics in the following:

Among the curiosities of literature and thought is the career of Lord Monboddo, *baronet,* author of a book called Of the Origin and Progress of Language. He believed that human speech came from the speech of animals, and imported an *orang-outang* into Scotland, assuming that the animal represented *the infantine state of our species.* The *chimp,* as the animal was called, was presumably a representative of "Pongo pygmaeus" or Simia satyris. Lord Monboddo taught the animal to play the flute, after a fashion, but in Monboddo's words, he *never learned to speak.* The lord patiently tried to teach the animal to say "hungry" and "eat," but without success. The learned journals of the day, periodicals like the Quarterly Review and Blackwood's Edinburgh Magazine ridiculed poor Monboddo, publishing articles with titles like Misguided Jurist and *This Monkey Business.* Not until long after the publication of Darwin's Descent of Man did students of modern thought realize that Lord Monboddo had been ahead of his day. Among the milder satirists of the radical jurist was Thomas Love Peacock, who made genial fun of Monboddo and his orang-outang by inserting into his book Melancourt, a satirical novelette, a certain Sir Oran Haut-ton, whose name was of course a pun upon the French haut-ton, that is, high-toned.

42. SPELLING

[*For Guide to Revision, see page 515*]

*Spelling can be improved. First analyze spelling habits;
then work systematically to overcome weaknesses.*

Whimsical spelling constitutes one of the great weaknesses of the English language. English vocabulary is large and precise; English grammar is flexible, but English spelling, though it is historical and revealing, is highly confusing to the beginner. Foreigners and natives alike groan over it.

Other linguistic groups have forcibly regularized their spelling. As a result learning to spell in Spanish or German, for instance, is relatively easy, but writers of English have never been willing to submit to regularization of their spelling. Perhaps the same spirit which has led the English-speaking peoples to defend traditional free speech has led them also to cherish traditional orthography. In any event, spelling is not easy to reform, and hasty efforts to simplify spelling have usually done more harm than good. Whatever the reason, English spelling is a troublesome subject, and an important one. Even though a student understands Sanskrit and thermodynamics, if he cannot spell he will not be considered an educated person or even a very intelligent one. This judgment may be illogical, but it is also inescapable.

Nor is there any substitute for ability to spell. An occasional person tries to avoid misspellings by using only familiar words. If he wishes to write, "Little Nancy was trudging up the path," and does not know how to spell *trudging,* he writes, "Little Nancy was walking up the path." Precise, vivid writing becomes flat and colorless because the writer cannot spell. This device leaves a bad speller a bad speller and encourages him to become a bad writer. No one with any pretense to an education can afford to spell badly, and anyone not moronic can learn to spell at least moderately well if he will try hard enough and approach the job in the right way.

42-1 Origin of spelling variations

Our spelling is not so haphazard as it may seem. Writers of English have always tended to indicate sound by spelling, but spelling is not always phonetic, partly because printing and writing have tended to crystallize spelling forms while usage and pronunciation have changed. In two ways, especially, order has developed into seeming confusion. First, words native to English and words which were borrowed early have generally kept the spellings they acquired in Middle English. Sometimes these spellings were haphazard or represented local practices, but often they reflected actual pronunciation or usage. For instance, Chaucer rhymed *sick* and *seek,* but would not rhyme *meet* and *meat.* Similarly, the *gh* of *night* or *thought* represents an earlier pronunciation.

Second, words borrowed during the last few hundred years have generally kept all or part of the spelling of the language from which they were borrowed. For instance, the old spelling demon *phthisic* is spelled phonetically, but in a spelling based upon the Greek; *schnapps* retains its German spelling. Thus if the student wishes to study enough of the history of the English language and then learn many foreign languages, English spelling becomes much more orderly, but most of us do not have the time to become linguists and philologists, even if we have the inclination.

42-2 Learning to spell

Fortunately, there are easier ways to learn to spell. Many people are sufficiently eye-minded so that they learn to spell unconsciously. By the time they have seen a word spelled correctly several times, they can tell how to spell it by writing it down. Other individuals are not so fortunate. They have to learn to spell. They are not stupid. They may have very good minds, but minds which do not record spelling automatically. Luckily, however, anybody who is normally intelligent can learn to spell, often much more easily than he supposes. A "bad" speller is usually only a person who does not spell without learning, who has never been properly taught, or who has never tried hard enough to learn.

In spelling, as in almost everything else, there is no substitute for a good background. The more a student reads, and the better writing he reads, the better he is likely to spell. Similarly, a knowledge of other languages and of etymologies will help. Anyone who knows that *license* is related to Latin *licere* will not spell it *lisence;* deciding whether *innocence* and *inoculate* have one or two *n's* is not difficult for the person who knows that the first was formed from *in* and the Latin *nocere* and the second from *in* and the Latin *oculare.* But building background is a slow process, and even learning etymologies takes time. Furthermore, the sad fact is that a writer may be very learned and yet spell badly.

42-3 Analyzing spelling difficulties

Most adults who must learn to spell go about the job in the wrong way. With commendable but misdirected zeal, they look up a list of words, and promptly forget them. Or they look up the same few words again and again, while telling themselves "I never could remember that word," and forget the words once more. Either approach is wearing and nearly worthless.

For most students who have reached college and still have spelling difficulties, the best method is to analyze the individual's spelling troubles and work systematically on the basis of the analysis. The first step is to find out what words a writer misspells and, if possible, why he misspells them. Here a good teacher can help, but the student must do most of the work, and often he can do it best—after all, he knows himself as nobody else is likely to. He should first make a list of all words he looks up in the dictionary in order to verify their spelling and of all words he misspells, including all repetitions in either class. Misspelled words can be collected from corrected themes or from letters which the recipient has been asked to correct and return. There is always a way to get a list of one's misspellings; it should be based upon one's normal writing and should be extensive enough to be typical. For diagnostic purposes, the student should record his misspellings, not the correct spellings of the words.

42-4 Habitual misspelling

Following is a list of misspellings collected from two themes of a student who had spelling difficulties:

> recieve, to (*for* too), planatarium, too (*for* to), seperate, to (*for* too), recieve, to (*for* too), seperate, too (*for* to), Phillippine, too (*for* to).

[509

Of course, good analysis requires a longer list, but even in so short a list the main difficulty is obvious. The student is misspelling the same few words over and over. All he has to do is to learn the difference between *to* and *too,* that *separate* is spelled *ar* instead of *er,* and that *receive* follows the rule of *e* before *i* after *c.* Anybody can learn that much in five minutes, and this "bad" speller could make a good start overnight by learning a few words.

Not every case of bad spelling is so simple as this or so easily helped. Most students with trouble not only misspell some words habitually but make errors for other reasons like those classified below.

42-5 Carelessness

Consider the following list of misspellings from one theme:

> effect (*for* affect), Tes of D'Ubervilles, Tess of D'Uberviles, inan (*for* inane), Tamos, usally, Tess of Durbervilles, disipated, Tes of D'Urbyvilles, tradgedy, to (*for* too), principle (*for* principal), Tess of DUrbeville, berth (*for* birth), Tess of D'Urberville.

The girl who wrote the paper managed to spell one title six different ways—all of them wrong. That she did not know how to spell the title is not surprising, but she could have looked it up if she were not careless or lazy or both. She probably knows how to spell *inane, dissipated, Thames, tragedy,* and other words in the list, but she was too careless to bother to spell them correctly.

Hesitating during composition to spell every word correctly may impede writing, but there is no excuse for leaving misspellings uncorrected after the writing is done. An uncertain speller should scrutinize every word before he lets any written work out of his hands.

42-6 Phonetics and spelling

Consider the following list of misspellings:

> to (*for* too), goverment, ast (*for* asked), tradegy, airfiel, seperate, intrest, athalete, Scananavian, constriction company, preform (*for* perform), half to, airplan, thing (*for* think), to (*for* too), affect (*for* effect), exackly, comdy, seperate, wend (*for* went)

There are some habitual misspellings—*to* (for *too*), *seperate,* but most of the remaining misspellings result from mispronunciations or from ignorance of phonetic values.

English spelling is not entirely phonetic. An ideal alphabet would have one letter for every sound and only one sound for each letter, but in English some letters may have many sounds, and some sounds can be represented in several ways. It is still true, however, that the phonetic value of the letters and the pronunciation of the words are, in general, the basis of spelling. No one who knows phonetic values and pronounces carefully need be in much doubt about how to spell *perform* or *government.* In the list above, words like *asked, tragedy, airfield, interest, athlete, Scandinavian, construction, think, exactly, comedy,* and *went* are misspelled probably because the writer did not pronounce them correctly, and possibly also because he was not sure of the phonetic value of the letters. Anyone who makes errors of this sort should first be sure he knows the sounds associated with each letter. He should then be careful to know the words he uses and to pronounce them precisely. Temporarily, to fix troublesome words in mind, a speller may wish to pronounce the troublesome syllable with exaggerated stress: *prePAration, audiENCE, ATHletic, govERNment.*

42-7 Spelling verbs

The spelling of familiar verbs does not bother most literate people, but verb forms may be troublesome, because misspelled verbs may result from several causes. Consider the following list.

> ast (*for* asked), lie (*for* lay), arnt (*for* aren't), don't (*for* doesn't), went (*for* gone), goes (*for* go), kill (*for* kills), can (*for* can't), goin (*for* going), layed (*for* laid), layed (*for* lain), ast (*for* asked).

Apparently, the writer does not know the principal parts of the verbs *lie* and *lay* and how these verbs should be used (see 29a). He may not understand the use of *s* in the present, as evidenced in confusion of *go, goes; kill, kills.* He seems unsure of the use of the apostrophe in contractions (see 42a). He may not pronounce carefully or know the phonetic value of letters (*ast, can* for *can't*). Most errors in verb forms will be corrected by understanding the use of verb forms (30). The remainder fall within one of the other categories of spelling mistakes examined above.

42-8 Indication of vowel sounds

Consider the following list:

> alright, geting, diner (*for* dinner), alright, doesnt, helpfull, combin, refering, occuring, excelence, noticeing, alright, permited, rideing, tradegy, laborously, Britanica, ninty, quanity, dominent, argueing, durring.

[511

Some old friends like *all right* appear in this, and there is a sufficient variety of misspellings so that a much longer list would be required to be sure which represent a tendency and which result from carelessness or are odd words habitually misspelled, but there is at least one noticeable tendency in this list. The writer does not accurately use consonants and vowels to indicate vowel sounds.

There are few reliable rules for the doubling of consonants and the use of additional vowels to indicate sounds, but there are tendencies which are consistent enough to be useful. Medieval scribes often doubled a consonant if they wished to indicate that a previous vowel was short, especially if the consonant was not final, and added an extra vowel if they wished to indicate that a vowel was long. The scribes were not consistent in their practice, and we have not been entirely consistent in preserving medieval spellings, but modern practice is consistent enough to be useful. For instance, *dine* is distinguished from *din* by the extra final vowel. The writer of the list of words above seems not to understand this practice; otherwise he would not have confused *diner* and *dinner,* which follow the rule, and he probably also would not have misspelled *getting, combine, helpful, referring, occurring, excellence, permitted, riding, Britannica, ninety, arguing,* and *during.* The rules covering these misspellings are somewhat complicated; the student who has difficulties of this sort should turn to 42d.

42-9 Special problems in spelling

The peculiarities of the language have given rise to special problems in English spelling. Consider the following list:

> lay (*for* laid), gread-grandfather, sensable, attendence, recieve, incidences, shipwreack, abbes (*for* abbess), recieve, sixty two, ponie's, dipthong, relient, primative, definate, dessert (*for* desert), playwrite, influance, perrequisites, presede, roll (*for* role), Britian, marketible, loose (*for* lose), recieve, lays (*for* lies), site (*for* cite), indistinguished.

There are several sorts of errors here, some of which, like the habitual misspelling of *receive,* have been mentioned above. Another type of error (*ponie's* and *sixty two*) results from ignorance of the plural forms in English (see 42c) and of the uses of the hyphen and apostrophe in spelling certain forms (see 42a, 42b). But the bulk of these errors come about through the confusion of words or parts of words which in some way resemble something else.

A few words the writer apparently does not understand. He wrote *gread-grandfather,* but he surely would not have written *gread mistake.* Similarly, he would not have referred to a collision on the highway as a *wreack,* nor would he have written *incidence* for a single happening. He is failing to understand the word or the parts of it, and his misspelling is a symptom of his poor grasp of vocabulary. Most of these words, however, present problems in spelling.

Some represent the confusion of homonyms, that is, of words having the same sound but different meanings, for example, *sight, site,* and *cite; to, too,* and *two; rite, write, right,* and *wright.* The cure for such errors is to look up all the homonyms in a good dictionary and learn enough about them to keep them separate, and then to find some way of associating the meaning with the spelling. Words which are not pronounced identically but are similarly spelled are confusing, especially if the difference in the spelling involves only a transposition or a doubling of a letter. Thus the following have always given trouble: *angle, angel; casual, causal; chose, choose; lose, loose; desert, dessert; canvas, canvass; accept, except; affect, effect.*

Spelling by analogy or etymology can be very helpful, but analogies may lead a writer astray, especially if they rest upon false assumptions. One of the most common misspellings is *definate* for *definite,* probably because of the large number of English words ending in *ate.* The misspellings like *pronounciation* and *renounciation* result from the analogy with the corresponding verbs. The spelling *primative* is probably influenced by the more common *primary.* The frequent misspellings *Britian* and *villian* are probably made by false analogy with many English words having *i* and *a* in this sequence, as in *Parisian, gentian, Martian.* Even very accomplished spellers will make occasional errors of this sort, but awareness of the problem helps to solve it, and thorough acquaintance with the word will cure individual difficulties.

The most numerous words which cause trouble through confusions are those that employ a syllable, often a prefix or a suffix, which can be spelled in several ways, or which differs but slightly from another syllable. Thus, *-ible* is confused with *-able,* and *-ents* with *-ence.* Is it *indistinguished* or *undistinguished, indistinguishable* or *undistinguishable?* Differences in meaning and use offer some help. The suffixes *-ents* and *-ants* are plurals, as in *residents* and *attendants; -ence* and *-ance* are evidences of an abstract noun, as in *residence* and

[513

attendance. Latin prefixes and suffixes tend to be used with Latin words, Anglo-Saxon affixes with Anglo-Saxon words. Thus we have *unable,* since both *un-* and *-able* come from Anglo-Saxon, against *indigestible,* since *in-, digest,* and *-ible* are Latin, but the rule is by no means consistent, as the confusion mentioned above in connection with words related to *distinguish* will illustrate. Frequently, *-able* follows words which are complete as they stand, whereas *-ible* follows syllables which have no meaning without the suffix (*acceptable, marketable,* but *terrible*), even though a silent *e* has been dropped from the word (*drivable*). Some tendencies can be observed, also, in the letters which suffixes follow, but many students find learning the words easier than learning the tendencies and the exceptions. For what the tendencies may be worth, here are the most common: *-able* usually follows hard *g* or *c* (*applicable*), *i* or *y* in the root word (*justifiable*); *-able* is common in words having a long *a* in a related word (*irritate,* and hence, *irritable*). The suffix *-ible* usually follows soft *c* or *g* (*tangible*), *miss* or *ns* (*sensible*); if the suffix can replace *-ion* in another word, without change of adjacent letters, *-ible* is usual (*perfection,* and hence, *perfectible*). The ending *-ar* is much less common than *-er* or *-or* (*grammar, calendar,* and a few others); *-er* is usual among words coming from Anglo-Saxon if the *-er* indicates a person's temporary or permanent occupation (*teacher, walker*); *-or* is the common ending, especially in words from Latin (*doctor, governor, motor*). Among the prefixes warranting unusual attention are the following:

per-	(meaning *through* as in *perfect,* carried through to the end)	pre-	(meaning *before* as in *prerequisite, predecessor*)
anti-	(meaning *against* as in *antitoxin, anti-Russian*)	ante-	(meaning *before* as in *antebellum, anterior*)
di-	(meaning *twice* as in *dibase, digraph*)	de-	(meaning *from* or *concerning, down* as in *depart, define*)

The endings *-cede, -ceed,* and *-sede* cause some confusion. The regular form in English is *-cede* (*concede, precede, recede*). The exceptions can be easily learned; one word ends *-sede* (*supersede*), and three end *-ceed* (*exceed, succeed, proceed,* but not *procedure*).

In modern English, especially in modern American English, all unaccented vowels tend to lose their quality and become a common vowel sound called *schwa,* the sound of the vowel in *the,* when *the* is not pronounced like *thee*. Thus, for many American speakers the vowel in the final syllable of *resident* and *attendant* has the same sound, which is the same sound they use for the next to the last vowel in *accommodate* and *government*. Since the same sound is here serving for *e, a, o,* and *er* (and it can serve, also, for *i, u, y,* and a number of others) phonetics will not help much directly. Indirectly, phonetics can help, however. The word in which the vowel has become *schwa* can sometimes be associated with a related word in which the vowel has retained the accent, and hence its quality. For instance, although the *e* has lost its quality for many speakers in *resident* it has kept its quality in *residential*. A writer has only to sound out *residential* to know that *residant* is incorrect. The pronunciation of *inferential* indicates the spelling of *inference*. Less can be done with the syllable written ʃʌn ʃən in phonetic script, which is variously represented in *shun, percussion, complexion, cushion, direction, Hessian, freshen*.

Obviously, spelling problems which rest upon any situation as complicated as that which gives us various uses for the same or similar sounds are not likely to find resolution by simple means. Even here, however, knowing one's weaknesses helps. The writer who knows that he is likely to confuse *-ence* and *-ance* can give special attention to words with these spellings, and eliminate the most troublesome, and he can make use of some special devices, distinguishing the meaning of homonyms, for instance, and associating words difficult to spell with related words which the writer knows already, or can "sound out."

42 Spelling   Sp

GUIDE TO REVISION:

Correct the misspelled word. Try to find out why you have made the error, and learn the correct form so thoroughly that you do not repeat your mistake.

Most misspellings involve one of the causes discussed above: (1) the writer is careless; (2) he habitually misspells certain words; (3) he has one or more of several different sorts of spelling difficulties, any of which can be cured or greatly reduced with a little attention.

For the first, the solution is obvious. For the second, there are also simple cures. Since relatively few words need be learned, they can be memorized. The writer can work from a list, eliminating words he knows. Furthermore, he can take advantage of some of our knowledge of how the mind learns. Anything repeated just before sleep is likely to be remembered in the morning. If the writer reminds himself just before going to sleep that *receive* is spelled *ei,* and does it on three successive nights, he is likely not to misspell it again. Anything repeated at intervals will be learned; a list of a few troublesome words can be repeated before every class, or every night while the writer is undressing. In a short time they will be learned for life, and the card with the list of words can be thrown away. A mnemonic device sometimes helps with particularly troublesome words. For instance, an old schoolboy device distinguishes *principal* and *principle* by suggesting that a high school *principal* might be a *pal* but a geometric *principle* could not. If the writer makes up his own device, it may work, no matter how silly it may sound. Often, learning many details about a word will make it easy to remember. The distinction between *affect* and *effect* is easier for the person who looks up the words in a good dictionary and understands all the differences between them.

Errors of the third sort are often more troublesome, but systematic work will decrease them. A first step is diagnosis of troubles (see 42-1 to 42-9). Some errors can be corrected by learning what are called "spelling rules," although strictly speaking these so-called rules are not rules at all, since spellings were not originally based on them. They are observations of spelling practice which has been more or less regular. All these rules have some exceptions, and for some rules the exceptions are so numerous that the rule is not worth learning. Rules in the sections below have enough application so that anyone who has difficulty spelling should simplify his problem by learning them.

42a The apostrophe   Sp a; Apos

The apostrophe is used to indicate an omission of one or more letters or figures.

> can't, isn't, o'clock, the gold rush of '49.

It is used also to indicate omissions in reports of dialectal speech.

> "I rec'leck how y'r paw come courtin' like 'twar yestiday," she said.

Avoid overuse of the apostrophe in recording dialect; apostrophes clutter the page and confuse the reader. A writer is usually wise to indicate with an apostrophe only the most noticeable omissions in pronunciation.

Some contractions give especial difficulty because they are readily confused with possessive forms of pronouns which do not require apostrophes. Note the following pairs:

Contractions	*Possessive pronouns*
it's (it is)	its (The cat carried its kittens.)
they're (they are)	their (They ate their lunch.)
you're (you are)	your (Mind your manners.)
who's (who is)	whose (Whose little boy are you?)

Original

You're supposed to pick it up by the back of it's neck.

[*The contraction* you're *requires an apostrophe; the possessive pronoun* its *does not.*]

"I'm go'n' t' d'vide m' w'rk int' a duz'n per'ods," he said.

[*Even though the omissions actually occur in speech, so many apostrophes confuse more than they clarify.*]

Revision

(1) You're supposed to pick it up by the back of its neck.

(2) You are supposed to pick it up by the back of its neck.

[*The contraction is suitable for informal writing only.*]

"I'm goin' to divide my work into a dozen periods," he said.

[*There is no right number of apostrophes, and transcription of dialect is always difficult; but the best writers try to suggest, not to reproduce.*]

The apostrophe is now most frequently used as a sign of the possessive or genitive case. In a curious blunder, Renaissance grammarians supposed that a form like *the kingis book,* an alternate medieval form for *the kinges book,* should actually read *the king, his book.* They assumed that an *h* had been omitted; accordingly they used an apostrophe. They were wrong, but the practice has become standard modern usage.

To show possession in singular nouns and indefinite pronouns, provided possession is not shown by the preposition *of,* add an apostrophe and *s.*

Paul's temper, the cat's tail, anybody's opinion

For plural nouns which end in *s,* add only an apostrophe.

the soldiers' rifles, the schoolgirls' idol

For plural and collective nouns which end with a letter other than *s,* add an apostrophe and *s.*

> the people's choice, all men's fate

Proper nouns ending in *s* follow the rule:

> Frances's earring, Carl Zeiss's best lens

but may have the extra *s* omitted if it would cause an awkward series of sounds.

> Xerxes' army, Moses' code, Keats' or Keats's poems

In compounds, the last part of the compound takes the possessive form.

> mother-in-law's visit, anyone else's rights

In words showing joint possession, only the last takes the sign of the possessive.

> Germany, France, and England's position; John and Robert's fight

A possessive form for each of two or more compound nouns indicates individual possession.

> Harry and Bert's bicycle (they own it together);
> Harry's and Bert's troubles (each has troubles of his own)

The apostrophe is often omitted in proper names which have become established.

> Columbia University Teachers College, Clayton County Old Folks Home

A few possessive forms, known as double possessives, use both the apostrophe and *of.*

> a friend of my father's, a cousin of Ann's

Nouns of specification in time, space, quantity, or value follow the rule for the apostrophe in the possessive.

> an hour's walk, a quarter's worth, Monday morning's *Journal,* five dollars' worth, at their wits' end.

An important exception should be noted. The possessive forms of personal and relative pronouns do not require the apostrophe. *His, hers, its, ours, yours, theirs,* and *whose* are used as possessives and do not have apostrophes.

518]

Original

When June went to Ball State Teacher's College for a years work, she found that the warm wind's there made her hair curl.

[*The apostrophe should be omitted from the proper name;* year's, *a noun of specification, requires the apostrophe;* winds, *a plural, does not.*]

Revision

When June went to Ball State Teachers College for a year's work, she found that the warm winds there made her hair curl.

The Jones's dog chased the Macks's cat.

[*The sense indicates that plural possessives are required.*]

The Joneses' dog chased the Macks' cat.

[*The apostrophe after the regular plural forms the plural possessive.*]

A publishers joke suggests that the ideal book title would be *Lincolns Doctors Dog.*

A publisher's joke suggests that the ideal book title would be *Lincoln's Doctor's Dog.*

I became interested in my brother's-in-law troubles.

I became interested in my brother-in-law's troubles.

42b Compounding; hyphenation   Sp b; Hy; ⊙

When two words combine in meaning, they are sometimes written as one word, sometimes as two words, and sometimes as a hyphenated word. They are combined when they join so closely that they function as a single new word. In the following sentences, for example, the difference is clear:

There are red buds on the redbud.

Blackbirds are so called because they are black birds.

All cases are not so clear as these. That we should write *pea soup* is obvious, because the soup is thought of as soup and it is made of peas. One would probably guess that we should write *peahen* because we have come to think of this word as the name of a particular fowl, and besides the hen is not made of peas. Then why should we write *pea jacket,* for the jacket is not made of peas either? There is no simple answer, and frequent use of the dictionary is necessary.

A few general principles help:

(1) Two words, one of which modifies the other, are separate (*main highway*), even though both would normally be considered noun forms (*Texas highway*).

(2) Any combination which has acquired a meaning of its own is one word (*highway, hydrobiplane, limehouse*).

(3) Words which have been combined but still retain their individual meanings are hyphenated (*law-hand, Dutchman's-breeches, sailor's-choice*).

(4) Verbs or modifiers which are combined for a particular usage should be hyphenated even though these words would not be hyphenated otherwise.

> Macbeth was not caught red-handed, but he had a red hand.
>
> This where-do-we-go-from-here attitude had distinguished their foreign policy.
>
> We hot-roll all metal and double-rivet the joints.

There are, however, many irregularities and a number of special uses:

Alternatives. If there are alternatives for the first element of a hyphenated compound, each of the alternatives may include a hyphen (*eight- and ten-paddle canoes; two-, three-, and four-ply roofing*). When the first of two modifiers can be thought of as modifying the second, the modifiers are not hyphenated, especially if the first is formed by adding *-ly*.

> The slowly moving truck pulled over to the right.
>
> The truck was slowly climbing the hill.
>
> *But,* Slow-moving traffic stays right; fast-moving traffic stays left.

Prefixes. Hyphens usually separate a prefix ending with a vowel from a word beginning with the same vowel (*pre-eminent, semi-independent, re-elected,* but *co-ordinate* or *coordinate*). Hyphens often separate other prefixes, especially *ex-, self-, all-, anti-, pro-,* to avoid confusion with other words (*re-cover* from *recover*), to stress the prefix, or separate a prefix and a name.

> ex-husband, self-government, all-America, self-contained, anti-Nazi, sub-subcommittee, ex-governor

Numbers. Compound numbers from twenty-one to ninety-nine are hyphenated. A fraction used as a modifier is hyphenated unless one element of it is already a hyphenated compound. Fractions used as nouns are usually not hyphenated.

520]

Twenty-seven cattle, nine hundred and ninety-nine, a four-fifths majority, four fifths of the class, a three-sixteenths drill, twenty-one thirty-seconds deep.

Hyphens are used to join the figures in inclusive dates (*1790–92, 1850–1900*) and to join inclusive figures when these appear in tabular form (*500-1000, 10,001-10,025*).

Original	*Revision*
The car sank hub-deep in the newly-made road.	The car sank hub-deep in the newly made road.
[Newly, *which modifies* made, *should not be hyphenated.*]	[Hub-deep *is hyphenated; two words have been joined to form a modifier.*]
Our slow baked bread has been slowly-baked.	Our slow-baked bread has been slowly baked.
Jim, back from the army, displayed his "ruptured duck" emblem.	Jim, back from the army, displayed his "ruptured-duck" emblem.
[*Combined as one modifier,* ruptured *and* duck *should be hyphenated.*]	
The alloy is rust, weather, and heat-resistant.	The alloy is rust-, weather-, and heat-resistant.
[*Alternatives should include the hyphen with each alternative.*]	

42c Plurals   Sp c; Pl; Sing

English vocabulary is made up mainly of (1) native words which have come from Anglo-Saxon, and (2) words borrowed from other languages. Roughly speaking, a piece of writing is likely to contain about equal quantities of each. The fact is of interest for spelling. Anglo-Saxon formed plurals in a variety of ways, but with few exceptions, all Anglo-Saxon nouns were reduced eventually to a single system, so that most native words form their plurals by adding -s or -es.

To form regular plurals, add s if the sign of the plural is not pronounced as a separate syllable (*boy, boys; regulation, regulations*); after a consonant, if the sign of the plural is pronounced as a separate syllable, add es (*grass, grasses; class, classes*); if the singular ends in e, add s (*house, houses; bridge, bridges*).

[521

Some few nouns were not regularized in Middle English and retain archaic forms (*ox, oxen; deer, deer; brother, brothers* or *brethren; child, children*). For such words, consult a good dictionary; the *New English Dictionary on Historical Principles* includes interesting histories. Words ending in *o* formerly regularly added *es* (*tomato, tomatoes; Negro, Negroes; motto, mottoes*), but words recently borrowed usually have only the *s* ending in the plural (*radio, radios; banjo, banjos; solo, solos*). Thus words ending in *o* do not follow a reliable rule; exceptions must be learned. Proper nouns ending in *y* form the plural with the addition of *s,* and the *y* is not changed to *i* (*two Marys, all the family of Frys*). For common nouns ending in *y,* see 42e. In nouns having a final *f* or an *f* before a final silent *e,* the *f* is often changed to *v* before the sign of the plural (*wife, wives; loaf, loaves*); there are so many exceptions to this practice that it cannot be thought of as a rule (*sheriff, sheriffs; belief, beliefs*).

Words borrowed from other languages offer special problems. The English vocabulary is one of the most extensive ever built up, partly because English-speaking people have borrowed words very freely. Furthermore, English speakers tend to change words slowly, to keep a word relatively long in the form in which it has been borrowed. Eventually, of course, if the word becomes common, it becomes Anglicized, which means, among other things, that the plural is formed by adding *-s* or *-es.* The transitional period does not greatly affect the plurals of words from German, French, and Spanish, most of which form plurals with *-s.* Words from Latin and Greek, however, are somewhat complicated because they sometimes retain endings from the complicated classical declensional systems. Latin words ending in *um* usually form the plural by changing the *um* to *a* (*datum, data; agendum, agenda*); *us* is changed to *i* (*focus, foci; cactus, cacti*); *a* is changed to *ae* (*alumna, alumnae*). Foreign words eventually acquire a plural form by analogy with English; that is, the plural ends in *-s* or *-es.* Thus, for a time, there are two current forms; *focuses* is now more common than *foci.* Sometimes foreign plurals are not recognized for what they are, and they are treated as though they were singulars. Thus one hears *This data is unreliable,* although *data* is properly plural and *is* is singular; and one hears *The committee made up its agendas,* although *agenda* is already plural without the *s.* Eventually these blunders may become standard speech (our accepted plural *children* results from a similar blunder), but careful writers will avoid such plurals until they are generally accepted.

Numbers, letters, symbols, and words spoken of as objects form their plurals by adding *'s* (*two 2's; a row of x's; there are no and's or but's about it*). This is the only plural form which resembles the possessive.

Original

High over our heads we saw dozen's of vapor trail's from the plane's.
[*The apostrophe is used with possessives, but not with regular plurals.*]

The louses were making life miserable for the deers.
[Deer *and* louse *have retained archaic plurals.*]

Be sure to dot your is and cross yours ts.
[*Numbers, letters, symbols, figures, and words out of context form the plural with* 's.]

The irate old man started throwing tomatos at all the radioes.
[*In general, words entering the language early, like* tomato, *form the plural with* es; *new words like* radio *add only* s.]

Mrs. Appleby brought all the little Applebies with her.
[*Proper names ending in* y *regularly do not change the* y *to* i *to form the plural.*]

Revision

High over our heads we saw dozens of vapor trails from the planes.

The lice were making life miserable for the deer.

Be sure to dot your *i's* and cross your *t's*.
[*Notice also that italics show that the letters are used out of context.*]

The irate old man started throwing tomatoes at all the radios.

Mrs. Appleby brought all the little Applebys with her.

42d Combinations of i and e **Sp d**

When *i* and *e* are combined to indicate the sound of *e,* the old rhyme reminds us

Put *i* before *e*
Except after *c.*

Thus we spell *relieve,* but *receive.* There are several exceptions, the most common of which can be kept in mind by remembering the following sentence: At his *leisure* the *sheik* will *inveigle* and *seize* the *weird* words *either* and *neither.* The standard spelling is *ei* when the symbol represents the sound of *a,* as in *weigh, neighbor.* In a few words having other sounds, *e* occasionally precedes *i,* as in *height, foreign, sovereign.*

42e Plurals with y   Sp e

A final *y* regularly changes to *i* before an ending beginning with a vowel (*ally, allies; cry, cries; lucky, luckier*). There are many exceptions, mostly for obvious reasons. If *y* is preceded by a vowel, it usually is not changed (*monkey, monkeys; destroy, destroyer*). If the ending begins with *i,* the preceding *y* is not changed (*fly, flying, flies; fry, frying*). For proper names ending in *y,* see 42c.

42f Double consonants, double vowels, final silent e   Sp f

In general, (1) consonants are doubled only after short vowels; (2) silent *e, o, a, i,* or *y* marks a preceding long vowel. This statement grows out of medieval practice, which was very irregular, and it cannot be used in determining all spellings, but it has sufficient application to help the memory. The first part of the rule is complicated by the fact that some consonants are never doubled (*q, v, j, h, w, x*); others are seldom doubled except before an ending (*b, d, g, m, n, r, t*). Some consonants are usually doubled but not always (*f, l, s, c*—double *c* being spelled *ck*). Thus, we spell *cuff, hill, spell, hack, hiss,* BUT, *bed, dog, man, cur, get.* The second part of the rule is complicated by the various means of indicating a long vowel (*hoed, hose, speak, cede, read, day, maid*), and by the fact that these same indications of a long vowel sometimes stand for a short vowel (*head, dead*). As usual, there are many exceptions (*add, axe*).

A final consonant in an accented syllable having a short vowel is regularly doubled before an ending beginning with a vowel (*forgot, forgotten; omit, omitting; hug, hugged; slur, slurred*); in unaccented syllables the consonant is not doubled (*counsel, counseled; benefit, benefited*). Alternate forms are often admissible but are discouraged in American spelling; *travelled, traveller,* and a number of other doublings are common in British spelling. American practice avoids unnecessary doubling. If the vowel in the syllable is long, a following

524]

consonant is not doubled (*ride, riding; eat, eaten; steal, stealing; hate, hated*).

Final silent *e* is usually retained before an ending which begins with a consonant (*bore, boredom; love, lovely*); and dropped before n ending beginning with a vowel (*hate, hating; cure, curable*). There re exceptións, usually for good reasons. If the final *e* is preceded by a vowel, it is usually dropped regardless, to avoid an awkward sequence of letters (*true, truly; argue, argument*). It is often dropped if it might lead to mispronunciation when retained (*whole, wholly*). If the final *e* is used to indicate that a preceding *c* or *g* has the soft sound, that is, if it occurs before *a, o,* or *u,* it is retained (*notice, noticeable; courage, courageous*). There are also exceptions to the exceptions. *Judgment* is preferred in the United States to *judgement;* the *d* is sufficient indication that the *g* is soft.

EXERCISE 42

A. In the following paragraph, identify the specified forms to fill the numbered blanks:

(1) _____ have long been intrigued by their (2) _____ peculiar habits. A (3) _____ year allows him some (4) _____ leisure, when he is likely to wonder what a (5) _____ mind is like, and spend long (6) _____ reading (7) _____ description of the social organization of the (8)_____ and (9) _____ *Entymology,* available in (10) _____ translation. Maeterlinck, alone, provides a long (11) _____ reading, or for that matter, several (12) _____ reading, and raises curious questions. Why, for instance, with (13) _____ reputation for industry, does a bee spend time on a sunny afternoon in what is called "play," when this time is (14) _____ for the using? The beekeeper was likely to answer, "Why, indeed?

(1) plural of *beekeeper,* (2) possessive plural of *bee,* (3) possessive singular of *beekeeper,* (4) form of *month* indicating extent, (5) possessive singular of *bee,* (6) plural of *evening,* (7) possessive singular of *Maeterlinck,* (8) plural form of *bee* in the possessive with *of,* (9) possessive singular of *Fabre,* (10) possessive singular of *Mattos,* (11) singular form of *evening* indicating extent, (12) plural form of evening indicating extent, (13)

[525

(15) _____ strange (16) _____ and (17) _____ no accounting for (18) _____ doing." But the (19) _____ work differently. (20) _____ method requires the collection and study of (21) _____; that is, in the case of the (22) _____, studying them when they were supposed to be at play. On any warm afternoon they can be observed before the hive in a sort of dance in the air, making figures like (23) _____ and (23) _____. The beekeeper had assumed a few bees had become tired of industry, and danced around a little to feel better, but the (24) _____ (25) _____ showed that these (26) _____ were returning workers, laden with honey, who with a series of (27) _____ were informing their fellow workers where they got the honey. In short, the supposed "play" is the (28) _____ way of giving directions, what might be called The (29) _____ Daily Market News.

possessive singular of *it*, (14) appropriate possessive singular of *it*, (15) contraction of *they are*, (16) plural of *creature*, (17) contraction of *there is*, (18) possessive of *they*, (19) plural of *scientist*, (20) possessive singular of *scientist*, (21) plural of *datum*, (22) plural form of *bee* for the possessive with *of*, (23) plural of *s* and *z*, (24) possessive plural of *scientist*, (25) plural of *record*, (26) plural of *bee*, (27) plural of *signal* used with *of*, (28) possessive singular of *bee*, (29) possessive plural of *honey-bee*, form suitable for a title.

B. In the passage below italicized words include several compounds. Which should be (1) combined into a single word, (2) hyphenated, or (3) left as they are? For each, decide whether the current form can be determined by rule or must be sought in a dictionary.

After the second *World War,* a German *displaced person* whom we shall call Hans found himself in a *base hospital* and also in a *semi rigid plaster cast*. He was *thirty one* years old, *brim full* of energy, was *naturally curious,* and had a *North German* horror of waste. He contemplated his cast with a *sadly jaundiced eye*. It was a *hand made* cast, intended to restrict his *inter costal* muscles, and it was *nicely calculated* to hold the *spinal column* while at the same time there was space enough to allow *abdomino thoracic* movement. In fact, by contracting his stomach muscles, Hans could enjoy a *side glimpse* of his own navel. There was enough space, he decided, to allow him to insert a *hen's egg*. He ordered a raw egg for his *mid morning* lunch, and proceeded to transform his cast into the equivalent of a *setting hen*, an *incubator cast*, if you will. That is, he tucked the egg under his cast, and it fitted nicely into his navel so long as he kept his *stomach muscles* contracted. But he was not a *mother hen* by nature. After *one day's* care, he relaxed and smashed the egg. He had the persistence of a *German born* scientist, however; he *back ordered* the egg, and was heard to remark, "I'll *mother hen* one of those things if I have to stay here until I've grown a *hen's nest* in my beard." Three weeks later he *hatched out* a little, downy, *baby chick*. He might, of course, have become a *duck incubator,* too, or started a *turkey flock,* even a whole barn yard, but he remembered that *turkey eggs* require a *five or six week* period, and he did not have room on his bed for a *duck pond*.

C. The most careful study of spelling yet attempted is that of Dean Thomas Clark Pollock of New York University, who has reported some of his findings in *College English,* XVI (1954), 102-109. The following words and word groups occur on his list of the hundred most frequently misspelled words in college, in high school, and in junior high school. They would seem to be the true "spelling demons." Everyone should know them infallibly.

acquaint	government	recommend
all right	grammar	separate
beginning	immediately	similar
believe	interest	studying
benefit, benefited	it's, its	surprise ·
business	lose, losing	their, there, they're
decision	necessary	to, too, two
definite	occasion	tries
describe	occur, occurred	weather, whether
experience	realize	writing
	receive	

Dean Pollock's most extensive summary to date concerns college misspelling, for which he used nearly 600 reports from college teachers, listing 31,375 misspellings, which included 4,482 different misspellings. Two salient facts emerge from this study: most words are misspelled very seldom, and most of the misspellings occur with relatively few words. More than a third of all the words were misspelled only once, but the 27 words misspelled more than 100 times each accounted for 5,097 misspellings; that is, less than 1 per cent of the words were involved in more than 16 per cent of the errors. Similarly, the 417 words misspelled more than 20 times accounted for more than half the misspellings. The moral of all this is that most young people who have trouble with spelling have their trouble with relatively few words, and learning to spell correctly may be easier than they think.

Following are the 417 word groups which account for twenty or more misspellings on Dean Pollock's list, printed in the order of the frequency with which the words were misspelled. They warrant careful study.

their	its	psychology	realize
they're	it's	psychoanalysis	really
there	privilege	psychopathic	led
two	environment	psychosomatic	loneliness
too	personal	analyze	lonely
to	personnel	analysis	prefer
receive	than	equipped	preferred
receiving	then	equipment	surprise
exist	principle	affect	explanation
existence	principal	affective	fascinate
existent	choose	rhythm	immediate
occur	chose	tries	immediately
occurred	choice	tried	interpretation
occurring	perform	weather	interpret
occurrence	performance	whether	thorough
definite	similar	forty	useful
definitely	professor	fourth	useless
define	profession	criticism	using
separate	necessary	criticize	noticeable
separation	unnecessary	apparent	noticing
believe	began	sense	probably
belief	begin	conscious	imagine
occasion	beginner	studying	imaginary
lose	beginning	varies	imagination
losing	control	various	marriage
write	controlled	category	prejudice
writing	controlling	embarrass	disastrous
writer	argument	excellent	passed
description	arguing	excellence	past
describe	proceed	grammar	acquire
benefit	procedure	grammatically	busy
benefited	achieve	repetition	business
beneficial	achievement	consistent	Negro
precede	controversy	consistency	Negroes
referring	controversial	prevalent	among
success	all right	intelligence	height
succeed	possess	intelligent	interest
succession	possession		

origin
original
conscience
conscientious
accommodate
comparative
decision
decided
experience
prominent
pursue
shining
practical
woman
acquaint
acquaintance
exaggerate
incident
incidentally
effect
government
governor
prepare
recommend
appear
appearance
convenience
convenient
mere
opinion
possible
ridicule
ridiculous
summary
summed
attended
attendant
attendance
coming
difference
different

hero
heroine
heroic
heroes
opportunity
paid
quiet
villain
accept
acceptance
acceptable
accepting
dominant
predominant
foreign
foreigners
independent
independence
particular
technique
transferred
discipline
disciple
humor
humorist
humorous
quantity
accident
accidentally
character
characteristic
characterized
hypocrisy
hypocrite
operate
planned
pleasant
athlete
athletic
challenge
fundamental
fundamentally

liveliest
livelihood
liveliness
lives
philosophy
speech
sponsor
unusual
usually
across
aggressive
article
disappoint
suppose
curiosity
curious
desirability
desire
knowledge
ninety
undoubtedly
optimism
permanent
relieve
religion
together
you're
familiar
suppress
where
whose
author
authority
authoritative
basis
basically
before
conceive
conceivable
consider
considerably

continuous
dependent
extremely
finally
satire
careless
careful
condemn
maintenance
parallel
permit
weird
efficient
efficiency
friendliness
friend
fulfill
piece
temperament
carrying
carried
carries
carrier
happiness
response
further
laboratory
oppose
opponent
propaganda
propagate
therefore
hindrance
approach
approaches
physical
advice
advise
entertain
influential
influence

[529

significance
exercise
involve
leisure
leisurely
sergeant
subtle
Britain
Britannica
completely
dealt
divide
excitable
favorite
interrupt
perceive
persistent
reminisce
suspense
amount
approximate
curriculum
disease
especially
fallacy
financier
financially
meant
politician
political
relative
scene
sophomore
guarantee
guaranteed
huge
indispensable
laid
length
lengthening

mathematics
remember
seize
several
substantial
tendency
whole
accompanying
accompanies
accompanied
accompaniment
hear
here
luxury
moral
morale
morally
phase
playwright
represent
schedule
source
capital
capitalism
certain
certainly
chief
counselor
counsel
council
divine
fictitious
primitive
regard
roommate
story
stories
strength
accustom
forward
pertain

safety
satisfy
satisfied
sentence
theory
theories
tremendous
vacuum
view
accomplish
arouse
arousing
despair
guidance
guiding
ignorance
ignorant
magnificent
magnificence
narrative
obstacle
shepherd
simply
simple
straight
synonymous
themselves
them
amateur
attack
attitude
boundary
clothes
expense
fantasy
fantasies
intellect
irrelevant
laborer
laboriously
labor

later
license
medieval
naturally
noble
peace
sacrifice
strict
symbol
actually
actuality
actual
adolescence
adolescent
against
appreciate
appreciation
experiment
field
hungry
hungrily
hunger
interfere
interference
likeness
likely
likelihood
magazine
maneuver
mechanics
medicine
medical
miniature
mischief
omit
persuade
those
thought
tragedy
yield

IX. The Research or Investigative Paper

Nothing's so hard but search will find it out.
—ROBERT HERRICK

What is the evidence? What does this evidence mean?

Our civilization is distinguished from others perhaps most sharply in this, that we have asked these questions more persistently than has any other group of people, and we have found generally more reliable answers. What degree of radioactive fallout is harmful, and how harmful is it? What sort of turbine engine is best adapted to automobiles? Which is the most advantageous site for a supermarket in Middletown? We tend to answer such questions by investigation, which provides evidence. This evidence becomes the basis for an interpretive report, founded on facts but leading to conclusions. More and more the world is requiring, and obtaining, such reports.

Practice in research, then, is not idle academic exercise. Research is the basis of most serious intellectual activity in commerce, in engineering, in science, in government. The lawyer preparing a case works through previous cases, using indexes and summaries, and applies the information he collects to his particular problems. The sales manager proposing a new campaign to his directors investigates the past records of his own company, the policies of other companies, and general economic and psychological conditions, and finds information which will help him plan his own project and predict its results. The techniques vary, of course, with the materials, but the essential process behind much of the world's activity is research—acquiring knowledge about a subject and applying it to new circumstances from the point of view of a new thinker. The student working on an investigative paper, whether he is getting a few facts for a short theme or preparing a thorough study of a limited subject, is learning a fundamental technique.

The investigative method is peculiarly the business of the sort of people who go to college, but it is also peculiarly important for life and success in college. Most of what a college teaches has been learned by investigation, and most of the skills a student learns— ability to handle language or figures or laboratory equipment—and most of the information he absorbs are designed in the end to equip him to find out more, and to report what he finds. The student in college is concerned to get practice in finding out about the world, about its past, its present, and its future, and with understanding of how to use evidence when he has it.

The longer investigative paper described in the following pages is, of course, only a more extensive project in research than many papers the student has already written. But the longer paper has certain advantages as practice in student writing. Much bad writing is bad because the writer has nothing to say; for the investigative paper the writer has only to study his subject enough and he will inevitably have something to say. More writing is bad because the writer does not provide objective details; again, in an investigative paper, industry and proper methods will produce details. Even the most elementary investigation requires some space if it is to be well reported, and thus the writer is forced to face the problems of organizing considerable bodies of material. To write the paper, the student must learn how to use a library, how to gather and assort evidence. Furthermore, since the investigative paper is an objective report, it teaches the kind of writing a highly civilized world increasingly requires in science, in business, in government, in the professions, in serious journalism, and in all complicated aspects of modern life, where more and more we require extensive, careful, reliable, objective reports.

43. PRELIMINARY INVESTIGATION

[For Guide to Revision, see page 547]

Careful, orderly, systematic investigation saves time and promotes accuracy in any research project.

Individual writers develop different systems of conducting their research, but some system is essential. The writer who takes notes on the back of matchbooks and old envelopes cannot keep enough material in order to finish an accurate paper. The procedures discussed here are standard and will give the writer methods for systematic work.

43-1 Choosing a subject

Choosing a subject for investigation presents the same problems involved in choosing any subject (see 1). Most beginners have no understanding of the great body of material available on almost all subjects. Thus, they are prone to choose a subject far too large. This subject can eventually be narrowed; but if it must be narrowed many times, the writer will find that he has done work which later proves unnecessary, or he starts to write and finds that he has to write such a long introduction that he never gets to the problem. *Physics* is obviously too broad; no human being, and certainly no beginner, could learn all that is to be known about physics. *Atomic Energy* is also too broad. *The Most Recent Atomic Energy Plant* may also be too broad, but this title suggests the sort of restriction which should be characteristic of all investigative subjects. Analysis is especially useful in reducing research topics. Ideally, for a research paper, the writer should have read everything that has ever been written on his subject, and have new material of his own. In an investigative paper for a college undergraduate course this ideal can seldom be realized, but the subject should be so restricted that the writer can read everything readily available to him and yet not be buried under material.

An investigative paper should be objective; that is, the writer should begin with an impartial attitude and try to find out the truth, which he will then endeavor to report. *Why I Am a Republican* is not a fit subject for an investigative paper. An interesting paper could be written on this subject, but not an investigative paper, since the subject cannot be investigated objectively. *Why I Am Against Fraternities and Sororities* is likewise unsuitable; the writer is starting with his mind made up. He is not prepared to make an objective investigation of the worth or the dangers of campus Greek-letter organizations. *Braking Power Required to Control the Streamliner "James Whitcomb Riley," The Early History of Bentonville, The Automobile Strikes of 1955* are fit subjects, at least in that they can be objectively investigated.

The subject should be one which the writer has some prospect of handling. Obviously, the subjects concerning atomic fission above are not suitable for anyone who lacks extensive technical knowledge of this subject. Even if the writer is expert in atomic fission, he may find that the most important information has been withheld for security reasons. *The Writings of Mariano Azuela* is not a good topic for anyone who does not know Spanish, because much of the pertinent material appears only in Spanish. *Early Newspapers in Southern Ohio* would require a library possessing extensive files of early newspapers in the area, and since these files would be rare and valuable, they probably would not be made available for a class exercise.

In spite of these limitations, there are innumerable subjects which can lead a writer into fascinating investigations.

43-2 Types of research material

Research material falls within several categories. Some research rests upon experiments. The research worker inserts cultures into hen's eggs under controlled circumstances, observes, records, and reports the results. Usually evidence of this sort requires more time and background than the beginning writer can afford. Some material can be gathered from living people, that is, from oral sources. Old Mary Judson, the first white child born in Crystal Springs Valley, may be an important source for the early history of that valley, but writers should avoid oral sources when written sources are available. Usually written sources are more reliable than oral sources—even

534]

though Mary Judson thinks the local school was built in 1871, if the *Mineral County Herald* for August 6, 1872, has a squib, "We hear that the Crystal Springs Valley folks just had a roof raising to get the school built in time for use this autumn," Mary is probably wrong. Your economics professor is probably right when he says, "Thorstein Veblen, although he sometimes shocked the neighbors, was one of America's most original social and economic thinkers," but the writer will usually do well to quote a written rather than an oral source.

The great body of material available for investigation and research is printed and is best available in large libraries. There is no substitute for a personal library, but very few persons can afford, in time, space, or money, to accumulate sufficient printed materials for extensive research. Most investigators rely mainly upon public and semipublic libraries for research, just as they rely upon public roads and common carriers for travel. Thus the problem of finding material usually resolves itself into the problem of using the research tools in a library.

Printed material is classified according to the manner of its publication. For purposes of arrangement, printed material is divided into books, periodicals, and pamphlets and bulletins. The investigator should satisfy himself as to which of these media will contain the material he wants, and use the appropriate tools to locate all the material of each sort which may be pertinent to his study.

43-3 Finding appropriate books

Most important material is eventually published in book form and is most readily available in that form The best tool for locating books is usually the card catalogue in the library, which for most libraries lists all available books (but *not* the articles in periodicals nor the pamphlets). Books in the library will be entered alphabetically by the last name of the author if the author is known, by the first letter (except *a, an,* or *the*) of the title, and by the subject of the book. For instance, Eric Partridge's *The World of Words* will be catalogued under *Partridge, Eric,* as author; under *World of Words, The,* as title; and under *Language and languages, English language—History, Americanisms,* and other divisions of learning as subject. If there is more than one author, a book will be entered once for each author; sometimes a book will be entered for an editor; usually a book will be entered for more than one subject, since most books discuss more than one. In fact, most books have so many subjects that only the most important can appear in the catalogue. The subject cards in a library catalogue are very helpful, but they can never be exhaustive, and the investigator must expect to use a card catalogue as a useful means of getting started, not as the final list of his appropriate books. The research worker should always look up several synonyms of his subject. For instance, if he is working on *words,* he should also try *language, speech, vocabulary, diction, etymology, usage* and the like.

43-4 Classification of books; card catalogues

So that they can be easily located, books in libraries must be arranged according to some system. Many American libraries use the Dewey Decimal System or a variation upon it. Large libraries often use the Library of Congress numbering system or a system adapted to their peculiar needs. The numbering and the classifications vary, but the theories of the systems are similar.

By the Dewey Decimal System, for example, all books are divided into ten groups (except fiction and biography, which are classified under *F* and *B* respectively), the first group being general books and the nine others books in nine general areas of knowledge which supposedly include all subjects. Each of these groups is in turn divided into ten, and this subdivision again into ten. Thus the top row of the number for Partridge's book would be 410. The number means that this book falls within the broad subject of language, 400 in the Dewey system; 1 as the second digit indicates the English language, and 0 as the third digit indicates that the book is general. The second row of the call number identifies the individual book, with a capital letter for the author's name, numbers to identify the book within the latter group, and the initial of the first important word of the title (*P259w*). A third line of the call number may add the date of first publication. Thus the call number of Partridge's book would be: 410
                                                    P259w
                                                    1944
This call number is put on the spine of the book itself and recorded on the book's catalogue cards; every book in the library can be identified and located by a call number.

Library cards provide a variety of information about the book and its author. A typical author card looks like the following:

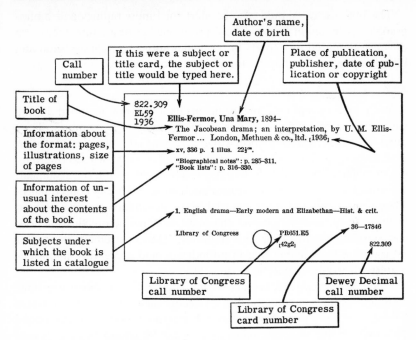

Author's name, date of birth

Call number

If this were a subject or title card, the subject or title would be typed here.

Place of publication, publisher, date of publication or copyright

Title of book

Information about the format: pages, illustrations, size of pages

Information of unusual interest about the contents of the book

Subjects under which the book is listed in catalogue

822.309
EL59
1936

Ellis-Fermor, Una Mary, 1894–
The Jacobean drama; an interpretation, by U. M. Ellis-Fermor ... London, Methuen & co., ltd. ₁1936₎

xv, 336 p. 1 illus. 22½ᵐ.

"Biographical notes": p. 285–311.
"Book lists": p. 316–330.

1. English drama—Early modern and Elizabethan—Hist. & crit.

Library of Congress   PR651.E5   36—17846
                                        ₁42g2₎   822.309

Library of Congress call number

Dewey Decimal call number

Library of Congress card number

43-5 Printed catalogues and bibliographies

If books are not available in the local library, they may be obtained from other libraries, borrowed by interlibrary loan, or if they are important and in print, purchased. For these purposes, printed catalogues of the great libraries and printed bibliographies are indispensable. Three are eminently the most useful for general work. The catalogue of the Library of Congress is available in some libraries on cards and has also been printed with supplements which bring the whole up to more than two hundred volumes. The catalogue of the British Museum has also been issued in supplements, though not yet brought down to date; it is excellent for older books, for British and Continental books, and for rare books. The *Cumulative Book Index* lists current books in English; in annual and cumulative five-year volumes it is known as the *U. S. Catalog of Books in Print*. Other bibliographies can be found through *Bibliographic Index: A Cumulative Bibliography of Bibliographies, 1938-* (New York, 1939-). Some libraries have a union card catalogue made up of cards for books in many libraries.

[537

The investigator should also be alert for bibliographies and bibliographic footnotes in books. These are often the best sources because
they are prepared by experts in particular subjects. A good beginning
bibliography can usually be found in a good encyclopedia.

43-6 Periodical indexes

With rare exceptions, magazine articles are not included in the
card catalogues of libraries nor in the general bibliographies. They
must be located through special indexes. Magazine articles are often
extremely important, more important than the writer who knows only
popular magazines is likely to expect. There are scholarly, technical,
scientific, and professional journals in all subjects of any consequence.
They print highly technical material, some of which is never reprinted
in book form, and they report the latest findings before this material
can possibly be incorporated in books. Thus, extremely important
information is available first in periodicals, and some very important
material is available only in periodicals.

Good periodical indexes are "cumulated"; that is, they are constantly re-edited and republished in accordance with a system which
keeps them up to date. For instance, the *Reader's Guide to Periodical
Literature,* which indexes relatively popular magazines, appears every
month. In February of any year, the library will receive a small number which indexes the January issues of magazines, and in March a
number which indexes the February issues. In April, however, a larger
number will arrive, in which all the issues of January, February, and
March have been re-edited into one list. Thereafter one-month numbers will continue, but in August there will be an issue for six months.
The following January there will be a number which cumulates the
entire preceding year. Similarly, there will be two-year, three-year,
and five-year cumulations, by which time the book has become so
large that the cumulation begins all over again. In this way, the index
can be kept constantly up to date, but the user does not have to
thumb through the numbers for each month. The investigator should
be sure, however, that he uses all the copies of the index to cover the
time in which he is interested. He should be sure, also, that the periodicals he needs are indexed in the periodical index he is using; there
will be a list somewhere, usually in the front of any volume. Most
periodical indexes use a highly skeletonized style; the user should
consult the list of abbreviations.

538]

The *Reader's Guide* indexes popular but relatively serious American periodicals. All libraries of any consequence have it. The *International Index* indexes more serious and technical American journals and the most important foreign journals. In addition to these two general indexes, there are specialized indexes for most fields of study. The research investigator should find out what specialized periodical indexes are available and use them. Most of them are arranged by subject; some also by author and title. The following are among the most useful:

Agricultural Index, 1916–. Annual volumes by subject, author, and title; monthly supplements only by title; includes, also, books and the very extensive body of pamphlets issued for agriculture by governmental and academic research groups. Very important.

Art Index, 1929–. Articles on the fine arts; listings by author and subject.

Book Review Digest, 1905–. Brief excerpts from important book reviews and references to others; treats general books. To use, look in the volume issued the year the book was first published or the year following.

Education Index, 1929–. Books and articles on education and related subjects, especially educational psychology; author and subject index.

Industrial Arts Index, 1913–. Lists books, articles, and pamphlets on a wide variety of subjects associated with industry, including technical subjects like geology and professional fields like engineering. Very important and useful for a wider field than its title may at first suggest.

London Times and *New York Times* Indexes. The indexes for these two newspapers have been made on different bases and are generally harder to use than the periodical indexes, but they open up mines of material not otherwise available. They can be used also as rough indexes to files of local papers, since all newspapers publish news on important events at about the same time.

43-7 Indexes to pamphlets

On many subjects material is not published in pamphlet form, but in some fields pamphlets are extremely important. Most government reports, for instance, come out as pamphlets or documents. Most of these are indexed in a series of volumes popularly known as the

United States Document Catalogue; the exact title has varied, and the details of publication are somewhat complicated. For a reliable description, see Constance M. Winchell, *Guide to Reference Books,* 7th ed. (Chicago, 1951), nos. F14-16. Some periodical indexes include pamphlets, among them the *Agricultural Index* and the *Industrial Arts Index* listed above. Some libraries make pamphlet collections, especially on local subjects.

43-8 Reference books

Some books are so useful for ready reference that most libraries keep them on special reference shelves or at a reference desk. The most important works in all fields, including reference works, can be located through Miss Winchell's *Guide to Reference Books,* cited in 43-7. Some reference works are so useful that everyone should know them without reference to Winchell.

Dictionaries. For the most important dictionaries of English, see 34-1.

Encyclopedias and specialized dictionaries. Encyclopedias and specialized dictionaries are good to start with but not to finish with. The writer who says, "Oh, yes, I found out all about it in the encyclopedia," knows very little about encyclopedias and still less about the wealth of information in the world. To make the situation worse, he has probably used an elementary encyclopedia like the *World Book.* Encyclopedic works should be used mainly to acquire a reliable introduction, for brief bibliographies, and to verify routine details. They should not be used as crutches to avoid serious investigation.

The best general encyclopedia in English is the *Encyclopaedia Britannica;* the work is continuously revised, but there is much material in the old thirteenth edition which was not retained in subsequent editions, and consequently most libraries keep both a recent edition and the thirteenth available. The *Encyclopedia Americana* and the *New International Encyclopedia* should also be consulted. For a one-volume work, *The Columbia Encyclopedia* is remarkably informative. There are excellent general encyclopedias in many languages, especially in Italian, German, French, and Spanish.

There are encyclopedic works, more or less useful, for most important fields; they can be located through Winchell or the subject cards in the library catalogue. Some are so broad in their subject matter that they approach general encyclopedias; these include the *Catholic*

Encyclopedia, The Jewish Encyclopedia, Hastings's *Encyclopedia of Religion, New Schaff-Herzog Encyclopedia of Religious Knowledge,* and *Encyclopedia of the Social Sciences.* For more specialized subjects, works like *Grove's Dictionary of Music and Musicians,* the *Oxford History of Music, Mythology of All Races,* and *Harper's Dictionary of Classical Literature* can save time and trouble.

Biographical dictionaries. Dictionaries of biography are generally of two sorts, those that include relatively long, serious considerations of very important people, and those that give brief biographical summaries of important living people; the latter are usually published periodically and are thus roughly up to date. In English the two most important of the first sort are the *Dictionary of National Biography* (called the *DNB*), which treats important British figures, and the *Dictionary of American Biography (DAB).* General works of the second sort in English are *Who's Who,* international but with a strong preference for British citizens, and *Who's Who in America.* Many other countries have similar works, and there are many more specialized dictionaries of biography: *Congressional Directory, Living Authors, Current Biography, Who's Who in the West, Directory of American Scholars, American Men of Science,* and others. Summary works include *Webster's Biographical Dictionary* and Volume IX of the *Century Dictionary.*

Handbooks and yearbooks. Some works bring within ready compass miscellaneous information, current statistics, cumulative statistics, and the like. Every writer should have on his desk, for instance, some such compilation as the *World Almanac* or the *Statesman's Yearbook.* The most extensive body of general statistical information readily available in English is to be found in the *Statistical Abstract of the United States.* There are annual supplements, surveys of the year, for the *Encyclopaedia Britannica,* the *Encyclopedia Americana,* and the *New International Encyclopedia. Facts on File* is a weekly digest under headings like *World Affairs* and *Sport;* it is cumulated in periods extending to a year. The *Abstract of Census* gives relatively detailed population figures for the United States.

43-9 The trial bibliography

The first step in any investigation is the preparation of a trial or preliminary bibliography. This bibliography has several uses. Through it the investigator discovers what has already been learned about his subject, and accordingly, what is left for him to do. It provides him with a general view of his subject and its relationships, with the titles of the most important works on his subject, and with an orderly way of working. Since he now has a list of all the best known works, he can start with the more general and the more important.

To make a trial bibliography, the investigator should make intelligent use of available bibliographical and reference tools. First, he should look up the subject in some general works, in encyclopedias, for instance. Next, he should consult the card catalogue, using first the subject entries. If there are general works on the subject, they should be consulted in a preliminary way for bibliography. Anyone who has written on the subject should be looked up in the card catalogue as an author; for if a man writes a book on a subject, he may include information on the same subject in another book, although too little to warrant a subject card in the catalogue. Meanwhile, the investigator should be considering other sorts of publications. Is the subject of such nature that there would be magazine articles on it? If so, what index would cover magazines that might include articles on the subject? Would there be pamphlets or documents on the subject?

For instance, let us assume that a writer has realized that the system of roads in the United States is one of the great achievements of man and has decided to learn more about road building. He looks up *roads, transportation,* and *road building* in several encyclopedias. He discovers that modern methods of building roads have developed in the last two centuries, and he then looks up social histories, like Trail's *Social England,* and books on transportation. In some of these he finds extensive bibliographies and bibliographical footnotes, and he makes cards for these (see 43-10). In one of them he notes that when Josiah Wedgwood's dishes became popular all over Europe, Wedgwood built private roads, because the public roads were so bad that he had to pack his dishes on muleback, and when packs slipped off mules, that was the end of the dishes. The writer is interested and tries to find out all he can about Wedgwood and his ware. He looks him up in the *DNB* and finds biographies of him and bibliographical suggestions for further investigation. He discovers that there is an elaborate series of British local histories, called the *Victoria County Histories,* and he surmises that the county history for Wedgwood's shire will tell him something about the roads of the area and probably refer to more detailed studies which will include Wedgwood's roads. By now the writer is well on his way to locating the material for an investigative paper on the manner in which ornamental vases contributed to the revolution in road building. From now on he has only to use reference works intelligently and faithfully.

Two things the investigator should not do. He should not begin by asking the librarian, "Is there anything in the library on building roads?" There are hundreds, thousands of works in any good library on building roads, but the librarian does not have time to prepare a list of them. That is the investigator's job, not the librarian's. Furthermore, if the librarian is intelligent—and librarians usually are intelligent—he will know that anybody who asks a question like that will not do much work. He will probably smile kindly and provide the most elementary encyclopedia that is handy. Similarly, the investigator should not try to get his work done for him by writing an authority for information. He should not write the county engineer, "Please tell me all you know about building roads"; he should not write Allis-Chalmers, "Please send me all the information you have on road-building machinery."

Some circumstances warrant a request for help. The librarian is ready to help anyone having trouble in using the card catalogue or a reference book or in locating material in the library. An investigator who has read everything he can get his hands on and needs certain limited information which somebody can supply and which is not available in print will probably find that a courteous letter receives a considerate answer. But most of what an investigator wants to know is in published form. The writer's job is to find it.

43-10 Bibliography cards

As fast as the investigator locates titles which may be pertinent to his subject, he should prepare his bibliography. The way not to do this is to scrawl something in a notebook, where it will probably be lost among other jottings; if it is ever resurrected, it will probably be incomplete and full of errors. Most competent investigators use a system something like the following:

They provide themselves with small cards or slips of paper of uniform size; three-by-five-inch cards are customary. They use one card and only one for each book, article, or pamphlet. On it they write the name of the author first, exactly as it appears on the title page except that the last name is put first. They write the title of the work accurately, underlining the title of a book or magazine, putting the title of an article in quotation marks. They record the bibliographical information in accordance with a style like that described below. They often add the library call number for the book, for their own convenience, and any brief comment they may wish for their later use. A bibliography card for a book looks like this:

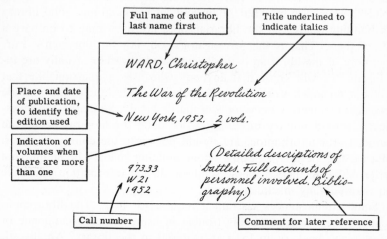

Some bibliographies include other information. The publisher may be added, but this is customary only for books recently published. The place and date of publication, however, are necessary to identify the edition; many books are published again and again, and the pagination changes from edition to edition, but few books are published in the same place twice in the same year.

A bibliography card for a magazine article looks like this:

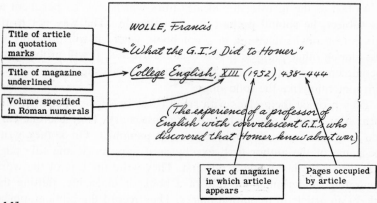

The month of issue and the number of the magazine are sometimes added.

A bibliography prepared on cards of this sort can be expanded indefinitely without becoming confused. The cards can be kept in a file drawer for ready reference. They are usually filed alphabetically by the author's last name (alphabetically by the first important word of the title if the work is anonymous).

43-11 Bibliographical form

A bibliography of the principal works consulted, including all those cited in the paper, is customarily appended to a documented composition. The entries should follow a standard form, and the form should be used in entering information on cards of the preliminary bibliography. Styles for bibliographies vary in details according to the field of investigation and the publication for which the paper is written. All publications of any consequence have a style sheet, which formalizes practice; if a writer knows he is writing for a specific publication, he should acquire the style sheet of that publication and follow it. Described here is one of the standard styles. Others vary in details, some using periods rather than commas between items or omitting the parentheses around publication data. But unless another style is specified, the following pattern should be used for bibliography cards and the final bibliography: author's last name, comma, remainder of author's name, comma, title in italics, space, parenthesis, place of publication, comma, date of publication, parenthesis, period. The entry looks like this:

> Peattie, Donald Culross, *An Almanac for Moderns* (New York, 1935).

If the book is so recent as to be in print, the publisher is often added; style is as follows:

> Rooke, Daphne, *Mittee* (Boston: Houghton Mifflin, 1952).

If the book runs to more than one volume, the number of volumes should be included in the bibliographical entry, even though only one of the volumes is cited in the paper.

> Ward, Christopher, *The War of the Revolution* (New York, 1952), 2 vols.

[545

Works by unknown authors may be entered under *Anonymous* but are usually entered under the first word (except *a, an,* or *the*) of the title:

> *Beowulf* and *The Fight at Finnsburg,* ed. Fr. Klaeber (New York, 1928).

Edited books of this sort may be entered under the name of the editor, especially if the edition is important, with the following form:

> Klaeber, Fr., ed., *Beowulf* and *The Fight at Finnsburg* (New York, 1928).

A subtitle is printed in italics but separated from the main title by a colon. The name of a series is also in italics. Information about the book may be abbreviated in the bibliographical entry, even though it is not abbreviated on the title page. Details of these sorts can be complicated, but see the following sample form.

> *Master Tyll Owlglass: His Marvellous Adventures and Rare Conceits,* ed. and tr. K. R. H. Mackenzie, *Broadway Translations* (London, n.d.).

Master Tyll Owlglass is the title; *His Marvellous Adventures and Rare Conceits* is the subtitle; *Broadway Translations* is the name of the series (if the series were numbered the entry would appear *Broadway Translations,* XXI); the abbreviations may be expanded to *edited, translated,* and *no date,* respectively. If a date of publication is inferred from the date of copyright or from some other source, the date is placed within brackets.

The basic style for a magazine article is as follows:

> Wolle, Francis, "What the G.I.'s Did to Homer," *College English,* XIII (1952), 438-44.

A few periodicals are not paged by volumes; for them the necessary information cannot be skeletonized, but it may be abbreviated:

> Marriott, Alice, "Beowulf in South Dakota," *The New Yorker,* XXVIII (1952), no. 24, pp. 42-45.

An article published in a book which is part of a series is treated as follows:

> Rippy, Pauline, "Language Trends in Oil Field Jargon," *American Dialect Society, Publications,* XV (1951), 72-80.

The bibliography is arranged alphabetically by the last name of the author, or by the first word of the entry if the author is unknown (see

546]

45-7). If there is more than one entry for an author, the name after the first entry is usually replaced by a long dash.

Bryant, Margaret M., *A Functional Grammar* (Boston, 1945).

Sapir, Edward, "Language," *Encyclopedia of the Social Sciences,* **IX** (New York, 1933), 155-69.

————, "Two Navaho Puns," *Language,* VIII (1932), 217-19.

43 *Preliminary investigation*   **Res**

GUIDE TO REVISION:

Make careful preparation for the investigative paper by refining the subject and finding appropriate and comprehensive sources of information.

The writing of any competent investigative paper requires time and patience. The investigator must expect to expend much time over a considerable period. Not infrequently, failure results from taking the assignment too lightly; the student, harried by other occupations, hopes to be able to work hard at the last minute and finish the job in a hurry. That hope usually leads to disaster. No good investigation can be conducted or reported in a hurry.

43a *Narrowing research topics*   **Res a**

Writers of relatively brief papers should always guard against topics which are too broad to permit adequate treatment, but this danger is usually acute in investigative papers, since there is more material available on most subjects than beginners expect. Usually a subject which is too broad can be restricted in time, space, application, or the like; see also 1, 43-1.

Original	*Revision*
The 1952 Campaign	Accuracy of the Polls in Forecasting the 1952 Campaign
History of Clarke County	Early History of Edmondsville
Travel in Space	Development of the Two-stage Rocket

[547

Original (*Cont.*)	*Revision* (*Cont.*)
Adolf Hitler	Recent Growth of the Hitler Legend
History of Musical Instruments	Musical Instruments that Chaucer Knew
Wonders of the West	The Geyser System of Yellowstone

43b Objective topics   Res b

For a research or investigative paper the subject should be appropriate for objective, factual investigation, and the writer should be prepared to investigate the subject impartially.

Original	*Revision*
Why I Like Hemingway	Contemporary Reviews of *The Old Man and the Sea*
Crime Never Pays	Findings of the Kefauver Committee
My Experience as an Oil Driller	Modern Methods of Submarine Drilling
The Communist Menace	How Extensive is Agrarian Reform in China?

43c Bibliography cards   Res c; Bibliog

Bibliography cards must be accurate and clear and must have information entered in the form in which it is to appear later in the bibliography of the paper (see 43-10, 43-11).

Original

Crutch, Joseph Wood
The Modern Temper: a study and
    a confession
Harcourt, Brace

[*The investigator has misspelled the author's name, forgotten to under-line the title, omitted capitals, omitted the date and place of publication, and failed to note the book's call number for future reference.*]

Revision

KRUTCH, Joseph Wood

The *Modern Temper*: a *Study* and a *Confession*

New York [*1929*]

190
K947
1929

EXERCISE 43

A. Correct the following bibliographical items for form:

1. Fong, Doreen Yen Hung. The Joy of Chinese Cooking, New York, Greenberg, publisher. It has no date, but it was new in 1951.

2. Otto Jespersen, *Language,* its nature, development, and origin, (New York, the MacMillan company, 1922, p. 85.

3. *This Was America,* edited by Oscar Handlin, True Accounts of People and Places, Manners and Customs, as Recorded by European Travellers to the Western Shore in the Eighteenth, Nineteenth, and Twentieth Centuries, Copyright 1949 by the President and Fellows of Harvard College, to Frederick Mark, Harvard University Press, Cambridge, 1949.

4. G. N. Clark, "Social and Economic Aspects of Science in the Age of Newton." Economic History 3 (1937) pp. 362-79.

5. Davidson, Martin: *The Stars and the Mind,* a study of the impact of astronomical development on human thought, (London: 1947), 210 pages long.

6. August Goll, *Criminal types in Shakespeare, Journal of Criminal Law and Criminology* 29 (1938), 492-516.

7. Ruth Leila Anderson, *Elizabethan Psychology and Shakespeare's Plays,* University of Iowa Humanistic Studies (1927) III, number 4.

8. Greenlaw, Edwin. The New Science and English Literature in the seventeenth century. Johns Hopkins Alumni Mag. XIII (1925) 331-54.

B. Below is a selection of entries from the *Reader's Guide to Periodical Literature*. Prepare appropriate bibliographical entries for each, expanding the abbreviations and making the whole entry conform to the style given in this book. If necessary, consult the list of abbreviations in a copy of the *Reader's Guide*.

> **MILLER, Henry,** 1891-
>> Coming into Poros harbor; excerpt from Colossus of Maroussi. Atlan 195:147-8 Je '55
>
> **MILLER, Hunt**
>> Pilot's choice; story. Scholastic 66:19 My 11 '55
>
> **MILLER, Lona Eaton**
>> Iris lover's own garden. Flower Grower 42:66-7+ Je '55
>
> **MILLER, Mitchell William**
>> Man who makes money records. G. Cook. il pors McCalls 82:20-2 Je '55
>
> **MILLIGAN, Robert**
>> Dog-ridden mail carrier. il pors Life 38: 127 My 23 '55
>
> **MILLIS, Walter**
>> Louisville's Braden case. Nation 180:393-8 My 7 '55
>
> **MILOSZ, Czeslaw**
>> Out of the fight for Warsaw. D. Bell. New Repub 132:41-2 My 16 '55
>
> **MILTON, Nerissa Long**
>> Know your congressman. Negro Hist Bul 18:168 Ap '55
>
> **MINIATURE electronic equipment**
>> New midgets join avionics lineup. il Aviation W 62:39 My 16 '55
>
> **MINING law**
>> Credit where credit is due. Am For 61:7 My '55
>> First step toward correcting abuses of mining laws. Am For 61:18-19+ My '55

C. Below are twenty titles of reference works and twenty questions which have answers in the books. For each question indicate which reference book would be likely to supply the answer.

1. *World Almanac*
2. *Statesman's Yearbook*
3. *Encyclopaedia Britannica*

4. *Dictionary of National Biography*
5. *Dictionary of American Biography*
6. *Catholic Encyclopedia*
7. *Statistical Abstracts*
8. *Facts on File*
9. *Hastings Encyclopaedia of Religion and Ethics*
10. *Harper's Dictionary of Classical Literature*
11. *Dictionary of Americanisms*
12. *New English Dictionary on Historical Principles*
13. Winchell, *Guide to Reference Books*
14. *American Men of Science*
15. *Bibliographic Index*
16. *Who's Who*
17. *Who's Who in America*
18. *New York Times Index*
19. *Mythology of All Races*
20. *Grove's Dictionary of Music and Musicians*

---

1. When was the sonata first popular as a type of musical composition?
2. What is the educational background of the present secretary of state of the United States?
3. What is the history of the word *mugwump*?
4. Who is currently head of the government of Venezuela?
5. Where is the original of the Magna Carta?
6. When did the term *sans-culotte* develop with a political meaning?
7. What is the title of a standard bibliography of English history?
8. When did a wrestling team from Notre Dame last compete at the University of Michigan?
9. What beliefs are associated with the god Krishna?
10. Who discovered electric welding?
11. What is the story told of the Virgin of Guadalupe?
12. Is it true that Watt became interested in steam engines while watching his mother's kettle?
13. Which college at Cambridge was attended by Sir Nicholas Bacon?
14. What were the twelve labors of Hercules?
15. Who were the Nobel Prize winners of 1955?
16. Is there a prepared bibliography on diamond cutting?
17. How does it happen that Buddhism has become common in China but has lost popularity in India?

18. What college or university did the head of your department of physics attend as an undergraduate?

19. What was the sixteenth-century meaning of the word *fond*?

20. What Greek plays deal with stories of the family of Atreus?

D. By using conventional reference aids, answer the following questions and specify where you found each answer.

1. What did Richard Lovell Edgeworth invent because of his interest in a horse race at Newmarket?

2. What is the most recent history of India in your library?

3. When the conflict between Juan Domingo Perón and the Roman Catholic Church led to fighting in the streets of Buenos Aires, which of the armed forces supported Perón?

4. Is there a concordance of Omar Khayyam? If so, when was it published?

5. To what position in the Virginia Council was William Byrd elected in 1743?

6. Locate and name two recent magazine articles on trout fishing.

7. When was the word *gig* current to refer to a rowing boat used for racing?

8. How many students attended the University of Wisconsin last year?

9. According to classical mythology, who was the great-great-grandfather of Jason?

10. What is the source of the quotation: "Great wits are sure to madness near allied"?

11. When did John Horne Tooke start sending correspondence to newspapers?

12. What was the height of the winning pole vault in the most recent Western Conference outdoor track meet?

13. What is the height of the tallest mountain peak in Europe?

14. In what city did the word *hoodlum* originate?

15. In Jewish religion, what is the length of the knife to be used in Shehitah, or the ritual slaughtering of animals?

16. What was the title of a catalog of English poets produced in 1802 by Joseph Ritson?

17. What was the maiden name of the wife of one of the senators of your state?

18. What is the most recent article published on methods of keeping bees from swarming?

19. Who are the authors of a bibliography of the writings of Washington Irving published in 1936?

20. Of what type is the government of Liberia?

44. COLLECTING MATERIAL

[For Guide to Revision, see page 558]

Take accurate, systematic notes, selecting wisely from available material.

Once a subject is chosen and the trial bibliography prepared, the interesting work begins. Most subjects are altered several times after they are started; the investigator finds that his subject is too big, or he discovers one aspect of it which is so interesting that he wishes to develop it, or he discovers that something he wanted to say is not so new as he thought it was, and he drops that part. The investigator should be alert for changes of this sort, but the principal occupation is now finding material, selecting it, recording it.

First, the investigator should have clearly in mind what he is doing. He is discovering things in order to report them later. He needs to find material which will permit him to write an adequate, objective treatment of a significant subject. He needs to put it in such shape that he will not be harassed to death when he comes to the exacting job of writing. Usually, investigative papers which are hard to write are hard because the collecting of material has been badly done. On the other hand, if the investigator adopts an orderly method of working, carries it through, and does his work carefully and intelligently, his material is then in such good order that his writing becomes easy. The first requirement of orderly investigation is use of a note-card system.

44-1 Note cards

The wrong way to take notes is to write them down consecutively in a notebook. They soon become a jumble. They occur in whatever order they occurred in the book from which the information was taken

—usually not the order which the investigator will require. They are unidentified. They cannot be classified, particularly if the investigator writes on both sides of a sheet of note paper. As a result, the investigator knows only that he "has that somewhere" and has to spend half his time hunting for notes he cannot find.

All notes should be taken on cards or slips, the same kind of three-by-five cards for the preliminary bibliography or larger ones if the investigator prefers. The card system takes a little time to learn, but it more than pays for itself. No matter how big the job, whether an investigative paper for a class, a doctoral dissertation, or a life work of many volumes, the card system will expand without confusion.

There are a few fundamental rules for using the system:

(1) *Put only one piece of information on a card.* If a card contains only a single piece of information, it can be classified by subject with cards containing similar information, no matter from what source it comes. Thus the investigator has all his material on one aspect of his subject filed together.

(2) *Identify the source of the information on the card.* The investigator needs to know from what work his information comes so that he can identify it as he proceeds. Probably the majority of research workers use the following system: they record the author's name and an abbreviated form of the title. A reference to page 166 of the first volume of Christopher Ward's *The War of the Revolution* might be identified on the note card as Ward, *Revolution,* I, 166.

(3) *Be sure to indicate clearly on the note cards any passages taken verbatim from the source.* Apparent plagiarism results if the investigator fails to mark a direct quotation on his note card, forgets that the passage was written by somebody else, and writes it into his paper as his own work. Whenever even a two- or three-word phrase is taken directly from a source, it should be enclosed in quotation marks on the note card.

(4) *Indicate with key words the nature or use of the material taken.* When the card is complete, it should be filed according to subject matter. For this purpose, the investigator should adopt a number of words under which material can be filed; usually these words are headings of his outline.

A good note card looks something like the following:

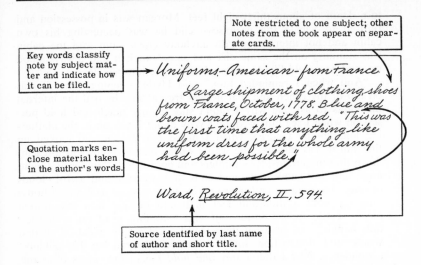

Note restricted to one subject; other notes from the book appear on separate cards.

Key words classify note by subject matter and indicate how it can be filed.

Uniforms—American—from France

Large shipment of clothing, shoes from France, October, 1778. Blue and brown coats faced with red. "This was the first time that anything like uniform dress for the whole army had been possible."

Quotation marks enclose material taken in the author's words.

Ward, Revolution, II, 594.

Source identified by last name of author and short title.

This card contains material for a paper on the importance of clothing and supplies in the Revolutionary War. Clothing and supplies, of course, are subjects of all the cards and need not be entered on any of them. One important subtopic of the subject, however, is the importance of uniforms. Thus *uniforms* becomes the first key word to identify the note. *American* subdivides the cards concerning uniforms, and *from France* further identifies this note.

44-2 Taking notes

Much of the labor of collecting material is routine; there are sound and unsound methods of working, and the investigator has only to use sound methods. But the selection of material is not routine. It requires understanding, alertness, and self-training. Consider the following passage from Mark Twain's *Roughing It.*

> He [Hyde] said it was pretty well known that for some years he had been farming (or ranching, as the more customary term is) in Washoe District, and making a successful thing of it, and furthermore it was known that his ranch was situated just in the edge of the valley, and that Tom Morgan owned a ranch immediately above it on the mountainside. And now the trouble was, that one of those hated and dreaded landslides had come and slid Morgan's ranch, fences, cabins, cattle, barns, and everything down on top of *his* ranch and exactly covered up every single vestige of his property,

to a depth of about thirty-eight feet. Morgan was in possession and refused to vacate the premises—said he was occupying his own cabin and not interfering with anybody else's—and said the cabin was standing on the same dirt and same ranch it had always stood on, and he would like to see anybody make him vacate.

"And when I reminded him," said Hyde, weeping, "that it was on top of my ranch and that he was trespassing, he had the infernal meanness to ask me why I didn't stay on my ranch and hold possession when I see him a-comin'! Why didn't I *stay* on it, the blathering lunatic—by George, when I heard that racket and looked up that hill it was just like the whole world was a-rippin' and a-tearin' down that mountainside—splinters and cord-wood, thunder and lightning, hail and snow, odds and ends of haystacks, and awful clouds of dust! Trees going end over end in the air, rocks as big as a house jumping 'bout a thousand feet high and busting into ten million pieces, cattle turned inside out and a-coming head on with their tails hanging out between their teeth!—and in the midst of all that wrack and destruction sot that cussed Morgan on his gatepost a-wondering why I didn't *stay and hold possession!* Laws bless me, I just took one glimpse, General, and lit out'n the country in three jumps exactly."

Let us assume that the investigator wishes to make use of this passage in a paper intended to reveal the peculiar qualities of Mark Twain's humor. He can, of course, copy out the whole passage as it appears here. That would take time. He might make a note like the following:

> T. makes a rancher called Hyde give very funny account of how another ranch landed on top of his. Good picture of way landslide came down mountain, using exaggeration and wild details.

A note like this is almost worthless. It is too general to be of use; Twain's humor has disappeared from it. Compare:

> T. makes rancher named Hyde tell how in a landslide "Morgan's ranch, fences, cabins, cattle, barns, and everything" slid down and "exactly covered up every single vestige of his property, to a depth of about thirty-eight feet." Morgan refused to vacate, saying cabin "was standing on the same dirt and the same ranch it had always stood on," and asked Hyde why he had left when he "see him a-comin'." What Hyde had seen was "just like the whole world was a-rippin' and a-tearin' down that mountainside," bringing with it "odds and ends of haystacks . . . trees going end over end in the air, rocks as big as a house jumping 'bout a thousand feet high and busting into ten million pieces, cattle turned inside out and a-coming head on with their tails hanging out between their teeth!" In the face of this, Hyde "lit out'n the country in three jumps exactly."

The quotation has been reduced to less than half, but the most picturesque details have been preserved. Furthermore, the material can be used without fear of plagiarism because material which has been quoted exactly has been kept within quotation marks.

Selection of the material to be recorded on note cards, then, depends first of all on the purpose of the investigator. He can select sensibly because he knows what he is looking for. A few basic rules, however, may help him to take notes adequately and efficiently.

(1) *Adopt a system and follow it scrupulously.* The investigator must doggedly resist the temptation to "just jot this one down in my notebook," or to "just remember this one until I get a chance to write it down."

(2) *Avoid taking unnecessary notes.* Hours spent collecting material not pertinent to the paper may be educational, but they do not get the job done. Some material important for a general understanding of the subject will soon become so familiar that the investigator will not need it in his notes. The sensible research worker reads generally upon a subject before starting to take notes, and skims through a book before collecting material from it.

(3) *If in doubt, take the note.* Taking just the right material, just enough material and no more, is hardly possible. The investigator will save time by taking too much rather than too little. Copying a few extra words takes a few minutes, but trying to get a book after it has been returned to the library and someone else has borrowed it may take hours.

(4) *Take concrete, specific, exact material.* Occasionally generalities are useful, but, on the whole, the more specific the notes, the more useful they will prove to be. Facts, figures, dates, statistics, verbatim quotations, or factual digests are useful. Most beginners are wont to collect too much general material, not enough concrete, objective material.

(5) *Distinguish sharply between material which you quote and material you digest; if you quote, quote exactly.* Often a beginner finds good material and starts putting it on his note cards, quoting some passages exactly. The process takes time, and the investigator starts summarizing some parts of a passage and quoting some, incorporating whole phrases and clauses into his summary without using quotation marks to distinguish them. Weeks later, when he writes his paper, he can no longer remember what he quoted and what he did

[557

not. He therefore writes down essentially what he has in his notes. He has then stolen another person's literary property and passed it off as his own. He is guilty of one of the worst sorts of dishonesty because he is stealing ideas, and ideas are more important and personal than money. Many a beginning writer is guilty of such plagiarism, not because he is so mean that he would pick a friend's pocket, but just because he was careless about using quotation marks.

Knowing when to take material verbatim and when to summarize is difficult. In general, however, the investigator may find that he wants word-for-word accounts of the following: material that has been very well phrased; material which is extremely important for the discussion; and controversial material, especially if the writer expects to examine the statement and comment upon it adversely.

(6) *Double-check every note card.* A wrong page number or an omitted title can cost hours of time and frustration in locating a quotation. And if the final paper contains misquotations, misspellings, or mispunctuation in copied material, the reader cannot be expected to have much confidence in any of the conclusions of the paper.

44 Collecting material   Mat

GUIDE TO REVISION:

> *Take careful, accurate notes and preserve them in an
> orderly way; prefer concrete and specific material.*

An accurate paper cannot be written from inaccurate notes; an interesting and informative paper cannot be written from notes consisting of dull generalities. No ingenuity in writing can save an investigative paper for which the collecting has been careless or inadequate. There is no single rule for a good note, but in practice many good note cards are good précis with key material quoted verbatim; for the précis, see 2-4.

44a Note cards   Mat a

Note cards should be legible and clear, should include an exact reference to the sources, should identify quoted material, and should be marked with key words for classification (see 44-2).

Original

```
Burkhart--

     Machines developed for mystery plays in
14th century to make figures rise and float
in the air--one of the chief delights of the
plays.  Brunellesco invented a marvelous
apparatus consisting of a heavenly globe sur-
rounded by two circles of angels, out of
which Gabriel flew down in a machine shaped
like an almond.
```

[*The note card lacks key words to classify the material; the writer has misspelled the author's name, has not identified the book from which he has taken the information, and has forgotten to note the page; he has failed to specify which portions of the note are quotation.*]

Revision

```
Staging--machinery

Machines developed for mystery plays in
14th century to make figures rise and
float in the air--"one of the chief de-
lights" of the plays.  Brunellesco invented
"a marvelous apparatus consisting of a heav-
enly globe surrounded by two circles of
angels, out of which Gabriel flew down in
a machine shaped like an almond."

Burckhardt, Renaissance, p. 249
```

[*The card contains a note for a paper on the mystery play in Renaissance Italy; it is part of an investigation of staging and therefore should have key words for classification. The revision makes needed corrections and additions, and uses quotation marks to indicate passages taken verbatim from the source.*]

Original

> Vogue of Ramism in England apparently
> associated with Sir Wm. Temple. See p. 149.
>
> From beginning of 16th C. humanists like
> Cadmon were studying the more classical
> writers. p. 253
>
> Hardin Craig, Enchanted Glass, Oxford U. P.,
> 1936, p. 149, 253.

[*The investigator apparently does not understand the method he is trying to use. He seems to confuse his note card with his bibliography cards, including data for the book. He has put two notes on one card and is therefore unable to include key words as guides for later use and classification. The card cannot be revised. The investigator needs to reconsider his method (see 44-2), determine whether his notes are valuable and what he wants each for, and then, if he wants the notes, make a new separate card for each.*]

44b Quoted material   Mat b

Check both note cards and the final draft of the paper to be sure that quoted material has been accurately copied.

Original

Kilhwch used vigorous methods to convince his unwilling prospective father-in-law. In Lady Charlotte Guest's translation, "Kaw of Brittain [Kilhwch's friend] came and shaved his [the father-in-law's] beard, skin, and flesh clean off to the very bone from ear to ear. 'Art thou shaved, man?' said Kilwch, 'I am shaved,' answered he. 'Is they daughter mine now? "She is thine, said he. . . ."

[*Lady Guest did not misspell* Kilhwch, Britain *and* thy *nor misuse punctuation marks.*]

560]

Revision

Kilhwch used vigorous methods to convince his unwilling prospective father-in-law. In Lady Charlotte Guest's translation, "Kaw of Britain [Kilhwch's friend] came and shaved his [the father-in-law's] beard, skin, and flesh clean off to the very bone from ear to ear. 'Art thou shaved, man?' said Kilhwch. 'I am shaved,' answered he. 'Is thy daughter mine now?' 'She is thine,' said he. . . ."

44c Material worth quoting   Mat c

Avoid quoting unimportant material; there is no need to make verbatim notes of information which is generally known or obvious.

Original

As the famous historian J. R. Green has written, "The city was divided into wards, each of which was governed by an alderman."
[*Green wrote the sentence, but he would not expect to have it quoted from him.*]

Revision

The city was divided into wards, with an alderman in charge of each.

According to Professor Warren in a recent lecture, the Declaration of Independence was signed July 4, 1776.

The Declaration of Independence was signed July 4, 1776.

44d Distinguishing quoted matter   Mat d

Distinguish sharply between material quoted verbatim and material summarized. If you summarize, summarize in your own words, not those of your source; if you quote his words, enclose them within quotation marks.

Original

According to Henry Adams, Jefferson was a tall, loosely built, somewhat stiff figure. He could be seen in the White House, in red waistcoat and yarn stockings, slippers down at the heel, sitting on one hip, with one shoulder high above the other, talking almost without ceasing to his visitors.
[*This passage contains much stolen matter, probably plagiarized innocently because the writer was careless about using quotation marks in his notes, but still plagiarized.*]

Revision

According to Henry Adams, Jefferson was a "tall, loosely built, somewhat stiff figure." He could be seen in the White House, "in red waistcoat and yarn stockings, slippers down at the heel . . . sitting on one hip, with one shoulder high above the other, talking almost without ceasing to his visitors. . . ."
[*The quotation marks and evidences of omission give Adams credit for his work and make the extent of the quoted matter clear to the reader.*]

That the "California toothpick" was a dangerous weapon can be

That the "California toothpick" was a dangerous weapon can be

Original (*Cont.*)	*Revision* (*Cont.*)
inferred from William Gilmore Simms's remark in 1856 that a hunter's knife was a most formidable weapon only inferior in size and weight to the modern 'California toothpick.' "	inferred from William Gilmore Simms's remark in 1856 that a hunter's knife was "a most formidable weapon only inferior in size and weight to the modern 'California toothpicks.' "
[*Carelessness with punctuation marks leaves the reader uncertain how much has been quoted.*]	[*For quotation marks within quotations, see 40a.*]

EXERCISE 44

Read carefully the following selection:

The silk craze swept the country in the late 1820's. Silk was a useful and valuable product. Silk came from cocoons of the silkworm. Silkworms lived on the mulberry leaf. The mulberry grew abundantly in the South and West. "Wherever the mulberry finds a congenial climate and soil, there, also, the silkworm will flourish. Such a climate and soil, and such a country is ours, throughout its whole extent, from its Eastern to its Western shores." [1] Therefore farmers could always be sure of one big cash crop. "How long will it be before the old fields of the middle and southern states will be converted into mulberry orchards, and the United States into an exporter instead of an importer of silk.— We answer, not twenty years!" [2] Every agricultural periodical printed dozens of articles annually on the culture and profits of silk. By 1839 there were at least five periodicals in the country devoted mainly or exclusively to silk growing,[3] besides numerous manuals on the subject. From these publications the newspapers regularly copied long extracts on silk and often added enthusiastic editorials and letters.[4] When the Ohio legislature appointed a committee to find a staple crop to enhance the state's wealth, the committee felt it could make no better recommendation than silk and sugar beets.[5] Apparently the great silk boom existed on paper rather than in reality, and the Midwest never became a serious competitor with the Orient.

—R. CARLYLE BULEY, *The Old Northwest Pioneer Period, 1815–1840,*
I, 186-87.

[1] *The American Silk Grower's Guide* (Boston, 1839), 25.

[2] *Cleveland Herald,* March 26, 1833, quoting the Baltimore *American Farmer.*

[3] *Ohio Farmer and American Horticulturist,* July 15, 1839. These were the *Journal of the American Silk Society and Rural Economist,* Baltimore; *The Southern Silk Grower,* Baltimore; the *American Silk Grower,* Philadelphia; the *Silk Culturist,* Hartford, Connecticut; and one at Keene, New Hampshire.

In 1826 silk was taken up seriously by Congress. The Secretary of the Treasury was ordered to prepare a manual on the growth and manufacture of silk, and in 1828 six thousand copies were printed. (U. S. *House Executive Documents,* 20 Congress, I session, No. 158.) In 1830 a national school was proposed by

Congress with M. D'Homergue, of France, as instructor in sericulture. The House of Representatives Committee on Agriculture issued a report on silk culture in 1830 (U. S. *House Reports,* 21 Congress, I session, No. 289), which included D'Homergue's directions. Reviewed by James Hall in *Illinois Monthly Magazine,* I (1830–31), 145-58.

⁴ For instance, the *Hamilton* (Ohio) *Advertiser,* May 4, 1827, ran a two-and-one-half-column editorial on silk culture.

⁵ *Cincinnati Daily Gazette,* February 20, 1837.

Now make the following note cards on the passage:

1. A card for a paper to be entitled "Early Agricultural Journalism in Maryland."
2. A card for a paper to be entitled "Federal Attempts to Aid the Farmer in the 1820's."
3. A card for a paper to be entitled "The Early History of Keene, New Hampshire."
4. A card for a paper to be entitled "D'Homergue in the New World."
5. A card for a paper to be entitled "Hartford as an Early Center of Culture."

Be sure to record the sort of concrete, specific material which will be useful in lively, objective composition. Be sure to get all titles and references exact. Be careful to use your quotation marks and your quotation marks within quotation marks so that you will later be in no doubt as to just what was quoted verbatim and from whom. Try your hand also at providing key words with which to file the cards.

If you were writing an article called "The Great Silk Craze," how many cards would you probably make for this single entry? What might be the key words for the different cards? Make one of the cards.

45. **WRITING THE INVESTIGATIVE PAPER**

[For Guide to Revision, see page 577]

Organize material carefully; write accurately and interestingly.

The report of any serious investigation usually requires a paper of some length and therefore presents problems of organization. This organization becomes relatively easy if the writer uses the methods recommended in 5 and has taken his material on cards as recommended in 43. He has now only to revise his outline, arrange his cards so that they follow the outline and write through the cards.

The writer must remember, however, that his paragraphs will lack unity and continuity if he follows slavishly the phrasing of his notes. If the style of the paper is to be clear and interesting, each paragraph must be thought out as a unit; the paper must be more than notes strung together without rewriting.

Furthermore, all serious expository or argumentative writing is documented; that is, the writer makes clear to his reader at all times where his information comes from and how reliable it is. Documentation can be more or less formal, but relatively formal and technical writing usually requires a bibliography and footnotes.

45-1 Footnotes

Footnotes permit the writer to let the reader know at all times what his authority is, without interrupting the flow of the prose. The reader can take the authority for granted, and read on, ignoring the footnotes; or at any moment he can find the authority; he can even obtain the source upon which the writer is relying and read more of it, or check the way in which the writer has used his source.

The ability to use footnotes deftly is one of the marks of a good research worker. In general, footnotes can be used for the following:

(1) *The source of a significant quotation.* In carefully documented writing, all direct quotations used as evidence should be identified with a footnote. Material quoted for embellishment need not be identified in a footnote. For instance, suppose a writer begins a discussion as follows:

> "In the beginning was the word"; whether or not we now accept this statement literally, words have been at the beginning of many ideas, and hence they have been at the beginnings of what grew out of the ideas.

The quotation from the New Testament does not require a footnote. Most readers would recognize it, and in any event it is only a stylistic device. If, however, the passage were used as evidence of the Greek veneration of language, it should carry a footnote.

(2) *The source of information not sufficiently familiar so that most readers would know it or be able to find it readily.* There need be no footnote for the date of Shakespeare's death or the name of the twenty-fifth president of the United States. Anyone who does not take the writer's word for such details can find them in dozens of reference works. But all major assertions in a serious discussion should be supported by footnotes.

(3) *Controversial matter and opposing views.* Any serious investigation is likely to lead the writer into fields where there are differences of opinion. Whether he takes sides or not, the writer should be sure that both sides are represented in footnote references.

(4) *Details or statistics that would interrupt the paper.* Statistics, figures, tables, or other supplementary data are sometimes placed in footnotes, where they are available for reference but do not interrupt the movement of the paper.

45-2 Style in the investigative paper

The handling of materials in any research report should be objective and relatively impartial, and the style should reflect this objectivity. If the writer has opinions to express, he should label his opinions clearly. In general, research reports are made in the third person. Best practice now allows the use of the first person to avoid excessive use of the passive voice where circumstances require some discussion of the author and what he did—for instance, in describing how equipment was set up, or why an investigation was conducted in a certain way—but a research report should be couched in generally objective terms.

One writing problem becomes acute in almost any research report, and the mastering of this difficulty gives the young writer excellent training. The reader of any difficult or controversial report wants always to know whether the author is sure that he is right, whether his evidence is sound. But writers cannot always be sure; they do not always have adequate evidence. Thus the writer should make clear what he knows certainly and why; he should also make clear what he is saying because the evidence is extremely good, although inconclusive; and he should identify any observations which are guesses, which he has made just because they are his best guesses, subject to revision. Identifications are not easy, but a skillful writer can make them, while attracting no attention to the machinery with which he keeps his reader informed. The beginning writer will do well to study competent pieces of serious writing, in magazines like *Harper's* and *The Atlantic,* for instance, and in scholarly and scientific journals.

Another problem bothers almost every beginning research worker: what should he do when the authorities disagree? They do disagree. Most important problems cannot be settled certainly and finally, and even for minor questions the evidence is often contradictory. If the writer finds no reason for preferring one of his disagreeing sources, he can present the evidence on all sides and cite all authorities in his footnotes. If he thinks one argument is better than the others, he can present it and then cite opposing evidence in a footnote. Even if he is sure that one side is right, he should cite any opposing opinions in footnotes.

45-3 Style for footnotes

The style for footnotes follows closely that for the bibliography, except: (1) that the name of the author is usually not reversed in the footnote, since no alphabetizing is involved, and (2) for books the page numbers referred to must be included, and for articles the page numbers of the citation replace the page numbers for the whole article. Form in footnotes varies slightly; if the writer knows that he is writing for a particular publication, he should obtain a style sheet and follow it. For class work, the style of this book is standard, unless other instructions are given. It is based upon styles common in good scholarly journals. Following are examples referring to several pages of a book, with mention of edition:

> Louis John Paetow, *A Guide to the Study of Medieval History*, rev. ed. (New York, 1931), pp. 139-41.

A work published in more than one volume:

> Christopher Ward, *The War of the Revolution* (New York, 1952), II, 86.

An article in a magazine:

> Francis Wolle, "What the G.I.'s Did to Homer," *College English*, XIII (1952), 441.

An anonymous article in a small newspaper:

> "Wm. Tell," *Indiana Journal* [Indianapolis], April 24, 1827, p. 2.

A signed article in a newspaper with complicated pagination:

> Brooks Atkinson, "Avon Bankside," *The New York Times*, June 19, 1955, sec. 2, pt. 1, p. 2, col. 3.

An article in a book, with a combination of forms:

> E. H. Clough, "The Bad Man from Bodie," *A Treasury of Western Folklore*, ed. B. A. Botkin (New York, 1951), pp. 60-61.

Material from source not available but quoted in secondary source:

> Thomas Sheridan, *British Education* (1756), p. xvii, cited in Albert C. Baugh, *History of the English Language* (New York, 1952), p. 322.

For common reference works known to all people who read, the usual bibliographical details may be omitted; if the work is arranged alphabetically, the alphabetical identification is sufficient, as follows:

> *Encyclopaedia Britannica*, 15th ed., under *Washington, George.*

For extremely familiar works having a highly formalized and standard means of division, a conventionalized form suffices, as follows:

> *Luke*, 9:2-4.   *Hamlet*, V, 1, 201-15.

After the first occurrence of a footnote reference to a given source, the citation may be abbreviated in a number of conventional ways, which can best be inferred from the list of abbreviations, 45-4, and from the sample paper in 45-7.

45-4 Abbreviations in footnotes

Some abbreviations and standardized forms are collected in the list below. Notice that some are abbreviations of foreign words, hence are printed in italics and should be underlined in manuscript.

p., pp.—page, pages.

l., ll.—line, lines.

v., vv.—verse, verses.

vol., vols.—volume, volumes.

no., nos.—number, numbers.

cf.—compare.

ibid.—in the same work or place; used with or without a page number to replace author, title, and publication data in a note referring to the work cited in the immediately preceding note. It is used without a page number if the reference is to the same page in the previously cited work; when the page number differs, it must be specified. Notice that *ibid.* abbreviates the Latin *ibidem* and is therefore underlined in manuscript for italics.

n.—note, footnote.

op. cit.—in the work cited; used in place of the title when a work has been cited but not in the immediately preceding note and when only one work of the author is cited in the paper. If more than one work of the author is used in the footnotes of the paper, then the *op. cit.* reference is insufficient to identify the title. Sometimes a short title for the work is used in all citations of a work after the first one, and publication data is omitted.

loc. cit.—in the place cited; used to refer to a specific passage already cited.

supra—above; preferred to *ante*.

infra—below; preferred to *post*.

c.—copyright; used when the date of a copyright is known but the date of publication is not.

c. ca.—circa, about; used in approximate dates (*ca.* 1888).

ff., *et seq.*—and following; not used in the best practice to complete a citation to pages; inclusive page reference (pp. 86-93) is preferable.

passim—at intervals through the work or pages cited.

sic—thus; may be used after an obvious error in a quotation to indicate that the error was in the original; best used sparingly; when inserted in a quotation, should be enclosed in brackets.

n.d.—no date.

ed.—editor, edited, edition.

tr.—translated by, translation.

rev.—revised.

45-5 Formal handling of footnotes

Footnotes are usually numbered consecutively through a brief paper or through a chapter of a long work. They are not now usually indicated by asterisks, daggers, and other printer's marks, because this system does not admit sufficient flexibility. Neither are footnotes now often numbered by pages; the numbers in the copy do not correspond with the numbers on the printed page, and mistakes are easy. Customarily a superior figure (made on the typewriter by turning the platen half a line) is placed in the copy directly after the word, passage, sentence, or paragraph to which the footnote refers. A similar number appears immediately before the footnote. The notes are then placed in one of three positions: (1) in the space immediately after the line containing the citation and ruled above and below; this system takes a little effort but is clearest for the reader and simple for the typist and the printer; (2) at the bottom of each page and ruled above; the system is difficult for the typist because he must estimate the space needed for notes at the bottom of each page; (3) at the end of the work or the chapter; this system is easy for the typist, a bother to the reader.

45-6 Pictures, graphs, tables

Graphs, tables, and other illustrations or tabulated inserts are imperative for many technical papers, and much complicated material is best shown in visual or tabular form. The writer should always consider whether a table or an illustration will not make his meaning clearer. Inserts of this sort should usually be labeled for ready reference in the text. Use *plate* to refer to a full page (Plate IX), *figure* for an illustration in the text (Figure 8), and *table* for a tabular or graphic arrangement (Table 3).

45-7 Sample investigative paper

The beginning of an investigative paper written by a college freshman may be used to illustrate the common problems encountered in reporting elementary research.

THE BOBBIN NET MACHINE

AND

FEMALE AMERICAN TASTE

An Investigative Paper

by

Vicky Vickrey

Theme Number 8
English 102
Section 8
Professor Morris
April 26, 19--

[The title page includes information to identify the paper.]

In the year of Our Lord, 1809, John Heathcoat, the son of an honorable British family, invented a bobbin net machine. No doubt he was proud of his device; like many another Briton of his day, he was lowering the price of dress goods, and bringing hitherto impossibly expensive articles within the reach of all sorts of people with lean

570]

The introduction leads directly into the subject and at the same time catches the reader's interest.

The first footnote serves two main pur-

purses. He probably thought of little but the commercial possibilities of his invention, and they were considerable, for he proposed making expensive lace for a few pennies a yard. By 1815, lace was being made with machines at Tiverton, Devonshire, and three years later at Medway, Massachusetts. Heathcoat may have dreamed that his invention was to become the "foundation of an enormous industry,"[1] but he probably did not

---

[1] Francis Morris, *Encyclopaedia Britannica,* 14th ed., under *lace.*

---

guess that he was to have a part, also, in a revolution in taste in women's clothes.

Until the nineteenth century all lace had been handmade, so that even when labor was cheap, lace was expensive.[2] Only the wealthy could own

---

[2] For the standard bibliography of lace making, see René Colas, *Bibliographie générale du costume et de la mode* (Paris, 1932). For briefer bibliographies more readily available, see *Encyclopaedia Britannica,* 14th ed., and *Encyclopedia Americana,* both under *lace.* Older but still useful is *A Reading and Reference List on Costume* (Brooklyn, 1909). Indispensable for locating costumes is Isabel Monroe and Dorothy E. Cook, *Costume Index: a Subject Index to Plates and to Illustrated Text* (New York, 1937).

---

it in any quantity, and wearing lace freely was a sure indication of wealth and was usually a mark of being well born. One has only to glance through histories of costume prior to 1800 to notice that, although at times it was used sparingly, lace in some quantity was usually one of the requirements of more elegant costumes.[3] But now there

---

[3] See, for example, James Robinson Planché, *Cyclopaedia of Costume: or Dictionary of Dress* (London, 1876–79), 2 vols., of which the second volume is a history of costume to 1760. For the United States, see Elizabeth McClellan, *Historic Dress in America, 1607–*

---

poses. It identifies the direct quotation. It also provides a source for most of the facts in the first paragraph.

The author does not say "according to the *Encyclopaedia.*" She was evidently aware that articles in encyclopedias are very uneven, but she noticed that this was signed F. Mo. In Volume I she found a list of contributors and learned there that the author was associate curator of the Metropolitan Museum. Accordingly, she quotes him with confidence.

Since lace is central to her paper, Miss Vickrey reveals at once the principal sources of her information. Note that even a little acquaintance with a foreign language opens important works to the investigator. The encyclopedias being well known, the customary bibliographical data are dispensed with.

Since eighteenth century costume is only background for the paper, Miss Vickrey treats it briefly, giving the reader a start but not cluttering the footnote with dozens of general works. The mention of relations of British and American costume is

1800 (Philadelphia, 1904). American styles generally followed British styles. Late in the eighteenth century there was a Georgian simplicity about much of the costumes, especially in the colonies, where lace was scarce; see figures 212-15.

---

were changes. The industrial revolution was altering the making of cloth from handicrafts into a machine industry, and leading the way to a new economic and industrial system which was to change the whole complexion of western society, and eventually, no doubt, of the world. But most women were presumably unaware of these great changes. What they knew was that suddenly the shops began to have cheap lace to sell.

The change came slowly at first. Lace was soon available in great quantities, but only narrow lace, suitable for edgings.[4] This narrow lace was

---

[4] Georgianna Hill, *A History of English Dress from the Saxon Period to the Present Day* (London, 1893), II, 319.

---

supplemented, through the ingenuity of a Munich engineer, with a very fine and relatively cheap lace, used especially for veils, called "caterpillar veils." To produce these, the engineer "having made a paste of the leaves of the plant on which the species of caterpillar he employs feeds, he spreads it thinly over a stone, or other flat substance of the required size. He then, with a camel-hair pencil dipped in olive oil, draws the pattern he wishes the insects to leave open."[5] The stone

---

[5] Charles Babbage, *On the Economy of Machinery and Manufacture,* cited in Hill, *op. cit.,* II, 319-20.

---

is then placed in a slanting position, and caterpillars are scattered along the bottom. Crawling up, they eat away all the paste except the part touched by the oil, leaving the pattern in gossamer. But even with the co-operation of caterpillars, large pieces of lace remained for a time "a costly luxury." The high prices of lace are presumably reflected in the styles of the time; fashion plates of the day show women loaded with flowing and bulging fabrics—the mills of Leeds, Nottingham, and Huddersfield were turning out

572]

pertinent, but not very pertinent. In a footnote, it does not interrupt the progress of the paper.

Miss Vickrey includes no footnote on the industrial revolution. Matters of common knowledge introduced for background should not be the occasion for cluttering the paper with needless footnotes.

This is a standard footnote, documenting information. Note the form for a book of more than one volume.

All quotations significant for the discussion should be documented. Footnote 5 may serve as an example of the treatment for material taken from a source not available to the writer, but quoted in a secondary work. If the passage had not been quoted verbatim, Miss Vickrey could have quoted Hill, and added something like, "Cited from Charles Babbage, *On the Economy of Machinery and Manufacture.*" Miss Vickrey cannot supply the usual bibliographical material and page references because they are not in Hill. If she had been able to get Babbage's book, she could

cloth by the ton—but the dresses mostly have relatively narrow edgings or no lace at all. Skirts ballooned so that women wore as many as eight petticoats to hold them out, and one woman is said to have worn thirteen.[6] Full skirts, however,

---

[6] Frank Alvah Parsons, *The Psychology of Dress* (Garden City, N. Y., 1920), p. 289.

---

did not prevent bare shoulders, as an anecdote from the *Gossip of Paris* illustrates.

It is not so very long since the Archbishop of Paris, having the private *entrée* given by an illustrious personage, entered by a door behind a crowd of ladies. In their efforts to make way for him, one said in an apologetic tone, "Your Grace must excuse us; really our dressmakers put so much material in our skirts—"

"That none remains for the corsage," interrupted the Bishop.[7]

---

[7] Anthony B. North, *Gossip from Paris* (New York, 1903), p. 35.

But not for long did the lace mills encourage restraint. There were improvements upon John Heathcoat's basic design, and soon the mills were producing lace in all sizes and in many patterns at very modest prices.[8] Now milady could revel in

---

[8] For a general sketch of the relations of fashion to cloth production throughout most of the century, see Millia Davenport, *The Book of the Costume* (New York, n.d. [1948]), 2 vols.

---

lace if she wished, and throwing off any lingering Georgian classic restraint, she did so. By the middle of the century, lace was common even in remote portions of the world like the United States. A relatively serious magazine like the newly founded *Harper's* took account of the influx of lace, initiating their first spring of publication as follows:

There is a decided tendency in fashion this season to depart from simplicity in dress, and to adopt the extreme ornamental elegance of the middle ages. Bonnets, dresses, and mantles

then have referred directly to Babbage, but courtesy would require that she add, "I owe the reference to . . ." and give a reference to Hill.

Observe in footnote 5 the form for a second citation from a work when another note has intervened. If Miss Vickrey were using two works by Hill, she could use a short-title form like the following: Hill, *History of English Dress*, II, 319-20.

Relatively long quotations may be typed single-spaced, indented, without quotation marks.

Since there is no date on the title page, the copyright date is used instead. If no date is discoverable in the book, the abbreviation, *n.d.*, is used for "no date." Sometimes library catalogues supply a date; a date of this sort should be inserted in brackets.

See footnote 9 for the form for an anonymous article. The quoted passage extends over two pages.

are trimmed all over with puffings of net, lace, and flowers.[9]

One reason this is a good investigative paper is this: Miss Vickrey has not been content to use only secondary works about costume, but has gone to the plates themselves and studied them with an observing eye.

[9] "Fashions for Early Summer," *Harper's Monthly Magazine,* I (1850), 142-43.

In the accompanying illustrations nearly half the costumes appear to be made mostly of lace. There is a ball dress with "three flounces of lace"; the dress seems to be lace from top to bottom in rosettes and flounces, and the accompanying text points out that some of this lace is machine imitation of *guipure.*[10] Very elegant indeed was a

[10] For genuine *guipure,* see *Larousse du xxme siècle,* under *dentelle.*

Miss Vickrey is making good use of her French.

"black lace jacquette." Nor had lace gone out of fashion for the more sober weeds of autumn. Most of the gowns shown to illustrate "Autumn Fashions" were well besprinkled with lace, and an autumn evening gown was described as follows:

> The skirts are all raised [there were five of them] at the sides with a large moss rose encircled with its buds . . . and they are worn over a petticoat of lively pink silk, so that the color shows through [the lace of] the upper fifth skirt.[11]

Brackets are used to enclose matter inserted within a quotation. Three periods, the ellipsis mark, indicate an omission of part of the original.

[11] "Autumn Fashions," *Harper's Monthly Magazine,* I (1850), 719-20.

Soon the use of lace became even more extensive, and some would say that taste in costume became even more debased, as fashions moved on into what one writer has characterized as the period of "sex-attraction by dumb-show." [12] This

Miss Vickrey appropriately gives credit. If she were less honest, she might have tried to appropriate the witticism.

[12] Davenport, *op. cit.,* II, 793.

was the great day of *Godey's Lady's Book,*[13]

[13] *Godey's* had several titles during its long history, 1830–98; see Frank Luther Mott, *A History of American Magazines, 1741–1885* (Cambridge, Mass., 1938–39), 3 vols. On *Godey's,* see also James Playsted Wood, *Magazines in the United States: Their Social and Economic Influence* (New York, 1949), 2 vols.

Miss Vickrey continues the sound practice of making all general references to *Godey's* in one place. Note the style for a book with a subtitle.

when L. A. Godey as publisher and Mrs. Sarah

Josepha Hale [14] dispensed dogmatic morality and

[14] She is now known mainly as the author of "Mary Had a Little Lamb." See Wood, *op. cit.,* I, 56.

lace-flounced fashions to tens of thousands of eager women. Godey was proud of the "embellishments" in his book, the steel engravings of flamboyant houses, the sentimental pictures, but especially he was proud of his hand-colored fashion plates. He boasted in an advertisement in the *Saturday Evening Post* of the day that he had spent $2000 in one year for these plates and added:

> To omit this is certainly a saving, but is it just to subscribers? Is it honorable? We cannot practice such deception. [15]

[15] *Ibid.,* I, 54.

Since the last reference was to the same source, Miss Vickrey can use *ibid.* and the volume and page number. Note that the abbreviation must be capitalized when it begins a sentence.

The *Broadway Journal* admitted, perhaps a little grudgingly, that "Godey keeps almost as many ladies in his pay as the Grand Turk," [16] hand-

[16] Mott, *op. cit.,* I, 592.

tinting his steel engravings. These ladies were extensively occupied tinting ribbons and flowers, set off by lace. For instance, in "Godey's Fashions for July 1867" two of the five dresses are heavy with imitation Cluny lace, and these were "short" dresses, that is, dresses which came only to the ground. [17] The leading evening gown of the month

[17] *Godey's Lady's Book and Magazine,* LXXV (1867), 92.

was notable since "the front of the dress is formed of rows of Cluny, and bands of straw," and the "Chitchat upon Fashions for July" had the following comment by the "fashion editress":

Notice the effectiveness of brief quotations run into the text.

Since the title of the article is included in the text, it can be omitted from the footnote. Footnotes should not be cluttered with useless information.

> Probably in no one article is female extravagance carried to greater extent than in the use of costly lace. The chief attraction now, in the lace department, is a white lace shawl, a mixture of *point appliqué* and old point valued at $2500. The groundwork is of exquisite fineness, while on it are worked bouquets and garlands,

For footnote 18 *ibid.* is sufficient; the quotation is from the same page of the same magazine as that cited in the immediately preceding footnote.

interwoven with borderings of scrolls and me-
dallions, each medallion differing from the
other, and a perfect study of itself.[18]

---

[18] *Ibid.*

The editress then explains the difference between
the two kinds of lace and enumerates the various
items for which each is used, which seem to include most of the items of female attire. She
closes, "Honiton, so fashionable a few years since,
is now rarely seen, and entirely out of date in the
stores."

By now Miss Vick-
rey is well on the
way. She might pleas-
antly spend a little
more time on *Godey's*
or on some magazine
like *Graham's*, move
on to chronicle the
decline of the fashion
for lace, and end with
an appropriate conclu-
sion.

At the end of her article, Miss Vickrey appended a bibliography
composed of all the books and articles she had cited, any books she
had not cited but found quite useful, but not books she had looked
at but found inappropriate to her study. For the section of her article
here reproduced, her bibliography would start with the items below.
Note that the names of authors are reversed so that the bibliography
can be alphabetized, and that the bibliography carries no pages, except inclusive page numbers of articles. The first entry gives the form
for an anonymous article; if the author were known, the article would
be alphabetized under his name. The second entry is a conventional
entry for a book, the fifth entry for a book of two volumes having no
publication date. The third entry follows the capitalization for a
French title. The fourth entry has a half title. The last two entries
are for encyclopedias, the *Americana* without mention of edition because the title page carries no indication of edition.

BIBLIOGRAPHY

"Autumn Fashions," *Harper's Monthly Magazine,* I (1850), 719-20.

Babbage, Charles, *On the Economy of Machinery and Manufacture*
(London, 1874).

Colas, René, *Bibliographie générale du costume et de la mode* (Paris,
1932).

Cook, Dorothy E., *Costume Index: A Subject Index to Plates and to
Illustrated Text* (New York, 1937).

Davenport, Millis, *The Book of Costume* (New York, n.d. [1948]), 2 vols.

Encyclopedia Americana (New York and Chicago, 1949), 30 vols.

Encyclopaedia Britannica, 14th ed. (Chicago, 1949), 24 vols.

45 *Writing the investigative paper* **Doc**

GUIDE TO REVISION:

* *Study the special forms for bibliographies and footnotes, the techniques for handling references and
quotations, and make your paper conform to standard
style.*

45a Footnote and bibliographic form **Doc a**

For some reason, even writers who are careful about details in the
body of the paper will forget special forms and even conventional
spelling, capitalization, and punctuation in footnotes and bibliographies. Documentation should be carefully checked for accuracy and
consistency.

Original	*Revision*
[1] Tyonbee, Arnold J., A Study of History, abridged by D. C. Somervill (NY and London, 1947) p. 87.	[1] Arnold J. Toynbee, *A Study of History,* abridged by D. C. Somervell (New York and London, 1947), p. 87.
[2] *ibid.* p. 138.	[2] *Ibid.,* p. 183.
[3] Orne Gerald, The Language of the Foreign Book Trade, Abbra., Terms, and phrases, (Chicago: 1949), P. 23.	[3] Jerrold Orne, *The Language of the Foreign Book Trade: Abbreviations, Terms, and Phrases* (Chicago, 1949), p. 23.
[4] Frederic Bracker, "Of Youth and Age. James Gould Cousins. *Specific Spectator* 5 (1951) 48 ff.	[4] Frederick Bracher, "Of Youth and Age: James Gould Cozzens," *The Pacific Spectator,* V (1951), 48-60.
[*These footnotes are seeded with errors and inconsistencies; see how many you can detect before comparing each with the revision in the right-hand column.*]	[*Some blunders apparently resulted from inaccurate bibliography cards, some from carelessness during composition or recopying.*]

45b Documenting appropriate material **Doc b**

Avoid footnoting material which is common knowledge or material
which can be readily verified and is not of major concern for the discussion in progress.

Original

As though there were a tendency among modern educators to agree with a British poet that "a little learning is a dangerous thing," [35]

[35] Alexander Pope, *Essay on Criticism,* 1. 12.

there seems now to be a drift in curricula toward specialization in certain fields.

[*The quotation is hackneyed and had best be avoided, but if the writer keeps it he need not make it more pompous with a footnote.*]

The "One Hundred Proverbs" of Mr. Tut-Tut [1] treat many of the

[1] *The Wisdom of China and India,* ed. Lin Yutang (New York, 1942), p. 1093.

usual sentiments, that old friends are best, [2] that silence is golden, [3]

[2] *Ibid.*
[3] *Ibid.*

and that. . . .

Revision

As though there were a tendency among modern educators to agree with Pope that "a little learning is a dangerous thing," there seems now a drift in curricula toward specialization in certain fields.

[*The quotation is not part of the argument and thus need not be documented. If anyone is curious to find any well-known passage there are always Bartlett,* Familiar Quotations, *and Mencken,* A New Dictionary of Quotations.]

The "One Hundred Proverbs" of Mr. Tut-Tut treat many of the usual sentiments, that old friends are best, that silence is golden, and that. . . .[1]

[1] *The Wisdom of China and India,* ed. Lin Yutang (New York, 1942), p. 1093.

[*The citation may be placed appropriately at the close of the evidence. Useless footnotes do not make a composition appear learned; they merely clutter the text.*]

45c Documenting crucial points   Doc c

Adequate reference, usually at least one reliable footnote, should support every statement that is vital to the discussion and depends on some authority.

Original

It is consistent with this negative attitude toward hoarding that in a period of panic following an earthquake, Zuni housewives gave away all their accumulated food.

[*This is strange behavior. Is the statement accurate? Is the evidence*

Revision

It is consistent with this negative attitude toward hoarding that in a period of panic following an earthquake, Zuni housewives gave away all their accumulated food.[77]

[77] Ruth Bunzel, *Zuni Texts, American Ethnological Society Publications,* XV (1933), 53.

Original (*Cont.*)

properly interpreted? The reader is
likely to be reluctant to accept the
statement, but with a reference he
may judge for himself.]

EXERCISE 45

A. Correct the following footnotes, which refer to works listed in the
bibliography in Exercise 43A:

   [1] Clark, G.M., "Social and Economic Aspects of Science, Economic
History 3 (1937) p. 371-72.

   [2] Clark G.M., op. cit. 371-72.

   [3] Feng, Doreen Yen Hung. The Joy of Chinese Cooking, p. 87.

   [4] Feng, ibid p. 87.

   [5] Greenlaw, New Sc. and Engl. Lit. in 17th, 18th, and 19th Cs.
John's Hopkin's Alumnis Mag. XII (1925) p. 349

   [6] ibid.

   [7] Clark, G. M., ibid.

   [8] Oscar Handlin, *This was America,* p. 1071-77.

   [9] Feng, loc. cit. 87.

   [10] Oscar, op. cit., 348.

B. Find a scholarly article in a periodical; there should be current numbers of many scholarly journals in the periodical room of your library.
Try to decide why the author has decided to document the passages
for which he has footnotes; observe the form of the notes; and observe
whether material other than references to books is included in the
footnotes. Then try to write a series of comments for the article similar to those which in this book accompany Miss Vickrey's paper.

46. REVISING AND CORRECTING THE THEME

[*For Guide to Revision, see page 583*]

> *Every piece of writing requires revision: convention-*
> *ally, a college composition needs at least two revi-*
> *sions, one before it is submitted and a second after*
> *the instructor returns it.*

A student learning composition is like a man thrown into mid-ocean to practice swimming. He has to write while learning to write. While he practices organization he must remember to spell and punctuate according to the conventions, and while he checks pronoun reference he must watch the development and coherence of his paragraphs. Nobody has found a simple solution to this dilemma, but careful and repeated revision helps.

46-1 Check chart for revision

A first draft, even a good first draft written by an accomplished writer, is seldom a finished composition. Warmed by the fire of composing, a writer can easily become uncritical of his product. When he has finished a draft, he will do well to check his own work by asking himself probing questions concerning it, even though he believes he has considered such questions in his original planning. Even well-laid plans can go imperceptibly awry. For a college theme, the student might well ask himself the following questions, checking back against his paper each time as objectively as he can.

1. Did the subject prove to be too big or too little, or unsuitable?

    a. Was it so broad that you could say very little that was specific?

    b. Was it so inconsequential that you found little to say?

    c. Was it suited to you? Did you know enough about the subject?

2. Have you brought the subject sharply into focus?

    a. As you now conceive the subject, is your original theme sentence, stating your main idea, as clear and exact as possible?

    b. Does your introduction introduce and your conclusion conclude?

    c. Examine your topic sentences. Do they introduce each paragraph and make the relationships clear between the paragraphs?

    d. Is your title adequate? interesting? the best you can think of?

3. Have you made each paragraph a developed unit?

    a. Are your paragraphs short and choppy, a sentence or two to each?

    b. Have you developed each paragraph with specific details, logical presentation of facts, illustrations, an example?

    c. Can you trace an orderly development in each paragraph?

4. Have you developed your subject adequately and logically?

    a. Can you trace a consistent growth of your idea in the paper?

    b. Are all parts of your paper pertinent, or could you cut some?

    c. Is not something lacking, a whole paragraph or the development of one part of your idea?

    d. Are parts of your composition in the best order?

5. What about style? point of view? tone?

    a. Are the sentences absolutely clear? Does the thought flow easily from sentence to sentence?

    b. Have you made frequent or awkward use of the passive voice, or of expressions like *there is?* Have you used expressive verbs wherever possible? Try rewriting each sentence by changing the order. Do you overuse forms like *is, are, was, were?*

    c. Have you adopted and kept an appropriate point of view?

    d. Is your tone suited to your material? Have you maintained it?

6. Have you chosen words carefully and well?

    a. Have you used words that mean what you want to say?

    b. Is your usage appropriate? Have you used slang inappropriately or scarred your prose with expressions not generally acceptable?

    c. Is your theme wordy, perhaps because your sentence structure is awkward or you have tried to be funny by using unnecessary words?

    d. Are words as concrete, specific, or vivid as you can make them?

7. Have you corrected your mechanics? (Make it your ideal to hand in papers without error.)

   a. Spelling? Be sure of each word, using your dictionary if necessary, and adding any word you misspell to your list.

   b. Sentence fragments? Check each sentence for completeness.

   c. Tense and number of verbs? Do verbs agree with their subjects?

   d. Pronouns? Does each pronoun refer clearly to an antecedent?

   e. Punctuation? Check especially any sorts of punctuation that have troubled you in the past.

The revision of a first draft may look something like this:

The ~~stock market~~ crash, *however,* ~~of 1929~~ was only the begin*n*ing ~~of the great de-~~ ~~pression~~; in the summer of 1932 the depression reached its lowest point, both economically and psychologically. The first signifi*c*ant event ~~to start the~~ ~~ball rolling for the epoch~~ of the great depression was the stock market crash in October, 1929. ~~The clerks in Wall Street~~ ~~brokers' offices worked late into the~~ ~~night posting records of an unprecedented~~ ~~volume of sales.~~ Apples began to ~~be sold~~ *sell apples* on the street. ~~by~~ unemployed citizens. In New York, as well as in other cities, bread lines appeared, displaying the extreme poverty suffered by some people.

As early as January, 1932, ~~there was a~~ demonstrat*ed*~~ion~~ at the national capital. ~~conducted by~~ 10,000 unemployed men. When destitute families lacked sufficient funds even to buy a few pounds of coal, *a relief bureau had to furnish* ~~they'll gave~~ them fuel. People began crowding into banks, fearing failures and hoping to rescue any savings they had.

The opening sentence is moved to improve continuity in the paragraph.

Spelling errors are corrected.

Unnecessary words are deleted.

A comma is supplied.

A sentence not relevant to the main idea of the paragraph is dropped.

Word order is changed to make the sentence active.

The sentence is shifted to regular actor-action order and moved to the end, where it provides a transition to the next paragraph.

The sentence is revised to correct vague pronoun reference.

When the draft has been thoroughly revised, it should be carefully and neatly copied, and then the final version should be checked for typographical errors or blunders introduced in the process of copying.

46   *Revising and correcting the theme*   **Rev**

GUIDE TO REVISION:

Even though the student has carefully revised his theme, the instructor is likely to add corrections and suggestions. Inside the front cover of this book is a chart of systems of numbers or abbreviations which may be used in correcting themes; an alphabetical list of the abbreviations will be found inside the back cover. A key to the rhetorical sections of the book appears on the back of the front end paper. To profit from his instructor's corrections, the student should correct his paper according to the following procedures:

1. If your instructor uses abbreviations to mark corrections, refer to the alphabetical list inside the back cover and find the number of the section to which each abbreviation refers.
2. If your instructor uses numbers as symbols, or after you have found numbers corresponding to his abbreviations, turn to the section of the book headed by each number indicated on the paper. To locate the sections, refer to the numbers at the tops of the pages.
3. Study the section of the book to which the instructor has referred you, comparing examples in the *Guide to Revision* sections of the book with your own paper until you are sure you understand his recommendation.
4. Then rewrite each passage as it should be written.

The student should note that profitable correction often requires more than rewriting misspelled words or changing punctuation. The writer derives the greatest benefit from carefully reworking sentences and paragraphs. A mark like *con* or *15* in the margin of the paper, for instance, indicates to the student that the portion of his theme so marked lacks sufficient continuity; it tells him to strengthen continuity between ideas, devote special study to Chapter 15 in the text, and to rewrite the passage so that it holds together. If the marks *sub* or *22* appear in the margin of the paper, the student needs to devote special study to Chapter 22, where he will find a discussion of methods for improving sentence structure through the proper employment of subordination; it is possible that to achieve this improvement he will need to combine

[583

two or three sentences by reducing a clause to a phrase or a single word. The following selection from a student theme has been marked with the abbreviations listed inside the back cover.

The public is fooled every day by a

Ref variety of people <u>ranging</u> from the glib

medicine man to people working for hi<u>gh</u>   *Hy*

geared political machines. The <u>inteligence</u>   *Sp*

SV of these people <u>vary</u> widely. The people

they fool are often more <u>inteligent</u> than   *Sp*

Run-on th<u>ey,</u> however, their skills are so great

that they overcome even the <u>inteligent</u>   *Sp*

Sp man. <u>Inteligence</u> is not acquired, but

Sp <u>knowlege</u> can be acquired, (due to) man's   *Rel*

ability to learn. Salesmen often state   *Con*

as fact information about their products.
Sub
Often these are untrue.

The opening for the theme is not promising, and frequent errors in structure and mechanics have been marked. To correct them, the student should check each abbreviation in the list inside the back cover. He will discover, for example, that *Ref* indicates faulty word reference and is discussed under 24 in the text. He can find 24 quickly by using the numbers at the tops of the pages. *Hy,* the student will find, indicates faulty hyphenation and is discussed under 42b, and *SV* refers to faulty agreement of subject and verb and is discussed under 31. The third sentence from the end is marked *Rel,* which refers to relevance and is discussed under 12, but it contains an expression, *due to,* circled and not otherwise marked. Whenever no abbreviation or number is used with a marked passage, the student should look up the marked expression in the glossary (47) or index, where he will find an explanation or a reference.

A theme may also be marked directly with the numbers which appear above portions of the book and at the tops of pages and are summarized in the chart inside the front cover. The following selection from the theme begun above has been marked with numbers.

Many methods are used to influence people. These methods include as one of the most popular the use of propaganda. **22a**

Pamphlets, newspapers, magazines, books, posters, billboards, radio, movies _and_ television are all mediums for the spread of propaganda. For example, know- **39c**

23c,
see also
19d

ing the kinds of things audiences want to hear, many facts are distorted by radio commentators. There are many kinds of in- **19b** formation which are distorted for propa-ganda purposes.

7, *see*
especially
7-1

The student can look up 22a and find a suggestion that the sentences be combined, with one subordinated to the other. The reference to 39c points out an omission of a comma in a series, and 23c marks a dangling modifier. The instructor has also suggested that the writer see 19d, which refers to overuse of passive sentences. The reference to 7 calls attention to a weakness that is apparent throughout the theme, overuse of general rather than specific development.

The instructor has used another kind of symbol here also, the hyphenated number 7-1. Hyphenated numbers head discussions of writing methods and procedures rather than specific instructions for improvement. Sometimes, however, an instructor may think that the writer could profit from study of these sections and will refer to them. A reference chart appears on the back of the front endpaper.

46a Record of themes and recommendations for revision

Mechanical proficiency alone will not make a writer competent, but mechanical proficiency is necessary. It can be acquired—if the writer will learn to understand his errors, will learn how to avoid them, and will concentrate on correcting habitual mistakes. The chart on the following page is intended to help the student analyze his weaknesses, to give him a guide for special study, and to help him know what to look for in theme revision. Use the blanks at the bottom of the chart for other subjects marked frequently in your papers.

THEME NUMBER	1	2	3	4	5	6	7	8	9	10	11	12	13	14	15
GRADE															
Organization, 5															
Development, 6-11															
Point of view, 13															
Paragraphing, 14															
Fragment, 17															
Run-on, 18															
Postponed subject, 19b															
Passive sentence, 19d															
Predication, 20															
Parallelism, 21															
Subordination, 22															
Dangling modifier, 23															
Reference, 24															
Pronoun form, 28															
Verb form, 29-30															
Verb agreement, 31															
Adjective, adverb, 32															
Articles, 33h															
Words, 34-37															
Punctuation, 38-40															
Manuscript form, 41															
Spelling, 42															
Possessive, 42a															

47 Glossary of usage

Gloss

GUIDE TO REVISION:

> *Use language appropriate in its context (see 37). The following list describes customary uses of certain troublesome expressions.*

A, An. Indefinite articles (see 33h).

Accent marks. Some foreign words, especially French words, retain in written English accent marks which are part of their spelling in the original language (*café, naïveté, suède*). The dictionary should be consulted for specific usages. Some words are used with or without the accent marks (*role, rôle*).

Accept, Except. To *accept* means "to receive"; *to except* means "to exclude."

> He decided *to accept* the bribe.

> They agreed *to except* the controversial paragraphs of the motion.

> *Except* is also a function word to indicate an exception.

> They all quit *except* Johnny.

Ad. Informal shortening of *advertisement,* not appropriate in standard English (see 37a).

A.D. Abbreviation of *Anno Domini,* in the year of Our Lord, used for dates after the birth of Christ when dates A.D. and B.C. could be confused. Being Latin, it preferably precedes the date (A.D. 43).

Adapt, Adept, Adopt. To *adapt* is "to adjust," "to make suitable."

> The children *adapted* their habits to their new home.

> *Adept* means "skilled, proficient."

> She is *adept* at typing.

> To *adopt* is "to accept" or "to take as one's own."

> The resolution was *adopted.*

> He *adopted* the mannerisms of his teacher.

Adviser, Advisor. Both spellings are in current use; the *-er* spelling is perhaps more usual.

Affect, Effect. *Affect* is a verb meaning "influence." *Effect* is usually a noun meaning "result," but it may be used as a verb meaning "cause" or "bring about."

> The weather *does not affect* her disposition.
>
> The weather has no *effect* on her disposition.
>
> The envoys tried *to effect* a compromise.

Aggravate. Used in standard English to mean "intensify" or "make worse." Used colloquially in the sense of "annoy" or "provoke."

> COLLOQUIAL: The children *aggravated* her.
>
> STANDARD: The children *annoyed* her.
>
> STANDARD: The new ointment only *aggravated* the disease.

Alibi. Formally used only in the legal sense, an indication that a defendant was elsewhere at the time of a crime; colloquially, "an excuse."

All (of). Constructions with *all of* followed by a noun can often be made more concise by omission of the unnecessary *of.* Usually *of* is retained between *all* and a pronoun.

> He could not bribe *all of them* with *all* the money in the world.

All right, Alright. Alright is a common misspelling for *all right,* accepted in modern dictionaries only with reservations.

Already, All ready. *Already* is a single modifier meaning "before some specified time." *All ready* means "completely ready."

> The team was *already* on the field.
>
> They were *all ready* for the kick-off.

Alumnus, Alumnae. An *alumnus* is a male graduate; *alumni* is the plural of *alumnus.* An *alumna* is a female graduate; *alumnae* is the plural form of *alumna.* The contraction, *alum,* is not acceptable in standard English.

Among, Between. The formal distinction that *between* is used of two and *among* of more than two has not been rigidly observed, at least informally, for *between.*

> The men divided the reward *between* Bob and me.
>
> The book records differences *among* (or *between*) synonyms.

Amount, Number. *Amount* indicates a sum or total mass or bulk. *Number* refers to a group of which individual parts can be counted; it is a collective noun, singular when designating a unit, plural when designating individuals.

> A *number* of friends were in the lobby.
>
> The *number* of his crimes is astounding.
>
> A large *amount* of wheat had been stored.

And, But, For. To begin sentences (see 33a).

And which. Proper only when the following clause is co-ordinate with a previous clause introduced by *which.*

> FAULTY: That was the first car I owned, *and which* I expected to cut down for a "hot rod."
>
> STANDARD: The car, which was the first I ever owned *and which* I expected to cut down for a "hot rod," was . . .

Angle. Currently popular in a number of colloquial expressions, rapidly becoming trite.

> SLANG OR COLLOQUIAL: He knew all the *angles.* What's the *angle* on this?

Anxious. Formerly restricted in meaning to "apprehensive," "worried"; still sometimes suspect formally in newer sense of "eager."

> FORMAL: He was *eager* (not *anxious*) to enter the game.

Anybody, Any body; Anyone, Any one. Combine the words to make the noun form; separate if the first portion is a modifier.

> *Anybody* may come.
>
> *Any body* in the burning ruins . . . .
>
> *Anyone* could do that.
>
> *Any one* infraction of the rule . . . .

Anywheres. Substandard; omit the *s.*
Apt. See *Liable.*
Around. Colloquial when used for *about.*

> There were *about* (not *around*) a thousand people present.

As. Useful as a conjunction indicating contemporary times but overused for *since, because, for,* or *that,* usually imprecisely.

> She was happy, *because* (not *as*) she had found the book.
>
> I do not know *that* (not *as*) I believe you.
>
> *As* I rounded the corner, the car stopped.
>
> COLLOQUIAL: *As* it was raining, we went inside.

For confusion of *as* and *like,* see 33c.
Aspect. Overused as a blanket term; see 35b.
As to. Awkward as a substitute for a more precise preposition such as *about* or *of.*

> He spoke to me *about* (not *as to*) the nomination.

At. Redundant and to be avoided in questions with *where.*

> Where was he? (not *Where was he at?* or *Where at was he?*)

Athletics. Plural in form, but often considered singular in number.
Auto. Not yet standard for *automobile.*

Awful, Awfully. Overworked as a vague intensive: *awfully good, awfully bad.* Since the words are overworked, their effectiveness is blunted. In formal English awful means "awe-inspiring."

Bad. When used as subject complement, sometimes confused with the adverb *badly* (see 32b).

> She felt *bad* (not *badly*) all day.

Basic. Often jargonic; see 36b.

B.C. Abbreviation of *before Christ,* used to mark dates that could be confused with dates in the Christian era. It appears after the date (52 B.C.)

Because. Not the most appropriate connective to introduce a noun clause (see 20c, 33d).

> The reason I ride the elevator is *that* (rather than *because*) I am lazy.
>
> I ride the elevator *because* I am lazy.

Being as, Beings as. Nonstandard usage for *since* or *because.*

> *Because* (not *being as*) I live here, I know what I am doing.

Beside, Besides. Beside is used as a preposition, meaning "by the side of." *Besides* may be an adverb or preposition, meaning "in addition to" or "except."

> He had to sit *beside* the teacher.
>
> It was too late to go to the dance, and *besides* I was tired.

Between. See *Among.*

Blond, Blonde. A tendency remains in writing to preserve the feminine *e* ending of the French word. As a noun *blond* refers to men, *blonde* to women.

Broke. Used to mean "out of money," *broke* is slang, not standard English; "financially embarrassed" as a substitute, however, is trite and affected.

Bunch. Colloquial and overused to mean "group."

> A *group* (not a *bunch*) of students . . . .
>
> A large *amount* (not a *bunch*) of material . . . .

Burst, Bust. Standard principal parts are *burst, burst, burst. Bust* or *busted* in the sense of "burst" is nonstandard.

But, Hardly, Only, Scarcely. Negative words which should not be used with another negative (see also *Double negative*).

> He *had* (not *didn't have*) but one alternative.
>
> He *knew* (not *didn't know*) only one answer.
>
> I *hardly* (not *don't hardly*) think so.

But that, But what. Used for *that, but that* is redundant and *but what* is nonstandard.

> He did not doubt *that* (not *but what* or *but that*) she would finally agree.

Can, May. In formal English, *may* refers to permission (*Mother,* may *I go swimming*) and *can* to ability (*I* can *swim across the pool*). Colloquially, *can* is commonly used for both meanings, and even formally *can* sometimes refers to permission to distinguish from *may* referring to possibility:

> I *can* (I have permission to) go swimming.
> I *may* (possibly I shall) go swimming.

Cannot, Can't help but. A double negative (see *But, Hardly,* etc.) used only colloquially.

> I *cannot help thinking* (not *cannot help but think*) she is honest.

Cannot. Also acceptably spelled *can not.*
Can't hardly. See *But, Hardly,* etc.
Case. Overworked and jargonic in expressions like "in this case" or "in the case of" (see 36c).
Censor, Censure, Censer. To *censor* means "to examine," especially to examine printed matter for possible objections. *To censure* means "to reprimand" or "to condemn." A *censer* is a receptacle for incense, especially in religious ceremonies.

> Half the story *was censored.*
> The students condemned their treasurer in a vote of *censure.*
> Choir boys carried the *censers.*

Certain. Redundant in expressions like "this certain person" or "in that certain instance."
Circumstances. Currently misused and overused in jargonic writing; use a more exact expression.

> He was *in great difficulty* (not *in very difficult circumstances*).

Cite, Sight, Site. To *cite* means to "refer to." *Sight* means "view" or "spectacle." A *site* means a "location."

> He *cited* an old legal document.
> The mountains below were a beautiful *sight.*
> We visited the *site* of the new building.

Claim. Overused as a blanket term; see 35b.
Combine. Colloquial as a noun meaning "combination."

> Several business houses *combined* (not *formed a combine*) to supply the needs of the new college.

[591

Complected. A dialect or colloquial substitute for *complexioned*.

She was *light-complexioned* (not *light-complected*).

Conscience, Conscious. *Conscience* is a noun referring to a sense of rightness. *Conscious* is an adjective meaning "awake" or "aware" or "active mentally."

Let your *conscience* be your guide.

I was not *conscious* of his fear.

Contact. Currently overused and loosely used, especially overworked as a verb synonym for *talk with, telephone, ask about, advise, inform, query, write to, call upon* (see also 26).

Continue on. Redundant as a verb with a separable suffix; omit *on*.

Could of. Sometimes, because of its sound, mistakenly written for *could have*.

He *could have* (not *could of*) looked up the word in the dictionary.

Council, Counsel, Consul. *Council* means "advisory board" or "group." *Counsel* means "advice" or, especially in law, "the man who gives advice." A *consul* is a "government official."

He was elected to the administrative *council*.

The dean *counseled* him to leave school.

He was American *consul* in Brazil.

Couple. Colloquial in the sense of "two" or "about two."

I gave him *two* (not *a couple of*) dollars.

Cunning. Once restricted to mean "shrewd" or "clever"; now extended to mean "attractive" or "pretty," but still questionable and often vague in the newer sense.

FORMAL: She bought an *attractive* (not *cunning*) gown.

Cute. Overworked colloquially as a vague way of expressing approval.

She was an *attractive* (or *charming* or *pleasant* or *lovely,* rather than *cute*) girl.

Data. Originally the plural form of Latin *datum,* often considered singular in colloquial usage, but still plural in standard English. *Strata* and *phenomena* are plurals of the same sort.

These (not *this*) data *confirm* (not *confirms*) the theory.

Date. A useful colloquialism meaning "appointment" or "to make an appointment," or "the person with whom an appointment is made"; the usage is rapidly becoming acceptable in standard English.

Deal. Currently overworked as a vague slang term for any transaction or arrangement or situation. A more specific term is preferable.

Definite, Definitely. Currently overworked as vague intensifiers in expressions like "a definitely fine party."

Didn't ought. See *Had ought,* etc.

Different than, Different to. Different from is the preferred idiom, although *different than* is recognized as common usage.

Do. An extremely useful verb sometimes carelessly used in idioms in which it cannot function (see 24h).

> Everyone has an ambition he wants to *fulfill* (rather than *do*).

Disregardless. Substandard; use *regardless.*

Don't. A contraction of *do not* not acceptable after *it* or *he* or *she*.

> It *does not* (or *doesn't* in conversation, not *don't*) seem wise to question the decision.

Double negative. Although a double negative is conceived in some languages as a device for enforcing the negative sense, two negatives are not used in the same negative statement in modern standard English.

> We *did* (not *didn't do*) nothing wrong.

> We did not see *anybody* (not *nobody*) on the pier.

Two negatives are used in the same statement in English to give varying emphasis to a positive idea.

> It was not impossible to see their meaning.

> I was not totally unimpressed by the speech.

Doubt. Doubt that implies a negative; *doubt whether* (colloquially *doubt if*) assumes that there is room for doubt.

> I *doubt that* he will come (presumably he will not).

> I *doubt whether* he will come (probably he will not, but he may).

Due to. Like *owing to* or *on account of, due to* is originally an adjective modifier (The delay was *due to* the icy roads). Its use as an adverbial modifier is not generally accepted as standard English, although it has long been common in introductory adverbial phrases (*Due to* unavoidable circumstances, the delivery has been delayed). *Because of* is the preferable adverbial idiom.

> *Because of* (not *due to*) the icy roads, the bus was late.

Each other, One another. Many careful writers distinguish, using *each other* to refer to only two and *one another* to refer to more than two.

Effect. See *Affect.*

Either, Neither. Usually singular in number (see 31b) and used to designate one of two, not one of more than two (see also *Each other*).

> *Neither* John nor Jack *is* eligible.

> *Any* (not *either*) of the three books has the information.

Enthuse. Colloquial and overworked for *be enthusiastic* or *make enthusiastic*.

Equally as. A wordy confusion of *as good as* and *equally*.

My cake was *as good as* Sue's.

The cakes were *equally* (not *equally as*) good.

Etc. Abbreviation for *et cetera* meaning "and so forth," appropriate only when statistics or lists justify abbreviations. *And etc.* is redundant, *et* means "and."

Except. See *Accept*.

Expect. Colloquial in the sense of "suppose" or "suspect."

I *suppose* (not *expect*) that his paper is finished.

Extra. Colloquial or dialectal in the sense of "unusually."

The coffee was *unusually* (not *extra*) good.

Fact, The fact that. Often overused as a roundabout way of saying *that*.

He was aware *that* (not *of the fact that*) everybody disliked his plan.

Factor. Often jargonic; see 36b.

Famed. Used for *famous* or *well known, famed* usually suggests journalese or amateur writing.

Farther, Further. A useful distinction, not universally made, prefers *farther* as the comparative form of *far* in expressions involving space and *further* to mean "in addition." Modern dictionaries recognize the interchangeable use of the two words.

Feature. Used to mean "emphasize" or "give prominence to," *feature* is becoming standard usage, but the word has been so overworked in this sense by journalists and press agents that it bears watching. Usually a more exact word is preferable. In expressions like "Can you feature that?" the word is slang.

Fellow. Colloquial in the sense of "man," "friend," "person," "individual."

Fewer, Less. *Fewer* is used in distinctions involving numbers of individuals, *less* in relation to value, degree, or quantity.

The course will not be offered for *fewer* than ten students.

The receipts were *less* than the expenditures.

Figure. Colloquial for *think, expect, suppose, conclude, believe*.

I did not *expect* (not *figure*) the course to be difficult.

Fine. Colloquial as an adverb.

She sang *well* (not *fine* or *just fine*).

Fix. In standard English a verb meaning "make fast" and, more recently, "repair." The word is colloquial as a noun meaning "predicament" and as a verb meaning "intend" or "prepare" (I was *fixing* to go).

Folks. Colloquial for *people* or *relatives.*

Force. Useful but often jargonic (see 35b).

Formally, Formerly. Formally means "in a formal manner"; *formerly* means "previously."

> We had to dress *formally* for the party.
>
> She was *formerly* a dress designer.

Fundamental. Useful but often jargonic; see 36b.

Funny. Colloquial, overused, and imprecise in the sense of "strange," "odd," "unusual," "perplexed." A more exact word is preferable.

Get, Got. Useful verbs and the basis of many standard idioms, but also used in many colloquial and slang expressions (The song *gets* me. The pain *got* him in the back. Better *get* wise). Used to mean "must" or "ought to," *got* is colloquial and usually redundant.

> We *must* (or *have to,* not *have got to*) finish by evening.

Good. An adjective, not to be confused with *well,* the corresponding adverb (see 32a).

Good and. Colloquial as an intensive.

> He was *very* (not *good and*) angry.

Gotten. Alternative form for *got* as past participle for the verb *get.*

Graduate. The idiom "to be graduated from" is sometimes preferred in formal English (He *was graduated from* Harvard in 1953). Informally the usual idiom is "graduate from" (He will *graduate from* high school in June).

Guess. Many dictionaries now accept *guess* in the sense of "believe," "suppose," "think," but some writers restrict it to colloquial usage.

Had of. Nonstandard for *had* (see also *Could of*).

> I wish he *had* (not *had of*) told me.

Had ought, Didn't ought, Hadn't ought. Nonstandard redundant forms for *ought* or *should.*

> He *ought not* (or *should not,* not *hadn't ought to*) speak disrespectfully to his mother.

Hang. Principal parts of the verb are *hang, hung, hung,* but to refer to death by hanging, they are *hang, hanged, hanged* in formal English.

> We *hung* the new picture.
>
> The murderer *was hanged.*

Hardly. See *But, Hardly,* etc.

Healthful, Healthy. A distinction gradually breaking down restricts *healthful* to mean "conducive to health" and *healthy* to mean "possessing health."

Heap, Heaps. Colloquial in the sense of "a great deal."

He made *a great deal* (not *a heap of* or *heaps of*) money.

Heighth. Common misspelling for *height.*

Hisself. Vulgate for *himself;* not acceptable.

Honorable. Used as a title of respect, mainly for people of prestige in political office. It is usually preceded by *the* and used only with a full name (*The Honorable John H. Jones* or *the Honorable Mr. Jones* not *Honorable Jones* or *the Hon. Jones*).

Human. Originally an adjective, *human* is now often used as a noun meaning "human being." Some modern dictionaries accept the noun use as standard, although others label it colloquial.

Idea. A handy word which careless writers readily overuse. A more exact word is often preferable.

My purpose (not *my idea*) is to become a nurse.

The theme (not *the idea*) of the book is that crime never pays.

If, Whether. *If* implies uncertainty; *whether* implies an alternative.

If he will trust me, I shall tell him.

I shall tell him, *whether* or not he believes me.

If is not used with *regardless.*

Even though (not *regardless if*) he is a doctor . . . .

Impersonal constructions. Impersonal constructions are troublesome in English; there is no one good solution. Constructions with *one* are permissible but sometimes confusing, because *one* is also a number. *One's* is especially awkward, but may be replaced by *his.* *They, it,* and *you* are often confusing because the reader does not know at once whether these words being used in an impersonal construction are personal pronouns having antecedents (see 24d). Constructions with *there* are uneconomical, but sometimes useful (see 19-3, 19b). Despite the weakness of the passive voice (see 19d), it often offers the best substitute for an impersonal construction. Often impersonal constructions can be recast in an active sentence.

IMPERSONAL: While traveling, one should be sure to learn the languages of the countries he visits.

ACTIVE: Travelers should be sure to learn the languages of the countries they visit.

For inconsistency in impersonal constructions, see 13b, 28j.

Imply, Infer. *To imply* is "to suggest a meaning"; *to infer* is "to draw a conclusion from evidence" (see also 35a).

The attorney *implied* that the witness was lying.

The jury *inferred* that the attorney was trying to discredit the witness.

In, Into. In implies rest or motion within a restricted area; *into* is preferable to indicate motion from the outside to the inside.

> She lives *in* town.
>
> We drove *into* town.

In back of. Redundant; prefer *behind.*

In regards to. Nonstandard; use *in regard to.*

Individual. Loosely used, and often overused, as a synonym for *person;* best used as a noun to emphasize that persons are separate and unique.

> Students are not merely names in a card file; they are *individuals.*

Infer. See *Imply.*

Inferior than. Nonstandard; use *inferior to.*

Ingenious, Ingenuous. Ingenious means "having or giving evidence of resourceful intelligence." It can be used of either persons (an *ingenious* strategist) or things (an *ingenious* device). *Ingenuous* means "naïvely frank." Except for things closely associated with people (an *ingenuous* proposal), it is used only of persons.

Inside of. Redundant as a compound preposition; omit *of.*

Invite. Restricted in standard usage to use as a verb, not acceptable as a substitute for *invitation.*

> I asked Joe for *an invitation* (not *an invite*) to the dance.

Irregardless. Nonstandard; use *regardless.*

It. Usually to be avoided in impersonal constructions, especially in locutions like *"It* says in the book . . . ," in which *it* seems to have an antecedent but does not (see 24a, 24c).

Its, It's. Its is a modifier, possessive form of *it. It's* is the contraction of *it is.*

Kind, Sort. Singular words, which formally can be modified only by singular demonstrative adjectives, *this* or *that.* Plural forms, *those kinds* or *these sorts,* are used, and colloquially *kind* and *sort* are commonly treated as if they were plural (*these kind*).

Kind of. Colloquial as the equivalent of *somewhat, rather.*

Kind of a. Colloquial.

Lay. For confusion of forms of *lay* and *lie,* see 29a.

Lead, Led. Lead is the present tense of the verb. Because of the similarity in pronunciation, the past tense, *led,* is often misspelled as *lead,* the name of the mineral.

> He *led* (not *lead*) the horse to water.

Less. See *Fewer.*

Let, Leave. Both are common in a few idioms (*leave* or *let it* alone), but in other idioms, especially when the verb carries a sense of permission, *let* is standard.

Let (not *leave*) the men stay.

Let us (or *let's,* not *leave us*) go soon.

Liable, Apt, Likely. Interchangeable informally, but often distinguished in careful writing.

She is not *likely* (rather than *liable* or *apt*) to tell her teacher.

Strictly, *liable* means "responsible for" or "subject to."

He is *liable* for the damage he caused.

Apt means "has an aptitude for."

Marie is an *apt* pupil.

Lie. For confusion of forms of *lie* and *lay,* see 29a.

Like. For misuse as a conjunction, see 33c.

Line. Jargonic or slang or redundant in certain current uses.

He sells books (not *Selling books is his line*).

I want to buy something *similar to* (not *along the lines of*) the dress in the window.

He *was deceiving her* (not *handing her a line*).

Literally. An antonym, not a synonym of *figuratively.* The student who wrote, "This was literally but not actually true," did not say what he probably meant.

Loan. Now generally accepted as a synonym of *lend*; many careful writers, however, use *loan* only as a noun and prefer *lend* as a verb.

Locate. Provincial as a synonym for *remember* or *take up residence.*

Lot(s) of. Colloquial as a synonym for *many.*

Love. Currently misused as a synonym for *like.* Use an exact word.

Lower case (lc). Letters which are not capitals; printers who set type by hand kept these letters handy in the "lower case" (see 41a).

Mad. Colloquial in the sense of "angry." Use *angry* or a more exact word like *vexed, furious, annoyed.*

Math. Clipped form of *mathematics,* not appropriate in formal writing.

Might of. Use *might have,* or for colloquial use its contraction, *might've* (see *Could of*).

Mighty. As a synonym for *very* not acceptable in standard English, although common in certain areas as a colloquialism.

She was a *very* (not *mighty*) pretty girl.

Moral, Morale. *Moral* is a modifier, concerning the preference of right over wrong; *morale* is a noun suggesting good spirits and a healthy attitude.

George Washington was a *moral* man.

The victory improved the soldiers' *morale.*

More than one. Logically plural, sanctioned by custom as singular except when the meaning clearly requires a plural verb.

> *More than one* man is eager to marry her.

> If there are *more than one* apiece, they should be divided as equally as possible.

Most. Colloquial as a synonym for *almost.*

> I am home *almost* (not *most*) every evening.

Movie. Gaining in popularity as a synonym for *motion picture* but not generally accepted for formal discourse.

Muchly. Nonstandard; use *much.*

Must. Currently overworked as a noun expression (see 26).

Myself. For misuse as a substitute for *I* or *me,* see 28h.

Names. Names of persons used in writing should be spelled correctly and should be given in full. Citation of an author in the text of a paper should include the first name, unless the person is so well known that there is no possibility of confusion (Shakespeare, Shelley, but Edwin Arlington Robinson, Bertrand Russell).

Nature. Jargonic in certain current wordy expressions (see 36c).

> The job was *difficult* (not *of a difficult nature*).

Neither. Used of two; see *Either.*

Neither . . . nor. Used as correlatives.

> She could *neither* set up her experiment *nor* (not *or*) conduct it.

Neologism. A new word, not yet accepted by standard dictionaries.

Nice. Colloquial as a synonym for *affable, agreeable, amiable, congenial, considerate,* and so on through the alphabet. Prefer a more exact word. Carefully used, *nice* means "precise," "exact," "discriminating."

Nice and. Colloquial as an intensive.

> The coffee was *pleasantly* (not *nice and*) hot.

Nominative absolute. A construction not part of the basic sentence pattern but having a verbal and a subject.

> *The three minutes having elapsed,* the umpire blew his whistle.

The construction readily becomes dangling, and should be used with caution (see 23c).

None. *None* as a subject takes a singular or plural verb depending upon its meaning.

> SINGULAR: *None* of you *is* to blame.

> PLURAL: *None* but the brave *deserve* the fair.

Not . . . as. Some writers on usage have objected to this construction. They prefer

He is *not so* (rather than *not as*) dull as his younger brother.

Either construction is now generally considered acceptable.

Nowheres. Substandard; omit the *s.*
Number. Use with caution.

> Many (*dozens* or *hundreds* or *thousands,* but not *a great number*) of students will participate.

> *Number* as a grammatical concept refers to singular and plural (see 42c).

Of. Confused with *have.* See *Could of, Might of.*
On the part of. Often a clumsy equivalent of *by;* see *Part.*
One. For *one* in impersonal constructions, see 13b, 28j and Impersonal constructions; see also *More than one.*
Only. For the position of *only,* see 23-5.
Out of. Prefer *out* (*out* the door; not *out of* the door).
Outside of. Redundant as a compound preposition (*outside* the barn, not *outside of* the barn). *Outside of* is colloquial in the sense of "except."

> He failed all his examinations *except* that in chemistry (not *outside of* chemistry).

Outstanding. An overworked blanket term; see 35b, 32e.
Over with. Colloquial in the sense of "done," "finished with," "ended," "completed."
Over-all. Useful as a synonym for *general,* but currently overused; accurately used in a phrase like *the over-all length.*
Part, On the part of. Often used in wordy writing.

> WORDY: There was some objection, *on the part of* the administration, to the moral tone of the skits.

> REVISED: The administration objected to the moral tone of the skits.

Party. Not usually acceptable in formal composition as a synonym for *person;* used in legal papers (party of the first part) and by telephone operators (Here is your party).
Past. Preferred to *passed* as a modifier or complement.

> His troubles were *past* (rather than *passed*).

Passed. Preferred to *past* as a verb form.

> She *passed* (rather than *past*) the examination.

Per cent. Acceptable forms either *per cent* or *percent.*
Per. The prefix *per-* should not be confused with *pre-* (see 42-9).
Phase. Often jargonic; see 36b.
Phenomena. Plural; the singular is *phenomenon* (see 42c).
Phone. Colloquial; in formal composition use *telephone.*

Phone up. Substandards; use *telephone, call on the telephone,* or for more familiar uses, *call up.*

Picture. Vague and usually jargonic.

JARGONIC:	I gave them the picture in a few minutes.
IMPROVED:	I described my troubles.
FURTHER IMPROVED:	I explained why I needed five dollars.

Piece. Colloquial in the sense "a short distance."

Plan on. Colloquial in some uses (*plan to go,* not *plan on going; plan to see,* not *plan on seeing*).

Plenty. Not acceptable as an intensive (*excellent,* not *plenty good*).

Point. Overworked as a blanket word.

He had many admirable *characteristics* (not *points*).

Poorly. Colloquial in the sense "in poor health."

Pre. The prefix *pre-* should not be confused with *per-* (see 42-9).

Prejudice. A noun, not to be confused with *prejudiced,* a modifier.

He was *prejudiced* (not *prejudice*) against John.

Presence. The noun form corresponding to *to be present* (The chairman requests your *presence* on the platform); to be distinguished from *presents,* plural of *present.*

Preposition with time word. Unnecessary prepositions with a time word are usually discouraged in formal writing.

I shall see you Saturday (rather than *on Saturday*).

Principal, Principle. The two words should be distinguished. *Principal* can be a modifier meaning "first in importance" (I answered his *principal* objections), or a noun naming somebody or something first in importance (a high school *principal,* the *principals* in the fight). *Principle* is always a noun (The law of the conservation of matter formulates a fundamental *principle* in physics; Machiavelli has been accused of having no *principles*). See also 35.

Prof. Slang when used as a common noun (I like the course, but not the *prof*). Acceptable in journalistic and informal writing as an abbreviation with a full name (*Prof.* George B. Sanders, but *Professor* Sanders). Best formal style requires that *professor* be written out in all titles.

Proved, Proven. Proved is the only form having historical foundation, and is preferred; *proven* is increasing, and is commonly accepted. The verb *to prove* is often used carelessly of statements which are not proved; often *to suggest, to imply,* or *to indicate* would be more accurate.

Providing. In older usage, not admitted as a synonym of *provided,* a conjunction meaning "on the condition."

Quite. Generally accepted, although often unnecessary, in the sense of "entirely" (*quite* dead, frozen *quite* to the bottom); colloquial in the sense "somewhat," "rather" (*quite* cold, *quite* a big job).

Raise. The forms of *raise,* meaning "to lift," are readily confused with those of *rise,* meaning "to stand up" or "to move against the direction of gravity" (see 29a). *Raise* is now generally accepted as a synonym of *rear* in the sense "bring to maturity," but many writers prefer *rear* when referring to human beings.

Rate. Currently overused and misused; slang in some usages (He does not *rate* with us).

Re. In the sense "about," used for formal purposes only in legal documents and skeletonized commercial writing.

Real. Colloquial as an intensive (It was a *real* nice clam bake). Use *really, very,* or a word expressive enough so that it needs no intensive.

Really. A useful word frequently overused and misused so that it clutters sentences.

> INEFFECTUAL: He had been *really* traveling.
>
> REVISED: He was gasping for breath.
>
> REDUNDANT: It was *really* true.
>
> REVISED: It was true.

Reason is because. A common but somewhat illogical expression avoided by careful writers (see 33d). A reason is a reason, it is not *because.* At best, the construction is wordy and awkward; often it results from choosing the wrong subject.

> AWKWARD: The reason I want to be an engineer is because I like mathematics.
>
> REVISED: I want to be an engineer because I like mathematics.

Reason why. Usually redundant (The reason why I like to swim. . . .); omit *why.* In many sentences *reason,* also, can be omitted and the structure strengthened.

> WORDY: The reason why I hate the sight of cows is that I had to milk so many of them.
>
> REVISED: I had to milk so many cows that I hate the sight of them; *or* I hate the sight of cows because I had to milk so many of them.

Reckon. Colloquial and inexact as a synonym for *believe, suppose, assume.*

Regard, regards. Often overused and jargonic; see 36b. *Regards* is nonstandard in constructions like *in regards to.*

Respectfully, Respectively. Respectfully means "in a respectful manner" (*respectfully* submitted); *respectively* means "in the specified order," "severally" (The balloons were identified as 4b, 5a, and 2g, *respectively*).

Reverend. Used in standard English with the first name or initials of the person described or with the title *Mr.* (see 41b), in formal usage preceded by *the.*

The Reverend William Dimity; the Reverend W. L. Dimity; the Reverend Mr. Dimity.

Right. Informal as an intensive in expressions like "right away"; prefer *immediately, at once, promptly,* etc. A localism in the sense of "very."

> It was a *very* (not *right*) good fight.

Rise. Forms of *rise* should not be confused with forms of *raise* (see *Raise* and 29a).

Said. Pseudo-legal affectation as a modifier; if necessary, use *this, that, these,* and the like.

> Having rejected *the motion* (not *the said motion*), the committee adjourned.

Same. As a pronoun used with *in, same* is sometimes useful in legal documents, but sounds affected in most writing.

> Having made his bed he must lie *in it* (not *in same*).

Scarcely. Not to be used with another negative (see *Double negative*).

> There *was scarcely* (not *was not scarcely*) any butter.

Seem. A useful word, often misused or overused, especially as a qualification in constructions like "it would *seem* that."

> The evidence *suggests* (not *would seem to suggest*) that Shakespeare was once a schoolmaster.

Seldom ever. Redundant; omit *ever.*

Set. Forms of *set* should not be confused with those of *sit;* see 29a.

Set-up. Slang in the sense of "an easy victory," and currently overused in jargonic writing to mean anything related to organization, condition, or circumstances (I liked the new *set-up*). Try to use an exact word.

Shall. Commonly indistinguishable from *will;* for the distinction maintained by many careful writers and speakers see 30g.

Shape. Colloquial in the sense of "condition," "manner."

> She was *well trained* (not *in good shape*) for the tournament.

Should. For distinctions between *should* and *would,* see 30g.

Should of. Mistaken form of *should have;* see *Could of.*

Show. Colloquial as a synonym for *chance, opportunity;* colloquial also as a synonym for *moving picture, play.*

Show up. Not acceptable in standard English in either the sense "arrive" (Jim did not *show up*) or the sense *"expose"* (He is no gentleman, and Mary *showed him up*).

Sic. For uses of *sic* see 45-4.

Sign up, Sign up for, Sign up with. Not acceptable in standard English.

Sit. Forms of *sit* should not be confused with those for *set* (see 29a).

Situated. Often used redundantly.

The house was *in* (not *situated in*) the tenement district.

Situation. Wordy and jargonic in expressions like "the team had a fourth-down situation."

Size. Not generally accepted as a modifier (*this size of dress,* not *this size dress*).

So. Avoid the excessive use of *so* to join independent clauses (see 22).

So as. Not to be confused with *so that* (see 33b).

Some. Not acceptable in standard English to indicate vague approval.

It was *an exciting* (not *some*) game.

Somebody's else. The sign of the possessive appears on the last word (see 42a). Use *somebody else's.*

Sometime, Some time. One word in the sense "occasion," "some other time"; two words in the sense "a period of time."

Come up to see me *sometime.*

The repairs will require *some time.*

Somewhat of. Avoid.

Sir Andrew *resembled* (not *was somewhat of*) a beanpole.

Somewheres. Substandard. Omit the *s.*

Sort. See *Kind.*

Sort of, Sort of a. Both are clumsy and colloquial as modifiers.

I was *rather* (not *sort of*) tired.

He was *an amateur* (not *a sort of a*) plumber.

Speak, Speech. The difference between the vowel sequence in the verb *speak* and the noun *speech* is fruitful of spelling errors.

State. Currently misused as a loose equivalent of *say, remark, observe, declare.* Carefully used, *to state* is "to declare in a formal statement."

The board *stated* that the coach's contract would not be renewed.

The coach *said* (not *stated*) that practice would be postponed until four-thirty.

Stationary, stationery. *Stationary* is a modifier meaning "not movable" or "not moving"; *stationery* is a noun meaning "writing materials." They can be distinguished by remembering that letters are written with stationery.

Stop. Colloquial in sense of "to stay."

Stress. A useful word, currently being overused, especially in journalism.

Such. Colloquial as an intensive.

COLLOQUIAL: It was *such* a warm day.

STANDARD: It was a very warm day *or* It was hot.

Careless use of *such* as a modifier encourages jargon.

604]

JARGONIC: Departments must restrict such expenditures to budgeted totals, and only such requisitions will be approved.

REVISED: Departments must stay within their budgets; requisitions will be approved only if they are backed by budgeted funds.

Suit, Suite. *Suit,* the commoner word, can be either a verb (*suit* yourself) or a noun (a tailor-made *suit*). *Suite,* only a noun, has several specialized uses. (The ambassador and his *suite* occupied a *suite* of rooms).

Suspicion. A noun, not appropriately used to supplant the excellent verb *suspect.*

Sure. Colloquial as an intensive.

He was *certainly angry* (not *sure sore*).

Swell. Not acceptable in standard English as a modifier; use *good, excellent,* or, preferably, some more exact modifier.

Take and. Colloquial in most uses.

He *whacked* (not *took and whacked*) down the hornet's nest.

Take sick. Not generally accepted in standard English; prefer *became ill* or a more exact expression.

Terrible, Terribly. Overused and misused; colloquial as general intensives (She is a *terribly* sweet girl) and as blanket words signifying anything unpleasant (I had been vaccinated and felt *terrible*).

Terrific. Recently misused and overused; not a general synonym for anything *large, impressive, dramatic, significant, dexterous,* or *important;* a word so abused that it can now scarcely be used in its standard meaning, "causing terror."

That. As a function word introducing a clause, *that* can often be omitted to good effect, especially in informal and colloquial English.

I told him he need not come (*that* not necessary).

In more complicated writing *that* can be omitted only with caution (see 25c). It is usually required with the second of two parallel clauses (see 21b). It is required when the clause comes first.

That he was crazy had not occurred to me.

That is usually necessary when preceded by an impersonal construction.

That there. Substandard; omit *there.*

Their, There, They're. Commonly confused in spelling. *There,* which can be remembered by its similarity to *where,* means "in that place" (Lie *there,* Nipper). *Their* is the possessive of *they* (see 28). *They're,* the contraction of *they are,* is not acceptable in formal composition.

These. *These* should be avoided as a substitute for *the* (see 33h).

[605

These kind, These sort. See *Kind.*

They're. See *Their.*

This. *This* should be avoided as a substitute for *the* (see 33h); for reference of *this,* see 24a.

This here. Substandard; omit *here.*

Tho. A variant spelling of *though,* not preferred for formal composition.

Those. Avoid *those* as an intensive with no reference.

> He looked back fondly on *his* (not *those*) old college days.

Through, Through with. Colloquial in the sense of "finished."

> *Have you not finished* (not *Aren't you through with*) the experiment?

Thusly. Vulgate; use *thus.*

To, Too, Two. Distinguish the function word *to* (*to* the game, learn *to* read) from the adverb *too* (*too* sick, *too* hot), and the numeral *two* (*two* seats on the aisle).

To be. For the faulty use of forms of *to be* in an equation see 20c.

Toward, Towards. Alternative forms; *toward* is more common in the United States.

Try and. *Try to* is preferred in standard English.

Type. In standard English, *type* is a noun or verb, although colloquially it is often an adjective (*a ranch-type house*).

> *This type of research* (not *this type research*) yields results.

Unique. For the use of *unique,* see 32e.

Up. Useful in verb-adverb combinations (see 29-4); can frequently be separated from the verb, but often the sense is clearer and the construction smoother if *up* is kept close to the verb.

> AWKWARD: He made his mind up.
>
> REVISED: He made up his mind.

Used to. The *d* is elided in speech but not omitted in writing.

> We *used to* (not *use to*) go to the beach every summer.

Used to could. Vulgate for *used to be able.*

Very. The most useful intensive, but since it is usually only an intensive, with relatively little meaning, it is as likely to weaken writing as to strengthen it. Most good writers use *very* sparingly. The older practice was to forbid the use of *very* before a past participle without an intervening *much* (*very much pleased,* not *very pleased*). The distinction is still maintained in much formal writing.

Video. Rapidly growing in popularity at this writing to pertain to the transmission of television images, but not yet accepted as standard English.

Vulgate English. English not generally accepted (see 37).

Wait on. Except in the sense of "serve," use *wait for.*

    We have been waiting *for* (not *on*) you.

Want for. In most constructions, omit the *for.*

    I *want* (not *want for*) you to meet her.

Want in, Want out. Not accepted in formal English.

    The cat *wants to get out* (not *wants out*).

Ways. Colloquial for *way* in the sense "a distance."

    It was a long *way* (not *ways*) to the road.

We. Used as an indefinite or editorial subject (see 13-2).

Weather. Frequently confused in spelling with *whether* (I asked him *whether* or not we could depend upon fair *weather*).

Well. An adjective in the sense "in good health," "cured" (The patient is now recovered, and is quite *well*); an adverb corresponding to the adjective *good,* but not to be confused with it (see 32b).

    She played her part *well* (not *good*).

    The blueprints look *good* (not *well*).

What. Should not be confused with *that* (see 28k).

When. Avoid the *when*-clause in a definition (see 33d).

Where. Colloquial when substituted for *that.*

    I noticed in the paper *that* Senator Jones is a candidate for re-election (*not* I see by the paper *where* Senator Jones is up for re-election).

Where at. In most constructions, omit the *at.*

    Where is he? (not *Where at is he?* or *Where is he at?*).

Whether. See *If.*

Which. For *which* after *and,* see *And which;* for the use of *which* to refer to human beings, see 28-3.

While. Often carelessly used as a synonym for *although* or *and* (see 33b).

Who, Whom. Pressure of sentence pattern encourages the replacing of *whom* by *who* (see 28g). For distinction between *who* and *which,* see 28-3.

Who's, Whose. Who's is the contraction of *who is; whose* is the possessive form of *who* (see 28-3). In all but the most formal contexts, *whose* may replace the awkward *of which.*

    The dog, *whose nose* (not *the nose of which*) was full of porcupine quills. . . .

Will. Sometimes distinguished from *shall;* for the distinction, see 30g.

Wire. Informal for either *telegram* or *telegraph.*

Without. Colloquial as a substitute for *unless.*

    I will not stay *unless* (not *without*) you raise my wages.

Wood, Woods. In the United States either is acceptable as a synonym of *forest.*

Worst kind, Worst way. Not acceptable in the sense "very much."

Worth-while. Overused blanket word; see 35b.

Would have. Often awkward.

If they *had* (not *would have*) done that. . . .

Would of. Mistaken form of *would have* (see *Could of*).

You. To be used with caution in impersonal constructions (see 13b, 28j, and Impersonal constructions).

You-all. Colloquial Southern form as the plural of *you;* not acceptable for formal composition.

INDEX

CORRECTION CHART 4·25

For an alphabetical list of correction symbols, see inside back cover. A chart of reference numbers to rhetorical and grammatical discussions will be found on the back of this page. Directions for the use of charts and symbols are in 46.

0b=Ev b Adequate Evidence	**11=Log** Logic	**11e=Log e** Assumptions	**12=Rel** Relevance	**13=PV** Point of View	**13a=Tone** Tone
5b=Tran Transitions	**16=Intro, Conc** Introduction; Conclusion	**16a=Intro a** Adequate Introduction	**16b=Intro b** Independent Introduction	**16c=Conc c** Adequate Conclusion	**16e=Intro e, Conc e** Apology in Intro., Conc.
19c=Em c Substitute Subject	**19d=Pass** Passive Sentences	**20=Pred** Predication	**20c=Eq** Equation with <u>to be</u>	**21=Paral** Parallelism	**21c=Paral c** Misleading Parallelism
23c=DM Dangling Modifier	**23e=Mod e** "Split" Constructions	**24=Ref** Reference	**24e=Ref e** Word Reference	**25=Inc** Incomplete Constructions	**25c=Inc Comp** Incomplete Comparisons
30e=Prin Principal Parts	**31=SV** Subject-verb Agreement	**32=Adj, Adv** Form of Modifier	**33=FW** Function Words	**33b=Conj b** Subordinating Conjunctions	**33h=Art** Articles
36a=Rep Careless Repetition	**36b=Red** Redundancy	**37=Us** Good Usage	**37a=Colloq** Colloquialism	**37b=Slang** Slang	**37c=Id** Idiom
38e=EPe,⊙ Semicolon	**39=Com,⊙** Comma	**39a=Com a** (See 18b) Co-ordinate clauses	**39b=Com b** (See 18c) Comma Fault	**39c=Com c** In Series	**39d=Com d** Non-restrictive Modifiers
39j=Com j Places, Dates, Measurement	**39k=Com k** Inappropriate Commas	**40a=Quot,∨** Quotation Marks	**40b=Dash,⊖** Dashes	**40c=Parens,( )** Parentheses	**40d=[ ]** Brackets
41f=Ital Italics		If an expression is circled or underlined without reference to the chart above, look it up in the index or in the Glossary (47).			
43c=Res c Bibliography Cards	**44=Mat** Adequate Material	**45=Doc** Adequate Documentation	**45a=Doc a** Footnote Form	**46 Rev** REVISION AND CORRECTION OF THEME	**47 Gloss** GLOSSARY

REFERENCE CHART TO DISCUSSION OF TECHNIQUES OF COMPOSITION

I	THEME TOPIC The theme 1-1 Limiting topic 1-2 Suggested topics 1-3	UNITY Stating idea 2-1 Main idea and unity 2-2 Devices for unity 2-3 Précis 2-4	ANALYSIS Scientific, literary 3-1 Structural 3-2 Chronological 3-3	CLASSIFICATION Basis 4-1 Co-ordination, subord- ination 4-2 In writing 4-3	ORGANIZATION Types 5-1 to 5-3 Outline 5-4 to 5-8
II	FACTS, DETAILS Fact, judgment 6-1 Limiting judgment 6-2 General, specific 7-1 Symbolization 7-2	ILLUSTRATION, DEFINITION Particulars 8-1 Examples 8-2 Incident 8-3 Analogy 8-4 Definition 9-1 to 9-3	INDUCTION Induction 10-1 Generalization 10-2 Induction in writing 10-3 Tests of evidence 10-4	DEDUCTION, RELEVANCE Induction, deduction 11-1, 11-2 Middle term 11-3 Reasoning 11-4, 11-5 Assumptions 11-6 Relevance 12-1, 12-2	POINT OF VIEW Tone 13-1 Person 13-2 Space 13-3 Time 13-4
III	STANDARD PARAGRAPH Brief compositions 14-1 Standard 14-2 Topic sentence 14-3	PARAGRAPH DEVELOPMENT Patterns 14-4 Types 14-5 to 14-11	CONTINUITY Main outline 15-1 Topic sentence 15-2 Transitions 15-3 to 15-6	INTRODUCTION Functions 16-1 Types 16-2 to 16-4	CONCLUSION Functions 16-5 Types 16-6 to 16-8
IV	SENTENCE PATTERN Grammatical devices 17-1 Basic pattern 17-2 Incomplete 17-6	SENTENCE PARTS Subject, verb comple- ment 17-3 Complements 17-4 Parts 17-5	COMBINING CLAUSES Clauses 18-1 Varieties of clauses 18-2 Distinguishing clauses 18-3	EMPHASIS Variations in order 19-1, 19-2, 19-6 Postponed subject 19-3 Substitute subject 19-4 Passive 19-5	PREDICATION Sense in pattern 20-1 To be equation 20-2
V	CO-ORDINATION Co-ordination 21-1 Parallel 21-2 Comparison 21-3	SUBORDINATION Style 22-1 Relationships 22-2 Emphasis 22-3 Contexts 22-4	MODIFIERS Types 23-1 to 23-3 Order of modifiers 23-4 Fixed modifiers 23-5 Sentence modifiers 23-6	REFERENCE Word reference 24-1 Reference signals 24-2 Reference patterns 24-3	INCOMPLETE CONSTRUCTIONS Incomplete construc- tions and sentence patterns 25
VI	PARTS OF SPEECH Form changes in grammar 26-1 Parts of sentence 26-2	NOUN EXPRESSIONS Types 27-1 to 27-2 Verbal nouns 27-3 Pronoun forms 28-1 Pronoun types 28-2 to 28-8	VERBS Classes 29-1 to 29-4 Principal parts 30-1 Forms 30-2 to 30-6 Agreement of subject and verb 31	MODIFIERS Adjective, adverb 32-1 Verbal modifiers 32-2 Other types 32-3 Comparison 32-4	FUNCTION WORDS Uses, types 33-1 to 33-3 Conjuctions 33-4 Conjunctive adverbs 33-5 Prepositions 33-6 Articles 33-7
VII	DICTIONARY Vocabulary 34-1 Using dictionary 34-2	WORD CHOICE Meaning 35-1, 35-2 Abstract, concrete 35-3 Denotation, connotation 35-4, 35-5 Contexts 35-6	ECONOMY IN WORDS Through structure 36-1 With words 36-2 Adequacy 36-3	USAGE Language and usage 37-1 Linguistic change 37-2 Dialect 37-3 Idiom 37-4	LANGUAGE LEVELS Levels and importance 37-6, 37-7 Standard English 37-8
VIII	END PUNCTUATION Structural 38-1 Styles 38-2	COMMA Structural 39-1 Conventional 39-2	FORMALITIES Formal punctuation 40 Manuscript 41	SPELLING Variations and diffi- culties 42-1, 42-2	SPELLING PROBLEMS Analyzing problems 42-3 to 42-9
IX	RESEARCH PAPER Subject 43-1 Types of material 43-2 Finding books 43-3, 43-4	BIBLIOGRAPHY Catalogues, indexes 43-5 to 43-7 Reference books 43-8 Trial bibliography 43-9 Cards 43-10 Form 43-11	MATERIAL Note cards 44-1 Taking notes 44-2	WRITING PAPER Footnotes 45-1 Style 45-2 Sample paper 45-7	DETAILS Footnote style 45-3 Abbreviations 45-4 Illustrations 45-6